KAPLAN BAR REVIEW

First Year

Course Materials

- ✓ Writing for an "A"
- ✓ Constitutional Law
- ✓ Contracts
- ✓ Criminal Law
- ✓ Federal Civil Procedure
- ✓ Real Property
- ✓ Torts

Special thanks to: Lauren Allen, Esq., Chris DeSantis, Esq., Adam Feren, Esq., Christopher Fromm, Esq., Elizabeth Horowitz, Esq., Steven Marietti, Esq., Adam Maze, Esq., Michael Merrill, Ph.D., Walter Niedner, Mike Power, Esq., Tammi Rice, Esq., Micol Small, Esq.

Published by Kaplan Bar Review, a division of Kaplan, Inc.

750 Third Avenue
New York, NY 10017

Printed in the United States of America

July 2016

TABLE OF CONTENTS

Writing for an "A"

STUDENT HANDOUT FOR WRITING FOR AN "A"

Part I: Rule & Counter-Rule

1. At common law, an offeror seeking a performance—i.e., proposing a "unilateral" contract—was free to revoke his offer at any time before the requested performance was complete. This created the so-called "flagpole" problem: I offer to pay you $10 to climb to the top of the flagpole. When you are half-way up, I shout, "I revoke." Because the performance is not complete—i.e., you didn't get to the top of the flagpole—you are out of luck (or "up a flagpole without a paddle").

2. The so-called "modern" approach is captured in Restatement (Second) of Contracts § 45(1): "Where an offer invites an offeree to accept by rendering a performance and does not invite a promissory acceptance, an option contract is created when the offeree…begins the invited performance…." The point of the option contract is to prevent the offeror from revoking when the offeree satisfies this test.

Part II: Sample Exam Question

Paul Patron offers Arlene Artiste $10,000 to paint a portrait of the Patron family. Artiste explains that her other commitments make it impossible for her to promise a completed work by a particular date, and Patron responds, "I don't *want* your commitment. I just want the portrait." After Artiste spends numerous hours doing preliminary sketches—but before she has put brush to canvas and begun the actual portrait—Patron advises her that he has changed his mind and is revoking the offer. Discuss the issues that are likely to arise in an action by Artiste against Patron.

The sample question—and several of the answers that follow—are drawn from Richard Michael Fischl and Jeremy Paul, *Getting to Maybe: How to Excel on Law School Exams* (Carolina Academic Press 1999).

Answer # 1

To make a contract, you need an offer and an acceptance. There are two kinds of contracts, bilateral contracts and unilateral contracts. With a bilateral contract, the offer seeks a promissory acceptance; with a unilateral contract, the offer seeks a performance. At common law, an offeror was free to revoke his offer any time before acceptance, and acceptance of a unilateral offer was defined as complete performance. Therefore, an offer to make a unilateral contract could be revoked at any time before performance was complete. The modern rule from Restatement § 45 is that an option contract is created once the offeree begins performance. Under the common law rule, the offeror in this case could revoke; under § 45 he couldn't.

Answer # 2

Patron has made an offer to Artiste: If Artiste will paint a portrait of the Patron family, Patron will pay her $10,000. Artiste is too busy to promise to meet a deadline, but that doesn't matter because Patron makes it clear that he doesn't want her to <u>promise</u> a portrait, he just wants her to <u>paint</u> one. She begins her work by doing a series of sketches and this takes her "numerous hours," but she hasn't actually begun work on the portrait itself when Patron calls her to tell her that he is revoking his offer. If Rest. § 45 applies, she hasn't started yet so Patron can revoke.

Answer # 3

Whether Patron can revoke his offer will depend on whether we apply the common law rule or the rule provided by § 45 of the Second Restatement. If we apply § 45, there will then be a second issue about whether Artiste's work so far counts as having begun performance.

Answer # 4

Patron can revoke if the old common law rule applies or, even if § 45 of the Restatement governs, if a court can be persuaded that Artiste has yet to begin performance. Patron's right to revoke under the common law is based on the fact that his offer seeks a performance (painting a portrait) rather than a return promise (he says he doesn't want a commitment); thus it constitutes an offer to form a unilateral contract. At common law, such offers can be revoked any time until performance is complete, and Artiste has not yet finished the painting. Section 45 of the Restatement replaces the common law rule with one more favorable to offerees in this context. It will prohibit revocation once Artiste has begun (as opposed to completed) performance. Artiste will contend that her sketchwork indeed constitutes a beginning of performance, and Patron will respond that they are "mere preparations" and thus he is still free to revoke.

Answer # 5

The first thing we need to know is whether the jurisdiction applies the common law rule (which permits the maker of an offer for a unilateral contract to revoke at any time before acceptance is <u>complete</u>) or the modern rule of Restatement § 45 (which prevents revocation once the offeree <u>begins</u> performance). This is pretty clearly a unilateral contract—Patron quite literally precludes acceptance via a promise ("I don't want your commitment")—and it is also clear that Artiste has not completed acceptance/performance (i.e., painting the portrait) at the point Patron tries to revoke. Accordingly, under the common law Artiste isn't going to have any rights against Patron. If the jurisdiction has not yet adopted the Restatement position, this would be a good case for urging it to do so, emphasizing Artiste's vulnerability given the fact that the performance in question is valuable only to Patron and his family (it's not like she can sell her work on their family portrait to someone else) and in addition citing the general trend in modern contract law toward protecting reliance even in the absence of an enforceable contract between the parties. Patron, in response, may be able to invoke the importance of following precedent (if there is in-jurisdiction law embracing the common law rule) and the unfairness of binding one only one party to a deal—which is what would happen if we say that Patron is under an obligation not to revoke while Artiste is under no such obligation to complete her performance.

If Restatement § 45 applies, the offer may not be revoked once the offeree begins performance, but it's not clear whether Artiste has met that requirement. On the one hand, Artiste can argue that she began the performance when she did the preliminary sketchwork. To an artist, such sketches are as much a part of portraiture as the brush strokes on the final canvas, and from that standpoint she "began the invited performance" at the moment she started work on her first sketch. But Patron can counter that he asked for a family portrait—not a series of sketches—in exchange for his promise of $10,000. From the customer's standpoint—and the customer is always right!—the "invited performance" is *the actual painting of the commissioned portrait*, and the preliminary sketches were "mere preparations" for that performance.

Artiste might turn to the underlying policy driving the distinction between "mere preparations" and "beginning of performance," arguing that "preparations" (like buying paintbrushes, paints, or canvas) can ordinarily be redirected to other endeavors, whereas "performances" (like sketches and the portraits) are frequently of value only to the offeror and would therefore represent a "dead loss" to the offeree if the offeror were permitted to revoke (once again, that's likely the case here). But Patron might challenge Artiste's claim "on the facts" (since the sketchwork of accomplished artists can command considerable sums) and challenge its relevance as well (since even a low value doesn't magically turn the sketchwork into the "portrait" that Patron expressly requested).

Answer # 6

Under the common law rule, Patron can revoke at any time before performance is complete, and since Artiste won't complete her performance until she actually finishes the portrait, Patron is free to revoke, no matter how much work she has done on the sketches. Even if Restatement § 45 applied—and it doesn't, because the Restatement is merely persuasive authority—Artiste is out of luck. Patron asked for "a portrait"—not sketches—so Artiste can't argue that she has "begun the invited performance" by doing the sketchwork; she won't begin the invited performance until she starts painting the actual portrait. So there is no option contract, and Patron is free to revoke the offer. Artiste is "up the flagpole without a paddle!"

| **KAPLAN** BAR REVIEW

Constitutional Law

Outline

TABLE OF CONTENTS

IX. **FIRST AMENDMENT FREEDOMS**

I. THE NATURE OF JUDICIAL REVIEW

A. **Organization of the Courts in the Federal System**
  1. **Federal Court System**
     a. **Source of Federal Judicial Power**
        (1) Article III, Section 1 provides that the "judicial power of the United States shall be vested in one Supreme Court and in such inferior Courts as the Congress may from time to time ordain and establish."
     b. **Scope of Federal Judicial Power**
        (1) Article III, Section 2 limits the jurisdiction of the federal courts to:
           (a) cases, in law and equity, arising under the U.S. Constitution, federal laws, and treaties;
           (b) cases affecting ambassadors, public ministers, and consuls;
           (c) cases of admiralty and maritime jurisdiction;
           (d) controversies to which the United States shall be a party;
           (e) controversies between two or more states;
           (f) cases between a state and citizens of another state; and
           (g) cases between citizens of different states (diversity of citizenship cases).
     c. The Eleventh Amendment prohibits the citizens of one state from suing their own state or another state on federal claims for money damages, in federal court or state court, without the state's consent.
        (1) The Eleventh Amendment recognizes the states and their governmental immunity.
        (2) It applies not only to diversity suits but to federal question cases as well.
        (3) The concept of **governmental immunity**, or **sovereign immunity**, means that the government may not be sued without its consent. However, subdivisions of a state (e.g., cities, towns, and counties) do not have immunity from suit under the Eleventh Amendment [Lincoln County v. Luning, 133 U.S. 529 (1890)].
        (4) Despite Congress's enumerated powers under Article I, Section 8, the Eleventh Amendment nonetheless prohibits federal court adjudication of claims by private parties against a state.

        EXAMPLE: Congress could not use Article I to circumvent the limitations placed on federal jurisdiction and, therefore, could not allow a Native American tribe to sue a state in federal court [Seminole Tribe of Florida v. Florida, 517 U.S. 44 (1996)].

           (a) However, pursuant to its enforcement powers under the post-Civil War amendments (Thirteenth, Fourteenth, and Fifteenth), Congress can authorize private suits by individuals to compensate for state violations of those amendments [Fitzpatrick v. Bitzer, 427 U.S. 445 (1979)].

(5)　Exceptions to the application of the Eleventh Amendment include:

(a)　suits against state officials for abusing their power in enforcing an unconstitutional state statute [Ex parte Young, 209 U.S. 123 (1908)];

(b)　federal suits brought by one state against another state, or suits brought by the federal government against a state; and

(c)　most suits for injunctions—e.g., a private citizen may sue to enjoin a state official from acting in violation of the plaintiff's federal constitutional rights.

EXAMPLE: State workers alleging age discrimination under the federal Age Discrimination in Employment Act may not sue their employers (i.e., the state) using the federal statute as a cause of action, because Congress lacks the power to override the state's Eleventh Amendment immunity from federal lawsuits in the absence of a pattern of unconstitutional action by the states violative of the Fourteenth Amendment [Kimel v. Board of Regents, 528 U.S. 62 (2000)].

(6)　A state may consent to suit in federal court if it clearly waives its Eleventh Amendment immunity and does so expressly and unequivocally (or by voluntarily invoking a federal court's jurisdiction). A state will not be held to have impliedly or constructively waived its immunity simply because Congress provides that a state will be subject to private suit if it engages in certain federally regulated conduct (such as infringing a federally granted patent) and the state voluntarily elects to engage in that conduct [College Savings Bank v. Florida Prepaid Postsecondary Education Expense Board, 527 U.S. 666 (1999)].

(7)　Complete preclusion of all jurisdiction may occur in certain instances.

EXAMPLE: Probation officers owed money under federal law cannot sue for it in either federal or state court.

EXAMPLE: States can infringe patents or copyrights and thus violate federal law, but cannot be sued in either federal or state court by private parties.

(a)　Remember, however, that state officials can be sued for injunctive relief, but injured private plaintiffs have no damage remedy against state governments.

2.　**Limitations on Jurisdiction of Federal Courts**

a.　**Case or Controversy**

(1)　Article III, Section 2 limits the jurisdiction of federal courts to "cases" and "controversies." A **case** or **controversy** is a real and substantial dispute that touches the legal relations of parties having adverse interests and that can be resolved by a judicial decree of a conclusive character [Aetna Life Insurance Co. v. Haworth, 300 U.S. 227 (1937)].

(a) The Supreme Court will not give advisory opinions to either the president or Congress concerning the constitutionality of proposed action or legislation.

NOTE ▸ State courts may be allowed to render advisory opinions.

(b) The prohibition against advisory opinions does not preclude federal courts from granting declaratory judgments. A **declaratory judgment** is a decision in which the court is requested to determine the legality of proposed conduct without awarding damages or injunctive relief. However, the plaintiff must meet the case or controversy tests, as well as the "RAMPS" requirements explained below.

Federal Court Jurisdiction RAMPS Up

Ripeness, **A**bstention & Adequate State Grounds, **M**ootness, **P**olitical Questions, **S**tanding

---

b. **Mootness**

(1) If a controversy or matter has already been resolved, then the case will be dismissed as **moot**. An actual case or controversy must exist at all stages of the litigation [Liner v. Jafco, Inc., 375 U.S. 301 (1964)].

(a) Although the principal issue in a lawsuit has been resolved, if a party still has an interest in resolving collateral (or lesser) matters, the case will not be dismissed.

EXAMPLE: A case about wrongful termination is not moot even though the plaintiff had his employment restored if issues of back pay remain [Powell v. McCormick, 395 U.S. 486 (1969)].

(b) The case will not be dismissed for mootness if the injury is "capable of repetition, yet evading review," meaning that it is a practical impossibility for there to be adjudication or appellate review before the claims of the plaintiff, or other individuals who are members of the class, become moot.

EXAMPLE: A pregnant woman's suit challenging the constitutionality of a state abortion statute was held not to be moot even though she was no longer pregnant at the time the case reached the Supreme Court. Pregnancy is "capable of repetition, yet evading review," for the plaintiff and for members of the class she represents [Roe v. Wade, 410 U.S. 113 (1973)].

c. **Ripeness**

(1) Whereas mootness bars consideration of claims after they have been resolved, **ripeness** bars consideration of claims before they have fully developed.

(a) Generally, a court may not review or grant a declaratory judgment of a state law before it is enforced or when there is no real threat the statute will ever be enforced [Poe v. Ullman, 367 U.S. 497 (1961)].

EXAMPLE: The Supreme Court dismissed a claim against the Army's data-gathering activities because there was no showing that the Army's surveillance system resulted in any specific present harm or threat of future harm to the complainants [Laird v. Tatum, 408 U.S. 1 (1972)].

EXAMPLE: The Supreme Court refused to grant equitable relief because there was no evidence that the pattern of allegedly unconstitutional racial discrimination in the bail and sentencing practices in the Cairo, Illinois court system threatened the plaintiffs, who were not in imminent danger of being prosecuted [O'Shea v. Littleton, 414 U.S. 488 (1974)].

EXAMPLE: The Supreme Court did rule on the constitutionality of a statute prohibiting the teaching of evolution in public schools even though the statute had not been enforced [Epperson v. Arkansas, 393 U.S. 97 (1968)].

(b) However, if the plaintiff can show, before enforcement of the law, that the law presents a specific or present harm or a threat of specific future and imminent harm, the court may grant a declaratory judgment [Abbott Laboratories v. Gardner, 387 U.S. 136 (1967)].

d. **Abstention**

(1) The federal court may **abstain**, or refuse to hear a particular case, when there are undecided issues of state law presented. The abstention doctrine permits the state court to resolve issues of state law, thereby making a decision of the constitutional issue unnecessary. Thus, proper deference is paid to the state court system and harmonious federal-state relations are furthered [Railroad Commission v. Pullman, 312 U.S. 496 (1941)].

(a) The federal court may abstain if the meaning of a state law or regulation is unclear. In this situation, the state court might interpret the statute so as to avoid the constitutional issue [Harris County Commissioners Court v. Moore, 420 U.S. 77 (1975)].

(b) Where state criminal proceedings are pending, the federal court will abstain in a suit seeking an injunction against the state prosecution, absent a showing of bad-faith harassment on the part of the state prosecutors [Younger v. Harris, 401 U.S. 37 (1971)]. This principle has been extended to cases:

1) where state civil proceedings had commenced (seeking an injunction against operation of a state public nuisance

statute used to close a pornography movie house) [Huffman v. Pursue, Ltd., 420 U.S. 592 (1975)]; and

2) where civil contempt hearings had begun [Judice v. Vail, 430 U.S. 327 (1977)].

e. **Standing**

(1) Article III requires a person litigating a constitutional question to show:

(a) injury-in-fact;

1) The plaintiff must show a direct and personal injury, actual or imminent, caused by the action that he is challenging. Where the plaintiff has not suffered any personal injury or harm, he does not have standing [Sierra Club v. Morton, 405 U.S. 727 (1972)].

(b) causation (the injury was caused by the challenged action); and

1) The injury must be caused by the violation of a duty affecting the plaintiff's rights arising under the constitution or federal law [Simon v. Eastern Kentucky Welfare Rights Organization, 426 U.S. 26 (1976)].

(c) redressability.

1) The plaintiff must show that he will benefit from the remedy sought in the litigation.

EXAMPLE: Environmentalists sued the government because they did not receive notice when the government sold burnt timber after a particular forest fire. After settling the suit, the environmentalists brought a second suit, asking the court to require the government to give notice before conducting any future timber-salvage activities. Held: The environmentalists had standing in the first action because they suffered the concrete harm of being excluded from the sale of particular burnt timber. However, they lacked standing in the second action, because there was no new imminent harm caused by the government's general policy of not giving notice before timber-salvage activities [Summers v. Earth Island Institute, 555 U.S. 488 (2009)].

(2) **Specialized Problems of Standing**

(a) As a general rule, federal taxpayers do not have standing to challenge allegedly unconstitutional federal expenditures on the grounds that their injury is comparatively minute and indeterminative, and their interest is too remote [Massachusetts v. Mellon, 262 U.S. 447 (1923)].

EXCEPTION: In 1968, the Supreme Court held that a federal taxpayer had standing to challenge federal expenditures to aid parochial schools where the taxpayer was challenging the expenditure of money by Congress under its taxing and spending power and the expenditure allegedly violated the Establishment Clause [Flast v. Cohen, 392 U.S. 83 (1968)].

NOTE ▶ The Flast v. Cohen principle has not been extended to other areas of government activity.

> **EXAMPLE:** Taxpayers did not have standing to challenge a transfer of valuable real estate, under the Property Clause, to a Christian college from a local government [Valley Forge Christian College v. Americans United for Separation of Church and State, 454 U.S. 464 (1982)].

> **EXAMPLE:** Citizens did not have standing to challenge a senator's or representative's service in the Armed Forces Reserve as violating Article I, Section 6, prohibiting a member of Congress from "holding any office under the United States" [Schlesinger v. Reservists Committee to Stop the War, 418 U.S. 208 (1974)].

(b) Under the traditional view, a litigant lacks standing to assert the rights of third parties not before the court [Tileston v. Ullman, 318 U.S. 44 (1943)].

1) The Supreme Court has permitted a party to raise the constitutional rights of a third party where he himself has suffered injury and:

a) a special relationship exists between the claimant and third party because of the connection between the interests of the claimant and the constitutional rights of the third person; or

> **EXAMPLE:** The Supreme Court acknowledged the right of a physician to raise the rights of his patients in challenging an abortion ruling because of the close relationship between the doctor and his patient, and also because the patient was unable to bring suit on her own behalf [Singleton v. Wulff, 429 U.S. 106 (1976)].

> **EXAMPLE:** A vendor of beer had standing to assert the rights of males under the age of 21 in a challenge to a law prohibiting the sale of beer to them [Craig v. Boren, 429 U.S. 190 (1976)].

> **EXAMPLE:** A seller of contraceptives had standing to assert the rights of potential purchasers against a law prohibiting the sale of such devices [Carey v. Population Services International, 431 U.S. 678 (1977)].

b) the third party is unable or finds it difficult to bring suit on his own behalf.

2) An association has standing to assert the claims of its members, even if the association has not suffered any injury itself, if [Hunt v. Washington Apple Advertising Commission, 432 U.S. 333 (1977)]:

a) the members would otherwise have standing to sue in their own right;

b) the interest asserted is germane to the association's purpose; and

c) neither the claim asserted nor the relief requested would require participation by the individual members in the lawsuit.

f. **Political Questions**

(1) Federal courts cannot hear cases involving political questions. A **political question** is a matter assigned to another branch by the constitution or incapable of a judicial answer. the Supreme Court set forth the following relevant factors to consider to determine if the political question doctrine applies [Baker v. Carr, 369 U.S. 186 (1962)]:

(a) whether there is a textually demonstrable constitutional commitment of the issue to a coordinate political department;

(b) a lack of judicially discoverable and manageable standards for resolving it;

(c) the impossibility of deciding without an initial policy determination of a kind clearly for nonjudicial discretion;

(d) the impossibility of a court's undertaking independent resolution without expressing lack of respect due coordinate branches of government;

(e) an unusual need for unquestioning adherence to a political decision already made; and

(f) the potential for embarrassment from multifarious pronouncements by various departments on one question.

(2) There are two principal factors related to the political question doctrine. First, considerations (a), (d), (e), and (f) enumerated above are rooted in the separation of powers. On the other hand, considerations (b) and (c) recognize the limitations of the judiciary in resolving certain types of controversies.

EXAMPLE: the ability of a grand jury to subpoena documents in the possession of the president against a claim of executive privilege does not present a political question apart from a claim based on national security [United States v. Nixon, 418 U.S. 683 (1974)].

(3) Other areas of political questions include decisions in regard to:

(a) the impeachment process;

(b) the amendment ratification process;

(c) the president's power to unilaterally terminate a treaty;

(d) foreign affairs; and

(e) Guaranty Clause issues under Article IV.

> **NOTE** A claim that a state has redrawn its electoral districts in a racially discrimi
> natory manner is not a political question. However, a claim that a state has
> redrawn electoral districts to benefit one political party is a political question
> and, therefore, is nonjusticiable. The Supreme Court has ruled that there are
> manageable judicial standards for deciding claims of race discrimination, but
> that there are no such standards for deciding when a political party has been
> unfairly advantaged when electoral districts are redrawn.

B. The United States Supreme Court

1. **Jurisdiction of the Supreme Court**

   a. Under Article III, Section 2, the Supreme Court has original jurisdiction "in all cases affecting ambassadors, other public ministers and consuls and those in which a state shall be a party." Congress may neither enlarge nor restrict the Supreme Court's original jurisdiction [Marbury v. Madison, 5 U.S. 137 (1803)].

   b. Article III, Section 2 further provides that "in all other cases before mentioned, the Supreme Court shall have appellate jurisdiction, both as to law and fact, with such exceptions, and under such regulations as the Congress shall make." The Supreme Court has the power to:

      (1) hold acts of the other branches of the federal government (the executive branch and Congress) unconstitutional [Marbury v. Madison, 5 U.S. 137 (1803)];

      (2) hold state statutes unconstitutional [Fletcher v. Peck, 10 U.S. 87 (1810)];

      (3) review state court decisions to ensure that the states act in conformity with the U.S. Constitution and federal statutes [Martin v. Hunter's Lessee, 14 U.S. 304 (1816)]; and

      (4) decide other state law questions.

         (a) In cases of diversity jurisdiction:

            1) the Supreme Court will defer to an existing state court interpretation of state law;

            2) the Supreme Court will interpret a state law which has not already been interpreted by the state court based on the Supreme Court's prediction of how the state court will interpret the statute; and

            3) the Supreme Court will abstain from a decision if the state court's interpretation of unsettled state law could end the dispute and the Supreme Court cannot predict how the state court will rule.

   c. Under federal law, there are two methods for invoking Supreme Court appellate jurisdiction [28 U.S.C. § 1257]:

      (1) by appeal (where jurisdiction is mandatory); and

(a) In 1988, an act of Congress reduced obligatory review on appeal to decisions of three-judge federal district courts.

(2) by writ of *certiorari* (discretionary review where four or more justices vote to hear the case).

(a) Since the two categories of decisions that were subject to obligatory review on appeal have been eliminated, practically all decisions from state supreme courts and federal courts are now reviewable by a writ of *certiorari*, except decisions made purely on state law.

(b) Grounds for *certiorari* include:

1) cases involving conflicts between different federal courts of appeal;

2) cases involving conflicts between the highest courts of two states;

3) cases involving conflicts between the highest state court and a federal court of appeals; or

4) cases from state courts or U.S. courts of appeal involving important, yet unresolved, issues.

d. **Adequate and Independent State Grounds**

(1) Although a state court decision may involve a federal question, if the state court judgment can be supported on an adequate and independent state ground, the Supreme Court will not take jurisdiction. To do so would be tantamount to rendering an "advisory opinion" [Herb v. Pitcairn, 324 U.S. 117 (1945)].

(a) Unlike other doctrines of judicial review, which apply to the entire federal judiciary, adequate state grounds apply only to the Supreme Court.

(2) Where a state court clearly states that a state law violates other state law or a provision of the state constitution, that decision will be an adequate and independent state ground (regardless of whether the opinion also decides that the state law violates a federal law as well).

(a) Where a state court holds that a state law violates both the state and federal constitutions, the doctrine of adequate state grounds will apply.

(3) Where a state court's decision is based upon a federal interpretation of a similar federal law, adequate and independent state grounds will not apply. The Supreme Court may review in this situation.

(4) Where it is unclear whether the state court made its decision based upon state or federal interpretations of statutes, the Supreme Court may take the case, although it also has the power in that situation to dismiss or remand the case for clarification from the state court.

(a) The independence prong focuses on whether it is "apparent from the four corners" of the opinion that the state court judgment was settled based on a state court interpretation of state law precedent or the state's constitution. If not, the Supreme Court may [Michigan v. Long, 463 U.S. 1032 (1983)]:

1) obtain clarification from the state court, or

2) presume that the state court decision was rooted—at least in part—in federal law, and review the case.

II. SEPARATION OF POWERS

A. **The Powers of Congress**
   1. **Legislative Power**
      a. Legislative power is primarily the power to make laws, but incidental to that power is the right to conduct investigations and hearings, consider matters upon which legislation may be enacted, and do all other things "necessary and proper" to the enactment of legislation [U.S. Const. art. I, § 1].
         (1) Congress has enumerated powers to collect taxes and spend money for the general welfare, to borrow money on the credit of the United States, to regulate commerce with foreign nations and among the several states, to declare war, and to raise and support the army, navy, and militia [U.S. Const. art. I, § 8].
         (2) The Necessary and Proper Clause gives Congress the implied power "to make all Laws which shall be necessary and proper for carrying into Execution the foregoing Powers, and all other Powers vested by this Constitution in the Government of the United States, or any Department or Officer thereof" [U.S. Const. art. I, § 8].
         (3) The Enabling Clauses of the Thirteenth, Fourteenth, and Fifteenth Amendments give Congress the power to enforce those amendments by "appropriate legislation."
   2. **Commerce Power**
      a. Despite the broad language used by the Supreme Court in Gibbons v. Ogden [22 U.S. 1 (1824)], subsequent cases used various criteria to restrict the power of Congress to regulate "commerce which concerns more states than one." Today, Congress can regulate:
         (1) channels of interstate commerce (i.e., highways, waterways, and air traffic);
         (2) instrumentalities of interstate commerce (i.e., cars, trucks, ships, and airplanes); and
         (3) activities that "substantially affect" interstate commerce.
            (a) Under the **affectation doctrine**, Congress now has the power to regulate any economic activity, whether carried on in one state or many, that has a substantial effect (whether directly or indirectly) upon interstate commerce.
               1) This doctrine was first formulated in National Labor Relations Board v. Jones and Laughlin Steel Co. [301 U.S. 1 (1937)], which upheld the constitutionality of the Wagner Act in requiring collective bargaining in all industries "affecting" interstate commerce.
            (b) The affectation doctrine was expanded upon by the **cumulative effect doctrine**, in which the Supreme Court held that the federal commerce power permitted regulation of the amount of wheat a farmer could grow on his own land, for

his own consumption, because his activity, together with that of other growers of wheat for their own consumption, had a substantial cumulative effect upon interstate commerce [Wickard v. Filburn, 317 U.S. 111 (1942)].

(c) Congress's plenary commerce power is not without limits. In United States v. Lopez [514 U.S. 549 (1995)], for the first time in more than half a century, the Supreme Court struck down a federal law that made it a crime for any individual knowingly to possess a firearm in a school zone. Since gun possession near schools is neither itself an "economic" activity nor an activity that "substantially" affects interstate commerce, and since no "jurisdictional element" connecting particular gun possession to interstate commerce was expressed in the language of the statute, the Supreme Court held that Congress was acting beyond the limits of the Commerce Clause.

> **NOTE** To validly exercise its Commerce Clause power under the "substantial effects" test, Congress must now show: (1) that the regulated activity is "economic" in nature; and (2) that the regulated activity (when taken cumulatively throughout the nation) has a substantial effect on interstate commerce.

(d) The Commerce Clause has been used as the vehicle to uphold laws aimed at barring racial discrimination in activities connected with interstate commerce.

EXAMPLE: Congress may prohibit racial discrimination in private restaurants if a substantial portion of the food consumed traveled in interstate commerce [Katzenbach v. McClung, 379 U.S. 294 (1964)].

EXAMPLE: The Court has upheld provisions of the Civil Rights Act of 1964 barring discrimination in places of public accommodation (e.g., as applied to a motel) as "affecting" interstate commerce [Heart of Atlanta Motel v. United States, 379 U.S. 241 (1964)].

(e) The Supreme Court has upheld, under the commerce power, a federal law prohibiting extortionate credit transactions (i.e., loan sharking) on the grounds that such transactions provide a major source of revenue for organized crime, and that organized crime, in turn, has an adverse effect upon interstate commerce [Perez v. United States, 402 U.S. 146 (1971)].

(f) The Tenth Amendment, which provides that powers not delegated to the federal government are reserved to the states, or to the people, serves as a very weak limitation on the federal commerce power today. Generally applicable federal laws that regulate the states (state businesses and/or employees) do not violate the Tenth Amendment [Garcia v. San Antonio Metropolitan Transit Authority, 469 U.S. 528 (1985)].

> **NOTE** The Tenth Amendment does prevent Congress from interfering with a state's lawmaking processes. Congress may not commandeer the legislative processes of the states by directly compelling them to enact and enforce a federal regulatory program.

> **EXAMPLE:** The Supreme Court has held invalid as violating the Tenth Amendment a federal law that required the state of New York to pass legislation to arrange for the disposal of radioactive waste generated within its borders [New York v. United States, 505 U.S. 144 (1992)].

> **NOTE** The Tenth Amendment also prevents Congress from commandeering state executive officials. That is, Congress may not order state officials to act as administrators of federal programs.

> **EXAMPLE:** The Supreme Court held unconstitutional the federal Brady Handgun Violence Protection Act, because it commandeered state and local law enforcement officers for performance of various acts required by federal legislation [Printz v. United States, 521 U.S. 898 (1997)].

3. **Taxing Power**

   a. Congress has the power to lay and collect taxes, duties, imposts, and excises to pay the debts and provide for the common defense and general welfare [U.S. Const. art. I, § 8].

> **EXAM TIP** A congressional act purporting to be a "tax" should be upheld as a valid exercise of the taxing power provided that it does, in fact, raise revenue (the **objective test**) or that it was intended to raise revenue (the **subjective test**).

> **NOTE** The Sixteenth Amendment gives Congress the power to collect taxes on incomes derived from any source.

   b. Congress has used its taxing power as a necessary and proper means of achieving a regulatory effect. Generally, as long as Congress has the power to regulate the activity taxed, the tax can then be used as a regulating device rather than for revenue-raising purposes.

   EXAMPLE: The Supreme Court sustained a tax on coal producers who violated a fair competition law, even though it was clearly designed to be a penalty rather than revenue-raising [Sunshine Anthracite Coal Co. v. Adkins, 310 U.S. 381 (1940)].

      (1) Even when Congress does not have power to regulate the activity taxed, the tax will nevertheless be upheld if its "dominant intent" is revenue-raising. Thus, even though the tax may have a substantial regulatory effect, if the tax in fact raises revenue, it will be valid.

EXAMPLE: The Supreme Court upheld as revenue-raising a discriminatory tax on colored oleomargarine, even though Congress did not have the power to regulate its production directly [McCray v. United States, 195 U.S. 27 (1904)].

(2) As a general rule, the modern judicial trend is to uphold any tax as valid if it is, in fact, a revenue-raising measure.

EXAMPLE: Although a tax on bookmaking activities had a regulatory effect, it was upheld as producing revenue (albeit negligible in amount) [United States v. Kahriger, 345 U.S. 22 (1953)].

4. **Spending Power**

a. Congress has the power to lay and collect taxes "to pay the Debts and provide for the common Defense and General Welfare of the United States" [U.S. Const. art. I, § 8, cl. 1].

(1) The Supreme Court has construed the General Welfare Clause as a limitation on Congress's taxing and spending powers and not as an independent source of congressional power. In other words, Congress's power to tax and spend must be exercised for the "general welfare" of the United States [United States v. Butler, 297 U.S. 1 (1936)].

EXAMPLE: The Federal Election Campaign Act, which limited the amount a candidate could spend if he accepted money from the federal government, is a valid exercise of the power to spend for the "general welfare." The Supreme Court sustained the power of Congress to finance elections because this would reduce the harmful effect of candidates' reliance on large private contributions [Buckley v. Valeo, 424 U.S. 1 (1976)].

(2) By exercising its spending power, Congress can require states to comply with specified conditions in order to qualify for federal funds.

EXAMPLE: Congress conditioned further grants of highway funds upon the resignation of a state highway administrator who was also the state Democratic Party chairman [Oklahoma v. Civil Service Commission, 330 U.S. 127 (1947)].

(3) The Supreme Court held that Congress may place a condition on the receipt of federal funds by a state if [South Dakota v. Dole, 483 U.S. 203 (1987)]:

(a) the spending serves the general welfare;

(b) the condition is unambiguous;

(c) the condition relates to the federal program;

(d) the state is not required to undertake unconstitutional action; and

(e) the amount in question is not so great as to be considered coercive to the state's acceptance.

EXAMPLE: The Supreme Court rejected South Dakota's Tenth and Twenty-First Amendment arguments and upheld Congress's withholding of federal highway funds from states permitting the purchasing of alcoholic beverages by individuals under age 21.

5. **War and Defense Powers**

   a. Congress may [U.S. Const. art. I, § 8]:

      (1) declare war;

      (2) raise and support armies;

      (3) provide and maintain a navy; and

      (4) organize, arm, discipline, and call forth a militia.

   b. The war power confers upon Congress a very broad authority to initiate whatever measures it deems necessary to provide for the national defense, in peacetime as well as in wartime.

      (1) Thus, the military draft and selective service systems have repeatedly been upheld [United States v. O'Brien, 391 U.S. 367 (1968)].

      (2) Similarly, the power of Congress to initiate wage, price, and rent control of the civilian economy during wartime has been sustained [Yakus v. United States, 321 U.S. 414 (1944)].

      (3) The exclusion of civilians from certain restricted areas during wartime has been approved [Korematsu v. United States, 323 U.S. 214 (1944)].

   c. Congress has the power to establish military courts and tribunals. Since military courts are not Article III courts, the accused in court-martial proceedings is not entitled to the same procedural safeguards set forth in the Bill of Rights (e.g., the right to jury trial or grand jury indictment). Rather, an accused is safeguarded by the procedures provided in the Uniform Code of Military Justice [U.S. Const. art. I, § 8, cl. 14].

      (1) Military courts have jurisdiction over offenses committed by servicemen on a military post or in an area under military control. Jurisdiction is determined by the status of the individual as an armed service member, not the connection between service and the offense [Solorio v. United States, 483 U.S. 435 (1987)].

      (2) Military courts also have jurisdiction over current members of the armed forces, even while on a pass or on leave, for nonservice matters.

      (3) As long as civilian courts are available, military courts are denied jurisdiction over civilians and their dependents unless Congress has affirmatively granted such jurisdiction.

EXAMPLE: The Supreme Court held that, absent military exigency, the president may not try alleged terrorists in special military courts if Congress has enacted a statute denying the president that authority. Congress, however, may affirmatively grant that authority to the president [Hamdan v. Rumsfeld, 548 U.S. 557 (2006)].

(4) Although civilian courts have no general power of review over court-martial proceedings, there can be a limited examination of the regularity of such proceedings by a civilian court [Burns v. Wilson, 339 U.S. 103 (1950)].

6. **Investigatory Power**

a. Although Congress does not have any express constitutional power to investigate, the Necessary and Proper Clause permits Congress to conduct investigations incident to its legislative power [McGrain v. Daugherty, 273 U.S. 135 (1927)].

(1) Congress's investigatory power is broad, and it may extend to any matter within a "legitimate legislative sphere."

(2) If a witness fails to appear after being summoned before a congressional committee or fails to answer a question posed by such a committee, Congress may either:

(a) cite the witness for contempt; or

(b) refer the matter to the U.S. attorney general for prosecution.

(3) Generally, a witness can raise as a defense:

(a) the privilege against self-incrimination;

(b) lack of due process safeguards; or

(c) interference with the First Amendment rights to privacy and freedom of association.

> **EXAMPLE:** The Supreme Court upheld the refusal of a member of the NAACP to release membership lists to a legislative committee because there was not a sufficient nexus between the investigation and the records sought [Gibson v. Florida Legislative Committee, 372 U.S. 539 (1963)].

7. **Property Power**

a. Congress has the power "to dispose of and make all needful Rules and Regulations respecting the Territory or other Property belonging to the United States" [U.S. Const. art. IV, § 3].

8. **Power of Eminent Domain**

a. Although the Constitution does not expressly give Congress the power of eminent domain, the power to take property is "implied in aid of the other powers granted to the federal government" [Kohl v. United States, 91 U.S. 367 (1876)].

b. This power is limited, however. The Fifth Amendment provides, in part, that private property shall not be taken for public use without just compensation.

EXAM TIP ▶ Be sure to consider and include an analysis under the Takings Clause.

9. **Admiralty and Maritime Power**

a. The Supreme Court has determined that the Necessary and Proper Clause gives Congress complete and plenary power to fix and determine the maritime laws throughout the country [Southern Pacific Co. v. Jensen, 244 U.S. 205 (1917)].

10. **Bankruptcy Power**

    a. Congress has the power "to establish uniform Laws on the subject of Bankruptcies throughout the United States" [U.S. Const. art. I, § 8, cl. 4].

11. **Postal Power**

    a. Congress may establish post offices and post roads [U.S. Const. art. I, § 8, cl. 7].

> **NOTE** The post office has now been moved out of the Cabinet and is a self-operating entity within the government.

12. **Copyright and Patent Power**

    a. Congress may "promote the Progress of Science and useful Arts, by securing for limited Times to Authors and Inventors the exclusive Right to their respective Writings and Discoveries" [U.S. Const. art. I, § 8, cl. 8].

13. **Speech and Debate Clause**

    a. "The Senators and Representatives…for any Speech or Debate in either House…shall not be questioned in any other Place" [U.S. Const. art. I, § 6, cl. 1].

    b. The Speech and Debate Clause protects legislators and their aides against criminal or civil proceedings for "legislative acts" [United States v. Johnson, 383 U.S. 169 (1966); Gravel v. United States, 408 U.S. 606 (1972)]. Members of Congress, however, can be liable based on defamation for issuing press releases or newsletters that injure reputation [U.S. Const. art. I, § 6, cl. 1].

        (1) The clause insulates members of Congress for "acts that occur in the regular course of the legislative process," but does not bar prosecution for taking a bribe to influence legislation [United States v. Brewster, 408 U.S. 501 (1972)].

        (2) The Speech and Debate Clause forbids the courts from enjoining members of Congress or their aides from issuing subpoenas or conducting their inquiry [Eastland v. United States Servicemen's Fund, 421 U.S. 491 (1975)].

14. **Civil War Amendments**

    a. Congress has the power to enforce:

        (1) the Thirteenth Amendment, banning slavery;

        (2) the Fourteenth Amendment, prohibiting the states from violating protections regarding due process, equal protection, and privileges and immunities; and

        (3) the Fifteenth Amendment, prohibiting the states from discriminating in voting rights.

    b. To validly enforce the Fourteenth or Fifteenth Amendment, Congress must show that:

(1) state governments have engaged in widespread violations of the amendment; and

(2) the legislative remedy is "congruent with and proportional to" the violations.

c. Congress may enforce the Thirteenth Amendment ban on slavery even when the state governments have not violated the amendment. However, Congress may enforce the Fourteenth and Fifteenth Amendments only when state governments have widely violated those Amendments.

B. Executive Power

1. Chief Executive

a. "The Executive Power shall be vested in a President of the United States." This provision confers broad authority in the president to execute the laws of the United States. There are few enumerated powers expressly granted to the president under Article II. Many of the president's domestic and foreign powers are implied. The Supreme Court has held that the president has no power to make laws, but has the power to execute them [U.S. Const. art. II, § 1].

(1) **Appointment Power**

(a) Article II gives the president the power, "with the Advice and Consent of the Senate," to nominate and appoint all "Ambassadors, other public Ministers and Consuls, Judges of the Supreme Court, and all other Officers of the United States, whose appointments are not herein otherwise provided for" [U.S. Const. art. II, § 2].

NOTE The presidential appointment power should be construed as a limitation on the congressional appointment power. Although Congress can appoint officials to its legislative committees, it cannot appoint members to any agency or commission with administrative powers.

EXAMPLE: An attempt to vest the power to appoint members of the Federal Elections Commission in the speaker of the House of Representatives was held unconstitutional [Buckley v. Valeo, 424 U.S. 1 (1976)].

(b) The president, therefore, has the exclusive power to nominate high-level officials such as cabinet members, ambassadors, and heads of agencies. The Senate, however, has the power to confirm or reject the president's nominees for such high-level appointments.

(c) Congress can delegate the appointment of "inferior" officers (including special prosecutors) to:

1) the president;

2) the judiciary; or

3) heads of departments.

(2) **Removal Power**

    (a) Although the U.S. Constitution is silent with respect to removal power, it is generally agreed that the president may remove any executive appointee (e.g., an ambassador or cabinet member) without cause.

    (b) However, the president must have cause (i.e., good reasons) to remove executive officers having fixed terms and officers performing judicial or *quasi*-judicial functions (e.g., a member of the Federal Trade Commission).

    (c) Congress has no power to summarily remove an executive officer [Bowsher v. Synar, 478 U.S. 714 (1986)].

    (d) Federal judges cannot be removed by either Congress or the president during "good behavior"; formal impeachment proceedings are required for removal.

(3) **Veto Power**

    (a) Once Congress has passed legislation and presented it to the president, the president has 10 days in which to act upon it. Unless he vetoes it within the 10-day period, the proposed legislation will become law [U.S. Const. art. I, § 7].

    (b) The president can **pocket veto** a bill passed within 10 days of the end of the congressional term by not signing it.

    (c) Congress has the power to override a veto by a two-thirds vote of both the Senate and House of Representatives [U.S. Const. art. I, § 7].

    (d) A **line-item veto**, which gives the President the power to cancel particular provisions of new federal legislation, has been held unconstitutional as a grant of power to the president to amend a statute. Amendments are valid only when Congress enacts a new statute followed by a presidential signature [Clinton v. City of New York, 524 U.S. 417 (1998)].

(4) **Congressional Legislation and Presidential Power**

    (a) The president may exercise only those powers expressly or impliedly granted by the Constitution or an act of Congress. Moreover, if Congress validly exercises one of its powers and overrides the president, then Congress prevails over the president.

    EXAMPLE: The president may not validly use his power as commander-in-chief to seize a factory in order to prevent a strike during wartime if Congress opposes such action [Youngstown Sheet and Tube Co. v. Sawyer, 343 U.S. 579 (1952)].

    (b) Congress can enact legislation that delegates rulemaking power to an executive or administrative agency in some designated subject area (such as securities law, labor law, environmental law, and so on), creating a huge exception to the general rule that the executive branch may not make law.

(5) **Pardon Power**

    (a) The president may "grant reprieves and pardons for offenses against the United States, except in cases of impeachment" [U.S. Const. art. II, § 2].

(6) **Executive Privilege**

    (a) The president has an absolute privilege to refuse to disclose information relating to military, diplomatic, or sensitive national security secrets.

    (b) Other confidential communications between the president and his advisors are presumptively privileged [United States v. Nixon, 418 U.S. 683 (1974)]. The presumption is overcome when confidential communications are subpoenaed as evidence in a criminal trial.

(7) **Obligation to Report**

    (a) The president "shall from time to time give to the Congress Information of the State of the Union, and recommend to their Consideration such Measures as he shall judge necessary and expedient." This obligation has evolved into the annual "State of the Union" address given by the president [U.S. Const. art. II, § 3].

2. **Commander-in-Chief**

  a. "The President shall be the Commander in Chief of the Army and Navy of the United States, and of the militia of the several States when called into the actual service of the United States by Congress" [U.S. Const. art. II, § 2].

    (1) **Military Powers**

      (a) The president has the power to deploy military forces without a formal declaration of war in response to an attack upon the United States (as determined by the Prize Cases) [Brig Amy Warwick, 67 U.S. 635 (1863)].

      (b) He additionally has the power to seize private property during wartime unless Congress denies him that power [United States v. Pewee Coal Co., 341 U.S. 114 (1951)].

      (c) However, the president does not have the power to declare war.

    (2) **Unsettled Areas**

      (a) Clearly, the president may commit troops to repel a sudden attack on the United States. However, certain issues remain unclear, such as:

        1) whether the president may commit forces without congressional approval to aid a U.S. ally under attack (although provisions in certain defense treaties would authorize such intervention); and

        2) whether the president may order a preemptive strike in anticipation of an enemy attack.

3. **International Affairs**

   a. **Treaty Power**

      (1) The president has the power to make treaties with foreign nations "by and with the Advice and Consent of the Senate" [U.S. Const. art. II, § 2, cl. 2]. Treaties require consent of two-thirds of the Senate before they can be enacted.

         (a) A treaty is **self-executing** when it takes effect without the necessity of any further action by Congress beyond consent or ratification [Missouri v. Holland, 252 U.S. 416 (1920)].

         (b) A treaty is not self-executing when it requires Congress (or state legislatures) to pass legislation to implement its provisions—i.e., requiring a change in either federal or state law which would enable fulfillment of treaty obligations.

      (2) In accordance with the Supremacy Clause, treaties are "the supreme Law of the land; and the Judges of every State shall be bound thereby, any Thing in the Constitution of Laws of any State to the Contrary notwithstanding" [U.S. Const. art. VI, cl. 2].

         (a) Self-executing treaties are considered the supreme law of the land, whereas treaties which are not self-executing become part of the supreme law of the land, and thus supersede existing federal and state statutes, only when further legislative action is taken by Congress.

> **NOTE** Treaties take precedence over any conflicting state law regardless of whether a treaty precedes or follows the enactment of the state law [Nielsen v. Johnson, 279 U.S. 47 (1929)]. However, when a treaty and federal statute conflict on the issue in question, time determines the controlling authority—the last-in-time will prevail.

   b. **Executive Agreements**

      (1) The president has the power to enter into executive agreements and compacts with foreign nations. Such agreements are valid and prevail over inconsistent state law [United States v. Belmont, 301 U.S. 324 (1937)].

      (2) Executive agreements are the sole responsibility of the president, and need not be ratified by Congress.

      (3) Executive agreements do not prevail over federal statutes.

TREATIES AND EXECUTIVE AGREEMENTS: PRECEDENCE CHART			
	U.S. Constitution	**Federal Law**	**State Law**
Treaties	Constitution prevails.	Last-in-time prevails.	Treaty prevails.
Executive Agreements	Constitution prevails.	Conflicting federal statute prevails.	Executive agreement prevails.

C. **Interbranch Checks upon the Exercise of Federal Power**

1. **Congressional Limits on the Executive**

   a. **Foreign Affairs**

      (1) If Congress is acting within its constitutional powers, Congress may block the president from acting.

   b. **Impeachment Power**

      (1) "The President, Vice President, and all civil Officers of the United States shall be removed from Office on Impeachment for, and Conviction of, Treason, Bribery or other high Crimes and Misdemeanors" [U.S. Const. art. II, § 4].

         (a) The House of Representatives has the sole power to impeach.

         (b) The Senate has the sole power to try impeachments. A two-thirds vote in the Senate is required for conviction.

   c. **Legislative Veto**

      (1) A legislative veto occurs when Congress enacts a law containing a provision that Congress can change the law without a new Congressional vote or presidential signature.

      (2) The Supreme Court has held that a legislative veto violated the constitutional requirements of bicameralism and presentment to the president [Immigration & Naturalization Service v. Chadha, 462 U.S. 919 (1983)].

   d. **Investigative Power**

      (1) As indicated earlier, under the Necessary and Proper Clause, Congress has the implied power to conduct investigations concerning all matters over which Congress has jurisdiction.

   e. **Delegation to Executive**

      (1) On numerous occasions Congress has delegated to the executive branch the authority to make rules having the power of law (through rulemaking by such agencies, such as the Department of Health, Education, and Welfare; the Environmental Protection Agency; and the Nuclear Regulatory Commission).

   f. **Appropriations Power**

      (1) Where Congress by legislative act explicitly directs the president to spend appropriated money, the president has no power to impound (i.e., refuse to spend or delay spending) the authorized funds.

2. **Presidential Limits on Congress**

   a. Every act of Congress must be approved and signed by the president before it can become law, or, being disapproved, must be passed by a two-thirds vote of each House [U.S. Const. art. I, § 7].

3. **Judicial Limits on Congress and the President**

   a. The federal judiciary is the ultimate arbiter of cases whose disposition depends upon construction of the Constitution, an act of Congress, or a federal treaty [U.S. Const. art. III, § 2].

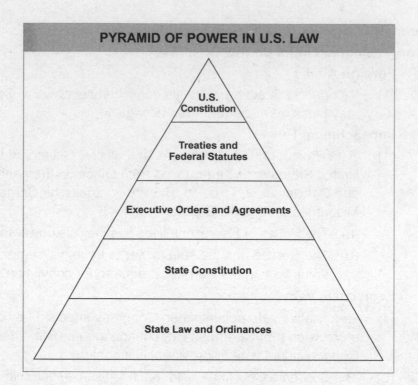

III. THE RELATION OF THE NATION AND THE STATES IN THE FEDERAL SYSTEM

A. **Nature and Scope of Federal and State Powers**

1. The fundamental principle of federalism is the co-existence of the national government and the state governments.

2. The Tenth Amendment provides that "[t]he powers not delegated to the United States by the Constitution, nor prohibited by it to the States, are reserved to the states respectively, or to the people."

3. While each state has a general police power, there is no federal police power. The federal government must legislate through one of its enumerated powers, whereas the states may regulate any health, safety, welfare, moral, or aesthetic interest through their respective police powers.

4. The U.S. Constitution limits the state's police powers by:

   a. reserving certain enumerated powers exclusively for the federal government;

   b. restricting both the federal and state governments from acting in violation of constitutional provisions; and

   c. providing under the Supremacy Clause that if Congress enacts legislation with the intention of preempting state law, the congressional regulation will control.

B. **Intergovernmental Immunities**

1. **Immunity of the Federal Government**

   a. The federal government and its agencies are immune from suits by private individuals except where they allow themselves to be sued (e.g., the Federal Tort Claims Act).

   EXAMPLE: The U.S. Postal Service is part of the federal government rather than a separate antitrust "person" under the Sherman Act, and, therefore is not subject to antitrust liability [U.S. Postal Service v. Flamingo Industries (USA) Ltd., 540 U.S. 736 (2004)].

   b. **Taxation of the Federal Government by a State**

      (1) In accordance with McCulloch v. Maryland [17 U.S. 316 (1819)], the federal government and its agencies are immune from state taxation and state regulation. States may nevertheless collect a nondiscriminatory tax on persons who deal or contract with the federal government.

         (a) A nondiscriminatory gross-receipts tax applied to a contractor performing work for the federal government has been upheld [James v. Dravo Contracting Co., 302 U.S. 134 (1937)].

         (b) A state's sales tax on goods purchased by a contractor, even if the goods will eventually be sold to the United States, is valid. In a "cost-plus" contract with the federal government, the tax will be part of the cost [Alabama v. King & Boozer, 314 U.S. 1 (1941)].

1) However, such a sales tax is invalid if it falls upon the federal government itself.

(c) A state property tax is valid when applied upon a building owned by the United States but used by a contractor [Detroit v. Murray Corp., 355 U.S. 489 (1959)]. Likewise, a building owned by a contractor doing work for the United States will be subject to a property tax.

(d) A state income tax applied to employees of the United States domiciled within that state is valid [Graves v. O'Keefe, 306 U.S. 466 (1939)].

c. As a general rule, the Supremacy Clause impliedly prevents the states from regulating the activities of agents or instrumentalities of the federal government if the regulation will interfere with the government's ability to carry out its federal functions [Johnson v. Maryland, 254 U.S. 51 (1920)].

(1) Congress has the power "to dispose of and make all needful rules and regulations respecting the territory or other property belonging to the United States." Thus, federal lands (e.g., military bases, Indian reservations, FBI offices, etc.) are subject to the authority of the federal government, except to the extent that Congress has ceded jurisdiction to the state [U.S. Const. art. IV, § 3, cl. 2].

EXAMPLE: States cannot require a federal contractor to obtain a state license to construct facilities at an Air Force base located within the state [Miller Inc. v. Arkansas, 352 U.S. 187 (1956)].

2. **Immunity of State Governments**

a. The federal government, or one of its agencies or instrumentalities, may sue a state without its consent. In this case, the Supreme Court has original, but not exclusive, jurisdiction.

b. A state may be sued by a sister state without its consent. In this case, the Supreme Court has original and exclusive jurisdiction.

c. As a general rule, the Eleventh Amendment prohibits citizens of one state from suing another state in federal court. This rule has been extended to prohibit suits by a citizen of a state against his own state. However, some exceptions do exist to this rule. In particular [Ex parte Young, 209 U.S. 123 (1908)]:

(1) a state may be sued if it consents to the suit; and

(2) a state officer may be sued for injunctive relief on the theory that his allegedly unlawful conduct was beyond the scope of his authority.

d. Congress is generally limited to the powers granted to it by the Constitution and, as explained above, is prohibited by the Tenth Amendment from "commandeering" state governments. The Supreme Court has attempted to limit Congress' use of the Commerce Clause to regulate integral operations in areas of traditional government functions [National League of Cities v. Usery, 426 U.S. 833 (1976)].

(1) However, Usery was overruled in 1985 by a decision in which the Supreme Court found that drawing immunity boundaries around "traditional government functions" was unworkable and "inconsistent with established principles of federalism" [Garcia v. San Antonio Metro. Transit Auth., 469 U.S. 528 (1985)].

e. A state now enjoys immunity from federal taxation if the tax is applied to either:

(1) unique state activities; or

(2) essential governmental functions.

NOTE ▶ Where a state engages in a proprietary business (i.e., one similar in nature to a business operated by a private individual), then the state may be taxed to the same extent as the private citizen.

C. **Authority Reserved for the States**

1. **The Tenth Amendment**

a. The Tenth Amendment provides that the "powers not delegated to the United States by the Constitution, nor prohibited by it to the states, are reserved to the states respectively, or to the people."

EXAM TIP ▶ The Tenth Amendment is frequently a "red herring" wrong answer choice except when the facts show the federal government "commanding" the states.

b. The Constitution specifically prohibits any state from [U.S. Const. art. I, § 10]:

(1) making treaties with other nations;

(2) coining money;

(3) passing a bill of attainder;

(4) enacting an *ex post facto* law;

(5) impairing the obligation of contracts;

(6) laying any duty on imports or exports, except where necessary for executing its inspection laws;

(7) engaging in war; or

(8) maintaining a peacetime army.

c. The Tenth Amendment prohibits the federal government from using an enumerated power to force a state legislature to pass a law or a state executive official to administer a federal program. This is known as the **anti-commandeering doctrine**.

2. **The Dormant Commerce Clause**

a. The Commerce Clause gives Congress the power to regulate interstate commerce. Where Congress has not enacted legislation, the states are free to regulate local transactions affecting interstate commerce, subject to certain limitations. These limitations are generally known as the **dormant Commerce Clause**, or the **negative implications doctrine**.

b. If a state law discriminates on its face between in-state and out-of-state economic actors, the state must show that:

    (1) the regulation serves a compelling state interest; and

    (2) the regulation is narrowly tailored to serve that interest.

c. If a state law merely incidentally burdens interstate commerce, the court will apply a balancing test and the law will be upheld unless the burden imposed on interstate commerce clearly outweighs the local benefits [Pike v. Bruce Church, Inc., 397 U.S. 137, 142 (1970)].

d. There are some exceptions to the dormant Commerce Clause which should be noted:

    (1) Congress may affirmatively authorize states to legislate in areas that would violate the dormant Commerce clause; and

    (2) when states act as market participants, they may discriminate between in-state and out-of-state businesses.

e. Traditionally, it is within the state's police power to enact legislation for the protection of the health, safety, and welfare of its citizens.

EXAMPLE: A Detroit smoke-abatement ordinance that affected ships traveling in interstate commerce was upheld as a valid health measure [Huron Portland Cement Co. v. City of Detroit, 352 U.S. 440 (1960)].

f. If a state regulation furthers no ostensible benefit and imposes a substantial burden on interstate commerce, it will likely be held unconstitutional.

EXAMPLE: An Illinois statute requiring all trucks to be equipped with a new type of contour mudguards (instead of the flat mudguards permitted in all other states) was declared unconstitutional because it placed an undue burden on interstate carriers [Bibb v. Navajo Freight Lines, Inc., 359 U.S. 520 (1959)].

EXAMPLE: A state law limiting the length of trucks traveling on state highways or trains rolling through the state is unconstitutional because the regulation unduly burdened interstate commerce, and the state failed to demonstrate any significant safety benefit [Raymond Motor Transportation, Inc. v. Rice, 434 U.S. 429 (1978)].

g. Generally, public health measures (e.g., quarantine and inspection laws) are upheld so long as they do not discriminate against or unduly burden interstate commerce [Hannibal & St. Joseph Railroad v. Husen, 95 U.S. 465 (1877)].

D. Reserved State Power in Taxation

1. As a general rule, state taxation of interstate commerce is permissible as long as the tax does not discriminate against or unduly burden interstate commerce. In determining the validity of a state tax affecting interstate commerce, the court will generally consider the following four factors [Complete Auto Transit, Inc. v. Brady, 430 U.S. 274 (1977)]:

a. there must be a substantial nexus between the activity taxed and the taxing state;

    (1) In other words, the taxpayer must have "sufficient contacts" or presence within the taxing state.

    (2) "Substantial nexus" is more than "minimum contacts" under the Due Process Clause.

    EXAMPLE: The solicitation by mail and shipping of goods by common carrier or postal service, although enough to show "minimum contacts," does not satisfy the "substantial nexus" requirement [Quill Corp. v. North Dakota, 504 U.S. 298 (1983)].

> **NOTE** A regular operation within a state, despite owning no property, is enough to show "substantial nexus"—for example, an airline operating regularly scheduled flights from a rented station [Braniff Airways, Inc. v. Neb. Bd. of Equalization, 347 U.S. 590 (1954)].

b. the tax must be fairly apportioned;

    (1) The taxpayer has the burden of proving unfair apportionment.

    EXAMPLE: The Supreme Court invalidated an apportionment based upon track mileage within the state, as compared with total track mileage, which resulted in a disproportionate tax because the railroad had an unusually large amount of track in the taxing state [Norfolk & Western Railway v. Missouri Tax Commission, 390 U.S. 317 (1968)].

c. the tax must not discriminate against interstate commerce; and

    (1) A tax favoring local commerce over interstate commerce will be invalidated under the Commerce Clause unless it is authorized by Congress [Prudential Insurance Co. v. Benjamin, 328 U.S. 408 (1946)].

    (2) Article IV, Section 2 (the Privileges and Immunities Clause) prohibits state taxes that discriminate against nonresidents [Austin v. New Hampshire, 420 U.S. 656 (1975)].

d. the tax must be fairly related to the services provided by the taxing state.

THE STATE TAX ON INTERSTATE COMMERCE IS VALID IF...

- It is not preempted by federal law.
- It does not discriminate against interstate commerce.
- It has a substantial nexus.
- There is a fair apportionment and relationship.

---

2. **Various Types of State Taxes**

a. States are not permitted to levy an *ad valorem* tax on "goods" that happen to be in the taxing state on the tax day if those goods are still in the course of transit [Standard Oil Co. v. Peck, 342 U.S. 382 (1952)]. However, the validity of such *ad valorem* property taxes as applied to "instrumentalities of commerce" (e.g., airplanes or railroad cars) depends upon:

(1) whether there is a taxable *situs* (or nexus) within the state; and

(2) whether the tax is fairly apportioned to the amount of time the equipment is in the state.

b. A **sales tax** is a tax upon the transfer of title of goods consummated within the state.

(1) If the sale is consummated within the state (even though the buyer takes the goods outside the state), a sales tax is valid. If, however, the sale is made to a buyer outside the state (i.e., if the seller delivers the goods to an out-of-state buyer), then the sales tax is invalid.

c. On the other hand, a **use tax** is a tax upon the use of goods within the state that were purchased outside the state.

(1) The ability of a state to collect a use tax usually depends upon whether the interstate seller, who receives goods from outside the state, has a sufficient nexus within the taxing state.

(a) Where the seller maintains offices within the taxing state (or even sends salespeople into the state as employees or independent contractors), there is a sufficient nexus even though the use tax was imposed on interstate mail-order sales [National Geographic Society v. California Board of Equalization, 430 U.S. 551 (1977)].

(b) In contrast, if no sales office is maintained in the state and all selling is done by mail, there is not a sufficient nexus with the taxing state to justify the collection of a use tax [National Bellas Hess, Inc. v. Department of Revenue, 386 U.S. 753 (1967)].

d. **Doing-business taxes** (variously referred to as "privilege," "occupa-tion," "franchise," "license," "gross receipts" or "net income" taxes) can be measured by either a flat annual fee or a graduated rate based in proportion on the amount of revenue derived from the taxing state. As a general rule, such taxes must "relate to the benefits" conferred by the taxing state upon the interstate business.

EXAMPLE: A fee applied to airport users was held constitutional because it bore a reasonable relationship to use of the facilities by the passengers [Evansville-Vanderburgh Airport Authority v. Delta Airlines, Inc., 405 U.S. 707 (1972)].

e. **Net income taxes** may be applied by the state upon a company engaging in interstate commerce or on a nonresident engaged in business in the taxing state. A net income tax is valid only as long as the tax is fairly apportioned, has a significant nexus, and is nondiscriminatory [Northwestern States Portland Cement Co. v. Minnesota, 358 U.S. 450 (1959)].

f. A **flat license fee** is generally unconstitutional. This is a fee levied by the state upon drummers, or solicitors who solicit local orders and then fill them out-of-state and ship them through interstate commerce [Nippert v. Richmond, 327 U.S. 416 (1946)].

g. A **license tax** on a peddler, or itinerant salesperson, is valid when a state levies it upon a seller who actually sells and delivers the product within the state. A license is valid as nondiscriminatory only as long as the tax is fairly apportioned with an equal application to local salespeople.

IV. TYPE OF ACTION GOVERNED BY THE CONSTITUTION

A. **State Action versus Private Action**

1. In order to show a constitutional violation either by the state or federal governments, the plaintiff must first show that there is governmental action. Constitutional rights can be violated only by governmental actors, not by private actors. This is called the **state action requirement**. In this context, **state action** is a term of art referring to governmental action either by the federal or state governments.

2. **Fourteenth and Fifteenth Amendments**

   a. The Fourteenth Amendment says, "No State shall make or enforce any law which shall abridge the privileges or immunities of citizens of the United States; nor shall any State deprive any person of life, liberty or property without due process of the law; nor deny to any person within its jurisdiction the equal protection of the laws."

   b. The Fifteenth Amendment prohibits the state and federal governments from denying the right to vote based on race.

   c. The Fourteenth and Fifteenth Amendments therefore prohibit governmental conduct, and not private conduct which infringes upon protected individual rights.

3. **Federal Violation of Constitutional Rights**

   a. Private actors cannot violate the Bill of Rights and other constitutional amendments that constrain the federal government. The federal government, but not private actors, can violate those individual rights.

4. **Exceptions**

   a. There are two exceptions to the rule that constitutional rights can be violated only by governmental action. State action can be found in the actions of private actors under:

      (1) the **public function theory**, where a private entity is carrying on activities traditionally and exclusively performed by the government; or

      (2) the **significant state involvement, endorsement, or encouragement theory**, where the government and private entity are so closely related that the action by the private party fairly can be treated as action by the government.

5. **Examples of State Action**

   a. **Where the Private Activity Performs an Exclusive Public Function**

      (1) In Marsh v. Alabama [326 U.S. 501 (1946)], a private company owned an entire town. A member of the Jehovah's Witnesses was arrested and convicted of violating a state trespass law that made it a crime "to enter or remain on the premises of another." The Supreme Court reversed the trespass conviction because the town's streets, although privately owned, were the functional equivalent of city streets. The Supreme Court held that the company's actions were in violation of the First and Fourteenth

Amendments because neither a state nor a private owner can totally ban the expression of free speech.

> **NOTE** The Supreme Court has ruled that the "company town" rationale did not apply to a privately owned shopping center [Hudgens v. National Labor Relations Board, 424 U.S. 507 (1976)].

      (2)   In Smith v. Allwright [321 U.S. 649 (1944)], the Supreme Court held that because holding an election is a public function, a political party could not racially discriminate against blacks by excluding them from voting in a primary election.

   b.   Where there is "significant state involvement" in private discrimination, the constitutional right of equal protection may be applicable.

EXAMPLE: A restaurant owner, whose business was located in a building owned by the city, was prohibited from discriminating against racial minorities. The Court found that there was a "symbiotic relation-ship" between the city and the restaurant [Burton v. Wilmington Parking Authority, 365 U.S. 715 (1961)].

EXAMPLE: State court enforcement of restrictive covenants prohibit-ing the sale of property to blacks was held to involve sufficient state involvement so as to constitute state action [Shelley v. Kraemer, 334 U.S. 1 (1948)].

EXAMPLE: However, state action was not found in granting a liquor license to a private club that racially discriminated against blacks [Moose Lodge No. 107 v. Irvis, 407 U.S. 163 (1972)].

EXAMPLE: More recently, the Supreme Court found state action be-cause of the "entwinement" between a state and a private organization that regulated interscholastic athletic competitions among public and private secondary schools [Brentwood Academy v. Tennessee Second-ary School Athletic Association, 531 U.S. 288 (2001)].

6. **Thirteenth Amendment**

   a.   The Thirteenth Amendment prohibits slavery and involuntary servitude. The amendment has been interpreted as providing Congress with the power to pass legislation prohibiting badges and incidents of slavery, and thus can be used to proscribe purely private acts of forced labor without the requirement of state action.

B. **National Power to Override State Authority**

1. **Supremacy Clause**

   a.   The Supremacy Clause provides that the Constitution, treaties, and laws of the United States are "the supreme Law of the Land." In general, a federal law will supersede any state law with which it is in direct conflict. Furthermore, Congress can preempt any state law in an area in which the exercise of federal power is constitutional [U.S. Const. art. IV, § 2].

(1) Where Congress does not intend to occupy a field completely, and state laws are not otherwise preempted, the states may enact similar legislation.

EXAMPLE: A state statute prohibiting racial discrimination was held valid even though there was a substantially identical federal law [Colorado Anti-Discrimination Commission v. Continental Air Lines, Inc., 372 U.S. 714 (1963)].

(2) Greater state protection is also permitted. Where Congress has legislated to establish minimum standards (such as in the areas of health and safety requirements pertaining to food and drugs or the regulation of roads and highways), then the states are free to enact more stringent standards than those mandated by federal law.

EXAMPLE: A municipal smoke-abatement statute was held valid even though it imposed stricter standards than the federal regulation [Huron Portland Cement Co. v. City of Detroit, 362 U.S. 440 (1960)].

V. DUE PROCESS AND THE INCORPORATION OF PORTIONS OF THE BILL OF RIGHTS

A. **Incorporation of the Bill of Rights**

1. As originally enacted, the Bill of Rights (the first 10 amendments to the U.S. Constitution) was applicable only to the federal government, not to the states. In 1868, the Fourteenth Amendment was adopted, which provided: "No State shall make or enforce any law which shall abridge the privileges or immunities of citizens of the United States; nor shall any State deprive any person of life, liberty, or property, without due process of law; nor deny to any person within its jurisdiction the equal protection of the laws."

2. **Fourteenth Amendment Privileges and Immunities Clause**

   a. A few years after the Fourteenth Amendment was adopted, the Supreme Court held that the fundamental rights set forth in the Bill of Rights were not privileges and immunities of national citizenship [Slaughter-House Cases, 83 U.S. 36 (1873)].

   b. In 1999, the Supreme Court held that under the Fourteenth Amendment Privileges and Immunities Clause (along with the fundamental right to travel), new residents could challenge a state's denial of full unemployment benefits until a specified waiting period had been satisfied.

   c. The Court struck down a California law that limited the payment of welfare benefits for first-year residents to the amount they would have received from their former state. The law violated the right to travel freely from state to state, which the Court said is protected by the Fourteenth Amendment Privileges and Immunities Clause as a right of national citizenship [Saenz v. Roe, 526 U.S. 489 (1999)].

3. **Fourteenth Amendment Due Process Clause**

   a. Although the Supreme Court rejected the argument that the Due Process Clause incorporated all of the Bill of Rights, under the **doctrine of selective incorporation**, the following specific provisions are now applicable to the states [Adamson v. California [332 U.S. 46 (1947)]:

      (1) the First Amendment freedom of speech and freedom of press, the right to assemble and petition the government for a redress of grievances, the right to free exercise of religion, and the prohibition against the establishment of religion;

      (2) the Fourth Amendment provisions guaranteeing the right to be free from unreasonable searches and seizures [Ker v. California, 374 U.S. 23 (1963)];

      (3) the Fifth Amendment protection against double jeopardy [Benton v. Maryland, 395 U.S. 784 (1969)], privilege against self-incrimination [Malloy v. Hogan, 378 U.S. 1 (1964)], and requirement of just compensation when private property is taken for public use;

      (4) the Sixth Amendment rights guaranteeing the accused in criminal prosecutions a speedy and public trial [Klopfer v. North Carolina,

386 U.S. 213 (1967)], the right to confront and cross-examine witnesses [Pointer v. Texas, 380 U.S. 400 (1965)], the right to counsel [Gideon v. Wainwright, 372 U.S. 335 (1963)], and the right to a jury trial in criminal cases [Duncan v. Louisiana, 391 U.S. 145 (1968)];

(5) the Eighth Amendment prohibition against cruel and unusual punishments; and

(6) the Supreme Court recently held that, in addition to applying to the District of Columbia, the Second Amendment right to keep and bear arms applies to state and local governments.

EXAMPLE: A Chicago law banning possession of handguns by almost all private citizens was found to be invalid. In *dictum*, however, the Court said that many traditional state gun regulations will still be upheld [McDonald v. City of Chicago, 130 S. Ct. 3020 (2010)].

b. Major rights not incorporated include:

(1) the Fifth Amendment right to a grand jury in criminal cases; and

(2) the Seventh Amendment right to a jury trial in civil cases.

THE BILL OF RIGHTS STOPS HERE!	
The Fourteenth Amendment extends the Bill of Rights EXCEPT:	
NO RIGHT TO	• Prevent quartering soldiers in your home (Third). • Grand jury indictment (Fifth). • Civil jury trial (Seventh). • Prevent excessive fines (Eighth).

c. **Scope of the Due Process Clause**

(1) The Due Process and Equal Protection Clauses of the Fourteenth Amendment protect the rights of "persons," and not merely "citizens."

(2) A corporation is considered a "person" for purposes of due process and equal protection. Note, however, that a corporation is not entitled to the privilege against self-incrimination.

(3) Aliens are considered "persons" for purposes of due process and equal protection.

B. **Procedural Due Process**

1. Both the Fifth and Fourteenth Amendments protect against the deprivation of life, liberty, or property without the due process of the law. Where there is a deprivation of one's "life," "liberty," or "property" interests, the individual is entitled to fundamentally fair procedural safeguards (e.g., some form of notice and a meaningful hearing within a reasonable time).

2. **Deprivation of Liberty**
   a. Acts that invade a liberty interest include:
      (1) freedom from bodily restraints;
         (a) A state must grant a parolee an evidentiary hearing before it revokes parole or probation [Morrissey v. Brewer, 408 U.S. 471 (1972)].
      (2) physical punishment; and
         (a) Corporal punishment of pupils in a public school is valid, although a liberty interest exists [Ingraham v. Wright, 430 U.S. 651 (1977)].
      (3) commitment to a mental institution.
         (a) An adversary hearing must be provided to adults before they are committed to a mental institution against their will. Minor children have a liberty interest in not being confined unnecessarily for medical treatment. In the case of minor children, a screening by a neutral fact-finder is required [Parham v. J.R., 442 U.S. 584 (1979)].
   b. Acts that do not invade a liberty interest include:
      (1) injury to reputation; and
         (a) Injury to one's reputation in the absence of a related harm to a more tangible interest (such as an employment opportunity) is not a deprivation of a liberty interest [Paul v. Davis, 424 U.S. 693 (1976)].
      (2) forced administration of medicine.
         (a) The federal government may administer antipsychotic drugs against a defendant's will in order to render him competent to stand trial, as long as the treatment is medically appropriate, does not cause substantial side effects, and is necessary to significantly further important governmental trial-related interests [Sell v. United States, 539 U.S. 166 (2003)].

3. **Property Interests**
   a. **Public Education**
      (1) There is a constitutionally protected property interest in the statutory entitlement to continued attendance at a public school [Goss v. Lopez, 419 U.S. 565 (1975)].
      (2) On the other hand, no prior evidentiary hearing is required when a student is dismissed for academic reasons [Board of Curators of University of Missouri v. Horowitz, 435 U.S. 78 (1978)].
   b. **Continued Welfare Benefits**
      (1) A property interest is created by a statutory entitlement to continued welfare benefits [Goldberg v. Kelly, 397 U.S. 254 (1970)].
   c. **Retention of Driver's License**
      (1) A state may not revoke a driver's license without a hearing [Bell v. Burson, 402 U.S. 535 (1971)].

d. **Public Employment**

    (1)   There is a property interest in a person keeping his job if the employment is under a tenure system or there is a clear understanding, either express or implied, that the employee can be terminated only for "cause" [Perry v. Sindermann, 408 U.S. 593 (1972)].

    (2)   However, the Supreme Court has held that there was no property interest where a police officer held his position "at the will of" the public employer [Bishop v. Wood, 426 U.S. 341 (1976)].

    (3)   Furthermore, there is no property interest when a state refuses to renew a fixed-term contract [Board of Regents v. Roth, 408 U.S. 564 (1972)].

e. **Prejudgment Garnishment**

    (1)   Prejudgment attachment or garnishment of wages, without notice or hearing, violates procedural due process [Sniadach v. Family Finance Corp., 395 U.S. 337 (1969)].

    (2)   A due process property interest does not arise when an individual is first applying for employment. However, if the person has already been getting employment benefits, he has a property interest in continuing the receipt of those benefits.

f. **Forfeiture of Property**

    (1)   Due process is satisfied where the government sends a certified letter to prison to notify an inmate that property seized will be forfeited, because such an action is "reasonably calculated, under the circumstances, to apprise interested parties of the pendency of the action and afford them an opportunity to present their objections." Actual notice is not required; constructive notice will suffice [Dusenbery v. United States, 534 U.S. 161 (2002)].

g. **Business Licensing**

    (1)   The First Amendment and due process require that a licensing scheme for adult businesses provide applicants with "prompt judicial determination" of their claim that the government unconstitutionally denied a license, as opposed to mere prompt access to judicial review [City of Littleton v. Z.J. Gifts D-4, L.L.C., 541 U.S. 774 (2004)].

> **NOTE**   As with any other constitutional right, procedural due process is not required where there is no "state action" [Flagg Brothers v. Brooks, 436 U.S. 149 (1978)].

4. **Life Interests**

a. Capital punishment is clearly a deprivation of a life interest, and rigorous due process protections are applicable. When life interests have been claimed in other contexts, such as in abortion or right-to-die situations, the Supreme Court has addressed it under other provisions of the Constitution.

5. **Type of Process Required**

a. Once it is determined that there is a sufficient deprivation of life, liberty, or property, the next step is to decide what process is required. In order to determine what procedural safeguards are necessary, the Supreme Court set forth the following factors to look at [Mathews v. Eldridge, 424 U.S. 319 (1976)]:

(1) the private interest that will be affected by the official action,

(2) the risk of an erroneous deprivation of this interest through the procedures used, and the probable value of additional or substitute procedures; and

(3) the government's interest in streamlined procedures, including the function involved and the fiscal and administrative burdens that the additional or substitute procedural requirements would entail.

EXAMPLE: The Supreme Court held that a full hearing was not required for the dismissal of a medical student from a state medical school for academic deficiency because the decision was an evaluative one, made by faculty officers and outside practitioners [Bd. of Curators of Univ. of Missouri v. Horowitz, 435 U.S. 78 (1979)].

EXAMPLE: The Supreme Court held that it was not necessary for a public school to give a student a hearing before imposing corporal punishment [Ingraham v. Wright, 430 U.S. 651 (1997)].

EXAMPLE: The Supreme Court ruled that a temporary suspension of a driver's license without a hearing, where the driver refused to take a breathalyzer test, was valid, because he had a right to an immediate hearing following the suspension [Mackey v. Montrym, 443 U.S. 1 (1979)].

b. Due process requires a judge to recuse himself when the judge has a pecuniary interest in the case, such that an average judge would "possibly be tempted" to render an "imbalanced or untrue" judgment.

EXAMPLE: If one party to a case had a "significant and disproportionate influence" in getting the judge elected, then due process requires that the judge recuse himself. Such a disproportionate influence exists when, for example, an appellant contributed more than 50% of all campaign contributions to the appellate judge's election campaign [Caperton v. A. T. Massey Coal Co., 556 U.S. 868 (2009)].

6. **Irrebuttable Presumptions**

a. In recent cases, the Supreme Court has held that irrebuttable presumptions violate procedural due process.

b. **Civil Proceedings**

(1) The Supreme Court held that a statutory presumption that a pregnant schoolteacher was physically incapable of performing her duties was unconstitutional [Cleveland Board of Education v. LaFleur, 414 U.S. 632 (1974)].

(2) A state law requiring children of unwed fathers to become wards of the court was invalidated because its statutory effect was to create a conclusive presumption that unwed fathers were unfit parents [Stanley v. Illinois, 405 U.S. 645 (1972)].

c. **Criminal Cases**

(1) A statutory presumption that possession of marijuana was conclusive proof that the drug had been imported was invalidated, because marijuana is frequently grown in the United States as well as abroad [Leary v. United States, 395 U.S. 6 (1969)].

CONSTITUTIONAL LAW ANALYSIS TIPS	
when you see this...	**...remember this**
Thirteenth Amendment	• Best answer when private individuals, who do not qualify as state actors, discriminate.
Fourteenth Amendment	• All the elements of the Constitution incorporated into the amendment are, hence, protected by it. • Frequently best answer when First Amendment right of free speech or freedom of religion is not offered as a choice.
Commerce Clause	• Grants Congress the power to enact legislation that affects interstate commerce. • Important source of congressional power over civil rights. • Does not empower Congress to push states into acting.
Contract Clause	• Can be an issue where the state revokes a contract to which it is a party.
Dormant Commerce Clause	• Legal doctrine inferred from Commerce Clause. • Prohibits a state from passing legislation that improperly burdens or discriminates against interstate commerce.

Due Process Clause	• Best choice for an unconstitutional argument when:
	  1. state acts; or
	  2. state does not grant a hearing or invades privacy rights.

Equal Protection Clause	• Best option when state action interferes with a fundamental interest (e.g., right to vote or travel, or classifications by race, alienage, or sex).
General Welfare Power or Spending Power	• Congress' power to spend treasury funds, but not to regulate activity. • Best answer when voluntary cooperation by party with federal government is the ONLY way to reach result.
Police Power	• Can be the answer only when state action versus federal action.
Privileges and Immunities Clause	• Bars states from discriminating against nonresidents on fundamental matters, unless the regulation in question specifically targets a problem arising from such nonresident's behavior. • The Privileges and Immunities Clause of the Fourteenth Amendment is almost never a correct answer.

CONSTITUTIONAL LAW ANALYSIS TIPS	
when you see this...	**...remember this**
Supremacy Clause	• Not a congressional power. • Not a good choice unless there is a congressional statute or provision conflicting with a state activity.
Taxing Power	• Allowed for regulatory purposes if there is a revenue-raising function. • Best answer if Commerce Clause isn't available.

EXAM TIP When answering a question involving the various arguments that can be used to attack the constitutionality of a statute regulating economic activity, you should still consider the argument that it violates substantive due process, especially if the statute operates in an arbitrary and unreasonable manner and there is no legitimate reason for the legislature to pass the statute.

WHEN SHOULD THE SUPREME COURT AVOID A CONSTITUTIONAL DECISION?

1. When there is no issue in controversy—no adversarial conflict between the parties.
2. When the complainant cannot show injury by the statute in question.
3. When the issue isn't ripe and the Supreme Court doesn't feel the issue has arisen yet.
4. When the decision requires a ruling broader than the facts of the case.
5. When the complaint can be resolved in a nonconstitutional manner (e.g., by a statute).
6. When the Court can determine a statutory construction that avoids constitutional analysis.
7. When the complainant benefited from the statute it now argues is unconstitutional.

C. Substantive Due Process

1. **Economic Regulation**

   a. In the past, the doctrine of substantive due process was frequently used to protect rights of property and contract and to invalidate legislation that regulated economic activity. However, this approach to substantive due process was abandoned by the Supreme Court in the 1930s.

   b. The Supreme Court held that challenges to economic regulation are to be subjected to deferential rational basis scrutiny, with a challenger having the burden of proving that a regulation lacks a rational connection to a legitimate government interest. As a result, since the New Deal, the Supreme Court has not struck down any economic regulation on substantive due process grounds.

   c. Such an economic regulation will be upheld if it is rationally related to a legitimate government interest.

2. **Fundamental Rights**

   a. The substantive due process doctrine is now used to evaluate governmental regulations that affect fundamental rights of personhood, rather than rights of property. Strict scrutiny review, or other forms of heightened scrutiny, apply to laws that burden the exercise of fundamental rights, including the right to vote, the right to travel, the right to privacy, First Amendment rights, family rights, and other rights referred to as fundamental rights.

   b. The following are some of the categories that fall under the penumbra of privacy rights.

   c. **Contraceptives**

      (1) The Supreme Court invalidated a state law prohibiting the use of contraceptive devices, thus recognizing a right of marital privacy [Griswold v. Connecticut, 381 U.S. 479 (1965)].

      (2) The Supreme Court later expanded the Griswold decision and held that the right to use contraceptives belonged to single as well as married persons [Eisenstadt v. Baird, 405 U.S. 438 (1972)].

      (3) In Carey v. Population Services International [431 U.S. 678 (1977)], the Supreme Court invalidated a state law that prohibited the sale of contraceptives to minors except through a licensed pharmacist.

   d. **Marriage**

      (1) The right to marry is deemed fundamental. Any substantial interference with that right must be necessary to further a compelling interest [Zablocki v. Redhail, 434 U.S. 374 (1978)].

   e. **Abortion**

      (1) Planned Parenthood of Southeastern Pennsylvania v. Casey [505 U.S. 833 (1992)] modified the Supreme Court's approach to reproductive freedom that was established in Roe v. Wade [410 U.S. 113 (1973)]. The Casey holding rejected the trimester approach of Roe and instead adopted an "undue burden" standard.

         (a) A woman has a protected privacy interest in choosing to have an abortion before the fetus is viable.

         (b) During the first two trimesters (that is, before viability), the government may regulate (but not ban) abortion in the interest either of the mother's health or of the potential life of the fetus. The regulation may not impose an "undue burden" on the woman's right to choose an abortion.

         (c) For the period of time subsequent to viability, the Supreme Court reaffirmed Roe in concluding that a state may "regulate, and even proscribe, abortion except where it is necessary…for the preservation of the life or health of the mother."

      (2) **Consent Requirements**

         (a) Neither spousal notification nor spousal consent may be required before a woman may obtain an abortion [Planned Parenthood of Missouri v. Danforth, 428 U.S. 52 (1976)].

      (b) However, parental consent may be required before an unemancipated woman under the age of 18 obtains an abortion if the state establishes a "judicial bypass" procedure through which a minor may obtain an abortion with the consent of a judge [Hodgson v. Minnesota, 497 U.S. 417 (1990)].

    (3) **Public Funding**

      (a) There is no constitutional right for indigent women to obtain government funding for abortions [Maher v. Roe, 432 U.S. 464 (1977)]. Furthermore, a state may prohibit the use of public facilities and publicly employed staff in performing abortions [Webster v. Reproductive Health Services, 492 U.S. 490 (1989)].

    (4) **Late-Term Abortion**

      (a) Where a Nebraska statute prohibited "deliberately and intentionally delivering into the vagina a living unborn child, or a substantial portion thereof, for the purpose of performing a procedure that the person performing such procedure knows will kill the unborn child and does kill the unborn child," such a statute was unconstitutional because it did not provide an exception for the health of the mother and because it prohibited the dilation and evacuation procedure used in most second-trimester abortions, as well as the less frequently used "partial-birth" procedure [Stenberg v. Carhart, 530 U.S. 914 (2000)].

      (b) Subsequently, the Supreme Court upheld a federal ban on partial-birth abortions [Gonzales v. Carhart, 550 U.S. 124 (2007)]. The Court rejected a facial challenge to a prohibition against use of this particular type of abortion procedure, but left open the possibility of challenges to the act as applied to specific individuals.

f. **Family Relations**

    (1) A fundamental right exists for related persons to live together. A zoning ordinance prohibiting members of an extended family from living in a single household has been subjected to heightened scrutiny and held unconstitutional [Moore v. City of East Cleveland, 431 U.S. 494 (1977)].

NOTE This fundamental right does not apply to unrelated persons [Belle Terre v. Boraas, 416 U.S. 1 (1974)].

g. **Sexual Orientation**

    (1) In Lawrence v. Texas [539 U.S. 558 (2003)], the Supreme Court applied a stringent form of rational basis scrutiny and held that a statute making it a crime for a person to engage "in deviate sexual intercourse with another individual of the same sex" furthered no legitimate state interest.

    (2) Parents were held to have a protected liberty interest concerning the control of visitation with their children by others, including grandparents [Troxel v. Granville, 530 U.S. 57 (2000)].

h. **Private Education**

(1) Parents have a right to privately educate their children outside the public school system [Pierce v. Society of Sisters, 268 U.S. 510 (1925)].

i. **Obscene Material**

(1) The right to possess obscene material in the privacy of one's home is protected [Stanley v. Georgia, 394 U.S. 557 (1969)].

(2) However, the government can severely restrict the sale, purchase, receipt, transport, and distribution of obscene materials, both in stores and through the mail. Furthermore, the state can criminalize even the private possession of child pornography [Osborne v. Ohio, 495 U.S. 103 (1990)].

j. **Right to Die**

(1) The right of a terminally ill or comatose person to choose to die is not presently a fundamental right.

(2) Nevertheless, a person has a well established due process "liberty" interest in not being forced to undergo unwanted medical procedures, such as life-support [Cruzan v. Missouri Department of Health, 497 U.S. 261 (1990)].

(3) However, the state has a countervailing interest in preserving life. A terminally ill patient has no right to assisted suicide [Washington v. Glucksberg, 521 U.S. 702 (1997)].

k. **Right to Travel**

(1) The Privileges and Immunities Clause of Article IV, Section 2 and the Commerce Clause mutually enforce the right of every citizen to travel freely from state to state [Griffin v. Breckenridge, 403 U.S. 88 (1971)].

(2) Durational residency requirements for dispensing government benefits are subject to strict scrutiny.

EXAMPLE: A one-year waiting period before receiving welfare benefits or state-subsidized medical care is invalid.

EXAMPLE: Reasonable residency requirements are valid for obtaining a divorce as well as for obtaining reduced tuition at state universities.

(3) The right to international travel is not absolute and may be subject to reasonable restrictions, and Congress may authorize the president to restrict travel to certain countries or danger areas [Zemel v. Rusk, 381 U.S. 1 (1965)].

EXAM TIP The Privileges and Immunities Clause of the Fourteenth Amendment has frequently been a wrong answer on the MBE. Almost all the privileges and immunities are protected by the Commerce Clause, Due Process Clause, or Equal Protection Clause. However, the Privileges and Immunities Clause is not entirely dead: In Saenz v. Roe [526 U.S. 489 (1999)], the Supreme Court ruled that it was an alternative to an Equal Protection Clause protection with regard to the right to travel.

I. **Right to Vote**

(1) The fundamental right of U.S. citizens over age 18 to vote extends to all federal, state, and local elections, as well as to primaries. Strict scrutiny review is used to adjudicate restrictions on the right to vote.

(2) However, government regulations of ballot-access by candidates–based upon age, duration of residency, or payment of filing fees–require only minimum rational basis scrutiny.

    (a) In addition, voter registration requirements and regulation of the time, place, and manner of casting ballots are valid so long as they do not impose an "undue burden" on the right to vote.

(3) A rule of "one-person, one-vote" is generally followed. Whenever the government attempts to establish a new apportionment or redistricting scheme, fairly exact mathematical equality between districts is required so as not to dilute the fundamental right to vote.

(4) There must be equality in the distribution of the right to vote.

EXAMPLE: Imposition of a poll tax as a prerequisite to vote violates equal protection and is unconstitutional [Harper v. Virginia Board of Elections, 383 U.S. 663 (1966)].

EXAMPLE: Limiting voting for school board elections to parents of schoolchildren and/or property owners is unconstitutional [Kramer v. Union Free School District, 345 U.S. 662 (1969)].

EXCEPTION: Voting can be limited to landowners for a special purpose "water-storage district" (which cannot enact laws or perform government functions) [Ball v. James, 451 U.S. 355 (1981)].

D. **Takings Clause**

1. The Fifth Amendment provides that private property shall not be taken for public use without just compensation. This prohibition also applies to the states through the Due Process Clause of the Fourteenth Amendment.

2. In Agins v. City of Tiburon [447 U.S. 255 (1980)], the Supreme Court held that a taking of property occurs if a regulation of private property "does not substantially advance legitimate state interests."

    a. Agins was overruled in Lingle v. Chevron U.S.A., Inc. [544 U.S. 528 (2005)], in which the Supreme Court held that the extent to which a regulation advances a legitimate state interest is not a relevant factor in determining if a taking has occurred.

3. Property can be taken by a variety of means, including:

    a. direct government appropriation;

        (1) Where the state validly regulates for health, safety, or welfare purposes under its police power, the government action merely

amounts to a regulation, and payment of just compensation is not required. However, a taking does occur where there is an actual appropriation of one's property [Loretto v. Teleprompter Manhattan CATV Corp., 455 U.S. 904 (1982)].

b. a regulatory taking;

(1) Any permanent, physical invasion, no matter how minor, will constitute a taking.

(2) A land-use regulation is a taking if it denies an owner all reasonable, economically beneficial uses of his land.

(3) To analyze regulations that merely decrease economic value, the court may use a balancing test to determine if there is a taking [Pennsylvania Coal Co. v. Mahon, 260 U.S. 393 (1922); Penn Central Transportation Co. v. New York, 438 U.S. 104 (1978)].

EXAMPLE: A state zoning law was passed after the owner purchased the property, and was held to constitute a taking because the law precluded the owner from erecting any permanent structure on his land [Lucas v. South Carolina Coastal Council, 505 U.S. 1003 (1992)].

c. temporary restrictions; or

(1) When considering whether a taking has occurred, a court will look at both the dimensions of a property interest (metes and bounds) and the term of years.

EXAMPLE: A temporary restriction causing a diminution in value (such as a 32-month moratorium on development in an area) is not a taking of the parcel as a whole because the property will recover value when the prohibition is lifted, and thus the regulation will not "permanently deprive" the owner of "all economically beneficial uses" of his land [Tahoe-Sierra Preservation Council, Inc. v. Tahoe Regional Planning Agency, 535 U.S. 302 (2002)].

d. conditional permits.

(1) The government can place a condition on the grant of a permit for land development if [Nollan v. California Coastal Commission, 483 U.S. 825 (1987); Dolan v. City of Tigard, 512 U.S. 374 (1994)]:

(a) there is a logical nexus between the condition and the governmental purposes; and

(b) there is rough proportionality between the impact on the proposed development and the governmental objectives served by the condition.

4. The Supreme Court has interpreted the "public use" language of the Takings Clause to mean "public purpose," and held that a city has the power to take private property and transfer it to a private developer because of the public benefits of the proposed development [Kelo v. City of New London, 545 U.S. 469 (2005)].

VI. EQUAL PROTECTION OF THE LAWS

A. **Constitutional Basis**

1. The Fourteenth Amendment provides that no state shall "deny to any person within its jurisdiction the equal protection of the laws." The Supreme Court has ruled that equal protection also applies to the federal government under the Due Process Clause of the Fifth Amendment.

2. The guarantee of substantive due process assures that a law will be fair and reasonable, not arbitrary; equal protection review is triggered where persons similarly situated are treated differently.

    a. Substantive due process review applies where a law affects the rights of all persons with respect to a specific activity (e.g., a state law prohibits the sale of birth control devices except by prescription).

    b. Equal protection review applies where a law affects the rights of some persons with respect to a specific activity (e.g., a state law prohibits the sale of birth control devices to unmarried persons except by prescription).

B. **Standards of Review**

1. Under the **strict scrutiny standard**, the burden of persuasion is on the government to prove that the measure being challenged is necessary to further a compelling interest.

    a. The word **necessary** means that there is no less restrictive alternative means available. There must be a very close "fit" between the means and the end.

    b. The government usually fails to prove its burden under strict scrutiny, so an equal protection challenge to a law is generally successful (i.e., the law is presumptively invalid).

    c. Strict scrutiny review applies to government action that uses suspect classifications—race, alienage, and national origin.

2. Under the **intermediate scrutiny standard**, the burden of persuasion is placed on the government to prove that the measure being challenged is substantially related to the achievement of an important governmental interest.

    a. The key term, **substantially related**, means that an exceedingly persuasive justification must be shown. Intermediate scrutiny is much closer to strict scrutiny than it is to rational basis.

    b. Intermediate scrutiny applies to government action using *quasi*-suspect classifications—gender and illegitimacy.

3. Under the **rational basis standard** of review, the burden of persuasion is on the plaintiff to show that the measure being challenged serves no legitimate government interest or is not rationally related to any legitimate interest.

    a. **Rational relationship** is a minimal requirement which means that the law cannot be arbitrary or unreasonable.

b.   Practically any police power regulation which furthers a health, safety, or welfare purpose will be found "legitimate." For this reason, laws scrutinized under rational basis are almost always upheld. From the plaintiff's standpoint, an equal protection challenge under rational basis is generally unsuccessful.

c.   Rational basis review applies to all classifications not falling under strict or intermediate scrutiny, such as classifications based on age, poverty, wealth, disability, and need for necessities of life (food, shelter, clothing, medical care).

THE THREE STANDARDS OF SCRUTINY		
Rational Basis	**Intermediate Scrutiny**	**Strict Scrutiny**
The plaintiff must prove **no legitimate** governmental interest.	The government must prove its classification is substantially related to an **important** government interest.	The government must prove its classification is **necessary** to achieve a **compelling** government interest.

C. Proving Discrimination

1. **Discriminatory intent**—purposeful discrimination—must be shown to trigger strict or intermediate scrutiny. Mere discriminatory effect is insufficient. Discriminatory intent may be shown facially, as applied, or where a discriminatory motive exists.

a.   **Facial discrimination** arises where a law, by its very language, creates distinctions between classes of persons (e.g., "only white, male U.S. citizens may apply for positions with the state police department").

b.   Where a law that appears neutral on its face but in its application has a disproportionate effect on a particular class of persons, strict or intermediate scrutiny will apply only if the court finds a discriminatory purpose exists.

EXAMPLE: The fact that black applicants scored lower than white applicants on a police qualifying test did not *per se* prove a discriminatory purpose in hiring practices, so strict scrutiny review was not triggered and no equal protection violation was found [Washington v. Davis, 426 U.S. 229 (1976)].

c.   A facially neutral law can be applied in a discriminatory manner. Where the challenger can show a discriminatory purpose, the law will be invalidated.

EXAMPLE: Where a law prohibited the operation of laundries in wooden buildings, most of which were owned by Chinese individuals, and government officials granted discretionary exemptions to white-owned laundries, the Supreme Court found that purposeful discrimination in the application of the law violated equal protection [Yick Wo v. Hopkins, 118 U.S. 356 (1886)].

D. Suspect Classifications

1. **Strict Scrutiny**

   a. Strict scrutiny applies to classifications based on race, alienage, and national origin. Such laws will be presumptively invalid absent a showing by the state that the measure is necessary to achieve a compelling state interest.

      (1) A state law prohibiting interracial marriages was held unconstitutional [Loving v. Virginia, 388 U.S. 1 (1967)]. Similarly, a state law prohibiting interracial cohabitation was held invalid [McLaughlin v. Florida, 379 U.S. 184 (1964)].

      (2) Deliberate *de jure* segregation violates equal protection [Brown v. Board of Education, 347 U.S. 483 (1954); Plessy v. Ferguson, 163 U.S. 537 (1896)].

         (a) Various plans to hinder desegregation have been deemed unconstitutional, including the closing of all public schools [Griffin v. County School Board of Prince Edward County, 377 U.S. 218 (1964)].

         (b) The Supreme Court has held that public aid to private, segregated schools—such as tuition grants and the exclusive use of public facilities—was unconstitutional [Norwood v. Harrison, 413 U.S. 455 (1973)].

         (c) School boards have an affirmative duty to eliminate the intentional racial segregation of schools.

            1) Court-ordered busing is constitutional where it is implemented to remedy past discrimination in a particular school system, rather than to attract nonminority students from outside districts to achieve integration. Court-ordered busing is a temporary measure that must be terminated once the vestiges of past discrimination have been eliminated [Board of Education v. Dowell, 498 U.S. 237 (1991)].

      (3) Where it can be shown that race was the "predominant factor" in defining the borders of new election districts (rather than contiguity, compactness, or community interest), then such a plan will be subject to strict scrutiny [Miller v. Johnson, 515 U.S. 900 (1995)].

   b. The Court will generally apply strict scrutiny when a state law discriminates against aliens.

      EXAMPLE: A state law prohibiting aliens from owning land was invalidated [Oyama v. California, 332 U.S. 633 (1948)].

      EXAMPLE: A state law denying commercial-fishing licenses to resident aliens who were ineligible for citizenship was held invalid [Takahashi v. Fish & Game Commission, 334 U.S. 410 (1948)].

      EXAMPLE: The Supreme Court invalidated a state law that excluded financial assistance for higher education to aliens who were eligible for

U.S. citizenship as not furthering any "compelling state interest" [Nyquist v. Mauclet, 432 U.S. 1 (1977)].

(1) States may discriminate against aliens in activities where participation in the functioning of government is involved.

    (a) A New York statute requiring state police officers to be citizens was held valid, under what is called the "**government function test**" [Foley v. Connelie, 435 U.S. 291 (1978)].

    (b) Aliens also may be denied positions as public school teachers because they influence students' views toward government and the political process [Ambach v. Norwick, 441 U.S. 68 (1979)].

(2) The Supreme Court has not held illegal aliens to be a suspect class; the rational basis analysis will apply.

    (a) However, in Plyler v. Doe [457 U.S. 202 (1982)], the Court determined that illegal alien children have a right to free public elementary and secondary education. The Court used a stringent version of the rational basis scrutiny test and held that the discrimination against the children "can hardly be considered rational unless it furthers some substantial goal of the state."

NOTE ▶ Federal laws that discriminate against aliens are not subject to the strict scrutiny test because Congress has broad plenary power to regulate immigration.

2. **Intermediate Scrutiny**

a. Distinctions drawn between legitimate and illegitimate children are subject to an intermediate, or "*quasi*-suspect," standard [Mathews v. Lucas, 427 U.S. 495 (1976)]. As a result, it is now close to the "almost suspect" standard used for gender discrimination [Mills v. Habluetzel, 456 U.S. 91 (1982)].

(1) Classifications must be "substantially related to an important state interest" [Id.].

(2) Classifications that favor legitimates and disfavor illegitimates are generally struck down because the overriding government interest in this area is not to punish the offspring of an illicit relationship.

EXAMPLE: In Levy v. Louisiana [391 U.S. 68 (1968)], the Supreme Court struck down a state law that permitted legitimate children, but not illegitimate children, to maintain a wrongful death action.

EXAMPLE: Similarly, the Supreme Court invalidated a state law that excluded illegitimate children from sharing equally with other children in worker's compensation death benefits [Weber v. Aetna Casualty and Surety Co., 406 U.S. 164 (1972)].

EXAMPLE: Likewise, illegitimate children are entitled to welfare benefits [New Jersey Welfare Rights Organization v. Cahill, 411 U.S. 619 (1973)].

b. As with federal laws that discriminate against aliens, the Supreme Court has been more lenient in applying an intermediate standard of scrutiny to illegitimacy under federal law than under state law. The Supreme Court upheld a federal law granting immigration preferences to legitimate children as within Congress's plenary power to regulate immigration [Fiallo v. Bell, 430 U.S. 787 (1977)].

c. Classifications based on gender are "*quasi*-suspect" and violate the Equal Protection Clause unless they "serve important governmental objectives and [are] substantially related to achievement of those objectives" [Craig v. Boren, 429 U.S. 190 (1976)]. In Craig, an Oklahoma statute permitted the sale of beer to females who were 18 years of age or older, but prohibited the sale of beer to males under 21 years of age. The statute was held unconstitutional because it was not substantially related to any important government objectives.

  (1) Intermediate review applies whether the classification is **invidious** (intended to harm) or **benign** (intended to help or to remedy past discrimination). Intentional, or purposeful, discrimination is required to trigger middle-tier scrutiny; discriminatory effect alone is insufficient.

  (2) Statutes that reinforce archaic, gender-based stereotypes will almost certainly be struck down.

  EXAMPLE: The Supreme Court required a state to show an "exceedingly persuasive justification" for its gender discrimination in admissions to the Virginia Military Institute. This language reflects the rigorous nature of the Craig v. Boren intermediate-level test [United States v. Virginia, 518 U.S. 515 (1996)].

  (3) In recent decisions, the Court has held unconstitutional, under equal protection, all laws discriminating against women.

  EXAMPLE: A state law giving preference to men over equally qualified women to be administrators of decedents' estates was held unconstitutional [Reed v. Reed, 404 U.S. 71 (1971)].

  EXAMPLE: Discrimination in military benefits to servicewomen was held invalid [Frontiero v. Richardson, 411 U.S. 677 (1973)].

  (4) Similarly, the Supreme Court has held unconstitutional under an equal protection analysis laws discriminating against men [Craig v. Boren, 429 U.S. 190 (1976)].

  EXAMPLE: The Court struck down a law authorizing alimony payments upon divorce to women but not to men [Orr v. Orr, 440 U.S. 268 (1979)].

  EXAMPLE: A New York law that permitted an unwed mother, but not an unwed father, to block the adoption of their child was held to be invalid [Caban v. Mohammed, 441 U.S. 380 (1979)].

EXAMPLE: The Supreme Court held that the exclusion of males from a state nursing school violated a male applicant's right to equal protection [Mississippi University for Women v. Hogan, 458 U.S. 718 (1982)].

EXAM TIP ▶ In some cases, laws discriminating against men have been upheld when they are "substantially related to the achievement of an important government interest."

EXAMPLE: The Supreme Court has upheld the registration of males but not females for conscription by the military because Congress, pursuant to its military powers, had determined that this was necessary to further important government interests [Rostker v. Goldberg, 453 U.S. 57 (1981)].

EXAMPLE: Statutory rape laws that punished the male participant, but not the female accessory, were upheld because they furthered the important state interest in preventing teenage pregnancy [Michael M. v. Sonoma County Superior Court, 450 U.S. 464 (1981)].

3. **Affirmative Action**

   a. Affirmative action measures based on race must pass strict scrutiny.

      (1) The only justifications for affirmative action that have been upheld are:

         (a) remedying the effects of past or present discrimination in a particular institution; and

         (b) achieving a diverse student body in an institute of higher education.

      (2) A school district may not assign individual students to schools based on race in order to achieve "voluntary integration" or "racial balancing" when school segregation is caused by social factors (*de facto* **segregation**) and not caused by past or present government action (*de jure* **segregation**) [Parents Involved in Cmty. Schools v. Seattle School Dist. No. 1, 551 U.S. 701 (2007)].

         (a) However, a school district is permitted to carry out such voluntary racial balancing by "structural" measures, such as redrawing school zones or building new schools.

      (3) Affirmative action measures based on race must be narrowly tailored to achieve their goals. The institution that adopts such a program must show that available, workable, non-racial alternatives do not suffice.

   b. Affirmative action based on gender need only pass intermediate scrutiny.

EXAMPLE: Social Security statutes and tax exemptions that entitle women to greater benefits have been upheld [Califano v. Webster, 430 U.S. 313 (1977)].

EXAMPLE: A U.S. navy discharge procedure that required male officers twice denied promotion to be automatically discharged, whereas female officers were not, was upheld because in the past, men had been afforded greater promotional opportunities than women [Schlesinger v. Ballard, 419 U.S. 498 (1975)].

c. In Richmond v. Croson [488 U.S. 469 (1989)], the Supreme Court first held that minority set-asides ("affirmative action") established by state or local governments for construction projects—i.e., programs where a fixed percentage of publicly funded money is awarded to minority-owned businesses—are subject to strict scrutiny review, and must be narrowly tailored to justify a compelling interest.

   (1) In Adarand Construction, Inc. v. Pena [515 U.S. 200 (1995)], the Supreme Court set forth a clear rule that any race-based affirmative action program designed to remedy past discrimination—whether enacted by a state municipality or even the federal government—is subject to strict scrutiny.

   (2) This rule applies to any "benign," or compensatory, program by any government entity that either favors or discriminates against racial or ethnic minorities. Other general principles include the following:

      (a) remedying past discrimination in a particular government institution is generally viewed as a compelling interest, but attempting to remedy general societal injustice through affirmative action is not;

      (b) race or ethnic origin may be considered as a "plus" factor in admissions programs, for the purpose of achieving a diverse student body [Regents of University of California v. Bakke, 438 U.S. 265 (1978)]; and

         1) Bakke was affirmed in Grutter v. Bollinger [539 U.S. 306 (2003)], whereby the Supreme Court held that a school may take race into account as one of many factors in making admissions decisions.

         2) However, a school may not use an admissions system that gives a set number of admissions points to each minority applicant, even if the purpose is to create a diverse student body [Id.].

      (c) discrimination by private employers is not subject to equal protection review.

4. **Other Classifications**

   a. Age is neither a "suspect" nor a "*quasi*-suspect" classification. Thus, laws and other governmental actions against the elderly are judged by the traditional (or rational basis) test.

      EXAMPLE: The Supreme Court upheld the validity of a Massachusetts statute requiring police officers to retire at age 50 even though they may be as physically fit as younger officers [Massachusetts Board of Retirement v. Murgia, 427 U.S. 307 (1976)].

   b. The Supreme Court has held that "poverty standing alone is not a suspect classification" [Harris v. McRae, 448 U.S. 297 (1980)].

   c. Mental retardation is not a "*quasi*-suspect" classification, and the rational basis standard of review is applicable [City of Cleburne v. Cleburne Living Center, 473 U.S. 432 (1985)].

EQUAL PROTECTION CHALLENGES		
Rational Basis	Intermediate Scrutiny	Strict Scrutiny
• Age • Alienage (some) • Disability • Sexual orientation • Wealth • All else	• Gender • Illegitimacy • Undocumented alien children	• Alienage • Domestic travel • National origin • Race • Voting

VII. PRIVILEGES AND IMMUNITIES CLAUSES

A. **Privileges and Immunities under the Fourteenth Amendment**

   1. The Fourteenth Amendment provides that no state shall make or enforce any law which abridges the privileges or immunities of citizens of the United States.

   2. The Supreme Court ruled early on, in the Slaughter-House Cases [83 U.S. 36 (1873)], that the Privileges and Immunities Clause of the Fourteenth Amendment had very limited application. Among the protected privileges and immunities of national citizenship are the rights [Twining v. New Jersey, 211 U.S. 78 (1908)]:

      a. to travel from state to state;

      b. to petition Congress for redress of grievances;

      c. to vote for national offices;

      d. to enter public lands;

      e. to be protected while in custody of U.S. Marshals; and

      f. to assemble peaceably.

> **NOTE** Corporations and aliens are not protected under the Fourteenth Amendment Privileges and Immunities Clause.

B. **Privileges and Immunities under Article IV, Section 2**

   1. Sometimes referred to as the Comity Clause, Article IV, Section 2 provides: "The Citizens of each State shall be entitled to all Privileges and Immunities of Citizens in the several States."

   2. This clause prohibits states from discriminating against nonresidents (based upon the fact that they do not reside in the state) with respect to rights and activities that are fundamental to the national union. Corporations and aliens are not "citizens" for purposes of the Article IV Privileges and Immunities Clause.

      a. The following have been held to be invalid forms of nonresident discrimination:

         (1) a state statute requiring a nonresident commercial fisherman to pay a $2,500 license fee to fish offshore, while a resident fisherman paid only a $25 license fee [Toomer v. Witsell, 334 U.S. 385 (1948)];

         (2) a commuter tax applied to nonresidents who entered New Hampshire to work, while New Hampshire residents were exempt from the tax [Austin v. New Hampshire, 420 U.S. 656 (1975)];

         (3) a state statute imposing residency requirements on women seeking an abortion, which was held invalid because an individual has a fundamental right to seek medical care [Doe v. Bolton, 410 U.S. 179 (1973)]; and

         (4) a state law requiring employers to give hiring preference to state residents [Hicklin v. Orbeck, 437 U.S. 518 (1978)].

      b. The Privileges and Immunities Clause does not protect a nonresident against all forms of discrimination. The following types of nonresident discrimination have been upheld:

(1) a state statute requiring a nonresident to pay $225 for a recreational hunting license, while a resident hunter paid only a $9 license fee, because it is within a state's police power to regulate recreational, noncommercial activities [Baldwin v. Montana Fish and Game Commission, 436 U.S. 371 (1978)]; and

(2) discrimination against nonresidents will be given special consideration if its purpose is the preservation of natural, state-owned resources [Sporhase v. Nebraska, 458 U.S. 941 (1982)].

EXAM TIP Discrimination against citizens or residents in regards to an essential economic right or liberty triggers the Article IV Privileges and Immunities Clause, whereas general economic discrimination against a business or entity is more often viewed using Commerce Clause analysis.

VIII. RETROACTIVE LEGISLATION

A. **The Contract Clause**

1. "No state shall...pass any...Law impairing the Obligation of Contracts" [U.S. Const. art. I, Section 10].

   a. The principal reason for the inclusion of the Contract Clause in the Constitution was to prevent state legislatures from passing retroactive laws impairing an existing contractual obligation. Therefore, the Contract Clause applies only to state legislation and not to state court decisions. Similarly, the Contract Clause does not apply to the federal government.

   b. A private contract can be modified by the legislature under its police power when it is necessary to serve an important and legitimate public interest and the regulation is a reasonable and narrowly tailored means of promoting that interest.

   (1) Thus, during the Great Depression, a statute imposing a moratorium on mortgage foreclosures was upheld [Home Building & Loan Association v. Blaisdell, 290 U.S. 398 (1934)].

   (2) In determining whether a contract may be modified, the Court will consider [Allied Structural Steel Co. v. Spannaus, 438 U.S. 234 (1978)]:

   (a) the severity of the impairment; and

   (b) the importance of the public interest to be served.

   EXAMPLE: New York and New Jersey violated the Contract Clause by permitting the Port Authority to use funds to subsidize public transportation in violation of a previous statutory covenant to private bondholders [United States Trust Co. v. New Jersey, 431 U.S. 1 (1977)].

   EXAMPLE: The Supreme Court recognized the validity of police power limitations on the Contract Clause and invalidated state pension reform legislation which increased the obligation of companies under preexisting pension plans [Allied Structural Steel Co. v. Spannaus, 438 U.S. 234 (1978)].

B. *Ex Post Facto* **Laws**

1. There are two *ex post facto* clauses in the Constitution that prevent both the state and federal governments from passing retroactive criminal laws. Article I, section 9, clause 3 provides: "No...*ex post facto* Law shall be passed"; and Article I, Section 10, Clause 1 provides: "No State shall pass any...*ex post facto* law."

   a. In general, a statute retroactively alters the criminal law if it:

   (1) makes criminal an act that was not a crime when committed;

   (2) prescribes greater punishment for a crime after its commission;

   (3) decreases the amount of evidence required for conviction; or

(4)   extends the statute of limitations for a crime as to which the previously applicable statute of limitations has already expired.

C. Bills of Attainder

1.   A **bill of attainder** is a legislative act that inflicts punishment without a judicial trial upon named individuals or an easily ascertainable group for past conduct.

2.   Article I, Section 9, Clause 3 states: "No bill of attainder…shall be passed"; and Article I, Section 10, Clause 1 provides: "No state shall pass any Bill of Attainder." These two provisions prevent both federal and state legislatures from passing bills of attainder.

    a.   The Supreme Court held that a provision in the Landrum-Griffin Act making it a crime for a member of the Communist Party to act as an officer of a labor union was the equivalent of legislative punishment, and hence a bill of attainder [United States v. Brown, 381 U.S. 437 (1965)].

    b.   However, the Court later held that legislation authorizing government control of various presidential papers and tape recordings did not constitute a bill of attainder, because the act was nonpunitive [Nixon v. Administrator of General Services, 433 U.S. 425 (1977)].

IX. FIRST AMENDMENT FREEDOMS

A. **Freedom of Religion and Separation of Church and State**

1. The First Amendment provides that "Congress shall make no law respecting an establishment of religion, or prohibiting the free exercise thereof."

2. **Establishment Clause**

    a. Where a government program prefers one religion or religious sect over others, strict scrutiny analysis will be applied [Board of Education v. Grumet, 512 U.S. 687 (1994)].

    b. Where the legislation or government program contains no religious or sect preference, the Supreme Court will follow the following three-part test under Lemon v. Kurtzman [403 U.S. 602 (1971)]:

        (1) the statute must have a secular legislative purpose;

        (2) the principal or primary effect or purpose must neither advance nor inhibit religion; and

        (3) the statute must not foster an excessive government entanglement with religion.

    c. **Religious Activities Conducted at Public Schools**

        (1) As a general rule, religious activities conducted in public schools violate the Establishment Clause because their primary purpose is to promote religion.

        (2) The following practices in public schools have been held to be invalid:

            (a) prayer and bible reading in public schools [Engel v. Vitale, 370 U.S. 421 (1962)];

            (b) an Alabama law authorizing a period of silence "for meditation or voluntary prayer" [Wallace v. Jaffree, 472 U.S. 38 (1985)];

            (c) posting the Ten Commandments on the walls in public school classrooms [Stone v. Graham, 449 U.S. 39 (1980)]; and

            (d) a public school sponsoring a rabbi or other cleric to conduct even a nondenominational prayer as part of a graduation ceremony [Lee v. Weisman, 505 U.S. 577 (1992)].

                1) A state legislature may employ a chaplain to conduct an opening day prayer [Marsh v. Chambers, 463 U.S. 783 (1983)].

                2) However, a state court judge may not conduct such a daily prayer [North Carolina Civil Liberties Union Legal Foundation v. Constangy, 947 F.2d 1145 (4th Cir. 1991)].

        (3) High school students being allowed to vote on whether a student-delivered "invocation" or "message" would take place at school football games is impermissible, as such an activity would be forced on all those present at a school-sponsored event [Santa Fe Independent School District v. Doe, 530 U.S. 290 (2000)].

(4) A state university regulation prohibiting the use of school facilities by a registered student religious organization (whereas facilities were available to other student groups) was held to be in violation of the freedom of free speech under the First Amendment [Widmar v. Vincent, 454 U.S. 263 (1981)].

(5) The Supreme Court has held that prohibiting a religious club from meeting in a public school amounted to religious viewpoint discrimination and violated the Free Speech Clause of the First Amendment. Furthermore, the Court ruled, permitting the club to meet on school grounds would not be in violation of the Establishment Clause [Good News Club v. Milford Central School, 533 U.S. 98 (2001)].

(6) The University of California required student groups to open their membership to "all comers." The university denied funding to the Christian Legal Society on the grounds that it refused membership to gays and lesbians. The Court upheld the university's rule against a First Amendment challenge on the grounds that it was a viewpoint-neutral restriction. The Court ruled that, in the academic context, the rule was reasonable in light of the goals of ensuring all students are included in the student group program, avoiding the need for the University to inquire into the groups' motives for excluding members, bringing together diverse students, and complying with state antidiscrimination rules [Christian Legal Society v. Martinez, 130 S. Ct. 2971 (2010)].

(7) Other decisions regarding religious activities in public schools include:

(a) a prohibition against showing religious films at a school violated free speech [Lamb's Chapel v. Center Moriches Union Free School District, 508 U.S. 387 (1993)];

(b) a university's refusal to fund a student publication because it addressed issues from a religious perspective violated free speech [Rosenberger v. Rector and Visitors of the University of Virginia, 515 U.S. 819 (1995)]; and

(c) a state university's viewpoint-neutral allocation of mandatory student activities fees to political and ideological groups as part of a program to facilitate extracurricular student speech did not violate the First Amendment rights of students who objected to subsidizing those groups' activities [Board of Regents of University of Wisconsin System v. Southworth, 529 U.S. 217 (2000)].

d. **Public School Curriculum**

(1) Anti-evolution laws prohibiting the teaching of Darwinian principles in public schools are unconstitutional [Epperson v. Arkansas, 393 U.S. 97 (1968)].

e. **Other Government Endorsement of Religion**

(1) Displays that celebrate the holiday season without favoring one religion over another are generally upheld. The government

cannot permit the type of display that a reasonable observer would conclude constitutes an endorsement of religion. The context surrounding the display is a key factor in determining its validity [Lynch v. Donnelly, 465 U.S. 668 (1984)].

    (a) The display of a creche as part of a Christmas display in a park passes the Lemon test, but a creche with no other symbols nearby—i.e., a "Season's Greetings" banner or Chanukah menorah—and prominently displayed by a private religious group in the county courthouse violated the Establishment Clause [County of Allegheny v. ACLU, 492 U.S. 573 (1989)].

(2) Placing a cross in a state-owned park immediately in front of the State Capitol was held to not violate the Establishment Clause; there was no endorsement of religion because the park had long been used by a variety of groups to conduct expressive activities [Capitol Square Review Board v. Pinette, 515 U.S. 753 (1995)].

(3) Placement of the Ten Commandments on the walls of court-houses was unconstitutional because there was no secular purpose [McCreary County v. ACLU, 545 U.S. 844 (2005)].

    (a) However, having the Ten Commandments carved on a six-foot-high granite monument in a 22-acre park surrounding the Texas State Capital, and surrounded by 37 other monuments, was held to be constitutional [Van Orden v. Perry, 545 U.S. 677 (2005)].

    (b) The crucial difference between the cases was the extent to which an objective observer would have perceived each display of the Ten Commandments as a governmental endorsement of religion.

(4) Sunday closing laws have been upheld as a governmental action with a mere incidental benefit to religion [McGowan v. Maryland, 366 U.S. 420 (1961)].

    (a) Blue laws or state statutes giving churches and schools the power to veto applications for liquor licenses within a 500-foot radius of the church or school were held unconstitutional because of "excessive government entanglement" [Larkin v. Grendel's Den, Inc., 459 U.S. 116 (1982)].

f. **Tax Deductions for Religious Institutions**

(1) The Supreme Court has upheld the validity of a property tax exemption for religious institutions as the equivalent of exempting other charitable organizations [Walz v. Tax Commission of New York, 397 U.S. 664 (1970)].

(2) A tax exemption from sales and use taxes available only for the sale of religious magazines and books violates the Establishment Clause as an endorsement of religion [Texas Monthly v. Bullock, 489 U.S. 1 (1989)].

g. **Government Aid to Religious Schools**

(1) Most government programs providing direct aid to parochial elementary and high schools have been held to violate the Establishment Clause because they involve "excessive government entanglement" with religion.

(2) Programs that provide aid to all elementary and secondary students (including parochial school students) have been held to "pass" the three-prong test.

(3) Providing bus transportation to and from school for all students (including those attending parochial schools) was held valid [Everson v. Board of Education, 330 U.S. 1 (1947)].

    (a) It was also held that necessary municipal services (e.g., police and fire protection) can be provided to churches and church-related institutions.

(4) If a tax deduction is given to all parents based on actual expenditures for children attending any public, private, or religious school, it will be upheld [Mueller v. Allen, 463 U.S. 388 (1983)].

(5) The Supreme Court permitted the state to furnish textbooks to all students, including those attending parochial schools, because there was little entanglement, and the primary effect was secular [Board of Education v. Allen, 392 U.S. 236 (1968)].

(6) Furnishing standardized secular examinations to parochial school students was held valid because the materials did not contain any religious content [Wolman v. Walter, 433 U.S. 229 (1977)].

(7) Public health services, including a school lunch program, can be provided to all students, since their purpose and effect are secular [Lemon v. Kurtzman, 403 U.S. 602 (1971)].

(8) The Supreme Court stated that Chapter 2 of the 1981 Education Consolidation and Improvement Act, which channels federal funds to local education agencies to acquire, for use in public and private schools, instructional and educational materials, including library and media materials and computer software and hardware, had a secular purpose and did not have the effect of advancing religion either by resulting in governmental indoctrination or by defining recipients by reference to religion, and therefore did not violate the First Amendment's Establishment Clause [Mitchell v. Helms, 530 U.S. 793 (2000)].

(9) A public school may pay for an interpreter for a deaf child at a religious high school in a program that aids both public and private school disabled students without reference to religion [Zobrest v. Catalina Foothills School District, 509 U.S. 1 (1993)].

    1) Grants to parochial schools for salaries of teachers of secular subjects have been held invalid, because of the risk of "excessive government entanglement" [Lemon v. Kurtzman, 403 U.S. 602 (1971)].

        (a)   In contrast, grants to church-related colleges are permissible because their instructors are thought to be restrained by the various academic disciplines (e.g., sociology, biology, etc.), and their students are older, more mature, and less susceptible to indoctrination.

            1)   A state statute permitting all parents, in computing their state income tax, to deduct expenses incurred in providing "tuition, textbooks and transportation" for their children in elementary and secondary schools, including parochial schools, was upheld [Mueller v. Allen, 463 U.S. 388 (1983)].

            2)   Giving tax deductions or tuition grants only to parents whose children attend parochial schools was held unconstitutional as violating the Establishment Clause [Committee for Public Education v. Nyquist, 413 U.S. 756 (1973)].

            3)   A voucher program that allows parents to send their children to parochial or religious schools with state aid instead of to failed public schools is allowed because the aid is neutral with respect to religion to a broad class of citizens, the program is defined without reference to religion, and parents direct aid to religious schools as a result of their own independent and private choice [Zelman v. Simmons-Harris, 536 U.S. 639 (2002)].

  h.   **Providing Public Services through Religious Institutions**

      (1)   Federal grants to church-affiliated hospitals for maintenance and care of indigent patients have been held valid [Bradfield v. Roberts, 175 U.S. 291 (1899)].

3. **Free Exercise Clause**

  a.   A person's religious beliefs are absolutely protected. The government may not punish an individual by denying benefits or imposing burdens based on religious belief [Cantwell v. Connecticut, 310 U.S. 296 (1940)].

      (1)   A state cannot require a person to carry a message on his license plate (e.g., New Hampshire's "Live Free or Die") which offends his religious belief [Wooley v. Maynard, 430 U.S. 705 (1977)].

      (2)   The government may not determine the truth or falsity of a person's religious beliefs, but it may determine a person's sincerity in his claim of religious belief [United States v. Ballard, 332 U.S. 78 (1944)].

      (3)   Public employment may not be conditioned on taking an oath based on a religious belief.

  b.   Where an individual's conduct is motivated by his religious beliefs, the state may regulate or prohibit the activity if the regulation is neutral in respect to religion and is of general applicability.

      (1)   In Employment Division v. Smith [494 U.S. 872 (1990)], the State of Oregon criminalized the possession of peyote, and no

exemption was made for American-Indians who use peyote for their religious rituals. The Supreme Court upheld the law, and held that a neutral law of general applicability does not violate the Free Exercise Clause, even if it prohibits or punishes conduct engaged in as a religious observance or practice.

c. The approach taken by the Supreme Court in Smith is consistent with all but two of the earlier cases:

(1) a state law outlawing polygamy was upheld [Reynolds v. United States, 98 U.S. 145 (1878)];

(2) the Court struck down a free exercise challenge by a Jewish Air Force doctor who violated uniform dress requirements by wearing a yarmulke while on duty [Goldman v. Weinberger, 475 U.S.503 (1986)];

(3) the Social Security tax applied to an Amish employer was held constitutional even though his religious beliefs prohibited him from making payments and from receiving benefits [United States v. Lee, 455 U.S. 252 (1982)];

(4) a state cannot deny unemployment compensation benefits to a person whose religious faith commands the observance of Saturday as the Sabbath [Sherbert v. Verner, 374 U.S. 398 (1963)];

(a) This approach by the Supreme Court to denials of unemployment compensation benefits is inconsistent with, but not overruled by, Smith. In light of Smith, it should be viewed as precedent only for cases involving very similar facts.

(5) the Court required that Amish children be exempt from a state law requiring all children to attend high school [Wisconsin v. Yoder, 406 U.S. 205 (1972)];

(a) This case is also inconsistent with Smith, but has not been overruled.

(6) the Court upheld Sunday closing laws because they further the state interest in providing a common day of rest [Braunfeld v. Brown, 366 U.S. 599 (1961)]; and

(7) a state-funded scholarship program for which devotional theology majors were ineligible did not suggest animus toward religion or impose more than a relatively minor burden on program participants [Locke v. Davey, 540 U.S. 714 (2004)].

d. Where the government purposely interferes with particular conduct because it is dictated by religious beliefs, strict scrutiny analysis will be applied and the law will be held unconstitutional unless it can be justified through proof of a compelling state interest served by narrowly tailored means.

EXAMPLE: A city ordinance banned all animal sacrifice done in a public or private ritual not for the primary purpose of food consumption ("kosher" slaughter was permitted). The primary purpose of the law was not to prevent cruelty to animals, but to abolish the sacrificial rituals of a particular Cuban Santeria religious sect. This purposeful interference with religious observance and practice was held unconstitutional by the Court [Church of the Lukumi Babalu Aye, Inc. v. Hialeah, 508 U.S. 520 (1993)].

B. Freedom of Expression

1. The First Amendment provides: "Congress shall make no law…abridging the freedom of speech, or of the press; or the right of the people peaceably to assemble, and to petition the government for a redress of grievances."

   a. The First Amendment was held applicable to the states through the Due Process Clause of the Fourteenth Amendment [Gitlow v. New York, 268 U.S. 652 (1975)].

2. The government may neither censor all categories of speech nor engage in content-based discrimination among different categories of speech (even if that speech is offensive), with some exceptions.

3. **Exceptions to Freedom of Speech**

   a. **Strict Scrutiny**

      (1) The regulation of speech is allowable if it passes strict scrutiny.

      EXAMPLE: A provision of the District of Columbia Code prohibiting signs within 500 feet of a foreign embassy that tended to bring the foreign government into "public odium" or "public disrepute" was held unconstitutional as a content-based regulation of political speech that could not be justified by proof of a compelling governmental interest served by narrowly tailored means [Boos v. Barry, 485 U.S. 312 (1988)].

      EXAMPLE: Congress banned corporations and unions from using their general treasury funds to advocate the election or defeat of a candidate within 30 days of an election. Citizens United wanted to run a television show that was critical of presidential candidate, Hillary Clinton, shortly before the primary election. The Court ruled that corporate spending on speech merits the same First Amendment protection as speech by natural persons. Hence, Congress could not censor such corporate speech [Citizens United v. Federal Election Commission, 130 S. Ct. 876 (2010)].

      EXAMPLE: In Washington State, citizens may put a referendum on the ballot if they can get a certain number of signatures on a petition. Washington publicly disclosed the signers of a petition seeking a referendum on the rights of same-sex partners. The Court ruled that the First Amendment rights of the signers were not violated, at least in the absence of any showing that the disclosure caused specific harm to the signers. The disclosure requirement served the goal of maintaining the integrity of the electoral process [Doe v. Reed, 130 S. Ct. 2811 (2010)].

b. **Conduct Regulation**

(1) A law which regulates conduct but creates an incidental burden on speech is allowable if [United States v. O'Brien, 391 U.S. 367 (1968)]:

(a) the regulation furthers an important or substantial government interest that is unrelated to the suppression of free expression; and

(b) the incidental restriction on speech is no greater than is essential to the furtherance of that interest.

EXAMPLE: Students wearing black armbands to protest the Vietnam War was held to be protected speech [Tinker v. Des Moines Independent Community School District, 393 U.S. 503 (1969)].

EXAMPLE: A Texas prohibition against desecrating an American flag was held unconstitutional as applied to an individual who burned a flag as a form of political expression. Strict scrutiny was applied because the Texas statute was intended to control expression [Texas v. Johnson, 491 U.S. 397 (1989)].

EXAMPLE: A federal statute, the Flag Protection Act of 1989, was subjected to strict scrutiny and held unconstitutional as a content-based regulation of political speech [United States v. Eichman, 496 U.S. 310 (1990)].

EXAMPLE: Virginia's prohibition of cross-burning with the intent to intimidate was not unconstitutional since it banned conduct rather than expression. While cross-burning could constitute expression, such expressive conduct was not proscribed unless it was done with the intent to intimidate, and targeting cross-burning was reasonable because burning a cross was historically a particularly virulent form of intimidation. A plurality of the Supreme Court, however, found the law to be a facially unconstitutional restraint on speech, to the extent it had the effect that any cross-burning could, *prima facie*, be sufficient evidence from which the jury could infer the required intent to intimidate [Virginia v. Black, 538 U.S. 343 (2003)].

c. **Government as Speaker**

(1) Where the speaker is the government rather than a private actor, the government may discriminate based on the content of the speech.

EXAMPLE: A city erects several permanent monuments in a public park. Some of the monuments were donated by private organizations. A religious organization asks the city to erect a monument containing the Seven Aphorisms of Summum. The city refuses. The organization sues the city, alleging the violation of the organization's right of free speech. The Supreme Court held that there was no violation of the First Amendment. The permanent monuments constituted speech by the government, even if the monuments were donated by private organizations. When the government speaks, it may favor some views and disfavor others [Pleasant Grove City v. Summum, 555 U.S. 460 (2009)].

EXAMPLE: If private individuals or organizations engage in direct communication in a public park (for example, making speeches or distributing leaflets, as opposed to donating permanent monuments) then, of course, the government may not discriminate among the speakers based on the content of their message, since the communication is by private actors and not by the government.

EXAMPLE: Pursuant to the First Amendment, a city must allow the KKK to temporarily erect a cross on a public park when other groups have been permitted to temporarily erect installations. Temporary installations by private organizations constitute private speech, while permanent installations constitute government speech even if donated by private organizations.

d. **Unprotected Speech**

(1) A regulation which relates to unprotected speech is permissible.

(2) **Unprotected speech** includes:

(a) speech that advocates violence or unlawful action;

    1) The constitutional guarantees of free speech do not permit state regulation of the advocacy of the use of force or of violation of law, "except where such advocacy is directed to inciting or producing imminent lawless action and is likely to incite or produce such action" [Brandenburg v. Ohio, 395 U.S. 444 (1969)].

    EXAMPLE: A Virginia's statute which stated, "Any such burning of a cross shall be *prima facie* evidence of an intent to intimidate a person or group of persons," was found to be unconstitutional. The Court held that this provision was unconstitutional because of its "indiscriminate coverage." However, it ruled that a state "may ban cross burning carried out with the attempt to intimidate." The state must prove the intent to intimidate [Virginia v. Black, 538 U.S. 343 (2003)].

(b) fighting words;

    1) Words likely to incite an ordinary citizen to acts of immediate physical retaliation may be punished [Chaplinsky v. New Hampshire, 315 U.S. 568 (1942)].

    2) To fall within this category, the speech must be more than annoying or offensive; there must be a genuine likelihood of imminent violence by a hostile audience.

    3) "Fighting words" statutes are subject to facial invalidity if the conduct proscribed is vague (e.g., a law prohibiting "opprobrious words") or overbroad.

4) "Fighting words" statutes designed to punish certain viewpoints are unconstitutional [R.A.V. v. St. Paul, 505 U.S. 377 (1992)].

(c) hostile audience speech;

1) Speech which elicits an immediate violent response against the speaker by an audience may be grounds for prosecution. The police, however, must make reasonable efforts to protect the speaker, to guard against a "heckler's veto" of unpopular speech.

(d) obscene speech; and

1) For speech to be considered **obscene**, the following three-part test must be satisfied [Miller v. California, 413 U.S. 15 (1975)]:

a) the average person, applying contemporary community standards, would find that the work, taken as a whole, appeals to the prurient interest (a national standard is not used);

i) The manner in which allegedly obscene materials are advertised and sold may be probative of their "prurient" appeal [Ginzburg v. United States, 383 U.S. 463 (1966)].

b) the work depicts or describes, in a patently offensive way, sexual conduct specifically defined by the applicable state law; and

c) the work, taken as a whole, lacks serious literary, artistic, political, or scientific value.

i) A national standard is used to determine this value [Pope v. Illinois, 481 U.S. 497 (1987)].

2) Child pornography is unprotected speech. It may be regulated even without satisfying the Miller test because of the state's compelling interest in protecting minor children.

a) The sale and distribution of visual depictions of sexual conduct involving children may be prohibited [New York v. Ferber, 456 U.S. 942 (1982)].

b) A state may criminalize the private possession of child pornography in one's home [Osborne v. Ohio, 495 U.S. 103 (1990)].

c) Recently, the Supreme Court held that a statute which outlawed not only actual child pornography but also virtual child pornography (in which no real children were depicted) was overly broad and violated the First Amendment [Ashcroft v. Free Speech Coalition, 535 U.S. 234 (2002)].

i) However, in a follow-up case, the Court upheld a congressional statute that punished those who solicited or distributed pornography while believing it depicted real children, even if in fact it did not [United States v. Williams, 553 U.S. 285 (2008)].

    (e) defamatory speech.

        1) Constitutional restrictions apply to defamatory speech where the plaintiff is either a public official or public figure, or where the defamatory statement involves a matter of public concern.

        2) When the plaintiff is a private person and the subject of the statement is a matter of purely private concern, such as the operations of a credit-reporting agency, the plaintiff need not prove actual malice or negligence, and may recover according to common law defamation principles [Dun & Bradstreet, Inc. v. Greenmoss Builders, Inc., 472 U.S. 749 (1985)].

        3) When the plaintiff is a private person and the subject of the statement is a matter of public concern, the plaintiff need not prove actual malice, but must prove negligence about the truth or falsity of the statement.

        4) When the plaintiff is a public official or public figure, the plaintiff must prove the state law requirements of defamation plus **actual malice**, defined as knowledge of the falsity or reckless disregard of the truth or falsity of the statement. This rule holds whether the allegedly defamatory statement is a matter of public or private concern [New York Times v. Sullivan, 376 U.S. 254 (1964)].

        5) The Supreme Court held that a private plaintiff suing a media defendant for false-light invasion of privacy concerning a matter of public interest must prove actual malice [Time, Inc. v. Hill, 385 U.S. 374 (1967)].

            a) Note that this standard is higher than in cases where a private plaintiff sues for defamation over matters of public interest; in the latter cases, the plaintiff need only prove negligence.

            b) In addition, the Court said that a newspaper or broadcaster cannot be held liable for publishing truthful information obtained from the public record [Cox Broadcasting Co. v. Cohn, 420 U.S. 469 (1975)].

        6) Pure opinion may be actionable if it reasonably implies a false and defamatory fact [Milkovich v. Lorain Journal Co., 497 U.S. 1 (1990)].

  (3) Certain categories of speech receive lower levels of protection, however, including:

    (a) commercial speech; and

        1) A state may prohibit commercial advertising of matters that are illegal (e.g., prostitution) or advertising that is

untruthful, misleading, or deceptive [Pittsburgh Press Co. v. Pittsburgh Commission on Human Relations, 413 U.S. 376 (1973)].

2) Commercial speech is protected by the First Amendment if it is not false or deceptive and does not relate to unlawful activity. If commercial speech satisfies these requirements, government regulation of the speech must satisfy the three-part test set forth in Central Hudson Gas v. Public Service Commission [447 U.S. 557 (1980)]. The regulation must:

a) serve a substantial governmental interest;

b) directly advance the substantial governmental interest; and

c) not be more extensive than is necessary to serve that interest.

3) A state cannot place an absolute ban on the advertisement of drug prices by a pharmacist [Virginia State Board of Pharmacy v. Virginia Citizens Consumer Council, Inc., 425 U.S. 748 (1976)].

4) A federal law making it a crime to send unsolicited advertisements for contraceptive devices was held unconstitutional [Bolger v. Youngs Drug Products Corp., 463 U.S. 60 (1983)].

5) A state cannot prohibit attorneys from advertising routine legal services at stated fees [Bates v. State Bar of Arizona, 433 U.S. 350 (1977)]

a) Similarly, a state supreme court rule prohibiting an attorney from mailing new-office-opening announcements to persons "other than lawyers, clients, friends or relatives" was held to be unconstitutional [In re R. M. J., 455 U.S. 191 (1982)].

6) A state may discipline lawyers for "in-person" solicitation of clients for personal gain because of the potential for overreaching [Ohralik v. Ohio State Bar Association, 436 U.S. 447 (1978)].

7) A state can prevent doctors from claiming to be "board certified" in a medical specialty unless the certifying organization meets certain state standards because the commercial speech doctrine does not protect fraudulent speech, and because such a statute reasonably advances the state's interest in protecting the public [American Academy of Pain Management v. Joseph, 353 F.3d 2020 (9th Cir. 2004)].

8) It is within a state's police power to prohibit billboards carrying commercial advertising [Metromedia, Inc. v. City

of San Diego, 453 U.S. 490 (1981)]. It is unclear, however, whether a total ban on billboards would be upheld.

9) A city ban on newsracks placed on sidewalks to distribute commercial publications (while allowing newsracks to sell newspapers) was held invalid, because there was no reasonable "fit" between the type of publication being regulated and the state interest in reducing litter and promoting aesthetics [Cincinnati v. Discovery Network, Inc., 507 U.S. 410 (1993)].

10) Clearly, advertising of unlawful products can be prohibited. However, as to advertising of harmful, yet lawful, products—i.e., "vice advertising," such as advertising for cigarettes, liquor, and gambling—it seems unlikely that the government can completely ban truthful advertising.

    a) The Supreme Court held that a ban prohibiting all advertisement of liquor prices except for price tags displayed on the merchandise, enacted in order to protect the public and decrease alcohol consumption by discouraging price wars, was held unconstitutional [44 Liquormart, Inc. v. Rhode Island, 517 U.S. 484 (1996)].

    b) The Twenty-First Amendment, which allows the states to regulate liquor and liquor establishments within the state's borders, may not be used as a constitutional basis to override the protection on commercial speech afforded by the First Amendment.

    c) A federal ban prohibiting beer bottle labels from displaying alcoholic content was held unconstitutional as a violation of the brewer's free speech rights. Because the law applied only to labels, not to advertising, and only to beer, not to wine and spirits, it did not directly advance the government's interest in preventing "strength wars" [Rubin v. Coors Brewing Co., 514 U.S. 476 (1995)].

(b) sexual speech.

1) Regulation of sexual speech must serve a substantial government interest and leave open reasonable alternative channels of communication.

EXAMPLE: A ban on public nudity, including nude dancing in adult entertainment establishments, was held constitutional, with a plurality opinion focused on the need to protect the important government interests in societal order and morality [Barnes v. Glen Theatres, Inc., 501 U.S. 1030 (1991)].

> **EXAMPLE:** A majority opinion of the Supreme Court held that a similar ban on nude dancing was content-neutral and constitutional because its purpose was to deal with the secondary effects of establishments where there is nude dancing, such as prostitution and other forms of criminal activity [City of Erie v. PAP's A.M., 529 U.S. 277 (2000)].

e. **Time, Place, Manner**

   (1) Reasonable regulation of the time, place, or manner of speech is allowed.

   (2) The government may place reasonable restraints on the time, place, and manner of speech in public areas, such as streets, sidewalks, and parks—places historically associated with expressive conduct (e.g., picketing, leafleting, and broadcasting). The focus is not on the "content" or "message" of the speech, but rather its "conduct" or "method."

   (a) A three-part test is used to determine the constitutionality of time, place, or manner regulations of speech and assembly in public places. The regulation must:

   1) be content-neutral as to both subject matter and viewpoint (i.e., the regulation cannot prefer some messages over others);

   2) be narrowly tailored to serve a significant (important) government interest; and

   3) leave alternative channels of communication open.

> **NOTE** This test is very much like the test for intermediate scrutiny under equal protection.

   (b) The Court has held that a complete ban on door-to-door solicitation is unnecessary, because a homeowner can protect his privacy by posting a "No Solicitors" sign [Martin v. Struthers, 319 U.S. 141 (1943)].

   (c) An ordinance requiring door-to-door solicitors, or canvassers, to identify themselves to local authorities was upheld in the interests of crime prevention [Hynes v. Mayor of Oradell, 425 U.S. 610 (1976)].

   (d) A city may not require persons canvassing door to door to register with the mayor's office and receive a permit where the canvassing consists of religious proselytizing (such as that done by Jehovah's Witnesses), anonymous political speech, or the distribution of handbills [Watchtower Bible & Tract Soc. of N.Y., Inc. v. Village of Stratton, 536 U.S. 150 (2002)].

   (e) Charitable solicitations for funds in residential neighborhoods are generally protected [Schaumburg v. Citizens for a Better Environment, 444 U.S. 620 (1980)].

      (f)   Face-to-face solicitation of funds at an airport terminal, which is a non-public forum, may be prohibited, but a total ban on distribution of literature may not be [International Society for Krishna v. Lee, 505 U.S. 672 (1992)].

      (g) The Supreme Court has upheld the constitutionality of a federal law that permits the post office, upon a householder's request, to order a mailer to stop all future mailings to that addressee [Rowan v. United States Post Office, 397 U.S. 728 (1970)].

  (3)   Speech-related activities at non-public forums, such as military bases, jails, government workplaces, and mailboxes, can be regulated by reasonable time, place, and manner regulations. The test used by the Court requires a government regulation to be:

      (a) viewpoint-neutral; and

      (b) reasonably related to a legitimate interest.

  (4)   A state may prohibit demonstrations on jailhouse grounds [Adderley v. Florida, 385 U.S. 39 (1966)].

  (5)   Military bases may be closed to political speeches and distribution of leaflets [Greer v. Spock, 424 U.S. 828 (1976)].

  (6)   A city may sell space for commercial advertising on city buses but refuse to sell such space for political advertising [Lehman v. Shaker Heights, 418 U.S. 298 (1974)].

  (7)   A public school may not deny use of its facilities to religious groups if other public and private groups are allowed similar access [Lamb's Chapel v. Center Moriches Union Free School District, 508 U.S. 672 (1992)].

  (8)   The owner of a private shopping center is not required by the Constitution to allow access for purposes of picketing and/or leafleting [Hudgens v. NLRB, 424 U.S. 507 (1976)].

      (a) However, a state's constitution may be interpreted to protect such expressive activity [Pruneyard Shopping Center v. Robins, 447 U.S. 74 (1980)].

4. **Freedom of Association**

  a.   There is a close "nexus" between the freedoms of speech and association. The Supreme Court has acknowledged that "state action which may curtail (or have the effect of curtailing) the freedom to associate is subject to the closest scrutiny."

    (1)   Under the freedom to associate, the Court has struck down laws that prevented the NAACP from assisting individuals and that prevented a labor union from assisting its members in retaining lawyers [NAACP v. Button, 371 U.S. 415 (1963); Brotherhood of Railroad Trainmen v. Virginia, 377 U.S. 1 (1964)].

    (2)   It is unconstitutional for the government to order the Boy Scouts of America to allow homosexuals to participate in the organization. The organization's view that homosexual conduct was

inconsistent with the values it sought to instill in youth members fell within its First Amendment right of expressive association [Boy Scouts of America v. Dale, 530 U.S. 640 (2001)].

    (a) The Supreme Court refused to extend First Amendment protection to a high school student's lewd and offensive campaign speech delivered at a school assembly [Bethel School District No. 403 v. Fraser, 478 U.S. 675 (1986)].

5. **Public Employment**

  a. In general, an individual cannot be denied public employment based upon membership in a political organization unless the position is a high-level policy-making position [Keyishian v. Board of Regents, 385 U.S. 589 (1967)].

    (1) The Court invalidated political patronage dismissals by the Democratic sheriff of Cook County [Elrod v. Burns, 427 U.S. 347 (1976)].

    (2) The Court held that party affiliation is not an appropriate requirement for the position of public defender [Brand v. Finkel, 445 U.S. 507 (1980)].

  b. An individual may be deprived of public employment for political association if [Scales v. United States, 367 U.S. 203 (1961)]:

    (1) he is an active member of a subversive organization;

    (2) such membership is with knowledge of the illegal aims of the organization; and

    (3) he has a specific intent to further those illegal ends (e.g., violent overthrow of the government).

EXAMPLE: A provision of the Subversive Activities Control Act was held unconstitutionally overbroad by denying members of the Communist Party "employment in any defense facility" [United States v. Robel, 389 U.S. 258 (1967)].

  c. In the past, the Court has chosen to deal with loyalty oath qualifications under the "vagueness" and "overbreadth" doctrines.

EXAMPLE: An Arkansas statute requiring teachers to file an affidavit listing "every organization to which they have belonged or regularly contributed within the preceding five years" was invalidated as overbroad [Shelton v. Tucker, 364 U.S. 479 (1960)].

EXAMPLE: Similarly, the Supreme Court invalidated a Florida statute requiring public employees to swear, "I have not and will not lend my aid, support, advice, counsel or influence to the Communist Party" as vague and ambiguous [Cramp v. Board of Public Instruction, 368 U.S. 278 (1961)].

    (1) On the other hand, an oath that public employees will "support the Constitution of the United States and will oppose the overthrow of the government of the United States by force, violence, or by any illegal or unconstitutional means" was held valid in part; the portion of the oath requiring the employees to swear that they would support

the Constitution was held constitutionally valid. However, the part of the oath requiring them to swear that they do not believe in the violent overthrow of government was held invalid as providing for the employee's dismissal without inquiry or hearing as required by due process [Connell v. Higginbotham, 403 U.S. 207 (1971)].

6. **Prior Restraint**

 a. As a general rule, the government cannot suppress or restrain speech in advance of its publication or utterance.

 b. There is a strong presumption against the constitutional validity of any system of prior restraint of expression.

 (1) The Supreme Court refused to permit the government to enjoin the publication of the Pentagon Papers [New York Times v. United States, 403 U.S. 713 (1971)].

 (2) Confiscation by the post office of mailed materials determined by the postmaster general to be "obscene" was held invalid [Bantam Books, Inc. v. Sullivan, 372 U.S. 58 (1963)].

 (3) A restraining order issued by a trial judge to limit media reporting of a criminal trial was held unconstitutional [Nebraska Press Association v. Stuart, 427 U.S. 539 (1976)].

 c. There are some exceptional cases in which prior restraints are allowed, including:

 (1) a government agency can require prepublication review of writings related to employment of past or present employees where such a review is necessary to protect national security [Snepp v. United States, 444 U.S. 507 (1980)];

 (2) classified military information; and

 (3) any case involving a search and seizure is governed by the Fourth Amendment.

 (a) Thus, any "large scale" seizure of allegedly obscene materials must be preceded by a full adversary hearing, and a judicial determination of obscenity [Quantity of Books v. Kansas, 378 U.S. 205 (1964)].

 (b) However, the seizure of a single book or film to preserve it as evidence in a criminal proceeding need only be made pursuant to a warrant based on a determination of probable cause by a neutral magistrate [Heller v. New York, 413 U.S. 483 (1973)].

 d. The Supreme Court required trial judges to consider three factors in determining if a restraining order against pretrial publicity is appropriate:

 (1) the nature and extent of the pretrial publicity;

 (2) the availability of other measures to mitigate the effects of pretrial publicity; and

 (3) the likely effectiveness of the restraining order.

 e. Another form of prior restraint is the censorship or licensing of motion pictures prior to their exhibition. The Court has held that statutes requiring films to be submitted to a Board of Censors before showing them are constitutional if the following requirements are met [Freedman v. Maryland, 380 U.S. 51 (1965)]:

(1) the standards for the denial of a license are narrowly drawn and reasonable;

(2) when a license is denied, the censor promptly seeks an injunction [Teitel Films v. Cusack, 390 U.S. 139 (1968)];

(3) the burden of proving that the material is "obscene," or otherwise unprotected, is on the censor; and

(4) a prompt judicial determination is provided.

f. A method the government frequently uses for regulating the time, place, and manner of speech is to require a license or permit for such activities as a parade, demonstration, or rally.

(1) Such a licensing statute is valid provided that it:

(a) is content-neutral as applied (i.e., for protected speech, the message of the petitioners cannot be considered in granting or denying the permit); and

(b) does not give licensing officials "unfettered discretion" to determine who may receive a permit.

EXAMPLE: A parade permit that required applicants to pay up to $1,000 per day to cover anticipated costs of police security was held void on its face as a prior restraint. Also, as applied to a white supremacy group, the ordinance was not content-neutral, because unpopular speech is met with greater hostility, thus requiring more police protection [Forsyth County v. Nationalist Movement, 505 U.S. 123 (1992)].

(2) Where a statute is facially void (i.e., it gives the licensing officials unrestricted discretion), a speaker need not even apply for a permit. In this case, one may exercise his First Amendment rights on the public property without a permit [Staub v. Baxley, 355 U.S. 313 (1958)].

(3) On the other hand, if a statute is valid on its face (i.e., it contains narrowly defined standards as to time, place, manner, and duration), then the applicant must seek a permit. If the permit is denied, even arbitrarily, the applicant must appeal the adverse ruling to the proper administrative or judicial body [Poulos v. New Hampshire, 345 U.S. 395 (1953)].

g. As a general rule, if one is enjoined from speaking, he must either obey the injunction or appeal it, unless the licensing statute is facially void or the timing is such that an appeal would effectively frustrate the exercise of his rights [Walker v. City of Birmingham, 388 U.S. 307 (1967)].

7. **Overbreadth**

a. When a state has the power to regulate an area dealing with free speech, it must not do so "by means which sweep unnecessarily broadly and thereby invade the area of protected freedoms" [NAACP v. Alabama, 377 U.S. 288

(1964)]. Thus, the wording of a statute must be narrow and specific, and not overly broad so as to have a "chilling effect" upon protected speech.

(1) The Supreme Court has held that "the overbreadth of a statute must not only be real, but substantial as well" [Broadrick v. Oklahoma, 413 U.S. 601 (1973)].

(2) The Supreme Court further explained that "there must be a realistic danger that the statute itself will significantly compromise recognized First Amendment protections of parties not before the Court for it to be facially challenged on overbreadth grounds" [Members of City Council v. Taxpayers for Vincent, 466 U.S. 789 (1984)].

EXAMPLE: An ordinance making it unlawful "to curse or revile or to use obscene or opprobrious language toward or with reference" to a police officer performing his duties was held invalid because the ordinance effectively punished all vulgar and offensive speech, even though some of this speech may be protected by the First Amendment [Lewis v. City of New Orleans, 415 U.S. 130 (1974)].

EXAMPLE: An ordinance prohibiting speech that "stirs the public to anger, invites dispute, brings about a condition of unrest, or creates a disturbance" was held to be overbroad and unconstitutional [Terminiello v. City of Chicago, 337 U.S. 1 (1949)].

8. **Vagueness**

a. The vagueness doctrine is closely related to the overbreadth doctrine. In NAACP v. Button [371 U.S. 415 (1963)], the Court admonished that governmental regulations must be drawn "with narrow specificity." The following statutes have been ruled "void for vagueness" under due process inquiries:

(1) a statute making it a crime to "publicly mutilate, trample upon, deface or treat contemptuously the flag of the United States" [Smith v. Goguen, 415 U.S. 566 (1974)];

(2) a municipal vagrancy ordinance defining vagrants to include "rogues and vagabonds,…lewd, wanton, and lascivious persons,…[and] persons wandering or straying around from place to place without any lawful purpose or objective" [Papachristou v. City of Jacksonville, 405 U.S. 156 (1972)]; and

(3) a city ordinance that defined loitering as "to remain in any one place with no apparent purpose" and gave police officers absolute discretion to issue dispersal orders to groups of two or more persons seen loitering in a public place if the officer reasonably believed that one of them was a criminal street gang member, and which made it a criminal offense to disobey such order [City of Chicago v. Morales, 527 U.S. 41 (1999)].

9. **Press**

a. The press has no greater freedom to speak than any ordinary member of the general public does. Also, the press has no special right of access to government information.

(1) The First Amendment guarantees both the public and the press a right to attend criminal trials. However, this right is not absolute and may be outweighed where the judge finds an "overriding" interest that cannot be accommodated by less restrictive means [Richmond Newspapers v. Virginia, 448 U.S. 555 (1980)].

(2) A **gag order**—a pretrial order prohibiting the press from publishing certain types of information—will almost never be held constitutional because the trial judge has other alternatives at his disposal (e.g., a change of venue, postponement of the trial, careful *voir dire*, or restricting statements of the lawyers, police, and witnesses) [Nebraska Press Association v. Stuart, 427 U.S. 539 (1976)].

(3) A newsperson has no First Amendment right to refuse to testify before a grand jury [Branzburg v. Hayes, 408 U.S. 665 (1972)].

(4) In general, radio and television broadcasting can be more closely regulated than the press, due to the limited number of airwaves available. A radio broadcast of "patently offensive sexual and excretory speech" (even if not "obscene" under the Miller test) can be sanctioned to protect the privacy interests of children likely to be listening [FCC v. Pacifica Foundation, 438 U.S. 726 (1978)].

(5) The Court has held that cable television receives First Amendment protection somewhere between that of broadcast television and newspapers.

(6) Where cable television operators are subjected to content-neutral regulations, intermediate scrutiny is applied [Turner Broadcasting System, Inc. v. FCC, 512 U.S. 622 (1994)].

(7) On the other hand, where content-specific regulation is imposed, the Court has yet to select a standard of review. However, the Court allows cable television operators the right to ban "indecent" programming that describes sexual activities in a patently offensive manner when in programming on channels that are leased outright to unaffiliated third parties (but not to public access channels) [Denver Area Educational Telecommunications Consortium, Inc. v. FCC, 518 U.S. 727 (1996)].

(8) The Supreme Court held that where a radio commentator played a tape on his talk show that he had legally obtained, but which had been recorded by another person in violation of the law, such a publication was protected under the First Amendment. The Court reasoned that a stranger's illegal conduct does not suffice to remove the First Amendment shield from speech about a matter of public concern [Bartnicki v. Vopper, 535 U.S. 514 (2001)].

(9) As a general rule, any prior restraint of publication will be deemed illegal. This does not mean that, after publication, there may not be civil or criminal consequences from the publication itself. Consider the timing of the action in question and determine if it takes place before or after publication.

10. **Bar Admission**

    a.   The state is permitted, under the Due Process Clause, to inquire into the qualifications and fitness of candidates for admission to the bar.

        (1)   A candidate cannot be denied admission for past membership in the Communist Party [Schware v. New Mexico Board of Bar Examiners, 353 U.S. 232 (1957)].

        (2)   However, the state can refuse bar membership to an applicant who refuses to answer questions (e.g., regarding past Communist Party membership) if his refusal obstructs the bar examiner's investigation of his qualifications [Konigsberg v. State Bar of California, 366 U.S. 36 (1961)].

        (3)   Reaffirming the validity of Konigsberg, the Court held that a state can inquire into knowing membership in subversive organizations in screening its applicants for the bar. Thus, the First Amendment does not extend unlimited protection to a bar applicant who refuses to disclose his political affiliations [Law Students Civil Rights Research Council, Inc. v. Wadmond, 401 U.S. 154 (1971)].

        (4)   A residency requirement by the New Hampshire state bar requiring a Vermont resident to establish a home address in New Hampshire prior to being sworn in was held to violate of the Privileges and Immunities Clause of Article IV, Section 2 [Supreme Court of New Hampshire v. Piper, 470 U.S. 274 (1985)].

Issue-Spotting Exercises

Question 1

In recent years, a city has been plagued by teenage violence. There have been numerous incidents of sporadic shootings and stabbings. Unfortunately, even innocent bystanders have fallen victim to this violence. In an effort to alleviate the problem, the city has opened a teenage dance club where local youths can mingle and dance while under adult supervision. Only teenage boys and girls between the ages of 13 to 19 are permitted to enter the dance club.

When the dance club first opened, an unexpected problem presented itself. There were a lot more male teenagers frequenting the club than females. This resulted in much harassment and many fights, which only contributed to the girls' staying away. In order to try to correct this situation, the city council passed an ordinance that provided that any male teenager desiring to enter the dance club must be accompanied by a female.

After this ordinance went into effect, an 18-year-old teenager was denied admission to the dance club because he came alone. He then filed suit in federal court challenging the constitutionality of the city ordinance. Before his suit came to trial, the teenager got married. Also, a city councilwoman has now indicated that she is considering to propose a resolution repealing the ordinance.

What action should the court take?

Question 2

In order to resolve a long-standing territorial dispute with an Indian tribe, Congress enacted a statute conveying 1,000 acres of federal land to the Indian tribe. The statute provided that the land in question would be sold to the tribe for the price of one dollar. After enactment of this statute was made public, many other Indian tribes protested the government's action. In particular, one of the other tribes claimed title to a large tract of federal land in their state and were angered because no similar land conveyance was made to them. The other Indian tribe brought suit in an appropriate federal district court challenging the constitutionality of this federal statute.

Is the act of Congress constitutional?

Question 3

A hurricane struck the coast of a state with devastating force and caused more than $100 million in damage. Farmers in the state were especially hit hard by the hurricane, which destroyed more than 30 percent of the state's citrus crops. As a consequence, Congress passed an emergency farm aid bill providing $50 million in subsidies to the state's orange growers to compensate them for their economic losses.

The state's economy is very much dependent upon the orange industry, which is its largest staple crop. The federal farm aid bill, however, did not provide any compensation to state farmers growing crops other than oranges. A papaya farmer in the state suffered substantial economic loss when his entire crop was destroyed by the hurricane. The papaya farmer challenges the constitutionality of the aforementioned federal law.

Is this act of Congress constitutional?

Question 4

In an effort to attract a major league baseball team to a city, the city council, with the approval of the state legislature, passed an act that authorized and required the mayor and sports commission to acquire land at a designated area and to develop and construct a ballpark. It also incorporated an express finding that the construction of a baseball park was a municipal use for the citizens of the city.

A group of owners of property in the primary ballpark site filed suit in an appropriate state court seeking to enjoin the city from proceeding with plans to acquire land on that site, including the use of eminent domain to acquire the said property. The property owner's principal argument is that the taking of their land would violate the public use clause of the Fifth Amendment, even if they are paid a fair price for their loss.

Who has the burden of persuasion, and what is the appropriate standard whether property taken by the government satisfies the public use requirement?

Question 5

As a part of its annual ceremony, a religious group gathers on the highest mountaintop in the vicinity for a day of prayer and chanting. The ceremony culminates in an evening bonfire during which the religious group believes the sins of the world are expunged. The religious group applied for a permit to hold its annual ceremony on top of a mountain in a federal park. The chief ranger denied the permit, citing the serious fire risk posed by the bonfire. A federal regulation permits the appropriate federal official to deny such permits if the official has reason to believe that any person or group could cause any environmental harm to the federal park. The chief ranger had been quoted in the local newspaper making various derogatory remarks about cults and had denied day-use permits to other unorthodox groups in the past.

What is the most likely result when the religious group challenges the chief ranger's denial of a permit?

| **KAPLAN** BAR REVIEW

Essays

Constitutional Law

In Class

Suppose a state passes the following statute:

1. *Marriage shall be defined as "the union of one man and one woman." It is a compelling interest of this state to preserve the moral integrity of the institution of marriage, and to preserve the institution as one in which children are born and raised in accordance with our historical traditions.*

2. *It shall be a felony for any man to intermarry or attempt to intermarry with any other man.*

3. *It shall be a felony for any woman to intermarry or attempt to intermarry with any other woman.*

The statute was passed after being lobbied for by a number of "pro-family" groups, including one group called "Protect Our Families from Gays and Lesbians." When it was introduced before the state legislature, its sponsor gave a long speech talking about the "threat" that homosexual activity posed to the institution of marriage. There is also some social science evidence that if members of the same sex were allowed to marry in the state, 60% of the likely unions would involve members of racial minority groups.

You are a junior attorney for a civil rights organization considering making a constitutional challenge to the statute. Write a memorandum assessing the constitutionality of this statute under Section 1 of the 14th Amendment. You have been asked to identify as many possible constitutional defects in the statute, under a variety of theories and different standards of review.

Constitutional Law

In Class

I. **If the right to marry a same-sex partner is considered a fundamental right, does the statute violate the Due Process Clause?**

   A. **(Rule)** Fourteenth Amendment protects against the deprivation of "life, liberty, or property without the due process of the law"
      1. Guarantee of substantive due process assures that a law will be fair and reasonable, and not arbitrary
      2. Substantive due process review applies where a law affects the rights of all persons with respect to a specific activity
      3. Strict scrutiny standard applies to laws that burden a person's exercise of fundamental rights
      4. Under the strict scrutiny standard, the burden of persuasion is on the government to prove that the measure being challenged is necessary to further a compelling state interest
         a. "Necessary" means that there is no less restrictive alternative means available
         b. Strict scrutiny standard demands proof that the restriction of a fundamental right is necessary to serve that interest
   B. **(Application)** Right to marry is recognized as a fundamental right by tradition
      1. Not all marriage restrictions fall under strict scrutiny
         a. Age restrictions and consanguinity limits
      2. State must prove that it is necessary to prohibit same-sex marriages in order to serve a compelling state interest
   C. **(Conclusion)** Yes, the statute violates the Due Process Clause
      1. Preservation of the moral integrity of marriage is not a sufficiently compelling state interest
      2. Alleged threat to the moral integrity of marriage if members of the same-sex are allowed to marry is pure speculation

II. **If the right to marry a same-sex partner is not considered a fundamental right, does the statute violate the Due Process Clause?**

   A. **(Rule)** Courts have applied the rational basis plus standard to cases involving discrimination against gays and lesbians
      1. Traditional rational basis standard- the burden of persuasion is on the plaintiff to show that the measure being challenged serves no legitimate government interest or is not rationally related to any legitimate interest
      2. Rational basis plus standard- closer scrutiny of the measure being challenged and the government's interest
   B. **(Application)** Statute fails the rational basis plus test because protecting the institution of marriage is not a sufficiently legitimate government interest
      1. Restriction is purely based on irrational fear and not fact
   C. **(Conclusion)** Yes, the statute violates the Due Process Clause
      1. No evidence to support that gay marriage will harm or threaten heterosexual marriage

III. **If the right to marry a same-sex partner is considered a fundamental right, does the statute violate the Equal Protection Clause?**

    A. **(Rule)** Fourteenth amendment provides that no state shall "deny to any person within its jurisdiction the equal protection of the laws"

      1. Equal protection review is triggered where persons similarly situated are treated differently- where a law affects the rights of only some persons with respect to a specific activity

      2. As discussed under I, the right to marry is recognized as a fundamental right by tradition, but not all marriage restrictions fall under strict scrutiny

    B. **(Application)** Sexual orientation in general is not a suspect class, but discriminating against gays and lesbians with respect to the enjoyment of a fundamental right (the right to marry) will be reviewed under a strict scrutiny standard

    C. **(Conclusion)** Yes, the statute violates the Equal Protection Clause and is unconstitutional

IV. **Does the statute violate the Equal Protection Clause as a result of sexual orientation discrimination?**

    A. **(Rule)** As discussed above, equal protection review is triggered where persons similarly situated are treated differently- where a law affects the rights of only some persons with respect to a specific activity

      1. Courts have applied the rational basis plus standard to cases involving discrimination against gays and lesbians as a result of sexual orientation

    B. **(Application)** Statute denies gay and lesbian couples the legal benefits of marriage

      1. Obvious denial of the equal protection of the law

      2. Justification for this discrimination is the threat that homosexual activity will impose on the institution of marriage, but this threat is not a sufficiently legitimate state interest to justify discrimination

    C. **(Conclusion)** Yes, the statute violates the Equal Protection Clause and is unconstitutional

V. **Does the statute violate the Equal Protection Clause as a result of gender discrimination?**

    A. **(Rule)** Intermediate scrutiny standard- burden of persuasion is placed on the government to prove that the measure being challenged is substantially related to achievement of an important governmental interest

      1. "Substantially related" means that an exceedingly persuasive justification based on real differences and not prejudice or stereotypes must be shown

    B. **(Application)** Purpose of the statute is not an important governmental interest

      1. Even if it is found that this is an important governmental interest, barring same-sex marriages is not substantially related to the goal of the statute

      2. No evidence to support that gay marriage will harm or threaten the institution of marriage

        a. Fear is based on prejudice and stereotypes about gays and lesbians which is not an "exceedingly persuasive" justification

    C. **(Conclusion)** Yes, the statute violates the Equal Protection Clause and is unconstitutional

Constitutional Law

In Class

This sample answer would be considered above the standard expected of a 1L student.

MEMORANDUM

To: Civil Rights Organization
From: Junior Attorney
Re: Constitutionality of Statute

Your organization can argue that this statute violates the Due Process and Equal Protection Clauses of the 14th Amendment by depriving the state's citizens of a fundamental liberty interest and by discriminating on the basis of sexual orientation and gender.

I.   Due Process—Fundamental Right

The 14th Amendment protects against the deprivation of "life, liberty or property without the due process of the law." The guarantee of substantive due process assures that a law will be fair and reasonable, and not arbitrary. Substantive due process review applies where a law affects the rights of all persons with respect to a specific activity.

The ability to choose whom to marry is essential to self-identification and happiness in life. As such, the freedom to choose a marriage partner is a fundamental liberty right protected by substantive due process against unjustified state restriction. The strict scrutiny standard applies to laws that burden a person's exercise of fundamental rights. However, while the right to marry is recognized as a fundamental right by tradition, not all marriage restrictions fall under strict scrutiny. For instance, the Court may distinguish between regulations that temporarily limit the right to marry (age restrictions) or those that remove possible partners to marry (consanguinity limits), and those that effectively exclude some people from marrying at all, which a same-sex marriage ban does for gays and lesbians. Here, instead of focusing on the narrow right of heterosexual marriage, the right at issue encompasses the fundamental right of all individuals to make personal decisions about marriage partners.

Under the strict scrutiny standard, the burden of persuasion is on the government to prove that the measure being challenged is necessary to further a compelling state interest. The word "necessary" means that there is no less restrictive alternative means available. There must be a very close "fit" between the means and the end.

Here, the state must prove that it is necessary to prohibit same-sex marriages in order to serve a compelling state interest. The facts indicate that the state's interest in preventing same-sex marriage is "to preserve the moral integrity of the institution of marriage, and to preserve the institution as one in which children are born and raised in accordance with our historical traditions." Under the strict scrutiny standard of review, the preservation of the moral integrity of marriage is not a sufficiently compelling state interest.

Even if preserving the moral integrity of marriage was found to be a compelling state interest, the strict scrutiny standard demands proof that the restriction of a fundamental right is necessary to serve that interest. Here, the alleged threat to the moral integrity of marriage if members of the same sex are allowed to marry is pure speculation.

II. Due Process—Liberty Interest

Even if it is found that the right to choose a same-sex partner to marry is not a fundamental right, denying gays and lesbians this liberty would be reviewed under a rational basis plus standard. The courts have applied the rational basis plus standard to cases involving discrimination against gays and lesbians.

Under the traditional rational basis standard, the burden of persuasion is on the plaintiff to show that the measure being challenged serves no legitimate government interest or is not rationally related to any legitimate interest. However, under a rational basis plus standard, there is closer scrutiny of the measure being challenged and the government's interest.

Here, the statute fails this test because protecting the institution of marriage is not a sufficiently legitimate government interest. Further, there is no evidence to support that gay marriage will harm or threaten heterosexual marriage. The restriction is based purely on irrational fear and not fact.

III. Equal Protection—Fundamental Right

Denying gay and lesbian couples the right to participate in the legal institution of marriage also violates the Equal Protection Clause.

The 14th Amendment provides that no state shall "deny to any person within its jurisdiction the equal protection of the laws." The Supreme Court has ruled that equal protection also applies to the federal government under the due process clause of the 5th Amendment. Equal protection review is triggered where persons similarly situated are treated differently - where a law affects the rights of only some persons with respect to a specific activity.

As discussed above, the right to marry is recognized as a fundamental right by tradition, but not all marriage restrictions fall under strict scrutiny. While sexual orientation in general is not a suspect class, discriminating against gays and lesbians with respect to the enjoyment of a fundamental right (the right to marry) will be reviewed under a strict scrutiny standard (defined above), and found unconstitutional.

IV. Equal Protection—Sexual Orientation

The statute denies gay and lesbian couples the legal benefits of marriage. This is an obvious denial of the equal protection of the law. This denial will be reviewed under a rational basis plus standard (defined above). The only justification for this discrimination is the threat of homosexual activity to the institution of marriage. However, the threat of homosexual activity to the institution of marriage is not a sufficiently legitimate interest to justify discrimination under the Equal Protection Act.

V. Equal Protection—Gender Discrimination

The statute states that only a couple of the opposite gender may marry - it treats couples unfairly based on the gender of the couple. Under the intermediate scrutiny standard, the burden of persuasion is placed on the government to prove that the measure being challenged is substantially related to achievement of an important governmental interest. "Substantially related" means that an exceedingly persuasive justification based on real differences and not prejudice or stereotypes must be shown.

Here, the purpose of the statute, "to preserve the moral integrity of the institution of marriage, and to preserve the institution as one in which children are born and raised in accordance with our historical traditions" is not an important governmental interest. Even if it is found that this is an important governmental interest, barring same-sex marriages is not substantially related to the goal of the statute. As stated above, there is no evidence to support that gay marriage will harm or threaten the institution of marriage. Rather, this fear is based on prejudice and stereotypes about gays and lesbians which is not an "exceedingly persuasive" justification.

VI. Conclusion

Your organization has a number of constitutional challenges that it can argue under the Due Process and Equal Protection Clauses of the 14th Amendment.

Constitutional Law

In Class

This sample answer would be considered below the standard expected of a 1L student.

<u>Due Process</u>

The 14th Amendment protects against the deprivation of "life, liberty or property without the due process of the law." The ability to choose whom to marry is essential to self-identification and happiness in life. As such, the freedom to choose a marriage partner is a fundamental liberty right protected by substantive due process against unjustified state restriction. However, while the right to marry is recognized as a fundamental right by tradition, not all marriage restrictions fall under strict scrutiny.

The strict scrutiny standard applies to laws that burden a person's exercise of fundamental rights. Under the strict scrutiny standard, the burden of persuasion is on the government to prove that the measure being challenged is necessary to further a compelling state interest.

The state must prove that it is necessary to prohibit same-sex marriages in order to serve a compelling state interest. Under the strict scrutiny standard of review, the preservation of the institution of marriage (a tradition), is not a sufficiently compelling state interest. Even if preserving the institution of marriage was found to be a compelling state interest, the strict scrutiny standard demands proof that the restriction of a fundamental right is necessary to serve that interest.

Even if it is found that the right to choose a same-sex partner to marry is not a fundamental right, denying gays and lesbians this liberty would be reviewed under a rational basis plus standard. Here, the statute fails this test because protecting the institution of marriage is not a sufficiently legitimate government interest. The restriction is based purely on irrational fear and not fact.

<u>Equal Protection</u>

The 14th Amendment provides that no state shall "deny to any person within its jurisdiction the equal protection of the laws." The Supreme Court has ruled that equal protection also applies to the federal government under the Due Process Clause of the 5th Amendment.

As discussed above, the right to marry is a fundamental right. Denying gay and lesbian couples the right to participate in the legal institution of marriage also violates the Equal Protection Clause.

The statute denies gay and lesbian couples the legal benefits of marriage. This is an obvious denial of the equal protection of the law. This denial will be reviewed under a rational basis plus standard. The only justification for this discrimination is the threat of homosexual activity to the institution of marriage. However, the threat of homosexual activity to the institution of marriage is not a sufficiently legitimate interest to justify discrimination under the Equal Protection Act.

Strict scrutiny review applies to classifications based on race. Race is a suspect class and, as stated above, such laws will be presumptively invalid, absent a showing by the state that the measure is necessary to achieve a compelling state interest. The facts state that if same-sex couples were allowed to marry, social science evidence shows that 60% of the unions would involve members of racial minority groups. Preventing the marriage of members of the same sex who are also members of racial minority groups is not a compelling state interest. Even if the state argues that it is trying to preserve the institution of marriage, and this is found to be a compelling state interest, the strict scrutiny standard of review demands proof that restriction of a fundamental right is necessary to serve that interest.

Constitutional Law

Homework Question 1

Compare individual rights and states' rights. Which are more in need of judicial protection? Which, based on the Constitution, can judges more legitimately protect? In which context have judges come closer to imposing their policy preferences in the guise of constitutional law?

Constitutional Law

Homework Question 1—Outline

Judicial Protection of Individual Rights v. States' Rights

I.   **Which are more in need of judicial protection- Individual Rights or States' Rights?**

   A.   **(Rules)**
   1.   States' rights are represented in the federal government via the Senate, but no such representation exists to similarly safeguard individual rights
   2.   After the 17th Amendment, senators no longer represented the states as states
   3.   Unlike states, individuals are not adequately represented to protect themselves through the political process

   B.   **(Application)** Differences between individuals and states that make oppression of individuals more likely
   1.   There are racial minorities who might be victims of discrimination, whereas there are no minority states
   2.   Extent to which a state legislature is likely to oppress or neglect some subgroup of citizens is probably greater than the extent to which Congress might oppress or neglect some subgroup of states
   3.   In the original constitutional design, the states were actually supposed to protect individual rights against the federal government
       a.   States are now perceived as more of a threat to individual rights, especially for minorities (the Reconstruction paradigm)

   C.   **(Conclusion)** Courts must seek to preserve individual rights against any overstepping by the federal and state governments; individual rights are in greater need of judicial protection from encroachment by the other branches of government
   1.   Judges (and possibly Congress) need to get involved and not afford such great latitude to the states

Judicial Protection of Individual Rights v. States' Rights Based on the Constitution

I.   **Which, based on the Constitution, can judges more legitimately protect?**

   A.   **(Rules)**
   1.   Individuals enjoy a variety of rights that are clearly enumerated in the Constitution, its Amendments, and the Bill of Rights, whereas states do not have much in the way of textual rights
   2.   States' rights are protected by the 11th Amendment, which prohibits federal courts from exercising jurisdiction over state governments in certain circumstances
       a.   Although Eleventh Amendment does not grant the states true immunity, it requires that some types of suits against states be brought initially in state rather than federal court, unless the state waives its immunity
       b.   Also, individual suits for money damages against states cannot be brought in state court

B. **(Application)**

1. Supreme Court decisions (Alden decision) establishing and expanding state immunity have gone well beyond the text of the 11th Amendment
2. Cases (Printz and New York) brought under the guise of a federalism question are examples of judges proceeding in the absence of any constitutional text

C. **(Conclusion)** Based on the Constitution, judges can more legitimately protect individuals' rights

Policy Preferences of Judges in the Guise of Constitutional Law

I. **In which context have judges come closer to imposing their policy preferences in the guise of constitutional law?**

A. **(Rule)** Judges protecting states' rights cannot select a policy outcome the way they can when protecting an individual's rights

1. The most judges may do in the context of states' rights is to shift decision-making power from the federal government to the states

B. **(Application)** A judge accepting an individual rights claim, such as the right to an abortion, can render a judicial decision that implements a policy choice

1. If he favors the right to abortion, he can grant that right to everyone
2. A judge accepting a states' rights claim, such as the claim that the Gun-Free School Zones Act exceeded Congress' power under the Commerce Clause, cannot similarly implement a policy choice

   a. If he strikes down the federal law, states may simply enact their own state-level versions

C. **(Conclusion)** Judges have come closer to imposing their policy preferences in the guise of constitutional law in the context of individual rights

Constitutional Law

Homework Question 1—Sample Answer

This sample answer would be considered above the standard expected of a 1L student.

Judicial Protection of Individual Rights v. States' Rights

Individual rights are in greater need of judicial protection from encroachment by the other branches of government. While states are represented in the federal government (via the Senate), no such representation exists to similarly safeguard individual rights. After the 17th Amendment, senators no longer represented the states as states. Unlike states, individuals are not adequately represented to protect themselves through the political process. Accordingly, the courts must seek to preserve individual rights against any overstepping by the federal and state governments.

There are also differences between individuals and states that make oppression of individuals more likely, with a concomitantly greater need for judicial protection. For instance, there are racial minorities who might be victims of discrimination, whereas there are no minority states. Although there may exist states with unique economic interests, the problem of discrimination is not as acute. Thus, the extent to which a state legislature is likely to oppress or neglect some subgroup of citizens is probably greater than the extent to which Congress might oppress or neglect some subgroup of states.

Finally, in the original constitutional design, the states were actually supposed to protect individual rights against the federal government (the Founding paradigm). However, in light of a modern shift in our view of states, states are now perceived as more of a threat to individual rights, especially for minorities (the Reconstruction paradigm). As such, judges (and possibly Congress) need to get involved and not afford such great latitude to the states.

Judicial Protection Based on the Constitution

Based on the Constitution, judges can more legitimately protect individuals' rights. Individuals enjoy a variety of rights that are clearly enumerated in the Constitution, its Amendments, and the Bill of Rights, whereas states do not have much in the way of textual rights.

States' rights are protected by the 11th Amendment, which prohibits federal courts from exercising jurisdiction over state governments in certain circumstances. Although the 11th Amendment does not grant the states true immunity, it does require that some types of suits against states be brought initially in state rather than federal court, unless the state waives its immunity. After Alden v. Maine, individual suits for money damages against states cannot be brought in state court either. Supreme Court decisions establishing and expanding state immunity have gone well beyond the text of the 11th Amendment. Alden is an example of such, since the amendment plainly talks about federal court and not state court. It also talks about a state being sued by citizens of another state, not its own citizens, but the Court has extended immunity to own-citizen suits.

Similarly, cases brought under the guise of a federalism question are examples of judges proceeding in the absence of any constitutional text, such as in Printz and New

York where the federal government attempted to rely on an enumerated power to commandeer the legislative processes of the states to enact a federal regulatory program.

Policy Preferences in the Guise of Constitutional Law

Judges have come closer to imposing their policy preferences in the guise of constitutional law in the context of individual rights. This is so because judges protecting states' rights cannot select a policy outcome the way they can when protecting an individual's rights. The most judges may do in the context of states' rights is to shift decision-making power from the federal government to the states.

A judge accepting an individual rights claim, such as the right to an abortion, can render a judicial decision that implements a policy choice. If he favors the right to abortion, he can grant that right to everyone. A judge accepting a states' rights claim, such as the claim that the Gun-Free School Zones Act exceeded Congress' power under the Commerce Clause, cannot similarly implement a policy choice. If he strikes down the federal law, states may simply enact their own state-level versions.

Constitutional Law

Homework Question 2

You are a legislative assistant to a senator from Pennsylvania. The senator is fond of late-night brainstorming sessions and frequently comes to you seeking your input on various proposals. One night she offers some thoughts on the economy.

*"I think I know what we need to get America going again. (We'll call this bill GAGA.) First, we need to help people get back on their feet. **A.** Congress should award an unrestricted grant of $500 million to all states that amend their unemployment laws so as to add $50 per month to their unemployment compensation. Of course, I've heard that some governors don't want to accept this aid on that condition. So maybe we should **B.** just pass a law saying that they have to amend their laws and giving them the money."*

   I.   *Is A. constitutional? Is B.? Is there a better way to achieve the senator's goal?*

"Second, we need to stimulate the economy. I have several ideas.

   A.   *"Back to the free market. **A1.** Congress should prohibit the states from making or enforcing any minimum wage laws. If they do, **A2.** any person subjected to that law should be able to get money damages from the state.*

   B.   *"Clean out the deadwood. Congress should require states to impose a mandatory retirement age of 70 in all jobs, public and private.*

   C.   *"Children are our future. Congress should **C1.** require state universities to accept any student from the top 5% of the graduating class of any public high school in that state. I know that will achieve racial diversity in some states, and that's what I want to do. But it won't work everywhere. So let's also say **C2.** that any state that implements the 5% plan and still, at its most selective public university, has a student body containing less than 20% minority group members (we'll take the definition from Croson, p.1082 in that casebook you love so much), will get a million dollars for that university for every percentage point it increases minority representation, up to 20%. I don't care how they do it."*

   II.   *Are these various ideas constitutional? If not, do you have alternative suggestions?*

Constitutional Law

Homework Question 2—Outline

Part I

I. **Does the proposed grant violate Congress' spending power?**

    A. **(Rule)** Article I, section 8 provides Congress with power to lay and collect taxes "to pay the Debts and provide for the common Defense and General Welfare of the United States"

        1. Pursuant to its spending power, Congress can require states to comply with specified conditions in order to qualify for federal funds

        2. Congress may impose condition if: 1) the spending serves general welfare; 2) the condition is unambiguous; 3) the condition relates to federal program; 4) the state is not required to undertake unconstitutional action; and 5) the amount in question is not so great as to be considered coercive to state's acceptance

    B. **(Application)** Conditioning grant upon additional $50 per month in a state's unemployment compensation is proper exercise of Congressional spending power

        1. Condition is unambiguous, relates to the federal program, and does not require a state to undertake unconstitutional action

        2. Unrestricted grant of $500 million is not coercive; states may freely opt out of such aid

    C. **(Conclusion)** Congress has constitutional basis for awarding unrestricted grant to all states that amend their unemployment laws

        1. Valid exercise of Congress' power to spend for the "general welfare"

II. **Does the proposed bill requiring states to amend their unemployment laws violate the Tenth Amendment?**

    A. **(Rule)** Tenth Amendment prevents Congress from interfering with states' lawmaking processes

        1. Prohibits federal government from using an enumerated power to force a state legislature to pass a law or a state executive official to administer a federal program

        2. Known as the anti-commandeering doctrine; Congress may not "commandeer the legislative processes of the states by directly compelling them to enact and enforce a federal regulatory program"

    B. **(Application)** Congress may not coerce a state to implement a federal regulation

    C. **(Conclusion)** Congress overstepping boundaries set forth in the Tenth Amendment by imposing new state unemployment laws under the guise of its spending power

        1. Proposed bill violates the Tenth Amendment

III. **Can the Senator's goal of jumpstarting the economy be achieved in a better way?**

    A. **(Rule)** Sixteenth Amendment gives Congress the power to collect taxes on incomes derived from any source

1. Congressional act purporting to be a "tax" will be upheld as a valid exercise of Congress' taxing power provided it raises revenue or was intended to raise revenue

B. **(Application)** Rather than distributing the grant as an incentive to states, Congress could distribute the money to all states while imposing a tax on states that refused to contribute additional funds to their unemployment compensation

   1. Congress has used its taxing power as a necessary and proper means of achieving a regulatory effect
   2. As long as Congress has power to regulate the activity taxed, the tax can then be used as a regulating device rather than for revenue-raising purposes
   3. In Sunshine Anthracite Coal Co. v. Adkins, 310 U.S. 381 (1940), the Court sustained a tax on coal producers who violated a fair competition law, even though it was designed to be a penalty rather than revenue-raising
      a. Even when Congress does not have power to regulate the activity taxed, the tax will nevertheless be upheld if its "dominant intent" is revenue-raising

C. **(Conclusion)** Better way to achieve Senator's goal is to exercise Congress' taxing power, not spending power

Part II

Minimum Wage Laws

I. **Does a federal prohibition against state minimum wage laws violate the Tenth Amendment?**

   A. **(Rule)** Fundamental principle of federalism is the co-existence of the national government and the state governments
      1. Tenth Amendment provides that "The powers not delegated to the United States by the Constitution, nor prohibited by it to the States, are reserved to the states respectively, or to the people"
      2. While each state has a general police power, there is no federal police power
      3. Federal government must legislate through one of its limited, enumerated powers, whereas the states may regulate any health, safety, welfare, moral, or aesthetic interest through their respective police powers

   B. **(Application)** Federal government is exercising its commerce clause power
      1. Proposed legislation is regulating commercial activity
      2. Congress has the power to impose a national minimum wage

   C. **(Conclusion)** Proposed legislation falls within the ambit of Congress' commerce power
      1. Federal prohibition will preempt any state legislation pertaining to minimum wage

II. **May the federal government properly enforce the minimum wage legislation against states that are in violation of it?**

   A. **(Rule)** Proposed legislation is a permissible exercise of Congress' commerce power, but not permissible enforcement legislation
   B. **(Application)** There is no right Congress can claim to be enforcing

1. The right that Congress would purportedly be enforcing would be something along the lines of liberty of contract
2. However, such a right is not really recognized anymore

C. **(Conclusion)** Congress would not have a proper constitutional basis for enforcing such legislation

Mandatory Retirement Age

I. **Does a federal law imposing a mandatory retirement age of 70 on all states violate the Fourteenth Amendment?**

A. **(Rule)** Fourteenth Amendment requires that states provide citizens with equal protection under the law
1. Age discrimination is subject to rational basis scrutiny: regulation will be upheld if it is rationally related to a legitimate government interest
2. Burden of proof is on the injured party, and the government action is almost always upheld

B. **(Application)** Law discriminates on the basis of age by forcing all public and private employees to retire at the age of 70
1. Government interest is to "clean out the deadwood" and ensure all employees are capable of performing requisite duties while maintaining productivity
2. Governments have legitimate interest in regulating for the health, safety, and moral welfare of their citizens
3. Mandatory retirement age is rationally related to government interest

C. **(Conclusion)** Mandatory retirement law would not violate the Equal Protection Clause

II. **Does the federally-mandated retirement law imposed on all states violate the Tenth Amendment?**

A. **(Rule)** Tenth Amendment prohibits the federal government from using an enumerated power to force a state legislature to pass a law or a state executive official to administer a federal program
1. Known as the anti-commandeering doctrine

B. **(Application)** Congress overstepping its boundaries by commandeering states to pass mandatory retirement legislation for private jobs
1. States would be required to pass a law instructing private employers to impose a mandatory retirement age of 70
2. Same analysis may not apply to public jobs because the state might accept requirement as federal directive to fire employees at 70 without any legislation

C. **(Conclusion)** Proposed legislation will not pass constitutional muster.
1. Must be fixed by either: 1) using Congress' spending power to induce states to implement such a mandatory retirement law; or 2) simply bypassing the states and imposing a national mandatory retirement age as a matter of federal law

Admissions Policy at State Universities

I. **May Congress dictate a state university's admission policy?**

   A. **(Rule)** While this may be possible since there is economic activity involved, the Lopez court seemed to think that direct federal control of state education was beyond the pale
   B. **(Application)** Federal control of state education admissions policies exceeds the constitutional scope of Congress' power
   C. **(Conclusion)** Such activity by Congress lacks a proper constitutional basis

II. **Does federal legislation requiring state universities to accept the top 5% of high school graduates violate the Equal Protection Clause?**

   A. **(Rule)** Law affecting a group that is not a suspect classification only requires a rational relationship to a legitimate governmental interest
      1. Plaintiff must prove no legitimate governmental interest
   B. **(Application)** Academically superior students graduating in the top 5% of their high school class do not constitute a suspect classification
      1. Requiring that state universities admit students with stellar marks is rationally related to a governmental interest in education
      2. Dissidents must show absence of any government interest
      3. Senator has identified a race-specific goal, even though she is using a facially race-neutral device to achieve it
      4. Constitutes intentional discrimination; disparate impact with intent to achieve that impact
   C. **(Conclusion)** Proposed legislation violates Equal Protection

Federal Spending Program

I. **May Congress implement a federal spending program as incentive for state universities to increase racial diversity?**

   A. **(Rule)** Fourteenth Amendment requires that states provide citizens with equal protection under the law
      1. Racial discrimination is subject to strict scrutiny: government must prove the action is necessary to achieve a compelling government interest
      2. Government action that favors racial minorities is subject to the same level of scrutiny as government action that discriminates against racial minorities
      3. Supreme Court has upheld college application systems which took minority status into account but state may not use a quota
   B. **(Application)** Senator's proposed plan does not impose a quota; rather, it rewards racial diversity in a mechanical way while not talking about broader diversity, which is problematic
      1. Federal government is engaged in classification in order to determine what percent of the school consists of minority students

2. Proposed legislation will fail because it is not aimed at enhancing diversity; instead, simply racial balancing
3. Legislation is further problematic in that Senator stated "I don't care how they do it"
   a. She is willing to have payments go to states that employ quotas or other unconstitutional methods
C. **(Conclusion)** Federal spending program is unconstitutional

Constitutional Law

Homework Question 2—Sample Answer

This sample answer would be considered above the standard expected of a 1L student.

Part I

A. Congress would have a constitutional basis for awarding an unrestricted grant of $500 million to all states that amend their unemployment laws so as to add $50 per month to their unemployment compensation. Article I, Section 8 provides Congress with the power to lay and collect taxes "to pay the Debts and provide for the common Defense and General Welfare of the United States." By exercising its spending power, Congress can require states to comply with specified conditions in order to qualify for federal funds. The Supreme Court held that Congress may place a condition on receipt of federal funds by a state if: 1) the spending serves the general welfare; 2) the condition is unambiguous; 3) the condition relates to the federal program; 4) the state is not required to undertake unconstitutional action; and 5) the amount in question is not so great as to be considered coercive to the state's acceptance.

Here, the unrestricted grant of $500 million, which limits receipt of the funds to those states that amend their unemployment laws, is a valid exercise of Congress' power to spend for the "general welfare." The intent and purpose of this bill is to help Americans get back on their feet during a period of financial hardship. Conditioning the grant upon the addition of $50 per month to a state's unemployment compensation in order to qualify for the federal funds is a proper exercise of congressional spending power. In particular, the condition is unambiguous, relates to the federal program, and does not require a state to undertake unconstitutional action. Moreover, an unrestricted grant of $500 million is likely not to be deemed by the courts as coercive. Indeed, states may freely opt out of receipt of such aid should they choose not to accept the condition. Thus, the proposed grant would be upheld as a permissible exercise of Congress' spending power.

B. On the other hand, Congress does not have a constitutional basis for requiring states to amend their unemployment laws while imposing receipt of the federal funds. The issue is whether the proposed legislation's obligation on states violates the 10th Amendment. The 10th Amendment prevents Congress from interfering with a state's lawmaking processes. The 10th Amendment prohibits the federal government from using an enumerated power to force a state legislature to pass a law or a state executive official to administer a federal program. This is known as the anti-commandeering doctrine in that Congress may not "commandeer the legislative processes of the states by directly compelling them to enact and enforce a federal regulatory program." Here, Congress would clearly be overstepping the boundaries set forth in the 10th Amendment by attempting to impose new state unemployment laws under the guise of its spending power. Congress may not coerce a state to implement a federal regulation. Yet this is precisely what Congress would be attempting to effectuate here. Therefore, the proposed bill violates the 10th Amendment.

C. A better way to achieve the senator's goal may have been to exercise Congress' taxing power, instead of its spending power. Rather than distributing the grant as an incentive to all states that amended their unemployment laws, Congress could, instead, seek to distribute the money to all states while imposing a tax on those states that refused to contribute additional funds to their unemployment compensation. The 16th Amendment gives Congress the power to collect taxes on incomes derived from any source. A congressional act purporting to a "tax" will be upheld as a valid exercise of its taxing power, provided that it does, in fact, raise revenue or that it was intended to raise revenue. Congress has used its taxing power as a necessary and proper means of achieving a regulatory effect. Generally, as long as Congress has the power to regulate the activity taxed, the tax can then be used as a regulating device rather than for revenue-raising purposes. Indeed, in Sunshine Anthracite Coal Co. v. Adkins, 310 U.S. 381 (1940), the Supreme Court sustained a tax on coal producers who violated a fair competition law, even though it was clearly designed to be a penalty rather than revenue-raising. Thus, even when Congress does not have power to regulate the activity taxed, the tax will nevertheless be upheld if its "dominant intent" is revenue-raising. Even though the tax may have a substantial regulatory effect, if the tax in fact raises revenue, it will be valid.

Part II

A.

1. The issue is whether the prohibition against state minimum wage laws violates the 10th Amendment and a state's general police power. The fundamental principle of federalism is the co-existence of the national government and the state governments. The 10th Amendment provides that "The powers not delegated to the United States by the Constitution, nor prohibited by it to the States, are reserved to the states respectively, or to the people." While each state has a general police power, there is no federal police power. The federal government must legislate through one of its limited, enumerated powers, whereas the states may regulate any health, safety, welfare, moral, or aesthetic interest through their respective police powers.

   Here, the federal government is exercising its commerce clause power. The proposed legislation is regulating commercial activity. Congress has the power to impose a national minimum wage. Thus, the legislation falls properly within the ambit of Congress' commerce power. As such, it will preempt any state legislation pertaining to a minimum wage.

2. The issue is whether a person may file suit against a state for enforcing its minimum wage laws and recover money damages from the state. Although the proposed legislation is a permissible exercise of Congress' commerce power, it is not permissible enforcement legislation. There is no right Congress can claim to be enforcing. The right that Congress would purportedly be enforcing would be something along the lines of liberty of contract. However, such a right is not really recognized anymore. Thus, Congress would not have a proper constitutional basis for enforcing such legislation.

B. The issue is whether the imposition of a mandatory retirement law on all states is a proper exercise of congressional power.

The 14th Amendment requires that states provide citizens with equal protection under the law. The standard by which the court will examine a state action depends on the basis upon which the state is discriminating between classes of persons. Age discrimination is subject to rational basis scrutiny: the regulation will be upheld if it is rationally related to a legitimate government interest. For rational basis scrutiny, the burden of proof is on the injured party, and the government action is almost always upheld.

In this case, the law discriminates on the basis of age by forcing all public and private employees to retire at the age of 70. The government interest in this case is to "clean out the deadwood." Presumably this entails a concern for ensuring all employees are capable of performing the requisite duties of their jobs while also maintaining an optimal level of productivity. This interest is legitimate because state and local governments have the power to regulate for the health, safety, and moral welfare of their citizens. The mandatory retirement age is rationally related to the government interest because physical abilities tend to decline with age. There are other ways that the government could ensure the fitness of its employees but, under rational basis scrutiny, the government need not show that there is no better way to address the interest in question. Thus, the mandatory retirement law would not violate the Equal Protection Clause because it is rationally related to a legitimate government interest.

However, the issue then becomes whether Congress may impose such a requirement on the states. The 10th Amendment prevents Congress from interfering with a state's lawmaking processes. The 10th Amendment prohibits the federal government from using an enumerated power to force a state legislature to pass a law or a state executive official to administer a federal program. This is known as the anti-commandeering doctrine in that Congress may not "commandeer the legislative processes of the states by directly compelling them to enact and enforce a federal regulatory program."

Here, Congress would certainly be overstepping its boundaries by commandeering the states to pass such mandatory retirement legislation for private jobs. The states would be required to pass a law instructing private employers to impose a mandatory retirement age of 70. However, the same analysis may not apply to public jobs because the state might simply accept the requirement as a federal directive to fire employees at 70 without the need for any legislation. The proposed legislation as is will not pass constitutional muster. It needs to be fixed by either: 1) using Congress' spending power to induce states to implement such a mandatory retirement law; or 2) simply bypassing the states and imposing a national mandatory retirement age as a matter of federal law.

C.

1. The issue is whether Congress may require state universities to accept any student from the top 5% of the graduating class of any public high school in the state. There are several issues at play here in determining the constitutionality of such legislation.

   First, the issue is whether Congress has the power to dictate who state universities must admit. While this may be possible, since there is economic activity involved, the Lopez court seemed to think that direct federal control of state education was beyond the pale.

   Next, the issue becomes whether the proposed legislation violates the Equal Protection Clause. A law affecting a group that is not a suspect classification only requires a rational relationship to a legitimate governmental interest. A plaintiff must prove no legitimate governmental interest. Here, academically superior students graduating in the top 5% of their high school class do not constitute a suspect classification. Requiring that the student body at state universities consist of students with stellar marks is rationally related to a governmental interest in education. Dissidents of this proposed legislation would have to show the absence of any government interest in order to warrant a finding of unconstitutionality.

However, a different equal protection problem is called into question because the senator has indicated that she has a race-specific goal in mind, even though she is using a facially race-neutral device to achieve it. According to standard doctrine, that should count as intentional discrimination since it essentially constitutes disparate impact with an intent to achieve that impact, although several of the conservative justices have seemed to assume that 5% plans are race-neutral. Thus, the proposed legislation violates the Equal Protection Clause.

Accordingly, the proposed legislation would likely fail as an unconstitutional exercise of Congress' power.

2. The issue is whether Congress has a constitutional basis for implementing a federal spending program that rewards state universities for increasing racial diversity.

The 14th Amendment requires that states provide citizens with equal protection under the law. The standard by which the court will examine a state action depends on the basis upon which the state is discriminating between classes of persons. Racial discrimination is subject to strict scrutiny: the government must prove the action is necessary to achieve a compelling government interest. Government action that favors racial minorities is subject to the same level of scrutiny as government action that discriminates against racial minorities. The Supreme Court has upheld college application systems in the past that took an applicant's minority status into account, but it has held that a state may not use a quota to allocate 20% of the student body to minorities.

Here, the senator's proposed plan does not attempt to impose a quota; rather, it rewards racial diversity in a mechanical way while not talking about broader diversity, which is likely to be problematic. It is further problematic in that the senator has stated, "I don't care how they do it." Now, it sounds as though she is willing to have the payments go to states that employ quotas or other unconstitutional methods. Thus, the legislation is likely unconstitutional because it seems to induce state constitutional violations.

The issue is further complicated in that the legislation makes it possible for the states, who are the ones running the admissions program, to use a constitutionally acceptable holistic, individualized assessment. On the other hand, the federal government uses a cruder approach, but only to reward states, not to actually run the admissions policy. Thus, the federal government is engaged in classification because it has to classify students in order to determine what percentage of the school consists of minority students. For that reason, the grant must meet strict scrutiny. The proposed legislation will fail because it is not aimed at enhancing diversity. Instead, it is simply racial balancing.

As a result, the senator's proposed federal spending program will fail for want of constitutionality.

Multiple-Choice Questions

POWERS OF CONGRESS

Question 1

A state has a total population of one million people, of whom only 4% are black. The question of whether to celebrate Martin Luther King Day was put on the ballot and failed to pass by the narrowest of margins. To ensure its passage in the next election, a local pastor sought to relocate elderly citizens to the state with "Friends of the King Holiday," a citizens' group operating in the state. The state has a 90-day residency requirement before a person can vote, and a one-year residency requirement before a person can receive state-funded medical assistance. An elderly woman relocated to the state two months before the election. She liked the state so much that she decided to remain permanently, and she applied for medical assistance the same day that she attempted to register to vote. The woman's application for state-funded medical assistance was denied, and the town clerk refused to allow her to register to vote.

If the woman sues for medical benefits and the right to vote, what is the most likely outcome of the action?

(A) The court will order that the woman receive medical benefits.

(B) The court will order that the woman receive medical benefits and be permitted to register to vote, because she is a member of a suspect class.

(C) The court will deny the woman's claim for medical benefits and the right to vote, because she has resided in the state for only two months.

(D) The court will order that the woman be permitted to register to vote, because voting is a fundamental right that is not subject to state restrictions.

Question 2

According to law enforcement officials, a shocking abduction and murder in the state could have been prevented if the vehicle in which the victim was kidnapped had had an unobstructed sight line into the interior. Heavily tinted glass prevented officers from seeing the victim's signals for help. In response to complaints by law enforcement agencies throughout the state, the legislature enacted a law prohibiting the use of tinted glass that obscured the interior from view in passenger and commercial vehicles. The law exempted livery services from the prohibition, and also allowed tinted glass along the upper edge of the windshield. A trade association whose members received a significant percentage of their income from installing tinted glass challenged the constitutionality of the state law.

When the case reached the Supreme Court, the law was upheld on the grounds that the prohibition of tinted glass was rationally related to public safety concerns and did not unduly burden commerce. After the court handed down the decision, Congress enacted legislation permitting the use of tinted glass in all vehicles. A police officers' association from the original state now challenges the federal law.

How will a court most likely rule on the constitutionality of the federal law?

(A) Upheld, because Congress acted within its power to regulate for the general welfare.

(B) Upheld, because Congress acted within its power under the Commerce Clause.

(C) Struck down, because the highest court in the land upheld the prohibition of the use of tinted glass in motor vehicles.

(D) Struck down, because the state legislature acted within its police power to protect public safety.

Question 3

Congress recently enacted the Reproductive Health Act, and appropriated funds for the implementation of health education and clinical programs associated with sex education and pregnancy-related medical treatments. The sex-education programs were to provide clients with information about the prevention of sexually transmitted diseases, as well as information about all aspects of pregnancy prevention and termination. The president, who felt that homosexuality was immoral, ordered all executive branch personnel to refrain from discussing AIDS-related aspects of health care on the job. A physician's assistant working for the National Centers for Disease Control challenged the constitutionality of the president's order.

How is the court likely to find on the question of the constitutionality of the president's order?

(A) The order is constitutional, because the president has authority over executive branch employees.

(B) The order is constitutional, because the president has substantial discretion in executing the laws.

(C) The order is unconstitutional, because it violates the president's duty to faithfully execute the laws.

(D) The order is unconstitutional, because the president cannot refuse to spend funds as appropriated.

Question 4

The Experimental Drug Commission (EDC) is a federal agency authorized to promulgate rules governing the allocation of federal funds for clinical trials of experimental drugs. State medical facilities apply to the EDC for matching funds for cancer treatment programs serving local communities. The EDC's enabling statute provides that it is run by an executive appointed by the president. The executive, in concert with a 15-member panel of appointed officials, promulgates all rules relating to grants distributed to the experimental cancer drug program. Pursuant to the enabling statute, the executive decision on rules governing the allocation of funds may be blocked by the congressional Joint Committee on Health Care Financing.

In a constitutional challenge to the statutory provision allowing the committee to block the EDC rules on allocating funds, how will the court most likely find the provision?

(A) Invalid, because it violates the constitutional standards by which legislative action is observed.

(B) Invalid, because it violates the equal protection rights of the vast majority of members of both houses of Congress.

(C) Valid, because Congress may condition the receipt of federal funds under a regulatory scheme.

(D) Valid, because Congress has authority under the Necessary and Proper Clause to choose the means by which the purposes of the FDA are accomplished.

Question 5

Congress recently declared war on a foreign republic. In pursuit of this war, Congress enacted a law that instituted rent controls for the duration of the wartime period. The statute provided that the law would be administered by a rent control board. A group of landlords sued the administrator of the rent control board, contending that the rent control law was unconstitutional.

Assuming proper standing and jurisdiction, how should the court rule?

(A) In favor of the landlords, because the rent control statute violates the Contract Clause of the Constitution.

(B) In favor of the landlords, because Congress unconstitutionally abrogated its power to the administrator of the rent control board.

(C) In favor of the administrator of the rent control board, because Congress has the power to initiate wage, price, and rent control of the civilian economy during wartime pursuant to the War Powers Clause.

(D) In favor of the administrator of the rent control board, because Congress has the power to initiate wage, price, and rent control of the civilian economy during wartime pursuant to the Necessary and Proper Clause.

EQUAL PROTECTION

Question 6

Citizens of a state were horrified by the disappearance of a young schoolteacher, who had been vacationing in the state and vanished while jogging along a popular waterway frequented by residents and visitors alike. Local and regional news stations and the local press followed the developing story closely, and a website was created that tracked tips, leads, and search developments. One week after her disappearance, friends conducting their own search located her remains in a shallow grave several miles from where the woman was last seen. At the time the friends were searching, a local news team was following and filming them for a news update planned for the six o'clock broadcast.

The day after the woman's body was found, the state's largest circulation newspaper published a still photograph of the woman's remains taken from the film shot by the broadcast news team. In a front-page article below the photograph, it was reported that the woman had been sexually assaulted and that the cause of death was asphyxiation by garroting. The woman's sister and only surviving family member was appalled at the insensitivity of the newspaper, and brought suit for invasion of privacy against the newspaper for its publication of the picture.

If the newspaper raises the First Amendment as a defense, which statement correctly describes the standard that the court will apply in examining the merits of the case?

(A) The First Amendment protects the publication of truthful information of facts from the public record, such as the manner and cause of death of a person.

(B) The First Amendment protects the publication of truthful depictions of newsworthy events, even if offensive to some sensibilities.

(C) The First Amendment right to free speech guaranteed by the Constitution outweighs the right to privacy guaranteed by tort law.

(D) The First Amendment protects the publisher from liability when the information at issue is truthful.

Question 7

A city became a haven for protests of all kinds. Some of the protests and parades in the city had spawned counter-demonstrations, and on a couple of occasions, violent incidents erupted. The city council became worried when a budgetary analysis showed that the city spent $2,000,000 for extra police protection on weekends on which parades and rallies were held. Therefore, the city council passed an ordinance that provided that groups who applied for a permit to hold a parade or rally in the town could be charged up to a maximum of $2,500 for a permit, to be determined by the city manager, based on how much police protection was anticipated to be needed. A group of radical environmentalists applied for a permit to hold a parade in the town. Knowing that one of the largest employers in a town was a lumber company, the city manager expected a counter-demonstration, and so he imposed a $1,000 fee for the permit. The environmentalists sued to enjoin the enforcement of the ordinance.

How should the court rule?

(A) In favor of the city, because the fee was not based on the content of the message, was narrowly tailored to serve a significant governmental interest, and left open ample alternatives for communication.

(B) In favor of the city, because the ordinance was a valid use of the city's police power to regulate for the city's safety and welfare.

(C) In favor of the environmentalists, because the statute was facially void, not content-neutral, and gave the city manager overly broad discretion as to the price of the permit.

(D) In favor of the environmentalists, because although the ordinance was content-neutral, it gave the city manager overly broad discretion as to the price of the permit.

Question 8

A hearing officer has worked for a federal agency for 17 years. A federal statute provides that hearing officers and all other court employees, with the exception of Article III judges, must retire at age 70. The hearing officer, who is 69, is a highly productive employee, in good health, and could work for several years.

If the hearing officer seeks a declaratory judgment prohibiting her termination at age 70, which of the following is the strongest constitutional argument that the mandatory retirement statute is invalid?

(A) The statute violates the powers granted to Congress under Article I.

(B) The statute violates the Fourteenth Amendment Due Process Clause by depriving the hearing officer of a property right.

(C) The statute violates the Fifth Amendment Due Process Clause by discriminating against the elderly.

(D) The statute violates the Privileges and Immunities Clauses of Article IV and the Fourteenth Amendment.

Question 9

A maintenance worker was hired by a city's parks department and is now in his third consecutive one-year contract. According to a city ordinance, he cannot acquire tenure until after five consecutive annual contracts. In his third year, the maintenance worker was notified that he was not being re-hired for the following year. Applicable state law and city department rules did not require either a statement of reasons or a hearing, and, in fact, neither was offered to him.

Which of the following, if established, most strongly supports the parks department in refusing to give the maintenance worker a statement of reasons or an opportunity for a hearing?

(A) The maintenance worker's performance had been substandard.

(B) A speech he made that was critical of parks department policies violated a department regulation concerning employee behavior.

(C) The maintenance worker worked at the parks department for less than five years.

(D) The maintenance worker could be replaced with a more competent maintenance worker.

Question 10

An historic town had grown rather shabby over the years, with people having a hard time keeping up some of the grand houses. Without any citizen input, the city council decided to apply for the state's historic preservation district status, which would come with some help in bringing back the town's grandeur. When the preservation district status went into effect, the city was suddenly subject to many new ordinances about what colors houses could be painted, what kinds of decorations could be put up, and the design and size of business signs. Although people in the town were accustomed to putting up campaign signs, the city council now banned them, insomuch as their eye-catching graphics did not fit the town's new look. When a political activist insisted on putting up a small, discreet campaign sign, he was fined by the town inspector. The city council then filed for an injunction to remove the activist's sign.

Is the city council likely to obtain injunctive relief?

(A) No, because the activist's sign complies with the town ordinance.

(B) No, because the activist is exercising a protected speech right.

(C) Yes, because the sign is not the only way to publicize the political campaign.

(D) Yes, because the town ordinance does not violate the First Amendment.

FEDERALISM

Question 11

An army fort had been used as a military outpost for more than 100 years. Following the end of the Cold War, the federal government closed the fort and sold half of the property to the state, which used the land to build a university. The population at the school is now double the population that had existed at the base, straining the available water supply. The water source, while located on the land purchased by the state, supplies water to both halves of the property.

As a humanitarian gesture in response to global events, the federal government agreed to take in 200 refugees from a war-torn country, and decided to place them in the barracks that remained on the portion of the land which the federal government still owned. The state then brought suit in federal court to prevent the refugee relocation, claiming that there would not be enough water for the existing population.

What is the most likely outcome of the suit?

(A) The state will prevail, because a state may assert its regulatory authority over the federal government.

(B) The state will prevail, because the source of the water is on state property.

(C) The state will not prevail, because of the Supremacy Clause.

(D) The state will not prevail, because a state may not assert its regulatory authority over a natural resource to be used by the federal government for the benefit of aliens.

Question 12

For more than 100 years, the premier manufacturers of boats in the nation carried on their businesses in one particular state. There was little competition until recently, when out-of-state manufacturers began to take a significant portion of the boat-building business. At the same time, a global economic downturn affected the retail market for boats. Sales of boats manufactured in the state plummeted, layoffs followed on a massive scale, several builders closed their businesses permanently, and the surviving boat manufacturers turned to their state legislators for help.

The legislature responded by enacting an excise tax on all boats purchased in the state but manufactured elsewhere. The amount of the tax on each boat was a percentage of its purchase price, with luxury vessels paying an additional surcharge. A manufacturer of recreational and luxury crafts in a bordering state had acquired a large market share of the retail boat business in the state prior to the tax being passed.

In a challenge to the excise tax by the boat manufacturer in federal court, which of the following is the strongest constitutional argument against enforcement of the tax?

(A) The tax violates the Privileges and Immunities Clause.

(B) The tax imposes a burden on interstate commerce.

(C) The tax violates the Due Process Clause of the Fourteenth Amendment.

(D) The tax violates the Equal Protection Clause of the Fourteenth Amendment.

Question 13

After an anhydrous ammonia leak on a city railway line led to the deaths of three dozen people, the mayor had little trouble convincing the city council to ban the transportation of poisonous gases on that railroad line. Several other communities within the state followed suit, until carriers transporting such gases could no longer traverse the state legally. However, the state is small and not centrally located, so other railway lines in neighboring states allowed the carriers to reach their intended destinations without an unreasonable burden.

Although the inconvenience was minor, a group of carriers challenged the city bans in federal court. When the case reached the U.S. Supreme Court, the Court applied the rational basis test to find that the city bans on the transportation of poisonous gases did not impose an undue burden on interstate commerce.

If Congress were to thereafter enact legislation prohibiting states from banning the transportation of poisonous gases by rail or other channels of commerce, would the federal legislation be valid?

(A) Yes, because the state law would have to give way to the federal law under the Supremacy Clause.

(B) Yes, because the federal law, enacted under Congress's Commerce Clause power, intends to occupy the field.

(C) No, because the highest court in the land has authorized the states to ban the transportation of poisonous gases within their borders.

(D) No, because the equal protection rights of state carriers are violated by the federal prohibition against banning the transportation of poisonous gases within the state's borders.

Question 14

A state owned and operated several landfills, which were filled to 80% of capacity. There was little appropriate land in the state available to establish another landfill. The state legislature passed a statute that placed a $50-per-ton tax on rubbish transported from outside the state to the state's landfills. The governor signed the bill into law. The state's powerful federal congressional delegation, including its two very important senators, exerted their influence upon Congress, and Congress soon passed a bill that validated state taxes on out-of-state rubbish transported into a state if that state's landfills were more than 75% filled. The president signed the bill into law. An out-of-state rubbish-hauling company sued the state, contending that the tax was unconstitutional.

Assuming proper standing, how should the court rule?

(A) In favor of the out-of-state rubbish hauler, because the state tax discriminated against interstate commerce.

(B) In favor of the out-of-state rubbish hauler, because Congress unconstitutionally delegated its authority over interstate commerce to the states.

(C) In favor of the state, because Congress may validate a state tax that discriminates against interstate commerce.

(D) In favor of the state, because the tax did not discriminate against interstate commerce.

Question 15

A Native American reservation is located in the middle of a state. The reservation is large, and Native Americans actually occupy only a small portion of the reservation, which is rich in natural resources. Moreover, a large river flows through the reservation, and many merchants use the river to ship goods between states. A foreign country has offered to purchase a portion of the reservation from the United States—specifically, the portion not occupied by the Native Americans. However, the river flows through this portion of the reservation. By selling the land, Congress will be able to eliminate a substantial portion of the national deficit. Some of the surrounding states are upset over the possible sale of the land, and seek to block the sale.

Does Congress have the power to sell the Native American reservation land to the foreign country?

(A) Yes, because under a balancing test, Congress's interest in selling the land outweighs the states' interest in keeping the land.

(B) Yes, because Congress has the power to dispose of property belonging to the United States.

(C) No, because there is a compelling state interest to not sell the reservation.

(D) No, because Congress does not have the power to sell a portion of a state.

JUDICIAL REVIEW

Question 16

Two women, domestic partners, wished to have a child together. One of the women had had a hysterectomy, but the other hoped to carry a child to term after conceiving through artificial insemination. When attempts to conceive through this method failed, the woman's doctor told her that her only chance to conceive was through *in vitro* fertilization. However, the woman's health insurance carrier denied her request for coverage, claiming that covered fertility treatments were limited to families consisting of a male and female partner. The women decided to explore adoption, but the father of one of the women, outraged at the insurance company's discrimination against his daughter and her partner, filed suit in federal court challenging the insurer's action as a violation of the women's substantive due process right to privacy.

How will the court proceed with the case?

(A) The court will hear the case on the merits, because a special relationship exists between the father and the persons harmed as a result of the insurance company's decision.

(B) The court will hear the case on the merits, because the suit raises a federal question.

(C) The court will dismiss the case, because the father does not have third-party standing.

(D) The court will dismiss the case, because there is no constitutional right to have a grandchild.

Question 17

An employer refused to hire a disabled applicant. The applicant sued the employer for violating the state's Disabled Employees' Act and the Americans with Disabilities Act. The state law was analogous to the federal law, but had different filing and timing requirements. The state trial court found in favor of the employer, but the state appellate court reversed, finding that the employer had violated both the state and federal laws, in light of its interpretation of federal precedent regarding the Americans with Disabilities Act. The state supreme court affirmed the reversal. The employer filed a petition for a writ of *certiorari*.

Which of the following correctly describes how the U.S. Supreme Court will respond to the petition?

(A) It must grant the petition, because Article III, Section 2 of the Constitution gives federal courts jurisdiction over federal questions.

(B) It may grant the petition, because the state decision rested on the interpretation of federal precedent.

(C) It may grant the petition, because the state decision determined that the employer violated a federal law.

(D) It will refuse to grant the petition, because adequate and independent state grounds supported the state court judgment.

Question 18

A state legislature enacted the Health and Safety in Marriage Testing and Education Act, which required all persons applying for a marriage license to undergo a screening for human papilloma virus (a sexually transmitted disease that is frequently asymptomatic and can lead to cervical cancer) and for hepatitis C (a communicable disease that can lead to liver failure). Under the act, all applicants for a license are also required to attend a Saturday class to learn how to prevent the spread of these diseases from one partner to the other. The purpose of the act is to provide prospective spouses with information about two diseases that have severe health consequences and to slow the rates of the diseases in the state population. A resident of the state applied for a marriage license, but his application was denied because he refused to submit to testing for the two diseases, although he was willing to attend the class.

If the resident challenges the act in federal court on constitutional grounds, who bears the burden of proof?

(A) The state, to show that there is a compelling government interest in testing and educating prospective spouses about the two diseases.

(B) The state, because the act substantially affects the class of people seeking to marry.

(C) The resident, because legislative enactments are presumed constitutional.

(D) The resident, to show that the state has overstepped its Tenth Amendment police power to regulate for the health, safety, and welfare of its citizens.

Question 19

On the last day of its legislative session for 2009, a state legislature enacted the following statute, to go into effect on January 1, 2010: "Recycling creates many jobs in our great state, but many state citizens could benefit from increased demand for recycled products. Therefore, all offices in the state must use only 100% recycled paper in their copiers and printers." The governor signed the bill into law. On November 1, 2009, the state Chamber of Commerce filed a complaint in state court challenging the constitutionality of the new law. The state filed a motion to dismiss.

Which argument would best support the state's motion?

(A) The statute is constitutional, because the state's police power includes the authority to enact legislation for the health, welfare, and safety of its citizens.

(B) The Chamber of Commerce does not have third-party standing.

(C) The matter is not ripe for adjudication.

(D) The complaint asks for an advisory opinion, which state courts are not permitted to render.

Question 20

State law requires that any alcohol sold in the state must be sold through state-operated liquor stores. Recently, many of the stores in the state have had problems with employees belonging to a particular racial minority group. State legislators, aware that members of this minority group rarely graduate from college, passed a law that no person may apply for a job in a state-operated liquor store without a college degree. Members of the minority group who applied for jobs with the liquor stores and who were rejected on the basis that they lacked college degrees challenged the law as being discriminatory on the basis of race.

Which of the following correctly describes the level of scrutiny the court should use?

(A) Strict scrutiny, because the classification is based on race.

(B) Strict scrutiny, because even though the law is facially neutral, the state had a discriminatory purpose.

(C) Strict scrutiny, because the law has a discriminatory effect against members of the racial minority.

(D) Rational basis scrutiny, because the law is facially neutral and a mere discriminatory effect is insufficient to trigger strict scrutiny.

Answer Grid

1 (A)(B)(C)(D)		5 (A)(B)(C)(D)		9 (A)(B)(C)(D)		13 (A)(B)(C)(D)		17 (A)(B)(C)(D)
2 (A)(B)(C)(D)		6 (A)(B)(C)(D)		10 (A)(B)(C)(D)		14 (A)(B)(C)(D)		18 (A)(B)(C)(D)
3 (A)(B)(C)(D)		7 (A)(B)(C)(D)		11 (A)(B)(C)(D)		15 (A)(B)(C)(D)		19 (A)(B)(C)(D)
4 (A)(B)(C)(D)		8 (A)(B)(C)(D)		12 (A)(B)(C)(D)		16 (A)(B)(C)(D)		20 (A)(B)(C)(D)

Contracts

Outline

TABLE OF CONTENTS

VII. DEFENSES

VIII. REMEDIES

IX. THIRD-PARTY BENEFICIARIES

X. ASSIGNMENT OF RIGHTS AND DELEGATION OF DUTIES

I. SOURCES OF CONTRACT LAW

A. **In General**

1. There are two principal sources of contract law: Article 2 of the Uniform Commercial Code ("UCC") and state common law.

2. In deciding which source of contract law applies, first look for the subject matter covered by the UCC. If the UCC does not apply, then common law will apply.

B. **The Uniform Commercial Code**

1. The UCC governs "sales of goods." If the UCC would apply to a contract, then UCC provisions will trump any contrary common law rules.

   a. **Sales** are any transactions in which the seller transfers title of goods to the buyer.

      (1) Leases, bailments, and any other types of transactions that involve goods are not considered sales.

   b. **Goods** are broadly defined under the UCC to mean any "movable item."

      (1) Examples of goods are ball bearings, Hummers, processed foods and produce, the Mona Lisa, clothing, carpeting, furniture, and everything on the shelves of Wal-Mart. The UCC also specifically defines the following as goods: growing crops, unborn animals, and "identified things attached to realty," such as uncut timber or tobacco.

      (2) Intangibles (e.g., the "goodwill" of a business), currency, stock, bonds and other securities, the assignment of a legal claim, real property, services (e.g., construction and repair projects, landscaping, dry cleaning) are not goods.

   c. In **hybrid** cases, which involve both the sale of goods and a services contract, the question arises as to which source of contract law should apply.

      (1) The majority rule is that the appropriate source is determined by the predominant purpose of the transaction.

         (a) To determine the predominant purpose of a contract, the following factors are used:

            1) the language of the contract;

            2) the nature of the supplier's business; and

            3) the relative values of the good versus the service.

      (2) The minority rule involves partitioning the contract, applying the UCC to the sale of the goods portion of the contract, and then applying common law to the services portion of the contract.

         EXAMPLE: Both the sale and installation of an audio system for an automobile and the sale of a car with a long-term service agreement involve goods and services.

(3) **Services Contract with Incidental Goods**

    (a) A rendition of services with goods incidentally involved, such as a contract with an artist to paint a portrait, would be governed by common law.

(4) **Sale of Goods with Incidental Services**

    (a) A sale of goods with services being incidentally involved, such as the sale and installation of a water heater, would be governed by the UCC.

d. **Computer Software and Other Electronic Information**

(1) The majority of courts treat computer software and other electronic information as goods governed by the UCC.

(2) In Maryland and Virginia, the UCC has been displaced by the Uniform Computer Information Transactions Act for transactions involving electronic information.

EXAM TIP The UCC governs the sale of all goods, not just the sale of goods priced at $500 or more. The UCC's Statute of Frauds [§ 2-201] applies only to the sale of goods for a price of $500 or more, requiring that a writing be signed by the party against whom enforcement of the contract is sought, but the rest of the UCC applies to the sale of all goods.

EXAM TIP The UCC governs all sales of goods, not just sales of goods involving merchants. The UCC has a number of provisions that create special rules for merchants (e.g., Section 2-205—only a merchant can make a firm offer; Sections 2-314 and 2-315—the merchant warranty provisions). Although the sale of goods by and between consumers is beyond the scope of the special merchant provisions, such sales are governed by all the other provisions of the UCC.

C. **The Common Law of Contracts**

1. Contracts that do not involve the sale of goods are covered by the common law of contracts. Frequently encountered examples are service contracts, contracts involving real property, and assignments of legal claims.

2. **Interplay Between Sources**

a. **Common Law Filling in the Gaps of the UCC**

(1) In cases involving the sale of goods, the UCC supplies the primary law and displaces contrary common law rules. However, where the common law rules are not displaced, those rules will supplement the UCC and fill in its "gaps."

EXAMPLE: An example of a UCC provision displacing a common law rule would be Section 2-205, the firm offer rule. The firm offer rule eliminates the common law requirement of consideration by allowing a merchant to make a firm offer that will remain open by requiring a signed writing to that effect.

EXAMPLE: Another example of UCC provisions displacing the common law rules would be Section 2-207, the battle of the forms provision which overrules the common law's mirror image rule, and Section 2-209, the rule governing midterm modifications which eliminates the common law preexisting duty rule.

EXAMPLE: Some examples of common law gap-filling include the common law doctrines of fraud, duress, and incapacity of minors and/or the mentally infirm. These common law rules apply even where the sale is otherwise governed by the UCC.

b. **UCC by Analogy**

(1) For cases that do not involve the sale of goods, the UCC does not apply. However, courts will frequently use its provisions "by analogy" in developing common law.

D. **Basic Definitions and Concepts of Contract Law**

1. **Contractual Obligations**

a. There are three general categories of contractual obligations:

(1) **Express contractual obligations** are found where the parties make oral or written "expressions" of their commitments.

EXAMPLE: A written contract, an exchange of e-mails, or a face-to-face oral agreement.

(2) **Implied-in-fact contractual obligations** are consensual agreements that fail to express the agreement of the parties in its entirety.

EXAMPLE: The most common implied-in-fact contractual obligation is the duty to pay the "reasonable value" of services rendered or of goods delivered where price is not discussed by the parties in advance.

EXAMPLE: Homeowner hires a plumber to fix a leak, but because of the urgency of the service, the parties do not discuss the price of the work performed. Upon completion of the work, Homeowner has an implied-in-fact obligation to pay the plumber the reasonable value of the services rendered.

(3) An **implied-in-law contractual obligation** arises where there is an equitable imposition of a would-be contract. It is an equitable remedy available to prevent unjust enrichment, and arises in situations where one party bestows a benefit on the other. An implied-in-law obligation is also commonly referred to as a *quasi-*contractual obligation or a restitutionary obligation.

(a) In many cases, the courts will conclude that the bestowal of the benefits unjustly enriched the recipient and will accordingly impose an implied-in-law obligation on the part of the recipient to restore the value of the benefits conferred to the other party.

EXAMPLE: Emergency services are a typical *quasi*-contract area, i.e., a surgeon who performs emergency surgery on an unconscious patient creates an implied-in-law obligation to the patient.

EXAMPLE: Another common situation is where contractual benefits have been conferred by mistake, i.e., a merchant who mistakenly delivers goods to the wrong party may create an implied-in-law obligation on the benefiting party.

EXAMPLE: A third frequent *quasi*-contract situation is where contractual benefits have been conferred via an unenforceable contract, i.e., a would-be buyer of real property who makes improvements on the land before closing and whose oral contract turns out to be unenforceable under the Statute of Frauds may create an implied-in-law obligation on the seller.

b. ***Quantum meruit*** is a means of enforcing both implied-in-fact and implied-in-law contractual obligations.

EXAMPLE: The plumber who was hired to fix Homeowner's leak without first discussing the price may enforce Homeowner's implied-in-fact obligation to pay the reasonable value of the goods delivered via a *quantum meruit* action.

EXAMPLE: A supplier mistakenly delivers goods intended for his buyer to another merchant, who in turn sells them to her customers. The supplier may seek to enforce the merchant's implied-in-law obligation to pay a reasonable value of the goods delivered via a *quantum meruit* action.

c. **Signed Writing Requirements**

(1) A number of rules in contract law require a "signed writing" in order to create an enforceable legal obligation.

EXAMPLE: The Statute of Frauds under both the common law and the UCC bars enforcement of certain contracts unless the party against whom enforcement is sought has signed a writing evidencing the underlying agreement.

EXAMPLE: The UCC requires that firm offers must be made in writing and signed by the offeror in order to be enforceable.

(2) Electronic signatures are legally effective in the vast majority of U.S. jurisdictions under the terms of the Uniform Electronic Transactions Act.

(3) The majority of courts have held that e-mail and the like are sufficient to satisfy the writing requirements of contract law.

II. CONTRACT FORMATION: OFFER AND ACCEPTANCE

A. In General

1. In many cases, parties to a would-be contract negotiate in advance of reaching agreement, engaging in a communications "volley" where inquiries, proposals, and counterproposals are exchanged. The law of "offer and acceptance" provides the rules for determining the point at which the parties have a legally enforceable contract.

B. The Offer

1. In order to constitute an offer, a party's communication must meet two requirements:

   a. an outward manifestation; and

      (1) The manifestation can be oral, written, or made via conduct.

      EXAMPLE: A newspaper seller stands on the corner with a stack of newspapers and hands them to people who pay the posted price.

      (2) Inward thoughts or subjective intentions are irrelevant unless they are reasonably apparent to the other party.

      EXAMPLE: A seemingly serious offer to sell real property made in secret jest is nonetheless an offer.

      EXAMPLE: A proposal to sell at a price that a reasonable person would regard as "too good to be true" (e.g., "new HDTVs for $8.99") does not constitute an offer.

   b. the signal that acceptance will conclude the deal.

      (1) An offer must signal to the would-be offeree that the latter's agreement will conclude the deal. The key inquiry is whether the party making the communication expressed a willingness to commit without further assent.

      EXAMPLE: "I will sell you my car if you'll pay me $2,000 cash." This is an offer because it expresses a willingness to conclude the deal if the other party pays the required $2,000.

      EXAMPLE: "Yes, I'd be willing to sell you my car, but what are you willing to pay for it?" This is not an offer because the communicating party is obviously reserving the right to decide whether she likes the price suggested by the other party. She is thus withholding the privilege of further assent, or she is reserving the right to assent (or not assent) to the other party's proposal.

      (2) Communications that withhold the privilege of further assent fall short of constituting an offer.

         (a) A **preliminary negotiation** is a generic term that applies to the give-and-take that occurs during bargaining.

EXAMPLE: "We're willing to consider that price if you can be more flexible on the warranty and the payment terms."

(b) An **invitation for an offer** is an advanced stage of preliminary negotiations, where the communicating party is closing in on a deal but wants the other party to commit first.

EXAMPLE: "Okay, we're in agreement on everything but price now. What's the best price you can give me?"

2. **Multiple Offerees**

  a. When a question involves a party's communication proposing a deal to two or more persons at the same time, a **multiple offeree** issue arises.

  b. There are three situations where this can occur:

  (1) **commercial advertisements**, where possible offers occur in catalogs, price lists, and circulars;

  (a) Under the American advertising rule, advertisements addressed to multiple recipients are generally treated as invitations for offers rather than offers. The reason is that responses from recipients of the advertisement may exceed the available supply of goods or services; allocating the goods or services among the responding parties will necessitate further assent from the advertising party.

  EXCEPTION: Language in the advertisement such as "first-come, first-served," or "first 10 customers only," identifying the means by which the goods or services will be allocated in the event of an excess of demand, eliminates the need for further assent from the advertiser and, thus, constitutes an offer.

  (2) **reward offers**, which are general offers that name a price for a service but do not specify an offeree, such as "Will pay $100 reward to the person who finds my lost dog"; and

  (a) Generally, reward offers are treated as offers because they are considered communications that promise a bounty in exchange for the performance of a specified task. There are two types of reward offers:

  1) **Self-limiting rewards** are reward offers that indicate the task to be rewarded can possibly be performed only once. They are typically treated as offers that can only be accepted by the first person to render the requested performance in accordance with the terms of the offer.

  EXAMPLE: "Will pay $100 for finding my lost dog."

  2) **Open-field rewards** are reward offers that indicate that the task to be performed can potentially be performed by multiple parties.

EXAMPLE: The Carbolic Smoke Ball case, where the purveyor of a medical preparation promised to pay $100 to anyone who used the preparation as directed and, nonetheless, came down with the flu.

   a) Unless otherwise specified in the offer, open-field rewards can be accepted by any and all persons who render the requested performance in accordance with the terms of the reward.

   EXAMPLE: "Free Joe Six-Pack Action Figure! Send us proof of purchase labels from six cases of your favorite Anheuser-Busch product together with a self-addressed, stamped envelope. Offer good while supplies last!" Because of the limitation stated in the offer, the power of acceptance exists only so long as supplies last.

(3) **auctions**, which are situations where an item is sold to the highest bidder.

   (a) The general rule is that the auctioneer is inviting offers, and the responsive bids are the offers.

   EXCEPTION: Where the auction is "without reserve," then the auctioneer is making an offer to sell to the highest bidder.

3. **The Legal Effect of an Offer**

   a. An offer creates the power of acceptance in an eligible offeree. This gives the offeree the power to create a contract simply by accepting the offer.

   b. When an eligible offeree exercises the power of acceptance before that power is terminated, a legally binding contract is formed between the parties.

   c. Generally, there are four ways to terminate the power of acceptance: lapse of time, the death or incapacity of either party, revocation by the offeror, and rejection by the offeree.

   (1) **Lapse of Time**

       (a) An offeree's power of acceptance terminates at the time stated in the offer. If the offer does not specify the time of termination, then the power of acceptance will terminate after a reasonable time. The reasonable time determination is based on the following factors:

       1) subject matter and market conditions; and

          a) What is considered a reasonable time will vary depending on the subject matter and the relevant market conditions.

          EXAMPLE: A reasonable time would be shorter for an offer to sell stock in a wildly fluctuating market than for an offer to sell real estate in a dormant market.

2) the degree of urgency communicated by the means of transmission.

EXAMPLE: A reasonable time period would be shorter for an offer sent via e-mail than for an offer sent via postal mail.

   (b) **Face-to-Face Conversation Rule**

      1) An offer made by one person to another in a face-to-face conversation is ordinarily deemed to remain open only until the close of the conversation.

(2) **Death or Incapacity of Either Party**

   (a) The supervening death of either the offeror or offeree will terminate the power of acceptance with respect to the offer.

   (b) The supervening incapacity of either the offeror or the offeree, as evidenced by adjudication or the appointment of a guardian, will terminate the power of acceptance.

(3) **Revocation by Offeror**

   (a) Under the rule of free revocability in American contract law, the offeror is free to revoke an outstanding offer, terminating the offeree's power of acceptance, at any time and for any reason, so long as the revocation:

      1) occurs prior to acceptance; and

      2) is effectively communicated.

   (b) There are two methods of communicating a revocation.

      1) **Direct Revocation**

         a) Typically, revocation occurs and terminates the offeree's power of acceptance when the offeror communicates directly with the offeree and advises the latter that the offer has been revoked.

      2) **Indirect Revocation**

         a) In some cases, the offeree will learn of the offeror's intention to abandon the deal from a third-party source, and this will also terminate the offeree's power of acceptance where two conditions are met:

            i) the offeror has taken definite action inconsistent with the intention to enter the proposed contract (such as by selling offered real estate to a third party); and

            ii) the offeree acquires reliable information of the offeror's inconsistent action (such as learning of the sale from a real estate broker).

   (c) **Revocation of an Offer Made to Multiple Offerees**

      1) Under the Second Restatement of Contracts, where an offer is made by advertisement in a newspaper or other general notification to the public or some segment

thereof, the power of acceptance is terminated when the notice of revocation is communicated by advertisement or other general notification equivalent to that used for the offer and no better means of notification is reasonably available (the **functional equivalents rule**).

2) In such a case, a particular offeree loses the power of acceptance, even if he is utterly unaware of the revocation.

(d) **Option Contracts and Firm Offers**

1) An offeror is free to revoke an offer any time before acceptance. Under the common law rule of Dickenson v. Dodds (1876), the offeror can revoke even if he has expressly promised the offeree that he would hold the offer open. Under contemporary law, there are two ways to prevent revocation of an offer: a common law option contract or a firm offer under the UCC.

2) Three elements are required for an enforceable option contract:

a) an offer;

b) a subsidiary promise to keep the offer open; and

  i) A "sell-by" date in an offer is not necessarily a promise to keep the offer open. It can also constitute an express lapse provision, establishing a deadline for when the power of acceptance will terminate.

  EXAMPLE: "I hereby offer to sell you Blackacre for $10,000. This offer expires in 30 days." This language would not indicate an option contract but instead simply an offer with an express date of termination.

c) some valid mechanism for securing enforcement of the subsidiary promise.

  i) The most common way to secure enforcement of the subsidiary promise to keep the offer open is by giving consideration in return.

  ii) Consideration can be in the form of a performance (e.g., payment for the option) or a promise of performance (e.g., where a buyer of real estate promises his best efforts to obtain financing in exchange for the option).

  EXAMPLE: An offer stating, "I hereby offer to sell you Blackacre for $10,000, and in consideration for the $100 received, I hereby grant you a 30-day option on the deal," would meet these three requirements as follows: the offer is the proposal to sell Blackacre for $10,000;

the grant of a 30-day option on the deal; and the payment of $100 to the offeror.

3) A minority of courts have held that revocation of an offer can be prevented where the offer is in writing and signed by the offeror, recites the purported consideration for the promise to keep the offer open, and proposes an exchange on fair terms within a reasonable time.

EXAMPLE: "I hereby offer to sell you Blackacre for $10,000, and in consideration for the $100 received, I hereby grant you a 30-day option on the deal" will create an enforceable option contract under the minority rule, even if the offeree never paid the $100.

4) Under promissory estoppel, courts will sometimes enforce a subsidiary promise to keep an offer open where the offeree has foreseeably and reasonably relied on the option, and injustice can only be avoided by enforcing the promise.

5) **Special Rule for Construction Contracts**

   a) A general contractor bidding on a construction project solicits bids from different subcontractors, such as plumbers, electricians, or glazers. The general contractor must then use these bids in formulating his own bid, but cannot as a practical matter accept those bids unless and until the general contract is awarded.

   b) The problem occurs when a subcontractor revokes his bid (offer) after the general contractor has relied on it to make his own bid on the primary contract, and the general contractor is then awarded the contract based on that bid.

   c) The majority rule is that where a general contractor uses a particular subcontractor's bid to formulate his own, an implied option contract is created via promissory estoppel. This prevents the subcontractor from revoking the bid despite the fact that the subcontractor hasn't promised to keep the bid and the general contractor hasn't provided any consideration to keep the bid open.

6) **The UCC "Firm Offer" Rule**

   a) Under the UCC, a merchant can make a firm offer (an irrevocable offer) to either buy or sell goods without consideration so long as [§ 2-205]:

      i) the offer is made by a merchant;

      ii) the offer is made in a writing signed by the merchant; and

      iii) the offer expressly states by its terms that it will be held open.

b) Note that the UCC defines a **merchant** in terms of his special knowledge or skill with respect to the practices or goods involved in a transaction. It is important to note that a person may be considered a merchant even if he only has knowledge of the goods, or knowledge of the practices.

c) A firm offer that meets all of the above requirements becomes irrevocable either for the period of time stated in the firm offer or for a reasonable time if no time is specified.

d) Under the UCC, the shelf life of a firm offer can be **no more than three months**. Any firm offers that state a time longer than three months will only be irrevocable for the first three months. The offer would then become revocable, but still enforceable.

e) A merchant selling or buying goods can establish an irrevocable offer for longer than the three-month period stipulated in the UCC by creating a valid common law option contract. This means that the requirements of a subsidiary promise to keep the offer open, as well as some consideration in return, must also be present.

(4) **Rejection by the Offeree**

(a) The power of acceptance can also be terminated if the offeree refuses to accept the offer. There are three ways that rejection can be effected:

1) outright rejection;

a) The offeree's power to accept an offer is terminated by his rejection of the offer. The offeree has the power to accept the offer, but the offeree cannot change his mind and try to accept the offer once he has rejected it.

2) rejection via a counteroffer; and

a) A counteroffer made on the same subject matter operates to simultaneously reject the initial offer.

b) Not all statements or questions about an offer are considered counteroffers. An offeree may test the waters by making a "mere inquiry" about the offeror's willingness to negotiate without creating a counteroffer and terminating the power of acceptance.

EXAMPLE: "I am not willing to pay $10,000 for the car, but I would happily buy your car for $9,000." This statement would rise to the level of a counteroffer because the terms of the initial offer, to purchase the car at $10,000, have been modified by the offeree to $9,000. As a result, the offeree made a counteroffer which at the same time rejected the offeror's initial offer.

EXAMPLE: "$10,000 isn't out of the question, but it is a little high, given the age of the car. Would you be willing to consider a lower offer?" This language would not rise to the level of a counteroffer because the offeree is only asking if the offeror is willing to negotiate the terms, and not proposing a different deal.

3) rejection via nonconforming acceptance.

   a) At common law, the **mirror image rule** requires that acceptance must mirror the terms of the offer, and any variation results in a counteroffer and rejection of the initial offer. Despite the mirror image rule, a *de minimis* variation in the terms of the acceptance may likely constitute acceptance in some situations.

      i) If a court concludes that the minor variation was implicit in the offer, or merely a suggestion for the addition of a new term, then the response may constitute acceptance mirroring the offer, creating a contract.

      ii) If the purpose of raising the issue is to attempt in bad faith to back out of the contract, a *de minimis* variation in the terms of the acceptance may still constitute acceptance.

   b) The UCC rejects the common law mirror image rule and recognizes a binding contract despite the presence of a nonconforming acceptance in two sets of circumstances: the shipment of nonconforming goods and the battle of the forms. Each of those circumstances is discussed below.

(b) **Revival of the Offer**

   1) The maker is the master of the offer. Therefore, an offeror has the power to revive an offer that the offeree has rejected, and with it the offeree's power of acceptance, and he can likewise revive an offer that has lapsed; all he must do is communicate the revival to the offeree. This can be accomplished by restating the offer or giving the offeree more time to make a decision.

4. **Offer and Acceptance under Unilateral Contracts**

   a. An offer can require acceptance by either a promise or a performance.

   EXAMPLE: If A makes an offer to sell his car to B for $10,000, A could request a promissory acceptance from B, which would require B to say something to the effect of, "I accept your offer, and promise to pay you

$10,000." Alternatively, A could request a performance as acceptance from B, which would require B to pay A the actual $10,000.

(1) An offer seeking a promissory acceptance is an offer to enter into a **bilateral contract**. A promise is being exchanged for a promise. Under a bilateral contract, the offeree can accept the offer by making the requested promise. In this situation, both parties are bound by the terms of the contract once the mutual promises are exchanged.

EXAMPLE: When A promises the car to B, B accepts by promising A the money.

(2) An offer seeking performance in return is an offer to enter into a **unilateral contract**.

EXAMPLE: A promises B the car, and B can only accept the offer by paying A the money directly.

  (a) Under a unilateral contract:

    1) the offeror is bound only when the offeree completes performance in accordance with the terms of the offer; and

    2) the offeree is never bound to perform because he has never promised to perform. It is entirely up to him whether to perform or not, which accounts for the description of the contract being unilateral. However, he will not be entitled to the benefits of the offeror's promise unless and until he renders the required performance.

(3) Where an offer does not specify whether it must be accepted by a promise or a performance, the offeree is free to choose the means of acceptance. However, the offeree must accept via performance where the terms of the offer or the surrounding circumstances make it clear that a performance is required.

EXAMPLE: A says to his old friend B, "I'll sell you my car for $10,000." B may choose the form of acceptance in this case. B is free to accept the car by either promising to pay A the money, or actually paying A the money. In this case, B's acceptance would dictate the type of contract created, because the terms of A's offer did not specify.

  (a) In practice, true unilateral contracts, or those stemming from a unilateral offer, are relatively rare and typically fall into two categories.

    1) A **reward offer** is a type of unilateral offer where the offeror offers to pay a reward for the successful performance of some act. Ordinarily, the act in question requires some effort on the part of the offeree, and the latter's ability to perform it may be uncertain. The key factor is that the offeror will not settle for a promise and is instead seeking the actual performance before binding himself to the deal.

EXAMPLE: "I'll pay you $100 if you find my lost dog" or "We'll pay $1,000,000 to the first person who proves Fermat's Last Theorem."

2) Rather than a promise to sell a house, most real estate brokerage agreements include a promise by the owner to pay a fee in exchange for the actual sale of the property, which would constitute performance.

(b) **Revocation of the Offer in a Unilateral Contract**

1) Under common law, the offeror was free to revoke the unilateral offer up until the moment that the offeree actually completed performance. The modern rule, which appears in the Second Restatement but which has not yet been adopted by a majority of courts, is that once the offeree begins performance, an option contract is created and the offeror may not revoke.

EXAMPLE: If A offers to pay B $100 to climb to the top of the flagpole, then once B starts climbing the flagpole, A cannot revoke her offer under the modern rule.

EXCEPTION: An offeror may revoke under the modern rule where the offeree is engaged in "mere preparations" to perform rather than the beginning of performance itself.

EXAMPLE: A offers B $100 if the latter can "ride my horse Bronco" for a full minute, but A revokes when B is saddling the horse. Revocation is permissible because the required performance consisted of riding the horse, and saddling was merely preparation.

2) Although the offeror cannot revoke once the offeree has begun performance, acceptance of the offer is still effective only upon the completion of the performance. The task must be completed in accordance with the terms of the offer in order for the offeree to accept the offer and bind the offeror to his performance obligation. In other words, the offeree who gets close to the top of the flagpole but doesn't actually reach it has not yet accepted the offer, and the offeror need not pay him a penny.

3) The offeree of a unilateral contract is free to abandon the performance at any time and even to not undertake performance at all.

NOTE If an offer to enter a unilateral contract was mailed to the offeree, then the offeror may revoke the offer even if the offeree has placed the acceptance in the mail. The mailbox rule (discussed later in this outline) only applies to bilateral contracts, and so dispatch could not constitute acceptance to create a unilateral contract.

C. Acceptance under Common Law

1. There are only two general requirements to constitute effective acceptance:

    a. under the mirror image rule, the acceptance must mirror the terms of the offer; and

    b. the acceptance must be communicated to the offeror.

2. **Communicating Acceptance**

    a. Once again, the maker is the master of the offer, and if the offer stipulates a particular means of communicating acceptance, then the offeree must utilize those means in order to make an effective acceptance. If the offer is silent as to the means of communication, then the offeree is free to use any reasonable means of transmission.

        (1) Unless the circumstances indicate otherwise, a means of transmission is reasonable if it is:

            (a) the means used by the offeror;

            (b) the means customarily used in similar transactions; or

            (c) a means of communication that is equivalent in expeditiousness and reliability to the means used by the offeror.

    b. There are three instances where the requirement that acceptance be communicated to the offeror may not apply:

        (1) acceptance by silence;

            (a) Generally, an offeree's silence in response to an offer cannot constitute acceptance except in the following three circumstances:

                1) where the offeree takes the benefit of the offeror's services with a reasonable opportunity to reject them and with reason to know the offeror's intention;

                2) where the offeror has given the offeree reason to understand that acceptance may be communicated by silence, in which case the offeree's silence will operate as acceptance if he intends as such; and

                EXAMPLE: An insurance company notifies A that his policy will be automatically renewed unless it hears otherwise from him. A remains silent, intending to accept the offer of renewal. Accordingly, his acceptance is affected by his silence.

                EXAMPLE: Same facts as above, except that A does not intend to accept. In these circumstances, his silence will not operate as acceptance. This is a rare instance in which contractual liability depends on the subjective intentions of the party rather than his outward manifestation.

                3) where, because of previous dealings or other circumstances, it is reasonable that the offeree should notify the offeror if he does not intend to accept, in which case his silence will operate as acceptance.

> **EXAMPLE:** A newspaper sends a written notice that it will continue delivering the paper after the subscription has expired unless it hears otherwise from A. When the subscription has previously been renewed in this manner without incident, A's silence in the face of notice will constitute acceptance.

(2) acceptance by performance; and

    (a) The maker is the master of the offer and, accordingly, the maker of an offer to enter a unilateral contract is free to make communication of acceptance a part of the required performance. But if he fails to do so, then acceptance is effective upon the offeree's completion of the requested performance whether or not the offeree so notifies the offeror.

(3) acceptance by mail or other correspondence.

    (a) Under the common law **mailbox rule**, which is the rule in every American jurisdiction except the federal court of claims, acceptance by mail is effective upon dispatch so long as the acceptance is properly posted, with the correct address and postage amount.

        1) The mailbox rule applies only to acceptances and not to any other communication between contracting parties. Thus, offers, revocations, rejections, and counteroffers are all effective only upon receipt by the other party.

        2) Once the offeree dispatches his acceptance, he thereby creates a binding contract.

            a) The offeror may not revoke an offer once acceptance has been dispatched.

> **EXAMPLE:** While B was considering A's offer, A had a change of heart and sent B a revocation. However, B dispatched his acceptance before receiving A's revocation. The parties have a contract because A's revocation was not effective until receipt by B and B's acceptance was effective upon dispatch, which was prior to his receipt of the would-be revocation.

            b) Once the offeree dispatches his acceptance, the parties have a binding contract and the offeree may not withdraw his acceptance.

> **EXAMPLE:** B dispatches her acceptance of A's offer and then has a change of heart, telephonically notifying A of the fact while the acceptance is still in transmission. The parties have a binding contract because B's acceptance was effective upon dispatch, and it is too late for either party to back out because the contract has been formed.

    c)   The parties are bound even if the acceptance is lost in transmission and the offeror has no knowledge of that acceptance.

3)   The mailbox rule applies to acceptances sent by any means of transmission which involves a foreseeable delay between the time of dispatch by the offeree and the time of receipt by the offeror.

    a)   This definition would include a private overnight delivery service.

    b)   This would not include an instantaneous means of communication, such as a facsimile.

    c)   Its application to e-mail is still undecided.

4)   The mailbox rule is only a default rule, meaning that it only applies if the offeror is silent on the question of when acceptance will be effective. As always, the maker is the master of the offer, and thus the offeror is free to establish his own rules for effective acceptance.

EXAM TIP In a situation where the parties simultaneously dispatch identical offers, remember that offers are not effective until received, and the only effect an offer has once received is to create the power of acceptance in the offeree. Accordingly, unless and until one of the parties receives and accepts one of the offers passing in the night, there is no contract.

5)   According to the Restatement, acceptance under an option contract is effective upon receipt by the offeror, but the case law on this question is limited. Some authorities have rejected this approach and held that the mailbox rule applies in this context as well.

6)   **Mailbox Rule Does Not Apply**

    a)   Two situations under the mailbox rule involve an offeree who dispatches two responses to an offer: the first purporting to reject the offer, and the second purporting to accept it. In these cases, the mailbox rule does not apply.

    b)   The parties' obligations will depend on which of the offeree's communications reaches the offeror first:

        i)   If the acceptance reaches the offeror first, then the acceptance is effective upon receipt and the parties are bound to the contract.

        ii)   If the rejection reaches the offeror first, then the offeree's power of acceptance is terminated and the subsequently arriving acceptance becomes a counteroffer, which the original offeror is free to accept or reject.

D. Acceptance and the UCC

1. Unless the contract language or circumstances unambiguously indicate otherwise, acceptance may be made in any manner and by any medium reasonable under the circumstances [§ 2-206(1)(a)].

2. The UCC rejects the common law mirror image rule and recognizes a binding contract despite the presence of nonconforming acceptance in two situations: the shipment of nonconforming goods and the so-called "battle of the forms."

3. **Seller's Shipment of Conforming and Nonconforming Goods**

   a. Under the UCC, a seller can accept a buyer's offer to purchase goods for prompt or current shipment in one of three ways:

      (1) a promise to ship goods in conformity with the terms of the offer, such as an acknowledgment of order form sent to the buyer;

      (2) a prompt or current shipment of the goods in conformity with the terms of the offer; or

      (3) the seller can also accept the buyer's offer by shipping nonconforming goods.

         (a) In contrast to common law, under which the nonconforming shipment would have constituted a counteroffer which the buyer would have been free to accept or reject, the UCC specifies that the shipment constitutes a valid acceptance and creates a binding contract between the parties.

         EXCEPTION: Under the UCC, the shipment of nonconforming goods will not constitute acceptance if the seller notifies the buyer that the shipment is offered only as an "accommodation" to the buyer. In such circumstances, the shipment constitutes a counteroffer which the buyer is free to accept or reject.

         EXAMPLE: Buyer orders 1,000 widgets from Seller for immediate delivery. Seller responds by shipping 800 widgets with an accompanying notice to Buyer explaining that Seller did not have adequate inventory to ship 1,000 widgets and was thus shipping 800 widgets as an accommodation to Buyer in light of Buyer's urgent need. The nonconforming shipment would not constitute an acceptance of Buyer's offer in this case.

         (b) Absent accommodation, the seller's shipment of nonconforming goods constitutes acceptance of the buyer's offer under the UCC. It also constitutes a breach of the resulting contract under the perfect tender rule, which is described in detail later.

4. **The Battle of the Forms**

   a. UCC Section 2-207 is designed primarily to deal with difficulties created by the application of the common law mirror image rule to commercial settings, in which parties typically transact business via the use of preprinted forms.

b. A so-called "battle of the forms" may occur when a buyer places an order (the offer) and the seller's acceptance form contains terms which differ from the buyer's order or are not addressed in the order at all.

(1) Note that these rules apply regardless of which party (buyer or seller) is the offeror or offeree.

c. Because the seller's acceptance contains terms that vary from the buyer's offer, the seller's response constitutes a **nonconforming acceptance**. The UCC deals with two issues in a manner different from the common law.

(1) First, in many circumstances the UCC rejects the common law mirror image rule and treats a nonconforming acceptance as a legally effective acceptance, thus binding both parties to the contract despite the differing forms.

(2) Second, the UCC rejects the common law last shot doctrine in determining the terms that will govern a contract formed via mismatching forms.

d. Unless acceptance is expressly made conditional on assent to the additional or different terms (a **conditional acceptance**), the nonconforming acceptance will operate as an effective acceptance of the offer, forming a valid and enforceable contract. Once the contract is formed, the next step is to determine the effect of the new or additional terms.

EXAMPLE: Buyer sends Seller a purchase order for 1,000 widgets at the advertised price of $10 each. Seller sends Buyer an "Acknowledgment of Order Form" that promises delivery of the widgets at the stated price, but also contains boilerplate language negating warranties and limiting remedies in the event of breach. Seller's form will operate as acceptance of Buyer's offer and create a binding contract despite the presence of terms that vary from Buyer's purchase order.

(1) **Dickered versus Boilerplate Terms**

(a) Typically, the forms will be in agreement as to the **dickered terms**—those specific to the transaction—but may vary with respect to the **boilerplate terms**—standard terms that appear on the parties' respective forms regarding issues such as arbitration and warranties.

e. **Nonconforming Acceptance or Confirmation**

(1) When a contract is formed by an offer followed by a nonconforming acceptance, the treatment of additional or different terms depends on the identities of the parties.

(2) **Transaction Involving a Consumer**

(a) When at least one party to the transaction is not a merchant, the additional or different terms are construed as proposals for addition to the contract. Thus, they are not part of the contract unless the offeror expressly agrees to the additional terms [§ 2-207(2)].

(3) Transactions Where Both Parties Are Merchants

    (a) In a transaction between merchants, there is a distinction between additional terms and different terms.

        1) A nonconforming acceptance contains **additional terms** when its provisions address an issue or topic not addressed in the original offer.

           EXAMPLE: Buyer's offer is silent on the question of arbitration, and Seller's acceptance purports to require arbitration of all claims.

        2) A nonconforming acceptance contains **different terms** when the offer says one thing about a particular issue and the would-be acceptance says something else.

           EXAMPLE: Buyer's offer requires arbitration of claims, and Seller's acceptance precludes it.

    (b) Additional Terms

        1) Additional terms become part of the contract unless [§ 2-207(2)]:

           a) the offer expressly limits acceptance to the terms of the offer;

               EXAMPLE: "This order expressly limits acceptance to the terms stated herein."

           b) the offeror objects to the additional terms within a reasonable time after receiving notice of them; or

               EXAMPLE: This could be accomplished through language to the effect of: "We do not accept the binding arbitration provision set forth in your Acknowledgment of Order."

           c) the additional terms would materially alter the contract.

        2) **Materially Altering Terms**

           a) Under Section 2-207, terms that **materially alter** the contract are those that would result in surprise or hardship if incorporated without the express awareness of the other party [§ 2-207, cmt. 4].

           b) Examples of clauses that would materially alter the contract include [Id.]:

               i) a clause negating standard warranties, such as that of merchantability or fitness for a particular purpose in circumstances in which either warranty normally attaches;

               ii) a clause requiring that complaints be made in a time materially shorter than customary or reasonable; and

       iii) any clause that would vary in a significant way an established usage of trade or a course of past dealing between the parties.

EXAMPLE: Buyer sends Seller a purchase order for 1,000 widgets at the advertised price of $10 each. Seller sends Buyer an Acknowledgment of Order that promises delivery of the widgets at the stated price and includes boilerplate language that negates all warranties and requires payment for the order to be complete within 30 days of delivery, which is standard in the widget trade. The negation of warranties will not be considered part of the contract because it would serve to materially alter the contract. The 30-day payment deadline would be considered part of the contract because it would not materially alter the terms of the contract.

  (c) **Different Terms**

    1) With respect to different terms, the majority of decisions employ the **knockout rule** and omit both the offeror's original provision and the offeree's differing provision from the resulting contract.

EXAMPLE: Buyer's purchase order contains a choice-of-law provision stating that California law will govern disputes arising from the transaction, and Seller's order acknowledgment states that New York law will govern. Neither provision will be part of the parties' contract; if the parties desire a choice-of-law provision, they will have to negotiate one from scratch.

    2) A minority of decisions treat a different term appearing in the acceptance as a mere proposal for alteration of the contract, which the offeror is free to accept or reject.

EXAMPLE: On the same facts as immediately above, the buyer's California law provision would govern the contract unless he expressly agreed to the seller's contrary provision.

  (4) **Written Confirmations**

    (a) Another situation governed by the battle of the forms rules occurs when parties enter a contract—typically in real-time via face-to-face or telephonic communications—and then one or both of the parties follow up with a written confirmation containing terms additional to or different from the terms of the original deal.

        (b)   As is the case for a contract formed by an offer followed by a nonconforming acceptance, the treatment of the additional or different terms depends on the identity of the parties

            1)   If at least one of the parties to the transaction is a consumer, then any additional or different terms are mere proposals for addition to the contract which the receiving party is free to accept or reject.

            2)   If the transaction is between merchants:

                a)   any additional terms are automatically part of the contract unless:

                    i)   they would materially alter the contract; or

                    ii)   the receiving party objects to them within a reasonable time;

                b)   any terms in a confirmation that differ from the terms of the prior agreement are proposals for inclusion in the contract, which the receiving party is free to accept or reject; and

                c)   if both merchants send written confirmations and those confirmations contain conflicting terms, then the knockout rule applies and neither party's term is in the contract.

                    i)   All jurisdictions agree that the knockout rule applies to written confirmations.

        (c)   Because the parties already have a binding contract in this situation—formed prior to the sending of any written confirmation(s)—a written confirmation cannot constitute a conditional acceptance and, accordingly, the parties are bound to the contract irrespective of any differences between their prior agreement and the forms.

    f.   **Conditional Acceptance**

        (1)   Under the UCC, a definite and seasonable expression of acceptance will operate as an acceptance even though it states additional or different terms, unless acceptance is expressly made conditional on assent to the additional or different terms [§ 2-207(1)].

        (2)   However, if the acceptance is made expressly conditional on assent to the additional or different terms, the nonconforming acceptance will not be effective to form a contract.

            (a)   In this situation, no contract is formed until the offeror expressly assents to the additional or different terms.

        (3)   **What Constitutes a Conditional Acceptance?**

            (a)   Under the majority rule, a would-be acceptance which tracks the language of the exception as set out in Section 2-207 constitutes a conditional acceptance if the language in question is clear and conspicuous.

EXAMPLE: Buyer sends Seller a purchase order for 1,000 widgets at the advertised price of $10 each. Seller sends Buyer an Acknowledgment of Order form that promises delivery of the widgets at the stated price, but also contains boilerplate language negating warranties and limiting remedies in the event of breach. Seller's form also contains the following language in large bold font: "Our acceptance of your order is expressly conditional on your assent to the additional or different terms that appear in this acknowledgment." Under the majority rule, Seller's form constitutes a conditional acceptance of Buyer's order, and thus does not operate as a legally effective acceptance. Thus, the exchange of forms does not create a contract. Either party is free to back out of the deal prior to the buyer's assent to the additional or different terms.

(b) Under the minority rule, a would-be acceptance constitutes a conditional acceptance only if it clearly communicates that the offeree is unwilling to do business with the offeror unless and until the offeror agrees to the offeree's terms.

EXAMPLE: Buyer sends Seller a purchase order for 1,000 widgets at the advertised price of $10 each. Seller responds to Buyer's order with an e-mail saying, "We are in receipt of your order for 1,000 widgets at the advertised price of $10 each, and we will be happy to fill it. However, before we can do so, we must require you to agree to the following terms." The message then sets forth terms negating warranties and limiting remedies and concludes, "Upon receipt of your reply to this message stating your agreement to these terms, we will immediately ship your order." Under the minority rule, this exchange of forms would constitute conditional acceptance. By contrast, the proviso tracking language in the form used in the previous example would not constitute conditional acceptance.

g. **Other Situations Governed by the Battle of the Forms Rules**

(1) **Contracts Formed by Conduct**

(a) The UCC also provides that the parties' conduct in recognizing the existence of a contract is sufficient to establish a contract, even though their writings do not otherwise establish a contract [§ 2-207(3)].

EXAMPLE: Buyer sends a purchase order to Seller, Seller responds with a conditional acceptance containing a negation of warranties, and the parties have no further communications. Seller nevertheless ships the ordered goods, and Buyer accepts and pays for them. Although the parties' writings do not form a contract—because Seller sent a conditional acceptance—a binding contract is formed by their conduct.

(b) If a contract is established in this way, the terms of the contract will be the terms on which the writings of the parties agree, together with the implied terms or default rules established by the UCC for warranties, remedies, party performance, and other topics. (The UCC's default rules are discussed at length below in the section on contract interpretation.)

EXAMPLE: On the same facts as above, the parties' contract will include all the terms on which their respective forms agree—typically, the dickered terms such as product description, price, and quantity. Seller's negation of warranties would not be included in the contract because it does not appear in Buyer's form. The UCC's implied warranties would therefore govern the transaction despite Seller's attempt to negate them.

(2) **Transactions without Preprinted Forms**

(a) Although most situations governed by these rules will involve transactions consummated via preprinted forms, the same rules apply to any sale of goods in which an offer is followed by a nonconforming acceptance (e.g., an exchange of transaction-specific e-mails or letters) or a real-time contract is followed by confirmation(s) (e.g., a follow-up letter confirming the details of a deal reached over lunch).

(3) **Shrink-Wrap Contracts**

(a) The authorities are divided on whether the rules of Section 2-207 apply to so-called shrink-wrap contracts (i.e., agreements that consumers find "shrink-wrapped" to computers and other high-tech goods once they open the boxes containing them).

  1) The courts that apply Section 2-207 typically conclude that the boilerplate terms in such agreements are mere proposals for additions to the contract, following the usual rules governing transactions that are not "between merchants."

  2) Other courts have held that Section 2-207 does not apply and that the consumer's retention and use of the goods constitutes an acceptance of the shrink-wrap terms.

III. CONSIDERATION AND PROMISSORY ESTOPPEL

A. **Consideration and Bargain**

1. The general rule in American contract law is that a promise is unenforceable unless it is supported by consideration. The promise has some value and must be exchanged for something else of value, such as a counterpromise or performance given to the promisor by the promisee as *quid pro quo* for making the promise.

2. The exchange of promise for consideration is called a **bargain** or **bargained-for exchange**. The requirement of consideration is easily fulfilled in most contract situations, since there is almost invariably a *quid pro quo* (e.g., goods for money) establishing a bargained-for exchange.

3. However, in some promissory transactions, no exchange is contemplated or the existence of *quid pro quo* is questionable. Many of these situations involve intrafamilial transactions, but they occur in the commercial world as well. The problem arises because the promisee has neither promised nor given anything in return to the promisor, leaving the consideration requirement unsatisfied. These transactions are called **gratuitous promises**, which are generally unenforceable under the doctrine of consideration.

   EXAMPLE: A invites his newly widowed sister-in-law, who lives 60 miles from A's farm, to come and live in his guest house without charge so that she'll have a safe place to raise her family, explaining that he is eager to help her in her time of dire need. Because the sister-in-law neither promised nor gave anything in return for A's promise, A's promise is gratuitous and unenforceable.

4. **Insufficient Consideration versus Failure of Consideration**

   a. **Insufficient Consideration**

      (1) A promisor defending against an attempt to enforce a gratuitous promise can state his defense in several ways:

         (a) the promise is not supported by consideration;

         (b) there is a want of consideration, or consideration is lacking; or

         (c) there is legally insufficient consideration.

   NOTE ▶ These terms are not to be confused with a failure of consideration.

   b. **Failure of Consideration**

      (1) A **failure of consideration** is a claim that the party has not performed in accordance with his promise.

      EXAMPLE: If A promises to deliver a horse to B in exchange for B's promise of payment and A then fails to deliver the horse, then there is a failure of consideration. However, we would not say that the consideration for B's promise was lacking, since A's original promise of performance constituted consideration for B's promise of payment.

5. **Bargained-For Consideration**

    a. The majority of jurisdictions evaluate consideration based on the bargained-for exchange inquiry. A minority of jurisdictions use a benefit/detriment analysis instead. Under this test, consideration is evaluated based on whether there is a benefit to the promisor or a detriment to the promisee.

        (1) There are also jurisdictions that use a hybrid evaluation combining the bargained-for exchange inquiry with the benefit/detriment analysis to define consideration as requiring a promise in exchange for a detriment.

        (2) Whether courts are applying the benefit/detriment test or the hybrid "promise in exchange for a detriment" test, the question of whether a particular performance by the promise constitutes a "detriment" is answered by the application of the so-called **legal detriment test**.

            (a) Under this test, the question is not whether the promisee will actually suffer or end up with some sort of net loss due to the transaction. Rather, the question is whether the promisee is doing something he had a legal right not to do or is forgoing some activity in which he had a legal right to engage.

                EXAMPLE: Playing a concert at Carnegie Hall may well be thrilling for a musician, but it would still constitute a legal detriment because the musician has a legal right not to play the concert. Likewise, giving up smoking and drinking may well be good for one's health, but it would still constitute a legal detriment because the abstainer is forgoing activities in which he has a right to engage. Accordingly, promises to pay the musician and the abstainer for their respective efforts would be enforceable under the legal detriment test. These activities would likewise meet the majority bargained-for exchange definition of consideration, for they would each constitute a performance given in exchange for a promise.

6. **Inadequacy of Consideration**

    a. The modern rule is that courts do not police the equivalence of bargained-for exchanges via the consideration doctrine. In other words, the supposed inadequacy of consideration is no defense to a breach of contract claim.

        EXAMPLE: If A promises his birthright for a mess of pottage from B, B has nonetheless provided consideration for the promised birthright no matter how meager the value of the pottage.

        EXCEPTION: If A promised to sell Blackacre to B for a meager sum and then refused to deliver, some courts would refuse to grant B specific performance because of inadequate consideration and, instead, limit B's remedy for breach to money damages.

b. Do not confuse "insufficient consideration" with "inadequate consideration."

   (1) **Insufficient consideration** is an increasingly archaic way of saying that there was no consideration for a particular promise.

   EXAMPLE: A promises his sister-in-law a place to raise her family and seeks nothing in return.

   (2) By contrast, a claim of **inadequate consideration** assumes that there is consideration but argues that it is too small in comparison with the value of the promise for which it is exchanged.

c. Modern courts do not police the fairness of bargains via the consideration doctrine. However, a party may be able to defeat the enforcement of an excessively one-sided bargain through the defense of unconscionability, discussed later.

7. **Illusory Promises**

a. A promise to perform that leaves performance to the discretion of the promising party is an **illusory promise** and won't constitute consideration.

   EXAMPLE: Thus, if A says to B, "I'll sell you as many widgets as you want to order within the next two weeks for $5 a piece," and B agrees to buy at that price as many widgets as he decides to order from A, B's promise is illusory and will not constitute consideration for A's promise.

8. **Bargain**

a. Consideration requires a bargain, but does not require bargaining. Thus, there is no requirement that the parties actually negotiate before reaching a deal. "Take it or leave it"-styled transactions are just as enforceable as those following extensive rounds of negotiation. In other words, the bargain requirement refers to the presence (or absence) of an exchange between the parties, not the process of reaching the deal.

b. In contemporary language, bargain may mean that something of greater value was acquired for lesser value, and implies that the transaction was beneficial to the recipient. For purposes of the consideration doctrine, though, **bargain** merely indicates an exchange, which could be beneficial or detrimental.

9. **Gratuitous Promises**

a. **Executed Gifts Distinguished**

   (1) Although gratuitous promises are unenforceable under the consideration doctrine, gratuitous transfers are legally binding upon satisfaction of the requirements of a gift.

   (2) In most states, delivery of the would-be gift combined with a present intention to bestow the gift constitutes a legally binding gratuitous transfer.

   EXAMPLE: If John promises Kirsten a new car for her birthday, that would constitute a gratuitous promise and would be unenforceable if John declines to follow through. However, if John gives Kirsten a new car for her birthday, then the transfer is legally binding, and John cannot later change his mind and take back the car.

b. **Bargains Distinguished**

(1) Certain considerations will determine whether an exchange is a bargain or a gratuitous promise.

(a) **Recitals of Consideration**

1) The requirement of consideration is not satisfied by a false recital.

EXAMPLE: A wants to make a binding promise to give his young granddaughter $10,000 on her 21st birthday and, accordingly, gives her a note that reads: "For value received, I promise you $10,000 upon your 21st birthday." If no value was received in exchange for the promise, the recital would not satisfy the consideration requirement and the promise would be unenforceable.

EXCEPTION: Some courts will enforce option contracts on the basis of a signed writing with a false recital of consideration.

2) A condition on a gratuitous promise also does not satisfy the requirement of consideration. A condition is something a promisee must do to avail himself of the promisor's benevolence.

EXAMPLE: A invites his newly widowed sister-in-law, who lives 60 miles away from his farm, to come and live in his guesthouse without charge so she'll have a safe place to raise her family, explaining that he is eager to help her in her time of need. The promisee here won't be able to take advantage of A's offer unless she moves her family the 60 miles to A's farm. However, the move is merely a condition of the gratuitous promise, not consideration.

3) Distinguishing consideration from a condition on a gratuitous promise can be accomplished using three factors:

a) the language of the parties;

   i) Words suggesting benevolence rather than self-interest, such as "gift," may indicate a gratuitous promise that has a condition rather than consideration.

b) commercial versus charitable or familial context; and

   i) Bargains are standard operating procedure in the commercial context, and gratuitous promises in that setting are rare. By contrast, gratuitous promises are made in the family and charitable context more regularly.

c) the benefit to the promisor.

   i) In case of doubt, the most important factor in determining whether a particular performance is consideration or a mere condition on a gratuitous promise is whether the promisor benefits from the performance.

EXAMPLE: Consider again the situation in which A invites his newly widowed sister-in-law, who lives 60 miles from A's farm, to come live in his guest house without charge so the she'll have a safe place to raise her family, explaining that he is eager to help her in her time of need. The 60-mile move is a condition on a gratuitous promise rather than consideration because A's explanation suggests a benevolent purpose, the transaction occurs in the familial context, and it is the promisee-widow and her family, not A, who will benefit from the move.

10. **Alternatives in the Absence of Consideration**

   a.   There are two sets of circumstances in which a promisee may be able to enforce a promise that is not supported by consideration.

   (1) **Past or Moral Consideration**

   (a) As a general rule, a promise given in exchange for something already given or already performed will not satisfy the bargain requirement.

   EXAMPLE: In Mills v. Wyman [20 Mass. (3 Pick.) 207 (1825)], the court refused to enforce the father's after-the-fact promise to compensate a Good Samaritan for nursing his dying son, and the case would likely come out the same way today.

   (b) Two exceptions to the past consideration rule were available at common law and continue to apply today:

   1)   a written promise to pay a debt barred by the statute of limitations is binding; and

   2)   a written promise to pay all or part of an indebtedness that has been discharged in bankruptcy is binding.

   (c) A minority of jurisdictions, supported by Section 86 of the Second Restatement, will enforce a promise made in recognition of a past benefit conferred so long as:

   1)   the promisee conferred the benefit on the promisor and not on a third party; and

   2)   the benefit is material.

   EXAMPLE: A sees that B is in grave danger and heroically intervenes to save the latter, injuring himself in the process. B gratefully promises to compensate A for his efforts. These are the facts of Webb v. McGowin [168 So. 196 (Ala. Ct. App. 1935)], where the court enforced the promise because A's efforts bestowed a material benefit (the saving of a life) on B.

EXAMPLE: Because the Good Samaritan in Mills v. Wyman bestowed the benefit of nursing services on the promisor's son rather than on the promisor, the promise would not be enforceable.

EXCEPTION: Where the promisor makes a promise in recognition of benefits that the promisor received under the terms of a contract, the promise is not enforceable.

EXAMPLE: Employer promises a retiring employee a pension worth half the latter's salary in recognition of the latter's many years of hard and loyal work. Although the employee's past work no doubt bestowed material benefits on the employer, the work was done under contract (i.e., the employee was paid for it under the terms of the employment agreement), and accordingly, the employer's promise is not enforceable.

(2) **Promissory Estoppel**

(a) A promisee that reasonably relies to his detriment on a gratuitous promise may be able to enforce that promise. The doctrine of **promissory estoppel** allows for the enforcement of certain promises even where there is no consideration in return.

(b) There are four requirements that must be met in order for promissory estoppel to be available:

1) a promise;

    a) Clearly, in order for promissory estoppel to be available, there must be a promise on which the claim is based. Statements of present intention or vague statements about the future would not qualify as a promise. The statement must contain an unambiguous assurance of future action to be considered a promise.

    EXAMPLE: Statements like "I would like to give you some money to help you with college" would be considered too vague to be an actual promise. Alternately, "I will give $25,000 toward your tuition this fall" would be specific enough to qualify as a promise.

2) foreseeable reliance;

    a) The promisee's reliance must be reasonably foreseeable to the promisor at the time of the promise

    EXAMPLE: The widow's move to her brother-in-law's farm on the faith of his promise would have been reasonably foreseeable to the brother-in-law at the time he made her the promise. However, if the widow had purchased a high-end SUV to facilitate the move, this would likely not have been foreseeable.

3) actual reliance; and

    a) The actual reliance must be induced by the promise. This means that the action or reliance cannot be taken on account of other factors.

    EXAMPLE: If the widow had already decided to make the 60-mile move before her brother made her the promise, then this would not be actual reliance.

4) injustice without enforcement.

    a) A promise that meets the other elements required by promissory estoppel will be binding if injustice can be avoided only by the enforcement of the promise.

    b) Although this requirement may sound vague and open-ended, most courts take it seriously and are willing to use promissory estoppel to depart from the general rule that gratuitous promises aren't enforceable only where the prospect of injustice is convincingly established.

    c) There are several factors that a court analyzes.

        i) The court will consider the strength of the case as a whole, and where there is substantial proof of the other elements, the claim that injustice cannot otherwise be prevented is strengthened. Alternately, where there is weak evidence of the other elements, it is less likely that the court will find that injustice could not otherwise be prevented.

        ii) The court will consider the blameworthiness of the breach. Thus, a willful breach provides a stronger case for promissory estoppel than a breach occasioned by circumstances beyond the promisor's control.

        iii) The court will consider the **balance of equities** between the parties. Thus, the requisite injustice is easier to establish the greater the harm of nonenforcement to the promisee is, and more difficult to establish the greater the harm of enforcement to the promisor is.

        EXAMPLE: An uncle's promise to give his nephew $100,000 upon graduation from a specific school is more likely to be enforced if the nephew turned down scholarship opportunities at other schools in order to attend the school of the uncle's choosing, or if the school would have been out of the nephew's reach but for the uncle's promise to pay. It is less likely that a court would enforce an uncle's promise to pay $100,000 upon graduation from law school if the nephew has a lucrative job and the uncle's family has in the meantime suffered serious financial setbacks since making the promise.

iv) The more detrimental a promisee's reliance, the easier it is to establish the requisite injustice. Some courts treat detrimental reliance as an independent requirement to be established in order to prove promissory estoppel.

EXAMPLE: Consider an alternative to the preceding example of the uncle who promised to pay the nephew $100,000 upon graduation from law school. The nephew in reliance on the promise decided to borrow his way through a top-ranked school in a distant state, giving up a chance to attend a lesser-ranked, less expensive state school. In this case, it is very possible that the nephew's job prospects and earning potential upon graduation from the high-ranked school are dramatically improved, and a court might find that his reliance on his uncle's promise was, in fact, beneficial and not detrimental. As a result, this would prevent the promise from being enforced.

v) Some courts treat enforcement of a gratuitous promise as a last resort. In those jurisdictions, enforcement via promissory estoppel is barred where other alternatives that could prevent injustice exist. However, all courts would find the existence of options short of enforcement of the promise to be a highly relevant factor in deciding the nature of the injustice at risk.

IV. STATUTE OF FRAUDS

A. In General

1. The general rule in contract law is that a contract need not be in writing and that oral and written agreements are equally enforceable.

2. However, the Statute of Frauds provides an important exception to that rule and makes some classes of contracts unenforceable unless reflected in a signed writing. The Statute of Frauds was originally an English statute and has been adopted in every U.S. jurisdiction through either legislation or common law.

3. The Statute of Frauds can be divided into two general areas of application:

   a. certain sales of goods; and

      (1) The Statute of Frauds governs certain sales of goods in every jurisdiction except Louisiana [§ 2-201].

   b. certain transactions not involving the sales of goods.

      (1) Other types of transactions that do not fall under Section 2-201 of the UCC may still be governed by the Statute of Frauds where states adopted the original Statute of Frauds or some modified version of it.

B. The Statute of Frauds in Operation

1. The Statute of Frauds applies to certain categories of contracts, such as contracts for the sale of real estate or contracts lasting more than one year.

2. For these contracts, the Statute of Frauds requires that the contract be evidenced by a writing signed by the party against whom enforcement is sought.

3. In the context of litigation, the Statute of Frauds is a defense which, if available, may be raised against a party who has claimed breach of contract.

   a. The defense is available to the breaching party when the transaction in question falls within one of the categories governed by the Statute of Frauds, and the required writing is absent or deficient.

C. Evaluating Statute of Frauds Issues

1. The general rule is that a contract within the Statute of Frauds is not enforceable absent a writing signed by the party against whom the enforcement is sought. The most efficient way to analyze a Statute of Frauds problem is by analyzing three questions in the following order:

   a. **Does the agreement fall within the Statute of Frauds?**

      (1) The Statute of Frauds only governs certain categories of contracts/agreements; thus, if the subject matter of the agreement does not fall under the Statute of Frauds, then the Statute of Frauds will not apply.

      (2) If the agreement does fall under the Statute of Frauds, it is necessary to proceed further with the analysis.

b. **Is the Statute of Frauds satisfied?**

    (1)   If an agreement is within the Statute of Frauds, then the key question is whether the Statute's writing requirement is met.

        (a)   If the signed writing requirement is met and the Statute is satisfied, then the Statute of Frauds will not render the contract unenforceable.

        (b)   If the contract is within the subject matter of the Statute of Frauds but the Statute is not satisfied, then the party seeking to enforce the contract will lose.

c. **Is alternative enforcement available?**

    (1)   If the contract is within the Statute of Frauds, but the Statute is not satisfied, the party seeking to enforce the contract will have to use another theory of enforcement, such as promissory estoppel or *quasi*-contract, in order to protect its interests. The final step in the Statute of Frauds analysis is to look for any of those alternative theories that could apply.

D. Analyzing Problems under the Statute of Frauds

1. **Specific Coverage under the Common Law Statute of Frauds**

a. In most states, six categories of agreements are governed by the Statute of Frauds:

STATUTE OF FRAUDS

MY LEGS

Marriage, Year, Land, Executor, Guarantee, Sale of goods

---

    (1)   a contract upon consideration of marriage;

    (2)   a contract that will not be completed within one year of the formation of the contract;

    (3)   a contract for the sale of an interest in land;

    (4)   a contract of an executor or administrator to answer for a duty of the decedent;

    (5)   a contract of guarantee or suretyship; and

    (6)   a contract for the sale of goods at a price of $500 or more.

        (a)   This category is governed specifically by Section 2-201 of the UCC.

b. Individual states have added additional categories to the six conventional ones. Two common additional categories are real estate brokerage agreements and nonmarital cohabitation agreements.

c. In the typical case, there is little difficulty in determining whether a particular contract falls under the Statute of Frauds. However, some categories have specific limitations within them that narrow the reach of the Statute of Frauds.

d. **Promise to Marry**

(1) Most states have abolished the cause of action for breach of a promise to marry, though it still exists in some jurisdictions. In jurisdictions that recognize this claim, the coverage of the Statute of Frauds has been narrowed as follows:

(a) A promise to marry that has been given in exchange for dowry or other settlement is governed by the Statute, and there must be a signed writing in order to secure enforcement of either party's obligations.

(b) An exchange of promises to marry is not governed by the Statute of Frauds and does not need signed writing to secure enforcement.

e. **Performance within One Year**

(1) The year at issue under the one-year provision is measured from the date of the contract's formation rather than the date of the beginning of performance. A contract that contemplates a duration of less than a year may nonetheless fall under the Statute of Frauds if performance is not to be completed until more than one year after the contract's formation.

EXAMPLE: In June of her first year of law school, Law Student enters an oral agreement with Law Firm to work for the firm during June, July, and August of her second summer. Although the duration of the contemplated performance is only three months, the performance will not be complete until 14 months after the making of the agreement. Accordingly, the contract is governed by the one-year provision, and a signed writing is required in order to secure enforcement.

(2) When a contract does not specify a date by which performance is to be completion, the question of whether a particular contract is to be performed within one year of the making thereof is answered by determining whether it is at all possible to complete the required performance within a year's time.

EXAMPLE: It is highly unlikely that the construction of an oil-producing facility in a war-ravaged country would be completed within a year. But because the performance is possible within that time—even if exceedingly unlikely—the agreement is not governed by the one-year provision, and no signed writing is required.

EXAMPLE: One of the parties to an oral construction agreement attempts to back out 14 months into the project and raises the Statute of Frauds as a defense. Because the prospect of performance is measured from the point of making the contract (when completion within a year was possible) rather than from the time of the dispute (when completion within the first year is clearly no longer possible), the agreement is not governed by the one-year provision and no signed writing is required.

EXAMPLE: A three-year exclusive representation agreement between a professional athlete and his agent cannot be performed within a year, no matter how diligently the agent works. Accordingly, the agreement is governed by the one-year provision, and a signed writing is required.

(3) Virtually any contract can be breached or excused within a year of its formation. However, courts typically hold that a breached or excused contract would not be a fully performed contract for purposes of the one-year provision.

EXAMPLE: Although a two-year contract for an employee's services might be breached by the employee's poor performance at some point during the first year, the contract is nevertheless governed by the one-year provision because full performance will take two years.

(4) Under the majority rule, a lifetime or permanent contract of employment is not governed by the one-year provision because the employee's death is possible within the first year, resulting in termination of the contract without breach. The minority does treat these types of contracts as falling within the one-year provision.

f. **Land-Sale Contracts**

(1) The land provision has been modified under some circumstances.

(2) The land provision governs contracts for the sale of an interest in land, and most courts take the expression "contract for sale" literally, thus distinguishing between a contract for a future sale and a present conveyance.

 (a) The contract for future sale is governed by the land provision and requires a signed writing. The present conveyance of land promised for money is held to be outside the land provision.

(3) Although real estate brokerage agreements certainly contemplate the sale of an interest in land, most courts treat brokerage agreements as falling outside of the land provision. The reason is that the brokerage agreement is really a service contract and not a contract for real estate.

 (a) Some jurisdictions have resolved this by adding a separate category to their Statute of Frauds specifically for brokerage agreements.

(4) Most courts treat a lease of real property as a contract falling within the land provision because a leasehold is an interest in land. Other jurisdictions exclude short-term leases of a year or less from the Statute of Frauds.

g. **Guaranty / Suretyship Agreements**

(1) The general rule that a promise to answer for the debt of a third party—a suretyship or guaranty agreement—is subject to the Statute of Frauds has two critical exceptions.

(a) When the creditor discharges the original debtor from his obligation on the faith of a guarantee by a third party to pay the debt, these agreements are not governed by the Statute of Frauds and do not require a signed writing by the guarantor.

(b) Under the **main purpose exception**, if the main purpose of the guarantor's promise is to protect or promote his own economic interests, rather than the interests of the debtor, then the agreement is not within the Statute of Frauds and no signed writing is required.

1) The mere presence of a selfish interest is not sufficient to trigger this exception; it must be central to the promise.

h. **Sale of Goods over $500**

(1) This category is discussed under "Analyzing Problems under the UCC Statute of Frauds."

2. **Satisfaction of the Statute of Frauds**

a. If a contract falls within the Statute of Frauds, then the general rule is that the contract is unenforceable unless evidenced by a writing signed by the party against whom enforcement is sought. In essence, there are two requirements for satisfaction of the Statute: a writing, and that the writing be signed.

b. **The Writing Requirement**

(1) There is no requirement that the parties put their actual agreement in writing; rather, all that is necessary is that the writing be a memorandum thereof, which can be prepared before, during, or after contract formation. Under the common law, the following memoranda have been held to satisfy the writing requirement:

(a) a letter from one of the parties to a third party describing the agreement;

EXAMPLE: "Dear Carville: You'll be delighted to know that I finally convinced Matalin to sell her car to me, and she was willing to do so for only $8,000."

(b) the written offer, acceptance of which formed the contract; and

EXAMPLE: "I will sell you my CD collection for $5,000, but you'll need to move fast because other would-be buyers are interested."

(c) a letter from one of the parties to the other party repudiating, and so admitting, the agreement.

EXAMPLE: "Dear Tony: I regret to inform you that I can't go through with the sale of my racehorse to you. Although the $100,000 you agreed to pay is very generous, my accountant has advised me of the tax implications of the sale, which I hadn't considered, and so I must regretfully bow out."

    (2)   The memorandum need not document the transaction in detail. Only the following terms are required:

        (a)   the identity of the parties to the transaction;

        (b)   the nature and subject matter of the contract; and

        (c)   the essential terms of the unperformed promises in the agreement.

    (3)   **Required Description in Cases under the Land Provision**

        (a)   The case law is split on the kind of description you need to satisfy the land rule under the Statute of Frauds, with some cases holding that an address or its equivalent will do the trick and others requiring a full legal description.

    (4)   Most courts treat electronic documentation, such as e-mail, as satisfying the writing requirement.

c.   **The Signature Requirement**

    (1)   The actual signature of the party against whom enforcement is sought is not necessary. Any symbol, including initials; typed, stamped, or preprinted signatures; or letterhead, if used with the intention to authenticate the writing, will suffice.

    (2)   Most states have adopted the Uniform Electronic Transactions Act ("UETA"), pursuant to which electronic signatures are considered to satisfy any legal writing requirements.

    (3)   **"Tacking Together" Multiple Documents**

        (a)   The writing need not be a single document; a party may satisfy the Statute by tacking together several documents which, once combined, satisfy all the necessary requirements for the Statute of Frauds.

            1)   If all of the documents are signed by the party against whom the contract is being enforced, or if a signed document incorporates unsigned documents by reference, then the signature requirement is satisfied.

            2)   If unsigned documents are not incorporated by reference in a signed document, "tacking together" the signed and unsigned documents to satisfy the Statute of Frauds is nevertheless permissible if:

                a)   there is at least one signed writing unambiguously establishing a contractual relationship between the parties;

                b)   the signed and unsigned documents clearly refer to the same subject matter; and

                c)   there is clear and convincing evidence of acquiescence to the unsigned documents by the party against whom enforcement is sought.

d. **Performance**

(1) The Statute of Frauds may be satisfied with respect to some of the categories of governed contracts via part performance.

(2) **Land Contracts**

(a) Part performance will make an oral contract for the sale of land enforceable in two situations:

1) in an action by the buyer against the seller, but not in an action by the seller against the buyer; and

2) in an action for specific performance, but not in an action for money damages.

(b) Part performance requires a showing of any combination, or all three, of the following:

1) payment of all or part of the purchase price;

2) taking of possession; and

3) making substantial improvements to the property.

(3) **One-Year Contracts**

(a) Full performance of an oral contract for services by the party performing the services will make the contract enforceable against the paying party. On the other hand, part performance is not compensable on the contract. However, the performing party may be able to recover for the reasonable value of the services actually rendered via *quantum meruit*.

(4) **Sale of Goods Contracts**

(a) The UCC Statute of Frauds may be satisfied by part performance of a sale of goods contract, and the rules governing such satisfaction are discussed later.

3. **Enforcement Where the Statute of Frauds Is Not Satisfied**

a. If the contract is within the Statute of Frauds but the Statute is not satisfied because the breaching party never signed a written document, the aggrieved party may nevertheless be able to secure some protection for his interests via an action for restitution or promissory estoppel.

b. **Recovery for Benefits Conferred**

(1) Where one party bestows benefits upon another in connection with an oral contract, even if the enforcement of that contract is barred by the Statute of Frauds, the aggrieved party may recover something. The party has the option of filing a cause of action for restitution, seeking to recover the value of the benefits that he conferred. Alternatively, if services are involved, the party may recover on a theory of *quantum meruit*, meaning he could sue to recover the reasonable value for the services he rendered.

EXAMPLE: A spends three months working for B under an oral two-year employment contract. If B fires A and successfully raises a Statute of Frauds defense against enforcement of the oral contract, A may nonetheless be able to recover from B the reasonable value of the services rendered in *quantum meruit*.

c. **Promissory Estoppel**

(1) Where a party suffers losses in reliance on an oral contract, but the enforcement of that contract is barred under the Statute of Frauds, the party may be able to recover damages via promissory estoppel.

EXAMPLE: Where a party to an oral contract within the Statute of Frauds promises the other party that he has created or will create a signed writing evidencing the parties' agreement, and the other party relies on that assurance by failing to take other steps to satisfy the Statute of Frauds, most courts will find promissory estoppel against the party who falsely made assurances of a signed writing.

EXAMPLE: In many cases, however, there is no assurance that a writing has been or will be created, and the reliance at stake will instead be based on the very contract whose enforcement is barred by the Statute of Frauds—as would be the case, for example, for an employee who leaves his current job and moves across the country based on an oral two-year employment contract, only to be dismissed before he starts his new job. Invoking promissory estoppel in this setting is both more controversial and more difficult.

(2) Some courts hold that promissory estoppel is available to protect reliance on a contract whose enforcement is barred by the Statute of Frauds. Other courts have held that the common law promissory estoppel doctrine is preempted by the Statute of Frauds.

(3) Among those courts that do recognize promissory estoppel, some will impose stiffer requirements on the claimant than those applicable under an ordinary promissory estoppel action. In particular, courts will look for:

(a) the definite and substantial character of reliance, and its relationship to the remedy sought;

(b) the extent to which the reliance is corroborated by the evidence of the formation and terms of the contract; and

(c) the extent to which the formation and terms of the contract are otherwise established by clear and convincing evidence.

E. **Analyzing Problems under the UCC Statute of Frauds**

1. **Specific Coverage under the UCC Statute of Frauds**

a. The UCC Statute of Frauds is Section 2-201, which by its terms governs agreements "for the sale of goods for the price of $500 or more."

(1) With regard to agreements for which the price is payable in some form other than money (e.g., goods), the monetary value of the consideration must be determined in order to apply the $500 rule.

(2)   For agreements contemplating the sale of multiple goods, calculation of the price will depend on whether the transaction constitutes a single contract or a series of separate contracts. When an agreement falls within the UCC Statute of Frauds and the Statute is not satisfied, the entirety of the contract is unenforceable, not just the portion of the contract which exceeds $499.99.

b.   The UCC Statute of Frauds also applies if a contract as modified falls within the Statute (e.g., the contract is modified such that the price of the goods has gone from $300 to $600) [§ 2-209(3)]. By the same token, if the newly modified contract now falls outside of the Statute of Frauds, it does not apply.

2.   **Satisfaction of the UCC Statute of Frauds**

   a.   There are five ways to satisfy the UCC Statute of Frauds.

      (1)   **Signed Writing**

         (a)   The easiest way to satisfy the UCC Statute of Frauds, a signed writing requires:

            1)   a writing;

               a)   Although the UCC defines **writing** as "any intentional reduction to tangible form," which clearly covers everything from quill and parchment to computer printouts, a more difficult question is presented by electronic documentation (e.g., e-mail). A majority of courts have concluded that electronic documentation satisfies the writing requirement of the UCC.

               b)   The proposed revisions to UCC Article 2 replace the word "writing" with the word "record" for the express purpose of covering electronic documentation in the UCC Statute of Frauds and other provisions.

            2)   that is signed by the party against whom enforcement is sought; and

               a)   The UCC broadly defines "signed" as "any symbol executed or adopted by a party with present intention to authenticate a writing," which covers the same variety of "signings" effective under the common law Statute of Frauds.

                  EXAMPLE: The party's initials; a typed, stamped, or printed signature; or a memorandum written on preprinted letterhead would all suffice.

               b)   Most states have adopted the UETA, under which electronic signatures satisfy legal writing requirements.

            3)   which is "sufficient to indicate that a contract for sale has been made between the parties."

               a)   The Official Comment to UCC Section 2-201 states, "All that is required is that the writing afford a basis for believing that the offered oral evidence rests on a real transaction," a very relaxed standard.

> **EXAMPLE:** A enters an oral agreement with B to sell the latter a speedboat for $10,000. B writes a check that contains A's name as the payee, B's name as payor, $10,000 as the amount, and the word "speedboat" in the notation space. Although the writing does not use the word "agreement" or "contract," it is clearly "sufficient to indicate that a contract of sale has been made" between A and B and would, therefore, satisfy the writing requirement of the UCC Statute of Frauds against B, the signing party.

(b) Satisfaction of the UCC Statute of Frauds requires the term indicating the quantity of goods sold in the transaction.

   1) The contract is unenforceable beyond the quantity of goods shown in the writing, irrespective of the parties' actual agreement.

   2) If there is no quantity term, the contract is altogether unenforceable, subject to two exceptions:

   a) where other language in the writing provides an unambiguous basis for measuring quantity; and

   > **EXAMPLE:** "My 2009 sweet basil crop" or "my 1998 Honda Odyssey."

   b) in the case of output and requirements contracts, the expression "output," "requirements," or their equivalent satisfies the quantity requirement under the UCC.

   3) Apart from the quantity term, no other term is required in the writing. Moreover, it doesn't matter if a term is incorrectly stated. However, a writing can have so few terms that it will no longer be "sufficient to indicate that a contract for sale has been made between the parties."

   > **EXAMPLE:** A and B enter an oral agreement under the terms of which A is to sell B five tobacco barns for a total of $5,000. After they shake hands, A takes out a piece of paper, writes "five barns," signs it, and gives it to B. If A subsequently backs out of the deal, he will have a successful Statute of Frauds defense against B despite the fact that he signed a writing with a quantity term, because the writing, taken as a whole, is insufficient to indicate that a contract for sale has been made between A and B.

(c) Despite the fact that the rules under the UCC Statute of Frauds are generally more easily satisfied than the common law Statute of Frauds rules, a written offer that will satisfy the latter may not be enough under the UCC.

1) Because the UCC's writing requirement says that the writing must be "sufficient to indicate that a contract for sale has been made between the parties," the plain language suggests that only a writing that is contemporaneous with or subsequent to contract formation will satisfy the test.

2) However, a written offer that proposes a sale of goods at a price of $500 or more that meets the requirements of the UCC firm offer rule is enforceable against the signing merchant. In such a case, the UCC Statute of Frauds is irrelevant, despite the fact that without documentary proof of acceptance, the offer is not sufficient to indicate that a contract for sale has actually been made.

(2) **Merchant's Confirmation**

(a) The UCC Statute of Frauds may be satisfied when two merchants enter an oral agreement and one of them sends the other a written confirmation of the agreement. In such a circumstance, the Statute is satisfied against the recipient merchant if the latter fails to object to the confirmation in a timely fashion.

(b) A valid merchant's confirmation requires a writing that [§ 2-201(2)]:

1) is "sufficient against the sender";

a) The question here is whether the confirmation meets the requirements of Section 2-201(1) (i.e., it must be signed by the sender, it must contain a quantity term, etc.).

2) is "in confirmation of the contract";

a) The authorities are divided on whether this language imposes a requirement on valid merchants' confirmations in addition to the requirement that the writing be "sufficient against the sender." Some courts hold that a writing that is sufficient against the sender under Section 2-201(1) is all that is necessary; other courts stress the "and" term and require express language confirming the existence of a prior oral agreement.

EXAMPLE: During a telephone conversation on March 8, A places an order and B agrees to fulfill it. A sends a signed letter to B that outlines the price, quantity, and delivery terms "per 3/8 discussion," and ends with the following language: "We look forward to you fulfilling our order per these terms." Because the signed writing would be sufficient to satisfy the UCC Statute of Frauds against sender A, some courts would hold that it would also be sufficient against the recipient. Other courts would require an express reference to the parties' preexisting "agreement" or "contract" in order to satisfy the "writing in confirmation of the contract" requirement of Section 2-201(2).

3) is "sent within a reasonable time" of the making of the oral agreement; and

4) the contents of which the receiving merchant has "reason to know."

(c) A confirmation that never reaches the intended recipient's place of business (e.g., because of postal misdirection) would not be valid against the recipient, since the latter would have no "reason to know" its contents. On the other hand, a confirmation that reaches the intended recipient's place of business but remains unopened through some neglect would meet the "reason to know" test.

(d) A confirmation that meets the foregoing requirements will satisfy the UCC Statute of Frauds against the recipient unless the recipient provides written notice of objection to the confirmation's contents within 10 days of receipt, but a would-be objection that is itself sufficient against the objector under Section 2-201(1) will satisfy the Statute against the objector.

EXAMPLE: A and B enter an oral agreement under the terms of which A is to sell B five tobacco barns for a total of $5,000. The following day, B sends a written confirmation of the agreement to A, and two days later B receives a signed reply that reads in pertinent part: "My understanding is that we don't have a contract between us, for as I mentioned, I am still entertaining other offers for the barns. My apologies for any confusion that may have been caused." Because A's reply objects to the confirmation's contents, the confirmation does not satisfy the UCC Statute of Frauds against A.

EXAMPLE: A's signed reply to B's confirmation reads: "I regret that I can't go through with the sale of my barns to you. Although the $5,000 you agreed to pay is very generous, my accountant has advised me of certain tax implications of the transaction that I hadn't considered, and I must therefore bow out." Because A's signed reply is itself sufficient to indicate that a contract for sale had been made between the parties—a contract from which A is now seeking to escape—the reply satisfies the UCC Statute of Frauds against A.

(3) **In-Court Admission**

(a) A third means of satisfying the UCC Statute of Frauds occurs when a party against whom enforcement is sought "admits in his pleading, testimony, or otherwise in court that a contract for sale was made."

1) This exception applies whether the admission in question is voluntary (as in pleadings) or involuntary (as on cross-examination).

2) A number of courts have held that the existence of this exception requires that Statute of Frauds claims be resolved at trial rather than at the pleadings stage, since the party against whom enforcement is sought might be persuaded to admit to the existence of a contract in open court.

3) Other courts have concluded that it would defeat the purpose of the Statute of Frauds to permit a party attempting to enforce a contract to "badger the defendant through discovery and trial simply because of the possibility of obtaining an admission."

4) The in-court admission exception will not secure enforcement of the contract in question "beyond the quantity of goods admitted."

(4) **Part Performance**

(a) Despite the absence of a signed writing, an otherwise valid contract is enforceable "with respect to goods for which payment has been made and accepted or which have been received and accepted."

(b) The part performance exception does not apply unless there are actions by both parties indicating that a contract for sale exists. Thus, a payment can constitute part performance only if the buyer makes the payment and the seller accepts it, and delivery of goods can constitute partial performance only if the seller makes the delivery and the buyer accepts the goods.

1) If a buyer pays cash, there is seldom any question whether payment has been made and accepted. Payment by check, however, is more complicated, with some courts holding that receipt of a check without indorsement or negotiation does not constitute acceptance, and other courts holding that mere retention of the check for a reasonable period constitutes acceptance.

2) Any act of dominion inconsistent with a seller's continued ownership of goods (e.g., moving them from the warehouse receiving area to a retail store) will constitute acceptance of the goods.

(c) **Divisible versus Indivisible Goods**

1) If the contract in question involves divisible goods (e.g., widgets), part performance secures enforcement for any quantity that has already been paid for by the buyer or

delivered by the seller; the contract is not enforceable beyond that quantity.

2) If the contract in question involves an indivisible good (e.g., a speedboat) the majority rule holds that partial payment secures enforcement of the entire contract, though a minority of courts refuses enforcement unless full payment has been made.

(5) **Substantial Reliance by the Seller of Specially Manufactured Goods**

    (a) A seller is unlikely to be able to sell specially manufactured goods to other buyers if a would-be buyer backs out, thus leaving the seller with a potentially large reliance loss. Also, the fact of manufacture according to specifications attributable to the buyer provides strong evidence that an oral contract actually exists between the parties.

    (b) Accordingly, an aggrieved seller can secure enforcement of an oral contract by establishing the following five elements:

        1) the goods are to be specially manufactured for the buyer;

        2) the goods are not suitable for sale to others in the ordinary course of the seller's business;

        3) the seller has substantially begun to manufacture, or made commitments to procure, the goods;

        4) the actions undertaken to begin to manufacture or procure occurred under circumstances that reasonably indicate that the goods are for the buyer; and

        5) the actions undertaken to begin to manufacture or procure occurred before the seller received notice of the buyer's revocation.

b. Authorities are divided on whether a party seeking enforcement of a sale of goods contract that is also within the common law one-year provision must satisfy both the UCC and the common law Statute of Frauds.

EXAMPLE: Merchants A and B enter an oral installment contract calling for A's delivery to B of 1,000 widgets per month for two years at a price of $1.00 per widget. A sends B a written confirmation of the oral agreement that meets the requirements of UCC Section 2-201(2), to which B does not respond. B backs out of the deal, A sues for breach of contract, and B defends via the Statute of Frauds. Although the written confirmation clearly satisfies the UCC Statute of Frauds, the contract will be nevertheless unenforceable in some jurisdictions because the agreement is also governed by the Common law one-year provision, which is not satisfied because the party against whom enforcement is sought (B) did not sign the writing.

3. **Enforcement Where the UCC Statute of Frauds Is Not Satisfied**

a. If a party has relied to its detriment on an oral contract whose enforcement is barred by the UCC Statute of Frauds, the aggrieved party may be able to secure a remedy via promissory estoppel.

       (1)   While some courts hold that promissory estoppel is available in appropriate circumstances to secure enforcement of a promise otherwise barred by the Statute of Frauds, other courts point to the express language of the UCC Statute of Frauds ("[e]xcept as otherwise provided in this section, a contract . . . is not enforceable"), and conclude that it precludes promissory estoppel, since that doctrine is not mentioned in Section 2-201.

       (2)   Among those courts that do recognize promissory estoppel, some impose enhanced proof requirements on the claimant, such as proving unconscionable injury or that the other party would be unjustly enriched without enforcement of the contract.

       (3)   Because of the unique vulnerability of construction contractors to revocation by their subcontractors, virtually all courts have protected a general contractor via promissory estoppel even if the oral subcontract in question is for goods at a price of $500 or more.

F.   Effect of Satisfying the Statute of Frauds

1.   An otherwise perfectly valid contract, possessing offer, acceptance, and consideration, can still be unenforceable under the Statute of Frauds. This can happen if the contract is covered by the Statute of Frauds, but does not satisfy the Statute.

2.   On the other hand, satisfaction of the Statute of Frauds does not ensure a "win"; the aggrieved party must still go on to establish both a valid contract and a breach thereof to succeed on his claim.

3.   Thus, satisfying the Statute of Frauds is necessary but not sufficient alone to enforce a contract.

EXAMPLE: A sues B for breach of an oral contract for the sale of land, and B raises the Statute of Frauds defense. A adduces the written offer signed by B and thus establishes that the Statute is satisfied. A may still lose on his breach of contract claim, however, if it turns out that the offer lapsed or was revoked before A accepted it or if for any other reason A fails to persuade the trier of fact that a valid contract existed between the parties.

G.   No Mutuality of Obligation under the Statute of Frauds

1.   It is possible for one party to prevail under a Statute of Frauds defense while, for the same transaction, the other party would be fully liable under the contract. This is a result of the fact that the Statute of Frauds does not require that both parties have signed a writing, only that the party against whom enforcement of the contract is sought has signed. If the writing evidencing the contract is signed by only one of the parties, the contract will be enforceable against the signing party but not against the non-signing party.

EXAMPLE: A and B enter an oral contract for the sale of land and the only signed writing between them is an offer signed by B. If B breaches, he will not have a Statute of Frauds defense because A will be able to adduce a writing signed by B. If A breaches, however, he will be able to raise a successful Statute of Frauds defense because he is the party against whom enforcement is sought and he didn't sign the writing.

    a.   An exception to this principle is created by the merchant's confirmation provision of UCC Section 2-201, under which a signed written confirmation sent by one party to the other will defeat a Statute of Frauds claim by the receiving party as well as by the sending party unless certain conditions are met.

H. Limitations on the Statute of Frauds

    1.   The only effect of a successful Statute of Frauds defense is to defeat enforcement of the contract against the non-signing party. The contract may still be valid and enforceable for other purposes, such as:

    a.   the contract may provide evidence in establishing an element of a legal claim apart from breach of contract;

    EXAMPLE: A brings an action against C for tortious interference with A's oral land contract with B. Although B would have a successful Statute of Frauds defense in a breach of contract action brought by A, the Statute will be irrelevant in A's tortious interference claim against C.

    b.   the contract may provide evidence establishing a defense to a legal claim apart from breach; and

    EXAMPLE: Under an oral contract for the sale of A's land to B, B takes possession. A reneges and brings a trespass action against B. Although A would have a successful Statute of Frauds defense in a breach of contract action brought by B, the Statute would be irrelevant to the validity of B's defense to A's trespass claim.

    c.   the contract may provide evidence of the value of the services already rendered.

    EXAMPLE: A spends three months working for B under an oral two-year employment contract. If B fires A and successfully raises a Statute of Frauds defense against enforcement of the oral contract, A may nonetheless be able to recover from B the reasonable value of the services rendered in *quantum meruit*. Moreover, he may offer the price agreed to in the oral contract as evidence of the value of the services rendered.

V. GAP-FILLERS, INTERPRETATION, AND THE PAROL EVIDENCE RULE

A. In General

1. Parties to a contract ordinarily reach explicit and unambiguous agreements on the essential issues of the contract, such as quantity and price. However, they frequently fail to be as explicit as to the details. This can result in either gaps in the contract or contractual language that is subject to more than one interpretation. This section deals with the rules courts use to fill contractual gaps and resolve contractual ambiguities.

B. Filling in the Gaps with Default Provisions

1. One of the principal ways that contract law deals with gaps in a contract is by supplying terms that govern areas where the contract is silent. Just as a word processing program has default settings for the margins and layout, the body of contract law has default provisions for contracts.

2. These provisions can be overridden where the parties provide for a different procedure, but if they do not, the default contract terms will supplement their contract. Standard rules automatically supply contract terms unless they are set aside by party action or agreement.

3. **UCC Default Rules for the Sales of Goods**

    a. **Implied Warranties**

       (1) **Warranty of Title and against Infringement**

           (a) For the sale of all goods, there is an implied warranty of good title to the goods, of the rightful transfer of the goods, and that no liens or other security interests are attached to those goods [§ 2-312].

           (b) This warranty can only be excluded or modified by [§ 2-312(2)]:

               1) specific language; or

               2) circumstances which give the buyer reason to know that the seller does not claim unencumbered title.

           (c) Unless otherwise agreed, a merchant regularly dealing in goods of the kind warrants that they are free of any rightful claim of a third person by way of infringement. However, a seller is not liable for such a claim if the buyer provides specifications to the seller and the claim arises out of compliance with the specifications [§ 2-312(3)].

       (2) **Warranty of Merchantability**

           (a) If the seller of the goods is a merchant with respect to goods of that kind under the UCC, then there is a warranty of merchantability for the sale of goods. The warranty guarantees that the goods are fit for the ordinary purposes for which those goods would be used [§ 2-314].

- (3) **Warranty of Fitness for a Particular Purpose**
  - (a) This warranty grants that the goods being sold are fit for the particular purpose for which the buyer intends to use them. The warranty only applies where, at the time of contracting, the seller has good reason to know [§ 2-315]:
    1) the particular purpose for which the goods are required; and
    2) that the buyer is relying on the seller's skill or judgment to select or furnish reasonable goods.
- (4) **Excluding or Modifying Implied Warranties of Merchantability and Fitness**
  - (a) The **implied warranty of merchantability** may be excluded or modified by language mentioning "merchantability" and need not be in a writing. However, if it is in a writing, it must be conspicuous [§ 2-316(2)].
  - (b) An **implied warranty of fitness** may be excluded or modified by language in a writing that is conspicuous. Language to exclude all implied warranties of fitness is sufficient if it states, for example, that "There are no warranties which extend beyond the description on the face hereof" [§ 2-316(2)].
  - (c) However, the above language is not necessary to exclude or modify the warranty if [§ 2-316(3)]:
    1) the contract includes an expression like "as is" or "with all faults" or other similar language that in common understanding calls the buyer's attention to the exclusion of warranties and makes plain that there is no implied warranty;
    2) the buyer has fully examined the goods before entering into the contract, or has refused to do so, in which case there is no implied warranty as to defects that should have been apparent from the examination; or
    3) course of dealing, course of performance, or usage of trade indicate that the warranty is excluded or modified.

b. **Express Warranties**
  - (1) Note that the UCC also provides that a contract can create express warranties. Express warranties by the seller are created as follows [§ 2-313(1)]:
    - (a) any **affirmation of fact or promise** made by the seller to the buyer that relates to the goods and becomes part of the basis of the bargain creates an express warranty that the goods will conform to the affirmation or promise;
    - (b) any **description of the goods** that is made part of the basis of the bargain creates an express warranty that the goods will conform to the description; and

(c) any **sample or model** that is made part of the basis of the bargain creates an express warranty that the whole of the goods will conform to the sample or model.

(2) The seller need not use formal words such as "warrant" or "guarantee," nor must the seller have a specific intention to make a warranty in order to create an express warranty. However, a mere affirmation of the value of the goods or a statement of the seller's opinion does not create a warranty [§ 2-313(2)].

(3) Words or conduct relevant to the creation of an express warranty and words or conduct tending to negate or limit warranty shall be construed wherever reasonable as consistent with each other [§ 2-316(1)].

(a) Where an express warranty conflicts with a limitation or disclaimer, the express warranty will prevail [Id.].

(4) The measure of damages for breach of warranty is the difference at the time and place of acceptance between the value of the goods accepted and the value they would have had if they had been as warranted [§ 2-714(2)].

c. **Missing Terms**

(1) Under the UCC, where there are pertinent terms missing, the following provisions will supplant the contract:

(a) The default rule for a missing **price term** is the reasonable price at the time established by the contract for the delivery of goods.

(b) A missing **time term** exists if the contract is silent as to the date of delivery or any other date by which action must be taken under the contract. The default rule for a missing time term is that contractual action must be performed within a reasonable time.

(c) The default rule for a missing **place of delivery term** is that the place of delivery will be the seller's place of business unless otherwise agreed.

4. **Common Law Default Rules for Service and Employment Contracts**

a. **Missing Price Term**

(1) If one party performs services at the request of another but no price is discussed in advance, then the default rule under common law will apply. The default rule for a missing price term is the reasonable value of the services rendered. This is typically available based on *quantum meruit*.

b. **Missing Duration Term**

(1) In practically every jurisdiction, the employment-at-will rule is the default rule for duration of an employment contract; absent an agreement to the contrary, an employer may dismiss, and an employee may quit, at any time for any reason.

(2) In a majority of jurisdictions, oral or written assurances of job security made to an individual employee, as well as assurances

contained in policy documents distributed to the workforce, may suffice to take the contract out of the default rule.

EXAMPLE: Statements made during a recruiting interview that make assurances of job security would displace the at-will rule. Alternatively, similar written assurances contained in a personnel handbook would also displace the rule.

EXCEPTION: Most courts will enforce a clear and conspicuous declaration in a personnel handbook or other employer policy statement to the effect that the employment relationship is "at will." However, a conflict between such a disclaimer and other written or oral representations by the employer will create a jury question on whether the employer has successfully opted out of the at-will default.

5. **The Obligation of Good Faith and Fair Dealing**

   a. Another source of gap-filling is the obligation of good faith and fair dealing. Both the UCC and the Restatement impose an obligation of good faith in the performance and enforcement of contracts. **Good faith** is generally defined as "honesty in fact in the conduct or transaction concerned" and, in the case of a merchant, good faith means "honesty in fact and the observance of reasonable commercial standards of fair dealing in the trade."

   b. The obligation of good faith may only be raised in regards to the performance and enforcement of contracts, but not to negotiations or other precontractual conduct. Challenges to unfair dealing in those settings must be made via claims of fraud, duress, or other defenses, discussed later.

   c. The good-faith obligation will also operate to ensure good faith where the terms of the contract leave a critical term, such as the price, satisfaction, or quantity, open to the determination of one party.

      (1) **Open Price Term**

         (a) If a contract leaves the price to be fixed by one of the parties, then the specified party must fix the price in good faith [§ 2-305(2)].

      (2) **Satisfaction Term**

         (a) A contract may contain a satisfaction clause, or similar term, whereby the determination as to whether a party's performance obligation is complete is left to the discretion of the other party. In those contracts, the good-faith obligation operates to require the party making that determination do so in good faith.

            EXAMPLE: A commercial developer and the seller of a piece of land enter into a contract. The developer places a condition on his purchase of the land that the seller first acquires "satisfactory leases" for the future occupancy of the land. The developer must determine in good faith whether or not the future leases are "satisfactory."

  (3) **Open Quantity Term: Output and Requirements Contracts**

   (a) An **output contract** is a contract in which the buyer agrees to purchase all of a seller's output for a particular good.

   (b) A **requirements contract** is a contract in which the seller agrees to supply the buyer with all of the buyer's requirements for a particular good.

   (c) Under the UCC, the party entitled to determine the particular quantity of goods to be sold—either the buyer demanding delivery of his requirements or the seller demanding purchase of his output—must make that determination is good faith [§ 2-306].

   (d) In addition to the good-faith requirement, the UCC prohibits any unreasonably disproportionate demand or tender, if there was either [§ 2-306(1)]:

    1) a stated estimate made between the parties; or

    2) in the absence of a stated estimate, any comparable prior outputs or requirements.

    EXAMPLE: Seller and Buyer are parties to a three-year contract obligating Seller to supply Buyer with the latter's upsidasium bearing requirements for Buyer's turbojet engine manufacturing plant. The market price for upsidasium suddenly skyrockets, and Buyer greatly increases its demand for bearings with the intention of selling them at great profit to third parties. Seller is not obligated to fill the order because Buyer's requirements demand was made in bad faith.

    EXAMPLE: The upsidasium market remains stable, but because of a decline in the commercial aviation industry, the demand for Buyer's engines declines precipitously and accordingly Buyer reduces its monthly demand for bearings by 90% in comparison with the previous 24 months. Although Buyer's reduced demand was made in good faith, it is unreasonably disproportionate to its prior requirements and, accordingly, violates Section 2-306.

C. Interpreting Ambiguous Language

 1. Where the parties did not fail to address an issue, but instead drafted the contract's language in such a way that the language could be subject to more than one interpretation, then a different type of analysis is needed in order for the courts to properly determine the meaning.

  a. **Objective versus Subjective Meaning**

   (1) The objectively reasonable meaning of a term at the time of contracting would control over a contrary subjective understanding of the term by one of the parties.

EXAMPLE: Contractor and Homeowner enter a contract for renovations to Homeowner's home. The contract incorporates by reference "the specifications dated 1/11/07," which had been prepared by Homeowner and were attached to the contract before signing. Contractor mistakenly thinks that the specifications referenced were an earlier version prepared by Contractor, and he signs the contract on that understanding. The specifications prepared by Homeowner and referenced in the contract are binding on both parties.

    (2)   This rule is subject to two exceptions.

        (a)   Where one party harbors a subjective understanding of a term that differs from the objectively reasonable meaning, typically the objective understanding will prevail. However, if the other party knows or has reason to know of the first party's subjective understanding, then that subjective interpretation will control.

             EXAMPLE: The facts being otherwise as stated in the previous example, just before the parties sign the contract, Homeowner overhears Contractor tell his business partner that he was glad Homeowner had agreed to Contractor's version of the specifications. Because Homeowner knew of Contractor's understanding of the contractual terms, that understanding controls.

        (b)   Where the evidence demonstrates that both parties shared the subjective understanding of the term at the time of contracting, the mutual subjective understanding will control.

             EXAMPLE: A general contractor is building a bridge. He hires a paving subcontractor to do work at a price to be calculated in accordance with the dimensions of the "concrete surface of the bridge deck." At the time of contracting, both of the parties understand that the concrete work included the sides and bottom as well as the "surface" of the bridge deck and, accordingly, that interpretation would be the controlling interpretation.

    b.   ***Contra Proferentem* and the Doctrine of Reasonable Expectations**

        (1)   Under the **rule of *contra proferentem***, if an ambiguous term is included in the contract, then it will be interpreted against the party who supplied the term during negotiations or drafting. Thus, if more than one meaning is possible, then the meaning more favorable to the other party will control.

            (a)   This rule of construction applies to contracts between bargaining equals as well as to contracts of adhesion, which are standard form (take-it-or-leave-it) contracts that a party with superior bargaining power uniformly imposes on its trading partners.

        (2)   Under the **doctrine of reasonable expectations**, even unambiguous terms may be interpreted against the drafting party if they conflict with the reasonable expectations of the other party.

(a) Most courts will apply the doctrine of reasonable expectations to insurance contracts, but its application is potentially available to all adhesion contracts.

(b) Under the doctrine, courts make a distinction between the dickered terms, which discuss the transaction-specific terms negotiated by the parties, and boilerplate terms, or those terms appearing in fine print. The court will apply the doctrine only to the boilerplate terms.

EXAMPLE: In an insurance contract, the coverage, deductibles, premium amounts, and policy periods are typically the dickered terms. The rest of the agreement, including specification of the claims process and exclusions, are typically set forth in boilerplate and are therefore subject to the doctrine of reasonable expectations.

(c) Under this doctrine, the parties' obligations consist of the dickered terms and only the boilerplate terms that would be consistent with the reasonable expectations of the purchaser. Unreasonable boilerplate terms are unenforceable.

EXAMPLE: Fertilizer Co. purchased from Allied Insurance Co. an insurance policy covering burglary with fine-print boilerplate language defining "burglary" as requiring "visible marks on" or "physical damage to" the exterior of the insured building. During the policy term, Fertilizer Co. was the victim of a theft in which the perpetrators were able to force open a Plexiglas door without leaving marks or damage, and Allied refused payment on the policy. Because the definition of "burglary" was a boilerplate term inconsistent with the reasonable expectations of the insured, the court interpreted the policy to cover the theft.

D. **Trade Usage, Course of Dealing, and Course of Performance**

1. Extrinsic evidence of trade usage, course of dealing, or course of performance will be available as an additional means of filling contractual gaps or resolving contractual ambiguities.

2. **Definitions under the UCC**

   a. A **usage of trade** is any practice or method of dealing having such regularity of observance in a place or trade as to justify an expectation that it will be observed with respect to the transaction in question.

   b. A **course of dealing** is a pattern of conduct concerning previous transactions between the parties that is fairly to be regarded as establishing a common basis of understanding for interpreting their subsequent expressions and other conduct.

   c. A **course of performance** is present when a particular contract involves repeated occasions for performance by a party and the other party, with knowledge of the nature of the performance and opportunity for objection to it, accepts the performance or acquiesces in it without objection.

3. Evidence of trade usage, course of dealing, or course of performance is admissible under the UCC and is typically available in common law cases as well.

    a. Such evidence may be used to supplement the express terms of a contract or to give meaning to a particular ambiguous term. However, it is not admissible to contradict the express terms of a contract.

        EXCEPTION: Course of performance evidence may be available to establish the waiver or modification of an express term.

    b. In the event of a conflict, course of performance prevails over course of dealing and usage of trade, and course of dealing prevails over usage of trade.

        EXAMPLE: A is one of many suppliers of upsidasium, and B is one of A's long-standing customers. A fills an order by B and demands immediate payment; B refuses. It is standard practice in the upsidasium industry for purchasers to pay invoices upon delivery, and, therefore, B's refusal to do so is in violation of the parties' contract.

        EXAMPLE: Same facts as the previous example except that in the past, A has regularly given B 30 days to pay for deliveries. Because this course of dealing between the parties trumps the payment-upon-delivery usage of trade, B has 30 days within which to make the required payment.

        EXAMPLE: Same facts as the previous example except that the parties' contract contains a provision requiring payment within seven days of delivery. Because the express terms of a contract override both course of dealing and usage of trade, B has seven days within which to make payment despite the past practice of paying in 30 days and the industry practice of immediate payment.

        EXAMPLE: Same facts as the previous example except that A and B are parties to an installment contract and B has paid 30 days after multiple deliveries without objection by A. This evidence of the parties' course of performance is admissible to establish that A has waived its contractual right to payment within seven days of delivery and/or that the parties have mutually modified that obligation.

E. The Parol Evidence Rule

1. In General

    a. Another source of evidence shedding light on the meaning of an agreement is the negotiations of the parties leading up to the execution of a written contract. The **parol evidence rule** governs efforts to introduce such evidence [§ 2-202].

    b. The rule governs:

        (1) both oral and documentary evidence of negotiations and other communications between the parties (e.g., an exchange of letters between the parties); and

(2) communications that took place prior to or contemporaneously with the execution of the written contract.

> **NOTE**   For ease of reference, courts refer to all such evidence as "parol evidence."

2. **Approaching a Parol Evidence Analysis**

    a. When a party seeks to introduce parol evidence, the court will determine the admissibility of the evidence based on two questions:

        (1) First, what is the purpose for which the evidence is being introduced?

        (2) Second, does the evidence relate to a term or contract which is integrated?

           (a) The integration analysis may focus on the term itself or the contract as a whole, depending on the purpose for which the parol evidence is being introduced.

3. **Integration**

    a. While the first step in the analysis is to determine the purpose for which the evidence is being introduced, the effects of these different purposes will depend upon the level of integration in the contract.

    b. **Full versus Complete Integration**

        (1) When a particular contract is **fully integrated**, it means that the terms contained within the contract are intended to be the final discussion of the parties as to those specific terms. It does not, however, mean that the parties have specifically excluded any provisions not contained within the agreement.

        (2) On the other hand, when a contract is **completely integrated**, the parties intend the contract to represent a "complete and exclusive statement of all the terms" [§ 2-202(3)]. When this is the case, only the terms contained within the written agreement are considered part of the contract.

    c. **Determining Full Integration and Complete Integration**

        (1) The question of whether the terms of a contract are fully integrated (i.e., final) and whether an integration is complete (i.e., exhaustive) is for the judge, not the jury, to decide.

        (2) In reaching decisions regarding whether the terms of a contract are fully integrated, the judge will rely on the following evidence:

           (a) The thoroughness and specificity of the written instrument in connection with the terms at issue are strong indicators that the parties intended the writing to represent their final agreement.

           (b) Parol and other extrinsic evidence are admissible. The determination is not made on the basis of an examination of the writing alone; "all the circumstances"—including the proffered parol evidence and other evidence extrinsic to the written contract—must be considered.

(3) In reaching decisions regarding the complete integration of a contract, the judge will rely on the following evidence:

    (a) **Merger Clause**

        1) The most important evidence that the parties intended their written agreement to represent an exhaustive account of their contractual obligations is the presence in the contract of a merger clause reciting that the writing "contains the complete and entire agreement of the parties" or other words to that effect. The authorities are divided, however, on whether a merger clause is conclusive or merely persuasive on the question of complete integration.

    (b) **Other Evidence**

        1) Additional factors which are important for determining whether a contract as completely integrated include the detail with which the contract sets forth its provisions, as well as the length of the agreement itself.

    (c) **Parol and Other Extrinsic Evidence Admissible**

        1) Once again, the question is subject to an "all the circumstances" test, and the proffered parol evidence as well as other extrinsic evidence may be considered in that connection.

        EXAMPLE: A and B have a written contract under the terms of which A agrees to sell B "all the uncut timber on my property." Evidence of conversations between the parties during a visit to the timber site is admissible to explain that "property" means A's country cottage and not A's home in the suburbs.

        EXAMPLE: A and B have a written contract under the terms of which A agrees to sell B "all the uncut timber on my property." Evidence of an exchange of letters between the parties in which they agreed that their agreement would not include the shady trees in the immediate vicinity of A's country cottage would contradict the written expression (i.e., that A had agreed to sell B "all the uncut timber on my property") and would therefore be admissible only if the court concluded that the quoted provision not intended by the parties to be the final word with respect to which timber would be cut (i.e., that the writing was not integrated). In making that determination, the court is free to consider the exchange of letters and other extrinsic evidence.

        EXAMPLE: A and B had a written contract under the terms of which A agrees to sell B "all the uncut timber on my property," and the contract contained detailed terms with respect to the felling and transportation of the timber as well as a merger clause stating that the contract was "a complete and exhaustive account of the obligations between the parties." Evidence of an oral agreement between the parties at the time of signing the contract that A would pay to have the trees inspected for termites before cutting would be admissible to supplement the agreement only if the court concluded that the contract was partially (rather than completely) integrated. Some courts would consider the merger clause to be conclusive on the question of complete integration and thus bar the evidence, but other courts would treat it as persuasive only, evaluate the proffered evidence of the supplemental oral agreement, and admit it if they concluded that the parties did not intend the previously drafted merger clause to bar it, despite their subsequent signatures on the contract.

EXAMPLE: Same facts as in the previous example, except A and B are logging companies, and B offers evidence that sellers doing business in the commercial lumber trade invariably pay to have the trees inspected for termites before cutting. This evidence would be admissible even if the court concluded that the contract was completely integrated because, under the UCC, uncut timber equals "goods," and usage of trade evidence is admissible to supplement a written agreement.

4. **Purpose for Which Evidence Is Introduced**

   a. The effect of the rule depends on the purpose for which the parol evidence is being introduced:

      (1) to explain or interpret the terms of the written contract;

      (2) to supplement the terms of the written contract; or

      (3) to contradict the terms of the written contract.

   b. **To Explain or Interpret Terms of a Written Contract**

      (1) In a majority of jurisdictions, parol evidence is always admissible for this purpose.

      (2) A minority of jurisdictions follow the traditional common law rule and require a threshold showing that the term in question is patently ambiguous (i.e., ambiguous on its face) before admitting parol evidence for this purpose.

   c. **To Supplement Terms of a Written Contract**

      (1) Parol evidence is admissible for this purpose unless the contract is completely integrated.

         (a) A completely integrated contract is intended by the parties to represent an exhaustive as well as final account of the parties' obligations.

    (2) **UCC Distinction**

      (a) Usage of trade, course of dealing, and course of performance evidence are admissible in sale of goods cases to supplement the terms of a written agreement.

  d. **To Contradict Terms of a Written Contract**

    (1) Parol evidence is admissible for this purpose unless the term(s) in question are fully integrated.

      (a) Integrated terms are terms intended by the parties to represent their final agreement on the subjects in question.

    (2) **UCC Distinction**

      (a) Course of dealing or course of performance evidence may be admissible in sale of goods cases to "qualify" the meaning of an integrated term.

5. **When the Parol Evidence Rule Will Not Apply**

  a. The parol evidence rule will not apply to the following types of evidence:

    (1) **Subsequent Agreements**

      (a) The parol evidence rule only applies to oral or written communications made prior to or contemporaneously with the execution of a written agreement. This means that it will not apply to subsequent agreements entered into after the execution of the written document.

      EXAMPLE: Buyer and Seller enter into a written agreement for the sale of 1,000 widgets. Two months before delivery is to be made, the parties orally agree to modify the agreement and specify the goods as nonstandard type-Y widgets, with Buyer agreeing to pay an additional cost. Evidence of this modification would not fall within the parol evidence rule, as it was made subsequent to the execution of the written agreement.

    (2) **Collateral Agreements**

      (a) The parol evidence will not affect agreements between the parties that are entirely distinct from the written agreement of the contract at issue. Evidence offered to prove or enforce such "collateral agreements" is admissible.

      EXAMPLE: A and B execute a detailed written contract, complete with a merger clause, by which A agrees to sell A's car to B. As part of the transaction, the parties orally agree that B may park the automobile in A's garage for one year, paying $25 per month. Despite the completely integrated writing, either A or B may adduce evidence of the parking arrangement under the collateral agreement rule.

    (3) **Attacks on the Validity of the Written Agreement**

      (a) The key predicate to the application of the parol evidence rule is that there is a valid written agreement. As a result, the parol evidence rule will not bar efforts to prove that the written agreement is invalid or unenforceable. The absence of an enforceable agreement may be proved by parol evidence or any other extrinsic evidence.

(b) A party can assert such a claim in one of the following ways:

1) **Failure of an Oral Condition Precedent to the Agreement**

    a) Evidence that the parties orally agreed to a condition precedent to the contract taking effect as well as further evidence that the condition failed would not be barred by the parol evidence rule where both parties' obligations would be discharged by the failure of that condition.

    EXAMPLE: The parties to a written contract for the sale of artwork orally agree that the sale will not take effect unless and until a certificate of authenticity is issued by a named art expert. Because authentication is a condition precedent to the sale, the parol evidence rule will not bar proof of the oral agreement.

2) **Absence of Consideration**

    a) Evidence that a written agreement lacks consideration or that there was a false recital of consideration is not barred by the parol evidence rule.

3) **Mistake or Duress**

    a) Evidence that the written agreement was formed from mistake or duress may be admissible to prove that there was never a contract.

4) **Fraud**

    a) The majority rule is that the parol evidence rule will not bar extrinsic evidence of fraud.

    b) The minority rule is that extrinsic evidence is inadmissible to prove fraud where the written contract expressly eliminates an element of the claim (e.g., "the parties agree that neither party relied in any way on representations made outside the four corners of this agreement").

5) **Reformation**

    a) The parol evidence rule is also inapplicable where a party to a written agreement alleges facts entitling him to reformation of the agreement. Reformation is based on the premise that the parties had reached an agreement concerning the instrument, but while reducing their agreement to written form, and as the result of mutual mistake or fraud, some provision or language was omitted from, inserted, or incorrectly stated in the instrument intended to be the expression of the actual agreement of the parties.

h) For the plaintiff to obtain reformation, it must be shown:

    i)   that there was an antecedent valid agreement;

    ii) which is incorrectly reflected in the writing (e.g., by mistake); and

    iii) proof of these elements is established by clear and convincing evidence.

VI. PERFORMANCE, MODIFICATION, AND EXCUSE

A. **Obligations under the UCC**

1. **In General**

a. The seller's obligation is to transfer and deliver, and the buyer's obligation is to accept and pay in accordance with the contract [§ 2-301].

2. **Seller's Obligations**

a. **Non-Carrier Cases**

(1) **Non-carrier cases** are contracts in which it appears that the parties do not intend for the goods to be moved by common carrier.

(2) In non-carrier cases, the seller has an obligation to tender delivery—that is, to put and hold conforming goods at the buyer's disposition and give the buyer any notification reasonably necessary to enable him to take delivery [§ 2-503(1)].

(3) Tender must be at a reasonable hour, and the goods must be kept available for the period reasonably necessary to enable the buyer to take possession [§ 2-503(1)(a)].

(a) However, unless otherwise agreed-upon, the buyer must furnish facilities reasonably suited to receiving the goods [§ 2-503(1)(b)].

b. **Carrier Cases**

(1) **Carrier cases** are contracts in which, due to express terms or due to the circumstances, it appears that the parties intend for the goods to be moved by common carrier.

EXAMPLE: Common carrier may include such means as freight train, boat, or parcel delivery service.

(2) Absent some other agreement, there is a presumption that the contract is a **shipment contract**, under which the seller is not obligated to deliver at a named destination, and bear the concurrent risk of loss until arrival, unless he has specifically agreed to do so or the commercial understanding of the terms used by the parties contemplates such delivery [§ 2-503, cmt. 5].

(a) Under a shipment contract, the seller need only put the goods in the possession of a carrier and make appropriate arrangements for them to be sent to the buyer, provide the buyer with any document necessary to enable him to obtain possession of the goods, and promptly notify the buyer that the goods have been shipped [§ 2-504].

(b) The seller's failure to notify the buyer of the shipment or to make a proper contract for the shipment is only grounds for rejection if material delay or loss ensues [Id.].

(3) In a **destination contract**, the seller has agreed to tender the goods at a particular destination.

    (a) If the contract requires the seller to tender delivery of the goods at a particular destination, the seller must, at the destination, put and hold conforming goods at the buyer's disposition [§ 2-503(1)].

    (b) The seller must also give the buyer any notice of tender that is reasonably necessary and provide the buyer with any documents of title necessary to obtain delivery. Tender of documents through ordinary banking channels is sufficient [§ 2-503].

(4) In contracts that specify that delivery is **free on board** ("F.O.B."), the F.O.B. point is the delivery point.

    (a) If the contract is F.O.B. the seller's place of shipment, the seller need only, at his expense and risk, put the goods in the possession of the carrier.

      EXAMPLE: Seller is a shirt manufacturer with a factory in Baltimore. He contracts to sell 2,000 shirts to Buyer, who runs a retail clothing store in Las Vegas. If their contract states that the goods are "F.O.B. Baltimore," Seller's risk and expense would end once he puts it in the possession of the carrier (e.g., The Quick-Ship Co.).

    (b) If the contract is F.O.B. the destination, the seller must, at his expense and risk, tender delivery of the goods at the destination location [§ 2-319(1)].

      EXAMPLE: If in the above example, the contract states that the goods are "F.O.B. Las Vegas," the Seller would continue to bear the expense and risk while the goods are being shipped by The Quick-Ship Co., until the goods are actually tendered for delivery at the destination location.

(5) In contracts that specify the delivery is **free alongside** ("F.A.S."), the seller must deliver the goods alongside the vessel (in the manner usual at the port of delivery) or on a dock designated by the buyer and obtain and tender a receipt for the goods [§ 2-319(2)].

3. **Buyer's Obligations**

  a. Unless otherwise agreed-upon, the buyer's tender of payment is a condition to the seller's duty to tender and complete delivery [§ 2-511(1)].

  b. A tender of payment is sufficient when it is made by any means or in any manner current in the ordinary course of business, unless the seller demands payment in cash and gives the buyer a reasonable extension of time to procure it [§ 2-511(2)].

  c. A buyer's payment by check is conditional and will be defeated if the check is not honored upon presentment [§§ 2-511(3); 2-511, cmt. 5].

  d. **Inspection of the Goods**

    (1) Generally, unless the parties agree otherwise, the buyer has a right to inspect goods upon tender or delivery before making payment or acceptance [§ 2-513(1)].

(2) If the contract requires payment before inspection, nonconformity of the goods will not excuse the buyer from making payment unless [§§ 2-512(1), 5-109(b)]:

(a) the nonconformity appears without inspection (i.e., it is evident merely from taking delivery); or

(b) despite tender of the required documents, the documents are forged or materially fraudulent such that an injunction against the issuer would be justified.

(3) Note that payment before inspection will not constitute an acceptance of the goods or impair the buyer's right to inspect or any of his remedies [§ 2-512(2)].

4. **Risk of Loss**

a. If the seller is required or authorized to ship the goods by carrier, the risk of loss passes to the buyer [§ 2-509(1)]:

(1) when the goods are delivered to the carrier if the contract does not require the seller to deliver the goods at a particular destination (i.e., under a shipment contract, which is the default presumption in carrier cases); or

(2) when the goods are tendered at a particular destination by the carrier so that the buyer is able to take delivery if the contract requires the seller to deliver the goods at a particular destination (i.e., under a destination contract).

b. If the goods are held by a bailee to be delivered without being moved, the risk of loss passes to the buyer [§ 2-509(2)]:

(1) when the buyer receives a negotiable document of title covering the goods;

(2) when the bailee acknowledges the buyer's right to possess the goods; or

(3) after the buyer receives a nonnegotiable document of title or other written direction to deliver the goods to the buyer, once the buyer has had a reasonable time to present the document or direction to the bailee.

c. In any other case [§ 2-509(3)]:

(1) if the seller is a merchant, the risk of loss passes to the buyer when the buyer receives (i.e., takes physical possession of) the goods; and

(2) if the seller is not a merchant, the risk of loss passes to the buyer upon tender of delivery.

d. **Effect of Breach on Risk of Loss**

(1) If the seller breaches the contract by making a nonconforming tender or delivery, the risk of loss remains on the seller until cure or acceptance [§ 2-510(1)].

(2) If the buyer rightfully revokes acceptance (as described below), the buyer may—to the extent of any deficiency in his effective

insurance coverage—treat the risk of loss as having been on the seller from the beginning [§ 2-510(2)].

(3) If the buyer breaches before the risk of loss passes to the buyer, the seller may—to the extent of any deficiency in his effective insurance coverage—treat the risk of loss as resting on the buyer for a commercially reasonable time [§ 2-510(3)].

B. Modification

1. At common law, parties were free to enter a contract on virtually any terms that they wished. Once they had entered the contract, however, the law made it very difficult for them to modify those terms.

2. The contemporary rules allowing for modification under the UCC and common law are more flexible. However, effective modification of a valid contract is still a burdensome project.

3. **Modification at Common Law**

   a. **The Preexisting Duty Rule**

   (1) At common law, a promise to increase compensation under an existing contract is an unenforceable modification to an existing contract because there is no consideration offered for the modification. A promisor cannot provide consideration where that consideration is a duty the promisor is already obligated to perform. This is known as the **preexisting duty rule**, and preexisting duties are not deemed consideration because the promisor must already perform that duty on the basis of the original contract.

   EXAMPLE: The captain of a fishing vessel promised to pay $100 to each of the sailors for their work on a fishing voyage. Midway through the voyage, the sailors threatened to cease work unless they were promised an additional $50 each, and the captain reluctantly agreed. At the end of the voyage, the captain paid each of them the originally promised $100 but refused to pay the $50 increase, so the sailors sued to recover the additional amount. Because the sailors were already obliged to perform the work in question under the terms of their original contract with the captain, his promise of an additional $50 is unenforceable under the preexisting duty rule.

   b. **Exceptions to the Preexisting Duty Rule**

   (1) **Mutual Modification**

   (a) A promise to increase compensation under an existing contract is enforceable as a mutual modification to the contract if:

   1) both parties agree to a performance that is different from the one required by the original contract; and

   2) the difference in performance is not a mere pretense of a newly formed bargain.

EXAMPLE: During the course of the fishing voyage, the ship's cook takes ill, and the captain instructs the youngest of the sailors to perform the cook's duties in addition to his fishing duties. The sailor refuses to perform the work unless the captain promises him an additional $50 in compensation, and the captain reluctantly agrees. The promise of additional compensation is enforceable as part of a "mutual modification" of the original contract.

EXAMPLE: Midway through the voyage, the sailors threaten to cease work unless they are promised an additional $50 each. The captain reluctantly agrees, and in exchange, the sailors promised to wake him each morning with a chorus of "Rule Britannia." Although there appears on the surface to be a "mutual modification" of the original contract, it is a "mere pretense" of a new bargain and, accordingly, the promised increase in compensation is unenforceable under the preexisting duty rule.

(2) **Unforeseen Circumstances**

(a) Where a promise of increased compensation is given in exchange for a performance, and that performance is rendered substantially more burdensome than reasonably anticipated by the parties when they entered the contract, then the preexisting duty rule will not apply.

EXAMPLE: Same basic facts as in the previous examples, but the fishing nets provided by the captain turn out to be defective and thus increase the workload of the sailors in a manner substantially in excess of what was reasonably contemplated under the original contract. The sailors threaten to cease the fishing unless they are promised an additional $50 each, and the captain reluctantly agrees. The promise is enforceable despite the preexisting duty rule in view of circumstances not reasonably anticipated by the parties at the time of contracting.

4. **Modification and the Sales of Goods under the UCC**

a. Under the UCC, the preexisting duty rule is abolished and an agreement modifying an existing contract for the sale of goods needs no consideration to be binding. Modifications must, however, meet the UCC's **good faith test**, and a failure to do so will render them unenforceable.

b. The good faith test for modifications applies even to modifications that are supported by consideration. Similar to the contemporary common law rule that requires more than mere pretense of a new bargain to secure enforcement of a mutual modification, a bargained-for modification is unenforceable under the UCC if the appearance of the mutual bargain is merely a pretext to hide a bad faith change of terms.

5. **Duress and Midterm Modifications**

   a. In addition to challenging a midterm modification under the rules just discussed, a party who agrees to a contractual modification in commercially extortionate circumstances may also be able to raise the defense of duress, discussed later in this outline.

   b. The duress defense is available not only in common law cases, but also in sales of goods cases governed by the UCC.

6. **Effect of "No Oral Modifications" Clauses**

   a. Unless required by the Statute of Frauds, modifications can generally be oral or written. However, the enforceability of an oral modification to an agreement may depend upon whether the contract contains a "no oral modifications" clause.

      (1) There is no specific language required for this type of provision. "No oral modifications," "all modifications must be in writing," or any such similar language would suffice.

   b. **Common Law Cases**

      (1) Originally, there was a common law rule that made oral modification clauses invalid, and even today most courts will refuse to enforce them where a party has reasonably relied on the oral agreement at issue. However, their enforcement is becoming more likely in modern cases, particularly in the construction context.

   c. **UCC Cases**

      (1) Under Section 2-209, clauses prohibiting subsequent oral modifications are presumptively valid.

      (2) An oral modification made in violation of such a clause may nevertheless be enforceable if the disadvantaged party relies on the modification or the parties perform in accordance therewith.

C. Excusing Performance Due to Faulty Assumptions

1. A party entering a contract is susceptible to making countless assumptions about the present and future circumstances in which performance will take place. When such assumptions turn out to be faulty, the doctrines of mistake, impossibility, impracticability, and frustration of purpose may be available to excuse the parties' obligations.

   EXAMPLE: A faulty assumption about the facts at the time of contracting would be that the stone in a ring the seller is selling is a diamond and not a topaz.

   EXAMPLE: A faulty assumption about the future facts in a contract would be the assumption that the cost of fuel won't increase beyond a certain range and triple the costs of the busing service whose bid was accepted by the school district.

2. Faulty assumptions about present facts, or the facts as they exist at the time of contracting, are dealt with under the doctrine of mistake. Faulty assumptions about future facts are dealt with via the doctrines of impossibility, impracticability, and frustration of purpose.

3. **Mistake**

a. When a party or parties make a faulty assumption about the present circumstances, and thus enter a contract on that basis, this is known as a **mistake**.

b. A mistake regarding the facts that exist at the time of contracting will excuse performance only where the mistaken facts are material to that contract. This requires that the mistaken facts will significantly impact the value of the transaction to one or both parties.

c. When only one of the parties to a contract is operating under a faulty assumption about material facts as they exist at the time of contracting, the situation is governed by the rules of unilateral mistake. When both parties labor under a common faulty assumption, the situation is governed by the rules of mutual mistake.

(1) **Unilateral Mistake**

(a) Under the rules governing unilateral mistake, a party operating under a faulty assumption about material facts as they exist at the time of contracting is not excused from his contractual performance unless:

1) the other party knew or had reason to know of the mistake; or

EXAMPLE: A agrees to sell B a cow, which A knows to be barren and, as the parties are writing up and signing the agreement, B asks A a series of questions about the care and feeding of pregnant cows. Because A has reason to know that B is mistaken with respect to the cow's capacity to bear calves, B's obligation to purchase the cow is excused on account of unilateral mistake.

2) the mistake was based on a clerical error.

a) The clerical error exception is not available in all jurisdictions, and where available, it is subject to the following exceptions:

i) where the error was caused by extreme negligence on the part of the party making the error; or

ii) where the other party has relied on the clerical error.

(2) **Mutual Mistake**

(a) Where both parties have labored under a common faulty assumption regarding the present facts, there is a mutual mistake. Under the rules of mutual mistake, the contract will be voidable by the disadvantaged party where:

1) the fact about which the parties were mistaken is essential to the contract (i.e., it goes to the very heart of the exchange);

2) both parties were mistaken; and

3) the disadvantaged party did not bear the risk of mistake under the parties' agreement.

EXAMPLE: A agrees to sell B a cow at beef cow prices because at the time of contracting, both parties were under the assumption that the cow was barren. A short time later, the cow was discovered to be with calf, which greatly increased her resale value. The contract is voidable at the option of A.

EXAMPLE: A agrees to sell B a cow at beef cow prices. At the time of contracting, both parties share the mistaken impression that the cow is barren. B tells A that he is still going to try to breed the cow in any case. In this case, A bears the risk of B's efforts succeeding, because if B succeeds, it will prove the parties' assumption that the cow was barren wrong. So A is accordingly bound by the contract even if the cow turns out to be fertile.

(3) **Application under the Common Law and the UCC**

    (a) The doctrine of mistake originated under common law, but is also available in sales of goods cases governed by the UCC.

4. **Impossibility, Impracticability, and Frustration of Purpose**

    a. Where the faulty assumptions of the parties relate to future facts, as opposed to existing facts, these issues are dealt with under the doctrines of impossibility, impracticability, and frustration of purpose.

    b. These doctrines may be used as a defense to a breach of contract claim. However, they can also be raised affirmatively for claims of rescission or cancellation of the contract.

    c. **Impossibility**

        (1) The **doctrine of impossibility** excuses both parties from their obligations under a contract if the performance has been rendered impossible by events occurring after the contract was formed.

        (2) Application of the doctrine of impossibility requires:

        (a) objectively impossible performance; and

           1) Objective impossibility occurs when the performance under the contract becomes literally impossible because of circumstances beyond the control of the parties.

           EXAMPLE: If X promises to sell Y his horse, but the horse dies before X can deliver it, then X's performance has become objectively impossible.

           2) Subjective impossibility occurs when the performance under the contract becomes impossible because of some failure or fault on the part of the performing party. Under those circumstances, the performance obligation is not excused and will be considered as a breach of the contract.

           EXAMPLE: The failure of a party to have enough money either to make a promised payment or to obtain the components required for the production of a promised product would be subjective impossibilities.

EXAMPLE: Dealer promises to sell Buyer 200 bushels of wheat, expecting to procure the wheat from Farmer. Just before harvest, Farmer's crop fails due to wheat blight. The impossibility of Dealer's performance is subjective. While it may be impossible for Dealer to deliver the promised bushels in a timely fashion, because his expected source dried up at the last minute, under the contract he was free to secure the wheat from any source. It was Dealer's selection of Farmer, and his failure to have a backup plan, that gave rise to the resulting situation. Accordingly, Dealer does not meet the legal test of impossibility.

    (b)   the occurrence of the contingency must not be known to the parties at the time of contracting. This can occur in one of two ways:

        1)   it may be a supervening contingency, whereby the performance was possible at the time of contracting, but afterward a contingency occurs that renders the performance impossible; or

        2)   it may be an existing contingency, whereby a contingency existed at the time of contracting, but was unknown to the parties until after the contract was formed.

(3) Exceptions

    (a)   The doctrine of impossibility will not apply where the parties have allocated the risk of the contingency and provided remedial measures in the event of its occurrence.

    (b)   If events render performance only temporarily impossible, then this will typically only suspend the obligations of the parties until the impossibility ends.

(4) Types of Impossibility

    (a)   There are three main categories of impossibility:

        1)   destruction of the subject matter of the contract;

           a)   Where the contract performance involves particular goods, a building or structure, or any other tangible item, the destruction of which occurs without the fault of either party, then the contract is discharged.

               EXAMPLE: Buyer promises to buy Farmer's 2008 wheat crop, the entirety of which is destroyed just before harvest by wheat blight. Farmer's performance is excused on the basis of impossibility.

        2)   death or incapacity; and

           a)   If the existence of a particular person is necessary for the performance of a contract (e.g., personal performance by an individual is required, or performance is to be rendered to a specific person) then that person's death or incapacity will trigger the doctrine of impossibility, and the parties' obligations will be dismissed.

    3)   illegality.

       a)   The doctrine of impossibility will discharge the parties' obligations if performance is prohibited by a change in a constitution, statute, administrative regulation, or municipal ordinance, or by judicial order.

d. **Impracticability**

  (1)   Courts are reluctant to excuse performance for any reason other than impossibility. However, under the **doctrine of impracticability**, a promisor may be excused from performance where unforeseen difficulties have made performance prohibitively expensive or otherwise extremely burdensome.

  (2)   The doctrine of impracticability has its source in Section 2-615 of the UCC, but has since been adopted in the common law of contracts as well.

  (3)   The following elements are required to show that performance under a contract would be impracticable:

    (a) the impracticability of the performance was caused by some unforeseen contingency;

    (b) the risk was neither assumed nor allocated by the parties; and

    (c) the increase in the cost of performance would be far beyond what either party anticipated.

      1)   Even the courts that have allowed relief due to impracticability have held that increased cost alone is not sufficient as an excuse.

  (4) **Impracticability under the UCC**

    (a) Under the UCC, a number of examples of contingencies that would not excuse performance are listed.

      1)   Increased cost alone does not excuse performance unless the rise in cost is due to an unforeseeable contingency and alters the essential nature of performance.

      2)   A rise or collapse in the market will not justify impracticability because those contingencies are exactly the types of business risks that fixed-price contracts are intended to account for.

    (b) The UCC also lists the following examples of contingencies that would trigger impracticability. All involve a severe shortage of raw materials or supplies:

      1)   where the shortage is caused by:

        a)   war or embargo;

        b)   local crop failure; or

        c)   unforeseen shutdown of major sources of supply; or

    2)   the shortage either caused a marked increase in cost or prevents the seller from securing the supplies necessary for his performance.

(5) **Contractual Allocation of the Risk of Non-Performance**

    (a)   The parties are free to allocate the risk of a contingency or to specify the remedial measure to dictate performance in the event of a contingency. Where they do so, the performance that would otherwise be excused by impracticability will be governed by their contractual agreement.

    (b)   The doctrine of impracticability thus operates as a default rule where the contract is silent as to the occurrence of a contingency.

    (c)   Whether the parties have provided for the contingency will depend on all of the circumstances, but some specific guidelines apply.

        1)   If the contingency was foreseeable at the time of contract and the contract is silent, it may suggest that the absence of a term excusing the performance was an affirmative decision to allocate the risk to the performing party.

        2)   The payment of a supra-market premium by the non-performing party might also reflect that the parties bargained for the contingency, and that the consideration in exchange for the premium would be the performance of the party in spite of the contingency.

        3)   Where evidence of a course of dealing or of trade usage reveals that it is customary for the performing party or others in a similar position to assume the risk of such contingencies.

(6) A performance obligation may be excused when the failure to perform is based on a good faith compliance with a foreign or domestic regulation or order.

e. **Frustration of Purpose**

    (1)   Where a contingency occurs that dramatically reduces the value of performance to the receiving party, the **doctrine of frustration of purpose** may be available to excuse the receiving party from its contractual obligations.

    EXAMPLE: The doctrine of frustration of contractual purpose has as its source the famous case of Krell v. Henry, which involved the owner of a London flat with a "ringside" view of the forthcoming coronation parade who agreed to lease the flat at premium prices to a lessee eager to witness the festivities. The parade was canceled when the king became ill, and the lessee's contractual obligations to the owner were excused on the grounds that going through with the rental agreement in the absence of its *raison d'être* "cannot reasonably be said to have been in the contemplation of the parties at the date of the contract."

(2) **Modern Test**

    (a) The contemporary version of this rule will discharge a party's contractual obligations when the following three conditions are met:

        1) the party's principal purpose in entering the contract is frustrated;

            a) This means that the frustration of incidental or non-material purposes would not qualify.

        2) there is substantial frustration; and

            a) Thus, a variation on Krell v. Henry in which the town erected bleachers that only partially obstructed the parade view from the apartment would not justify a finding of frustration.

        3) non-occurrence of the event precipitating frustration was a basic assumption of the contract.

(3) **Contractual Allocation of the Risk**

    (a) Where the parties contractually allocate the risk of the non-occurrence of the event, the doctrine of frustration of purpose will not be available.

    EXAMPLE: The facts otherwise being as they were in Krell v. Henry, assume that the parties' written agreement contained the following language: "The parties understand and agree that the flat owner will be arranging at great expense to move himself and his family to the countryside in order to permit occupancy by lessee and accordingly that lessee will be obligated under this agreement irrespective of whether the coronation parade takes place during the lease period." Since the contract allocated the risk of the contingency to the lessee, his obligations under the contract were not excused for frustration of purpose when the parade was postponed.

    EXAMPLE: The facts otherwise being as they were in Krell v. Henry, assume that all of London was abuzz with news of the new king's possibly serious illness during the days before the parties entered into their agreement. Because a postponement of the coronation parade was therefore foreseeable, the lessee's failure to secure language in the parties' agreement discharging his duties in the event of postponement constitutes evidence that the lessee bore that risk and remained fully obligated under the contract when it came to fruition.

(4) **Application under Common Law and the UCC**

    (a) The frustration of purpose doctrine is followed under common law.

    (b) The frustration of purpose doctrine is available to supplement the UCC in sales of goods contracts.

D. **Excusing Performance by Agreement of the Parties**

1. **Rescission**

   a. The parties may also agree to discharge each other's remaining duties of performance under an existing contract that is at least partly executory on each side [Restatement (Second) of Contracts § 283(1)]. Typically, consideration will be provided by each party's discharge of the other's duties [Restatement (Second) of Contracts § 283, cmt. a].

   b. The Statute of Frauds will not prevent an oral agreement of rescission that discharges unperformed duties from being enforced unless rescission of a transfer of property is involved [Restatement (Second) of Contracts § 283, cmt. b, 148].

2. **Accord and Satisfaction**

   a. The parties may make an **accord**, which is a contract under which the obligee promises to accept substituted performance in satisfaction of the obligor's existing duty. **Satisfaction**—performance of the accord—will discharge the original duty [Restatement (Second) of Contracts § 281].

   b. Accord alone will not discharge the original duty, but once the accord is made, the original duty will be suspended subject to the terms of the accord until the obligor has the chance to make the substituted performance [Restatement (Second) of Contracts § 281, cmt. b].

      (1) If there is such a breach of the accord by the obligor as to discharge the obligee's duty to accept the substituted performance in satisfaction, the obligee is no longer bound under the accord, and he may choose between enforcing the original duty or the duty under the accord [Id.].

      (2) If the obligee breaches the accord, the original duty is not discharged, but the obligor can seek specific performance of the accord (in addition to damages for partial breach) [Id.].

   c. **Validity of Accord—Consideration Required**

      (1) General contract law applies to accords, such that consideration is required [Restatement (Second) of Contracts § 281, cmt. d].

      (2) There may be sufficient consideration if the substituted consideration differs significantly from that required by the original duty, or because the original duty was doubtful or the obligor believed it to be doubtful [Id.].

      (3) Generally, there may be an accord and satisfaction when a creditor agrees to accept part payment of an unliquidated debt that the debtor tenders in full satisfaction of the debt; however, in order for part payment to constitute sufficient consideration on its own, there must be a *bona fide* or good faith dispute as to the debt [see 1 Am. Jur. 2d. Accord & Satisfaction § 39].

3. **Anticipatory Repudiation**

   a. Anticipatory repudiation occurs when, prior to the time that performance is due under the contract, a party announces his intention not to perform, or circumstances make such an intention reasonably clear to the aggrieved party.

b. Technically, anticipatory repudiation is not the same as a breach of contract because the party has not yet failed on its promise of performance. However, the aggrieved party is given the option to immediately treat the anticipatory repudiation as a breach of contract and to be entitled to the same rights and remedies.

c. Anticipatory repudiation may be established by:

   (1) a party's definitive statement indicating that he will commit a breach of contract; or

   (2) a party's voluntary or affirmative act that renders the party unable to perform or apparently unable to perform (e.g., the sale of the contracted-for item to a third party).

d. **Adequate Assurance of Performance**

   (1) If anticipatory repudiation cannot be established but there are reasonable grounds for insecurity (i.e., reasonable grounds to believe that the other party is unwilling or unable to perform), the insecure party may make a demand for **adequate assurance of performance**.

   (2) Adequate assurance of performance must be provided in the following forms:

      (a) the UCC requires that a demand for adequate assurance of performance on a sale of goods contract be made in writing [§ 2-609(1)]; and

      (b) under the Restatement of Contracts, an adequate assurance of performance may be made either:

         1) by oral communication; or

         2) in writing.

   (3) **Suspension of Performance by the Insecure Party**

      (a) Upon making a demand for assurances, a party with reasonable grounds for insecurity may suspend its own contractual performance so long as:

         1) suspension is commercially reasonable; and

         2) the insecure party has not yet received the agreed-upon return for the performance in question.

            EXAMPLE: If a seller reads about a planned bankruptcy filing by a buyer, the seller may, after demanding assurances, suspend delivery of goods for which the buyer has not already paid.

      (b) The insecure party may also suspend his own performance where the performing party:

         1) does not respond to a demand for assurances within a reasonable time (30 days under the UCC); or

2) does not respond in a manner that provides reasonable assurance to the other party.

    a) In this situation, the reasonableness of an assurance of performance is determined by:

       i) the circumstances;

       ii) the relationship between the parties;

       iii) the parties' past dealings; and

       iv) the nature of the insecurity requiring assurance.

  (c) The failure to respond with reasonable assurances constitutes a repudiation of the contract by the non-responding party.

e. **Rights of the Aggrieved Party upon Repudiation**

  (1) If the aggrieved party chooses to treat the anticipatory breach as a breach of contract, he may:

    (a) cancel the contract and terminate all rights and obligations under it; or

    (b) bring an action for damages or specific performance.

  (2) The aggrieved party may immediately resort to one of these remedies upon repudiation, or he may wait until performance should have occurred.

  (3) If an aggrieved party chooses to ignore a repudiation, then he is prevented from continuing to perform on the contract if performance would increase his damages from the contract.

  (4) If the aggrieved party can prove to the court that he was willing, ready, and able to render performance had the anticipatory repudiation not occurred, then the aggrieved party is relieved of:

    (a) performance of contractual obligations; and

    (b) performance of any conditions precedent.

f. **Retraction of Repudiation**

  (1) A party who has made an anticipatory repudiation to the other party may retract the repudiation unless and until the other party:

    (a) acts in reliance on the repudiation;

    (b) positively accepts the repudiation by signifying this to the breaching party; or

    (c) commences a suit for damages or specific performance.

E. Conditions

1. In some contracts, the obligation to perform is conditioned upon the happening of some event or upon action by the other party. The law regarding conditions governs two distinct issues: the order of parties' performances and the remedies where conditions to the contract have failed.

2. **Promissory versus Pure Conditions**

  a. A condition to contractual performance can be a condition controlled by the parties or can be a condition outside of either party's control.

(1) A **promissory condition** is where the contract performance is conditioned on the occurrence of the promised performance by the other party.

> **EXAMPLE:** A publication contract contains the following language: "Publisher's duty of payment is expressly conditioned on Author's timely completion of the promised manuscript." In this case, Author's timely delivery of the manuscript is a promissory condition on Publisher's contractual obligation of payment.

(2) **Pure conditions** are typically where contract performance is conditioned on the occurrence of events beyond the control of either party.

> **EXAMPLE:** Skyblasters, Inc. agrees by contract to provide a fireworks display for a holiday celebration sponsored by the Village of Remulak, and the contract contains a "weather permitting" provision. In this case, good weather is a pure condition on Skyblasters' performance obligation.

3. **Express versus Implied Conditions**

   a. **Express conditions** are those which the parties expressly include in provisions of the contract.

   > **EXAMPLE:** "Publisher's duty of payment is expressly conditioned on Author's timely completion of the promised manuscript." This would be an express condition to contract performance of payment because it is listed within the contract.

   b. **Implied conditions** are those created under common law or the UCC to address order of performance and rights upon breach when the parties haven't done so expressly. Implied conditions are those fairly to be inferred from evidence of the parties' intentions. They are often referred to as implied-in-fact, since their existence is determined by the process of contract interpretation rather than the express language of the contract.

4. **Rules Governing the Order of Performance**

   a. The rules regarding order of performance are dependent on whether the contract falls under common law or the UCC.

      (1) **Cases Governed by Common Law**

         (a) If the contract contains express conditions specifying the order of performance, then those specifications will control the order of performance.

         (b) If the contract is silent as to order of performance:

            1) Where one party's performance requires a period of time to be completed and the other party's performance does not, then the performance over time is treated as an implied condition of the latter.

            2) Where the parties can exchange performance more or less simultaneously, then the performances are treated as concurrent conditions of each other.

(2) **Sales of Goods under the UCC**

(a) Under the UCC, the parties are free to specify the order of performance, and where the contract contains those specifications, the performance obligations under that contract will be performed according to the contractual terms.

(b) Because sales contracts most commonly involve delivery and payment of goods, performance is treated as concurrent, and so each performance is conditioned on the performance of the other.

5. **Rules Governing the Failure of a Condition**

a. The default rules for a failed condition of the contract performance are dependent on whether the contract falls under the common law rules of contracts or under the UCC.

b. **Cases Governed by the Common Law**

(1) In common law cases, the rights of the parties in the event of a failed condition depend on whether the condition is express or implied.

(2) **Express Conditions**

(a) Where a party's performance under the contract is subject to an express condition, the failure of that condition will discharge the party's obligation to perform.

(b) **Identifying Express Conditions**

1) In some cases, the parties will use the magic words to describe a particular performance or event as a condition on a return performance.

EXAMPLE: "The party's duty to perform is expressly conditioned on the promised performance."

2) The term "expressly conditioned" does not have to be included, but language conveying the same idea will constitute an express condition as well.

EXAMPLE: "No obligation to proceed unless and until franchisee takes the following steps" or "payment due upon completion of second benchmark."

3) In the absence of clear language, an express condition may be established by trade usage, course of dealing, or course of performance evidence.

(c) **Excusing Failed Express Conditions**

1) Generally, a failure of the occurrence of an express condition will discharge the performance obligation of the party who stood to benefit from the condition.

2) Nevertheless, there are three situations in which the failure of the condition may be excused without discharging the beneficiary's performance obligation.

3) **Waiver**

   a) The party who has been discharged from performing by the failed condition may waive the right to discharge and perform anyway. When the party waives the condition, the waiving party's obligation becomes absolute because it is no longer subject to the condition.

   b) Some courts treat a waiver of condition as a midterm modification to the contract and require that additional consideration be given by the other party to give the waiver effect.

4) **Bad Faith Conduct**

   a) A condition will be excused on the basis of bad faith conduct by the beneficiary of the condition. Thus, bad faith conduct will excuse the condition where the benefitting party interferes with the fulfillment of a contract, or where the benefitting party fails to take steps necessary for the condition's fulfillment.

   EXAMPLE: In a contract for the sale of real property, a buyer's performance obligation is conditioned on his success in securing financing. If the buyer fails to apply for financing, this would be considered conduct in bad faith, and the buyer's performance obligation would become absolute.

5) **Avoiding Forfeiture**

   a) In some situations the fulfillment of a condition may result in a forfeiture or great loss to one of the parties. In those cases a court may excuse the condition to avoid forfeiture.

   b) In deciding to excuse a condition, the court will consider:

      i) whether the party favoring excuse will suffer a loss greatly disproportionate to the actual prejudice to the other party;

      ii) whether the failure of the condition is due to willfulness or serious neglect;

      iii) whether the other party played a role in bringing that failure about;

      iv) whether the condition relates to a minor term in the contract as opposed to a material one; and

      v) whether the fulfillment of the condition has not failed completely but has merely been delayed.

> **NOTE** There is another consideration that applies to insurance contracts only. In deciding to excuse a condition, courts will consider whether, where a contract for insurance benefits conditions benefits payments on timely notice of covered events, such notice is not provided because of circumstances outside the insured's control.

EXAMPLE: A failure to provide notice of a covered disability, where the disability itself has caused the failure of timely notice, would be a condition that would be excused.

EXAMPLE: Failure to provide timely proof of death, where the body is not discovered for an extended period of time, would be an excusable condition.

(3) **Implied Conditions**

    (a) When the breach in question relates to an express condition, courts will enforce the condition to the letter and discharge the conditioned performance obligation, absent an excuse such as waiver or bad faith.

    (b) When the possibility of breach is not addressed by an express condition, it is still a breach; however, under the law of implied conditions, courts can treat that breach in one of two ways: either as a material breach or as substantial performance.

    (c) **Material Breach versus Substantial Performance**

        1) If the breach is serious enough, the court will treat the breach in the same way it would treat a breach of an express condition (i.e., as relieving the aggrieved party of his own performance obligation). This is called **material breach**, and the aggrieved party is free to walk away from his own obligations and sue the breaching party for damages.

        2) In certain cases, if the breach is less serious, the court will treat the party's performance as "close enough," meaning that the party has rendered **substantial performance** of the condition. In these cases, the aggrieved party will not be discharged of his performance obligation. The doctrine of substantial performance applies to contracts for services and, in particular, to construction contracts.

        3) Even where the court finds substantial performance of a condition, the aggrieved party may still sue for damages as remedy for the breach.

        4) The Restatement of Contracts lists five factors that can help to distinguish between material breach and substantial performance:

            a) the extent to which the aggrieved party will be deprived of the benefit, which he reasonably expected under the terms of the contract;

            b) the extent to which the aggrieved party can adequately be compensated via damages for the defective performance;

            c) the extent to which the breaching party will suffer forfeiture if a material breach is found;

d) the extent to which the breach was willful or in bad faith, rather than merely negligent or innocent; and

e) the likelihood that the breaching party will cure his failure within a reasonable time and in a manner consistent with the reasonable purposes of the contract.

    i) The likelihood that the failure will be cured is a significant circumstance in determining whether the breach is material or non-material [Restatement (Second) of Contracts § 241].

EXAMPLE: Contractor builds a house for Landowner and—unbeknownst to Contractor—the plumbing subcontractor installs a brand of pipe that differs from the brand specified in the contract but is in every important respect the same quality. It would be an extremely expensive and burdensome task for Contractor to remove and replace the pipe. The use of the substitute pipe is a breach of the parties' contract, but Contractor has substantially performed because Landowner is deprived of merely a *de minimis* benefit since the substitute pipe is the functional equivalent of the brand required by the contract. Contractor will suffer an enormous loss if he is required to remove and replace the errant pipe; and the breach was at most negligent if the Contractor did not monitor the subcontractor closely enough, but in no way was the Contractor's breach willful or in bad faith.

EXAMPLE: Contractor builds a house for the Yuppies, a young couple who are foodies and love to entertain and, accordingly, their plans include a spacious kitchen. The Yuppies spend the year in Paris while the house is under construction, and in their absence and without prior consultation, Contractor decides to deviate from the plans and build a smaller kitchen, thus enabling Contractor to save significant construction costs. Contractor's improvisation is a material breach because it would deprive the Yuppies of a substantial benefit for which they had contracted; because money would not adequately compensate them for the diminished kitchen that was to be the centerpiece of their dream home; and because Contractor's breach was willful and in bad faith.

5) **Total Breach versus Partial Breach**

   a) A material breach can be treated as either a partial breach or a total breach.

      i) A claim for damages for **total breach** is one for damages based on all of the injured party's remaining rights to performance [Restatement (Second) of Contracts § 236].

      ii) A claim for damages for **partial breach** is one for damages based on only part of the injured party's remaining rights to performance [Id.].

   b) However, a non-material breach can only be a partial breach.

(4) **Failed Condition That Cannot Be Excused**

   (a) Where a condition has failed and cannot be excused, there are other methods of enforcement available to mitigate the consequences for the breaching party.

   (b) If a contract requires both parties to render a series of performances over a period of time, the contract may be divisible in the event of a failed condition.

      1) The failed condition must not be material to the contract itself, but must relate to a small portion of the contract performance in order for the contract to be severable into separate transactions, allowing the breaching party to recover for portions properly performed.

      2) The legal test for determining whether a contract is divisible is:

         a) Can the performance in question be apportioned into corresponding pairs of parties' performances?

         b) Can each pair be properly regarded as agreed equivalents?

> **NOTE** A helpful way to look at divisibility is by asking whether the contract is nothing more than the sum of its parts. If so, then the contract is divisible. If the contract involves more than the sum of its parts, then it is unlikely to be divisible.

EXAMPLE: A one-year cleaning service contract would be divisible if the services were provided and paid for on a monthly basis, as it would be easy to apportion the larger exchange into "pairs of part performance" that are "properly regarded as agreed equivalents" (i.e., a month's worth of cleaning in exchange for a month's pay). To put it another way, the one-year contract is merely the sum of the 12 monthly exchanges.

EXAMPLE: A contracts to build a house for B for $100,000, with progress payments of $5,000 due in monthly installments during construction and a balloon payment upon the architect's certificate of satisfactory completion. The contract is not divisible, for the performances and the progress payments are not "agreed equivalents," and the whole is greater than the sum of the parts, since no reasonable person would enter a freestanding contract for a month of construction work.

    (c) Where a party has failed to fulfill an express condition or is in material breach of the contract, he may still be able to recover in *quantum meruit* the value of benefits he has conferred to the aggrieved party during performance.

        1) The breaching party may recover the reasonable value of the benefits conferred under a theory of *quantum meruit*.

        2) The reasonable value of the benefits conferred will be reduced by the damages suffered by the aggrieved party due to the breach.

  c. **Sales of Goods Contracts under the UCC**

  (1) **Express and Implied Conditions in Relationship to the Perfect Tender Rule**

    (a) Under the **perfect tender rule**, the terms of a contract for the sale of goods are enforced exactly. Every contract term is thus treated as an express condition, and a breach of the performance obligation by the seller will relieve the payment obligation of the buyer.

        1) As a result, there is no need to distinguish between express and implied conditions because they will be treated in the same fashion.

    (b) The perfect tender rule enables a buyer to reject a seller's goods "if the goods or the tender of delivery fail in any respect to conform to the contract." Under this rule, any deviation from the performance specified by the contract (e.g., regarding the quality or quantity of the goods, or the time or manner of delivery) constitutes a breach by the seller.

    (c) If the seller fails to make perfect tender, the buyer has three courses of action available [§ 2-601]:

        1) **Reject the Goods**

            a) For a buyer to reject the goods, the buyer must exercise the right of rejection within a reasonable time after delivery and notify the seller of the rejection within a reasonable period of time [§ 2-602(1)].

            b) If the buyer rejects the goods, the buyer may bring an action for damages against the seller for imperfect tender, and the buyer must use reasonable care with respect to holding the goods for a time sufficient for the seller to remove them [§ 2-602].

    i)   If the seller gives no instructions within a reasonable time after notification of rejection, the buyer may store the goods for the seller's account, reship them to the seller, or resell them for the seller's account [§ 2-604].

    ii)   However, if the buyer is a merchant and the seller has no agent or place of business in the place where the goods were rejected, the buyer must follow any reasonable instructions received from the seller, and if none, must make reasonable efforts to sell the goods if they are perishable or their value will decline quickly [§ 2-603(1)].

    iii)   A merchant buyer who resells the goods after a rightful rejection is entitled to reimbursement for the reasonable expenses of caring for and selling the goods [§ 2-603(2)].

c)   If the buyer fails to state in connection with the rejection a particular defect, the buyer will be precluded from relying on the unstated defect to justify rejection if the defect is ascertainable by reasonable inspection, where [§ 2-605(1)]:

    i)   the seller could have cured the defect if it was stated seasonably; or

    ii)   between merchants, the seller after rejection made a written request for a written full and final statement of all defects on which the buyer proposes to rely.

d)   If a buyer does not effectuate rejection in the manner specified above, then he has made a failed rejection. A failed rejection will be deemed to be acceptance of the goods by the buyer.

2)   **Accept the Goods**

a)   The buyer may accept the goods, despite the improper tender. Acceptance occurs when the buyer has had a reasonable opportunity to inspect the goods and signifies acceptance either through:

    i)   stating to the seller that the goods conform to the contract;

    ii)   taking the goods despite their non-conformance;

    iii)   failing to make an effective rejection of the goods; or

    iv)   taking any action that would be inconsistent with the seller's ownership of the goods.

> **EXAMPLE:** Buyer puts the goods on display in the showroom.

    b) If the buyer accepts the goods, he has the following rights and duties:

        i) he must pay contract price for the goods;

        ii) he may seek damages against the seller for the nonconformity if he notified the seller of the nonconformity within a reasonable time after discovering it, the seller is not prejudiced by the lack of notice, or his rights would not be affected; and

        iii) he may revoke his acceptance if the nonconformity substantially impairs the value of the goods, and he was initially unaware of the nonconformity because of the difficulty of discovery or because his acceptance was predicated on the seller's assurances of conformity or that nonconformity would be cured.

NOTE ▶ The buyer must revoke his acceptance within a reasonable time after the buyer discovers or should have discovered the grounds for revocation, and before there is any substantial change in the condition of the goods (unless caused by their own defect). The revocation is only effective once the buyer notifies the seller of it [§ 2-608(2)].

    3) **Reject Part and Accept Part of the Goods**

        a) A buyer who has received improper tender may accept some of the commercial tender and reject the rest.

        b) The buyer will then have the rights and duties of acceptance for the goods he accepted, and the rights and duties of rejection for the goods he rejected (though this picking and choosing is limited to "commercial units"—e.g., a buyer of bread can reject individual loaves but not half loaves).

        EXAMPLE: Buyer's contract guaranteed that Seller would deliver 10 gross of quart-sized Mason jars, which are invariably boxed and sold by the gross in the Mason jar trade. If Seller's tender is imperfect (e.g., it is late or short), Buyer is free to accept some of the jars and reject the rest, but he must do so "by the gross."

  (d) **Seller's Ability to Cure**

    1) If a seller makes a nonconforming tender but the time of performance has not yet expired under the contract, then the seller may substitute conforming goods so long as:

> > a) the seller gives buyer seasonable notice of his intention to substitute; and
> >
> > b) the seller makes conforming delivery within the time specified in the contract.
> >
> > 2) If a seller makes a nonconforming delivery and had reasonable grounds to believe that delivery would be acceptable to the buyer, then he may substitute a conforming delivery if:
> >
> > > a) the seller gives buyer reasonable notice of his intention to substitute; and
> > >
> > > b) the seller makes conforming delivery within a reasonable time.
> >
> > 3) **Proof of Reasonable Grounds by Seller**
> >
> > > a) A seller may prove that he had reasonable grounds to believe that the buyer would accept nonconformity if he has evidence of:
> > >
> > > > i) express assurances to that effect from the buyer; or
> > > >
> > > > ii) trade usage, course of dealing, or course of performance evidence to that effect.

(2) **Special Rules for Installment Contracts**

    (a) Under the UCC, **installment contracts** are contracts that contemplate the delivery of goods in separate lots to be separately accepted by the buyer.

    (b) Because such contracts are performed in installments, the occasion of a nonconforming tender will almost invariably occur in connection with a particular installment. When that occurs, the rights of the buyer are as follows:

> 1) If the nonconforming installment substantially impairs the value of the whole contract, there is a breach of the whole contract [§ 2-612(3)].
>
> 2) If the nonconforming installment substantially impairs the value of that installment, and the seller cannot cure, the buyer may reject the installment. However, if the nonconforming installment does not substantially impair the value of the contract as a whole, and the seller gives adequate assurance that he will cure, the buyer must accept the installment [§ 2-612(2)].

VII. DEFENSES

A. **Incapacity**

1. **Infancy**

   a. Infancy is the time period before a person reaches the age of majority. An infant, commonly referred to as a minor, is any person who is under the age of 18.

   b. At common law, minors lacked the capacity to enter into a contract. The modern rule is that a minor may enter into a contract, but the contract is voidable at the option of the minor. However, in certain circumstances the contract may be ratified, or alternately, the minor may still be liable for the benefits received.

      EXCEPTION: In most states, minors enjoy the power of avoidance even if they are married or emancipated. However, a minority of jurisdictions deprive married or emancipated minors of the power of avoidance, making all contracts they enter into enforceable against them.

   c. **Power of Avoidance**

      (1) While minors have the capacity to enter a contract before they reach the age of majority, they also have the power to disaffirm contracts they enter into (the power of avoidance), with some exceptions.

      (2) The **power of avoidance** means that the minor has the option of voiding the contract. However, the contract is not void against the other parties to a contract, and so is enforceable against everyone but the minor.

         (a) There is an increasing trend toward limiting minors' use of the power of avoidance to a defense only. The minor is allowed to disaffirm a contract that the other party seeks to enforce against him. However, he may not use the defense to bring suit against the other party to secure restitution of monies already paid.

      (3) Upon exercising the right to disaffirm a contract, the minor is obligated to return to the other party any goods received under the contract.

         (a) The minor must return the goods if they are in his possession when he disaffirms the contract. However, he is not liable for damage, wear and tear, or any other depreciation in value of the goods.

         (b) If the minor is not in possession of the goods at the time of disaffirming the contract because he sold the goods, then the minor will be obligated to turn over the proceeds of the sale of the goods to the other party.

         (c) A contract between a minor and another party may be for something that cannot be returned, such as a services contract or a lease. In such a case, where the subject matter of the contract is non-returnable, the minor is under no further obligation to return or compensate the other party.

(d) In a minority of jurisdictions, a minor can only disaffirm a contract by making the other party whole. In these jurisdictions, the minor would be liable for depreciation, as well as compensating the other party for the services or other non-returnable items, in addition to returning possession or the proceeds of a sale for returnable items.

d. **Ratification**

(1) For most contracts that minors enter into before reaching the age of majority, the minor may **ratify** that contract upon reaching the age of majority.

(2) A minor may ratify most transactions entered into during infancy by making any manifestation to the other party of an intention to be bound by the original contract.

(a) The minor's silence regarding the contract after reaching the age of majority is not sufficient to constitute a ratification unless the minor continues to take advantage of goods or services provided under the contract.

(b) In a minority of jurisdictions, if a minor fails to disaffirm the contract within a reasonable time after reaching the age of majority, then the contract will be deemed ratified.

(c) Once a minor disaffirms a contract, a majority of jurisdictions consider the contract void, with title to the property revesting in the other party (where possible). Once disaffirmed, a minor can no longer ratify the contract. Ratification must occur prior to the minor's avoidance of the contract.

e. **Exceptions**

(1) **Necessaries**

(a) A minor's contract for necessaries is voidable. However, the other party has the right in *quasi*-contract to recover for the reasonable value of the goods or services provided.

(b) **Necessaries** are those items considered necessary for survival. Most basic categories of necessaries include things like food, clothing, shelter, and medical care.

1) In some jurisdictions, these items are only considered necessaries if provided to an emancipated minor whose parents cannot or will not provide them.

2) Courts are split on whether to include automobiles and/or education in the category of necessaries.

(c) The other party may secure the reasonable value of the goods or services only, not the contract price. Additionally, if the minor paid more than the reasonable value, then he is entitled to a refund of the difference between the amount paid and the reasonable value.

(2) **Misrepresentation by Minor**

   (a) In a minority of jurisdictions, if a minor has misrepresented his age to the contracting party in order to obtain the goods or services of the contract, he may be equitably estopped from proving his real age in court. This would deny the minor the defense of infancy and make the contract enforceable.

2. **Mental Incompetence**

   a. At common law, an insane person did not have capacity to enter a contract, and any contracts he made were void. Under modern rules, the bar for establishing mental incompetence is lower—a party need not be "insane" to invoke the doctrine—and the consequences of invocation depend on multiple factors.

      (1) The key in all cases is whether the person was incompetent at the time of contracting.

      (2) The party who becomes incompetent after entering a contract can escape contractual liability—if at all—via impossibility and related doctrines, discussed earlier.

   b. **Requirements for Mental Incompetence**

      (1) If a party is adjudicated incompetent and a guardian is appointed, then this adjudication will be sufficient to establish mental incompetence for contract cases.

      (2) Where there is no adjudication of mental incompetence by a court, then a party may still be declared mentally incompetent for the purposes of contract formation under the following circumstances:

         (a) **Cognitive Defects**

            1) In almost every jurisdiction, a person will be deemed mentally incompetent and lacking capacity to enter a contract if the person is unable to understand in a reasonable manner the nature and consequences of the transaction.

               EXAMPLE: A person who is operating under the influence of delusions or hallucinations will be deemed mentally incompetent based on cognitive defects.

         (b) **Volitional Defects**

            1) In many jurisdictions, mental incompetence can be established if:

               a) a person is unable to act in a reasonable mannor in relation to the transaction; and

               b) the other party has reason to know of this condition.

               EXAMPLE: A person who is a manic depressive would be able to avoid a contract if he was in a manic phase at the time of contract formation and if the other party had reason to know of that person's state based, for example, on his erratic behavior.

c. **Legal Consequences**
   (1) In most jurisdictions, a contract entered into by an incompetent person is voidable. This means that the contract is enforceable at the option of the incompetent party, rather than void, which would make it unenforceable by either party.
      (a) Some jurisdictions, as well as the Second Restatement, hold that a person adjudicated incompetent and under guardianship has no capacity to incur contractual duties, making such contracts void.
   (2) A party who is mentally incompetent at the time of contract may ratify the contract if he becomes competent at a later time. Ratification may be accomplished by an oral or written manifestation of the intention to be bound by the original contract.
   (3) If the mentally incompetent person exercises his power of avoidance and has received some benefit under the contract, then he is required to make the other party whole by paying the reasonable value of the goods or services rendered.
      (a) A mentally incompetent party will be responsible for damage, wear and tear, or any other depreciation in value of the goods.

      EXCEPTION: If the other party takes unfair advantage of the mentally incompetent person, and has knowledge of the person's incompetence, then the other party is entitled only to a return "as is" of any goods still in the possession of the mentally incompetent party and will have no right of recovery for goods or services already consumed.
   (4) The rules governing the liability of a mentally incompetent party for contracts for necessaries are the same as for minors. The mentally incompetent party will be liable to the other party for the reasonable value of those goods and services.
      (a) For mentally incompetent persons, necessaries include the retention of legal services in connection with adjudicating mental incompetence.

B. **Misrepresentation**
   1. Misrepresentation can play two roles in contract cases: it may be a "sword," as the basis for affirmative relief, or a "shield," a defense to enforcement.
      a. Misrepresentation can be used as a basis for affirmative relief under a tort claim brought by the aggrieved party in the form of an action for rescission and damages.
      b. Misrepresentation can be used as a defense to an effort to enforce the contract.
   2. **Misrepresentations** are untrue statements or assertions that relate to existing facts.
      a. Misrepresentations relate to existing facts, not to future conduct or action. If one says, "I'm going to do something," and doesn't do it,

that's a broken promise, not a misrepresentation. But, if one says, "I'm going to do X," and at the time he makes that promise he actually doesn't intend to do X, that may be actionable as promissory fraud.

b. Misrepresentations must relate to facts, not opinions. A statement that is based on a party's mere opinion, guess, or supposition will not be considered a misrepresentation.

   (1) Where one party disguises a fact as an opinion, then this will constitute a misrepresentation.

   EXAMPLE: An automobile dealer who tells a buyer that he thinks the car runs pretty well, even though he knows that the car does not run well, would be disguising a fact as an opinion, and thus be making a misrepresentation to the buyer.

   (2) Where a party holds himself out to have knowledge or special skill, and asserts an opinion on the basis of the skill or knowledge, then his assertions are held to relate to the underlying facts and, therefore, sufficient to establish misrepresentation.

   EXAMPLE: A certified mechanic who tells a buyer that he thinks the car runs pretty well, even though he knows that the car does not run well, would, in effect, be asserting facts about the state of the car and, thus, making a misrepresentation to the buyer.

3. **Types of Misrepresentation**

   a. **Fraudulent Misrepresentation**

      (1) To establish fraudulent misrepresentation, the following must be proved:

         (a) the defendant must have made an assertion that was inconsistent with existing facts;

            1) Most claims of fraudulent misrepresentation are based on oral or written statements.

               a) Statements that are "half-truths" can be misrepresentations as well.

                  EXAMPLE: An advertisement for real estate "suitable for commercial development," where applicable zoning regulations would prohibit such use.

            2) Misrepresentations can also be made through conduct.

               EXAMPLE: When a payor issues a check for a specified amount despite insufficient funds, he is representing that he has funds on deposit to cover the instrument.

               a) Active efforts to "cover up" the truth (termed **fraudulent concealment**) likewise constitute misrepresentations.

                  EXAMPLE: A seller of real estate undertakes efforts to hide termite damage from potential buyers.

(b) the state-of-mind element requires that there was both:

    1) scienter; and

        a) The scienter requirement relates to the defendant's state of mind with respect to the assertion. The defendant will satisfy the scienter requirement if either:

            i) he made the assertion knowing it to be false; or

            ii) he made the assertion knowing that he had no idea whether it was true or false.

            EXAMPLE: Scienter would be present where the auto dealer says, "This baby can go from zero to 70 in six seconds flat," if he either knows that the car can't accelerate that quickly or has no basis for knowing whether the car can accelerate that quickly.

    2) intent to mislead.

        a) The defendant will meet the requirement for intent to mislead if:

            i) he made the assertion for the purpose of misleading the aggrieved party; or

            ii) he made the assertion knowing there was a substantial likelihood that the aggrieved party would be misled.

(c) the misrepresentation must be material to the contract; and

    1) Materiality can be shown by either an objective standard or a subjective standard:

        a) Under an objective standard, a misrepresentation is material where such an assertion was likely to induce a reasonable person to enter into the contract.

        EXAMPLE: An assertion that a used car has been carefully inspected by an independent auto mechanic would appeal to a reasonable person and, thus, satisfy the objective materiality test.

        b) A misrepresentation is material under a subjective standard if assertion of such a fact was likely, for reasons known to the defendant, to induce the aggrieved party specifically into entering the contract.

        EXAMPLE: An assertion that the car was owned by Salman Rushdie when he was living incognito in the U.K. would be material if made to an individual whom the seller knew to be a Rushdie enthusiast.

(d) there must have been reasonable reliance on the representation.

    1) The standard for determining whether an aggrieved party's reliance on the defendant's misrepresentation is reasonable

is whether, under all of the same circumstances, a reasonable person would have relied on the assertion.

EXAMPLE: Reliance would be unreasonable if the aggrieved party has independent knowledge or reason to know that the perpetrator's statement is false.

EXAMPLE: Reliance would be unreasonable if the aggrieved party has reason to believe that the perpetrator is unreliable.

EXAMPLE: Reliance would be unreasonable if no reasonable person would have believed the assertion.

EXAMPLE: Reliance would be unreasonable if the aggrieved party could have easily ascertained the truth by cursory inspection of the goods.

2) Because of the "duty to read," it is generally not reasonable to rely on a trading partner's characterization of a writing's content. However, two situations in which reliance on the contents of a writing would be reasonable are:

a) if the defendant is a merchant and the aggrieved party is a customer; or

b) if the defendant induces the aggrieved party not to read the writing by some devious means.

EXAMPLE: The perpetrator induces the victim to sign a contract that the perpetrator knows to contain terms of which the victim is unaware and in circumstances in which the perpetrator know the victim won't have time to read the contract.

b. **Non-Fraudulent Misrepresentation**

(1) Non-fraudulent misrepresentation may either be negligent or innocent misrepresentation. For either claim, the following elements must be established:

(a) the defendant must have made an assertion that was inconsistent with existing facts;

(b) the misrepresentation must be material to the contract; and

(c) there must have been reasonable reliance on the misrepresentation.

(2) Because negligent or innocent misrepresentation is not intentional, there is no need to make a showing of the defendant's state of mind. Instead, the following factors are required:

(a) For negligent misrepresentation, the aggrieved party must show that the perpetrator would have known that the assertion was false had he exercised reasonable care.

(b) For innocent misrepresentation, the aggrieved party need only show that the perpetrator made an assertion not in accord with existing fact.

(3)	The same remedies are available to the victim of either negligent or innocent misrepresentation, so the difference between them is merely descriptive (i.e., what to call a particular misrepresentation) but has no further legal consequence.

c.	**Fraudulent Nondisclosure**

(1)	The wrong that must be committed under a claim of fraudulent nondisclosure relates not to an assertion made by the defendant, but to the defendant's silence where there was a duty to disclose.

(2)	To prove fraudulent nondisclosure, one must show that:

(a)	the nondisclosure was material to the contract, under either an objective standard or a subjective standard; and

(b)	there was reasonable reliance on the nondisclosure.

NOTE ▶ Because fraudulent nondisclosure is based on the defendant's silence rather than an assertion, there is no requirement that the defendant make an assertion.

(3)	Although there is generally no duty of disclosure to trading partners, if a party is aware of material facts that are unlikely to be discovered by the other party in the exercise of ordinary care and diligence, then there will be a duty to disclose that information in these circumstances:

(a)	where the parties enjoy a relationship of trust and confidence;

EXAMPLE: A relationship between family members or a professional's relationship with a client would be a relationship of trust and confidence.

(b)	if a party has made an assertion that was true at the time but has been rendered untrue by intervening events; or

EXAMPLE: If a person makes an assertion that an individual plans to keep property in an undeveloped state and later learns that the individual no longer intends to keep the property undeveloped, he would need to disclose this change.

(c)	if the obligation of good faith would require that the party disclose the information.

EXAMPLE: A seller of residential real estate who fails to disclose a termite infestation to the buyer would have a good-faith obligation to disclose the infestation to the buyer.

4.	**Remedies**

a.	Victims of fraudulent misrepresentation, non-fraudulent misrepresentation, and fraudulent nondisclosure may use those claims in two ways:

(1)	avoidance; or

(a)	All three claims give the victim the power of avoidance, which may be exercised to defend against a breach of contract claim brought by the misrepresenting party.

        (2)   rescission and reliance damages.

            (a)   All three claims enable the victim to bring a tort action to rescind the contract and collect damages for reliance on the misrepresentation, including consequential damages.

    b.   Victims of fraudulent and non-fraudulent misrepresentation have a third option: they may live with the contract and sue for the benefit of the bargain.

        (1)   The victim of fraudulent misrepresentation may bring a tort action seeking the benefit of the bargain. This would allow the victim to recover the difference between the value of the goods or services actually received and the value of the promised goods or services. This tort remedy is the functional equivalent of expectation damages, discussed later in this outline.

        (2)   This remedy is not available for claims of negligent or innocent misrepresentation. However, parties bringing such claims may be able to characterize the assertion contrary to fact as a warranty and thus obtain expectation damages by asserting breach thereof.

    c.   Because fraudulent misrepresentation is an intentional tort, the aggrieved party may secure punitive damages against the defendant to penalize the defendant on the basis of the fraudulent intention.

        (1)   Punitive damages are not available for claims of negligent or innocent misrepresentation or fraudulent nondisclosure.

C. Duress

  1.   At common law, the defense of duress was available in two circumstances:

    a.   physical compulsion; and

        (1)   A party could claim duress as a defense to contract liability if the party signed the contract under force of physical compulsion.

    b.   unlawful threat.

        (1)   A party could claim duress as a defense to contract liability if the party signed the contract under threat of unlawful activity against himself or his family.

  2.   Although the above two circumstances still constitute duress, the contemporary definition of the term has been relaxed to cover less egregious instances of coercive persuasion. Thus, under modern law, there are three elements to a defense of duress:

    a.   a threat;

        (1)   A **threat** made by the perpetrator is a manifestation of intent to inflict harm on the other person, made in words or by conduct.

            <u>EXAMPLE:</u> The words "your money or your life" would be considered a threat.

            <u>EXAMPLE:</u> An example of conduct considered a threat is the scene in "The Godfather" where the man wakes up with a horse's head in bed, which was placed there to induce him to sign the contract.

b. that is wrongful in nature; and

(1) A threat is wrongful in nature if it involves criminal or tortious conduct, whether the threat is itself unlawful (e.g., extortion or blackmail) or whether it is merely a threat to engage in future unlawful action (e.g., causing harm to a party's person, family member, or property).

(2) A threat to pursue criminal charges constitutes a wrongful threat, even if the perpetrator honestly believes that the target is guilty of that crime.

(3) A threat to bring a civil action is wrongful only if made in bad faith—that is, if the perpetrator does not honestly and reasonably believe that the target has civil liability.

(4) A threat is sufficient to constitute duress if what is threatened is a bad faith breach of contract. This is commonly known as economic duress.

(a) If a party refuses to perform unless he is awarded additional benefits, this may constitute a bad faith breach of contract.

1) Economic duress will usually arise where the threatened party acquiesces to the other party's demands at the time but then refuses to confer the additional benefits.

EXAMPLE: Sailors on a fishing voyage cease their work midway through the voyage and refuse to resume their duties unless the captain agrees to give them a raise. At the end of the voyage, the captain refuses to pay the higher amount, and the sailors sue.

(b) Not every demand for a change in contract price will be considered a bad faith demand. If the demand for a change in contract terms is due to the fact that performance under the terms of the contract has become extremely burdensome because of unanticipated circumstances, then there is no duress.

EXAMPLE: The sailors' demand for additional compensation in response to an unanticipated expansion of their workload due to faulty fishing nets would be a good-faith demand.

c. that leaves the aggrieved party with no reasonable choice but to succumb to the threat.

(1) The third element of duress is that the wrongful threat must leave the aggrieved party with the absence of reasonable choice except to agree to the contract or modification on which the perpetrator is insisting. This is seldom an issue when what is threatened is a crime or a tort, a criminal prosecution, or a bad faith civil suit, for risking the eventuality of any of those is scarcely a reasonable choice.

(2) Hard cases often arise in the context of economic duress (i.e., threatened breach of contract). Three common situations where this will arise are:

(a) when there are no adequate and reasonably priced substitutes for the services or goods the perpetrator is threatening to withhold:

EXAMPLE: The ship's captain is not in a position to find replacement sailors when already at sea, and so no adequate substitutes would be available.

(b) when the threatened breach would cause the aggrieved party to break his own contracts, especially if there is a prospect of substantial consequential or liquidated damages; or

EXAMPLE: If the purchaser of upsidaisium bearings needed for use in the manufacture of turbo-jet engines would, on account of the breach, be forced to breach its contract with an aircraft manufacturer.

(c) when the alternative of acquiescing to the threat and then suing for damages is inadequate to redress substantial harms to the aggrieved party.

EXAMPLE: Where the threatened breach would cause the aggrieved party to renege on its own commitments and thus harm its reputation and opportunities for future business, damages would be inadequate as a remedy.

NOTE A minority of jurisdictions add another element to the requirements for economic duress: the aggrieved party must protest the threatened breach rather than acquiesce without complaint in the demand for additional payment or other benefits with the secret intention of refusing to make the newly promised payment at contract's end. The courts that impose this additional requirement hold that the obligation of good faith requires the aggrieved party to speak up at the time of the threat.

3. **Third-Party Duress**
   a. If the wrongful threat is made by a third party, rather than the other party to the contract, the aggrieved party will still have a valid claim of duress unless:
      (1) the other party gives value or relies materially on the transaction; and
      (2) the other party is proceeding in good faith without reason to know of the duress.

4. **Remedies**
   a. Contracts made under physical compulsion are void.
   b. Contracts entered into under other forms of duress are voidable at the option of the aggrieved party.
   c. The aggrieved party is:
      (1) entitled to restitution of any benefits conferred under duress; and
      (2) required to return excess value of benefits to the perpetrator.

5. The common law defense of duress can be used in cases arising under the UCC as a supplementary provision.

D. Undue Influence

1. An aggrieved party may avail himself of the defense of undue influence when the circumstances reveal a vulnerable, but not incapacitated, party who succumbs to untoward bargaining tactics and pressures from the other party, where those pressures or tactics fall short of fraud or duress.

2. **Elements**

    a. There are two elements to the defense of undue influence:

       (1) unfair persuasion was used; and

           (a) Although the test for unfair persuasion is one that looks at all of the circumstances, courts have looked in particular to the following indicia of untoward pressure:

               1) discussion of the transaction at an unusual or inappropriate time;

               2) consummation of the transaction at an unusual place;

               3) insistent demands that the transaction or business be finished immediately;

               4) extreme emphasis on the untoward consequences of delaying the transaction;

               5) the use of multiple persuaders against the target of persuasion;

               6) absence of third-party advisers to the target of persuasion; and

               7) statements that there is no time to consult financial advisers or attorneys.

       (2) the other party was vulnerable to such persuasion.

           (a) A vulnerable party can be established in any of the following ways:

               1) where the mental infirmity is due to age or illness but falls short of mental incompetence;

               2) where the vulnerability is due to some recent trauma or event; or

               3) where the vulnerable party is reliant on the other party because of some relationship of trust or confidence with the other party.

3. **Remedies**

    a. Contractual obligations assumed under undue influence are voidable at the option of the aggrieved party.

    b. The aggrieved party is entitled to restitution of any benefits conferred on the other party, but must return the value in excess of those benefits to the other party.

    c. Where the vulnerable party suffers undue influence at the hands of a third party rather than the other party to the contract, the aggrieved party has the power to avoid the contract at his option, unless two conditions are met:

       (1) the other party gives value or relies materially on the transaction; and

       (2) the other party is proceeding in good faith without reason to know of the undue influence.

4. Like the other defenses, the common law claim of undue influence is available in cases arising under the UCC as a supplementary provision.

E. Unconscionability

1. Just as with undue influence, the defense of unconscionability may be available when a party uses inappropriate bargaining tactics to take unfair advantage of a vulnerable party. Unconscionability, however, focuses not only on the unfair process but also on the unfair results.

2. **Elements**

   a. There are two elements to a defense of unconscionability. In most jurisdictions, both of the following elements must be proved in order to succeed on a defense of unconscionability. However, where there is an extremely strong showing of one element, the party may be able to succeed on a defense of unconscionability despite a weaker showing of the other element. The elements are:

      (1) **procedural unconscionability**; and

         (a) This element can be met where the bargaining process that produced the contract in question created an absence of meaningful choice for the aggrieved party. The following are circumstances that may establish the absence of a meaningful choice:

            1) near-miss cases;

               EXAMPLE: When a party is vulnerable to the pressure of the other party, such as because of language barriers or advanced age, but the vulnerability falls short of mental incompetence or duress.

               EXAMPLE: When the victim is subjected to misleading or coercive sales tactics that fall short of actual fraud or duress.

            2) absence of bargaining power; and

               EXAMPLE: When the party is forced to accept proposed terms, as may be the case in standard form contracts with "take it or leave it" provisions which sellers and suppliers impose on all customers and that cannot be varied by bargaining, greatly limiting the other party's power to bargain.

               EXAMPLE: Where one party is weakened by poverty or language barriers, which greatly limits his ability to shop for alternative terms particularly with respect to necessaries.

            3) fine-print terms.

               EXAMPLE: Where the contract included complex or arcane terms hidden in the maze of the fine print in a lengthy standard form contract.

(2) **substantive unconscionability**.

    (a) The second element of unconscionability is met when the contract terms are unreasonably unfavorable to the aggrieved party.

    (b) Typical examples include:

        1) grossly excessive price;

        EXAMPLE: Where a pay-over-time plan requires the consumer to pay a total sum that is many times the value of the purchased goods, or where a bank charges an overdraft fee that is many times the bank's actual processing costs.

        2) grossly disproportional consequences for a minor breach;

        EXAMPLE: An add-on clause, pursuant to which a merchant is entitled to repossess multiple household items, including furniture, bedding, and a stereo, when a consumer missed a payment, despite the fact that the consumer had already paid nearly 80% of the monies owed for the various purchases.

        3) provisions binding one party but not the other; and

        EXAMPLE: An arbitration provision in an employment contract that requires the employee but not the employer to arbitrate any disputes, or that permits the employer but not the employee to amend the provisions of the agreement at will.

        4) provisions which are grossly unfair.

        EXAMPLE: In Brower v. Gateway 2000 [676 N.Y.S.2d 569 (N.Y. App. Div. 1998)], the court found unconscionable a binding arbitration clause that required consumers pursuing disputes with a merchant to pay a nonrefundable advance fee that exceeded the purchase price of the goods, travel to a distant city for the proceeding, pay the merchant's legal fees in the event of a loss, and file all correspondence in a foreign country.

3. **Remedies**

    a. Upon a finding of unconscionability, a court may:

        (1) refuse to enforce the contract;

        (2) excise the offending clause and enforce the remainder of the contract; or

        (3) limit the application of the offending clause as to avoid any unconscionable result.

4. **Application**

    a. The question of whether or not unconscionability is present is a question of law to be decided by the courts.

b. The question of whether a particular contract or clause is unconscionable is to be determined by the circumstances existing at the time of contract formation, not at the time the dispute arose.

c. A party claiming or resisting a claim of unconscionability is entitled to present evidence of the allegedly offending provision's commercial setting, as well as its purpose and effect.

   (1) To refuse a party the opportunity to present such evidence before granting summary judgment is a reversible error.

5. **Unconscionability under the UCC**

   a. The defense of unconscionability is specifically recognized as a defense under the UCC, and applies in the same manner as under the common law [§ 2-302].

F. **Public Policy**

1. The last of the defenses is called the public policy defense. It is a claim that courts should not enforce a contract because doing so would violate or undermine some important public policy.

2. Public policy may be raised as a defense to the enforcement of a contract in the following four contexts:

   a. where the subject matter of the contract itself is specifically prohibited by law;

      EXAMPLE: In most jurisdictions, a contract for prostitution, gambling, or bribery is illegal under the law and, accordingly, unenforceable in court.

   b. where a contract is formed for the purpose of committing a crime or violating a legal regulation;

      EXAMPLE: A contract between an employer and a hired assassin would be a contract for the commission of a crime.

   c. where the contract performance would not constitute a crime, but would constitute a tort; or

      EXAMPLE: A publicist being hired for the express purpose of spreading a defamatory story about a private citizen would be a contract for the commission of a tort.

   d. where the contract performance would violate certain values and freedoms designated by the state or jurisdiction.

      EXAMPLE: A contract that prohibits one party from marrying for an extended period of time would violate the public policy of promoting free and consent-based marriages.

3. **Sources of Public Policies**

   a. **Legislation**

      (1) Legislation is frequently the source of the "policy" invoked under the public policy defense.

EXAMPLE: Cases involving contracts prohibited by statutory law and cases involving contracts for the commission of a crime or the violation of a legal regulation.

b. **Judicial Decision**

(1) Where the subject matter of the contract is not specifically prohibited under law, then the public policy defense may operate to:

(a) fill gaps where there is no direct legislative warrant on point; and

(b) in most jurisdictions, promote larger notions of the public good.

(2) Judicially developed public policies include:

(a) policies grounded on moral and social values, such as the policy against the impairment of family relationships;

(b) policies based on economic considerations, such as the policy against restraints of trade; and

(c) policies designed to protect governmental processes and institutions, such as the policy of protecting the integrity of voting and elections.

EXAMPLE: A contract under which a private citizen agrees to vote a certain way in exchange for a year's supply of beer would violate the public policy of free and unrestricted exercise of the right to vote.

4. **Operation of the Defense of Public Policy**

a. The public policy defense is almost invariably invoked as a defense in an action by one of the parties seeking enforcement of a contract against the other. When it is successful, the defendant will win irrespective of whether he was the party who promised to perform the public policy violation or the party paying for it.

b. The idea here is not that the courts have any special solicitude for defendants, but rather that courts will refuse to play any role whatsoever in the enforcement of contracts violating public policy, with the result that the party attempting to enforce the contract will be out of luck.

EXCEPTION: An exception to the public policy defense may exist where one of the parties is more egregiously "in the wrong" than the other party. In the language of the courts, in such cases the parties are not *in pari delicto* ("equally at fault"), and the more innocent party may be able to secure restitution of any benefits conferred on the guiltier party despite the fact that the contract itself remains unenforceable.

(1) The *in pari delicto* defense is most commonly available when a particular statute has been enacted to protect a particular class of persons or actions.

EXAMPLE: A debtor may be entitled to restitution of insurance premiums, where the creditor coerced the debtor to purchase credit insurance and there is a statute on point that is designed to protect debtors from such creditor coercion.

b. A contract that is subject to the defense of public policy is not itself void as a matter of public policy. The defense only operates to treat the contract as voidable at the option of the defending party.

5. **Contracts Frequently Falling under the Public Policy Defense**

a. **Noncompetition Agreements**

(1) Many employment contracts, as well as contracts for the sale of a business, contain a provision that prevents one party from competing for a certain period of time or in a certain area. Where this provision is reasonable, the court will generally enforce it.

(a) However, where the noncompete provision imposes an unreasonable geographical barrier, duration, or term, then the enforcement of such a provision may be considered a violation of the public policy of promoting a citizen's freedom to work.

(b) Under the **blue pencil rule**, most jurisdictions remove the offending portion of the noncompetition clause while enforcing the remainder of it.

EXAMPLE: A court may enforce only the first two years of a five-year noncompete clause.

(c) A minority of jurisdictions will hold that the inclusion of such a provision invalidates the entire noncompetition clause.

b. **Sales of Goods via Bribery**

(1) If a contract for the sale of goods was based on bribery by any party, then the public policy defense could be used by the victim of the bribe to make the contract unenforceable.

EXAMPLE: Buyer sues Seller for breach of contract when Seller refuses to supply the specified quantity to Buyer at the agreed-upon price. Seller raises the defense of public policy because after the fact, Seller learns that Buyer bribed Seller's agent with a car in order to secure the unreasonably favorable contract terms.

c. **Sales of Goods Intended for Unlawful Use**

(1) If a contract is for the sale of goods that the seller knows the buyer intends for an unlawful use, then the public policy defense would be available to defeat an action either by the seller seeking payment or by the buyer seeking delivery.

d. **Liability-Limiting Provisions**

(1) When the provisions of a contract would limit a party's liability for tortious behavior by restricting the right of the injured party to pursue claims against the reckless or intentional harms caused by the party, the provision would not be upheld, because to do so would violate public policy.

(a) Provisions that limit liability for negligent (rather than reckless or intentional) tortious conduct are generally permissible.

e. **Unlicensed Goods or Services**

(1) When a contract is for unlicensed goods or services, then the contract may be rendered unenforceable by the public policy defense.

EXAMPLE: An unlicensed contractor could be prevented from recovering payment for his services if the homeowner invokes a public policy defense.

EXCEPTION: Because the homeowner is not *in pari delicto* with the unlicensed contractor, an action by the homeowner against the contractor for shoddy work might survive the public policy defense.

VIII. REMEDIES

A. Monetary Remedies for Breach of Contract

1. **Monetary Damages at Common Law**

   a. A party aggrieved by a breach of contract may be able to recover money damages calculated to protect that party's expectation interest, reliance interest, or restitutionary interest. A party may elect only one of these three remedies.

      (1) To compensate a party for his **expectation interest**, the court will calculate money damages designed to put the aggrieved party where he would be if the other party had fully and properly fulfilled the contract terms.

      EXAMPLE: A patient with a hand injury contracts with his doctor for hand surgery. The doctor promises him a "100% perfect" hand, but instead, the surgery makes the hand worse. The expectation interest of the patient is measured by the difference between the value of the promised "100% perfect" hand and the value of the hand worsened by surgery.

      (2) To protect an aggrieved party's **reliance interest**, a court will calculate the money damages designed to put the aggrieved party in the position he was before the contract was made.

      EXAMPLE: A agrees to buy B's car. On the faith of the promise, A pays B a $2,000 down payment for the car and enters a 12-month lease agreement with C for a parking space for $2,400. The reliance interest of A would be $4,400, the amount it would take to compensate A for what he's lost on the faith of B's promise.

      (3) To protect an aggrieved party's **restitutionary interest**, a court will calculate money damages designed to return to the aggrieved party the value of the benefit he conferred on the breaching party.

   b. **Expectation Damages**

      (1) The default rule for the proper measurement of damages in breach of contract cases is the expectation interest of the aggrieved party. This means the aggrieved party will be entitled to the amount that will restore him to the position he would have been in had the contract been fully performed.

      (2) The formula for expectation damages is:

Loss of value of the breaching party's performance
+ any incidental and consequential costs generated by the breach
- any payments received from the breaching party
- any costs saved as a result of the breach
= Expectation Damages of the Aggrieved Party

EXAMPLE: General Contractor repudiates its contract with Subcontractor when Subcontractor is halfway finished with its work under the subcontract. Subcontractor is entitled to seek from the breaching General Contractor an amount equal to: the contract price or the unrealized value of General Contractor's promised performance plus costs associated with storing, insuring, and/or returning materials and equipment secured by Subcontractor in the course of contractual performance (i.e., incidental costs generated by the breach), minus any progress payments already made by General Contractor and minus money Subcontractor may have saved on salaries and equipment rental by not having to complete performance.

(3) **Limitations on Recovery for Expectation Damages**

    (a) The aggrieved party may not be able to recover the full amount of expectation damages in the following situations:

        1) where the cost of performance greatly exceeds the market value of the performance;

            a) **Cost of performance** is the cost that would be incurred in an effort to perform as promised under the contract.

            b) **Market value of performance** is the net increase in the market value of finding substitute performance of the contract.

            EXAMPLE: In the infamous case of Peevyhouse v. Garland Coal & Mining Co. [382 P.2d 109 (Okla. 1962)], landowners entered into a contract with a coal-mining firm permitting the latter to strip-mine their farmland but requiring the firm to restore the land to its original state once the mining project was complete. When the firm breached by refusing to do the restoration work, there were two ways to measure the resulting expectation damages: the cost of performance (i.e., the costs that would be incurred in an effort to restore the land as promised in the contract), or the net increase in the market value of the property that would be realized if the restorative work had been completed as promised. Because restoration would have cost the mining firm $29,000 but increased the market value of the land by only $300, the court limited the landowners' recovery to the latter figure.

            c) Many courts would award cost of performance despite the disparity with market value on the view that expectation damages should be calculated, in the words of the Restatement Second, "on the basis of the value of performance to the injured party himself and not on its value to some hypothetical reasonable person or on some market."

2) where expectation damages cannot be calculated with reasonable certainty;

    a) While an aggrieved party does not have to calculate with mathematical precision to receive expectation damages, there must be some reasonable basis for calculation.

    b) Doubts in calculations will be resolved in favor of the aggrieved party.

    c) Requiring reasonable certainty of expectation damages may leave the aggrieved party uncompensated for losses that cannot be easily valued.

    EXAMPLE: A new business is unable to open because of a breach by a key supplier who has not completed promised work. Because there is no proven track record for the new business, it is difficult to establish with any certainty what profits would have been realized had it opened on time.

    d) Some jurisdictions apply the "new business" rule and automatically bar recovery, but most jurisdictions will evaluate the facts on a case-by-case basis and award expectation damages if a reasonable calculation is possible (e.g., on the basis of profit records for similarly situated ventures).

3) where damages are unforeseeable; and

    a) Under the **Hadley rule**, a breaching party will be liable for general damages (those damages that would foreseeably follow from the breach) but not for consequential damages (those damages that result from the particular circumstances of the aggrieved party and are therefore unforeseeable to the breaching party).

    b) The Hadley rule operates as another limitation on the right of an aggrieved party to recover expectation damages by denying recovery to the aggrieved party for consequential damages, even though those damages would not have occurred if the breaching party had fully performed on the contract.

    c) The rule barring recovery for consequential damages is a default rule, and the parties may opt out of its application to their contract and instead allow liability for consequential damages.

    d) The modern rule is that the breaching party will be liable for consequential damages if, at the time of contracting, the breaching party knew or had reason to know that the consequential damages would result from breach.

4) where damages can be mitigated.

    a) The aggrieved party may not recover for any losses it could have avoided without unreasonable risk, burden, or humiliation.

    b) The aggrieved party's duty to mitigate damages is limited to taking reasonable efforts to mitigate. If such reasonable mitigation efforts fail or cause additional expense, then the breaching party will be fully liable.

EXAMPLE: The liability of a breaching buyer of produce would be reduced if the seller permitted the produce to rot after breach rather than selling it to third parties; but if the seller is forced by the breach into a "fire sale" because of the short shelf life of the produce in question, then the breaching buyer will be fully liable for expectation damages—that is, for any difference between what the seller nets from the "fire sale" and what it stood to earn but for the broken contract.

EXAMPLE: The liability of an employer is reduced if an employee dismissed in breach of contract takes an extended vacation rather than seeking other work. But the aggrieved employee need only make reasonable efforts to secure a position that is reasonably equivalent to the job lost and, accordingly, she need not accept substitute work when it: is in a different field; offers significantly lower pay or less desirable terms and conditions of employment than those of the lost job; would entail more burdensome responsibilities than those of the lost job; or would damage the aggrieved party's career prospects (e.g., an A-list movie star would not be required to mitigate damages for a film producer's breach of contract by taking a lesser role in a B-grade film).

EXAMPLE: The liability of a breaching landowner to a construction contractor hired to erect a structure on the property is reduced where the contractor continues the building project after the landowner has repudiated the contract. But the liability of a buyer of goods ordered for special manufacture would not be reduced if the seller continues the manufacturing process after breach in order to finish the goods for possible sale to third parties.

c. **Reliance Damages**

   (1) Reliance damages may be available where expectation damages are not available.

   (2) The measurement of damages for the reliance interest of an aggrieved party is calculated by determining the amount of money necessary to restore the aggrieved party to the position he was in prior to the contract.

      (a) The reliance interest is compensated by the value lost to the breaching party, as well as any other value lost from the aggrieved party's reliance on the breaching party.

   (3) The aggrieved party's reliance interest is measured by any expenditures made in preparation for performance or in actually performing, less any loss which the breaching party can prove, with reasonable certainty, that the aggrieved party would have suffered even if the contract had been fully performed.

   (4) The most common use of reliance damages arises when the expectation damages would be uncertain or speculative, as where the breach would deprive the aggrieved party of opportunities to enter potential transactions with third parties.

      EXAMPLE: Inventor signs a contract with Railroad Co. for shipment of a new stove Inventor plans to display at a manufacturers' convention, and he pays fees to the convention hotel for a room and for display space, as well as an exhibition fee to the convention sponsor. If Railroad Co. breaches the contract by failing to deliver the stove until after the convention, Inventor will be unable to recover damages for opportunities he may have lost due to his inability to showcase the stove, as calculating the probability and value of those opportunities would be too speculative. However, Inventor would be entitled to reliance damages (i.e., a return of Railroad Co.'s fee, plus compensation for the amounts he paid to the hotel and convention sponsor).

d. **Restitutionary Damages**

   (1) A party aggrieved by a breach of contract is entitled to restitutionary damages rather than expectation damages at his option. If chosen, the aggrieved party may choose to recover the value of the benefits conferred on the breaching party by the aggrieved party during the course of the contract.

      (a) Restitutionary damages are available to both the breaching and aggrieved parties.

   (2) The aggrieved party's restitutionary interest will be measured by either:

      (a) the reasonable value of the benefit conferred upon the breaching party; or

         1) This is measured by the market value of the service(s) rendered, and not the price established by the parties in the contract.

2) The contract price may be admissible as evidence in calculating the restitutionary damages, as evidence of the price of retaining those services on the market.

EXAMPLE: Where General Contractor dismisses Subcontractor halfway through Subcontractor's performance, Subcontractor's restitutionary interest is measured by the market value of the services rendered thus far. The contract price may be admitted as relevant evidence for determining the market value for these services.

(b) the extent to which the breaching party's property has increased in value based upon the aggrieved party's performance.

EXAMPLE: Contractor built a Turkish bathhouse on Homeowner's property. The market value of the services is the cost to Homeowner of hiring another contractor to do the work, which equals $30,000. The value added to Homeowner's property is the net increase in the home's value from the addition of the bathhouse, which equals $20,000. A court calculating Contractor's restitutionary interest could award him either amount, considering what relevant precedents permit and what justice requires.

(3) An aggrieved party is likely to make this election if the restitutionary recovery would exceed the amount recoverable based on his expectation interest, and that situation is most likely to arise in the context of a "losing contract" (i.e., where the expectation interest would be less than zero because the aggrieved party would have actually lost money had the other party not breached).

EXAMPLE: General contractor breaches its contract with Subcontractor when Subcontractor is halfway finished with its work under the subcontract. Subcontractor is entitled to seek from the breaching General either expectation damages or restitutionary damages (i.e., the market value of the services already rendered at the time of breach). Even if Subcontractor had a "losing contract," it is nevertheless entitled to recovery of its restitutionary interest.

(4) In order to secure restitutionary damages, the party seeking the remedy must have conferred some benefit on the other party through either part performance or reliance.

(a) If the aggrieved party has fully performed under the contract, then the aggrieved party is limited to expectation damages.

EXAMPLE: Subcontractor completes contractual performance and General Contractor refuses to pay. Subcontractor has no right to seek restitutionary damages and is entitled to recovery of the contract price only.

e. **Liquidated Damages Provisions**

(1) Parties are free to include among the terms of their contract a **liquidated damages clause** designed to provide for damages of their own choosing in the event of breach.

(2) Such a provision is enforceable if the court finds it to be a valid liquidated damages clause, and unenforceable if the court finds that it constitutes a penalty.

(3) The basic idea here is that the parties are free to establish a regime of "home-made" damages designed to reflect the likely consequences of a breach in a manner suited to the peculiarities of their transaction, but that the parties are not free to threaten to punish a breach with harsh measures designed to give a potentially breaching party no choice but to perform.

   (a) A basic axiom of American contract law is that a party has a right either to perform on a contract or to pay damages, and a penalty clause is seen as interfering with that right.

(4) The test for determining whether a clause in a particular contract is a valid liquidated damages provision has three prongs:

   (a) Did the parties intend for the clause to operate as a liquidated damages clause or as a penalty?

      1) Evidence of specific or camouflaged effort to punish breach would support a claim that the clause was intended as a penalty.

      2) Modern decisions downplay the importance of this prong and emphasize the other two.

   (b) Was the clause reasonable at the time of contracting in relation to the anticipated harm?

      1) The key question is whether there was an anticipated harm that would be difficult to prove or for which no adequate remedy would be available.

      EXAMPLE: Repudiation of a commercial lease by an "anchor" tenant in a shopping mall is likely to cause reductions in pedestrian traffic to other stores as well as harm to the mall's reputation and attractiveness as a shopping "destination." Because the extent and monetary value of those harms would be difficult to establish in court, a liquidated damages clause designed to award the mall owner a sum that represents an inexact but reasonable forecast of those harms would be appropriate.

   (c) Was the clause reasonable in relation to the harm and losses that actually occurred due to the breach?

      EXAMPLE: If the shopping mall tenant repudiates the contract shortly after entering it, and the mall owner is able to secure a substitute "anchor" with minimal delay, a clause guaranteeing the owner significant liquidated damages would be unreasonable in relation to the actual harms caused by the breach.

    (5) **Anticipated versus Actual Harm**

        (a) When a particular clause satisfies the second prong of the test (it was reasonable at the time of contracting in relation to anticipated harms) but not the third prong of the test (it wasn't reasonable in relation to the harms actually suffered), some courts will uphold the challenged clause as a valid liquidation of damages with the view that a clause that satisfies either one of the prongs will be valid.

            1) Those courts would uphold the clause in the example immediately above because it was reasonable in relation to anticipated harms even though it wasn't reasonable in relation to the actual harms caused by the breach.

        (b) Other courts, however, will conclude that the clause is a penalty if it specifies damages that are "grossly disproportionate" to the actual harm, even if the clause was reasonable at the time of contracting.

            1) Those courts would declare the clause in the example immediately above to be a penalty, because it was excessive in relation to the actual harms, despite the fact that it was reasonable in relation to the harms anticipated at the time of contracting.

    (6) The party attempting to show that the liquidated damages clause is actually an unenforceable penalty has the burden of proof.

        (a) If the party fails to offer evidence of the unreasonableness of the provision, then the liquidated damages provision will be upheld.

    (7) If the court concludes that the liquidated damages clause is, in fact, a penalty, then the clause will be stricken from the contract.

        (a) If the clause is stricken from the contract, the aggrieved party is still entitled to recover whatever legal or equitable relief it would be entitled to under law.

2. **Monetary Damages under the UCC**

    a. Most of the rules governing remedies under the UCC reflect the same underlying principles that apply in common law cases—in particular, the right of an aggrieved party to expectation damages and the duty of an aggrieved party to mitigate damages—but they differ in their details because they are specifically designed for application to the sales of goods context.

    b. **Seller's Remedies**

        (1) Upon a buyer's breach of a contract for the sale of goods, the seller is free to cancel the contract and to withhold delivery of any yet to be delivered goods. In addition, the seller may have a right to recover money damages from the breaching buyer.

(2)   The nature of the seller's right to recover depends on whether the goods have been delivered.

   (a)   **Action for the Price**

      1)   If some or all of the goods have been delivered and accepted, the seller is entitled to collect the contract price for those goods [§ 2-709].

   (b)   **Damages for Nonacceptance or Repudiation**

      1)   If some or all of the goods have not been delivered—either because the buyer has rejected them, or in the context of anticipatory repudiation—the seller can recover damages with respect to them.

      2)   The measure of recovery will depend on whether the seller resells the goods to a third party.

         a)   **Seller Resells**

            i)   If the seller resells, he can recover the **contract-resale differential**—that is, the difference between the contract price and the resale price [§ 2-706].

            ii)   In order for the seller to recover, the resale must be made in good faith and in a commercially reasonable manner.

               EXAMPLE: A seller may not make a "sweetheart" deal to sell the goods at a below-market discount to a friend or a relative.

            iii)   The seller is not accountable to the buyer for any profit made on any resale [§ 2-706(6)].

         b)   **Seller Does Not Resell**

            i)   If the seller does not resell, he can recover the **contract-market differential**—that is, the difference between the contract price and the market value of the goods at the time and place of the promised delivery [§ 2-708].

      3)   **Whether or Not the Seller Resells**

         a)   Whether or not the seller resells, he is also entitled to recover **incidental damages**—that is, the costs associated with getting stuck with goods the seller thought he had sold as well as the costs of resale.

            EXAMPLE: Incidental costs associated with the seller remaining in possession of the goods include such things as storage and insurance. Incidental costs associated with the resale of the goods include costs incurred in the form of new advertisements and sales commissions.

b) However, the seller's damages will be reduced by an amount reflecting expenses avoided on account of the breach.

EXAMPLE: If the seller had expected to pay shipping costs in connection with the original contract, and instead incurs substantial savings by reselling to a local buyer, the seller's recovery will be reduced.

(3) **Lost Profits for Lost Volume Sellers**

(a) In the ordinary case, a seller's profit is built into the contract price and, accordingly, either the contract-market differential (if there is no resale) or the contract-resale differential (if there is a resale) will fully protect the seller's right to that profit in the event of breach by the buyer.

EXAMPLE: If Seller contracts to sell a boat to Buyer, Buyer subsequently reneges, and Seller's resale results in a lower price, Seller will get his anticipated profit by requiring the breaching Buyer to pay the difference between the contract price and the resale price.

(b) A different problem arises if the seller is a volume seller (i.e., if, instead of having a single object to sell, it makes repeated sales of the same goods, such as widgets). When a particular buyer breaches in this context, the seller has a "lost volume" problem—even if he sells the particular widget he expected to sell to the breaching buyer to another customer; but for the breach, at the end of the day, the seller would have made and profited from two sales rather than only one.

1) A **lost volume seller** is one whose supply of goods exceeds the demand for the same; that is, the seller can satisfy all potential buyers who may seek to deal with him.

EXAMPLE: BigBox, an electronics store, purchases from the manufacturer a particular brand of new televisions for $200, and resells them for $400. Buyer visits the store and, after shopping around, decides to purchase one of these new televisions as a gift for a friend. Buyer requests that the television be gift-wrapped, and the parties agree that Buyer will pay for the television two hours later, when he returns to pick up the television after it has been gift-wrapped. Buyer never returns. BigBox, the near the end of the day, sells a television of the same model to another purchaser for the same price. But for Buyer's breach, BigBox would have sold two televisions that day, rather than one.

(c) The UCC accordingly permits lost volume sellers to recover the profit they would have made on the lost sale rather than

...including them to either the contract-market or contract resale differential.

    (d) To recover lost profits, the seller must be able to show:

        1) that he could have made the sale to both the breaching buyer and resale buyer;

        2) that it would have been profitable for the seller to make both sales; and

        3) that he probably would have made the additional sale to the resale buyer even absent the buyer's breach.

c. Buyer's Remedies

    (1) Upon a seller's breach of a contract for the sale of goods, a buyer can either recover damages or seek specific performance.

    (2) There are two ways to measure a buyer's damages under the UCC, and the key factor is whether the buyer has **covered** (purchased replacement goods).

      (a) **If Buyer Covers**

        1) If the buyer covers, his damage measure is the **contract-cover differential**—that is, the difference between what the buyer would have paid under the contract and what he actually paid to secure cover [§ 2-712(2)].

        2) Cover must be made "in good faith and without unreasonable delay" [§ 2-712(1)].

            EXAMPLE: An aggrieved buyer cannot purchase substitute widgets from his brother-in-law at premium prices nor wait around until the market price of widgets has skyrocketed and purchase then.

      (b) **If Buyer Does Not Cover**

        1) If the buyer does not cover, he is entitled to the **contract-market differential**—that is, the difference between what the buyer would have paid under the contract and the market price of the goods at the time the buyer learned of the breach [§ 2-713].

      (c) **Whether or Not Buyer Covers**

        1) Whether or not the buyer covers, he is also free to seek incidental damages—the costs associated with securing cover—and consequential damages, as discussed earlier [§§ 2-712, 2-713].

        2) However, the buyer's damages will be reduced by an amount reflecting expenses avoided because of the breach.

    (3) **Difference in Value Damages**

      (a) This measure of damages available under the UCC is similar to the common law's expectation damages. It is available if the buyer receives nonconforming goods from the seller.

The buyer is entitled to recover damages for nonconforming goods based on the following:

(b) The difference in value damages does not require a showing of foreseeability—only that the goods did not conform to the goods specified in the contract.

Value of Goods Contracted For
− Value of Goods Received
───────────────────────────────
= Buyer's Recovery under Difference in Value Damages

---

(4) **Deduction of Damages from Price Still Due**

(a) A buyer may deduct all or any part of the damages resulting from the seller's breach of contract from any part of the price still due under the same contract. In order to make the deduction, the buyer must give notice to the seller of his intention to withhold all or part of the price [§ 2-717, cmt. 2].

B. **Equitable Remedies**

1. The typical remedy for contract claims is to award monetary damages. However, where an award of money damages would be inadequate to compensate the aggrieved party, a court may instead award an equitable remedy.

2. The most common equitable remedies in contracts cases are **specific performance** (which requires the breaching party to take some particular action) and **negative injunctions** (which prohibit the breaching party from a particular action).

3. **Specific Performance**

   a. Specific performance is an extraordinary remedy that is available to order a breaching party's performance only where a monetary award would be inadequate to grant relief to the aggrieved party.

   b. As a practical matter, specific performance is a remedy for paying, rather than performing, parties (e.g., buyers who pay money for goods, purchasers who pay money for real estate, and parties who pay money for services rendered).

      (1) When the paying party breaches, the remedy of money damages will, in the ordinary case, give the performing party the promised money, and so the availability of specific performance is a nonissue.

      (2) When the performing party breaches, however, the paying party may prefer to secure the promised performance itself rather than money damages; this raises the question of whether specific performance is available.

   c. **Cases Where Specific Performance is Generally Available**

      (1) At common law, money damages are presumed to be inadequate when a party is purchasing either:

         (a) unique objects; or

            EXAMPLE: Works of art and precious heirlooms.

(b) real property.

> **EXAMPLE:** At common law, Blackacre was presumed to be "unique," and such factors as location, natural resources, climate, and permissible uses justify that characterization even in contemporary real estate markets.

(2) **Equity Considerations**

(a) Specific performance is an equitable remedy, and a decision to grant or deny it is, accordingly, a decision for the court and not the jury.

(b) Whether to grant or deny specific performance is committed to the court's remedial discretion based on the competing equities in particular cases, and is not bound by hard-and-fast rules (such as those governing money damages).

(c) The court's determination is likely to take into account some or all of the following factors:

1) whether the aggrieved party has **clean hands** (has dealt fairly and in good faith with the breaching party);

2) whether the terms of the contract in question are sufficiently definite;

   a) Because a decree of specific performance is enforceable via contempt, courts are reluctant to issue an order that doesn't give the parties adequate guidance as to the conduct required.

3) whether performance by the aggrieved party can be reasonably assured;

   a) For example, performance could be assured by requiring tender of the aggrieved party's performance as a condition of the breaching party's obligations under the decree.

4) whether the terms of the contract are fair; and

   a) A court may deny specific performance where the underlying exchange is unfair even if the unfairness falls short of unconscionability or other doctrines that would excuse contractual performance altogether by the breaching party.

   b) In some jurisdictions, a party seeking specific performance of a contract for real property must plead and prove adequate consideration, despite the general rule that courts don't police the adequacy of contractual consideration.

5) whether specific performance would be in the public interest.

   a) Specific performance may be denied, for example, where the decree might have anticompetitive results.

d. **Contracts for Which Specific Performance is Not Available**

  (1) **Contracts for Personal Services**

  (a) Specific performance is not available to require a breaching employee or contractor to perform. Specific performance in such a case would violate the public policy prohibiting involuntary servitude, and it would be difficult to enforce.

  (2) **Contracts Requiring Ongoing Cooperation between Parties**

  (a) Specific performance is likewise disfavored in the context contracts that are not capable of immediate enforcement. Contracts that require a continuing series or acts or continuing cooperation between the parties for successful performance would present courts ordering specific performance with daunting problems of supervision similar to those in the personal services context.

e. **Sale of Goods Contracts under the UCC**

  (1) The UCC liberalizes the rules governing the availability of specific performance for sales of goods in two ways:

  (a) Specific performance may be permitted if the goods are unique or in "other proper circumstances" [§ 2-716(1)].

  1) Thus, the subject matter of a contract does not have to be unique in order to obtain specific performance; if the buyer has adequately searched but is unable to cover the breach, "other proper circumstances" may be present [§ 2-716, cmt. 2].

  (b) Specific performance is available even where ongoing cooperation would be required between the parties (e.g., in output or requirements contracts) so long as the requisite inability of a party to cover can be established.

  (2) **Replevin**

  (a) The buyer also has a right of **replevin**—which is an action to repossess property—for goods identified in the contract if [§ 2-716(3)]:

  1) after reasonable effort, the buyer is unable to cover;

  2) the circumstances reasonably indicate that an effort to cover will be unavailing; or

  3) if the goods have been shipped under reservation (i.e., the seller has reserved a security interest in the goods) and satisfaction of the security interest in them has been made or tendered.

4. **Negative Injunctions**

a. Negative injunctions are orders by the court prohibiting the breaching party from taking particular action. The limitations that apply to specific performance also apply to negative injunctions. Most commonly, negative injunctions are used to prevent employees from going to work for a competitor or competing with their former employer.

b. The availability depends on whether the former employer is seeking mid-term or post-employment relief.

(1) **Midterm Relief**

(a) When an employee is under contract for a specified period of time and the employee breaches the contract by departing before the end of that period, a negative injunction will be available to prevent the employee from competing directly or indirectly with his former employer if the employee's services are unique or extraordinary.

(b) Most of the cases finding that services meet this test involve professional athletes and entertainers.

1) Although the presence of a specific contractual provision establishing exclusive employment during the period of time in question will aid the employer in securing a negative injunction, most courts will imply such a term for the period of employment specified in the contract.

EXAMPLE: In the famous case of Lumley v. Wagner, an opera singer under contract to sing at Her Majesty's Theatre for a three-month period was persuaded to depart mid-contract to begin a concert series at a competing venue. Because her services were unique and extraordinary, the court granted a negative injunction barring her from performing at any competing venue for the duration of the contract term.

(2) **Post-Employment Relief**

(a) Enforcement of employment contract provisions that prohibit post-employment competition against the employer have become a common source of negative injunctions.

(b) The validity of such noncompetition clauses will depend on three factors:

1) most courts require a significant business justification for enforcing post-employment restraints;

a) An employer's need to protect confidential information would qualify, but some courts will allow little or no justification for enforcing such a provision.

2) most jurisdictions limit the scope of the enforcement of noncompetes to reasonable duration and geographical restrictions; and

a) However, the advent of the information age has prompted courts to broaden the definition of a reasonable geographical restraint, but at the same time, to lessen the amount of time considered to be a reasonable duration of restraint.

3) most courts will issue a negative injunction against a competing employee only if the employment contract

contains an express noncompetition agreement, but some courts have granted relief in the absence of such a provision based on the tort theory of inevitable disclosure of trade secrets.

C. Other Possible Remedies

1. **Promissory Estoppel**

    a. The type of interest a party may recover under a claim of promissory estoppel depends on the jurisdiction in which it brings suit. Courts are split:

    (1) some courts award expectation damages;

    (2) other courts, instead, favor reliance damages; and

    (3) other courts award damages on a case-by-case basis and tailor the remedy to the injustice at issue, where possible.

    (a) In doing so, the court will focus on:

    1) the strength of the proof for each of the individual elements of the claim;

    2) the blameworthiness of the breach;

    3) the extent of the detrimental reliance by the aggrieved party;

    4) the relative positions of the parties; and

    5) the availability of alternative options to granting full enforcement of the promise.

2. **Restitution and Unjust Enrichment**

    a. A party who bestows benefits on another may seek to recover the value of those benefits in an action for restitution. A party aggrieved by a breach of contract may have the option of electing a restitutionary, rather than expectation, recovery. However, there are many other contexts in contract law in which a party may be entitled to restitution pursuant to the policy of avoiding unjust enrichment.

    b. The following are contexts where restitution might be available:

    (1) **Benefits Conferred under a Failed Contract**

    (a) When a party bestows benefits on his trading partner in connection with what turns out to be a "failed" contract (e.g., unenforceable because of the Statute of Frauds or a failed condition, or voidable because of incapacity, fraud, duress, undue influence, or unconscionability), the party bestowing the benefits may ordinarily recover their value via restitution, subject to offset by any benefits received from the other party.

    EXAMPLE: A enters an oral contract to sell land to B, and prior to closing, B makes improvements on the land. If A reneges, B may be unable to enforce the contract because of the Statute of Frauds. However, B is entitled to recover the value of the improvements via an action for restitution.

(2) Benefits Conferred by a Breaching Party

(a) At common law, the breaching party was not entitled to receive any recovery for the benefits it may have conferred under the contract. The modern rule is that such a recovery is possible.

1) A breaching party may recover the amount of benefit he conferred on the aggrieved party less any damages to the aggrieved party as a result of the breach (otherwise known as the **right of offset**).

EXAMPLE: A works for B under a 12-month contract and, without advance notice, breaches the contract after 11 months in order to accept other employment. A is entitled to restitution of the reasonable value of the services rendered, subject to offset for B's damages—that is, the cost of hiring a replacement for A at the last minute.

(3) Emergency Benefits Conferred by a Health Care Professional

(a) The general rule is that a person who bestows benefits without request from the benefiting party is considered a volunteer or officious intermeddler who will not be entitled to any recovery.

(b) However, an exception applies to doctors and other health care professionals who provide emergency health care to a patient who is unable to consent. These health care professionals are entitled to the reasonable value of those services they have rendered, even where their efforts were unsuccessful.

NOTE This exception does not apply to non-medical persons whose life-saving efforts are deemed "gratuitous."

(4) Benefits Conferred by Mistake

(a) A party who mistakenly confers benefits to another party may be entitled to restitution. In this situation, the following will be considered:

1) the blameworthiness of the error;
2) whether the recipient was aware of the error in time to prevent it; and
3) whether the recipient availed himself of the benefits at issue.

EXAMPLE: After a hurricane, Owner hires Contractor to perform repairs on his storm-damaged home. Because of confusion caused by damage to street signs and mailboxes, Contractor performs the repairs on the wrong house. Contractor is entitled to restitution from the benefiting homeowner if the latter was aware of Contractor's mistaken efforts and remained silent.

3. **Agreed-To Remedies**

a. Parties to a contract may also contract out of the legal and equitable remedies available under the law, by specifying agreed-to remedies in the contract.

b. These remedies typically take two forms: liquidated damages provisions and provisions limiting or excluding damages.

c. **Provisions Limiting or Excluding Damages**

(1) The parties to a contract may limit or exclude the availability of certain damages. Thus, parties can limit their remedial rights to those provided for in the contract or exclude rights to remedies that it would otherwise be entitled to under law.

(2) There are different types of exclusive remedies provisions, including:

(a) provisions that limit or alter the measure of damages available; and

EXAMPLE: A provision limiting or excluding consequential damages.

(b) exclusive remedies provisions, in which the parties expressly agree that only one remedy, or certain specified remedies, will be available in the event of a breach.

EXAMPLE: A provision that limits the remedy available to the buyer for replacement goods or a "do-over" of services.

(3) Such provisions are enforceable unless they are unconscionable. Under the UCC, limitation of consequential damages for personal injury in the case of consumer goods is *prima facie* unconscionable [§ 2-719(3)].

IX. THIRD PARTY BENEFICIARIES

A. **In General**

1. In a typical contract, the parties promise performances to each other. If one party refuses to perform, the other has standing to bring a claim for breach because the parties are in contractual privity. In some contracts, however, one of the parties promises a performance that will benefit a third party (a third-party beneficiary).

   EXAMPLE: In exchange for B's promise of payment, A promises to deliver widgets to C. C is the third-party beneficiary of the contract between A and B.

2. The critical issue in third-party beneficiary law is the circumstances under which the third-party beneficiary has standing to enforce the contract against the promisor.

   a. Under common law, courts traditionally held that a third-party beneficiary did not have standing to sue the promisor because there was no contractual privity between them; however, under contemporary law, the privity requirement has been relaxed and third-party beneficiaries may have standing to sue the promisor for breach, even though the promise was made to the promisee and not to the third-party beneficiary.

B. **Classification of the Third-Party Beneficiary**

1. The right of an aggrieved third-party beneficiary to bring an action for breach of contract against a breaching promisor or promisee will depend upon the classification of the beneficiary. The First and Second Restatement each classifies beneficiaries differently.

   a. While the two Restatements use different terminology, the practical effect is the same under both nomenclatures.

2. **First Restatement**

   a. The First Restatement placed third-party beneficiaries into one of three categories:

      (1) when a promisee seeks a performance from the promisor that will benefit a third party, and the promisee's purpose is to satisfy a debt or other obligation owed by the promisee to the third party, the third-party beneficiary is a **creditor beneficiary**;

      EXAMPLE: A owes B $100 and enters a contract with C to whitewash C's fence in exchange for C's promise to pay B the $100. B is a creditor beneficiary because A's purpose in contracting with C is to satisfy his debt to B.

      (2) when a promisee seeks a performance from the promisor that will benefit a third party, and the promisee's purpose is to make a gift of that performance to the third party, the third-party beneficiary is a **donee beneficiary**; and

> **EXAMPLE:** Desiring to make a graduation gift to A, B agrees to pay C $100 in exchange for C's promise to whitewash A's fence. A is a donee beneficiary because B's purpose in contracting with C is to make a gift to A.

    (3)   third parties who will benefit from a promisor's performance as a practical matter, but who may not meet the test for creditor or donee beneficiaries under the First Restatement are **incidental beneficiaries**.

> **EXAMPLE:** A enters a contract with B whereby B is to erect a house on A's land. C owns land next to A, and the value of C's land will be enhanced by the building. C is an incidental beneficiary of B's promise to construct the house, and C has no rights under the contract.

3.   **Second Restatement**

    a.   The Second Restatement eliminates the "creditor" and "donee" beneficiary terminology, and instead puts third-party beneficiaries into one of two possible categories: intended beneficiaries and incidental beneficiaries.

    b.   **Intended beneficiaries** broadly fall into the same two categories utilized by the First Restatement, where the promised performance will satisfy an obligation of the promisee to pay money to the beneficiary (creditor beneficiaries) and where the promisee intends to give the beneficiary the benefit of the promised performance (donee beneficiaries). Many courts continue to use the older terms, however.

        (1)   The key factor in determining whether a party is an intended beneficiary is whether the promised performance is intended to benefit the third-party beneficiary. Courts are divided over whether the test for determining intent to benefit requires a mutual intention of the parties (the Second Restatement test) or merely a reasonably apparent purpose of the promisee (the First Restatement test).

> **EXAMPLE:** A hires Attorney B to draft A's will in accordance with A's instructions, which include a wish to make A's stepdaughter, C, a residual heir. Attorney B breaches the contract by neglecting to include the requested provision, and upon A's death, C brings a third-party beneficiary action against Attorney B for his breach. The intention of A to benefit C was "reasonably apparent" to Attorney B and, accordingly, would satisfy the "intent to benefit" test under the First Restatement. But because the benefit to C was a matter of indifference to Attorney B, there would be no "intent to benefit" her under the Second Restatement "intention of the parties" test.

    c.   **Incidental beneficiaries**, as under the First Restatement, are third parties who will benefit from a promisor's performance as a practical matter, but who may not meet the test for intended beneficiaries under the Second Restatement.

I. **Rights of Parties to Enforce the Contract**

1. **Third-Party Beneficiary's Rights**

   a. Under both the First and Second Restatement, an incidental beneficiary does not enjoy any right to seek enforcement of the contract from either the promisor or promisee to the original agreement.

   b. **Third-Party's Rights against the Promisor**

      (1) Any third-party beneficiary, other than an incidental beneficiary, has a right to secure enforcement of the agreement from a breaching promisor.

         (a) This applies to creditor and donee beneficiaries under the First Restatement and intended beneficiaries under the Second Restatement.

   c. **Third-Party's Rights against the Promisee**

      (1) Although a third-party beneficiary has rights against the promisor in connection with the promised performance, he has no rights against the promisee in the event that the performance is not forthcoming.

      EXAMPLE: Desiring to make a graduation gift to A, B agrees to pay C $100 in exchange for C's promise to whitewash A's fence. If C fails to whitewash A's fence, A has no recourse against B.

      (2) Instead, a third-party beneficiary will only have rights against the promisee resulting from the promisor's failure to perform based on whether or not there is an independent obligation between the promisee and the third-party beneficiary.

         (a) Thus, a First Restatement creditor beneficiary can elect to sue either the promisee on the prior obligation between the beneficiary and the promisee or the promisor on the third-party beneficiary contract. However, satisfaction of the claim by one operates as a release of the other's obligation.

         (b) Similarly, a Second Restatement intended beneficiary can only sue the promisee if the beneficiary would have fallen into the First Restatement's definition of a creditor beneficiary. That is, the intended beneficiary can only sue the promisor on the third-party beneficiary contract or the promisee if the promisee owes a separate obligation to the beneficiary, which the third-party beneficiary contract was intended to satisfy.

         EXAMPLE: A owes B $100 and enters into a contract with C to whitewash C's fence in exchange for C's promise to pay B the $100. In the event of nonpayment, B can elect to sue either A on the preexisting obligation or C as a third-party beneficiary, but payment of the $100 by either A or C will release the other from any further performance obligation to B.

      (3) The promisee's preexisting obligations to a creditor or intended beneficiary are not discharged by the formation of a third-party

beneficiary contract under which the promisor promises to fulfill the promisee's obligation to the beneficiary.

EXAMPLE: A owes B $100 and enters a contract with C to white-wash C's fence in exchange for C's promise to pay B the $100. C's obligation to pay B the $100 does not discharge A's preexisting obligation to B.

d. **Vesting of the Right to Sue**

(1) A third-party beneficiary does not automatically have the right to seek enforcement of the contract, or prevent the contract from being modified by the original parties, purely by virtue of the third-party beneficiary contract having been made.

(2) The parties to a contract are free to modify or rescind it by mutual consent, and they may modify or rescind a third-party beneficiary provision without the beneficiary's consent unless and until the beneficiary's rights under the contract have vested.

(a) Once the third-party beneficiary's rights vest, the ability of the original parties to make any future rescissions or modifications will be terminated.

(b) If the third-party beneficiary's rights under the contract vest before he is notified of any modification or rescission of the contract, the modification or rescission will be ineffective.

(3) Vesting occurs with regard to an intended beneficiary when:

(a) the beneficiary brings suit on the matter;

EXAMPLE: A contracts with B to pay B $2,000 in exchange for B doing renovations to C's house. B begins to perform, but ceases midway and informs C that he does not intend to complete the work. A and B agree to modify the original contract to instead have B do the renovation work on A's house, thereby eliminating C from the arrangement. Before being notified of the modification, C sues B to enforce the original contract based on B's anticipatory repudiation. C's filing suit vests his rights in the agreement, and A and B's modification will be ineffective.

(b) the beneficiary changes his position in justifiable reliance on the contractual promise;

EXAMPLE: As a birthday gift for his son B, A hires Contractor C to renovate B's home and advises B of the "gift" at a family party. In reliance on his father's promise, B lets an option expire on a new home he and his wife were intending to purchase. A and Contractor C can no longer modify B's rights under the contract.

(c) the beneficiary manifests his assent to the contract at the request of either the promisee or the promisor; or

EXAMPLE: A owes B $100 and agrees to whitewash C's fence in exchange for C's promise to pay B the $100. A asks B to assent to the contract; once B does so, A and C can no longer modify B's rights.

(d) the rights of the beneficiary have vested under an express term of the contract providing for such vesting.

EXAMPLE: Under the terms of his life insurance policy with Hartford Insurance, A's designations of beneficiaries become irrevocable upon A's demise or adjudication of incompetence. The rights of C, a designated beneficiary, against Hartford Insurance will vest upon the occurrence of either event.

e. **Defenses Available to Promisor**

(1) Because a third-party beneficiary's rights are entirely dependent on the underlying contract, any valid defenses the reneging promisor would have to the enforcement of the contract, such as impracticability, the failure of a condition, or a breach of the contract by the promisee, would also be effective against the beneficiary.

(2) The promisor may not assert defenses based on separate transactions with the promisee, such as a right to setoff arising in connection with a deal unrelated to the contract at issue, unless the contract expressly subjects the rights of the beneficiary to such a claim.

2. **Promisee's Rights against the Promisor**

a. When the promisor does not perform, the promisee has a claim for breach of contract against the promisor.

b. If the promisor's performance is intended to benefit a donee beneficiary, the promisee ordinarily will not have suffered any economic loss for the nonperformance and, therefore, may be unable to recover more than nominal damages. As a result, however, some courts consider the damage remedy inadequate and will order specific performance.

EXAMPLE: Desiring to make a donation to her alma mater, Laurie Lawyer promised to provide legal services to Nellie Merchant, a seller of computer hardware, in exchange for Merchant's promise to provide 100 free laptops to Nutmeg Law School. If Merchant fails to deliver the promised laptops, Lawyer can sue her for breach of contract, but because Lawyer has suffered no economic loss on account of the breach, she may be able to secure specific performance.

c. If the promisor's performance is intended to benefit a creditor beneficiary, the promisee may secure specific performance of the promisor's obligation.

(1) A claim for money damages would, however, expose the promisor to the possibility of double liability, since the promisor is also liable to the third-party beneficiary. Accordingly, some courts refuse to allow the promisee to recover damages against the promisor unless the promisee has already made payment to the beneficiary to cover the default.

X. ASSIGNMENT OF RIGHTS AND DELEGATION OF DUTIES

A. **Assignment of Rights**

1. An **assignment** is a transfer of a right to receive a performance under a contract.

2. Assignments typically have three relevant parties in a basic factual scenario: A and B have a valid contract, and B subsequently assigns his rights under the contract to C. In this scenario:

   a. A is the **obligor** (the party with the obligation to perform);

   b. B is the **assignor** (the party who assigned the right); and

   c. C is the **assignee** (the party to whom the right was assigned).

   EXAMPLE: A and B have a contract whereby B agrees to provide services to A in exchange for A's payment. B's right to A's payment may be assigned to C, a third party. Upon assignment, A has a payment obligation to C. In this transaction, B is the assignor, who assigned the right to receive payment; C is the assignee, to whom that right was assigned; A is the obligor, the party with the obligation to perform (here, to make the payment).

3. To make an effective assignment of a contract right, the owner of that right must:

   a. manifest an intention;

   (1) Manifestation of intention is ordinarily established by the oral or written words of the assignor.

   (a) There are no "magic words"—not even an express reference to "assignment"—required to make a manifestation effective.

   (b) Oral assignments are effective unless there is some independent applicable writing requirement, such as an assignment of a right to real property under a contract of sale, which must be in writing under the Statute of Frauds.

   b. to make a present transfer of the right without further action by the owner or the obligor.

   (1) A promise to transfer a currently existing right at a future date is not an effective assignment.

   (2) A promise to transfer a right that the assignor expects to acquire in the future is not an effective assignment.

   EXAMPLE: The statement "I will assign you 10% of the royalties when I obtain them" is not an assignment, as it expresses only an intent to assign in the future.

NOTE ▶ An "order" by an obligee directing an obligor to pay the debt to a third party is not an assignment. The most common example of an order is a check, which, under both common law and the UCC, does not operate as an assignment of the drawer's rights against the bank.

4. **Partial Assignments**

   a. A partial assignment is valid. Hence, there can be an assignment of a fraction of the assignor's rights.

   EXAMPLE: If A owes B $10,000 for goods B delivered to A, B may assign his right to $5,000 of that money to C.

   b. When suit is brought, however, all of the parties owning rights after the assignment must be joined in the action, unless joinder is not feasible and it is equitable to proceed without joinder.

5. **Rights to Be Assigned**

   a. The general rule is that all rights are assignable, subject to the following exceptions:

   (1) a right is not assignable if the assignment would materially alter the risks to or obligations of the other party to the contract;

   EXAMPLE: A and B are parties to a requirements contract under the terms of which A is obligated to supply B with B's monthly requirements for widgets. B's rights under the contract are not assignable to C if C's monthly requirements would greatly exceed B's.

   (2) a right is not assignable if the obligor has a personal interest in rendering the performance in question to the obligee and not to a third party;

   EXAMPLE: Nanny A's obligation under a contract to provide child-care services to B's family is not assignable to another family.

   (3) a right is not assignable if assignment would violate applicable law or public policy; and

   EXAMPLE: A state statute prohibiting assignment of wages.

   (4) a right is not assignable if assignment is prohibited by the contract. (Note that such provisions are strictly construed in both scope and effect.)

   (a) Although there is older precedent invalidating an assignment when the contract expressly states that attempted assignments are "void," most courts will treat an assignment in violation of contractual restriction as a breach of contract by the assignor—making him liable for any damages to the obligor—but not as a basis for nullifying the obligor's performance obligation to the assignee.

   (b) Absent contractual language or circumstances suggesting a contrary intention of the parties, a contractual prohibition against "assignment of the contract":

   1) will bar a delegation of contractual duties but not an assignment of contractual rights;

   2) will not apply to:

   a) rights that accrue to the assignor as a result of a breach of contract by the obligor; or

EXAMPLE: If A agrees to sell and B agrees to buy widgets under a contract prohibiting assignment, and A fails to deliver the promised widgets, giving rise to a claim for breach by B, B can assign his rights upon breach to C.

    b)   rights that accrue to the assignor upon complete performance by the assignor; and

EXAMPLE: If A agrees to sell and B agrees to buy widgets under the terms of a contract prohibiting assignment, and A delivers the promised widgets, A can assign his rights to B's payment to C.

    3)   can be invoked by the obligor (to resist making performance to the assignee) but not by the assignor (in an action brought by the assignee).

> **NOTE** An offer cannot be assigned, although an option can be.

EXAMPLE: If A has agreed to sell land to B and B has paid consideration to keep the offer open for six months, B can assign the option to C.

> **EXAM TIP** The right of a partner to share in the management of the partnership is not assignable, but the right to profits and to the partner's share in a dissolution is assignable.

6.   **Assignment for Value Contrasted with Gratuitous Assignment**

    a.   An **assignment for value**, where the assignee acquires the assignor's contractual right(s) in exchange for payment or a promise thereof to the assignor, is valid against the obligor and cannot be revoked by the assignor, although it may be modified like any other contract via mutual consent of the parties.

    b.   A **gratuitous assignment**, where the assignor assigns contractual rights to the assignee without consideration for such transfer, has the following legal effects:

        (1)   A gratuitous assignment is valid and binding against the obligor, who cannot raise the absence of consideration between the assignor and the assignee as a defense to any breach of his obligations to the assignee.

        (2)   Between the assignor and the assignee, the law of gifts governs the question of whether the assignor can revoke the assignment. A gift requires that there be donative intent and delivery.

            (a)   Because the assignment is a transfer of legal rights under a contract, it is impossible to physically deliver an intangible right. However, delivery of something representative or symbolic of an intangible right, such as a savings account book, is held to be sufficient to meet the delivery requirement.

(3) Even if there is no delivery, the assignment becomes irrevocable once payment of the obligation is made to the assignee.

(4) The assignor will be estopped from revoking the assignment if the assignee acts to his detriment in reliance upon the assignment.

7. **Rights and Obligations of the Parties after Assignment**

a. **Rights of Assignee against the Obligor**

(1) The basic rule is that:

    (a) an assignee gets whatever rights to the contract his assignor had; and

    (b) the assignee takes subject to whatever defenses the obligor could have raised against the assignor, such as a lack of consideration, incapacity, fraud, duress, or mistake.

(2) **Payment to Assignor**

    (a) If the obligor pays the assignor, this defense can be raised against the assignee, provided that payment was made before notice of the assignment was given to the obligor.

    (b) Once notice of the assignment is given, payment to the assignor is no defense.

    (c) If the obligor doubts whether the assignment was made, he can pay the money into court and interplead the assignor and assignee.

(3) **Setoffs and Counterclaims**

    (a) If the obligor has a right of setoff that could be raised against the assignor, such right can always be raised against the assignee if the alleged setoff arises out of the same transaction.

    (b) If, however, the setoff arises out of a separate transaction, it is available against the assignee only if the transaction which gave rise to the setoff arose before notice of the assignment was given to the obligor.

    (c) The obligor and the assignor may agree to an adjustment of their rights without consent of the assignee up until the time that the assignee has given notice of the assignment to the obligor.

(4) **Waiver of Defenses**

    (a) If one of the original parties to the contract agrees that he will not raise defenses against an assignee in the event that the rights are assigned, the agreement is enforceable with two limitations:

        1) defenses that are in the nature of "real defenses" under Article 2 of the UCC can still be raised; and

            a) These defenses include infancy, other incapacity that voids a contract, fraud in the execution, duress (when it removes the parties' capacity to contract), discharge in bankruptcy, and any other discharge of which the assignee has reason to know.

2) the agreement not to raise defenses is invalid if the obligor who signed the waiver was the buyer or lessee of consumer goods.

b. **Rights of Assignee against Assignor**

(1) Unless a contrary intention is manifested, one who assigns or purports to make an assignment for value impliedly warrants to the assignee:

(a) that he will do nothing to defeat or impair the value of the assignment and has no knowledge of any fact that would do so;

(b) that the right as assigned actually exists and is not subject to any limitations or defenses against the assignor other than those stated or apparent at the time of the assignment; and

(c) that any writing evidencing the rights that are being delivered to the assignee to induce him to accept the assignment is genuine.

> **NOTE** An assignment does not, in and of itself, operate as a warranty that the obligor is solvent or that the obligor will perform his obligation.

c. **Rights among Successive Assignees**

(1) A problem of rights among successive assignees may arise when the assignor, who is owed money by the obligor, assigns his right to the money to the first assignee, and then later assigns the same right to a second assignee. The assignor is liable to both assignees for assigning the same right twice.

(2) However, if the assignor is bankrupt or has fled the jurisdiction and both assignees attempt to collect from the obligor, the majority rule is that the first assignee prevails.

(a) There are various exceptions to the majority rule. In several jurisdictions, and under the Second Restatement, a subsequent assignee who has paid value and took the assignment in good faith will prevail if he [Restatement (Second) of Contracts § 342]:

1) obtains payment from the obligor;

2) recovers a judgment on the debt;

3) enters into a new contract with the obligor; or

4) receives delivery of a tangible token or writing from the assignor, the surrender of which is required by the obligor's contract.

B. **Delegation of Duties**

1. A **delegation** occurs when a third party agrees to satisfy a performance obligation owed by one of the parties to a contract.

2. Delegations typically have three relevant parties in a basic factual scenario: A and B have a valid contract, and B subsequently delegates duties under the contract to C. In this scenario:

a. A is the **obligee** (the party for whom the performance obligation is owed);

b. B is the **obligor** (the party with a performance obligation), and is also the **delegator** (the party who delegated his performance to a third party); and

c. C is the **delegatee** (the party to whom the performance obligation was delegated).

3. **Rights of the Obligee against the Delegator**

a. A delegation does not relieve the delegator from his obligations under the contract. Despite the delegator's delegation to the delegatee of the performance obligation owed to the obligee, the delegator remains liable for the performance.

   (1) Thus, while an assignment of rights effectuates a transfer of those rights to a third party (upon assignment, the assignee and not the assignor has rights under the original contract), a delegation of duties does not operate as a "transfer" of those duties from the delegator to the delegatee.

b. **Novation**

   (1) If there is a novation, the delegator is relieved from the obligations under the contract. This requires a clear promise by the obligee to release the delegator in return for the liability of the delegatee.

   (2) Simple assent to the delegation is not enough to effectuate a novation; there must also be a promise to release the delegator.

4. **Liability of the Delegatee**

a. When the delegatee has agreed to perform the delegator's contract obligations, he is liable to the delegator if he does not do so.

b. Under the third-party beneficiary theory, the delegatee is also liable to the obligee, because the obligee is an intended beneficiary of the promise made to the delegator.

   EXAMPLE: Joe Plumbing Co. enters a contract to provide plumbing services for Mondo Condo Association and subsequently hires a plumbing subcontractor, Elite Plumbers Inc., to perform the services in question. If Elite Plumbers Inc. fails to perform the delegated duties, it would be liable for breach of contract to both Joe Plumbing and Mondo Condo. Elite Plumbers would be liable to Mondo Condo because it is a third-party beneficiary of the Joe Plumbing-Elite Plumbers contract.

5. **Delegable Duties**

a. The general rule is that all obligations can be delegated.

b. The exceptions fall into the following two categories:

   (1) when the performance in question is personal and the recipient must rely on qualities such as the character, reputation, taste, skill, or discretion of the party who is to render the performance; or

   EXAMPLE: Nanny A is under contract to provide childcare services to B's family. Her performance obligation cannot be delegated to a third party.

        (2)   when the contract prohibits delegation.

           (a) Unlike prohibitions against assignments, contract provisions barring delegation are fully enforceable.

    c.   The effect of a party's attempt to delegate nondelegable duties differs depending on whether the contract is governed by the common law or the UCC.

        (1)   At common law, an attempted delegation of a nondelegable duty operates as an immediate breach of the contract and gives the other party an immediate right to sue.

        (2)   Under the UCC, any delegation of performance may be treated by the other party as creating reasonable grounds for insecurity, and the other party has a right to demand adequate assurances from the assignee without prejudicing his rights against the assignor [§ 2-210(5)].

Issue-Spotting Exercises

Question 1

A clothing store experiencing a downturn in their business decided to drum up new business by hiring circus performers and running advertising in the local paper for a one-day only Saturday sale. The store ran the following ad on Wednesday:

"This Saturday ONLY come on down, meet the clown, take advantage of the best deals in town! Men's and ladies' suits at ridiculous rates, only $49 each. They won't last at this price!"

On Saturday morning, after reading the advertisement, a couple went to the store to take advantage of the incredible deal. Once inside, they each picked out two suits and approached the counter. The clerk asked the couple for their phone number and realized they were already in the system. He then charged the couple the regular rate for the suits. The man mentioned the $49 ad in the paper. The clerk said, "I'm sorry, that was intended for new customers only, and because you are already in the system, you do not qualify."

If the couple sues the clothing store for breach of contract, for whom should the court rule?

Question 2

A cleetch is a custom-designed transmitter device that is used in wireless phones. A phone company has entered into a written contract with a cleetch manufacturer to purchase 1,000 cleetches for the total contract price of $100,000. After the 1,000 cleetches were manufactured, the phone company received a telephone call from the manufacturer. During their conversation, the manufacturer told the phone company that the manufacturer would not deliver the cleetches unless the phone company agreed to pay an additional $5 per cleetch. Reluctantly, the phone company agreed to pay the additional $5 per cleetch. Following their phone conversation, the manufacturer authorized the delivery of the 1,000 cleetches to the phone company. After the transmitter devices were accepted by the phone company, the phone company sent the manufacturer a check in the amount of $100,000. The manufacturer has made repeated demands for the additional $5,000, which the phone company refuses to pay.

The manufacturer filed suit against the phone company to recover the additional $5,000. What would be the best argument by the phone company that it is not obligated to pay the $5,000?

Question 3

An 80-year-old widow was confined to a wheelchair after undergoing a hip replacement operation. She lived in a remote rural town. Since she was unable to walk her son decided to hire a home health care worker to look after his mother. Thereupon, the son entered into an oral agreement with a certified health care worker to serve as a live-in companion for his ailing mother. According to their agreement, the health care worker would provide live-in care for the mother six days a week from Monday through Saturday with Sunday designated as her day off. The parties further agreed that the son would pay the woman $600 per week and that she would work for 10 months. The health care worker started to care for the mother on February 1 and worked continuously until July 1 when she gave notice that she would be quitting. Thereafter, the son learned that the health care worker had been hired away by the mother's invalid neighbor, who agreed to pay the health care worker $800 per week to care for her. The son then attempted to hire another home health care worker to care for his mother. He had trouble finding a replacement for the health care worker because of the remote locale of his mother's home.

The son brings suit seeking to enforce his employment agreement with the health care worker and enjoin her from working for the neighbor. Should the son prevail in his enforcement action?

Question 4

A 16-year-old high school junior had just received her driver's permit. One evening she was driving her mother's car when a heavy snow suddenly fell. The roadway became treacherous and the car got stuck in an embankment. Stranded in the forest, the girl began walking in the hopes of being rescued by another motorist. Miraculously, the girl came upon a motel that appeared to be open for business. She entered the lobby and told the owner about her predicament. Realizing that the girl had no place else to stay, the owner told her that he had a vacancy available and the room charge would be $200 per night (despite the fact that the standard room charge at the motel was $100 per night). The girl stayed two nights in the motel.

How much are the girl's parents liable to pay the motel owner for their daughter's two-night stay?

Question 5

A grain distribution company entered into a valid written contract with a farmer for 50 tons of corn at $1000 per ton. In late summer, the farmer was harvesting the corn and noticed that the crop was infested with aphids, which rendered it unsafe for consumption. This infestation commonly occurs in corn. The farmer called the grain distribution company the same day and informed them that due to the infestation he was unable to perform. The grain distribution company now brings suit.

How should the court rule?

|

Essays

Contracts

In Class

George was cleaning out his basement and came across a number of items he no longer needed. He decided to have a basement sale. He purchased ad space in the local papers and posted the following advertisement:

> Rock-Bottom Basement Sale!
> Saturday 9-5pm
> 123 Apple Street
> Phone: 123-456-7890
> Rain or Shine!
> Motorcycle—one available—$499!
> Also selling collection of spare tires, engine belts, automotive guide set from 1990-2010, and lots more. Everything must go!

George also posted copies of the advertisement in the local stores in town.

On Saturday at 9am, Carl came over and looked through the items for sale. He was very interested in the collection of spare tires and expressed his interest to George. Carl did not have any money, but was going to get paid at work later that afternoon at 2pm. George said, "No problem, buddy! I will sell you the collection of spare tires for only $250 as long as you come back with the money and pick up the collection by 4pm." Carl was very excited and stated, "I'll be back soon!" before he left.

Also at 9am, George got a call from Judy. Judy asked about the motorcycle for sale. George described the motorcycle to her. Judy came by a few minutes later and, after examining the motorcycle, she exclaimed, "This is exactly what I am looking for! I will buy the motorcycle for $499, but will return by 5pm with my truck and the money." Before George could say anything, Judy left.

At 11am, George's neighbor Larry came by and was very interested in the automotive guide set dating from 1990 to 2010. Larry was retired and on a fixed budget, and said to George, "I cannot justify spending $50 on the automotive guides because it is not in my budget." Larry often looked after George's house and pets while George was away. George told him, "I would like to sell the guides for $50 but since you always help me out, I would like to repay you. If they don't sell by 3:30pm, you can have them for free." Larry thanked George and went back home.

At 3:15pm, Sarah, a professional motorcycle racer, was at the local coffee shop and saw the ad for the motorcycle. She instantly fell in love with it. She stopped by the basement sale, handed George $499 and said, "I will buy the motorcycle for $499." George sold the motorcycle to Sarah.

At 3:30pm, Larry called George and asked if anyone had purchased the automotive guide set. George said, "No one has expressed much interest in the automotive guides yet. It looks like they will be yours." Larry responded, "Wonderful! I am going to run to the hardware store and buy some wood and supplies to build shelves for them."

A few minutes later, John, a collector of spare tires, stopped by George's basement sale and offered him $300 for the spare tire collection and $50 for the automotive guide set. George sold the spare tire collection and automotive guide set to John.

At 4pm, Larry stopped by George's basement sale after his trip to the hardware store. George told him that the automotive guide set had been sold.

Soon after, Carl came by with the money to pick up the spare tire collection. As he pulled up, he saw John loading his truck up with the spare tire collection. Carl ran inside to George, tried to give him the $250 and said, "We had a deal!" George refused the money.

Discuss whether Carl, Judy, and Larry had an enforceable contract with George. If George breached his contract with any party, discuss all available remedies.

Contracts

In Class

Carl v. George

I. **Was there a valid offer?**

   A. **(Rule)** Offer is an outward manifestation of the offeror's willingness to enter into a bargain, oral or written, that signals to the offeree that his assent to the bargain is invited and will conclude the deal
      1. Must consist of definite and certain terms, including identification of the goods, quantity, price, and parties
   B. **(Application)** George demonstrated a present intent to be bound when he told Carl "I will sell you the collection of spare tires for only $250…"
      1. Terms were definite and certain—goods, quantity, price, and parties identified
      2. Carl's assent invited to conclude the deal
   C. **(Conclusion)** There was a valid offer

II. **Was there an enforceable option contract?**

   A. **(Rule)** Option contract results when there is an offer, a subsidiary promise to keep the offer open, and a valid mechanism (consideration) for securing enforcement of the subsidiary promise
   B. **(Application)** Carl will argue that there is an option contract since George stated "…as long as you come back with the money and pick up the collection by 4pm"
      1. Carl did not give any consideration for the option contract
   C. **(Conclusion)** There was no enforceable option contract

III. **Was there a firm offer?**

   A. **(Rule)** Under U.C.C., a merchant can make a firm offer to sell goods without any consideration as long as the offer is in a writing signed by the merchant, and the offer expressly states in its terms that it will be held open
      1. U.C.C. defines a merchant as one with knowledge with respect to the goods involved in a transaction
   B. **(Application)** Carl may argue that George is a merchant selling goods of which he has special knowledge or skill
      1. Facts do not indicate that George has expertise in spare tires
      2. Act of owning a collection of spare tires does not make a person an expert or knowledgeable
      3. No writing signed by George stating the terms of the offer and that it will be held open
   C. **(Conclusion)** There was no firm offer

IV. **Was there a valid revocation?**

    A. **(Rule)** Revocation can be effectively communicated in two ways—directly or indirectly.

        1. Direct revocation—the offeror directly communicates with the offeree and revokes the offer

        2. Indirect revocation—the offeree learns of the offeror's intention to abandon the deal from a third-party

            a. This terminates the offeree's power of acceptance as long as the offeror has taken definite action that is inconsistent with the intention to enter the proposed contract, and the offeree acquires reliable information of the offeror's inconsistent action

    B. **(Application)** Carl returned to George's house and saw John loading up his truck with the collection of spare tires that George sold to him

        1. Carl's observation of John loading up his truck serves as reliable information of George's inconsistent action

    C. **(Conclusion)** There was a valid indirect revocation that terminated Carl's power of acceptance

Judy v. George

I. **Was the ad for the motorcycle an offer?**

    A. **(Rule)** "Offer" defined above

    B. **(Application)** George's advertisements were not an offer as not all of the terms of the contract were certain and definite

        1. Identified goods and quantity—one motorcycle

        2. Price—$499

        3. Parties not defined

    C. **(Conclusion)** There was no valid offer

II. **Did Judy make an offer?**

    A. **(Rule)** "Offer" defined above

    B. **(Application)** Judy showed intent to be bound by contract under the terms stated by her when she said to George, "This is exactly what I am looking for! I will buy the motorcycle for $499, but will return by 5pm with my truck and the money"

    C. **(Conclusion)** There was a valid offer

III. **Did George accept Judy's offer?**

    A. **(Rule)** Acceptance of an offer is a manifestation of assent to the terms thereof made by the offeree in the manner required (the mirror image rule), and the acceptance must be communicated to the offeror

    B. **(Application)** Judy left before George could respond to her offer

    C. **(Conclusion)** George likely retains the power to accept until 5pm, but he could reject the offer by selling the motorcycle to another party, which he did by selling to Sarah

        1. George never accepted—no enforceable contract

Larry v. George

I. **Did George make an offer?**

   A. **(Rule)** "Offer" defined above

   B. **(Application)** George's response "I would like to sell the guides for $50 but since you always help me out, I would like to repay you. If they don't sell by 3:30pm, you can have them for free" is an offer

     1. Statement exhibits George's intent to be bound

     2. Offer contains definite and certain terms

       a. Parties—George and Larry

       b. Price—free

       c. Goods and quantity—an automotive guide set

       d. Time for performance—by 3:30pm

     3. Offer also contains a condition precedent

   C. **(Conclusion)** Offer is only good if George cannot sell the automotive guide set for $50 by 3:30pm

II. **Did Larry accept the offer?**

   A. **(Rule)** "Acceptance" defined above

   B. **(Application)** Larry thanked George for his offer, which indicates acceptance of the terms of the offer

     1. Larry reinforced his acceptance when he called George at 3:30pm to see if the automotive guide set had sold

     2. George stated, "it looks like they will be yours"—the condition precedent was satisfied

   C. **(Conclusion)** Larry accepted George's offer

III. **Was there consideration present in the contract?**

   A. **(Rule)** Consideration is something that is bargained for and given in exchange for a return promise

     1. Past consideration will not satisfy the bargain requirement

   B. **(Application)** George will likely argue that his offer to give Larry the automotive guide set is gratuitous and there is no consideration present as George will receive no benefit

     1. Larry will argue that there was past consideration

   C. **(Conclusion)** There was no consideration

IV. **Is George's promise to Larry binding under the doctrine of promissory estoppel?**

   A. **(Rule)** Doctrine of promissory estoppel—a promisee that reasonably relies to his detriment on a gratuitous promise may be able to enforce that promise even if there is no consideration in return

     1. Four requirements that must be met:

       a. promise made by the promisor

       b. promisee's reliance must be foreseeable at the time of the promise

       c. actual reliance induced by the promise

        d.   if first three elements are satisfied, the promise will be binding if injustice cannot be avoided otherwise

B. **(Application)** George told Larry on the phone that "… it looks like they will be yours" and Larry responded to George, "Wonderful, I am going to run to the hardware store and buy some wood and supplies to build shelves for them"

    1.   George was aware that his promise to Larry had induced reliance by Larry

C. **(Conclusion)** George's promise to Larry is binding under the doctrine of promissory estoppel

V. **Can Larry seek specific performance?**

A. **(Rule)** Specific performance is an extraordinary remedy that is available to order a breaching party's performance only where a monetary award would be inadequate to grant relief to the aggrieved party

B. **(Application)** Automotive guide set is unique, Larry could seek specific performance

C. **(Conclusion)** Specific performance remedy is not practical since the automotive guide set was sold to John

VI. **Can Larry seek reliance damages?**

A. **(Rule)** Reliance damages are calculated by determining the amount of money necessary to restore the aggrieved party to the position he was in prior to the contract

B. **(Application)** Larry purchased wood and supplies in reliance on George's promise

C. **(Conclusion)** Larry will be able to recover the cost of the wood and supplies

VII. **Can Larry seek general damages?**

A. **(Rule)** Breaching party may be liable for general damages, which are damages that foreseeably follow a breach of contract

B. **(Application)** Larry may seek the value of the automotive guide set since specific performance is unlikely

C. **(Conclusion)** Larry will likely only receive reliance damages since the purpose of promissory estoppel is to avoid injustice

Contracts

In Class

This sample answer would be considered above the standard expected of a 1L student.

I.   Validity of Contract and Governing Law

A valid contract requires an offer, consideration, and acceptance. The determination of whether Carl, Judy, or Larry had an enforceable contract with George will be based on whether a valid contract was formed.

The U.C.C. governs all contracts for the sales of goods. Sales are any transactions in which the seller transfers title of a good to a buyer. Goods are defined under the U.C.C. as any "movable item."

II. Carl v. George for the Spare Tire Collection

A.   Was there an offer?

An offer is an outward manifestation of the offeror's willingness to enter into a bargain, oral or written, that signals to the offeree that his assent to the bargain is invited and will conclude the deal. The offer must consist of definite and certain terms, including identification of the goods, quantity, price, and parties.

When George told Carl, "I will sell you the collection of spare tires for only $250..." he demonstrated a present intent to be bound. The terms were definite and certain: the goods and quantity were identified as the collection of spare tires, the price was $250, and the parties were George and Carl. Further, Carl's assent was clearly invited to conclude the deal—all Carl had to do was comply with George's terms (show up by 4:00 with the money).

Accordingly, there is a valid offer.

B.   Was there an enforceable option contract or firm offer?

An option contract results when there is an offer, a subsidiary promise to keep the offer open, and a valid mechanism, typically consideration, for securing enforcement of the subsidiary promise.

Carl will argue that George's offer was an option contract because he stated, "...as long as you come back with the money and pick up the collection by 4pm." There did appear to be some indication that George would hold the offer open, since he stated that Carl could return by 4:00. However, Carl did not give any consideration for the option contract, so there is no enforceable option contract.

Carl may also argue that George is a merchant selling goods in which he has special knowledge or skill, and that a firm offer from a merchant does not require consideration.

Under the U.C.C., a merchant can make a firm offer to sell goods without any consideration as long as the offer is in a writing, signed by the merchant, and the offer expressly states in its terms that it will be held open. Further, the U.C.C. defines a merchant as one with knowledge with respect to the goods involved in a transaction.

Here, the goods are spare tires, and the facts do not indicate that George has expertise in spare tires. Furthermore, the act of owning a collection of spare tires does not make a person an expert or knowledgeable. In addition, there was no writing signed by George stating the terms of the offer and that it would be held open. Since George was not a merchant, and there was no signed writing, there is no enforceable firm offer under the U.C.C.

As a result, there is no option contract or firm offer, and George can revoke his offer at any time.

C. Indirect Revocation

A revocation can be effectively communicated in two ways: directly or indirectly. In a direct revocation, the offeror directly communicates with the offeree and revokes the offer, and in an indirect revocation, the offeree learns of the offeror's intention to abandon the deal from a third party. This terminates the offeree's power of acceptance as long as the offeror has taken definite action that is inconsistent with the intention to enter the proposed contract and the offeree acquires reliable information of the offeror's inconsistent action.

Here, Carl returned to George's house and saw John loading up his truck with the collection of spare tires that George sold to him. Carl's observation of John loading up his truck in combination with George's selling of the spare tire collection to John shows that George did not intend to enter into a contract with Carl.

Accordingly, there was a valid revocation, which terminated Carl's power of acceptance.

D. Conclusion

There is no enforceable contract between Carl and George.

III. Judy v. George for the Motorcycle

A. Was the ad an offer?

The term "offer" is defined above.

George's advertisements were not an offer, as not all of the terms of the contract were certain and definite. The identified goods and quantity was one motorcycle and the price was $499, but the parties were not defined.

Under the American advertising rule, advertisements that are addressed to multiple recipients are generally treated as invitations for offers rather than offers.

Accordingly, the advertisement is an invitation for offers.

Judy may further argue that the advertisement specifically stated the quantity of one motorcycle, the price ($499), and the time for acceptance of 9am to 5pm, and thus contained sufficient details to be considered an offer. In addition, since Judy called promptly at 9am and arrived at the sale shortly after, she may argue that it was an offer that was available for acceptance.

However, under the U.C.C., an offer must consist of definite and certain terms, including an identification of the goods, quantity, price, and parties. Here, the parties were not definite and, as a result, there is no valid offer.

B. Did Judy make an offer?

When Judy said to George, "This is exactly what I am looking for! I will buy the motorcycle for $499, but will return by 5pm with my truck and the money," she showed an intent to be bound by contract under the terms she stated. Her offer indicated that she was going to buy one motorcycle from George for $499 before 5pm. Further, all that was necessary was for George to say yes, and that would have concluded the deal.

There was a valid offer.

C. Acceptance of Judy's Offer

Acceptance of an offer is a manifestation of assent to the terms thereof made by the offeree in the manner required (the mirror image rule), and the acceptance must be communicated to the offeror.

Here, Judy left before George could respond to her offer. There was no acceptance at that point, since he had not manifested anything to her yet.

George likely retains the power to accept until 5pm, but he could reject the offer by selling the motorcycle to another party (which he did by selling to Sarah).

D. Conclusion

Since there was never an acceptance, there is not an enforceable contract between Judy and George.

IV. Larry v. George for the Automotive Guide Set

A. Offer

The term "offer" is defined above.

After George's neighbor Larry looked at the automotive guide set, he stated, "I cannot justify spending $50 on the automotive guides because it is not in my budget." This is not an offer, because it clearly states that Larry was not going to buy the automotive guide set. Larry did not state any willingness to enter into a bargain with George at that point.

However, George's response is likely an offer. George responded to Larry, "I would like to sell the guides for $50 but since you always help me out, I would like to repay you. If they don't sell by 3:30pm, you can have them for free." This statement shows George's willingness to give the automotive guide set to Larry, exhibiting George's intent to be bound. The offer contains definite and certain terms. The parties are George and Larry, the price is free, the identification of goods and quantity is an automotive guide set dating from 1990-2010, and the time for performance is by 3:30pm. However, the offer also contains a condition precedent that the offer is only good if George cannot sell the automotive guide set for $50 by 3:30pm.

B. Acceptance

The term "acceptance" is defined above.

Larry thanked George for his offer, which arguably indicates acceptance of the terms of the offer. Larry reinforced his acceptance when he called George at 3:30pm to see if the automotive guide set had sold. Larry was told by George, "No one has expressed much interest in the automotive guides yet. It looks like they will be yours." This statement indicates that the condition precedent has been satisfied.

Accordingly, there is acceptance.

C. Consideration

Consideration is something that is bargained for and given in exchange for a return promise. Typically, there is a benefit to the promisor or a detriment to the promisee.

George will likely argue that his offer to give Larry the automotive guide set is gratuitous and, as such, there is no consideration present, as George will receive no benefit.

Larry will argue that the consideration was stated by George when he said, "I would like to sell the guides for $50 but since you always help me out, I would like to repay you." However, past consideration will not satisfy the bargain requirement.

There is no consideration.

D. Promissory Estoppel

Under the doctrine of promissory estoppel, a promisee that reasonably relies to his detriment on a gratuitous promise may be able to enforce that promise even where there is no consideration in return. Under promissory estoppel, there are four requirements that must be met: (1) there must be a promise made by the promisor; (2) the promisee's reliance must be foreseeable at the time of the promise; (3) there must be actual reliance induced by the promise; and (4) as long as the first three elements are satisfied, the promise will be binding if injustice cannot be avoided otherwise.

Here, when George told Larry on the phone that, "… It looks like they will be yours," Larry responded to George, "Wonderful! I am going to run to the hardware store and buy some wood and supplies to build shelves for them." Consequently, George was aware that his promise to Larry had induced reliance by Larry. Larry, in fact, relied on the promise and purchased wood and supplies to build shelves for the automotive guide set. The first three requirements of promissory estoppel are satisfied and, thus, George's promise to Larry is binding.

Accordingly, George's promise to Larry will be binding under the doctrine of promissory estoppel.

E. Remedies

1. Specific Performance

Specific performance is an extraordinary remedy that is available to order a breaching party's performance only where a monetary award would be inadequate to grant relief to the aggrieved party.

Here, since the automotive guide set is unique, Larry could seek specific performance. However, this remedy is not practical since the automotive guide set was sold to John.

2. Reliance Damages

Reliance damages are calculated by determining the amount of money necessary to restore the aggrieved party to the position he was in prior to the contract.

Larry will be able to recover the cost of the wood and supplies he purchased in reliance on George's promise.

3. General Damages

A breaching party may be liable for general damages, which are damages that foreseeably follow from a breach of contract.

Here, since George breached his contract with Larry, Larry may seek the value of the automotive guide set, since specific performance is unlikely. However, it is likely that Larry will only receive reliance damages since the purpose of promissory estoppel is to avoid injustice.

Contracts

In Class

This sample answer would be considered below the standard expected of a 1L student.

A valid contract requires an offer, consideration, and acceptance. The U.C.C. governs all contracts for the sales of goods. Goods are defined under the U.C.C. as any "movable item."

Carl v. George

An offer is an outward manifestation of the offeror's willingness to enter into a bargain, oral or written, that signals to the offeree that his assent to the bargain is invited and will conclude the deal. When George told Carl "I will sell you the collection of spare tires for only $250…," he demonstrated a present intent to be bound. There was a valid offer.

An option contract results when there is an offer, a subsidiary promise to keep the offer open, and a valid mechanism, typically consideration, for securing enforcement of the subsidiary promise. Carl will argue that George's offer was an option contract because he stated, "…as long as you come back with the money and pick up the collection by 4pm." However, Carl did not give any consideration for the option contract, so there is no enforceable option contract.

Carl may also argue that George is a merchant selling goods in which he has special knowledge or skill, and that a firm offer from a merchant does not require consideration. Here, the goods are spare tires, and the facts do not indicate that George has expertise in spare tires. Furthermore, the act of owning a collection of spare tires does not make a person an expert or knowledgeable. In addition, there was no writing signed by George stating the terms of the offer and that it would be held open.

There was no option contract or firm offer, and George was able to revoke his offer at any time.

A revocation can be effectively communicated in two ways: directly or indirectly. Here, Carl returned to George's house and saw John loading up his truck with the collection of spare tires that George had sold to him. Carl's observation of John loading up his truck in combination with George's selling of the spare tire collection to John evinces that George did not intend to enter into a contract with Carl. There was a valid revocation.

There was not an enforceable contract between Carl and George.

Judy v. George

George's advertisements were not an offer as not all of the terms of the contract were certain and definite. The parties were not defined.

When Judy said to George, "This is exactly what I am looking for! I will buy the motorcycle for $499, but will return by 5pm with my truck and the money," she showed an intent to be bound by contract under the terms she stated. Her offer indicated that she was going to buy one motorcycle from George for $499 before 5pm. There was a valid offer.

Acceptance of an offer is a manifestation of assent to the terms thereof made by the offeree in the manner required (the mirror image rule), and the acceptance must be communicated to the offeror. Here, Judy left before George could respond to her offer. There was no acceptance.

There was no enforceable contract between Judy and George.

Larry v. George

After George's neighbor Larry looked at the automotive guide set, he stated, "I cannot justify spending $50 on the automotive guides because it is not in my budget." This was not an offer.

George's response is likely an offer. George responded to Larry, "I would like to sell the guides for $50 but since you always help me out, I would like to repay you. If they don't sell by 3:30pm, you can have them for free." The offer is good only if George cannot sell the automotive guide set for $50 by 3:30pm.

Larry thanked George for his offer, which indicates acceptance of the terms of the offer. Larry reinforced his acceptance when he called George at 3:30pm to see if the automotive guide set had sold. Larry was told by George, "No one has expressed much interest in the automotive guides yet. It looks like they will be yours."

Consideration is something that is bargained for and given in exchange for a return promise. George will likely argue that his offer to give Larry the automotive guides is gratuitous and, as such, there is no consideration present, as George will receive no benefit. Larry will argue that the consideration was stated by George when he said, "I would like to sell the guides for $50 but since you always help me out, I would like to repay you." However, past consideration will not satisfy the bargain requirement.

Under the doctrine of promissory estoppel, a promisee who reasonably relies to his detriment on a gratuitous promise may be able to enforce that promise even where there is no consideration in return. Here, when George told Larry on the phone that "...It looks like they will be yours," Larry responded to George, "Wonderful! I am going to run to the hardware store and buy some wood and supplies to build shelves for them." Consequently, George was aware that his promise to Larry had induced reliance by Larry. Larry, in fact, relied on the promise and purchased wood and supplies to build shelves for the automotive guide set. The contract is binding.

In terms of remedies, since the automotive guide set is unique, Larry could seek specific performance. However, specific performance is not practical since the automotive guide set was sold to John. Larry will be able to recover the cost of the wood and supplies he purchased in reliance on George's promise.

Contracts

Homework Question 1

Jack Bello operated a tiny, independent movie production company called "Indie Films." The company was a sole proprietorship, meaning it was owned entirely by Jack himself. Jack never made movies for wide studio release or with budgets much over $100,000. One of Jack's friends was a small-time actor, Brad Dapp. Brad was struggling to get roles, in order to get his acting career started, and Brad was also aware of the limited financial nature of Jack's past projects. Jack was getting ready to start making a new movie—a documentary about the plight of inner-city homeless people—and thought that Brad might be good for the primary narrator/protagonist role, so one day (it was May 1, 2005) he called Brad and asked him to come to the Indie Films office to discuss it.

When Brad got there, he smiled and shook Jack's hand. "Glad to hear from you, Jack," he said, "what role do you have for me?" Deciding to have a little fun, Jack said, "How does the role of Spider-Man a/k/a Peter Parker in the upcoming Spider-Man 4 sound? The pay is $15 million!" Brad laughed, and said, "I accept!" Then, after the laughing had died down, Jack stated, "Well, actually I am doing a documentary, and I thought you might be a good fit. What is your asking price these days?" "Well," Brad replied, "depending on the length of the job, I try not to get less than $10,000 for a complete film." "OK," Jack said, "I'll agree to pay you that right here and now—can you start next month?" "Thanks, Jack, I appreciate the opportunity," Brad said, "but can I have some time to think about it?" "Well," Jack responded, "we have a little bit of time. Shooting shouldn't take more than six months, but I want to be finished by the end of the year. So, just let me know in 10 days." Brad frowned, but said, "OK, I will be in touch," and then he left.

A week later, May 8, 2005, Brad was seriously considering calling Jack to do the documentary. He was at a coffee house that day, hanging out with one of his struggling, but trusted, actor friends, Rivers Gordon, discussing the project. Rivers suddenly interjected, "Oh man, Brad, I'm sorry, I thought you had heard. Jack discovered that Jon Voight was unexpectedly available for that documentary role—Voight was willing to do it for next to nothing, and Jack simply couldn't pass it up. Jack has signed him up to start shooting it next week." "You've got to be kidding!" Brad exclaimed, and raced over to a pay phone in the coffee house, and called Jack's phone number. There was no answer, and no answering machine, just constant ringing. "Figures," Brad mumbled, and ran the five blocks to the Indie Films offices, which were locked. Brad banged on the door, but no one answered because everyone was out for lunch. "I accept!!!" Brad shouted at the door at the top of his lungs. "Do you hear me, Jack, I accept your offer to do the film!!!" Then he went back to the coffee house, got a piece of paper, and wrote, "Jack: I'm doing the documentary. Plus, if you don't, we both know you owe me $15 million for the Spider-Man role you promised me! Sincerely, Brad Dapp." Brad signed the note, taped it on the door of the Indie Films office, and then went home.

Jack read Brad's note the next day. "Dang!" he said, "I forgot that I had a 10-day offer outstanding to Brad. And he's got to be kidding about the Spider-Man thing." Jack doesn't want to hire Brad, now that he has Jon Voight on board for the film, but thinks he may have legal troubles with Brad. So he comes to see you, a well-regarded entertainment lawyer.

Please discuss fully the contractual effect of all communications and actions that took place between Jack and Brad, and any other parties. In doing so, please discuss all legal issues that you see from these facts, from both Jack's and Brad's perspective. In doing so, discuss whether Jack is contractually obligated to Brad, including an assessment of whether Jack has any arguments against liability.

Contracts

Homework Question 1—Outline

I. **Was there a valid contract between Jack and Brad for the Spider-Man role?**

    A. **(Rule)** Objectively reasonable meaning of a term at the time of contracting controls over a contrary subjective understanding of the term by one of the parties

       1. If both parties shared the same subjective understanding of the term at the time of contracting, it controls

    B. **(Application)** Jack's offer was technically sound, and the ordinary rules of offer and acceptance were facially satisfied

       1. Apparent from the laughter during Brad's acceptance, and the additional laughter that followed from Jack that this was not a serious negotiation

       2. Reasonable person aware of Jack's limited budget and past projects would know that it was improbable that he had landed such a huge project

          a. Facts clearly state that Brad was aware of the limited financial nature of Jack's past projects

    C. **(Conclusion)** There was no contract between Jack and Brad for the Spider-Man role

II. **Was Brad's statement that he tries not to work for less than $10,000 per film an offer?**

    A. **(Rule)** Price quote is not an offer, but an invitation to the other party to make an offer

    B. **(Application)** Brad's statement indicating that he tries not to work for less than $10,000 per film was a direct response to Jack's question "What is your asking price these days?"

    C. **(Conclusion)** Brad's statement is not an offer, but rather an invitation to Jack to make an offer

III. **Was Jack's statement that he would pay Brad $10,000 an offer?**

    A. **(Rule)** Offer is an outward manifestation of the offeror's willingness to enter into a bargain, oral or written, that signals to the offeree that his assent to the bargain is invited and will conclude the deal

    B. **(Application)** Jack clearly manifested a willingness to enter into a deal when he stated "I'll agree to pay you that right here and now—can you start next month?"

       1. Further supported by his statement "...right here and now..."

    C. **(Conclusion)** Jack's statements in combination with the $10,000 price quote create an offer

IV. **Is Jack's promise to hold the offer open revocable?**

    A. **(Rule)** Rule of Free Revocability—the offeror is free to revoke an outstanding offer, terminating the offeree's power of acceptance, at any time and for any reason, as long as the revocation occurs prior to acceptance, and is effectively communicated

       1. Revocation can be effectively communicated in two ways—directly or indirectly

          a. Direct revocation—offeror directly communicates with the offeree and revokes the offer

          b. Indirect revocation—the offeree learns of the offeror's intention to abandon the deal from a third-party

       2. Two ways to prevent revocation of offer—firm offer or option contract

          a. Firm offer—applies only to the sale of goods

          b. Option contract—results when there is an offer, a subsidiary promise to keep the offer open, and a valid mechanism, typically consideration, for securing enforcement of the subsidiary promise

B. **(Application)** Jack orally granted Brad 10 days to think about the offer

       1. Oral contract, so nothing in writing

       2. No consideration given in exchange for this time period to think about the offer

       3. No firm offer and no option contract present

C. **(Conclusion)** Jack's offer is fully revocable

V. **Did Brad accept or reject Jack's offer in the May 1 conversation?**

A. **(Rule)** Acceptance of an offer is a manifestation of assent to the terms thereof made by the offeree in the manner required (the mirror image rule), and the acceptance must be communicated to the offeror

B. **(Application)** Brad asked for additional time to consider the offer when he said "Thanks, Jack, I appreciate the opportunity, but can I have some time to think about it?" and "OK, I will be in touch"

C. **(Conclusion)** Brad did not accept or reject the offer, but reserved his power of acceptance

VI. **Did Jack's offer survive the communication from Rivers to Brad?**

A. **(Rule)** Revocation can be effectively communicated in two ways—directly or indirectly (further discussed in IV above)

B. **(Application)** Brad did not have an enforceable option contract as there was no consideration present

       1. Brad's power of acceptance terminated when Rivers shared information with Brad about Jon Voight taking the role in Jack's documentary film

C. **(Conclusion)** Brad learning about Jon Voight's hiring through Rivers constitutes an indirect revocation of Jack's offer

VII. **Do any of Brad's actions after learning about Jon Voight's hiring from Rivers constitute acceptance of Jack's offer?**

A. **(Rule)** Once an offer is revoked, an offeree no longer has the power of acceptance

       1. Mailbox rule—acceptance of an offer is effective upon dispatch, and generally must be effectively communicated

B. **(Application)** After Brad found out that Jack hired Jon Voight to be in the documentary film, Brad tried to call Jack but failed to reach him, then he knocked on Indie Film's office door and yelled "I accept," before finally leaving a note of acceptance on the door

1. Brad's yelling was useless as there was no one at the office to hear it—notification to someone is required
2. Brad's post-it note on the door would not be effective acceptance either—mailbox rule would not apply
3. Even if Jack read the note—offer already revoked as a result of the information Rivers provided to Brad

C. **(Conclusion)** Brad lost his power of acceptance once Rivers informed him about Jon Voight—there is no acceptance

Contracts

Homework Question 1—Sample Answer

This sample answer would be considered above the standard expected of a 1L student.

I. <u>The issue is whether there is a valid contract created between Jack and Brad for the Spider-Man role.</u>

Typically, the objectively reasonable meaning of a term at the time of contracting would control over a contrary subjective understanding of the term by one of the parties. However, where the evidence demonstrates that both parties shared the same subjective understanding of the term at the time of contracting, the mutual subjective understanding of the term will control.

Here, Jack offered, "How does the role of Spider-Man a/k/a Peter Parker in the upcoming Spider-Man 4 sound? The pay is $15 million!" In response, Brad laughed and stated, "I accept!" After this exchange, more laughter ensued. While Jack's offer was technically sound, and the ordinary rules of offer and acceptance were facially satisfied, it was apparent from the laughter during Brad's acceptance, and the additional laughter that followed, that this was not a serious negotiation. Jack's follow-up of, "Well, actually I am doing a documentary…" further supports this conclusion. Both Jack and Brad had a mutual subjective understanding of this.

In addition, a reasonable person aware of Jack's limited budget and past projects would know that it was improbable that he had landed such a huge project. Here, the facts clearly state that Brad was aware of the limited financial nature of Jack's past projects.

Accordingly, there is no contract between Jack and Brad for the Spider-Man role.

II. <u>The issue is whether Brad's response indicating that he tries not to work for less than $10,000 per film is an offer.</u>

Similar to an advertisement, a price quote is not an offer, but rather an invitation to the other party to make an offer.

Here, Brad's statement indicating that he tries not to work for less than $10,000 per film was merely a direct response to Jack's question, "What is your asking price these days?"

Brad's statement is not an offer, but rather an invitation to Jack to make an offer.

III. <u>The issue is whether Jack's response that he would pay Brad $10,000 is an offer.</u>

An offer is an outward manifestation of the offeror's willingness to enter into a bargain, oral or written, that signals to the offeree that his assent to the bargain is invited and will conclude the deal.

Here, Jack clearly manifested a willingness to deal when he stated, "I'll agree to pay you that right here and now—can you start next month?" His willingness to enter into a bargain was further accentuated by his statement of, "…right here and now…." These statements in combination with the price quote of $10,000 create an offer.

IV. <u>The issue is whether Jack's promise to hold the offer open is revocable.</u>

Under the Rule of Free Revocability in American contract law, the offeror is free to revoke an outstanding offer, terminating the offeree's power of acceptance, at any time and for any reason, as long as the revocation occurs prior to acceptance, and is effectively communicated. Revocation can be effectively communicated in two ways: directly or indirectly. In a direct revocation, the offeror directly communicates with the offeree and revokes the offer. In an indirect revocation, the offeree learns of the offeror's intention to abandon the deal from a third party.

There are two ways to prevent revocation of an offer: a firm offer under the U.C.C. or an option contract. The firm offer rule applies only to the sale of goods. An option contract results when there is an offer, a subsidiary promise to keep the offer open, and a valid mechanism, typically consideration, for securing enforcement of the subsidiary promise.

Here, Jack orally granted Brad 10 days to think about the offer. This was an oral contract, so there was nothing in writing. There was no consideration given in exchange for this time period to think about the offer. Further, this offer was not a firm offer under the U.C.C. as it was an offer for services. Lastly, there was no option contract present since there was no consideration.

As a result, Jack's offer is fully revocable.

V. <u>The issue is whether Brad accepted or rejected Jack's offer in the original conversation that occurred on May 1.</u>

Acceptance of an offer is a manifestation of assent to the terms thereof made by the offeree in the manner required (the mirror image rule), and the acceptance must be communicated to the offeror. A rejection is a declination of the offer.

Here, Brad sincerely asked for additional time to consider the offer when he said, "Thanks, Jack, I appreciate the opportunity, but can I have some time to think about it?" and, "OK, I will be in touch." He clearly did not reject the offer. Brad's frown may be related to some disappointment about the offer, but it is not in itself evident of an express or implied rejection.

Accordingly, Brad did not accept or reject the offer, but reserved his power of acceptance.

VI. <u>The issue is whether Jack's offer survived the communication from Rivers to Brad.</u>

As stated in section IV above, a revocation can be effectively communicated in two ways: directly or indirectly. In a direct revocation, the offeror directly communicates with the offeree and revokes the offer, and in an indirect revocation, the offeree learns of the offeror's intention to abandon the deal from a third party. This terminates the offeree's power of acceptance as long as the offeror has taken definite action that is inconsistent with the intention to enter the proposed contract, and the offeree acquires reliable information of the offeror's inconsistent action.

Here, on May 8, seven days after the initial offer, Brad was still within the 10-day window to accept the offer. However, as discussed above, Brad did not have an enforceable option contract as there was no consideration present. Brad's power of acceptance terminated as soon as Rivers, a trusted friend, shared information with Brad about Jon Voight taking the role in Jack's documentary film.

Brad's learning about Jon Voight's hiring through Rivers constitutes an indirect revocation of Jack's offer, thus terminating Brad's power of acceptance.

VII. <u>The issue is whether any of Brad's actions after learning about Jon Voight's hiring from Rivers constitute acceptance of Jack's offer.</u>

Once an offer is revoked, an offeree no longer has the power of acceptance. In addition, under the mailbox rule, acceptance of an offer is effective upon dispatch, and generally must be effectively communicated.

Here, upon learning that Jack hired Jon Voight to be in the documentary film, Brad tried to call Jack but failed to reach him, then he knocked on Indie Films' office door and yelled, "I accept," and then he left a note of acceptance on the door. Even if Brad still possessed the power to accept, Brad's yelling was useless as there was no one at the office to hear it. Notification to someone is required to make a promise. Similarly, Brad's note on the door would not be effective acceptance either, as the mailbox rule would not apply. Even if Jack read the note, the offer was already revoked at this point as a result of the information Rivers provided.

Consequently, Brad lost the power of acceptance once Rivers informed him about Jon Voight and, as a result, there is no acceptance.

Contracts

Homework Question 2

Mary Minut is a high school senior and 17 years old. While at Facy's Department Store, Mary sees a handbag that she just has to have, but cannot afford. She stuffs the bag under her jacket and runs out of the store. Mary does not see her neighbor, Marla Farley, standing in the handbag section with a look of shock. Marla sees everything.

A week later, Mary has an argument with her parents about college. Her parents issue an ultimatum, and tell her that if she refuses to go to college, she must leave the house. Fortunately, she is able to stay at her friend's house, but has no transportation to get to work and school. She goes to Farley's Moped Shop to purchase a moped. Mike Farley, the owner of Farley's Moped Shop, is Marla's husband. After Marla saw Mary shoplift the handbag at Facy's, she came home and told her husband the entire story.

Upon entering the store, Mary starts looking at the mopeds in the used moped section and tells Mike that she needs a moped that will allow her to get around town and to school. She tells Mike that she only has about $300 to spend. Mike asks her age and she tells him she is 18, the age of majority. Mike starts to tell her about the used mopeds he has available. He points out a couple of options that would be an easy ride to get from place to place, but Mary is surprised at the cost of $650 for a used moped.

Mike then shows her a moped that his crew recently fixed up and tells her that this moped is like new and only $600. In reality, the moped had a broken chain mechanism, and Mike's crew repaired it just enough to make it appear intact to a casual rider. The chain mechanism is likely to break again after about 50 miles. Mary is hesitant to buy it as it looks older than most of the other used mopeds for sale, but she needs transportation and says to Mike, "I only have $300, will you take that?" Mike has had a slow week with no sales, so he tells Mary that he knows what she did at Facy's and if she does not quickly make up her mind to purchase this moped in the next minute, he will tell her parents and the police about her shoplifting the handbag. He then tells her that he can cut her a deal: $300 now and $75 a week for 4 weeks. Mary is scared and says to Mike, "I'll do it." She pays Mike the $300 and signs a contract agreeing to the terms discussed. She then races off to her friend's house on the moped.

Mary makes the payments to Mike over the next four weeks. She turns 18 between the third and fourth payments. As she is leaving the store parking lot after making the last payment, the moped chain mechanism breaks, and the moped is rendered inoperable. Mary pushes the moped home to her parents' house. She then confesses to her parents about shoplifting the handbag. Mary and her mother immediately go to Facy's and pay for the handbag. Mary also discusses her purchase of the moped with her parents.

Mary and her parents come to you to determine whether the contract with Farley's Moped Shop is enforceable and if there is any legal way for Mary to get out of the contract and get her money back. Discuss all legal theories completely.

Contracts

Homework Question 2—Outline

I. **Was there an enforceable contract between Mike and Mary?**

  A. **(Rule)** Contract requires offer, consideration, and acceptance
    1. Offer is an outward manifestation of the offeror's willingness to enter into a bargain, oral or written, that signals to the offeree that his assent to the bargain is invited and will conclude the deal
      a. Offer must consist of definite and certain terms, including identification of the goods, quantity, price, and parties
    2. Consideration is something that is bargained for and given in exchange for a return promise
    3. Acceptance is the manifestation of assent to the terms thereof made by the offeree in the manner required (the mirror image rule)
      a. Acceptance must be communicated to the offeror
  B. **(Application)** When Mary tells Mike that she needs a moped and that she has $300 to spend, she is inviting Mike to make her an offer
    1. Mike shows her a moped that costs $600—this is likely a price quote and not an offer because Mike is not offering the moped to Mary for $600
    2. Mary's statement "I only have $300, will you take that?" is an offer
    3. Mike's reply that he can take $300 now and $75 each week for four weeks, for a total of $600, is a counteroffer
    4. Consideration is present as there is the bargained-for exchange of money for the moped
    5. Acceptance of the terms when Mary says to Mike, "I'll do it," makes a payment of $300, and signs a contract stating the terms
  C. **(Conclusion)** There is an enforceable contract between Mike and Mary

II. **Can Mary raise a lack of capacity defense?**

  A. **(Rule)** Minor is any person who is under the age of 18
    1. Minor's contract for necessaries is voidable, but case law is split on whether to include automobiles in the category of necessaries
      a. Likely moped classified similarly as automobile
    2. Ratification—a minor may ratify a contract upon reaching the age of majority by making any manifestation to the other party of an intention to be bound by the original contract
  B. **(Application)** Mary only 17 when she entered into contract
    1. Mary made a payment to Mike after she turned 18—this constitutes ratification
  C. **(Conclusion)** Mary was a minor when she entered into the contract with Mike, but she later ratified it—the contract is not voidable based on a lack of capacity

III. **Can Mary raise a fraudulent misrepresentation defense?**

  A. **(Rule)** Misrepresentation is an untrue statement or assertion relating to existing facts

1. Fraudulent misrepresentation requires: (1) defendant to have made an assertion that is inconsistent with the facts; (2) state-of-mind elements of scienter and intent to mislead to have been established; (3) the misrepresentation to be material to the contract; and (4) reasonable reliance on the misrepresentation

B. **(Application)** Mike told Mary that the moped was recently fixed up and in like new condition
   1. Mike's statement was clearly false and made with the intent to mislead
   2. Mary relied on statement

C. **(Conclusion)** Contract is voidable based on Mike's fraudulent misrepresentation about the condition of the moped

IV. **Can Mary raise a duress defense?**

A. **(Rule)** Defense of duress arises when there is a threat that is wrongful in nature and leaves the aggrieved party with no reasonable choice but to succumb to the threat

B. **(Application)** Unclear whether Mike's implied threat to report Mary's shoplifting to the police and her parents was a wrongful threat
   1. Mike's threat is blackmail, which is clearly a wrongful threat
   2. Mike's threat is not wrongful, Mike should report shoplifting
   3. Mary agreed to the contract terms that Mike presented because she was scared

C. **(Conclusion)** Contract may be voidable under a duress defense since duress precluded Mary from exercising her free will—there was no true and free mutual assent

V. **Can Mary raise an undue influence defense?**

A. **(Rule)** Undue influence consists of: (1) unfair persuasion (2) against a vulnerable party
   1. Party can be vulnerable due to mental infirmity resulting from age or illness, a recent trauma or event, or because of reliance on the other party resulting from a relationship of trust or confidence

B. **(Application)** Mary is likely susceptible because of her age, and also because of the recent event of shoplifting
   1. Mike's reference to Mary's shoplifting and threat to report her is clearly unfair persuasion

C. **(Conclusion)** Contract is likely voidable based on the undue influence exerted on Mary by Mike

VI. **Can Mary raise a public policy defense based on illegality?**

A. **(Rule)** Public policy defense based on illegality may be raised where the subject matter of the contract itself is specifically prohibited by the law

B. **(Application)** Mary bargained for Mike's agreement not to report her shoplifting to the police. Shoplifting is an illegal subject matter

C. **(Conclusion)** Contract is likely voidable because of the illegality of the subject matter of the contract

Contracts

Homework Question 2—Sample Answer

This sample answer would be considered above the standard expected of a 1L student.

I. Validity of Contract and Governing Law

A valid contract requires an offer, consideration, and acceptance.

An offer is an outward manifestation of the offeror's willingness to enter into a bargain, oral or written, that signals to the offeree that his assent to the bargain is invited and will conclude the deal. The offer must consist of definite and certain terms, including identification of the goods, quantity, price, and parties.

Consideration is something that is bargained for and given in exchange for a return promise. Typically, there is a benefit to the promisor or a detriment to the promisee.

Acceptance of an offer is a manifestation of assent to the terms thereof made by the offeree in the manner required (the mirror image rule), and the acceptance must be communicated to the offeror.

The determination of whether there is an enforceable contract between Mike and Mary will be based on whether a valid contract was formed.

The U.C.C. governs all contracts for the sales of goods. Sales are any transactions in which the seller transfers title of a good to a buyer. Goods are defined under the U.C.C. as any "movable item."

The terms "offer," "consideration," and "acceptance" are defined above.

Here, when Mary tells Mike that she needs a moped and that she has $300 to spend, she is inviting Mike to make her an offer. Mike shows her a moped that costs $600. This is likely a price quote and not an offer because Mike is not offering the moped to Mary for $600. Mary's statement "I only have $300, will you take that?" is an offer. Mike's reply that he can take $300 now and $75 each week for four weeks, for a total of $600, is a counteroffer. Consideration is present as there is the bargained-for exchange of money for the moped. There is acceptance of the terms when Mary says to Mike, "I'll do it," makes a payment of $300, and signs a contract stating the terms.

There is an enforceable contract between Mike and Mary.

II. Mary's Defenses

A. Lack of Capacity

A minor is any person who is under the age of 18. At common law, a minor lacked the capacity to enter into a contract. Under modern rules, a minor can enter into a contract, but the contract is voidable at the option of the minor. This is the case even if a minor is emancipated.

Here, it is unclear whether Mike's implied threat to report Mary's shoplifting to the police and her parents was a wrongful threat. It can be argued that Mike's threat is blackmail, which is clearly a wrongful threat. However, it can also be argued that Mike's threat is not wrongful, as Mike should report shoplifting to the police. It is clear that Mary agreed to the contract terms that Mike presented because she was scared that he would report her shoplifting to the police and her parents. Mary's free will was overcome.

The contract may be voidable under a duress defense because duress precluded Mary from exercising her free will to agree to the contract; there was no true and free mutual assent.

D. <u>Undue Influence</u>

The defense of undue influence arises when the circumstances reveal a vulnerable but not incapacitated party who succumbs to untoward bargaining tactics and excessive pressures from another party, where those pressures or tactics fall short of fraud or duress.

The two main elements of undue influence are: (1) unfair persuasion; and (2) against a vulnerable party. A party can be vulnerable because of mental infirmity resulting from age or illness, a recent trauma or event, or because of reliance on the other party resulting from a relationship of trust or confidence with the other party.

Here, Mary is likely susceptible because of her age, and also because of the recent event of shoplifting. In addition, Mike's reference to Mary's shoplifting and threat to report her to the police and her parents if Mary did not decide to purchase the moped within a minute is clearly unfair persuasion.

The contract is likely voidable based on the undue influence exerted on Mary by Mike.

E. <u>Public Policy Defense Based on Illegality</u>

A public policy defense based on illegality may be raised where the subject matter of the contract itself is specifically prohibited by the law.

Here, it can be argued that in agreeing to purchase the moped, Mary bargained for Mike's agreement not to report her shoplifting to the police. Shoplifting is an illegal subject matter.

The contract is likely voidable because of the illegality of the subject matter of the contract.

III. <u>Conclusion</u>

Having established that a valid contract is present, I would advise Mary that we can try to invalidate the contract based on the defenses of fraudulent misrepresentation, duress, undue influence, and illegality. Her strongest arguments would be based on the defenses of fraudulent misrepresentation, undue influence, and illegality.

Multiple-Choice Questions

FORMATION

Question 1

An elderly man who lived by himself started repainting his house. Because the elderly man was having a difficult time with the project, his son hired a contractor to do the job. Their contract provided that the contractor would receive payment after completion of the work. When the contractor was halfway done with the job, the elderly man died.

Which of the following is correct?

(A) The contract is discharged and the contractor will receive no payments, because he did not complete the work.

(B) The contract is discharged, but the contractor will receive payment for work completed.

(C) The contract is not discharged, but the contractor must receive half of the payment before continuing work.

(D) The contract is not discharged, and the contractor must complete the repainting project.

Question 2

A young woman obtained used items of clothing from yard sales, swap meets, and similar sources, and then cleaned and refurbished them before selling them at her small shop. One day, an extremely well-to-do lawyer came into the woman's shop. The lawyer found nothing of interest in the clothing racks, but she noticed an odd-looking, canary-colored raincoat hanging from a hook on the wall.

Not realizing that the raincoat belonged to the young woman, the lawyer pointed to the raincoat and said, "I'll give you $25 for that hideous thing." Offended at the lawyer's condescending tone, the young woman replied, "That raincoat isn't worth a thing. Besides, you're far too corporate to wear a coat like that." The lawyer, now angry herself, replied, "I must have it." The young woman said, "Okay, it's yours for $550." "Done," said the lawyer.

Does an enforceable contract exist between the woman and the lawyer?

(A) Yes, because there was a bargained-for exchange of promises.

(B) Yes, because the raincoat was worth $550 to the lawyer.

(C) No, because the consideration supporting the woman's promise is insufficient.

(D) No, because the agreement between the parties is unconscionable.

Question 3

On January 1, a seller received an order in the mail from a buyer requesting shipment of its latest computer at the seller's current catalog price. The order specified that the seller could accept the offer either by shipping the goods or promptly notifying the buyer of acceptance. On January 2, the seller mailed to the buyer a letter accepting the order and assuring the buyer that the computer would be shipped on January 3. On January 3, the seller realized that he was out of that computer model, and instead shipped to the buyer a different computer model and a notice of accommodation. On January 5, the buyer received the seller's January 2 letter as well as the different computer model, but not the notice of accommodation.

Which of the following best states the parties' legal rights and duties?

(A) The buyer can either accept or reject the different computer model, and in either event, can recover damages, if any, for breach of contract.

(B) The buyer can either accept or reject the different computer model, but if he rejects it, he will thereby waive any remedy for breach of contract.

(C) The seller's prompt shipment of nonconforming goods constituted an acceptance of the buyer's offer, thereby creating a contract for sale of the replacement computer model.

(D) The seller's notice of accommodation was timely mailed, and his shipment of the different computer model constituted a counteroffer.

Question 4

On March 1, a manufacturer of valve stems offered to sell 5,000 valve stems to a manufacturer of car tires. On March 2, the manufacturer of car tires replied by letter informing the valve stem manufacturer that they accept the offer and that any disputes will be settled through mandatory arbitration.

What is the nature of the relationship between the parties as of March 2?

(A) There is no contract, because a necessary price term is missing.

(B) There is no contract, because the acceptance did not mirror the offer.

(C) There is a contract, which includes the arbitration clause.

(D) There is a contract, which does not include the arbitration clause.

Question 5

A businesswoman with dual citizenship in the United States and the United Kingdom decided to transfer her entire business overseas. She entered into a contract with a buyer for the sale of her home, which included a large home office, for $325,000. The contract further provided that the transfer of the deed, as well as the buyer's payment of the purchase price, would occur on May 1, one month from the date of the contract. After the signing of the contract, the businesswoman traveled to England to begin the process of setting up her headquarters there. She expected to stay for four weeks, and then return home the day before the closing date of the contract.

However, en route home to the United States, the businesswoman found herself stranded in Madrid, Spain, following a layover and several flight delays and cancellations. As a result, she did not arrive home until May 2, the day after the closing date. Upon her return, the businesswoman contacted the buyer to reschedule the closing. However, the buyer was highly offended at the businesswoman's failure to show up on the promised date or to contact him about the delay, and he informed her that he would be canceling the contract due to her breach.

If the businesswoman files an action seeking the buyer's specific performance of the contract, will she prevail?

(A) No, because unless otherwise provided in the terms of the contract, a party's failure to render performance on the date promised constitutes a repudiation of the contract.

(B) No, because specific performance is not an appropriate remedy for a buyer's breach of a contract for the sale of land.

(C) Yes, because the businesswoman's delay in performance was justified under the circumstances.

(D) Yes, because the contract did not provide that time was of the essence.

CONSIDERATION

Question 6

An uncle wanted his nephew to quit smoking, because smoking is unhealthy. The uncle attempted to convince the nephew to quit, but the nephew would not agree. The uncle then offered to pay the nephew $5,000 if the nephew quit smoking for one year. It was the uncle's hope that if he could get the nephew to stop smoking for one year, he would not pick up the unhealthy habit again. The nephew agreed, and signed a contract to that effect with the uncle. The nephew quit smoking for one year, but afterward, restarted smoking. He asked for the $5,000, but the uncle refused to pay. The nephew has now filed suit against the uncle.

What is the likely outcome of the case?

(A) The uncle is liable, because there was a bargained-for exchange.

(B) The uncle is liable, because the nephew relied to his detriment on the uncle's promise.

(C) The uncle is not liable, because the consideration was inadequate.

(D) The uncle is not liable, because the uncle did not receive a benefit and the nephew did not suffer a detriment.

Question 7

A man approached his neighbor, who was seven months pregnant, and said, "If you name your son after my father, I will pay you $200 per month for three years." The neighbor agreed and named her child after the man's father. Afterwards, the man reneged on his promise, and told his neighbor that he had decided not to pay her the money. The neighbor sued the man for breach of contract.

For whom should a court award judgment?

(A) The neighbor, because there was a bargained-for exchange.

(B) The neighbor, because her promise to name the child after the man's father was a condition of a gift made in consideration of carrying out a moral obligation.

(C) The man, because his promise to pay the neighbor was a mere gift promise unsupported by consideration.

(D) The man, because the neighbor did not experience any recognizable detriment in the naming of her child.

Question 8

A manufacturer of single-serving coffee makers mailed to a retailer of various household appliances the following written offer: "Will sell 50 single-serving coffee makers at our list price of $50 each. Available for immediate delivery. Please respond by return mail." Unaware of the manufacturer's offer, the retailer, on the same day, mailed a written letter to the manufacturer containing the identical terms: "Will purchase 50 single-serving coffee makers at your list price of $50 each." Both letters were mailed through the U.S. postal system.

Before either party receives the other's correspondence, which of the following accurately states the legal relationship between the manufacturer and retailer?

(A) Because there was a meeting of the minds, a contract was formed when the retailer mailed its letter.

(B) A contract exists, with UCC gap-filler provisions controlling for delivery and payment terms.

(C) A contract was formed when the retailer deposited its acceptance, because the crossing communications contained identical terms.

(D) No contract exists, because a posted offer has no legal effect.

Question 9

A hiker came across a cat while hiking in the woods. Not seeing an owner, the hiker decided to take the cat to the local animal shelter. As she was carrying the cat into the animal shelter, the hiker heard a man say, "I found you!" The cat's owner was so delighted to find his cat that he promised to pay the hiker $250 for her troubles. The hiker told him that that would not be necessary; she had picked up the cat out of her love for animals, and expected no reward. Later, however, the hiker received a large bill in the mail, and realized that she could really use the reward money. The hiker called the owner, but the man refused to honor his earlier offer.

If the hiker sues to collect the reward, what will she recover?

(A) Nothing, because there was no consideration for the reward.

(B) Nothing, because the hiker rejected the man's offer.

(C) $250, because the technical defense of the Statute of Frauds will be overcome by the fact that the hiker had fully performed.

(D) $250, because moral consideration is sufficient to support the promise of a reward.

Question 10

A business owner had 23 full-time employees working for her company, many of whom had been there for several years. One day, the business owner noticed that some employees were gaining weight and seemed to move about more slowly than they had in previous years.

In an effort to support her employees in improving and maintaining their health, she decided to buy any of them a bicycle if the worker would commit to riding it as a form of exercise at least 15 miles per week. She sent out a company memo informing her employees of this bonus and fun benefit and asked any workers who were committing to the 15-miles-per-week bicycling program to meet her at the locally owned mountain bike shop that Sunday before 1:00 p.m.

One of her newest employees was glad to learn of the 15-miles-per-week bicycling-for-exercise program, because he already biked to and from work daily, barring inclement weather. In fact, it was his example that had influenced and impressed the business owner to institute the new company bicycling program.

The following Sunday, the new employee rode his 10-speed bike to the mountain bike shop, arriving at 12:55 p.m. He saw the business owner there and waved hello to her. However, because the business owner was busy talking with several other employees who were also in the shop, the new employee locked up his bicycle and strolled through the shopping center for a few minutes until the other employees left the store.

Upon his return to the mountain bike shop at 1:05 p.m., the new employee asked the business owner for his free bike. The business owner told him that he did not qualify for the free bicycle offer because he already owned a bike and rode it to work. The business owner further stated that because the employee had been late arriving at the bike shop, he did not meet the timing condition of the company offer.

In a suit brought by the employee to recover the bonus mountain bike, which party is likely to prevail?

(A) The business owner, because there is substantial evidence that her offer did not induce the employee to commit to bicycling at least 15 miles per week for exercise.

(B) The business owner, because the employee failed to arrive at the store on time.

(C) The employee, under a quasi-contract theory.

(D) The employee, because his motives are irrelevant and he arrived at the mountain bike store to get a bike for the company's exercise program.

DEFENSES

Question 11

A woman had lived in Apartment 123 in the same apartment complex for six years. On many prior occasions, the woman had hired the same handyman to perform odd jobs in her apartment. The woman, who was leaving town on vacation, telephoned the handyman and said, "If you will replace the tile in my bathroom while I'm on vacation, I will pay you $700. You can get the keys from the superintendent." The handyman responded, "It's a deal." During their telephone conversation, the woman failed to tell the handyman that she no longer lived in Apartment 123, but had moved down the hall into Apartment 132.

The handyman came to the apartment complex, got the key for Apartment 123 from the superintendent, and re-tiled the bathroom. When the woman returned from her vacation, she noticed that her bathroom tile had not been replaced. She contacted the handyman, who then informed her that he had replaced the tile in Apartment 123. The handyman demanded that the woman pay him $700, but the woman refused.

If the handyman sues the woman for payment of the $700 and the woman claims mistake, for whom should the court award judgment?

(A) The handyman, because the woman should have realized that he would replace the tile in Apartment 123.

(B) The handyman, because even though no contract existed, he is entitled to quasi-contractual relief under the circumstances.

(C) The woman, because the handyman did not replace the tile in the woman's bathroom.

(D) The woman, because no contract existed due to the mutual mistake of the parties.

Question 12

Which of the following would not satisfy the applicable Statute of Frauds?

(A) An order form for 200 pairs of roller skates on the buyer's preprinted order form with the buyer's letterhead, but with no signature by an employee of the buyer. The lawsuit is against the buyer for refusal to accept the roller skates when delivered by the seller.

(B) A combined set of three writings stapled together by the buyer which, when all three are viewed together, supply all elements of the agreement. Only one of the three writings is signed by the buyer, who is the party being charged.

(C) A telegram sent by a buyer to a seller confirming a deal, with the buyer's name typed by the telegraph company. The suit is against the seller of real property.

(D) A letter from a buyer to her friend describing a deal the buyer recently entered into with a seller for a parcel of land. The seller is now suing the buyer for specific performance.

Question 13

A female horse won the most competitive horse race in the United States three years ago. Since her retirement, her owner has not been able to successfully breed her. A veterinarian who specializes in new techniques for breeding animals that have not been able to conventionally conceive approached the horse's owner with an offer to purchase the horse, explaining that he had always been a devotee of horseracing and had a lifetime ambition to own a winning horse. While the veterinarian's explanation was truthful, he did not tell the owner that he wished to try this technique on the horse.

The owner sold the horse to the veterinarian for $50,000, a generous price for a sterile, retired racehorse, but far less than the value of the horse if she could bear offspring. Soon after the veterinarian purchased the female horse, he extracted eggs from her ovary, fertilized them in a test tube, and implanted the fertilized egg in her womb.

When the owner learns that the female horse was pregnant and that the sire was another winner of the same competitive horse race, the owner sued the veterinarian to rescind the sale.

What is the most likely outcome?

(A) The owner will prevail, because his ignorance of the fact that the female horse was capable of being bred successfully constitutes a unilateral mistake.

(B) The owner will prevail, because there was a mutual mistake.

(C) The veterinarian will prevail, because attempts to breed the animal by him would be foreseeable to the owner.

(D) The veterinarian will prevail, because the owner has no legal basis on which to rescind this valid contract.

Question 14

A grain distribution company entered into a valid written contract with a farmer for 50 tons of corn at $1,000 per ton. In late summer the farmer was harvesting the corn and noticed that the crop was infested with aphids, which rendered it unsafe for consumption. This infestation commonly occurs in corn. The farmer called the grain distribution company the same day and informed them that due to the infestation, he would be unable to perform. The grain distribution company now brings suit against the farmer for breach of contract.

How should the court rule?

(A) For the farmer, due to impracticability of performance.

(B) For the farmer, due to impossibility of performance.

(C) For the grain distribution company, because the farmer failed to inspect the crops earlier.

(D) For the grain distribution company, because the farmer failed to deliver the corn at the agreed-upon time.

Question 15

A homeowner entered into a written contract with a local construction firm to build a 12'-by-12' addition onto the homeowner's house for $25,000, payable on completion. Under the terms of the contract, the homeowner's duty to pay the entire contract price was conditioned upon the construction firm's completing the job by March 30.

Shortly after the homeowner and the construction firm drew up their contract, the city in which the homeowner's house is located revised several zoning regulations. One of the revised regulations prohibited property owners in residential areas from building structures on their property less than three feet from their property line. To bring the project into compliance, the construction firm instead built the addition to measure 11' by 12'. The decrease in the size of the addition reduced the value to the homeowner by $1,000. The cost of paying another contractor to extend the room, assuming such an extension were legal, would be $5,000.

If the construction firm otherwise completed the project on time and conformed with all other contract specifications, to what amount is the construction firm entitled in payment?

(A) $25,000 minus the construction firm's cost and profit allocable to the "missing" foot.

(B) $25,000, because the constructive condition of complete performance by the construction firm was excused.

(C) $25,000 minus $5,000, because the construction firm substantially performed.

(D) $25,000 minus $1,000, because the construction firm substantially performed.

REMEDIES

Question 16

An inventor and owner of an innovative company that sells woodworking machinery and tools read an article about the hearing loss woodworkers commonly suffered due to the extremely loud machinery. He was struck with the "perfect" idea: a noiseless power saw, which would not only help humanity by helping to save the hearing of millions of woodworkers, but which would also be certain to yield a large profit. The inventor researched companies working to develop quieter engines and discovered a little-known manufacturer whose owner had invented an unusually quiet engine. The inventor believed it could be adapted for power saws and other machinery. His only concern was whether the "silent" engine would be powerful enough to cut through all types of wood.

After extensive negotiations, the inventor agreed to purchase 5,000 engines for $50 each, with the units to be shipped to the inventor's warehouse and his having prepaid the shipping costs. The purchase-and-sale agreement stipulated that each engine must be powerful enough to allow the saw to cut through both hard and soft woods of all types. The contract further provided that the manufacturer would deliver the engines in lots of 500 units each month, beginning on October 1, and that the inventor would pay for each lot within 48 hours of delivery.

After the first shipment of engines was delivered to the warehouse on October 1, the inventor sent the manufacturer a $25,000 check. However, after testing all 500 engines, the inventor found that not a single engine was capable of producing the power necessary to cut all types of wood. The inventor notified the manufacturer that he was hereby rejecting the engines already delivered and that he would reject all future deliveries as well, because the engines did not meet the minimum power requirements.

What amount of damages can the inventor recover and/or what remedies are available to him as to the 500 engines already delivered?

(A) Two-thirds of the $25,000 he paid for the engines.

(B) The entire $25,000 he paid for the engines, but he cannot resell them.

(C) The entire $25,000 he paid for the engines, or he can resell them.

(D) No damages.

Question 17

A whitewater rafting tour company and a state college faculty association arranged to rent all of the tour company's rafts for a faculty ride down the Rocopico River the first weekend of spring break. The contract price was set at $2,500, including a $1,000 nonrefundable deposit. The deposit was designated as "liquidated damages." The association paid the $1,000 and agreed to meet the tour company's owner and rafters at Avon on the Rocopico on March 18 at 7:30 a.m. The owner and his rafters showed up at Avon with their rafts in tow at 6:30 a.m. on the morning of March 18. By 10 a.m., however, no one from the faculty had shown up.

At 10:30 a.m., a group of students from the local elementary school showed up in Avon and became interested in a short ride when they saw the rafts were available. The tour company owner concluded that the association was not going to show up, so he arranged with the head teacher of the elementary school to take the students on a day trip for $2,000. The owner spent the rest of the day with the students on the river. The association requested a return of the deposit, but the tour company refused to return the deposit. The association has pursued a legal action to recover a refund of the $1,000 deposit.

Will the court enforce the liquidated damages clause?

(A) No, because $1,000 is an unenforceable penalty and damages are sufficient compensation for the breach.

(B) No, because the whitewater rafting tour company was able to mitigate its damages.

(C) Yes, because $1,000 was a reasonable estimate of damages in the event the association breached the contract.

(D) Yes, because the parties agreed to liquidated damages.

Question 18

A homeowner was very handy around the house. When he and his wife decided to add a wood deck and patio to their home, he made plans to construct it himself. He ordered the lumber necessary for the project from the owner and operator of a local lumber store. The lumber store required prepayment of the total amount owed prior to the homeowner's receipt and inspection of the lumber. The homeowner sent the owner of the lumber store a personal check in payment for the lumber, and several days later, the lumber was delivered to the homeowner.

Upon inspection of the lumber, however, the homeowner realized that the lumber store had sent him Grade 2 lumber instead of the Grade 1 lumber he had ordered. The homeowner returned the shipment to the lumber store and demanded a refund. The lumber store owner refused to return the homeowner's money, arguing that there was virtually no difference between the Grade 1 and Grade 2 lumber and that the Grade 2 lumber would be perfectly sufficient for the homeowner's purposes.

Is the homeowner permitted to resell the lumber?

(A) No.

(B) Yes, but only in a public sale.

(C) Yes, but only in a private sale.

(D) Yes, in a private sale, but only after notifying the lumber store owner of his intention to resell the lumber.

Question 19

A community theater received a request from a local opera company to stage a production at the theater the following January. The theater director agreed to have a local designer design the sets for the opera. They signed a written contract that promised the designer $5,000 for the sets. The director had some specific ideas and insisted on some detailed specifications for the sets. However, the theater stage was smaller than was really needed, and it would be difficult to fit everything the director wanted into the production. Under the agreement, the designer was to provide all material and labor, and would begin work on October 1. The $5,000 would be paid upon completion of the sets. The designer was going to make a profit of $1,000.

On September 15, the director called the designer and told her that it was impossible for the theater to stage the opera, and so she was going to cancel the production. Knowing that her contract was enforceable, the designer urged the director not to act hastily and to take some time to think about it. On September 17, the designer spent $1,500 on materials for the sets that she was to build according to the director's specifications. The materials were not suitable for anything other than the opera sets.

If the designer sues the director for breach for contract, what is she entitled to recover?

(A) Nothing, because she is estopped from recovering damages due to her failure to mitigate.

(B) $1,000, as expectation damages.

(C) $1,000 as expectation damages and $1,500 as reliance damages.

(D) $5,000, as expectation damages.

Question 20

A developer decided to build a major gas station and restaurant on a highway just outside of town. Studies showed that traffic would be increasing substantially along the highway during the next few years. The developer contracted with a construction company to build the facility for $3 million. Construction began in a timely manner on January 15. The County Board of Supervisors decided on April 10 to build a new highway bypass around the town, decreasing the traffic flow on the highway. On April 15, the developer ordered the construction company to cease all work, because they believed the facility was no longer going to have the traffic volume to make it economical to operate. By this time, the construction company had spent $2.25 million in construction costs. Because it was close to completion, the construction company went ahead and finished the facility, spending another $150,000. The total construction costs were $2.4 million. The construction company filed a breach of contract action against the developer.

How much will the construction company be able to recover?

(A) $2,250,000.

(B) $2,400,000.

(C) $2,850,000.

(D) $3,000,000.

Answer Grid

1 Ⓐ B C D	5 Ⓐ B C D	9 Ⓐ B C D	13 Ⓐ B C D	17 Ⓐ B C D
2 Ⓐ B C D	6 Ⓐ B C D	10 Ⓐ B C D	14 Ⓐ B C D	18 A B C Ⓓ
3 Ⓐ B C D	7 Ⓐ B C D	11 Ⓐ B C D	15 Ⓐ B C D	19 A B C Ⓓ
4 A B C Ⓓ	8 A B C Ⓓ	12 A B Ⓒ D	16 A B Ⓒ D	20 A B Ⓒ D

Criminal Law

Outline

TABLE OF CONTENTS

VI. DEFENSES

I. GENERAL PRINCIPLES

A. **Introduction and the Bases of Criminal Law (Common Law and Statutory Law)**

1. The substantive criminal law is defined by statute in most jurisdictions. To that end, some questions on the bar exam will include an excerpt from a statute.

2. Many jurisdictions follow the common law approach to criminal law when writing criminal statutes; a smaller number of jurisdictions choose instead to follow the approach of the Model Penal Code ("MPC").

3. The Multistate Bar Exam (MBE) generally tests the law "common to the states" (also referred to as "the generally prevailing view" or "the generally accepted view"). This means the **common law approach**. On some points of law, however, there is a divergence between the early common law approach and the modern trend among common law jurisdictions. This outline notes where modern statutes diverge from the common law. In all released questions available to date from the MBE, the bar examiners have either specified the approach in the question (the common law or the modern trend) or they have specified facts in the question that eliminate any possible differences in the answer to the question.

   EXAMPLE: At common law, burglary maintained the elements of the location being a dwelling and the timing being at night. The modern approach is to define burglary as including any structure and to include entries made during the day as well as at night. The question specified that the structure was a dwelling and was entered at night in order to eliminate the differences between the common law and the modern approach on this point.

4. With respect to essay questions, important distinctions relating to your jurisdiction's substantive criminal law will be covered in the state criminal law lecture.

B. **Types of Crimes**

1. **Felony**

   a. A felony is a crime punishable by death or by imprisonment for more than one year. At common law, burglary, arson, robbery, rape, larceny, murder, manslaughter, and mayhem were considered felonies.

2. **Misdemeanor**

   a. A misdemeanor is a crime punishable by imprisonment for less than one year or by a fine only. At common law, crimes not considered felonies were deemed misdemeanors.

3. ***Malum Prohibitum***

   a. *Malum prohibitum* is an act that is wrong only because it violates a statute (e.g., speeding or failing to register a firearm).

4. ***Malum In Se***

   a. *Malum in se* is an act that is inherently wrong or "evil"—an act that involves a general criminal intent or moral turpitude (e.g., murder, theft, and battery).

5. An infamous crime at common law involves fraud or dishonesty.

C. **Constitutional Issues**

1. **Void-for-Vagueness Doctrine**

    a. Under the Due Process Clause of the Fifth and Fourteenth Amendments of the United States Constitution, people must be on notice that certain conduct is forbidden. Therefore, the Supreme Court has required that criminal statutes be specific and give a person of ordinary intelligence "fair notice" of what conduct is prohibited. Furthermore, the **void-for-vagueness doctrine** requires statutes to be fair and consistent in their enforcement and not be arbitrarily or erratically enforced.

2. *Ex Post Facto*

    a. Under the Constitution, *ex post facto* laws are also prohibited. An *ex post facto* law is one that retroactively:

    (1) makes conduct criminal;

    (2) enforces a stricter punishment for the same conduct; or

    (3) alters procedural or evidentiary rules in such a way that the criminal defendant may be more easily convicted.

D. **Elements of Crimes**

1. Generally, the prosecution must prove the following elements:

    a. *actus reus* (a guilty act);

    (1) This element may be met by:

    (a) a voluntary act that causes an unlawful result;

    (b) an omission to act where the defendant is under a legal duty to act; or

    (c) vicarious liability where the defendant is responsible for the acts of another party.

    (2) Criminal liability can be imposed on a defendant for an omission to act where:

    (a) there is a legal duty to act; and

    (b) the defendant can physically perform the act.

    (3) Such a legal duty to act may arise in the following ways:

    (a) by statute (e.g., failure to file a tax return);

    (b) by contract (e.g., failure of a lifeguard, nurse, or guide on a hiking or river-rafting expedition to rescue);

    (c) based upon relationship (e.g., a parent for a child or a spouse for a spouse);

    (d) where a voluntary undertaking is begun (e.g., unreasonable abandonment of a rescue that could worsen a victim's plight is sufficient, even if done by a Good Samaritan); or

    (e) where someone creates a risk of peril to another.

    EXAMPLE: If a defendant pushes a victim into a swimming pool as a joke, but then realizes that the victim can't swim when the victim begins to drown, the defendant can be prosecuted for murder for failing to throw the victim a life preserver.

    (4)   Acts that are reflexive, convulsive, performed while unconscious, or otherwise involuntary are insufficient, as are mere bad thoughts unaccompanied by action. However, habitual acts that one is simply "unaware of" are considered conscious and voluntary (e.g., a chain smoker who lights a cigarette in a no-smoking area without realizing it can be successfully prosecuted).

b.   ***mens rea*** (a guilty mind);

    (1)   Virtually all crimes require some mental state (*mens rea*) with respect to some element of conduct (*actus reus*), and the definition of which mental state is required for which elements of conduct is often the key to successfully answering a question. In determining a defendant's criminal liability, the jury must look to the defendant's state of mind at the time of the commission of the crime. Except for a small category of strict liability crimes, a crime is committed only when a criminal act is coupled with a guilty mind; both the mental and physical elements must coexist.

    <u>**EXAMPLE:**</u> Grant took Foster's sunglasses believing they were his. No larceny has been committed since there was no intent to take someone else's glasses.

    (a)   A person acts **intentionally** when he desires that his acts cause certain consequences or knows that his acts are substantially certain to produce those consequences.

    (b)   A person acts **knowingly** when he knows the nature and/or result of his conduct. Lack of knowledge can often excuse criminal liability under the defense of mistake of fact. Traditionally, intent has been defined to include knowledge.

    (c)   A person acts **purposely** when there exists a conscious objective to engage in such conduct or to cause such a result.

    (d)   The term **willfully** encompasses the concepts of "intentionally" and "purposely," as opposed to accidentally or negligently, and has been used to imply evil purpose in crimes involving moral turpitude.

    (e)   A person acts **recklessly** with respect to a material element of an offense when he consciously disregards a substantial and unjustifiable risk that the material element exists or will result from his conduct. The risk must be of such a nature and degree that, considering the nature and purpose of the actor's conduct and the circumstances known to him, its disregard involves a gross deviation from the standard of conduct that a law-abiding person would observe in the actor's situation.

(f) **Criminal negligence** usually requires that the defendant's conduct create a high degree of risk of death or serious injury beyond the tort standard of ordinary negligence. The degree of that risk, however, has no precise, objective measure. It is more than mere ordinary negligence, but less than wanton and willful misconduct.

(2) A **specific intent** crime involves more than the objective fault required by merely doing the proscribed *actus reus*. A defendant will possess specific intent if:

(a) he wants, hopes, or wishes that his conduct will bring about a particular result, regardless of the objective likelihood of the result occurring (unless the result is inherently impossible); or

EXAMPLE: Joe wants to kill his cousin Mike, so at noon he tosses a brick off the 50-story building where Mike works, knowing that Mike is usually walking somewhere for lunch at that time. Despite the long odds, the brick actually hits Mike and kills him. Joe has the requisite specific intent to be charged with Mike's murder.

(b) he expects (i.e., is substantially certain) that his purposeful act will have that particular result, even though he does not necessarily want a particular result.

(3) Specific intent crimes include first-degree murder; theft crimes such as larceny, robbery, extortion, embezzlement, false pretenses, and receiving stolen property; burglary (but not arson, which is a "malice" crime); inchoate crimes (solicitation, conspiracy, and attempt); and assault.

(a) The typical criminal defenses apply to specific intent crimes.

(b) Voluntary intoxication and unreasonable mistake may negate requisite specific intent elements.

(4) A **general intent** crime merely requires commission of an unlawful act (e.g., nonconsensual intercourse) without a specific *mens rea*. A general bad state of mind will suffice where such a criminal act is committed voluntarily and purposely.

(a) Negligence or recklessness is a sufficient mental state for general intent crimes. While mere ordinary negligence (defined, as in tort, as the failure to use due care) does not amount to criminal negligence, negligence that causes a greater risk of harm than ordinary negligence or ordinary negligence where a defendant is consciously aware of the risk will amount to criminal negligence. Criminal negligence may also be called gross or culpable negligence.

(b) General intent crimes include rape, battery, kidnapping, false imprisonment, involuntary manslaughter, and depraved-heart murder.

> **EXAM TIP** If, on the exam, you encounter a criminal activity that does not appear by its classification (see classification chart below) to involve specific intent, the malice standard, or strict liability, and the question does not indicate or supply a mental state requirement, you should assume that for criminal culpability, general intent would be required. General intent is the "catch-all."

(5) The requisite intent for **malice** is met when a defendant acts intentionally or with reckless disregard of an obvious or known risk that the particular harmful result will occur.

    (a) Malice crimes are common law murder and arson.

(6) Under **strict liability**, culpability is imposed on a defendant merely for doing the act that is prohibited by statute. In other words, no particular mental state is required for at least some element of a strict liability crime.

EXAMPLE: State A has a statute that makes having sex with a minor under the age of 17 a strict liability crime. Joe meets Lolita in a bar and assumes that she is 21 because 21 is the drinking age in State A. Lolita also tells Joe that she is 21, and nothing about her appearance suggests she may be lying. She also presents to Joe a completely convincing piece of false identification that states a birth date that would make her 21. However, in reality, Lolita is only 15. If Joe has sex with her, he is guilty of violating the State A statute.

    (a) Strict liability crimes fall under the categories of:

        1) regulatory offenses (e.g., traffic violations, vehicle offenses, or administrative statutes);

        2) public welfare offenses (e.g., regulation of firearms, food, and drugs); and

        3) morality crimes (e.g., statutory rape, and bigamy).

    (b) The **transferred intent doctrine** preserves liability where a defendant intends criminal conduct against one party but instead harms another party, so that his actions bring about an unintended, yet still criminal, result.

CLASSIFICATION OF CRIMES			
Specific Intent Crimes	**General Intent Crimes**	**Malicious Crimes**	**Strict Liability Crimes**
• Attempt • Solicitation • Conspiracy • Larceny • Larceny by Trick • False Pretenses • Embezzlement • Forgery • Burglary • Assault • Robbery • Intent-to-Kill Murder • Voluntary Manslaughter	• Battery • Rape • Kidnapping • False Imprisonment • Involuntary Manslaughter • Depraved-Heart Murder	• Arson • Common Law Murder	• Regulatory offenses • Public welfare offenses • Morality crimes (such as statutory rape, or bigamy) • Selling liquor to minors

c. **concurrence in time** between the act and the requisite mental state; and

   (1)   It is not only necessary that the defendant's criminal intent occur at the time he commits the criminal act, but the mental state should also actuate, or put into action, the act or omission.

        EXAMPLE: In burglary, the "intent to commit a felony therein" must exist at the time of the breaking and entering.

d. some (but not most) crimes require the **occurrence of a result** for the crime to be complete (e.g., homicide crimes require that the victim die).

   (1)   For such crimes, causation between the defendant's act and the required result must be evident.

   (2)   The defendant's conduct must be both the actual and the proximate cause of the specified criminal result.

      (a)   **Actual cause** (also called cause-in-fact) may be satisfied by either of two tests:

         1)   if the criminal result would not have occurred absent the defendant's act, then the defendant's act is the actual cause of the criminal result; and

            a)   In other words, were it not for, or "but for" the defendant's actions, the criminal result would not have occurred.

         2)   when there are multiple causes or other parties responsible for the criminal result, courts will still find a defendant responsible if the defendant's act was a substantial factor causing the criminal result.

EXAMPLE: Defendant 1 stabs Victim in the heart with a knife. Simultaneous with this stabbing, Defendant 2 shoots Victim in the head. Medical testimony conclusively establishes that either the knife or bullet wound alone was sufficient cause to instantly kill Victim. Defendant 1's act can be considered the actual cause of Victim's death.

(b) To find **proximate cause**, the resultant harm must be within the risk created by the defendant's conduct in crimes involving negligence or recklessness, or sufficiently similar to that intended in crimes requiring intent, so as not to hold the defendant liable for extraordinary results (such as acts of nature or grossly negligent or intentional bad acts of third parties, including intentional medical mistreatment).

1) The tort maxim "you take the plaintiff as you find him" applies to crime victims as well. That is, if the harm results from a special sensitivity (such as hemophilia or another preexisting medical condition), the defendant's act is a proximate cause of the harm regardless of whether the defendant could have foreseen the unique medical condition.

(3) When the defendant's actions alone cause the harm, the defendant's act is the **direct cause**. It is very likely that the defendant will be held legally responsible.

(4) In **indirect cause** situations, the other force that combines with the defendant's act to bring about the harm is called an **intervening cause**.

(a) To relieve the defendant of liability and thus, in effect, break the chain of proximate cause, the other force must be a **superseding intervening cause**.

(5) The rules determining when an intervening cause is superseding (and thereby one that breaks the chain of causation) differ according to whether the intervening force is dependent on or independent of the defendant's act. An intervening force that is a result of or response to the defendant's act is a dependent intervening cause. An independent intervening cause is one that would have occurred regardless of the defendant's act.

(a) A **dependent intervening cause** will supersede the defendant's act only when it is a totally abnormal response to the defendant's act.

EXAMPLE: Defendant intentionally runs over Victim with Defendant's automobile, causing Victim to suffer serious (but not life-threatening) injuries. Victim is rushed to a hospital and given medical treatment. If the attending physician negligently treats Victim, resulting in Victim's death, and the negligent treatment is not considered abnormal, Defendant can be found to have proximately caused Victim's death.

(b) An **independent intervening cause** will normally supersede the defendant's act, except when the independent intervening force was foreseeable

EXAMPLE: Defendant, having planned to kill his wife, returns home late on a stormy night. Defendant drives into the driveway and notes that the entire house is surrounded by snow drifts from the storm. Defendant enters the home and pulls a gun on his wife. The wife struggles and manages to break free and get outside. She is dressed only in a nightgown and decides to hide from her husband and sleep in the doghouse rather than seek help in the bitter cold. She dies of exposure during the evening. Defendant's act might be sufficient to impose him to criminal liability due to the foreseeability of the wife's death from exposure.

II. CRIMES AGAINST THE PERSON

A. **Homicide**

1. A **homicide** results when there is a killing of a human being caused by another human being (i.e., the defendant). A more complete way of stating the rule is that a criminal homicide results from some action or actions of the defendant that cause the death of another human being, with criminal intent, and without legal excuse or justification.

2. The difference between the varying homicide crimes typically depends on the mental state the defendant had with respect to the conduct causing the death.

3. **Murder**

   a. At common law, **murder** is defined as the unlawful killing of a human being with malice aforethought.

   b. The *actus reus* may be a voluntary act, an involuntary act arising from a voluntary act (such as a person who has frequent seizures driving a car), or an omission to act where there is a legal duty to act.

   c. The act must actually and proximately cause the death of another living person. The common law requirement for a living person was one "born alive" (though a state may extend criminal liability to include a fetus after the first trimester).

   d. The death must be caused by someone other than the victim.

      (1) Suicide is not homicide because the death must be caused by another.

      (2) To persuade or aid another to commit suicide is a sufficient basis for murder in some jurisdictions.

   e. The defendant's conduct must be both the actual cause and a legal cause of the victim's death.

      (1) For common law murder, the "but-for" test applies. In other words, the fact finder must determine that the victim's death would not have occurred but for the defendant's actions. Even if the defendant's actions alone would be insufficient to cause the victim's death, but instead contributed to the death, a court may still find actual causation.

      (2) In situations when a victim is already dying, if the defendant's actions bring about the victim's death more quickly than if the defendant had not acted, the defendant's actions would be an actual cause of the killing.

      EXAMPLE: Disconnecting life support to a dying patient is an actual cause of the patient's death if she dies more quickly as a result.

      (3) Where the victim's death was a "natural and probable" consequence of the defendant's conduct, the defendant may be guilty of murder, even where he did not foresee the exact chain of events that resulted in the victim's death.

(4) Note that where an intervening act occurs that is outside the universe of foreseeable events caused by the defendant's acts, such an intervening act will sever the chain of causation, and the defendant will be acquitted of murder. Additionally, remember that a dead person cannot be killed. Thus, if an intervening cause kills the victim before the defendant can complete his act, he will be acquitted.

(5) At common law, if the victim died more than one year and one day after the defendant's act, the courts would rule that the defendant's act was not the proximate cause of the killing. Most states have either eliminated this rule or have extended the period within which the defendant is held legally responsible.

(6) Defendants who do not personally commit any acts sufficient to amount to actual cause may nonetheless be legally responsible for a killing in the following circumstances:

   (a) a defendant who is an accomplice to the killer may be held liable for a homicide even though only the killer actually acted to cause the victim's death;

   (b) where the reasonably foreseeable result of a conspiracy is a homicide, and that homicide was committed in furtherance of the conspiracy, then all members of the conspiracy can be held liable for the homicide regardless of which of the conspirators actually caused the killing;

   (c) where both a third party and the defendant together cause a victim's death, the causation question varies depending on whether the defendant's act was a direct or indirect cause; and

   1) When a victim would not have died "but for" the actions of both the defendant and a third party, both will be considered the direct causes of the death. The defendant's legal responsibility is superseded only by a dependent intervening act that is totally abnormal or an independent intervening act that is unforeseeable.

      EXAMPLE: Defendant shoots Victim in the shoulder, causing a serious but not life-threatening injury. Shortly thereafter, Third Party stabs Victim repeatedly in both feet, causing numerous bleeding wounds. Hours later, Victim dies from excessive blood loss. Both the shoulder and feet wounds caused the bleeding. Defendant and Third Party caused Victim's death.

   (d) where a defendant causes the death of another, even if not at his own hands, during the commission of or in an attempt to commit a felony (i.e., felony murder)

(7) As in tort situations of nonfeasance, people who fail to prevent injury or death are generally not criminally liable for the victim's condition unless they have a duty to act.

(8) Where a victim has an unusual condition that contributes to his death, a defendant can still be found guilty of murder. The defendant is said to "take the victim as he finds him."

f. At common law, the *mens rea* for murder was malice.

g. There are four distinct categories of mental states with respect to common law murder, all of which are sufficient to meet the malice standard required at common law. If any of the following mental states exist, it supports a murder conviction at common law:

(1) **intent to kill**;

    (a) Conduct where the defendant consciously desires to kill another person or makes the resulting death inevitable (absent justification, excuse, or mitigation to voluntary manslaughter) constitutes an intent to kill.

    (b) The defendant's own statements may provide proof of intent to kill.

    (c) Under the **deadly weapons doctrine**, an inference of intent to kill is raised through the intentional use of any instrument which, judging from its manner of use, is calculated to produce death or serious bodily injury.

    EXAMPLE: A defendant's intent to kill can be inferred from deliberately swinging a baseball bat at the victim's head.

    (d) Intent-to-kill murder is a specific intent crime.

(2) **intent to cause serious bodily harm**;

    (a) **Serious bodily injury**, also called "great bodily injury" or "grievous bodily injury," means significant but nonfatal injury. Intent-to-inflict-serious-bodily-injury malice, like intent-to-kill malice, can arise from a conscious desire or substantial certainty that the defendant's actions will result in the victim's injury.

    (b) Like intent-to-kill malice, intent to inflict serious bodily injury must be proved by examination of all the surrounding circumstances, including the words and behavior of the defendant. Similarly, the intentional use of any deadly weapon in a way that is likely to cause serious injury provides evidence of intent to inflict serious bodily injury.

    EXAMPLE: Defendant drives his car over Victim's legs, intending to break them. However, Victim ends up dying as a result of the injuries suffered. Defendant has the necessary *mens rea* for murder.

(3) **depraved-heart murder**; and

    (a) **Depraved-heart murder**, sometimes referred to as extreme recklessness murder, is an unintentional killing resulting from conduct involving a wanton indifference to human life and a conscious disregard of an unreasonable risk of death or serious bodily injury.

(b) A defendant may knowingly create a very high risk of death or serious bodily injury for a logical and socially reasonable purpose, in which case the conduct would not be considered depraved-heart murder.

EXAMPLE: Defendant thought it would be amusing to drive on the wrong side of the street, "like they do in England." He did so, at high speed, through a residential neighborhood and veered into children crossing at a crosswalk (who were looking the other way). Defendant likely will be found to have possessed the *mens rea* necessary for depraved-heart murder.

(4) **felony murder**.

(a) **Felony murder** is a killing proximately caused during the commission or attempted commission of a serious or inherently dangerous felony.

(b) Generally, it includes both intentional and accidental killings. The mental state required is an intent to commit the underlying felony, such as burglary, arson, robbery, rape, or kidnapping.

(c) The defendant must be guilty of the underlying felony. Any defenses to the felony will negate the felony murder.

(d) Several limitations have been placed on the scope of the felony-murder rule.

1) A majority of states have limited the felony-murder rule by requiring that the underlying felony be **collateral**. That is, the underlying felony must be independent of the homicide so that every felonious attack upon a victim (i.e., felonious assault) which is ultimately fatal does not become escalated to murder by the rule.

2) The felony must be an **inherently dangerous** one (i.e., burglary, arson, robbery, rape, or kidnapping).

3) The majority of states include both felonies which are:

a) dangerous by definition ("inherently" dangerous); and

b) felonies that are dangerous by the manner of their commission (in other words, any felony that is committed in a dangerous manner).

4) A minority of states still find the felony-murder rule applicable only in inherently dangerous felony situations.

EXAMPLE: Defendant pretended to be a doctor with a cancer cure and induced Victim to pay $5,000 for a medically worthless ointment that Defendant claimed would heal her. If Victim had received competent medical treatment, the cancer would have been cured. If Victim dies of cancer, Defendant can be charged with felony murder in a majority jurisdiction. A minority of states would not apply the felony-murder rule, though, as the act of selling a worthless ointment was not inherently dangerous.

5) The resulting death must be a **foreseeable outgrowth** of the defendant's actions. Note that most courts have generally been very liberal in applying the foreseeability requirement. Therefore, most deaths are considered foreseeable for purposes of felony murder.

6) The resulting death must occur during the commission or perpetration of the felony.

a) For purposes of felony murder, the felony starts when the defendant could be convicted of attempting the underlying felony. There is no requirement that the felony must be completed.

b) The felony is deemed to have terminated when the felon has reached a place of temporary safety. If the killing occurs after this point, the defendant can no longer be found guilty of felony murder.

> **NOTE** If a killing occurs while the defendant is fleeing from the scene of the felony, he may still be guilty of felony murder. The felony, and thus the possibility of committing a felony murder, does not terminate until the felon reaches a place of temporary safety.

(e) **Felony Murder Based on Vicarious Liability**

1) At common law, all felons were liable for any homicide that occurred during the perpetration of the felony. The common law did not make exceptions for homicides committed by non-felons (i.e., victims, bystanders, police officers, etc.).

2) Under the majority (**agency theory**) rule, there is no felony-murder liability when a non-felon causes the death. The agency theory posits that felony murder extends only when the killing is committed by one of the agents of the underlying felony.

3) Under the minority rule, felony-murder charges can be based on killings by non-felons, such as killings by victims of the crime, bystanders, and police officers.

a) Among jurisdictions that follow the minority rule, some extend an exception (the **Redline limitation**). Under this limitation, a co-felon is not guilty of felony murder where the killing constitutes a justifiable or excusable homicide. Such would be the case where, for example, the police or a victim shoots one of the co-felons, but not where the killing is done by one of the felons.

EXAMPLE: A bank robber would not be charged with felony murder under this limitation if his accomplice is justifiably killed by the police.

    b) Other minority rule jurisdictions follow common law felony murder principles.

  4) A large minority of jurisdictions allow an affirmative defense for nonviolent co-felons who were unarmed, unaware that violence would occur, and did not encourage the violence.

h. **Murder by Degrees**

  (1) While degrees of murder were not recognized at common law, most jurisdictions distinguish between different degrees of murder based on criteria identified in the given state's murder statute.

  (2) **First-Degree Murder**

    (a) **First-degree murder** includes intent-to-kill murder committed with premeditation and deliberation, felony murder, and, in some jurisdictions, murder accomplished by lying in wait, poison, terrorism, or torture. Some jurisdictions require little or nothing more than an intent to kill in order to find premeditation and deliberation, but most jurisdictions require more. Most jurisdictions require a reasonable period of time for premeditation and some evidence of reflection in order to distinguish first-degree murders from "spur-of-the-moment killings."

    EXAMPLE: Jerry walked into the ice cream shop and told Ben he'd just "scored" with Ben's new girlfriend. Ben, outraged, decided in that split second to beat Jerry to death and began pounding on Jerry's head with an ice cream scoop. Jerry dies as a result of the beating. Ben may have committed first-degree murder in a minority jurisdiction, but not in a majority jurisdiction.

    (b) If the defendant was voluntarily intoxicated—but still sober enough to form the intent to kill—he may be able to avoid liability for first-degree murder by proof that the intoxication precluded him from acting with premeditation or deliberation.

  (3) **Second-Degree Murder**

    (a) **Second-degree murder** is any murder that does not meet the requisite elements of first-degree murder. Examples include: a) where the defendant's malice is intent to inflict serious bodily injury; b) where the defendant acted with wanton and willful misconduct; or c) felony murder, where the underlying felony is not specifically listed in an applicable first-degree murder statute.

4. **Voluntary Manslaughter**

a. **Voluntary manslaughter** is an intentional killing mitigated by adequate provocation or other circumstances negating malice aforethought. Voluntary manslaughter is commonly called a **heat-of-passion killing**.

b. **Adequate provocation**, measured objectively, must be such that a reasonable person would lose self-control.

   (1) A causal connection must exist between the legally adequate grounds for provocation and the killing.

   (2) The time period between the heat-of-passion and the fatal act must not be long enough that a reasonable person would have cooled off.

   (3) Courts will commonly find that a defendant was adequately provoked when he killed after he was the victim of a serious battery or a threat of a deadly force or where he found his spouse engaged in sexual conduct with another person.

   (4) Where a defendant kills after an exchange of "mere words," courts generally will not find adequate provocation.

   (5) Courts do not find mitigating circumstances such that a defendant's criminal liability will be reduced from murder to voluntary manslaughter) where a defendant actually did cool off (even if a reasonable person would not have cooled off) or where a defendant, for any other reason, killed he was, subjectively, not in the heat of passion.

c. **Other Mitigating Circumstances**

   (1) Imperfect self-defense may mitigate murder to voluntary manslaughter where a defendant was either at fault in starting an altercation or unreasonably, but honestly, believed that harm was imminent or deadly force was necessary. Such mistaken justification has been applied to self-defense, defense of others, crime prevention, coercion, and necessity.

   (2) A minority of states allow diminished mental capacity short of insanity to reduce murder to manslaughter.

5. **Involuntary Manslaughter**

a. **Involuntary manslaughter** is an unintentional killing resulting without malice aforethought caused either by recklessness, criminal negligence, or during the commission or attempted commission of an unlawful act.

b. Examples of activities that may be deemed criminal negligence are the mishandling of loaded weapons or dangerous operation of a motor vehicle, including driving while intoxicated.

   (1) Gross negligence or criminally negligent conduct is required, but the majority of jurisdictions do not require that the defendant be consciously aware of the risk created.

c. An unintentional killing that occurs during the commission or attempted commission of a misdemeanor that is *malum in se*, or of a felony that is not of the inherently dangerous type required for felony murder, is classified as involuntary manslaughter under the so-called **misdemeanor-manslaughter rule**.

   (1) Whereas limitations do exist regarding the nature of the unlawful act and the causation between the act and the killing, the *malum in se* misdemeanor need not be independent of the cause of death, unlike felony murder.

    d. Death resulting from a *malum prohibitum* crime can only be sufficient for involuntary manslaughter when the killing is either a foreseeable consequence of the unlawful conduct or amounts to criminal negligence.

    e. Analogous in many respects to intent-to-kill or intent-to-cause-serious-bodily-injury murders, where the defendant intends to injure the victim to some "lesser" degree but this unexpectedly causes the death of the victim, an involuntary manslaughter results. Since such action is either a battery or an assault—both *malum in se*—application of the misdemeanor-manslaughter rule renders any resulting homicide an involuntary manslaughter. Common examples include inflicting a superficial cut upon a hemophiliac who dies from loss of blood or a simple battery that results in death because the victim had an "egg-shell" skull.

B. Assault and Battery

    1. Assault and battery were common law misdemeanors. Note that, at common law, because assault and battery were considered only misdemeanors, they could not be used as underlying felonies for purposes of felony murder. However, modern statutes have created aggravated forms of assault and battery, which are felonies.

    2. **Battery**

        a. **Criminal battery** is the intentional, reckless, or criminally negligent unlawful application of force to the person of the victim.

        b. Criminal battery is a general intent crime; a defendant may be guilty of battery where he acts:

            (1) recklessly;

            (2) negligently; or

            (3) with knowledge that his act (or omission) will result in criminal liability.

        c. The defendant's act of applying force may be direct or indirect.

            (1) Where the defendant puts a force in motion, the force need not be applied directly by the defendant.

                EXAMPLE: If John tells his attack bull terrier to charge at a visitor, John may be guilty of battery even though he did not personally touch the visitor.

                EXAMPLE: John, in a fit of rage, fires a gun at his ex-wife's new house. The bullet smashes the window and a shard of glass hits the ex-wife's new boyfriend in the eye. Regardless of whether John intended to shoot someone, this act would likely rise at least to the level of criminal negligence (creating a high degree of risk of death or serious injury) or even recklessness (conscious disregard of a substantial and unjustifiable risk). John would be guilty of battery.

        d. In most jurisdictions, certain circumstances cause a simple battery to be elevated to an aggravated battery. Most commonly, these circumstances include:

(1) the defendant causing the victim serious bodily injury;

(2) the defendant using a deadly weapon to commit the battery; or

(3) the defendant battering a woman, child, or law enforcement officer.

e. **Defenses**

(1) Consent may be a valid defense where it is not coerced or obtained by fraud, but it is no defense to a breach of the peace.

(2) Self-defense and defense of others are valid defenses to a battery charge.

(3) Where the defendant commits an offensive touching to prevent someone from committing a crime, this will be a defense to battery.

3. **Assault**

a. Generally, a defendant may commit **criminal assault** by:

(1) attempting to commit battery; or

(a) The majority of states define assault as an attempted battery. This type of assault requires an intent to commit a battery (i.e., an intent to cause physical injury to the victim). Thus, in those jurisdictions where an assault is limited to an attempted battery, an intent merely to frighten, though accompanied by some fear-producing act like pointing an unloaded gun at the victim, will not suffice. Additionally, since an intent to injure is required for an attempted battery, recklessness or negligence that comes close to causing injury (such as driving a car recklessly but just missing a victim) will not suffice for an assault.

(b) The fact that the victim was not aware of the attempted battery is no defense to this type of assault.

(c) Most states do not permit a defendant to avoid liability for "attempt" assault simply because the defendant lacked the present ability to consummate the battery (e.g., the defendant, with the intent to shoot the victim, pulls the trigger, but unbeknownst to the defendant, there are no bullets in the weapon). However, in the minority of states, there is an additional requirement imposed by statute or case law that the defendant have the present ability to commit the battery.

(2) intentionally causing the victim to fear an immediate battery.

(a) In this type of assault, the defendant must act with threatening conduct (mere words are insufficient) intended to cause reasonable apprehension of imminent harm to the victim. A conditional threat is generally insufficient unless accompanied by an overt act to accomplish the threat.

EXAMPLE: Defendant points a gun at Victim and says, "If you don't get over here right now, I am going to shoot you." Defendant has committed an assault.

(b) A defendant who is guilty of a "fear of battery" assault must intend to either cause the actionable apprehension or cause the victim to suffer bodily harm.

(c) **Reasonable Apprehension**

1) When a reasonable person would not expect imminent bodily harm, there is no criminal assault.

   EXAMPLE: Words alone are generally held insufficient to constitute an "apprehension" assault.

2) The element of **apprehension** in this type of assault connotes "expectation" more than "fear" (though the term "fear" is employed frequently in assault crime statutes). The victim does not have to actually be afraid but rather to simply (and reasonably) anticipate or expect that the defendant's act(s) will result in immediate bodily harm. Note that in this type of assault (unlike attempted battery assault), the fear or apprehension piece is a key element, so no assault has been committed where the victim is unaware of the threat of harm.

(d) The threat must be to commit a present battery; a promise of future action is generally not an assault.

(e) Any threatened contact, including one that is offensive or insulting, is sufficient to constitute an "apprehension" assault. There need be no actual pain or injury threatened.

(f) If the feared battery is accomplished, the assault and battery merge and the defendant is found guilty only of the battery.

b. A simple assault may rise to the level of an aggravated assault under certain circumstances. Most commonly, the circumstances include:

(1) where the defendant commits an assault with a dangerous weapon; or

(2) where the defendant acts with the intent to seriously injure, rape, or murder the victim.

C. Mayhem

1. The felony of **mayhem** at common law required an intent to maim or do bodily injury, accompanied by an act that either:

a. dismembered the victim; or

b. disabled his use of some bodily part that was useful in fighting.

2. In modern law, statutes have expanded the scope of mayhem to include permanent disfigurement.

EXAMPLE: In a California case, a middle school boy was convicted of mayhem when he spat a spitball at a fellow student, hitting the other child in the eye and disfiguring him.

3. Some states have abolished mayhem and treat it as a form of aggravated battery.

D. False Imprisonment

1. **False imprisonment** is the intentional, unlawful confinement of one person by another.

    a. The confinement must be intentional and must be against the law. If the defendant is privileged to confine the victim, such as a police officer or a private citizen making a valid citizen's arrest, no false imprisonment is committed.

    b. The victim must be fully confined. In other words, blocking one exit but leaving another open does not amount to false imprisonment.

    c. False imprisonment is not limited to one method of restraining the victim. For example, it may be accomplished by erecting physical barriers, applying force or threatening to apply immediate physical force, or invalidly asserting authority.

    d. Victims are not required to try to resist or attempt escape where the defendant has the apparent ability to effectuate threats. Victims are not "confined" if they are aware of a reasonable means of escape, but are not required to affirmatively search for potential escape routes.

    EXAMPLE: After discovering Diane cheating on him with another man, Jack left Diane in the bedroom and slammed the door, yelling, "Stay there until you're sorry. If you beg, I may let you out for breakfast." Though Jack intended to lock the bedroom door, he was so upset that he accidentally released the lock before slamming the door. Diane believed she was locked in and never checked the door herself. Jack may be guilty of false imprisonment.

E. Kidnapping

1. At common law, **kidnapping** consists of an unlawful restraint of a person's liberty by force or show of force so as to send the victim into another country.

2. Under modern law, it suffices that the victim be taken to another location or concealed.

3. A number of states define certain types of kidnapping as being of the aggravated type, and thus deserving higher punishment (e.g., where the kidnapper restrains a small child, is masked, holds the victim for ransom, or kidnaps for the purpose of committing a robbery or a sexual offense).

F. Rape

1. At common law, **rape** was the act of unlawful sexual intercourse by a male person with a female person without her consent. While penetration was required, emission was not.

    a. At common law, a man could not rape his wife. This is no longer the law in any state.

2. Intercourse accomplished by mere threats, rather than force, may also constitute rape.

3. In addition, if the victim is incapable of consenting, the intercourse is rape. Inability to consent may be caused by the effect of drugs or intoxicating substances or by unconsciousness.

   a. The modern trend is to require actual consent of the victim. If there is no consent, the sexual act is unlawful.

   b. Most courts do not recognize a mistake as to whether the victim consented as a defense, even a reasonable mistake.

   c. Consent is determined objectively from the observable circumstances. A victim's subjective lack of consent will not suffice if the objective circumstances suggest that consent existed.

   d. Under the traditional approach, force was required for rape to occur, and a victim had to resist to establish lack of consent. Under the modern approach, force is not always required, and verbal resistance (or in some jurisdictions the simple absence of affirmative consent) is sufficient for rape to occur.

4. Rape generally refers to penetration of the vagina of the female victim by the penis of the male perpetrator. The slightest penetration is sufficient to constitute the crime. Other nonconsensual sexual contact is generally covered under a separate crime of sexual assault, sexual contact, or sexual battery.

5. Where a female is under the statutorily prescribed age of consent (usually 16), an act of intercourse constitutes rape despite her apparent consent. A defendant's mistake as to the age of the victim is generally no defense to statutory rape. Where the parties are validly married, a husband cannot be convicted of "statutory" rape.

   a. A perpetrator can be guilty of both statutory and forcible rape. However, in most jurisdictions, he would be sentenced to the more serious crime of forcible rape because the less serious crime of statutory rape would merge.

6. At common law, males under 14 were conclusively presumed incapable of rape. Many modern jurisdictions maintain the presumption but make it rebuttable.

G. Other Crimes against the Person

1. **Bigamy** is the crime of marriage by one individual to more than one other person.

2. **Incest** is the crime of sexual relations between individuals who are closely related to one another. The degree of relationship required varies by state.

III. CRIMES AGAINST PROPERTY

A. **Theft Crimes**

1. Theft crimes are crimes that involve some taking of property from the victim by the defendant. The key to analyzing theft crimes and to distinguishing among them often depends on whether the defendant acquired custody, possession, or title to the property—larceny requires that the defendant obtain possession unlawfully, false pretenses that the defendant obtain title falsely, and embezzlement requires that the defendant convert (misuse) property that has already been entrusted to him.

B. **Larceny**

1. At common law, larceny is defined as:

    a. the taking;

        (1) The **taking** requires the assertion of dominion and control over the property by a defendant who does not have lawful possession, generally through trespass (i.e., without consent). When the taking is accomplished by trickery (i.e., where the victim consents to the defendant taking possession, but such consent is induced by misrepresentation), the crime is larceny by trick.

    b. and carrying away;

        (1) The carrying away (**asportation**) is complete upon even the slightest movement (e.g., six inches will suffice).

    c. of the tangible personal property;

        (1) Common law larceny was limited to tangible personal property.

        (2) Modern statutes have expanded the kinds of property to include theft of services and other intangibles (such as gas and electrical power and written instruments that represent property rights).

        (3) Abandoned property cannot be the subject of larceny, although lost or mislaid property can.

            (a) In order to be guilty of larceny for lost or mislaid property, there are two requirements. The finder:

                1) must intend to permanently deprive the owner of it; and

                2) must either know who the owner is or have reason to believe (from earmarkings on the property or from the circumstances of the finding) that he can find out the owner's identity.

    d. of another;

        (1) Because the property must be "of another," a good-faith claim of right is a valid defense. Larceny is a crime of possession, as opposed to ownership. Therefore, under certain circumstances, an owner can be guilty of larceny of his own property, such as when another is in lawful possession of the owner's property.

      (a) Generally, employees are said to have custody over their employer's property; however, the employee has possession—and thus could commit embezzlement—if:

          1) a third party gives property directly to an employee for the benefit of its employer; or

          2) the employee is in a high-level position (e.g., an office manager, bank president, or corporate official).

      (b) A bailee generally has possession.

          1) When a bailee opens closed containers and then misappropriates property, under the "breaking bulk" doctrine, constructive possession is said to exist in the bailor, and the bailee, thus having only custody of the property, is guilty of larceny.

e.   with the intent to permanently deprive the owner thereof.

    (1) Larceny, a specific intent crime, requires that the intent to permanently deprive the owner accompany the taking. Note that the intent to keep, destroy, or hold property for ransom will suffice to prove this element.

      (a) Where a defendant recklessly exposes property to loss or deals with property in a manner involving a substantial risk of loss, the intent to permanently deprive is satisfied.

    (2) If, at the time of taking, the defendant intends to return the property to the victim unconditionally and within a reasonable time, there is no intent to permanently deprive. The defendant must have the ability to return the property, even if something unanticipated stops the actual return of the property.

      (a) Intent is not conclusively established by proof that a defendant actually returned the property to the victim. If the taking occurred with the requisite intent to permanently deprive, a defendant will not be relieved of liability for larceny because the defendant later returns the property or if the victim later forgives the defendant.

    (3) Under the **doctrine of continuing trespass**, a person who takes another's property without authorization and intending only to use it temporarily before restoring it unconditionally to its owner may nevertheless be guilty of larceny if he later changes his mind and decides not to return the property after all.

      (a) As a general rule, the initial taking must be "wrongful"—i.e., without the owner's authorization. If the initial taking was wrongful, the trespass is said to continue until the time the intent to steal is formed.

    (4) The intent element will be satisfied where a defendant intends, when taking the property, to recklessly use it temporarily and then abandon it, hoping someone will return it to the victim, even if the property somehow does return to the victim.

(5) Defendants who pawn property may negate the intent to permanently deprive element by proof that, at the time of taking, they intended to redeem the property and return it to the victim.

(6) When the defendant takes property with the intent to later pay for it or later replace it, such intent may negate the intent to permanently deprive element if, for example, the property is easily replaceable (i.e., not unique).

EXAMPLE: Bill broke into Steve's home and took a computer. Bill took the computer and dumped it in a nearby alley, smashing it to pieces. Bill is guilty of larceny.

EXAMPLE: Same case, but Bill left the computer in his yard where it got rusted and dirty. One year later, Bill, feeling remorse, returned the computer to Steve. Bill will be guilty of larceny.

(7) Where a defendant, at the time of the taking, has a good-faith belief that he is entitled to possession, there is no intent to permanently deprive, even if that belief is both incorrect and unreasonable.

EXAMPLE: Dana accidentally takes someone else's umbrella upon leaving a restaurant. She is not guilty of larceny if she honestly (even if unreasonably) believed that it was not the property of another.

2. The taking and carrying away (asportation) must concur in time with the intent to permanently deprive (*animus furandi*).

C. Embezzlement

1. **Embezzlement** is a statutory crime defined as:

a. the fraudulent conversion or misappropriation;

(1) **Conversion** is some action toward property (such as selling, consuming, pledging, donating, discarding, heavily damaging, or claiming title to it), which seriously interferes with the rights of the owner. Slight movement or limited use, for instance, would not suffice, but use that deprives the owner of a significant portion of the usefulness of the object would be sufficient. Conversion is not fraudulent if the defendant honestly believed he had a right to so use the property.

(2) No direct personal gain need result to the defendant.

(3) The specific fraudulent intent required may be negated by a claim of right or by an intent to restore the exact property.

(4) A defendant who converts property but intends to later substitute it for equivalent property is guilty of embezzlement.

b. of the property of another;

(1) Embezzlement deals with tangible personal property, not services, although some modern statutes include real estate.

c. by one who is already in lawful possession.

2. In contrast to larceny, embezzlement involves misappropriation by a defendant who has lawful possession (as opposed to custody). So defined, embezzlement could not overlap with larceny.

3. Many embezzlement statutes require that the property be "entrusted" to the defendant. Such statutes have been construed as not applicable to defendants who come into lawful possession of property by finding it or by mistaken delivery (i.e., the property was not "entrusted" to the defendant because it was never intended that he be given possession). Fraudulent conversion by a co-owner of property is not embezzlement.

D. **Robbery**

1. **Robbery** was a common law felony consisting of all the elements of larceny, plus two additional elements:

   a. the taking must be from the person or presence of the victim (meaning an area within his control); and

   b. the taking must be accomplished either:

      (1) by force or violence; or

      (2) by intimidation or the threat of violence.

         (a) If the robbery is based on the threat of violence, the threat must place the victim in actual fear at the time of the taking.

EXAM TIP If the victim is placed in fear, though baseless, there may still be a robbery. In other words, fear based on lies qualifies as threats for constituting robbery.

         (b) The use of force must be contemporaneous with the taking (in other words, all part of one occurrence).

         (c) This element will be satisfied by slight force, but must be something more than what is required to just move the property.

2. If any of the elements of larceny are not met, a robbery did not occur.

3. Larceny, assault, and battery are all lesser-included offenses of robbery (which means that all of the elements of the lesser offense are included within the greater offense).

E. **Obtaining Property by False Pretenses**

1. The statutory crime of **obtaining property by false pretenses** consists of:

   a. a false representation of a present or past material fact by the defendant;

      (1) The representation must relate to a material fact, not opinion; "puffing" is insufficient.

   b. that causes the victim to pass title to his property;

      (1) The victim's reliance upon the representation must cause him to pass title. However, it does not need to be the only reason that the victim passes title.

      (2) The distinguishing characteristic of **false pretenses** is that title passes to the defendant even though it is voidable due to the defendant's fraud.

       (a) Where money is delivered to the defendant in a sale or trade situation by the person defrauded, title generally passes and the crime is false pretenses.

       (b) When a victim pledges money for security, bails money for safekeeping, or gives money to be used only for a specific purpose, and the victim takes such action as a result of the defendant's misrepresentations, the defendant acquires only possession and, thus, is guilty of **larceny by trick**.

          1) If, however, in response to the defendant's false representations, the victim lends money or grants title, the defendant is guilty of false pretenses.

          2) A defendant who pays for property with a worthless check is guilty of larceny by trick, since title does not pass until the check is cashed.

          3) Where money is exchanged by cheating at cards or betting, the defrauding party is receiving possession, not title, so the crime is larceny by trick.

       (c) The modern scope of false pretenses includes written instruments, stocks, bonds, notes, and deeds, as well as money and credit cards.

    (3) to the defendant;

    (4) who knows his representation to be false; and

       (a) The defendant must know that his representation is false at the time the victim transfers title to him.

    (5) intends thereby to defraud the victim.

F. Bad Checks

1. All jurisdictions have enacted **bad check legislation** to deal with no-account or insufficient-funds checks given with the intent to defraud. The giving of the check is an implied representation of sufficient funds, absent postdating or some other means of notification of inadequate credit by the drawer.

2. Bad check statutes generally do not require that any property be obtained from the victim as a result of issuing the bad check.

3. However, the requisite mental state of the drawer is often required to be that of knowledge of the insufficient funds and the intent to defraud.

G. Credit Card Fraud

1. Obtaining property by means of a stolen or unauthorized credit card is also a statutory crime in most jurisdictions.

H. Larceny by Trick

1. **Larceny by trick** is a form of larceny whereby the defendant obtains possession of the personal property of another by means of a representation or promise that he knows is false at the time he takes possession.

2. In larceny by trick, the defendant's fraud is used to cause the victim to **convey possession**, not title (as in false pretenses).

   a. In some states, there must be an intent to steal at the time of the induced delivery; a defendant who has some lesser (but still wrongful) intent and then subsequently converts the property to his own use may be guilty of embezzlement. In other states, the fraud will be construed as a "trespass," which continues until the time of "taking" and, therefore, a later misappropriation would still be considered larceny by trick.

3. Factual misrepresentations and false promises are typically deemed sufficient for the "fraud" element of larceny by trick.

False Pretenses	Larceny by Trick	Credit Card Fraud	Check Fraud
• Obtains title • By representation or promise he knows is fake	• Obtains possession • By representation or promise he knows is fake	• Obtains title • By stolen or unauthorized credit card	• Obtains title • By stolen check or on non-sufficient funds account

I. **Extortion**

1. **Extortion** was a common law misdemeanor involving the corrupt demand or receipt of an unlawful fee by a public official under color of his office.

2. Under modern statutory law, extortion is commonly called blackmail. **Blackmail** is defined as obtaining the property of another by the use of threats of future harm to the victim or his property.

   a. The threat is the essence of extortion, and includes threats to expose a person or his family to disgrace and threats to accuse the victim of a crime.

3. Some statutes consider the crime complete upon the making of the threats with the specific intent to obtain money or property, while other statutes require the threats to actually cause the victim to part with his property.

4. Unlike robbery, extortion does not require threats of immediate or imminent physical harm, and property does not need to be taken from the victim's person or presence.

5. The wrong that extortion statutes attempt to prevent is the taking of the victim's property by threat. Thus, even where a defendant's threat is to reveal factually correct information that the defendant is entitled to reveal, the crime of extortion may nonetheless be committed.

6. In many jurisdictions, threats made for the purpose of obtaining payment for a valid debt are not considered extortion. One rationale for this is that, since the defendant is entitled to the property, the defendant lacks the requisite intent to extort for gain. However, other states treat threats for debt collection as extortion to discourage creditors from using such methods to enforce their payment rights.

J. Receiving Stolen Property

1. Receiving stolen property was a common law misdemeanor.
2. As a modern statutory crime, it is defined as:
   a. the receiving of stolen property;
      (1) The receiving of physical possession of the property, while the most common situation, is not required, as long as the defendant exercises control over the goods.

      EXAMPLE: Arranging for a sale, having the thief place the goods in a designated place, or receiving the goods from another will all constitute exercising control sufficient for meeting this element.

   b. known to be stolen;
      (1) The defendant must either know or actually believe that the property is stolen. An honest but unreasonable belief that the property is not stolen would likely prevent a conviction for receiving stolen property.

   c. with the intent to permanently deprive the owner.
      (1) The defendant must, at the time he receives the stolen property, have the specific intent to permanently deprive the owner of that property. Where a defendant intends at the time of receipt to unconditionally return property to its owner, that defendant is not guilty of receiving stolen property. However, conditionally offering to return the property—such as upon payment of a reward—may evidence an intent to permanently deprive. The defendant does not have to be acting for personal gain.

K. Forgery

1. **Forgery** is defined as:
   a. fraudulent making;
      (1) The making element will be satisfied by the creation of a new document, the altering of an existing document (including improperly filling in a form), or by inducing someone to sign a document knowing that the person is unaware of the document's significance.
      (2) Completion of the "making" element completes the crime; the defendant does not have to actually use the forged document to be found guilty of forgery.
      (3) A defendant who actually acquires property by use of the forged document may be guilty of another crime, such as false pretenses.

      EXAMPLE: Dylan wrote a will and signed the name of his ailing Aunt Bunny. He then signed the names of two other family members whom Bunny would likely choose as witnesses. Dylan intended to use the document after Aunt Bunny died to claim a large part of her estate. The fake will is discovered before Bunny dies. Dylan is guilty of forgery.

b.   of a false writing with apparent legal significance; and

    (1)   Forgery is not merely including false information in an otherwise genuine document, but must involve a writing that is itself false.

    (2)   An alteration must be material (that is, change the legal meaning or effect of the document) to qualify the action as an element of forgery.

    (3)   For a writing to be one with apparent legal significance, the writing must have purpose or value beyond the document's own existence, such as a contract, will, negotiable instrument, deed, or mortgage. A document that is only valuable because of its existence, even one that is highly valuable (such as a painting or historical document), has no effect on legal rights or duties and does not fall within the definition of forgery.

        (a)   However, attempting to obtain money in exchange for an inherently valuable document may give rise to other crimes, such as false pretenses.

c.   with the intent to make wrongful use of the forged document.

    (1)   The defendant must act with an intent to make wrongful use, but not necessarily for monetary gain.

    (2)   Note that acting with an intent to reimburse the victim or to collect on a good faith claim of debt does not negate the intent element.

L. Crimes against the Habitation

1. Burglary

a.   The common law crime of **burglary** consists of:

    (1)   the breaking;

        (a)   This element typically required some use of force to create an opening. Today, some statutes have deleted the breaking element altogether.

        (b)   Under both the common law and modern statutes, this element may be satisfied where a defendant gains entry by fraud, deception, or threat of force (known as **constructive breaking**).

    (2)   and entering;

        (a)   Entry through an open door where the defendant later opens an inside closet door is sufficient.

        (b)   Breaking into a trunk or safe, or breaking to exit rather than to gain entry, is insufficient.

        (c)   Entry is achieved by placing any portion of the body inside the structure.

        (d)   Insertion of a tool is sufficient for an entry if it is used to accomplish the felony, but insufficient if it is used merely to gain entry.

           EXAMPLE: Inserting a tool merely to unlock the door is not an entry, as opposed to shooting a bullet through a window intending to kill the victim, which is an entry.

(e) Breaking and entering are two elements that may occur at different times but must be related.

EXAMPLE: If the defendant breaks a window with his gun, then sees an open window and climbs in, there would be no "breaking and entering." However, if that defendant breaks the window with his gun, then goes to buy a heavy jacket to wear so the broken glass will not hurt him, and comes back the next night wearing the jacket and climbs through the same broken window, there would be a breaking and entering.

(f) The breaking and entering must both be done without the occupant's consent (i.e., trespassory). Where someone with the authority to enter breaks and enters, this element will not be met. A business open to the public is generally deemed to have extended an open invitation to enter during regular business hours. There is a split of authority, however, regarding people who enter businesses with the intent to steal or commit other felonies. Some states find the entry nonetheless consensual, while others view the undisclosed intent to steal as a bar to consent and deem the entry a trespass.

(3) of the dwelling house;

(a) At common law, this element was interpreted literally. Only a structure used as a home where people slept would meet the definition. The dwelling could be occupied or unoccupied at the time of entry. This element also encompasses structures within the area immediately surrounding the dwelling (the "curtilage"), such as a storage shed or greenhouse. Modern statutes, however, extend this element to include most any structure regardless of whether it is a dwelling, and in some jurisdictions regardless of whether it has a roof, such as a fenced lumberyard.

(4) of another;

(5) in the nighttime; and

(a) At common law, burglary had to be done at night, between sunset and sunrise. However, modern statutes have largely eliminated this element.

(6) with the intent to commit a felony therein.

(a) Burglary requires that the breaking and entering be accompanied by a simultaneous felonious intent. Under some modern statutes, an intent to commit a misdemeanor will suffice. An intent formed after entry is insufficient, absent an additional "entry" once inside.

EXAMPLE: A defendant who has no intent to steal when entering a house but forms such intent once inside, and subsequently opens the bedroom door with the intent to steal items inside the bedroom has committed an additional "entry."

(b) A defendant who commits or attempts the intended felony can be convicted of both crimes. In addition, the burglary is complete once the defendant enters with felonious intent regardless of whether the defendant succeeds or even continues the effort to complete the intended felony.

2. **Arson**

    a. At common law, the crime of **arson** consists of:

        (1) the malicious;

            (a) The defendant need not have intended to burn the dwelling. Malice requires only that the defendant intentionally took an action that involved a substantial risk of burning.

        (2) burning;

            (a) With respect to the burning requirement, it was not necessary that the dwelling be substantially or totally damaged. Although a mere blackening of the surface was not enough, there must have been some charring (i.e., slight burning) of the premises. Additionally, mere burning of the furniture or other contents of the dwelling, without fire damage to the structure itself, is not arson.

        (3) of the dwelling;

            (a) Like burglary, the common law requirement of a dwelling has been expanded in a majority of states to include virtually any structure.

        (4) of another.

            (a) The "of another" requirement has been expanded to include finding guilt for arson where an owner maliciously burns his own structure (such as for insurance fraud).

IV. INCHOATE CRIMES

A. Solicitation

1. **Solicitation** was a common law misdemeanor including enticing, advising, inciting, inducing, urging, or otherwise encouraging another to commit a felony or breach of the peace.

2. The MPC defines solicitation broadly to include requesting another to commit any offense (including misdemeanors and felonies).

3. The solicitor must intend that the solicitee perform criminal acts (thus the solicitor must have a specific intent). Mere approval of the acts is not enough.

4. The offense is complete at the time the solicitation is made. In other words, completion of the offense solicited is unnecessary.

5. It is also unnecessary that the person solicited enter into an agreement to commit the requested crime. Indeed, a person solicited to do a crime may not even respond, but the solicitor will still be guilty of solicitation.

6. A solicitor is treated as an accessory before the fact, and thus will be guilty of any solicited crime (whether attempted or completed) by the solicitee.

7. The crime of solicitation, unlike conspiracy, merges with the target felony upon completion of the crime.

8. A solicitor may not be guilty of the offense if he could not be convicted of the underlying crime—for instance, where the solicitor is a member of the class of persons the law seeks to protect (e.g., a minor, in relation to statutory rape).

9. **Defenses**

    a. At common law, there were no defenses to solicitation if the elements described above were present. However, under modern statutes, specific intent defenses such as voluntary intoxication and unreasonable mistake of fact are legitimate defenses to solicitation.

    b. Even where it would be impossible for the solicitee to carry out the crime, such impossibility is no defense to the crime of solicitation. What matters is what the solicitor believes the circumstances to be, not what they actually are.

    c. Because the crime of solicitation is complete as soon as the solicitation is made, withdrawal cannot be a defense to the crime of solicitation. Even where the solicitor later changes his mind, the change of heart may be a defense to the underlying crime, but not to the solicitation crime.

B. Attempt

1. The crime of **attempt** consists of two elements:

    a. a specific intent to bring about a criminal result; and

    b. a significant overt act in furtherance of that intent.

2. Once the target crime is committed, the attempt merges into the target crime.

3. The **specific intent** requirement for attempt liability—the requirement that the defendant specifically intended to bring about a criminal

result—means that, in some cases, an attempt conviction requires more proof than a completed offense.

EXAMPLE: A and B attack C. A intends to kill C, but B intends only to seriously injure him. If C does not die, then only A can be convicted of attempted murder. Even in a jurisdiction that recognizes murder based on a *mens rea*, which itself does not require the specific intent to kill (e.g., murder based on the intent to seriously injure), to be guilty of attempted murder, one still must have a specific intent to kill.

4. The **significant overt act** must be an act (or act of perpetration) beyond an act of "mere" preparation.

   a. Several approaches are used to determine what constitutes a sufficient overt act.

   b. At common law, a defendant was required to have performed the "last act" necessary to achieve the intended result.

   c. Today, acts prior to the last act are usually sufficient. Many courts apply a **"proximity" test**, which asks how close in time and physical distance a defendant was to the time and place the target crime was to be committed. Some courts use an **"equivocality" test**, which requires that the defendant's conduct be such that it can have no other purpose than the commission of the crime attempted. Jurisdictions following the MPC require only an act that constitutes a substantial step toward the offense that corroborates the criminal intent required, such as scouting out the scene of the intended crime.

   EXAMPLE: Defendant intends to kill Victim by tying him up and pushing him into the pool. At common law, Defendant likely would have to push the tied-up Victim into the pool to be guilty of attempted murder. Today, tying up the Victim next to the pool without pushing him in would likely be sufficient under all of the tests discussed above.

5. **Defenses**

   a. **Abandonment**

      (1) At common law, abandonment is not a defense to attempt once the attempt is complete.

      (2) Many jurisdictions (including MPC jurisdictions) recognize a voluntary and complete abandonment as a defense.

         (a) **Voluntary** means a true change of heart, not simply giving up in the face of difficulties or an increased likelihood of being caught.

         (b) **Complete** means that the defendant is not merely postponing commission of the crime.

   b. **Legal Impossibility**

      (1) Legal impossibility is traditionally regarded as a defense to attempt and involves the situation where the defendant did all those things he intended to do, but his acts did not constitute a crime.

      (2) Factual impossibility (e.g., shooting into an empty house) is not a defense to attempt.

C. Conspiracy

1. A **conspiracy** is an agreement between two or more persons to commit a crime.

2. The agreement itself is the *actus reus* or conduct element of the offense of conspiracy.

   a. Actual agreement is required. Feigned agreement, as in the case of an undercover police officer, is insufficient.

   b. The agreement need not be express, but may be proved circumstantially, such as by conduct where the conspirators demonstrate over time that they intended to achieve the same objective and agreed to work together toward that end.

      (1) The agreement does not require a meeting of the minds, but merely a shared intent to pursue a mutual goal.

   c. The objective of the agreement must be to either commit a crime or to commit a lawful act by unlawful means.

3. Conspiracy is a specific intent crime. The mental state required is both the intent to agree and the intent to achieve the objective of the agreement.

4. **Overt Act Requirement**

   a. The majority rule is that an overt act in furtherance of the conspiracy is also required for conspiracy liability.

   b. This prevailing view reflects a change from the traditional common law rule, which had no such requirement (the agreement itself constituted the crime).

   c. The overt act requirement for conspiracy need not be criminal or unlawful, and need only be committed by one member of the conspiracy.

   d. Mere preparation will suffice.

      EXAMPLE: Purchasing matches in a conspiracy involving the burning of a building or driving by a house to observe if someone is home in a conspiracy involving theft.

5. Unlike attempt, conspiracy is a separate and distinct offense that does not merge upon completion of the target crime because criminal combinations are deemed to be dangerous apart from the underlying crime itself.

6. All jurisdictions recognize liability for crimes a conspirator aids and abets under the **doctrine of accomplice liability**.

7. Where a conspirator does not have the sufficient *mens rea* for liability as an accomplice, the **Pinkerton doctrine** provides that each conspirator is liable for the crimes of all the other co-conspirators where the crimes were both:

   a. a foreseeable outgrowth of the conspiracy; and

   b. committed in furtherance of the conspiratorial goal.

8. However, most jurisdictions have rejected the Pinkerton doctrine and will not impose liability upon a conspirator for crimes committed by other co-conspirators merely upon the basis of the agreement.

9. The nature of the agreement determines whether there is a single conspiracy or multiple conspiracies.

a. In a **chain relationship**, where several crimes are committed under one large scheme in which each member knows generally of the other parties' participation and a community of interest exists, one single conspiracy results.

b. Alternatively, in the so-called **hub-and-spoke relationship**, where one common member enters into agreements to commit a series of independent crimes with different individuals, multiple conspiracies exist.

10. **Procedural Issues**

a. An acquittal of one co-conspirator traditionally results in the acquittal of a single remaining co-conspirator because at least two guilty parties are required for a conspiracy conviction. However, it is not necessary to try more than one conspirator. Thus, a single conspirator could be tried and convicted of conspiracy if his co-conspirators were missing or dead.

b. The common law rule, followed by the majority of jurisdictions, is that no conspiracy exists if only one of the conspirators truly agrees and the other conspirator(s) feign agreement (i.e., there must be a "meeting" of at least two "guilty minds").

EXAM TIP ▶ The majority rule is that there are no "one-person conspiracies." Therefore, one criminal and one undercover police officer cannot conspire.

c. The MPC, however, follows the unilateral approach to conspiracy and dispenses with the requirement that two people actually agree. Under the unilateral approach, all of the co-conspirators, having feigned agreement or having been acquitted will not alone, prevent a defendant from a conviction for conspiracy.

d. The **Wharton Rule** states that in crimes where two or more people are necessary for the commission of the offense, there is no conspiracy unless the agreement involves an additional person who is not essential to the definition of that crime.

EXAMPLE: If A and B engage in a duel, they are guilty of the crime of dueling, but not of conspiracy to duel.

(1) Wharton Rule crimes include:
   (a) bigamy;
   (b) incest;
   (c) gambling;
   (d) giving and receiving bribes;
   (e) adultery; and
   (f) dueling.

e. Because a corporation and its agent are considered one person, no conspiracy can exist between them.

f. Likewise, a member of a legislatively protected class cannot be guilty of conspiracy to commit that crime (e.g., a minor female cannot conspire with a male to commit statutory rape) or of being an accessory to a crime.

      g.   A person can be guilty of conspiracy to commit a crime that he could not commit himself.

11. **Defenses**

      a.   Impossibility is not a defense to conspiracy.

      b.   The general rule is that withdrawal is not recognized as a valid defense to conspiracy because the conspiracy is complete as soon as the parties agreed to commit the crime and an overt act is committed.

      c.   Withdrawal may cut off further liability for crimes committed in furtherance of the conspiracy if, however, the withdrawing conspirator communicates his withdrawal to each of the co-conspirators.

      d.   Under the MPC, withdrawal by a co-conspirator may be a valid affirmative defense to the charge of conspiracy itself where the renouncing party gives timely notice of his plans to all members of the conspiracy and performs an affirmative act to "thwart" the success of the conspiracy.

V. PARTIES TO CRIME; ACCOMPLICE LIABILITY

A. **Accomplice**

1. The common law traditionally distinguished between accessories before and after the fact and principals in the first and second degree.

2. The modern approach is to distinguish only between accomplices to a crime and accessories after the fact. Under the modern approach, an accomplice to a crime is fully liable for the crime being committed.

   EXAMPLE: An accomplice to a bank robbery is a bank robber.

3. An individual is criminally liable as an **accomplice** if he gives assistance or encouragement or fails to act where he has a legal duty to oppose the crime of another (*actus reus*), and purposefully intends to effectuate commission of the crime (*mens rea*).

4. **The Act Requirement**

   a. Even slight assistance or encouragement is sufficient, but the defendant must actually assist or encourage. The assistance or encouragement need not be a cause-in-fact of the commission of the crime.

      EXAMPLE: A flashes B a thumbs-up sign just before B beats C. B would have beaten C anyway, but A's act is sufficient for complicity if B saw it and felt even slightly encouraged.

   b. Mere presence does not make one an accomplice.

   c. Words alone may be sufficient if they assisted or encouraged.

   d. The MPC recognizes complicity liability for one who attempts to aid or encourage but does not actually aid or encourage.

5. **Mental State Requirement**

   a. At common law, the person must intend to commit the acts of assistance or encouragement and must further intend to encourage or assist another to commit the crime charged.

   b. A minority of modern statutes create accomplice liability with a lower mental state—that of knowingly assisting or encouraging a crime, such as in cases where a seller, knowing of the buyer's intent to commit arson, sells him an explosive device.

6. An accomplice is responsible not just for the crime assisted and encouraged but also for other crimes that are the natural and probable consequences of the crime assisted or encouraged.

   a. The MPC limits accomplice liability to only the crime assisted or encouraged.

      EXAMPLE: An accomplice to an armed bank robbery can be held responsible for the death of a bank teller who is shot by another defendant during the bank robbery.

7. A defendant may be guilty as an accomplice for crimes he could not commit alone.

8. An individual is not liable as an accomplice for the acts of a "false accomplice" (i.e., an undercover police officer).

9. **Withdrawal or Abandonment**

   a. An accomplice may sever liability for future crimes by withdrawal or abandonment.

   b. He must give no further assistance or encouragement.

   c. He must communicate his withdrawal to his accomplices.

   d. Many jurisdictions require him to make efforts to neutralize his prior assistance or encouragement, but he does not have to try to thwart the commission of the crime.

   <u>EXAMPLE:</u> A had agreed to lend his car to B so that B could rob a bank. A tells B that he changed his mind. A needs to get his car keys back from B to cut off accomplice liability in the event that B goes ahead with the robbery, but he does not need to call the police and tell them of B's plan.

B. **Principal in the First Degree**

   1. The actual perpetrator who performs the criminal act with the requisite mental state is known as the **principal in the first degree**. More than one person can perpetrate the same crime.

C. **Principal in the Second Degree**

   1. One who is present at the scene of the felony and aids, abets, or otherwise encourages the commission of the crime with the requisite intent is guilty as a **principal in the second degree**.

   <u>EXAMPLE:</u> A getaway car driver who waits outside during a bank robbery.

   a. Mere presence without assistance or assistance without intent, are both insufficient.

   b. A principal in the second degree may be punished to the same extent as the perpetrator.

D. **Accessory before the Fact**

   1. One who aids, abets, counsels, or otherwise encourages the commission of a felony, but is not present at the scene, is guilty as an **accessory before the fact**.

   2. An accessory before the fact may be punished to the same extent as a principal for all crimes committed within the scope of the conspiracy.

   3. **Conviction of the Principal**

      a. Under the majority view, the principal need not be convicted in order for the accessory before the fact to be convicted.

      b. At common law, conviction of the principal was required for conviction of an accessory.

E. **Accessory after the Fact**

1. The following three requirements must be met for a person to be an **accessory after the fact**:

   a. a completed felony must have been committed;

   b. the accessory must have known of the commission of the felony; and

   c. the accessory must have personally given aid to the felon to hinder the felon's apprehension, conviction, or punishment.

2. Whereas modern law has abolished the distinction between principals in the first and second degree, one who is an accessory after the fact is not an accomplice, nor is he punished to the same extent as prescribed for the parties to the felony.

3. Modern statutes largely focus on punishing one for his own actions (which these statutes classify as a separate crime called "obstruction of justice"), and not by holding the "accessory after the fact" vicariously liable for the underlying felony.

VI. DEFENSES

A. Responsibility

1. **Insanity**

   a. If the defendant is insane at the time of his criminal act, no criminal liability will be imposed. Four tests for insanity are followed in various jurisdictions.

      (1) The **M'Naghten test** focuses on the defendant's reasoning abilities. Under this test, a defendant is relieved of criminal responsibility upon proof that, at the time of commission of the act, he was laboring under such a defect of reason from a disease of the mind as not to know the nature and quality of the act he was doing, or if he did know it, not to know that what he was doing was wrong.

         (a) **Disease of the mind** includes all mental abnormalities, but not a psychopathic personality.

         (b) There is a split of authority in M'Naghten jurisdictions as to whether "wrong" includes both legal and moral wrongs. Some jurisdictions will find that a defendant is not insane where, even though the defendant believes the act was not morally wrong, he knows it to be illegal. Others will find defendants who do not know an act was morally wrong to be insane, regardless of their belief as to the act's legality.

         <u>EXAMPLE</u>: Following what Defendant actually believed to be a higher power's command to kill all law professors, Defendant waited outside his criminal law final exam to kill his professor. Defendant is considered insane under the M'Naghten test.

      (2) Under the **irresistible impulse test**, a defendant will be found not guilty where he had a mental disease that kept him from controlling his conduct.

      (3) Under the **Durham** (or **New Hampshire**) **rule**, also known as the "product" rule, a defendant is not criminally responsible if his unlawful act was the product of a mental disease or defect (meaning it would not have been committed "but for" the defect or disease).

      (4) Under the **Model Penal Code test** (or **substantial capacity**), a person is not responsible for criminal conduct if, at the time of such conduct, as a result of mental disease or defect, he lacked substantial capacity to appreciate the criminality (wrongfulness) of his conduct or to conform his conduct to the requirements of law. It is typically easier to establish MPC insanity because it does not require the total or absolute loss of cognitive ability or volition, only that the defendant lacked substantial capacity in these areas. It also combines a cognitive component (not knowing) with a volitional component (not controlling) and allows a verdict of insanity for either one.

(a) "Mental disease or defect" does not include abnormalities manifested only by repeated criminal or otherwise antisocial conduct.

EXAMPLE: Kleptomania (a compulsion to steal) will not constitute a mental disease or defect under the MPC test.

b. **Procedural Issues**

(1) A defendant is presumed sane until such time as he goes forward by raising evidence as to his sanity.

(2) A not guilty plea at arraignment does not waive the right to raise the insanity defense at a later time.

2. **Competency**

a. Competency to stand trial is very different from a mental incapacity.

b. **Incompetency** typically refers to a doctrine that prevents defendants from being tried, convicted, or punished unless they have the sufficient present ability to consult counsel with a reasonable and rational understanding of the proceedings.

c. If a defendant is found incompetent, he can later be tried and punished if competency is restored.

d. Insanity concerns the defendant's mental state at the time the offense is committed; competency is assessed at any time during the pendency of the criminal case in court.

3. **Diminished Capacity**

a. Some jurisdictions allow the defense of **diminished capacity**, which is short of insanity, to prove that as a result of a mental defect, the defendant did or did not have a state of mind that is an element of the offense.

b. When pleading diminished capacity, the defense is used to negate a specific mental state required for the particular crime.

4. **Intoxication**

a. Voluntary or involuntary intoxication (whether brought about by alcohol or by narcotic drugs) is a defense to a crime when it negates the existence of an element of the crime.

(1) Under the prevailing view, **voluntary intoxication** may be a valid defense for a specific intent crime if it negates the requisite mental state, and may negate a purposeful or knowing mental state. However, voluntary intoxication is not a defense to general intent crimes and will not negate recklessness, negligence, or strict liability.

(2) **Involuntary intoxication** is a defense to a crime, even if it does not negate an element of the crime, under the same circumstances as insanity.

(3) The excessive use of alcohol or drugs may bring about real insanity, in which case the rules concerning insanity as a defense to crime govern.

EXAMPLE: Defendant voluntarily drank himself silly, then drove down to the harbor and snuck aboard Victim's yacht. Victim ordered Defendant off the boat. In a rage-filled response, Defendant grabbed some rope and strangled Victim to death. Defendant will not be excused.

5. **Infancy**

    a. At common law, a complete defense due to incapacity existed for children under seven years of age. Children between the ages of seven and 14 were rebuttably presumed to lack criminal capacity. Children over age 14 were held responsible as adults.

    b. Many states have abolished the common law presumptions and established a specific minimum age required for a criminal conviction.

B. Justification

1. Where an act is justified, no crime has been committed, notwithstanding what might otherwise be a criminal result.

2. **Self-Defense**

    a. If a person has a reasonable belief that he is in imminent danger of unlawful bodily harm, he may use that amount of force in self-defense that is reasonably necessary to prevent such harm, unless he is the initial aggressor.

        (1) Keep in mind that the force must be proportional to the initial attack, and the initial attack must be wrongful.

    b. **Deadly force** is that which threatens death or serious bodily harm.

        (1) Deadly force can only be used in self-defense in response to an attack that threatens death or great bodily injury.

    c. **Non-deadly force** threatens only bodily harm.

    EXAMPLE: If Abe takes a swing at Bob, Bob is legally justified in fighting back with non-deadly force. If Abe swings with a butcher knife, Bob is legally justified in shooting Abe with a gun if he cannot avoid the potentially lethal harm through non-deadly force.

    d. **Reasonable force** is that amount of force that is necessary to avoid the threatened harm. In other words, if non-deadly force would stop a deadly attack, responding with deadly force is not reasonable.

    e. An **aggressor** is one who strikes the first blow or commits a crime against the victim. The aggressor can regain the right of self-defense in either of two ways:

        (1) upon complete withdrawal perceived by the other party; or

        (2) escalation of force by the victim of the initial aggression.

        EXAMPLE: If Abe takes a swing at Bob, and Bob responds by shooting at Abe with a gun, Abe is legally justified in swinging his butcher knife at Bob.

    f. The general rule is that a person who did not initiate conflict has no duty to retreat in the face of a deadly attack.

    g. However, a number of jurisdictions do require retreat if it is feasible and can be done in safety before using deadly force.

(1) Those jurisdictions that require retreat before using deadly force do not require retreat if it cannot be done safely or if the defendant is in his own home, auto, or workplace. Even if in one of these places, however, a defendant in a retreat jurisdiction must retreat before using deadly force if the defendant is the aggressor.

(2) Retreat jurisdictions are split as to whether one must retreat in one's own dwelling if attacked by a co-dweller.

h. It is never self-defense to kill in order to retaliate or seek revenge for a wrongful attack once the attack is over.

3. **Defense of a Third Person**

a. Generally, a person is justified in using force to defend a third person to the same extent that that person would be justified in using force to defend himself.

b. Using lethal force is lawful when necessary to defend a third person who is facing an immediate and wrongful deadly attack. As with self-defense, however, the amount of force used must be proportional to the initial attack. In other words, if something short of deadly force would effectively ward off the attack, deadly force is not necessary and, therefore, not reasonable.

c. The majority rule focuses on the reasonableness of the defendant's belief that the third person was being unlawfully attacked. If the third person is also the aggressor or a felon resisting lawful arrest, and the defendant reasonably but mistakenly uses lethal force against the victim to protect that third person, the defendant may nonetheless claim the justification of defense of others. The minority rule is that the defendant has no more right to use deadly force than the third person ostensibly being protected.

d. Under most modern laws, the third person does not have to have a special relationship to the defendant; a defendant may use deadly force to protect a total stranger.

EXAMPLE: For no reason, Greg pulled a knife and attacked Peter. Peter struggled with Greg and succeeded in disarming Greg. Just as Peter was obtaining control of the knife, Bobby walked around the corner, saw his friend Greg, and reasonably thought that Greg was about to be stabbed by Peter. Bobby pulled a pistol and shot and killed Peter. In a minority jurisdiction, Bobby would not be excused.

4. **Defense of Property**

a. Reasonable, non-deadly force is justified in defending one's property from theft, destruction, or trespass where the defendant has a reasonable belief that the property is in immediate danger and no greater force than necessary is used.

(1) This means that the use of non-deadly force is improper where a request to desist would suffice.

b. **Non-deadly force** is also proper when used to reenter real property or regain possession of wrongfully taken personal property upon "immediate pursuit."

    c.   **Deadly force** may never be used to merely defend property.

        (1)   However, deadly force may be used where the defender reasonably believes an entry will be made or attempted in his dwelling by one intending to commit a felony therein.

5.   **Necessity**

    a.   Reasonable force is justified to avoid imminent injury resulting from natural (non-human) forces or where an individual reasonably believes that his criminal conduct is necessary to avoid a "greater harm" that would result from compliance with the law (e.g., A kills B to save C and D).

        (1)   This defense also protects military personnel acting within their duties and public executioners.

        EXAMPLE: A pilot is generally legally justified in crash-landing his disabled plane on a highway, even knowing it will kill several motorists.

    b.   There is no defense of necessity where the defendant is at fault in creating the perilous situation.

    EXAMPLE: If the pilot failed to ensure proper maintenance of his plane, he may be criminally liable for harm to others in a crash landing.

6.   **Law Enforcement Defenses**

    a.   **Police**

        (1)   A police officer may use that amount of non-deadly force that he reasonably believes necessary to effect a lawful arrest or prevent the escape of the arrestee.

        (2)   A police officer may use deadly force only to prevent the commission of a dangerous felony or to effectuate an arrest of a person reasonably believed to have committed a felony where it reasonably appears necessary to the officer.

    b.   **Private Citizens**

        (1)   A private citizen is privileged to use that amount of non-deadly force that reasonably appears necessary to prevent the commission of a felony or a misdemeanor amounting to a breach of the peace.

        (2)   A private citizen may use non-deadly force to make an arrest if the crime was, in fact, committed, and he reasonably believes the person against whom he uses the force committed the crime.

        (3)   A private citizen may use the same amount of deadly force as a police officer only if a dangerous felony is involved and the person against whom he used the force is actually guilty of the crime.

        (4)   A proper mistake—meaning one that is both made in good faith and reasonable—as to the use of lethal force may justify a homicide committed in self-defense or to prevent the commission of a dangerous felony. However, a private citizen-defendant who mistakenly uses deadly force to prevent the escape of a fleeing felon is not justified. Thus, if no dangerous felony has actually been committed, or if the victim was not actually the felon, the defendant will be criminally liable.

NOTE ▶ Unlike private citizens, police officers who mistakenly use deadly force in such fleeing felon situations may be justified.

    o.   **Resisting Unlawful Arrest**

        (1)   A defendant may use reasonable, non-deadly force to resist an unlawful arrest. A minority of jurisdictions do not permit even non-deadly force in order to resist an unlawful arrest. Most jurisdictions permit an individual to use force to resist an arrest made with excessive force, especially if the individual fears injury.

        (2)   An individual may only resist a lawful arrest by a police officer where the individual does not know that the other person is a police officer.

  7. **Duress**

    a.   The defense of **duress** justifies criminal conduct where the defendant reasonably believes that the only way to avoid unlawful threats of great bodily harm or imminent death is to engage in unlawful conduct. For duress, the threat comes from human forces rather than from forces of nature.

    b.   Duress, or coercion, is not available as a defense to murder.

  8. **Public Duty**

    a.   A public official, police officer, or private citizen offering assistance is justified in using reasonable force against another or in taking the property of another provided that he is acting within his authority pursuant to a law, court order, or process that is valid or that he reasonably believes to be valid.

  9. **Domestic Authority**

    a.   The parents of a minor child, or one *in loco parentis*, may justifiably use reasonable force on the child to promote the child's welfare.

    b.   **Reasonableness** is determined in light of the child's age, sex, health, and particular misconduct based on the totality of the circumstances.

    c.   This defense is available in some other situations where similar responsibility lies, such as a ship's captain for his crew or a warden for his prisoners.

C. Entrapment

  1. The defense of **entrapment** exists where the criminal act is the product of creative activity originating with law enforcement officials and the defendant is in no way predisposed to commit the crime.

  2. Government officials may, however, encourage criminal activity by providing the opportunity or the equipment for the commission of a crime.

  3. A defendant's past criminal record is relevant in proving predisposition.

D. Mistake

  1. **Mistake of Fact**

    a.   **Mistake of fact** is a defense where it negates the existence of a mental state required to establish a material element of the crime. In other words, there would be no crime if the facts were such as the defendant thought them to be.

        (1)   To negate the existence of general intent, a mistake of fact must be reasonable to the extent that, under the circumstances, a reasonable person would have made that type of mistake.

        (2)   To negate the existence of specific intent, a mistake of fact need not be reasonable. It may be unreasonable, provided it is honest.

    b.   Mistake or ignorance of fact is not a defense to a strict liability crime, which itself requires no mental state.

        EXAMPLE: It is not a defense to statutory rape that the defendant thought the victim was of age.

2.   **Mistake of Law**

    a.   Generally, where the defendant is unaware that his acts are criminally proscribed, such ignorance of the law is not a defense.

    b.   Exceptions include situations:

        (1)   where a statute proscribing the defendant's conduct has not been reasonably made available or where the defendant has reasonably relied on a statute or judicial decision that is later overruled or declared unconstitutional;

        (2)   where a defendant relies in good faith upon an erroneous official statement of law contained in an administrative order or in an official interpretation by a public officer or department; and

        (3)   where some element of a crime involves knowledge or awareness of the law by the defendant.

E.   Consent

1.   Consent of the victim is not a defense to a crime except when it negates a specific element of the offense, such as in rape or kidnapping.

F.   Condonation

1.   Subsequent forgiveness by the victim is generally not a defense to the commission of a crime.

INTENTIONAL KILLING: THINK MURDER, THEN LOOK FOR AN ERASER	
Common Law	**Model Penal Code**
Murder: Unlawful Killing **with** Malice EXPRESS MALICE: • Intent to kill—PURPOSE OR KNOWLEDGE • Intent to inflict grievous bodily harm	Murder: • Killing done with "purpose" • Killing done with "knowledge of substantial probability of death"
DEGREE MURDER AN EXPRESS MALICE MURDER, **PLUS** • Premeditation and Deliberation, OR • Proof Murder falls into Statutory Category of 1st Degree • REMEMBER VOLUNTARY INTOX MAY ERASE P&D	NO DEGREES OF MURDER: GRAVITY OF MURDER IS DETERMINED ON A CASE BY CASE BASIS
Voluntary Manslaughter: A PRESUMPTIVE murder **DOWNGRADED** BECAUSE MALICE IS ERASED BY: • Provocation producing: SUDDEN HEAT OF PASSION • Diminished Mental Capacity	Voluntary Manslaughter: A PRESUMPTIVE murder **DOWNGRADED** DUE TO EVIDENCE OF EXTREME EMOTIONAL DISTURBANCE
UNTENDED KILLING RESULTING FROM UNJUSTIFIED RISK CREATION: THINK MANSLAUGHTER, THEN LOOK FOR AN ESCALATOR	

Murder:
 	
IMPLIED MALICE
 	
• Reckless (knew risk and ignored) or Negligent (should have known risk) Conduct, PLUS
  • Evidence Proving a WANTON DISREGARD FOR HUMAN LIFE (Evidence proves D ACTED WITH A BLACK/MALIGNANT HEART)
• Felony Murder
  • Malice Implied from *Malum in Se* Conduct: BARRK Crime Causes Death
	Murder:
	
	Killing resulting from:
	
	• Reckless conduct, **PLUS**
	• AN EXTREME INDIFFERENCE TO HUMAN LIFE
	  • IN AN MPC JX, THERE IS NO FELONY MURDER, BUT CAUSING DEATH DURING COMMISSION OF A *MALUM IN SE* FELONY IS **PRESUMED** EXTREME INDIFFERENCE

Involuntary Manslaughter: Unlawful Killing **Without** Malice • A killing resulting from RECKLESS conduct *THAT DOES NOT* manifest a wanton disregard for the value of human life • A killing that results from CRIMINAL/CULPABLE NEGLIGENT CONDCUT (gross negligence)	Involuntary Manslaughter: • A killing resulting from RECKLESS conduct *THAT DOES NOT* manifest Extreme Indifference to the value of human life Negligent Homicide: Killing caused by Gross Negligence

KILLINGS ATTRIBUTED TO FELON(S) FOR F.M.

COMMON LAW HOMICIDE BY THE BUCKETS

DEGREE JURISDICTION HOMICIDE BY THE BUCKETS

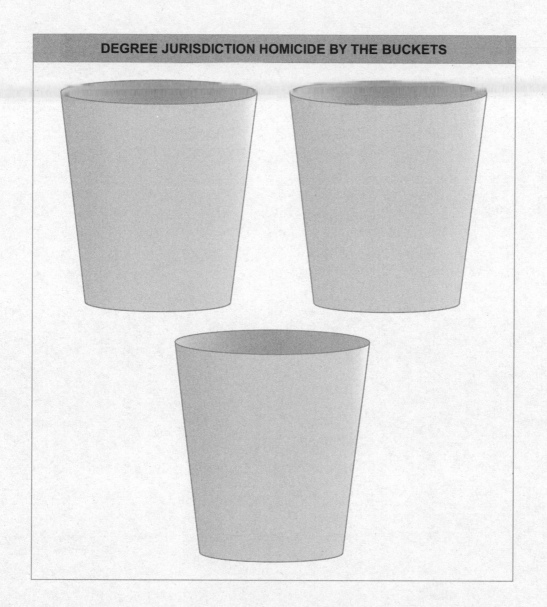

| **KAPLAN** BAR REVIEW

Issue-Spotting Exercises

Question 1

A state has enacted a criminal law statute making it unlawful to knowingly possess, sell, or transport narcotics and other controlled dangerous substances. A reputed drug dealer who lived in the state oftentimes would hire drivers to transport drugs across the Southwest.

One day the drug dealer approached an acquaintance and offered to pay him $250 to drive a van to another city located in the state. The acquaintance, who was unemployed and needed the money, agreed. The drug dealer then explained to the acquaintance that he would be transporting a package to a friend of the drug dealers. The drug dealer placed the package in the glove compartment of the van. The acquaintance neither asked nor was told what was contained in the package. The package contained a kilo of cocaine.

During the ten-hour drive, the acquaintance deliberately refrained from looking in the glove compartment and inspecting the package because he knew what the drug dealer did for a living. When the acquaintance arrived at the friend's residence, he was greeted by the friend who removed the package from the glove compartment. Moments later, police arrived at the scene and arrested both the acquaintance and the friend.

If the acquaintance is charged with violating the aforementioned state statute, will he be found guilty?

Question 2

A defendant and one of his co-workers had recently been terminated from their jobs. As they were commiserating about their misfortune, the co-worker thought of a great get-rich-quick scheme to defraud his insurance company. The co-worker told the defendant he was insured under an insurance policy covering personal injuries. He suggested that the defendant shoot him in the arm in a fake robbery attempt so that he could file a phony insurance claim to recover damages for his injury. In this jurisdiction, it is a felony to file a false insurance claim.

As part of their scheme, the defendant went to the co-worker's home one evening with a loaded gun. They were standing together in the kitchen discussing how to best implement their plan. Finally, the co-worker told the defendant to shoot him in the arm and then flee from the residence. After being shot, the co-worker planned to call 911 and have an ambulance transport him to the hospital where he would be treated for his wound. Following the co-worker's instruction, the defendant proceeded to shoot the co-worker in the arm. Thereupon, the co-worker telephoned 911 to report the shooting and requested an ambulance immediately be sent to his home.

Believing that the co-worker only suffered a superficial arm wound, the defendant drove home after the shooting. The bullet, however, severed an artery and the co-worker began to bleed profusely. Before the ambulance arrived, the co-worker lost consciousness from the loss of blood and passed out on the kitchen floor. When the paramedics arrived, they were unable to revive him and he was pronounced dead at the scene.

What is the most serious crime for which the defendant properly could be convicted?

Question 3

As part of a plan to rob a bank, two men would enter the bank while a woman would drive the getaway car. As they were driving to the bank on the morning of the robbery, one of the men saw a hitchhiker thumbing a ride. He ordered the woman to stop the car and pick up the hitchhiker. When the hitchhiker entered the car, the man asked him where he was going. The hitchhiker responded that he was going to a town that was located about five miles north of the bank.

A few minutes later, the car pulled up in front of the bank, and the man turned to the hitchhiker and said, "Listen, buddy, we're going inside and rob this place. I want you to stay in the car with the woman and help her keep a lookout for any cops." Startled by the chain of events the hitchhiker feigned agreement by nodding his head.

The two men then entered the bank, and brandishing their weapons, they ordered everyone on the floor. They went to the nearest counter and commanded the teller to fill a bag with all the cash she had in the drawer. After they were handed the money, the two men fled to the car and made a hasty getaway. While the bank robbery was in progress, the hitchhiker remained in the car and sat silently in fear. The group then sped toward the town where their hideout was located. Upon reaching the town, they drove the hitchhiker to his destination. As he was leaving the vehicle, one of the men gave him a $100 bill and thanked him for his help.

What, if any, crimes has the hitchhiker committed?

Question 4

A customer went to a store to buy some suntan oil, which she expected to use on her vacation the following week. She found the brand she wanted and decided to browse around. As she walked down the next aisle, she saw an expensive camera she really liked, though she could not afford to pay for it. She picked up the camera, examined it, and decided to steal it. She put the camera underneath her sweater, but noticed an employee watching her from the back of the store. Because she feared getting arrested for shoplifting, she quickly removed the camera from her sweater, put it back on the shelf, and left the store. She had put the suntan oil in her pocket and inadvertently forgot to pay for it. When she got home, she realized her mistake and decided to return to the store and pay for the suntan oil.

For what crimes can the customer be convicted?

Question 5

A compulsive gambler owed a large amount of money to a man who ran an illegal bookmaking operation. When the gambler was unable to pay his gambling debt, the man hired an enforcer to threaten the gambler. Late one evening, the enforcer went to the gambler's home and rang the doorbell. When the gambler opened the door, the enforcer pushed him aside and entered the home. The enforcer then slapped the gambler's face and said, "You better pay the man his money...or I'll be back and break your legs." As the enforcer was leaving, he saw the gambler's watch lying on a table in the hallway. The enforcer took the watch and left.

What, if any, crimes has the customer committed?

Essays

Criminal Law

In Class

Paul and Ringo are New Orleans police officers. On the third day following the flooding of that city by Hurricane Katrina, they were on patrol duty together, patrolling an area of the city in which there had been sporadic looting and gunfire since the hurricane. They had been on 12-hour shifts since the day prior to the hurricane and were working the noon-to-midnight shift on this day. Paul and Ringo were each eight-year veterans of the force.

Their shift began at noon, and by 7 P.M. they had encountered very little trouble. While on foot patrol, they often lost radio communications with their precinct headquarters, known at the time as "Fort Apache." As they were patrolling, Ringo and Paul noticed that a local bar—which they also knew was also a clandestine brothel—had a generator running and was occupied by a number of locals. Ringo and Paul decided that it was time they took a break to get some "refreshments." Once inside, Ringo and Paul started drinking beer and each also had two shots of whiskey. It was apparent that the local regulars at the bar certainly knew both officers as many greeted them. It was also apparent that most of the women working at the bar knew the officers.

Within about an hour, it was obvious to the bartender that Ringo and Paul were both getting drunk. The bartender told investigators later that he saw a woman who worked at the bar, who he knew was a prostitute, approach Paul and heard her bantering with him as if they knew each other. Paul suggested that they have a few drinks "in private," and then the bartender heard Paul say to the woman, "I hope I don't have to worry about any price gouging from you because of the hurricane?" The woman responded, "Don't worry about that; but hey, don't you think it would be worth it?" Paul laughed, and Ringo told Paul to "go for it." Paul went upstairs with the woman. About 30 minutes later Paul came down and announced, "That was the best money I have spent all week". At that point, Ringo said, "Let's get going," and the two officers left the bar to return to their patrol.

After they had walked for about five minutes, Paul exclaimed, "Where the hell is my pistol?" In a panic, he and Ringo looked around the area where they had been walking, but they did not find the weapon. They deduced that Paul must have left it in the room in which he had enjoyed his liaison, and he decided to return to the bar to retrieve it. By this time, it was very dark because there was no power and little moonlight. When they returned to the bar, they could not find the pistol, and no one would admit to taking it in spite of their demands. Paul threatened to tear the place up, but Ringo figured they would not be able to explain why they were there in the first place, and he convinced Paul to leave so they could figure out what to do.

Once outside, Ringo and Paul discussed their predicament. They were particularly worried about Paul getting in to serious trouble for losing his weapon. Also, they both knew there was no way they would be able to tell the truth about how it was lost and that they would also be in trouble for spending time at the bar. Paul said they needed to figure out some explanation for how the weapon was lost. Ringo said he had an idea. He would fire a few shots into the air so that they could make a false report that they had gotten into a brief exchange of fire with some unidentified looters. Ringo said that if questioned, they should both say that Paul chased the shooter in the dark, that somewhere along the chase route, his weapon must have fallen out, and that they were unable to find it in the darkness. Ringo looked at Paul, and Paul announced, "Okay, let's do it."

Ringo then removed his 9 mm service pistol and fired five shots randomly into the air. The duo then raced back to "Fort Apache." When they arrived, the Captain on duty asked to speak with the two of them. He asked where they had been and why they had not called in for so long. Ringo told him the false story. The Captain then said, "Well, that explains it." Ringo responded, "That explains what?" The Captain then said, "We just dispatched an ambulance to the area where you had the firefight to pick up a seven-year-old girl who was hit in the chest by a stray bullet while she was sitting out on her balcony." About that time, a radio report came in indicating that the girl was dead when the ambulance arrived, and that the cause of death was blood loss due to a single gunshot wound to the chest. The Captain instructed the ambulance to bring the deceased child to the medical examiner's building for an autopsy. In accordance with department policy, he then told Ringo to turn in his weapon (so it could be examined) and draw a new pistol.

Subsequent investigation establishes that the bullet recovered from the girl's body was fired from Ringo's pistol; that the girl died as the result of blood loss from the gunshot wound; that the girl would have survived had the ambulance arrived 20 minutes earlier; that the ambulance was delayed because it had to travel slowly because of the lack of street lighting and the amount of debris blocking many streets. The bartender is a cooperating witness for the prosecution. During questioning by internal affairs, Paul provided the details of the plan he and Ringo hatched when the realized the pistol was lost. The district attorney now wants to bring appropriate charges against the officers for the incident. Assume the jurisdiction follows the common law.

THE FOLLOWING RELEVANT STATUTES ARE IN FORCE IN THE JURISDICTION (CONSIDER ONLY THESE STATUTES IN YOUR ANALYSIS):

Conspiracy:

Any person who conspires with another person to commit any offense made punishable by this code shall be guilty of conspiracy.

Felony Solicitation of Prostitution:

Any person who solicits any other person to engage in sexual relations in exchange for payment of any kind shall be guilty of solicitation of prostitution and shall be sentenced to no more than five years in prison and/or no more than a $10,000.00 fine.

Unlawful Discharge of a Firearm:

Any person who, without legal authority or justification, willfully discharges a firearm shall be guilty of a misdemeanor.

Murder:

Murder is:

a. The unlawful killing of a human being with malice; or

b. The unlawful killing of a human being during the perpetration of an inherently dangerous felony.

The Jurisdiction applies the Abstract Theory of Inherent Dangerousness.

Manslaughter:

Manslaughter is the unlawful killing of a human being without malice.

There is no Misdemeanor Manslaughter statute in the jurisdiction.

Part 1:

Assume (for this question only) that we do not charge Ringo with felony murder. The DA wants to charge Ringo with criminal homicide. Propose the homicide offense you believe Ringo should be charged with, explain why you chose the offense, and analyze any issues related to proving the offense.

Part 2:

If we charge Ringo with felony murder, will the charge withstand (survive) a motion to dismiss for failure to allege a valid offense?

Part 3:

What other crimes are supported by these facts, who may be charged, and why?

Criminal Law

In Class

I. **Homicide Charge**

  A. Was Ringo legally responsible for causing an unlawful killing?

    1. **(Rule)** To prove defendant is guilty of criminal homicide, prosecution must prove beyond a reasonable doubt that defendant was the actual and proximate cause of victim's death and that act causing death concurred with criminal state of mind

      a. Act is actual cause if it is the but-for cause, or if multiple causes or parties, if it was a substantial factor

      b. Act is proximate cause if was within foreseeable risk created by conduct

        i. Dependent intervening cause supersedes liability only when abnormal

        ii. Independent intervening cause supersedes liability only when unforeseeable

    2. **(Application)** Ringo's firing of the pistol was the but-for cause of the victim's death and also the proximate cause because the delayed ambulance was a foreseeable independent intervening cause

      a. Bullet and Paul's statement establish that Ringo's firing the pistol was but-for cause of victim's death

      b. Ambulance's delay was intervening cause because had ambulance been timely, victim would have survived

      c. Ambulance's delay was independent of Ringo's act, and because of post-hurricane conditions, delay was foreseeable

      d. Firing the weapon was the reckless act

    3. **(Conclusion)** Ringo's act was the actual and proximate cause of unlawful killing and his act was reckless

  B. What culpable mental state is established by the evidence?

    1. **(Rule)** Murder is unlawful killing of human being with malice; manslaughter is unlawful killing of human being without malice

      a. For murder, malice may be express or implied

        i. Express malice means defendant intended to kill his victim or inflict grievous bodily harm or knew with substantial certainty that actions would result in victim's death or injury

        ii. Implied malice means defendant caused death as result of unjustified risk creation that manifests wanton disregard for value of human life; requires proof that defendant caused extreme risk to others as result of unjustified risk creation and/or that risk was result of base antisocial motive

      b. For manslaughter, crime is caused either by recklessness or criminal negligence

    2. **(Application)**

      a. No express malice, because Ringo did not even know girl was on balcony

      b. Implied malice may be present

        i. Firing deadly weapon into the air without legal justification in populated area creates risk to human life and demonstrates recklessness

       ii. Ringo's motive for firing weapon was base antisocial motive because he was covering up for professional dereliction

    c. If no implied malice, Ringo is subject to charge of manslaughter and has no applicable defenses

  3. **(Conclusion)** Ringo should be charged with murder but may be convicted only of manslaughter if malice cannot be shown

II. Felony Murder

A. Was Ringo guilty as co-felon under accomplice liability rules?

  1. **(Rule)** Defendant must have committed underlying felony to be convicted of felony murder

    a. Person is liable as accomplice if gives assistance or encouragement or fails to act where he has legal duty to oppose crime of another and purposefully intends to effectuate commission of crime

  2. **(Application)** Ringo provided encouragement to Paul to commit solicitation and he had legal duty to oppose the crime

    a. Ringo assisted Paul in covering up the felony

    b. Ringo can assert his encouragement came too late

  3. **(Conclusion)** Ringo will likely be found guilty of the felony as an accomplice

B. Does felony solicitation of prostitution fall within felony murder?

  1. **(Rule)** Felony murder is killing proximately caused during commission or attempted commission of serious or inherently dangerous felony

    a. Inherent dangerousness determined by applicable statute or whether felony is dangerous by definition—i.e., whether felony can be committed without causing inherent danger to human life

  2. **(Application)** Solicitation of prostitution is not inherently dangerous

    a. Does not carry inherent risk of injury or death

    b. Can be and normally is committed without endangering human life

  3. **(Conclusion)** It is unlikely that solicitation would be sufficient to charge Ringo with felony murder

C. Was the death foreseeable?

  1. **(Rule)** Death must be a foreseeable outgrowth of defendant's actions

    a. Most deaths considered foreseeable

  2. **(Application)** Death was only peripherally related to felony

    a. Ringo fired shots as result of Paul losing his weapon, not due to solicitation itself

    b. However, courts take liberal view of foreseeability

  3. **(Conclusion)** Although not really an outgrowth of felony, liberal view could conclude there was foreseeability

D. Did the murder occur in the commission of the felony?

  1. **(Rule)** Death must occur during commission of perpetration of felony

    a. Can occur while defendant is fleeing from scene of felony

    b. Felony has terminated if defendant has reached place of temporary safety

  2. **(Application)** Felony apparently terminated by time murder occurred

    a. Death occurred after officers took several actions subsequent to the felony

    b. Officers not in flight when Ringo fired pistol

      c. Prosecution could argue felony was ongoing until officers recovered weapon

  3. **(Conclusion)** Felony probably terminated by time of murder but possible court could find felony was ongoing

III. **Other Crimes**

  A. Felony Solicitation of Prostitution

    1. **(Rule)** Felony solicitation of prostitution is soliciting any other person to engage in sexual relations in exchange for payment of any kind

      a. Solicitation is specific intent crime which is complete at time solicitation is made

      b. No defense based on impossibility or withdrawal, but may defend on basis of voluntary intoxication

      c. Accomplice liability exists if defendant gives encouragement or assistance to crime

    2. **(Application)** Paul suggested encounter to prostitute in exchange for payment, and Ringo encouraged Paul to commit the solicitation

      a. Paul knew bar was a brothel and suggested to prostitute that they meet in private

      b. Paul's intoxication did not appear to affect intent

      c. Ringo encouraged Paul to "go for it" and then helped with cover-up

      d. Ringo can argue encouragement came to late

      e. Ringo's intoxication did not appear to affect intent

    3. **(Conclusion)** Paul can likely be charged with felony solicitation, and Ringo can possibly be charged as well

  B. Unlawful Discharge of Firearm

    1. **(Rule)** Person commits misdemeanor by willfully discharging firearm without legal authority or justification

      a. "Willfully" encompasses "intentionally" and "purposely"

      b. Accomplice liability exists if defendant gives encouragement or assistance to crime

    2. **(Application)** Ringo lacked legal authority or justification to fire the weapon, and Paul encouraged Ringo to commit the offense

      a. As a police officer, Ringo has the legal authority to carry a firearm, but here he did not have the authority or justification to discharge it

      b. Paul encouraged Ringo by saying "Okay, let's do it," and Paul had a statutory duty to prevent the crime

    3. **(Conclusion)** Paul and Ringo can likely both be charged with unlawful discharge of a firearm

  C. Conspiracy to Commit Unlawful Discharge of a Firearm

    1. **(Rule)** A conspiracy is an agreement between two or more persons to commit a crime

      a. Actual agreement is required, but need not be express

      b. Required mental state is intent to agree and intent to achieve objective of agreement

      c. Overt act in furtherance of conspiracy is required, but need only be committed by one member and mere preparation suffices

      d. Conspiracy does not merge into target crime

      e. Conspirators are liable for co-conspirators' crimes where crimes were foreseeable outgrowth of conspiracy and committed in furtherance of conspiracy

2. **(Application)** Ringo and Paul agreed to have Ringo fire shots into the air
   a. Paul's statement of "Okay, let's do it" constituted agreement to the plan
   b. Paul had an interest in executing plan, so there was shared intent to commit offense
   c. Ringo removing his pistol was the overt act
   d. Killing was possibly foreseeable, but was inadvertent and not committed in furtherance of the conspiracy
3. **(Conclusion)** Both parties can be convicted of conspiracy, but Paul will not be liable for killing pursuant to the conspiracy

Criminal Law

In Class

This sample answer would be considered above the standard expected of a 1L student.

Part 1

In order to determine what homicide charge to bring against Ringo, it is necessary to first determine whether Ringo is legally responsible for causing an unlawful killing, and if so, to next determine what culpable mental state the evidence establishes.

Proof of Causation

In order to prove that a defendant is guilty of criminal homicide (either murder or manslaughter), the prosecution will need to prove beyond a reasonable doubt that the defendant was the actual and proximate cause of the victim's death, and that the act that caused the death concurred with his criminal state of mind. The defendant's act is the actual cause of the victim's death if either the death would not have occurred but for the defendant's act, or, where there are multiple causes or other parties responsible for the death, if the defendant's act was a substantial factor causing the death. In order for the defendant's act to be the proximate cause of the victim's death, the death must be within the foreseeable risk created by the defendant's conduct.

Here, there is sufficient evidence to prove actual causation. But for Ringo's firing the pistol, the victim would not have died. This is established by evidence that the bullet recovered from the victim's body was fired from Ringo's pistol, and Paul admitted the details of the plan to the police. As discussed further below, the prosecution will also be able to show that Ringo's act concurred with his criminal state of mind, inasmuch as firing the weapon was the reckless act. The question of proximate cause is more complex. The investigation established that the victim would have survived had the ambulance arrived sooner, and the ambulance's delay was due to the debris and darkness caused by the hurricane. Therefore, the ambulance's delay could be seen as an intervening cause responsible for the victim's death.

Because there is an intervening cause, the prosecution must prove that it was foreseeable, and therefore does not cut off Ringo's legal responsibility for the death. This is known as proximate cause analysis. In order to determine whether the intervening cause (the delayed ambulance) was a superseding cause, the jury will consider whether it was dependent or independent. A dependent (responsive) intervening cause supersedes liability only when it is abnormal; an independent (coincidence) intervening cause supersedes liability only when it is unforeseeable. Here the delay to the ambulance was independent of Ringo's act—nothing Ringo did caused the delay. As a result, it is an independent intervening cause. Only if the delay was unforeseeable will it supersede Ringo's liability. Because of the conditions in New Orleans at the time of the shooting, there was nothing unforeseeable about an ambulance's being delayed by lack of street lights, debris, and flooding. Accordingly, as a foreseeable intervention, the delay does not supersede as the cause, and Ringo's actual cause is also the proximate cause of death.

Mens Rea: The Key to Determine the Crime With Which Ringo Should Be Charged

The key to assessing liability for criminal homicide is determining what mental state the evidence supports. Murder is the unlawful killing of a human being with malice. In order to convict Ringo of murder, the evidence must establish beyond a reasonable doubt that Ringo acted with malice when he caused the death. If the prosecution can prove that the only fair and rational hypothesis supported by the evidence is that Ringo acted with malice, it has met its burden of proving the requisite mental state to convict for the crime of murder. If, however, the prosecution is unable to prove Ringo acted with malice but nonetheless committed an unlawful killing, it has proved the mental state to support conviction of the lesser offense of manslaughter.

The malice required for murder may be express or implied. In order to prove Ringo acted with express malice, the prosecution must prove that he intended to kill his victim (meaning it was his conscious objective to kill her or that he knew with substantial certainty that his conduct would cause death), or that he intended to inflict grievous bodily harm on the victim (meaning the defendant had a conscious desire to inflict serious bodily injury, which is significant but non-fatal injury, or a substantial certainty that the defendant's actions would result in the victim's injury). The facts do not support proof of express malice, as there is no indication that Ringo even knew the girl was on the balcony. Instead, the facts indicate that the killing was unintentional, requiring analysis of implied malice.

It is also possible to prove malice for an inadvertent or unintended killing. Malice may be implied when the defendant causes death as the result of unjustified risk creation that manifests a wanton disregard for the value of human life. Often referred to as depraved-heart murder, because malice is the requisite mental state to convict for murder, that element is established even when the defendant's malice is implied. Proving implied malice requires proof that the defendant caused an extreme risk to other human beings as the result of his unjustified risk creation, and/or that the risk he created was the result of a base antisocial motive.

The evidence in this case supports a charge for implied malice murder. The prosecution will be able to prove Ringo created an unjustifiable risk to human life. Firing rounds wildly into the air with no legal justification in a populated area always creates risk to human life, because a pistol is a deadly weapon. Although it is reasonable to infer that the population had been reduced as the result of the hurricane, the fact that the officers were on patrol and that there were patrons at the bar indicates that the officers knew there were still residents in the area. The evidence indicates that Ringo was reckless, as it is reasonable to infer from the fact that as an experienced officer he was familiar with the neighborhood, that he knew firing a weapon into the air created risk, but that he ignored that risk. Had he fired the pistol into the dirt, that might have substantially reduced the risk, but he chose to endanger human life by firing into the air. The fact that the power was out and the weather was hot further supports this inference because these are circumstances from which the jury may infer Ringo knew residents would be seeking relief from the heat by staying outside, including on their balconies. Although the risk was not extreme (for example, like driving a car on a sidewalk with many pedestrians), it was unjustified.

Furthermore, the reason Ringo created this risk is highly relevant to proving implied malice. Ringo was covering up for his professional dereliction and to help his partner cover up his commission of the felony of soliciting prostitution. This was a base antisocial motive inasmuch as Ringo put other human beings at risk to protect himself after engaging in wrongdoing. The fact that he is a police officer only exacerbates the impact of this motive. As an officer, he was sworn to protect the public, not to endanger them unjustifiably in order to protect himself from professional and possible criminal sanction for his dereliction. When Ringo's motive is added to the equation, it transforms what is normally just recklessness into malice, and therefore supports a charge and conviction for murder.

Under the statute, manslaughter is the unlawful killing of a human being without malice. In the case of manslaughter, the crime is caused either by recklessness or criminal negligence (or, in jurisdictions with a misdemeanor-manslaughter statute, during the commission or attempted commission of a misdemeanor). It must be noted that proving implied malice is always a challenge because it is difficult to convince the finder of fact that a defendant who kills unintentionally is guilty of murder. If the jury determines that the evidence does not prove Ringo acted with a wanton disregard for the value of human life, and therefore acted without malice, Ringo's reckless conduct supports a conviction of the lesser-included offense of manslaughter.

Because there is no evidence to raise a defense of justification or excuse, Ringo's conduct was unlawful within the meaning of the law. Ringo may seek to raise the defense of voluntary intoxication. However, recklessness is the key mental element to either implied malice murder or manslaughter. Because this is a general intent mental state, and voluntary intoxication is relevant only to negate specific intent, Ringo will not be permitted to offer this evidence because it is irrelevant.

Based on this evidence, Ringo should be charged with murder (based on an implied malice theory). However, it is very likely that even if he is charged with murder, Ringo will be convicted of the lesser-included offense of manslaughter. The evidence establishes that the killing resulted from Ringo's recklessness in disregarding the known risk that firing a weapon into the air in that area at that time could cause the death of a human being. Whether the evidence also supports the conclusion that his recklessness also manifested a wanton disregard to human life is a closer call.

Part 2

The issues are (1) whether Ringo would be guilty as a co-felon under accomplice liability rules; (2) whether felony solicitation of prostitution is a felony that falls within the felony-murder rule; (3) whether the death was foreseeable; and (4) whether the murder occurred in the commission of the felony.

Felony murder is a killing proximately caused during the commission or attempted commission of a serious or inherently dangerous felony. It includes both intentional and accidental killings. It also includes liability for the acts of one's accomplices during the commission of such a felony. The felony must be an inherently dangerous one. There are two ways to assess inherent dangerousness. First, if the felony is listed in the statute, the requirement is conclusively satisfied. However, this jurisdiction does not include a list of felonies, but instead references any inherently dangerous felony. Normally, felonies within this category include *malum in se* felonies such as burglary, arson, robbery, rape, or kidnapping. States that follow the Abstract Theory of Inherent Dangerousness include only felonies that are dangerous by definition, and not those that are dangerous only by the manner of commission. This test asks whether there is any way to commit the felony without causing an inherent danger to human life. If the answer is yes, the felony is not considered inherently dangerous and may not be used as a predicate offense for felony murder.

To establish felony murder, the resulting death must be a foreseeable outgrowth of the defendant's actions; however, most deaths are considered foreseeable for purposes of felony murder. In addition, the resulting death must occur during the commission or perpetration of the felony. If a killing occurs while the defendant is fleeing from the scene of the felony, he may still be guilty of felony murder. However, if he has reached a place of temporary safety, the felony is deemed to have "terminated," and the defendant can no longer be found guilty of felony murder.

Under the rules of accomplice liability, an accomplice to a crime is fully liable for the crime being committed. An individual is criminally liable as an accomplice if he gives assistance or encouragement or fails to act where he has a legal duty to oppose the crime of another and purposefully intends to effectuate commission of the crime.

In order to charge and convict for felony murder, it is not necessary to prove the defendant acted with malice. However, it is necessary to prove the defendant committed the underlying (predicate) felony. To convict Ringo of felony murder, this means the prosecution must prove Ringo committed the felony solicitation of prostitution. Here, although Ringo did not use the services of the prostitute, he is nonetheless guilty of felony solicitation as an accomplice. Ringo provided encouragement to Paul to commit the crime and then gave assistance in covering up the felony by developing and implementing the plan to create an explanation for how Paul's weapon was lost. Ringo, however, could argue that he told Paul to "go for it" only after Paul had committed the solicitation offense, which was too late to satisfy the encouragement element for accomplice liability.

Assuming the evidence proves Ringo was an accomplice to the felony, the prosecution must still satisfy three requirements. First, felony solicitation of prostitution does not appear to be a felony that would fall within the felony-murder rule as it is applied in this jurisdiction. Solicitation of prostitution is defined as soliciting any other person to engage in sexual relations in exchange for payment of any kind. Unlike felonies recognized as inherently dangerous, such as burglary, arson, and rape, solicitation of prostitution does not carry an inherent risk of injury or death. Felony solicitation of prostitution is not inherently dangerous pursuant to the abstract test. There are numerous ways in which this offense can be (and normally is) committed without endangering human life. Accordingly, it fails the abstract test, and a felony murder charge based on this felony is defective and will be dismissed. Therefore, it is unlikely that this felony would be sufficient to charge Ringo with felony murder.

Second, in the unlikely event that a court will conclude the felony is inherently dangerous, Ringo could argue that the resulting death was not foreseeable. Here, Paul solicited the prostitute at the bar, and Ringo's conduct of shooting his pistol into the air after he and Paul left the bar was a result of Paul's having left his weapon behind, not of the solicitation itself. This seems only peripherally related to the felony transaction, and therefore unforeseeable. However, as courts generally take a liberal view of foreseeability, it is possible that the victim's death could be deemed foreseeable.

Third, even if felony solicitation of prostitution were deemed to fall within the felony-murder rule, the prosecution would still need to prove that the murder occurred during the attempt, commission, or immediate flight from the felony. The facts suggest that the felony had terminated by the time the murder occurred. The officers left the bar, walked for several minutes, looked for the weapon, went back to the bar to look further, left the bar again, and discussed a plan, and only then did Ringo fire the shot that appears to have killed the victim. However, the prosecution might argue that until the officers recovered the weapon the felony was still ongoing. This is not a strong argument, and because the officers were not in flight in any way at the time Ringo fired the pistol, it is unlikely the death will properly be attributed to the felony.

Although the prosecution might be able to establish that Ringo is liable for the felony itself, that the murder was foreseeable, and that the murder occurred during the commission of the felony, the felony-murder charge would be unlikely to survive a motion to dismiss because felony solicitation would not be found to fall within the felony-murder rule.

Part 3

There are several other crimes with which Paul and Ringo may be charged.

Felony Solicitation of Prostitution

Paul, and potentially Ringo, may be charged with felony solicitation of prostitution.

In this jurisdiction, felony solicitation of prostitution is defined as soliciting any other person to engage in sexual relations in exchange for payment of any kind. Solicitation is a specific intent crime, under which the solicitor must intend that the solicitee perform criminal acts. The offense is complete at the time the solicitation is made. Neither impossibility nor withdrawal is a defense to solicitation.

As noted above, under the rules of accomplice liability, an accomplice to a crime is fully liable for the crime being committed. An individual is criminally liable as an accomplice if he gives assistance or encouragement or fails to act where he has a legal duty to oppose the crime of another, and purposefully intends to effectuate commission of the crime.

Voluntary intoxication may be a valid defense for a specific intent crime if it negates the requisite mental state, and may negate a purposeful or knowing mental state.

Here, Paul can be charged with felony solicitation of prostitution. Paul went into the local bar, knowing it was a clandestine brothel, and then suggested to the prostitute that they have a few drinks "in private." Paul also mentioned price to her—in making a joke about price gouging—and after their encounter, stated that "that was the best money" he had spent all week. Paul had the specific intent to have the woman engage in prostitution, and the solicitation was complete prior to the actual encounter itself. While Paul can argue that he was intoxicated, and therefore did not have the requisite intent to commit the crime, he does not seem to have been so impaired by alcohol that he lacked the specific intent to commit solicitation.

Ringo may also be charged under the rules of accomplice liability for felony solicitation of prostitution. He encouraged Paul to "go for it," and then assisted Paul afterwards in covering up the crime. Ringo had a duty to stop Paul from committing the crime, but instead he offered assistance and encouragement. However, as noted above, Ringo could argue that he told Paul to "go for it" only after Paul had committed the solicitation offense, which was too late to qualify as proof of accomplice liability. Finally, like Paul, Ringo can argue that his intoxication negated his intent to assist Paul in the solicitation, but there are no facts to indicate that Ringo's intoxication was so great as to negate his intent.

It is likely that both Paul and Ringo can be charged with felony solicitation of prostitution, although the case is certainly stronger against Paul.

Unlawful Discharge of a Firearm

Ringo, and potentially Paul, could be charged with unlawful discharge of a firearm.

In this jurisdiction, a person will be guilty of a misdemeanor if he willfully discharges a firearm without legal authority or justification. The term "willfully" encompasses the concepts of "intentionally" and "purposely," as opposed to accidentally or negligently. As noted above, under the rules of accomplice liability, an accomplice to a crime is fully liable for the crime being committed. An individual is criminally liable as an accomplice if he gives assistance or encouragement or fails to act where he has a legal duty to oppose the crime of another, and purposefully intends to effectuate commission of the crime.

Ringo can be charged with unlawful discharge of a firearm. Although Ringo has the legal authority to carry his firearm and to fire it under appropriate circumstances while on duty, in this particular situation, Ringo did not have legal authority or justification to discharge his firearm. He fired the shots into the air on purpose, in order to make the cover-up plausible.

Paul may also be charged with unlawful discharge of a firearm as an accomplice. Paul and Ringo discussed their predicament, and once Ringo told Paul of his idea for explaining how Paul lost his weapon—which would include Ringo's firing shots into the air—Paul replied, "Okay, let's do it." Paul's statement is evidence of encouragement and proves his intent that Ringo commit the offense. Although Paul may argue Ringo needed no encouragement to commit the offense, this is irrelevant. The encouragement need not be a causal factor in the commission of the offense; it is sufficient that the accomplice did some act of facilitation with the intent to bring about the target offense. Furthermore, as a police officer Paul had a statutory duty to prevent the commission of a crime, even by his partner. His failure to intervene to do so, when coupled with this statutory duty, also supports convicting him as an accomplice by omission.

It is likely that both Paul and Ringo can be charged with unlawful discharge of a firearm.

Conspiracy to Commit Unlawful Discharge of a Firearm

Both Paul and Ringo can potentially be charged with conspiracy to commit unlawful discharge of a firearm.

As noted above, this jurisdiction's statute provides that any person who conspires with another person to commit any offense made punishable by the code is guilty of conspiracy. A conspiracy is an agreement between two or more persons to commit a crime. An actual agreement is required, but the agreement need not be express. Rather, it may be proved circumstantially by conduct where the conspirators demonstrate over time that they intended to achieve the same objective and agree to work together toward that end. Conspiracy is a specific intent crime. The mental state required is both the intent to agree and the intent to achieve the objective of the agreement. An overt act in furtherance of the conspiracy is required for conspiracy liability. The overt act need only be committed by one member of the conspiracy and may be trivial; mere preparation will suffice. Conspiracy does not merge into the target crime upon completion.

Here, Paul and Ringo discussed their predicament, and Ringo told Paul of his idea for explaining how Paul lost his weapon, which would include Ringo's firing shots into the air. When Paul said, "Okay, let's do it," he implicitly—if not explicitly—agreed to the plan. Furthermore, the evidence indicates Paul had an obvious interest in executing the plan as it was his weapon that was lost during his dereliction. This evidence can be used to infer a shared intent to commit the offense. As soon as Ringo removed his pistol, the overt act requirement was satisfied. Because an agreement need not be explicit, Paul's conduct and statement can be interpreted as an implicit agreement to the plan of having Ringo fire his weapon. This evidence satisfies all the elements of conspiracy, and both parties are guilty.

In addition, it is possible that Paul could be liable for the killing under the theory of liability for a co-conspirator's crimes. The Pinkerton doctrine provides that each conspirator is liable for the crimes of all the other co-conspirators where the crimes were both a foreseeable outgrowth of the conspiracy and committed in furtherance of the conspiratorial goal. However, while the death might be deemed to be foreseeable under the liberal approach taken by the courts, it was not committed in furtherance of the conspiratorial goal; rather, it was an inadvertent and unintended outcome of the conspiracy. Thus, Paul would be unlikely to be liable for the killing pursuant to the conspiracy.

Criminal Law

In Class Question

This sample answer would be considered below the standard expected of a 1L student.

Part 1

The prosecution will need to prove beyond a reasonable doubt that the defendant was the actual and proximate cause of the victim's death, and that the act that caused the death concurred with his criminal state of mind. The defendant's act must be the "but for" cause of the victim's death. Proximate cause must also be established.

Here, the victim would not have died if Ringo did not fire the pistol. However, it is hard to say whether there is proximate cause because of the delay of the ambulance. The fact that the ambulance was delayed by the darkness and debris could mean that Ringo's conduct did not actually cause the resulting death—the delayed ambulance did. But, if Ringo could have foreseen the delay, then he will still be responsible, unless he can show that he was so drunk that he couldn't form the intent to commit the homicide.

As to the offense with which Ringo should be charged, we must determine whether Ringo is legally responsible for causing an unlawful killing. If so, we then have to determine what culpable mental state the evidence establishes.

Murder is the unlawful killing of a human being with malice. If the prosecution can prove that Ringo acted with malice, it has met its burden of proving the requisite mental state to convict for the crime of murder. If the prosecution can only prove Ringo committed an unlawful killing, it has proved the mental state to support conviction of the lesser offense of manslaughter.

There is no evidence to raise a defense of justification or excuse, so Ringo's conduct was unlawful. The malice required for murder may be express or implied. The facts do not support proof of express malice, inasmuch as there is no indication that Ringo even knew the girl was on the balcony. Instead, the facts indicate that the killing was inadvertent. Malice may be implied when the defendant causes death as the result of unjustified risk creation that manifests a wanton disregard for the value of human life. This is often referred to as depraved-heart murder, which requires proof that the defendant caused an extreme risk to other human beings as the result of his unjustified risk creation. Here, Ringo's behavior created a risk to human life, and he was reckless.

Ringo could also be charged with manslaughter, if the evidence is not sufficient to prove malice. The evidence establishes that the killing resulted from Ringo's recklessness in disregarding the known risk that firing a weapon into the air in that area at that time could cause the death of a human being, but it is not clear if he also had a wanton disregard for human life.

Part 2

Felony murder is a killing proximately caused during the commission or attempted commission of a serious or inherently dangerous felony. It includes liability for the acts of one's accomplices during the commission of such a felony. A felony described in a statute as sufficient for felony murder is deemed inherent danger-ousness. There is no statute here, though. States that follow the Abstract Theory of Inherent Dangerousness include only felonies that are dangerous by definition, and not those that are dangerous only by the manner of commission. In addition, the resulting death must be foreseeable. Also, it must occur during the commis-sion or perpetration of the felony.

An accomplice to a crime is fully liable for the crime being committed. An individual is criminally liable as an accomplice if he gives assistance or encouragement or fails to act where he has a legal duty to oppose the crime of another and purpose-fully intends to effectuate commission of the crime.

To convict Ringo of felony murder, the prosecution must prove Ringo commit-ted felony solicitation of prostitution. Here, Ringo is guilty of felony solicitation because he encouraged Paul to commit the crime and then gave assistance in covering up the felony by developing and implementing the plan to create an explanation for how Paul's weapon was lost. If Ringo was an accomplice to the felony, the prosecution must still show that felony solicitation of prostitution falls within the felony-murder rule. Solicitation of prostitution does not carry an inherent risk of injury or death. Therefore, it is unlikely that this felony would be sufficient to charge Ringo with felony murder.

If a court will conclude the felony is inherently dangerous, Ringo could argue that the resulting death was not foreseeable. Here, Paul solicited the prostitute at the bar, and Ringo fired the shots because Paul forgot his gun. This question would depend on how strictly the court interprets the foreseeability requirement.

Part 3

Paul may be charged with felony solicitation of prostitution. Felony solicitation of prostitution is defined as soliciting any other person to engage in sexual relations in exchange for payment of any kind. The offense is complete at the time the solicitation is made. Voluntary intoxication may be a valid defense for this crime.

Paul went into the local bar and suggested to the prostitute that they have a few drinks "in private." Paul also mentioned price to her, and after their encounter, he stated that "that was the best money" he had spent all week. Paul had the intent to have the woman engage in prostitution, and the solicitation was complete prior to the actual encounter itself. Paul can argue that he was intoxicated, and therefore did not have the requisite intent to commit the crime, but he does not seem to have been so impaired by alcohol that he lacked the intent to commit solicitation.

Ringo, and potentially Paul, could be charged with unlawful discharge of a firearm. A person will be guilty of a misdemeanor if he willfully discharges a firearm without legal authority or justification. An accomplice to a crime is fully liable for the crime being committed. An individual is criminally liable as an accomplice if he gives assistance or encouragement or fails to act where he has a legal duty to oppose the crime of another.

Ringo can be charged with unlawful discharge of a firearm. Although Ringo has the legal authority to carry a firearm because he is a police officer, here, Ringo did not have legal authority or justification to discharge his firearm. He fired the shots into the air on purpose, in order to make the cover-up plausible.

Paul may also potentially be charged with unlawful discharge of a firearm as an accomplice. After Ringo told Paul of his idea for explaining how Paul lost his weapon, Paul replied, "Okay, let's do it." Paul encouraged Ringo. Paul might be able to refute this charge by arguing that Ringo needed no encouragement to commit the offense. But, as a police officer, Paul also had a statutory duty to prevent the commission of a crime, even by his partner. His failure to intervene to do so suggests he should be convicted as an accomplice.

Criminal Law

Homework Question 1

Dennis and his friend are at a fast-food restaurant late one evening. They are from out of town. While Dennis and his friend are eating, a group of locals comes in and starts harassing them. When Dennis and his friend exit the restaurant, the locals follow them and about 10 of the locals attack Dennis and his friend. The locals beat them with fists and kicks (but no weapons) severely. Dennis is able to break free and run to his SUV while being chased by the group. When he gets in, he sees his friend on the ground being kicked by about four locals. Dennis slams on the gas and runs right into the group. He runs over two of the locals and his friend. All three are killed from the collision/being run over. Dennis then exits the parking lot at high speed. A few blocks later, he sees a cop. He pulls over in a panic. The cop asks Dennis, "What happened?" Dennis responds, "All I can say is that I hope I killed those bastards."

This jurisdiction recognizes the "imperfect self-defense rule," under which a defendant may be charged with a lesser offense than the one committed if he makes an honest but unreasonable mistake that force is necessary to repel an attack and uses such force. This jurisdiction is a degree jurisdiction.

You are the prosecutor handling Dennis's case. What should you charge Dennis with and what do you think he will be convicted for?

Criminal Law

Homework Question 1—Outline

I.   Did Dennis have the required mental state for first-degree murder?

    A.   **(Rule)** First-degree murder requires proof of malice and the additional mental state of premeditation and deliberation

        1.   Premeditation is quantity of thought and requires appreciable period of time

        2.   Deliberation is quality of thought and requires that defendant rationally reflected on choice to kill

    B.   **(Application)** Although Dennis killed with purpose, his killing was not premeditated or deliberate

        1.   Dennis's statement to the cop is evidence that he had intent to kill at least some of his victims

        2.   Even if small amount of time Dennis had to contemplate his decision was sufficient to prove premeditation, his state of agitation and confusion disabled his ability to contemplate killing rationally

        3.   Time between breaking away and driving into the group was brief

            a.   May be insufficient for premeditation

    C.   **(Conclusion)** A first-degree murder charge is untenable

II. Did Dennis have the required mental state for second-degree murder?

    A.   **(Rule)** Second-degree murder is a killing with malice where the additional elements of premeditation and deliberation cannot be proven

        1.   Includes intent to kill formed in spur of the moment or where defendant's mental process was compromised, and all other types of murder

    B.   **(Application)** Dennis acted with purpose to kill without premeditation or deliberation, but heat of passion may negate malice

        1.   Dennis's statement shows he acted with purpose to kill; even without statement, Dennis likely knew with substantial certainty that driving SUV into crowd would cause death

        2.   Dennis's conduct was at least intended to inflict grievous bodily harm

        3.   However, Dennis formed intent to kill during sudden heat of passion resulting from adequate provocation, so no malice

    C.   **(Conclusion)** Dennis can be charged with second-degree murder but a conviction is uncertain due to possible lack of malice

III. Did Dennis have the required mental state for voluntary manslaughter?

    A.   **(Rule)** Voluntary manslaughter is an intentional killing committed during sudden heat of passion resulting from adequate provocation negating malice; transferred intent doctrine preserves liability where defendant intends criminal conduct against one party but instead harms another party

        1.   Adequate provocation must be such that reasonable person would lose self-control

        2.   There must be a causal connection between legally adequate grounds for provocation and killing

      3. Time period between heat of passion and fatal act must not be long enough that reasonable person would have cooled off

      4. Intent is established by proving defendant intended to kill a human being, not a particular human being

          a. Transferred intent doctrine prevents defendant from avoiding criminal responsibility when he intended to produce a result, but harm inflicted on wrong victim

B. **(Application)** Dennis was adequately provoked and had not cooled off at time of killing

      1. Dennis was victim of serious battery, which could be adequate provocation

      2. Committed killing moments later, before he had cooled off

      3. Dennis did not intend to kill his friend, but he can be liable because he intended harm to others

C. **(Conclusion)** Dennis could be convicted of voluntary manslaughter

IV.   Was Dennis justified in using self-defense?

A. **(Rule)** Using lethal force is justified when necessary to defend oneself or a third person from imminent threat of death or grievous bodily harm

      1. Amount of force used must be proportional to the initial attack

B. **(Application)** Dennis could have honestly believed driving his SUV into the crowd was necessary to protect himself or his friend, but may not have been reasonable

      1. Dennis was safe in his SUV when he drove into the crowd

      2. But, could be objectively reasonable to believe driving into crowd was only viable means of defending his friend from death or grievous bodily harm

C. **(Conclusion)** Dennis might be justified by self-defense or defense of others, depending on whether his belief that deadly force was necessary was reasonable

V.   Does the imperfect self-defense rule apply to mitigate murder to voluntary manslaughter?

A. **(Rule)** Imperfect self-defense may mitigate murder to voluntary manslaughter where defendant was either at fault in starting an altercation, or unreasonably, but honestly, believed harm was imminent or use of deadly force was necessary

      1. Defendant's honest but unreasonable judgment as to necessity may apply to self-defense, defense of others, crime prevention, coercion and necessity

B. **(Application)** Dennis may have honestly but unreasonably believed deadly force was necessary

      1. Dennis was probably unreasonable because had reached apparent safety of car

      2. Driving SUV into crowd may be excessive in response to beating with no weapons

C. **(Conclusion)** Dennis has a good likelihood of prevailing on an imperfect self-defense argument

Criminal Law

Homework Question 1—Sample Answer

This sample answer would be considered above the standard expected of a 1L student.

Dennis can potentially be charged with first-degree murder, second-degree murder, or voluntary manslaughter of the two locals and his friend. The issues are whether Dennis's state of mind satisfied the standard for first-degree murder, second-degree murder, or voluntary manslaughter, and if he could be charged with murder, whether imperfect self-defense could mitigate murder to voluntary manslaughter.

First-degree murder includes intent-to-kill murder committed with premeditation and deliberation. All murder requires proof that the defendant killed with malice. First-degree murder requires proof of the additional mental state of premeditation and deliberation. Most jurisdictions define premeditation as quantity of thought, and require an appreciable period of time to satisfy premeditation (although there is no defined time). Deliberation is defined as quality of thought, and requires proof that the defendant rationally reflected on the choice to kill. In order to prove first-degree murder, intent to kill means only purpose to kill, inasmuch as deliberation necessarily requires a purpose to kill. A defendant can kill intentionally without premeditation and deliberation when he kills in the "spur of the moment." Second-degree murder is any killing with malice where the prosecution cannot prove the additional elements of premeditation and deliberation. This includes intent to kill formed in the spur of the moment or when the defendant's mental process was compromised, and all other types of murder.

Voluntary manslaughter is an intentional killing committed during a sudden heat of passion resulting from adequate provocation negating malice; it is commonly called a "heat-of-passion killing." Adequate provocation, measured objectively, must be such that a reasonable person would lose self-control. A causal connection must exist between the legally adequate grounds for provocation and the killing. The time period between the heat of passion and the fatal act must not be long enough that a reasonable person would have cooled off. Courts will commonly find that a defendant was adequately provoked when he killed after he was the victim of a serious battery or a threat of deadly force.

Using lethal force is justified and therefore lawful when necessary to defend oneself or a third person from an imminent threat of death or grievous bodily harm. The amount of force used must be proportional to the initial attack. In other words, if something short of deadly force would effectively ward off the attack, deadly force is not necessary and, therefore, not reasonable. Imperfect self-defense may mitigate murder to voluntary manslaughter where a defendant was either at fault in starting an altercation, or unreasonably, but honestly, believed that harm was imminent or that use of deadly force was necessary. The defendant's honest but unreasonable judgment as to necessity has been applied to self-defense, defense of others, crime prevention, coercion, and necessity.

In addition, the transferred intent doctrine preserves liability where a defendant intends criminal conduct against one party but instead harms another party. The law requires proof of intent to produce a result. When it is intent to kill, the element is established by proving that the defendant intended to kill a human being, not a particular human being. The transferred intent doctrine accounts for this by preventing a defendant from avoiding criminal responsibility when he intended to produce a result, but the harm was inflicted on the wrong victim. Although the defendant may not have intended to harm the actual victim, as long as the proof establishes he intended to harm a victim, the intent element is satisfied

Here, Dennis likely cannot be charged with first-degree murder. The evidence does suggest that Dennis killed with purpose; without his statement, it would be uncertain whether he acted with intent to kill or intent to inflict grievous bodily harm (which would be insufficient to prove first-degree murder). However, Dennis's statement to the cop after the collision is evidence that he had intent—i.e., purpose—to kill at least some of his victims. Nonetheless, there is insufficient evidence to prove the killing was premeditated or deliberate. After being beaten by the locals, Dennis broke free and ran to his car, and then, seeing his friend continuing to be attacked, he slammed on the gas pedal and hit the group. Even if the small amount of time Dennis had to contemplate his decision was sufficient to prove premeditation, his state of agitation and confusion disabled his ability to contemplate the killing rationally. Furthermore, the time between his breaking away and driving into the group was brief, and it may be insufficient to prove the necessary time for Dennis to consider the situation or plan to commit murder. Therefore, a first-degree murder charge is untenable.

Dennis may be charged with second-degree murder, although conviction for that offense is far from certain. A second-degree murder conviction requires proof that Dennis killed with malice but without premeditation and deliberation. This means that if Dennis killed his victims intentionally, but without time to rationally decide to do so, he should be charged with second-degree murder. Dennis's statement indicates he acted with the purpose to kill (without premeditation or deliberation). Even if this is not proven, it is reasonable to infer that Dennis knew with substantial certainty that driving his SUV into the crowd would cause death. It is also reasonable to infer that Dennis's conduct was, at a minimum, intended to inflict grievous bodily harm. Second-degree murder is supported by proof of any one of these criminal mental states.

However, even if the proof is sufficient to establish intent to kill, this does not automatically prove malice. Here, the evidence suggests Dennis formed his intent to kill during a sudden heat of passion resulting from an adequate provocation. If the prosecution is unable to disprove this, then it cannot prove malice, for intent formed in a sudden heat of passion is not malice. An unlawful killing without malice is manslaughter, and, therefore, unless the prosecution is able to disprove sudden heat of passion, the most serious offense Dennis will be convicted of will be voluntary (intentional) manslaughter. Here, Dennis was the victim of a serious battery, which could be deemed adequate provocation such that Dennis could lose self-control. As he ran to his car, he was being chased, and he was clearly strongly affected by the battery (although at common law observing a friend (and not a close family member) being victimized by an unlawful act is not considered an adequate provocation). He committed the killing just moments after he and his friend were beaten, and he could not have cooled off during that very brief period, and the facts indicate that he did not cool off; when he pulled over after the collision, he was in a "panic." Furthermore, he intended to kill his provoker, which satisfies another element of adequate provocation. Thus, the facts strongly indicate that the prosecution will not be able to disprove sudden heat of passion, and therefore will fail in their burden to prove malice. Although Dennis did not intend to kill his friend (and, in fact, appeared to act in his defense), the transferred intent doctrine permits liability for a party that the defendant did not intend to harm.

However, Dennis could successfully defend against a second-degree murder or voluntary manslaughter charge by arguing that his behavior was justified in self-defense or defense of a third person. If the finder of fact determines that Dennis honestly and reasonably believed deadly force in the form of driving his SUV into the crowd was necessary to protect himself or his friend from an imminent threat of death or grievous bodily harm, Dennis will have a complete defense by legally justifying the killings. This will require Dennis to convince the finder of fact that his judgment of necessity (his conclusion that he and/or his friend faced imminent threat of death or grievous bodily harm and that his action of driving into the group was a proportional response to this threat) was objectively reasonable. Because Dennis was safe in his SUV when he drove into the crowd, it is unlikely he will prevail on a self-defense theory. However, his claim of defense of others is more viable. If the finder of fact concludes that a reasonable person in Dennis's position would conclude that driving the SUV into the crowd was the only viable means of defending his friend from death or grievous bodily harm, Dennis will have an absolute defense and should be acquitted. The prosecution will likely argue that the amount of force was objectively unreasonable because it was excessive, and that Dennis should have tried to scare the locals by threatening to run into them. Ultimately, this will be a very difficult determination, and could go either way.

If the finder of fact concludes that Dennis made an honest but unreasonable judgment of necessity to defend himself or his friend, Dennis will have a viable claim of imperfect self-defense and defense of others. This means that even if the finder of fact rejects the sudden heat-of-passion theory, Dennis would still be acquitted of murder and convicted of the lesser offense of voluntary manslaughter. Here, the evidence on perfect self-defense is uncertain enough where this outcome appears particularly viable. Dennis may have honestly but unreasonably believed that deadly force—hitting the locals with a car—was necessary to prevent deadly force from being used on himself or his friend. Given that Dennis had reached the apparent safety of his car, he probably was unreasonable in believing deadly (or perhaps any) force was needed to protect himself. The finder of fact may also conclude that driving an SUV into a group of human beings was an excessive use of force in response to a beating with fists and feet. However, if it is determined that Dennis nonetheless believed his conduct was necessary and proportional, then malice will be nullified, and Dennis will be guilty of voluntary manslaughter.

Based on this evidence, Dennis should be charged with second-degree murder, but will most likely be convicted of voluntary manslaughter, with a reasonable chance of a total acquittal based on the conclusion his conduct was legally justified.

Criminal Law

Homework Question 2

Suzy, an 18-year-old Riverton High School (RHS) senior and member of the soccer team, was hanging out with Tony, the RHS girls' soccer coach (who also refereed the boys' soccer games) after practice one day. Tony tended to spend more time with his players outside of practice than was typical of the other coaches. Tony mentioned to Suzy that he'd overheard a few kids talking about using fake IDs to get into a local bar, Delmonico's, that weekend. Thinking of his own not-too-distant days of underage drinking, Tony remarked, "You know, it's easy to make those things. Any kid with a scanner, a laminator, and half a brain can make a fake ID and earn a quick $50." Suzy answered, "Oh, wow, that's a good idea!"

After leaving the field where she had been talking with Tony, Suzy went home. Her dad, who had recently been laid off, was lounging on the couch watching sports. Still thinking about what Tony had said, Suzy remembered that her mom used a laminator to make posters for her hand-knitted scarf business. She asked her dad if he could lend her some money, thinking she could go buy a scanner, but he said he didn't have any cash. Suzy left the house and walked to a nearby electronics store, which was closed. Suzy walked around back and found a door that was slightly ajar. She pushed the door open, went inside, and used a stapler she found by the register to break the display glass and grab a scanner. Carrying the scanner, Suzy left the electronics store using the same door through which she had entered.

In the meantime, Tony left RHS and headed home. As he was walking, he passed a group of high school boys in soccer uniforms. He heard one of them shout, "Hey! That guy refereed our soccer game last week and called us off-sides when we totally weren't. Get him!" Tony panicked and ran across the street, shoved a young man who was getting into his pickup truck out of the way, and jumped into the driver's seat. He jammed his foot on the accelerator, which caused the truck to fly forward and hit one of the players, despite Tony's effort to slam on the brakes. The player was killed.

What charges can be brought and what defenses can be raised?

Criminal Law

Homework Question 2—Outline

I. **Suzy**

    A. Burglary

        1. **(Rule)** Common-law crime of burglary requires breaking and entering of dwelling of another at night with intent to commit a felony therein

            a. Today, breaking only requires slight enlargement of opening

            b. Entry is achieved by placing any part of body inside structure

            c. Today, dwelling house includes most structures

            d. Nighttime requirement has been eliminated

        2. **(Application)** Suzy broke into and entered store by pushing door open and walking inside with intent to commit larceny

            a. Under modern statutes, these actions are sufficient to constitute burglary

        3. **(Conclusion)** Suzy can be charged with burglary

    B. Larceny

        1. **(Rule)** Larceny is taking and carrying away of tangible personal property of another with intent to permanently deprive owner thereof

        2. **(Application)** Suzy broke into store, broke display case, and took scanner from the case, then left the store with the scanner

            a. Elements are met and Suzy has no plausible defenses

        3. **(Conclusion)** Suzy can be charged with larceny

II. **Tony**

    A. Battery

        1. **(Rule)** Criminal battery is intentional, reckless, or criminally negligent unlawful application of force to person of the victim

            a. Battery is general intent crime

            b. Force may be direct or indirect

            c. Use of force in self-defense is permitted if person has reasonable belief that he is in imminent danger of unlawful bodily harm

        2. **(Application)** Tony shoved young man in order to steal his truck; he intentionally applied force to the young man

            a. Tony can argue he committed battery in self-defense from soccer players

            b. Tony can also argue he committed batter out of necessity

         3. **(Conclusion)** Tony can be charged with battery

    B. Larceny or Robbery

        1. **(Rule)** Larceny is taking and carrying away of tangible personal property of another with intent to permanently deprive owner thereof; robbery consists of elements of larceny plus (1) taking must be from person or presence of victim; and (2) taking must be accomplished either by force or violence, or by intimidation or threat of violence

            a. Larceny and battery are both lesser-included offenses of robbery

        2. **(Application)** Tony took truck from the presence of the victim by force and drove it away with no intent to return it

            a. Tony may raise self-defense and necessity as defenses under reasoning described above

       b. Tony may also argue he lacked intent to permanently deprive man of truck because he simply wanted to escape from soccer players and planned to return truck once threat had subsided

      3. **(Conclusion)** Tony can be charged with robbery

  C. Felony Murder or Manslaughter

      1. **(Rule)** Felony murder is killing proximately caused during commission or attempted commission of serious or inherently dangerous felony; involuntary manslaughter is unintentional killing resulting without malice aforethought, caused by recklessness or criminal negligence or during commission or attempted commission of an unlawful act

       a. For felony murder, resulting death must be foreseeable outgrowth of defendant's actions, and must occur during commission or perpetration of felony

       b. Felony murder includes both intentional and accidental killings

      2. **(Application)** Tony killed soccer players in the course of committing a robbery, which is an inherently dangerous felony, but if death was not foreseeable, Tony at least acted recklessly

       a. Tony may argue death was not foreseeable outgrowth of robbery or that robbery was already complete when death occurred

       b. Tony acted recklessly by pushing hard on gas pedal, which caused truck to hit player and kill him; can raise defenses of self-defense and necessity, under same reasoning stated above

      3. **(Conclusion)** Tony can be charged with either felony murder or manslaughter

III. **Soccer Players**

  A. Assault

      1. **(Rule)** A person may commit criminal assault by attempting to commit battery or intentionally causing victim to fear an immediate battery

      2. **(Application)** One of the players taunted Tony verbally and a number of them chased him such that he could reasonably fear battery

      3. **(Conclusion)** Soccer players may potentially be charged with assault

Criminal Law

Homework Question 2—Sample Answer

This sample answer would be considered above the standard expected of a 1L student.

<u>Suzy</u>

There are several potential charges that may be brought against Suzy. First, Suzy may be charged with burglary.

The common-law crime of burglary consists of the breaking and entering of a dwelling house of another in the nighttime with the intent to commit a felony there-in. Under modern criminal codes, the required elements have eased somewhat. Today, breaking usually requires only the slightest enlargement of an opening. Entry is achieved by placing any portion of the body inside the structure. A dwelling house today typically includes most structures, regardless of whether they are dwellings. Also, most modern statutes have eliminated the requirement that the breaking and entering occur at night.

Here, Suzy broke into and entered the electronics store by pushing the door open and walking inside with the intent of committing the felony of larceny. Suzy might argue that her acts do not satisfy the elements because she entered through an open door, the structure was an office, and she did not enter at night. However, under modern statutes, this behavior would suffice to meet the required elements of burglary.

Suzy may also be charged with larceny. At common law, larceny is defined as the taking and carrying away of the tangible personal property of another with the intent to permanently deprive the owner thereof.

Here, Suzy broke into the electronics store, broke the glass of the display case, and took a scanner from the case. She then left the store, taking the scanner with her. The elements of larceny are met, and Suzy does not have any plausible defenses.

<u>Tony</u>

Tony may be charged with battery, larceny or robbery, and felony murder or manslaughter.

Criminal battery is the intentional, reckless, or criminally negligent unlawful application of force to the person of the victim. Criminal battery is a general intent crime. The defendant's act of applying force may be direct or indirect. If a person has a reasonable belief that he is in imminent danger of unlawful bodily harm, he may use that amount of force in self-defense that is reasonably necessary to prevent such harm, unless he is the initial aggressor. Reasonable force is justified to avoid imminent injury resulting from natural forces or if an individual reasonably believes that his criminal conduct is necessary to avoid a "greater harm" that would result from compliance with the law.

Here, the elements of battery appear to be satisfied. Tony shoved the young man in order to steal his truck; he intentionally applied force to the young man. Tony might argue that he committed the battery in self-defense because he was trying to protect himself from the soccer players who were chasing him. He might also argue that he committed the battery out of necessity for the same reason.

Tony may also be charged with larceny or robbery. As noted above, at common law, larceny is defined as the taking and carrying away of the tangible personal property of another with the intent to permanently deprive the owner thereof. Robbery is a common-law felony consisting of all of the elements of larceny, plus two additional elements: (1) the taking must be from the person or presence of the victim (meaning an area within his control); and (2) the taking must be accomplished either by force or violence, or by intimidation or the threat of violence. Larceny and battery are both lesser-included offenses of robbery.

Tony took the young man's truck and drove it away, with no apparent intent to return it, such that the elements of larceny are satisfied. In addition, Tony took the truck from the presence of the victim, and did so by force because he shoved the man. Therefore, Tony can be charged with robbery. As with battery, Tony may raise self-defense and necessity as defenses under the reasoning described above. Tony may also be able to argue that he lacked the intent to permanently deprive the man of his truck because he simply wanted to escape from the soccer players and planned to return the truck once the threat had subsided.

Finally, Tony may be charged with felony murder or involuntary manslaughter. Felony murder is a killing proximately caused during the commission or attempted commission of a serious or inherently dangerous felony, such as burglary, arson, robbery, rape, or kidnapping. The resulting death must be a foreseeable outgrowth of the defendant's actions, and it must occur during the commission or perpetration of the felony. Felony murder includes both intentional and accidental killings. Involuntary manslaughter is an unintentional killing resulting without malice aforethought, caused either by recklessness or criminal negligence or during the commission or attempted commission of an unlawful act.

Here, Tony may be charged with felony murder because he killed the soccer player in the course of committing a robbery, which is an inherently dangerous felony. Tony may argue that the death was not a foreseeable outgrowth of his robbery of the truck, or that the robbery was already complete when the death occurred. Should either of these defenses succeed, Tony may still be charged with involuntary manslaughter, which requires only that Tony have acted with recklessness or criminal negligence. Tony acted recklessly by pushing hard on the gas pedal, which caused the truck to hit the player and kill him. Tony could again raise the defenses of self-defense and necessity, under the same reasoning stated above.

Soccer Players

The soccer players may potentially be charged with assault. A person may commit criminal assault by attempting to commit battery or intentionally causing the victim to fear an immediate battery. Here, one of the players taunted Tony verbally, and a number of them chased him such that he could reasonably fear battery. There are no plausible defenses apparent from the fact pattern

Multiple-Choice Questions

HOMICIDE

Question 1

A lawyer was livid after he was unexpectedly laid off from his longtime job with a prestigious firm. The next day, he returned to the firm and fired shotgun rounds into the air. Unfortunately, one of the bullets ricocheted off the wall and killed the lawyer's former secretary. The lawyer later testified, without contradiction, that he had not intended to kill anyone, but simply sought to exact revenge on the firm's managing partner by scaring everyone so badly that they would leave work for the day, thereby causing the firm to miss a critical deadline in a case that the partner was working on.

The crimes below are listed in descending order of seriousness. What is the most serious crime of which the lawyer may properly be convicted?

(A) Murder.

(B) Voluntary manslaughter.

(C) Involuntary manslaughter.

(D) Assault.

Question 2

A married couple was waiting in line for tickets to a movie. A man waiting ahead of them was quite overweight. The husband made several comments to his wife about how fat the man was, which the man overheard. He confronted the husband and demanded an apology. The husband refused. The man again demanded an apology, and threatened to punch the wife if he did not get one. To show he was serious, the man pushed the wife and waved a closed fist in her face. Fearing that his wife would suffer a heart attack from shock, the husband reached down, grabbed a pipe lying nearby on the ground, and beat the man in the head with it repeatedly. The man died from his injuries.

If the husband is prosecuted for criminal homicide, should the court instruct the jury on voluntary manslaughter in addition to murder?

(A) No, because the husband clearly intended to kill or at least seriously injure the man.

(B) No, because the husband was the initial wrongdoer, having provoked the man with his rude comments.

(C) Yes, because the jury could reasonably conclude that the husband lacked the intent to kill or injure and was merely engaged in reckless conduct.

(D) Yes, because the jury could find that the husband unreasonably, but honestly, believed that deadly force was needed to defend his wife.

Question 3

A former minor league baseball pitcher was convicted of steroid use. As required by the terms of his parole, he was prohibited from ever playing baseball again in any form or fashion. One day, as the pitcher was passing by a park, a group of people, knowing of his athletic prowess but not his criminal history, begged him to join their baseball game. He reluctantly agreed to play.

The score was tied and, as he was pitching to the best player on the opposing team, the minor league pitcher decided to throw his famous fastball. The other player, sensing a fastball, moved closer to the plate. The pitcher then threw the fastball and hit the batter in the head, killing him instantly. The pitcher is charged with murder.

How should the court rule?

(A) Guilty, because he was violating his parole at the time of the incident.

(B) Guilty, because a minor league pitcher throwing a ball at such a high rate of speed is reckless.

(C) Guilty, because a baseball is a deadly weapon.

(D) Not guilty.

Question 4

A man left work very late one night and walked to his car, which was parked in a parking garage. As the man neared his car, he heard noises and what sounded like scuffling. The man, who was an avid golfer, grabbed a golf club from his trunk and walked toward the area from where the noise was coming. When he reached the source of the noises, he saw a teenager with a knife in his hand kneeling over an unconscious woman on the ground. The man recognized the woman as his long-time secretary. Believing that the teenager was about to stab the woman, the man swung the golf club at the teenager, hitting him in the head. The teenager died from his injuries. It was later determined that the woman had suffered a seizure, and the teenager was going to use the knife to cut open her turtleneck so that she could breathe more easily.

Is the man guilty of murder for the teenager's death?

(A) Yes, because the man intended to either kill or seriously injure the teenager.

(B) Yes, because the man did not warn the teenager before swinging the golf club.

(C) No, because the man reasonably believed that his action was necessary to prevent the stabbing of the woman.

(D) No, because the man knew the woman and therefore had the right to use deadly force to defend her.

Question 5

One Saturday morning, a father took his 10-year-old son to a little league game. The son, who played center field, made several errors during the game. The coach benched the son and berated him for costing the team the game, driving the young boy to tears. The father got into a heated argument with the coach over his treatment of the boy. Bystanders eventually broke up the argument, and the father drove his son home. Later that night, while picking up take-out for the family's dinner, the father saw the coach in the restaurant's parking lot. Wanting to make the coach cry as the coach had done to his son, the father grabbed his son's baseball bat from the back seat of his car, came up behind the coach, and hit him in the head with the bat. The coach died from his injuries.

Is the father guilty of murder for the coach's death?

  (A) No, because the father acted in the heat of passion.

  (B) No, because the father did not intend to kill the coach.

  (C) Yes, because a baseball bat may be a dangerous instrumentality depending upon how it is used.

  (D) Yes, because at a minimum, the father intended to inflict serious injury upon the coach.

THEFT OFFENSES

Question 6

A woman and her best friend went out to lunch at a local restaurant. During their lunch, the friend received several calls on her cell phone, and the woman grew increasingly frustrated at the constant interruptions. When the friend stepped out to use the ladies' room, leaving her cell phone on the table, the woman took the phone, turned it off, and put it in her purse, planning to return it at the end of lunch. However, the woman forgot to return the phone to her friend and ended up taking it home with her.

If the woman is charged with larceny, should she be convicted?

  (A) No, provided the woman eventually gave the phone back to her friend.

  (B) No, because the woman did not intend to permanently deprive her friend of the phone.

  (C) Yes, because the woman knowingly deprived the friend of her phone.

  (D) Yes, because the woman purposely took and kept the friend's phone.

Question 7

A plumber had a dispute with a homeowner about the amount owed on a plumbing job. While the homeowner eventually paid what the plumber demanded, the plumber believed that the homeowner stole his drill as a way to get back at him. The plumber asked his attorney if it was illegal to enter a house to take something that he believed belonged to him. The attorney incorrectly told him that it was not.

The plumber then entered the homeowner's home one night without permission and found a drill, which he quickly realized was not the drill that belonged to him. Disappointed, the plumber left without taking anything, locking the door behind him. This jurisdiction follows the common law without modification.

Is the plumber guilty of burglary?

(A) No, because the plumber made a reasonable mistake of law.

(B) No, because the plumber made a reasonable mistake of fact.

(C) Yes, because larceny is a felony.

(D) Yes, because ignorance of the law is not a defense.

Question 8

A boyfriend stole a diamond necklace and gave it to his girlfriend as a birthday present. At the time that the boyfriend gave the necklace to his girlfriend, she did not know that it was stolen. Three weeks later, while she and her boyfriend were passionately kissing, she whispered into his ear, "Darling, I really love the diamond necklace you gave me. It must have cost you a fortune." The boyfriend responded, "Honey, the necklace didn't cost me a dime. I stole it." Startled by her boyfriend's confession, the girlfriend broke down and started crying. However, after regaining her composure, the girlfriend decided to keep the necklace.

The girlfriend is guilty of which, if any, of the following crimes?

(A) Receiving stolen property.

(B) Larceny.

(C) Larceny by trick.

(D) No crime.

Question 9

A robber walked into a jewelry store, fired a gun into the air, and told everyone to get down on the ground. While the robber cleared out the jewelry displays and the cash register, an employee tripped the silent alarm. The police soon surrounded the store. While the robber was trying to figure out how he was going to get out of the store, an elderly female hostage panicked, running to the front door of the store. The robber fired at the elderly woman but missed. However, the defendant's gunfire caused the police to respond by firing their weapons into the store, accidentally killing the woman. The police apprehended the robber. This jurisdiction follows the proximate cause theory of felony murder.

Should the robber be convicted of murder for the elderly woman's death?

(A) No, because the robber did not intend to kill the elderly woman.

(B) No, because the elderly woman was killed by the police.

(C) Yes, because the robber's wanton indifference to human life led to the elderly woman's death.

(D) Yes, because the elderly woman was killed during the commission of a felony by a robber.

Question 10

A businessman asked to see an expensive watch in a jewelry store. In conversation with the clerk, the businessman falsely claimed to be the son of the city's district attorney. When handed the watch, he asked if he could put it on, walk around a bit so he could see how it felt on his wrist, and then briefly step outside to observe it in natural light. The clerk agreed, saying, "I know I can trust someone like you with the merchandise." The businessman walked out of the store wearing the watch and never returned. A week later, the clerk was at a gathering when she spotted the businessman wearing the watch. She told him that he must either pay for the watch or give it back. The businessman pulled back his jacket to reveal the handle of a pistol that was tucked inside his waistband. The clerk immediately walked away.

Of which of the following crimes should the businessman be convicted?

(A) Robbery.

(B) Larceny.

(C) False pretenses.

(D) Embezzlement.

INCHOATE CRIMES

Question 11

An elderly man's house was frequently the target of vandalism by local teenagers. Tired of having to repair the damage they did to his home, the man decided to lie in wait for teenagers on the night before Halloween, when they often vandalized his home. True to form, teenagers in costume appeared and began spray-painting the man's house. Wanting to scare the teenagers, the man fired a shotgun over their heads. However, some of the shotgun pellets went through the top of a tall hat one of the teenagers, who was dressed as Abraham Lincoln, was wearing, though the pellets did not harm him. The man was subsequently arrested.

What crime, if any, did the man commit?

(A) Mayhem.

(B) Battery.

(C) Attempted murder, because a shotgun is an inherently dangerous weapon.

(D) No crime.

Question 12

After he was turned down for a promotion, a man decided to murder his boss. The man purchased a gun for this purpose and then invited his boss to his house for dinner. However, the day before the boss arrived at the man's house, the man changed his mind, and left the gun under his mattress. The man was subsequently charged with attempted murder.

Should the man be convicted or acquitted?

(A) The man should be acquitted, because the boss was unaware of the man's motives.

(B) The man should be acquitted, because his actions were not sufficient to constitute an attempt.

(C) The man should be convicted, because a person is presumed to intend the natural and probable consequences of his acts.

(D) The man should be convicted, because he purchased the gun with the intent to kill his boss.

Question 13

As a practical joke, a defendant took a small container, filled it with gas, and placed it in the wood-burning stove in the cabin owned by his neighbor. That evening, as the temperature dropped, the neighbor decided to light a fire in his wood-burning stove. The gas exploded, causing extensive injuries to the neighbor and a great deal of damage to his cabin. The defendant was subsequently arrested and charged with arson.

Will the defendant be convicted?

(A) No, because the defendant never intended to hurt the neighbor.

(B) No, because the cabin was unoccupied when the neighbor entered it.

(C) Yes, because the defendant's conduct was reckless.

(D) Yes, because the defendant's conduct was negligent.

Question 14

Late one evening, a teenage boy and his 15-year-old girlfriend were leaving a public library. As they walked through the dimly lit parking lot to get to their bikes, an adult man, who was visibly intoxicated, emerged from behind a parked car and ran up to them. The man knocked the boyfriend to the ground and hit him over the head with a wrench, causing the boyfriend to lose consciousness. The man then forced the girlfriend into his car. Moments later, the boyfriend regained consciousness, and the man fled the scene. The man was subsequently charged with assault with the intent to commit rape.

Which of the following would provide the man with his best defense?

- (A) The man thought that the girlfriend had consented.

- (B) The man did not intend to rape the girlfriend.

- (C) The man's intoxication at the time negated the required general intent.

- (D) It is impossible to prove that the man was the perpetrator, because the parking lot was dimly lit.

Question 15

A disgruntled employee decided to kill his boss. The employee planned to hide near his boss's house and shoot him when he arrived home from work. The employee positioned himself behind a small grove of trees about 500 yards away from the boss's front door. Shortly thereafter, the boss pulled into his driveway. As the boss exited his vehicle, the employee fired a single shot from his rifle, but the shot did not reach the boss. A neighbor heard the gunfire, however, and called the police, who later arrested the employee as he was fleeing the scene with his rifle. At the employee's trial for attempted murder, it was conceded, following the testimony of a ballistics expert, that it would have been impossible for the employee to hit his boss from that distance with the rifle he had used.

Is the employee guilty of attempted murder?

- (A) No, because at that distance, he lacked the requisite intent to kill his boss.

- (B) No, because it was legally impossible for the employee to kill the boss from that distance.

- (C) Yes, because it was merely factually impossible for the employee to kill the boss from that distance.

- (D) Yes, because the employee's actions were premeditated.

DEFENSES

Question 16

In which of the following situations is a defendant most likely guilty of the offense of false pretenses?

(A) A defendant falsely tells a car salesman that he is interested in buying a new car and receives permission to drive it for a short trip. The defendant drives the car to another state and does not return it.

(B) A defendant falsely represents to a victim that he is a friend of the victim's boss, that he is employed by a local company, and that he has just lost his wallet. The defendant obtains a loan of $100 from the victim and falsely promises to repay the loan the next day.

(C) A defendant rents a motorcycle from a dealer for one day. Later that day, a stranger asks the defendant how much he will sell the motorcycle for. The defendant sells the motorcycle to the stranger for $1,000. The defendant then falsely informs the dealer that the motorcycle was stolen.

(D) A defendant fills the gas tank to his car at a self-service station and drives off without paying.

Question 17

A defendant was wearing a grey raincoat when he entered a restaurant for dinner. He placed his raincoat on a coat rack located in the foyer of the restaurant. After his meal, the defendant picked up a similar grey raincoat, believing it to be his own. The raincoat that he took, however, belonged to another patron. The defendant left the restaurant and had walked a short distance when he realized that he had taken the wrong raincoat by mistake. He then returned to the restaurant and placed the other patron's raincoat back on the coat rack. He found his raincoat, which had been partially hidden under a stack of other coats. The defendant was later arrested and charged with larceny of the other patron's raincoat.

Which of the following would be the strongest argument for the defendant's acquittal?

(A) There was a mistake of fact.

(B) The defendant returned the raincoat after discovering his mistake.

(C) The defendant lacked the requisite state of mind.

(D) There was no fraudulent conversion.

Question 18

A homeowner was asleep in his second-floor bedroom when he heard noises downstairs in the living room. The homeowner took a loaded pistol from the night table and descended the stairs. He saw two burglars running out the front door. The homeowner ran outside trying to catch them. Simultaneously, an off-duty plainclothes police officer was driving his car past the home when he saw two suspicious men running down the street. The police officer stopped his car in front of the house and pulled out his gun. The police officer got out of the car and started walking toward the homeowner, who was standing on the front lawn. The homeowner then saw the police officer with his gun drawn. Not knowing that he was an off-duty police officer, the homeowner shot him with his pistol. The police officer was wounded, but survived the shooting.

If the homeowner is prosecuted for assault with a deadly weapon, which of the following would provide him with his best defense?

(A) The homeowner shot the police officer only after seeing him with his gun drawn and walking toward him.

(B) The homeowner reasonably believed that his life was in danger when he shot the police officer.

(C) The homeowner reasonably believed that the police officer was one of the participants who was involved in the burglary.

(D) The victim did not identify himself as a police officer.

Question 19

A defendant had been dating her boyfriend for more than a year. One day, the defendant was walking in the park when she noticed her boyfriend sitting next to a woman on a park bench. The defendant observed her boyfriend kissing the woman. Despondent about her boyfriend's public display of infidelity, the defendant began aimlessly wandering around the vicinity of the park. As she passed by a bar, the defendant decided to go in and have a drink.

After guzzling down a couple of beers, she started conversing with the customer seated next to her. The two women began commiserating about their relationships with unfaithful boyfriends. As they talked, the defendant and the woman continued to drink beer, with an occasional shot of tequila thrown in as well. They soon became intoxicated. As they discussed ways to get back at the boyfriend, the woman suggested that they set fire to his home. With the defendant in agreement, the two women staggered from the bar and went to the boyfriend's home.

Under the cover of night, the defendant and the woman picked up little twigs and tree branches and stacked them along the outside of the boyfriend's home. The defendant then lit them with her cigarette lighter. As the branches ignited in flames, the defendant and the woman hurriedly ran away. Seeing smoke from his bedroom window, the boyfriend ran outside and immediately extinguished the fire with a garden hose. The fire slightly charred a small section of the exterior of the boyfriend's home, but did not cause any significant damage.

If the defendant is prosecuted for common law arson, will she be found guilty?

(A) Yes, because voluntary intoxication is no defense, inasmuch as she knew she was setting fire to the dwelling house of another.

(B) No, because her intoxication negated her criminal intent.

(C) No, because her malicious intent was formulated as a result of her intoxication.

(D) No, because the fire only slightly charred the exterior of the home.

Question 20

In which of the following situations could a court, applying the common law doctrine, most likely convict the defendant of the crime charged despite the defendant's mistake?

(A) A defendant was charged with assault with intent to commit rape. He admittedly ripped off the victim's underwear after mistakenly believing that she had consented to engage in sexual intercourse with him.

(B) A defendant was charged with murder. He shot and killed the victim after a barroom argument. The defendant mistakenly thought that the victim had raised his hand to shoot him when, in fact, the victim was shaking his fist at the defendant to frighten him.

(C) A defendant was charged with burglary. She broke into her old boyfriend's home and took a painting that she erroneously believed he had given her before their relationship ended.

(D) A defendant was charged with bigamy. She married a man five years after her husband was reported missing following a boating accident. Thereafter, her husband, who had been rescued, returned alive. A state statute provides that a person is presumed dead after six years of unexplained absence. The defendant mistakenly believed that the statutory period was four years.

Answer Grid

1 (A) B C D   5 A B C D   9 A B C D   13 A B C D   17 A B C D
2 A B C (D)   6 A B C D   10 (A) B C D   14 A B C D   18 A (B) C D
3 A B C (D)   7 A B C D   11 A B C D   15 A B C D   19 (A) B C D
4 A B (C) D   8 A B C (D)   12 A (B) C D   16 A (B) C D   20 A B C (D)

Federal Civil Procedure

Outline

TABLE OF CONTENTS

I. JURISDICTION AND VENUE

A. **Federal Subject-Matter Jurisdiction**

1. **Federal Question Jurisdiction**

   a. Federal district courts have original jurisdiction over all civil actions "arising under the Constitution, laws, and treaties of the United States" [28 U.S.C. § 1331]. A case arises under federal law if the federal question appears on a fair reading of a well-pleaded complaint.

      EXAMPLE: The Mottleys had free passes on the Louisville & Nashville Railroad. They lost those passes when Congress passed a law that banned free passes to railroads. The Mottleys brought suit in federal court, but the Supreme Court ruled that the federal court did not have subject-matter jurisdiction over the case because the case "merely arose under federal law," which was insufficient to establish federal question jurisdiction [Louisville & Nashville Railroad Company v. Mottley, 211 U.S. 149 (1908)].

   b. The Constitution or federal statutes may create a right of action. In that case, federal courts have jurisdiction to hear those suits.

   c. A defendant's use of federal law as the basis for her defense will not, by itself, create federal question jurisdiction. Under the **well pleaded complaint rule**, to create federal question jurisdiction, the federal question must arise within the plaintiff's affirmative claim—regardless of any defense the defendant might raise.

   d. A violation of a federal statute does not create a federal cause of action unless the statute also provides a remedy for the violation.

   e. A state question that involves a question of federal law may be sufficient to create federal question jurisdiction. The mere presence of federal law in a claim is insufficient to create jurisdiction. The federal law must have a substantial impact on the state law issue.

      EXAMPLE: Federal question jurisdiction was found to arise in a landowner's state law claim to quiet title against someone who had purchased the land at auction, because embedded in that claim was an argument that the Internal Revenue Service had given him inadequate notice of the sale [Grable & Sons Metal Products, Inc. v. Darue Engineering & Mfg., 545 U.S. 308 (2005)].

      EXAMPLE: Federal question jurisdiction did not arise in a legal malpractice claim in which the plaintiff alleged that his attorney did not raise a defense under federal patent law. The disputed issue of federal law was not substantial in any relevant sense [Gunn v. Minton, 133 S. Ct. 1059 (2013)].

   f. Federal courts have original jurisdiction over admiralty or maritime cases.

      (1) Admiralty jurisdiction requires that a case have a "maritime nexus." A maritime nexus requires that the incident giving rise to the case had a "potentially disruptive effect on maritime commerce," and the general character of the activity giving rise to the incident shows a "substantial

relationship to traditional maritime activity" [Jerome B. Grubart, Inc. v. Great Lakes Dredge & Dock Co., 513 U.S. 527 (1995)].

    (2)   Plaintiffs may pursue maritime claims as common law claims in state courts, however, remedies that are specific to admiralty courts will not be available [28 U.S.C. § 1333].

  g. Federal courts have subject-matter jurisdiction to review the state court conviction of a prisoner through a writ of *habeas corpus,* challenging the confinement of the prisoner on federal constitutional grounds [28 U.S.C. § 2254(a)].

    (1)   A petition for a writ of *habeas corpus* is a civil cause of action brought against the jailor or custodian of a person currently under confinement.

    (2)   A writ of *habeas corpus* is not an appeal, and it does not continue the criminal case against the prisoner in any manner. The writ does not make a determination of the prisoner's guilt or innocence.

    (3)   A petition for a writ of *habeas corpus* may be based only on the following grounds:

      (a) violation of the Due Process Clause of the Fifth and Fourteenth Amendments;

      (b) violation of the prohibition of compelled self-incrimination of the Fifth and Fourteenth Amendments;

      (c) violation of the protection against double jeopardy of the Fifth and Fourteenth Amendments; or

      (d) violation of the right not to be subject to cruel and unusual punishment under the Eighth Amendment.

    (4)   *Habeas corpus* relief is only available when the state court's determination was contrary to, or involved an unreasonable application of, clearly established federal law as determined by the Supreme Court of the United States.

    (5)   In order to seek a writ of *habeas corpus* from a federal court, the prisoner must have exhausted all remedies available at the state level, including all state appellate review.

    (6)   A petition for a writ of *habeas corpus* must be brought within one year of the final judgment of custody [28 U.S.C. § 2244(d)].

      (a) A prisoner may not file successive petitions for *habeas corpus* relief without the approval of the U.S. Court of Appeals.

2. **Diversity Jurisdiction**

  a. Federal district courts have original jurisdiction over matters involving litigants who are citizens of different states, U.S. citizens and citizens of a foreign country, or a foreign state and a U.S. citizen, if the amount in controversy is more than $75,000 [28 U.S.C. § 1332].

  b. The amount in controversy between the litigants must exceed $75,000, exclusive of the costs and expenses associated with the litigation.

    (1)   If the suit is based on a contract or statute that allows a winning party to collect attorney's fees, the amount in controversy includes the likely amount of those fees.

(2)   A suit in which the amount in controversy is *exactly* $75,000 does not meet the diversity jurisdiction requirement.

(3)   An action based on diversity will be dismissed if it appears "to a legal certainty" that the plaintiff's claim does not exceed $75,000. The burden falls on the defendant to prove that the amount in controversy is not more than $75,000.

(4)   There is a split of authority among the circuits regarding how the amount in controversy is determined.

(a)   Under the majority rule, which is the rule followed in most circuits, the amount in controversy is determined according to the amount sought by the plaintiff. This is referred to as the "plaintiff's viewpoint" rule.

(b)   Under the minority rule, known as the "either viewpoint rule," the amount in controversy is not necessarily the amount sought or recovered, but it is the value of the consequences which may result from the litigation.

(5)   A plaintiff may meet the amount in controversy requirement by combining or aggregating the total claims against the defendant. Claims against multiple defendants may not be aggregated to meet the threshold unless the claims are common and undivided.

(a)   Multiple plaintiffs cannot aggregate their claims for purposes of 28 U.S.C. § 1332. The U.S. Supreme Court 5-4 decision in Exxon Mobil Corp. v. Allapattah Services, Inc., 545 U.S. 546 (2005), held that a federal court has supplemental jurisdiction over claims of other plaintiffs who do not meet the jurisdictional amount for a diversity action, when at least one plaintiff in the action does satisfy the jurisdictional amount. So we need at least one plaintiff with a claim over $75,000.

(6)   If the suit seeks an injunction, the amount in controversy is either the injunction's worth to the plaintiff, or the cost of the injunction to the defendant [JTH Tax, Inc. v. Frashier, 624 F.3d 635 (4th Cir. 2010)].

c.   Diversity jurisdiction requires complete diversity, meaning a dispute that involves citizens of different states. There will be no diversity jurisdiction if any plaintiff and any defendant share citizenship of the same state.

(1)   Diversity must be met only at the time the suit is filed. If a defendant moves to the same state as the plaintiff after the suit has been commenced, diversity will not be destroyed. However, if a complaint is amended to add or dismiss a party, this can affect jurisdiction.

(2)   A party is considered to be a citizen of her state of domicile. Domicile is not the same as residence. **Domicile** requires a physical presence in the state and the intent to remain in that state indefinitely.

EXAMPLE: A and B, a married couple, live in Alabama. They are registered to vote there, have a car registered there, and own a home in that state. A and B are domiciled in Alabama. If A were to take a long-term work assignment in Texas, but she intended to move back to her home in Alabama with B, she would not be domiciled in Texas.

    (3)   **Alien** refers to an individual who is a citizen of a foreign country. For diversity purposes, if an alien is admitted to permanent residence in the United States (i.e., that person has a green card), he is a citizen of the state in which he is domiciled. Therefore, diversity is improper if a permanent resident alien is a resident of the same state of the citizen whom he is suing or is being sued by. In such a situation, there is no diversity jurisdiction.

    (4)   A corporation is a citizen of both the state or foreign country of its incorporation and the state or foreign country where it has its principal place of business. A corporation may only have one principal place of business. The principal place of business is the state in which the corporation has its "nerve center," or the place from which the corporation's high-level officers direct, control, and coordinate the corporation's activities [Hertz Corp. v. Friend, 130 S. Ct. 1181 (2010)].

    EXAMPLE: ABC Corporation is incorporated in Delaware, but has its principal place of business in New York. If ABC brought suit against a competitor, XYZ, which has its principal place of business in New Jersey, but which is also incorporated in Delaware, there would be no diversity jurisdiction.

    (5)   The citizenship of an unincorporated association, such as a partnership or limited liability company, is the citizenship of all of the members of the association. For purposes of class actions, however, an unincorporated association is a citizen of the state under whose laws the association is organized, and the state in which it has its principal place of business.

    d.   There is an exception to the complete diversity requirement for class actions. In class actions where the class contains over 100 persons and the amount in controversy exceeds $5,000,000, diversity need only be "minimal," meaning that federal jurisdiction exists if any single member of the class is diverse from any single defendant.

    3.   **Supplemental Jurisdiction**

        a.   **Supplemental jurisdiction** allows a federal district court to hear claims over which it would not ordinarily have jurisdiction (e.g., state law claims that do not involve diversity jurisdiction) [28 U.S.C. § 1367]. Supplemental jurisdiction permits a claim falling outside of federal question jurisdiction or diversity jurisdiction to "piggy back" on a claim that does fall within one of those jurisdictions.

        b.   To exercise supplemental jurisdiction over an additional claim, there must be a claim over which a court has original jurisdiction [Id.]. In other words, supplemental jurisdiction is only available over a claim if the claim arises out of the same transaction or occurrence as a claim over which the court would have federal question or diversity jurisdiction.

    (1)   Claims arise out of the same transaction or occurrence if they arise out of a common nucleus of operative fact.

        EXAMPLE: C was injured when he was wrongfully arrested by a police officer. The federal courts have jurisdiction to hear his claim for violation of his federal constitutional rights [42 U.S.C. §1983]. The federal courts have supplemental jurisdiction to hear his state law claim against the arresting officer for battery arising out of the same incident.

  c.   Supplemental jurisdiction may include claims that involve the joinder or intervention of additional parties, even if there would not otherwise be federal jurisdiction over those parties.

    (1)   In a diversity case, supplemental jurisdiction may be exercised over the claims of a party other than the plaintiff if the only reason the other party's claims do not qualify for diversity jurisdiction is the failure to meet the amount in controversy requirement.

        EXAMPLE: A nine-year-old child seriously injures her hand on a can of fish sold by a corporation incorporated and having its principal place of business in another state. The child's injuries meet the amount in controversy requirement. The child's mother also has a state-law claim against corporation, but the amount of her claim does not meet the amount in controversy requirement. The federal court may exercise supplemental jurisdiction to hear mother's claim along with child's claim.

    (2)   In a diversity case, a court may not exercise supplemental jurisdiction over a claim by a plaintiff proposed to be joined under Rule 19 (compulsory joinder), or a claim by a plaintiff seeking to intervene under Rule 24, when exercising supplemental jurisdiction would destroy complete diversity of the parties [28 U.S.C. § 1367(b)].

    (3)   Moreover, in a diversity case a court may not exercise supplemental jurisdiction over claims by plaintiffs against persons made party to the suit under Rule 14 (impleader) 19, 20 (permissive joinder), or 24.

    (4)   If non-diverse parties are joined to a case, and there is no supplemental jurisdiction to hear their claims, the court may dismiss only the claims of the non-diverse parties.

  d.   Even if the additional claim arises out of the same transaction or occurrence and the plaintiff is not trying to circumvent diversity jurisdiction, the court may (but is not required to) decline to exercise supplemental jurisdiction in the following situations:

    (1)   the state law claim raises a novel or complex issue of state law;

    (2)   the state law claim "substantially predominates" over the claim over which the district court has jurisdiction;

(3)   the court has dismissed all the claims over which it had jurisdiction; or

(4)   in "exceptional circumstances," there are other "compelling reasons" to decline jurisdiction.

4. **Concurrent Jurisdiction**

    a.   A federal court has concurrent jurisdiction over a particular case if the case could also have been brought in state court.

    b.   When a court has concurrent jurisdiction to hear a case, both state and federal laws or policies may apply, resulting in a conflict of laws.

5. **Removal**

    a.   A case that was originally brought in state court may be removed to federal court if the plaintiff could have brought the case in federal court [28 U.S.C. § 1441]. The defendant in such a situation has a right to remove or shift that case from state court to federal court.

        (1)   Note that removal is only an option for defendants; plaintiffs cannot remove a suit to federal court after having chosen state court.

    b.   If removal is based on diversity, all of the defendants must be diverse from the plaintiff. Removal on the basis of diversity will not be granted if any of the defendants is a citizen of the forum state.

        (1)   Under the **fraudulent joinder rule**, the right to removal will not be defeated if a defendant was fraudulently joined for the purpose of defeating diversity jurisdiction and preventing removal to federal court [Marshall v. Manville Sales Corp., 6 F.3d 229 (4th Cir. 1993)].

            (a) A party who claims fraudulent joinder has the burden of proving:

                1)   that there is no possibility the plaintiff would be able to establish a cause of action in state court against the in-state defendant; or

                2)   that there was outright fraud in the plaintiff's pleading of jurisdictional facts.

        (2)   The fraudulent joinder rule applies to defendants named in the original complaint, as well as to those joined as parties any time prior to removal [Mayes v. Rapoport, 198 F.3d 457 (4th Cir. 1999)]. In other words, if the removal is based on diversity, diversity is needed both at the time the original claim is filed and at the time when the notice of removal is filed.

    c.   The defendant has the right to remove when the plaintiff is suing the defendant in a jurisdiction that is not the defendant's home state. However, if the plaintiff is suing the defendant in state court located in that defendant's home state, there is no risk of being "homered." Therefore, that defendant cannot remove [28 U.S.C. § 1441(b)(2)].

    d.   If a plaintiff's suit is based on federal law, the defendant may have the case removed without a showing of diversity.

    e.   Removal is allowed only when at least one of the plaintiff's claims would fall within the subject-matter jurisdiction of the federal courts.

EXAMPLE: A files suit in her home state court against B, a citizen of another state. A's suit claims several violations of her home state's unfair trade practice laws. Her suit also alleges breach of contract, with a claim of $80,000 in damages. B may have the suit removed to federal court, and the federal court will hear her unfair trade practice claims.

EXAMPLE: C, a New York resident files suit against D, also a New York resident in a New York state court. C's complaint seeks $80,000 in damages. Two weeks later D gets a new job and moves to Florida, establishing residency and an intent to permanently live there. D may not have the suit removed to federal court because diversity must exist both at the time of filing and the time of removal.

f. If the basis for removal is federal question jurisdiction, and appended to the federal question claim is a state claim not within the original or supplemental jurisdiction of the district court or a claim that has been made non-removable by statute (i.e., a diversity claim against a defendant from the forum state or a claim as to which the defendant did not join in or agree to the removable notice), the entire case is removed to federal court [28 U.S.C. § 1441(c)].

   (1) Once in federal court, the federal district court judge must sever those non-removable pieces and remand them back to state court.

g. **Multiple Defendants**

   (1) In a case involving multiple defendants, all defendants who have been properly joined and served in the case must consent to or join in removal for removal to be proper [28 U.S.C. § 1446(b)].

   (2) Absent that unanimity, removal is improper.

h. **Procedure**

   (1) In order to remove a case, a defendant must file a notice in the federal district court in the district in which the action is currently pending.

   (2) The federal court will consider whether removal is proper. If removal is not proper, the court will remand the action to state court.

i. **Timing**

   (1) Notice must be filed within 30 days of service of the initial pleading. If a case is not removable when the initial pleading is filed, and the complaint is amended in a way that now makes the case removable, a notice of removal must be made within 30 days of service of the amended pleading.

      (a) Each defendant receives a 30-day period to decide whether to remove to federal court. This is important with respect to later-joined defendants.

         EXAMPLE: In the original lawsuit, the plaintiff is suing two defendants. Those two defendants have 30 days to decide whether or not to remove. If they do not remove and the plaintiff later joins a third defendant, that new defendant has

30 days to decide whether or not to remove. If that defendant decides to remove, the first two defendants who originally said they did not want to remove can join in the new request for notice of removal and the entire case will be deemed timely removed to federal court [28 U.S.C. § 1446(b)(2)(B), (C)].

(2) A case removable on the basis of diversity jurisdiction may not be removed more than one year after the commencement of the action (i.e., when the action was filed not served) [28 U.S.C. § 1446].

(a) However, if the plaintiff acted in bad faith so as to prevent the defendant from removing, that one-year time period can be relaxed.

j. The venue of a removed case is the district court where the state court is located.

k. Removal is allowed only for state court cases. Agency or administrative proceedings cannot be removed to federal court.

l. If a plaintiff believes that a case was improperly removed to federal court, she may bring a motion to remand the case to state court.

EXAMPLE: A consumer from State A brings a $100,000 products liability action in state court against the manufacturer of a product that injured her and the retailer from whom she bought the product. The manufacturer is a corporation that is a citizen of State B, while the retailer is incorporated in State C but has its headquarters in State A. The manufacturer and retailer have the case removed to federal court, based on diversity of citizenship and the amount in controversy. The consumer may bring a motion to remand to state court, on the grounds that retailer is not a diverse defendant.

(1) A motion to remand on the basis of any defect other than lack of subject-matter jurisdiction must be made within 30 days after the filing of the removal notice [28 U.S.C. § 1447(c)].

(a) Objections to subject-matter jurisdiction can never be waived and therefore a motion to remand based on lack of subject-matter jurisdiction is not subject to any time limit. If at any time before the final judgment a court lacks subject-matter jurisdiction, the case must be remanded [Id.].

(2) The defendant has the burden of showing that the removal was proper.

6. **Dismissal**

a. The court must dismiss an action if it determines that it does not have subject-matter jurisdiction over the case [Fed. R. Civ. P. 12(h)(3)].

b. Lack of subject-matter jurisdiction may not be waived by the parties.

B. **Territorial Jurisdiction**

1. **Territorial jurisdiction** is the authority of a court to bind a party to the action. There are three essential ways to establish territorial personal jurisdiction:

a. a federal court has territorial jurisdiction over the state in which that federal district is located;

b. a federal statute that creates a cause of action may provide that federal courts have nationwide jurisdiction; or

c. the "100 mile bulge" rule states that a federal court may exercise jurisdiction over a defendant outside the state in which the court is located if the defendant is joined under Rule 14 or 19 and is served within a judicial district of the United States not more than 100 miles from where the summons was issued [Fed. R. Civ. P. 4(k)].

   (1) In order for jurisdiction to be proper under this rule, the defendant must have the type of minimum contacts with the "bulge" that would support personal jurisdiction for a court in the "bulge."

C. Personal Jurisdiction

1. **Personal jurisdiction** refers to a court's authority over a defendant. Personal jurisdiction must be established separately for each defendant. There are three types of personal jurisdiction:

   a. *in personam* jurisdiction over the parties;

   b. *in rem* jurisdiction over the property that is the subject of the action; and

   c. *quasi in rem* jurisdiction over property that is attached to satisfy the judgment in an action.

2. ***In personam* jurisdiction** is jurisdiction over the parties to a lawsuit. The defendant typically is physically present in the forum state, or has some significant contacts with the state. To determine whether a federal court has personal jurisdiction over a particular party, the personal jurisdiction law of the state in which the federal court sits must be satisfied and the exercise of personal jurisdiction must comply with the United States Constitution.

   a. **State Long-Arm Statute**

      (1) For a federal court to have personal jurisdiction over a defendant, the state court in which the federal court sits must be able to exercise personal jurisdiction over that defendant.

         (a) If the state court could not assert personal jurisdiction, then the federal court may not assert personal jurisdiction either.

      (2) A state court may exercise personal jurisdiction over an out-of-state defendant if authorized by the state's long-arm statute. Long-arm statutes place limitations on the state's ability to establish personal jurisdiction by setting out the types of contacts that will support jurisdiction. Typically, the types of contacts that establish personal jurisdiction include the following:

         (a) the defendant transacts business within the state;

         (b) the defendant contracts to supply goods and services anywhere within the state; or

         (c) the defendant owns, uses, or possesses any real property within the state.

b. **Constitutional Considerations**

(1) Just because state law permits personal jurisdiction over a particular party does not mean that the federal court may automatically assert it. The federal court must also determine whether the state law is constitutional under the Due Process Clause of the Fourteenth Amendment.

> **NOTE** Many states authorize personal jurisdiction to the full extent of the Fourteenth Amendment. If a state does that, all you need to do is determine whether personal jurisdiction over a particular defendant is permissible under the Constitution. If it is, then both state law and constitutional law are satisfied.

(2) A state law will be constitutional if it authorizes personal jurisdiction in one of five following circumstances:

(a) residency;

(b) consent;

(c) service;

(d) minimum contacts; or

(e) substantial business.

(3) **Residency**

(a) If the defendant is domiciled in the forum state, personal jurisdiction over the defendant is constitutional. A person is domiciled in a jurisdiction if she:

1) resides in that jurisdiction; and

2) has expressed her intent to remain in that jurisdiction indefinitely.

(4) **Consent**

(a) If the defendant consents to the federal court's personal jurisdiction over him, personal jurisdiction is constitutional.

1) A person may expressly consent to personal jurisdiction by agreement with the other party. For example, parties to a contract often put a choice-of-forum clause in their contracts that specifies the forum in which any lawsuit arising from the contract must be litigated. If a defendant signs a contract with a choice of forum clause, she has consented to the power of the court specified in the clause.

EXAMPLE: A man obtains a line of credit from the bank. The credit agreement provides that all disputes relating to the agreement will be heard by the federal district court in Delaware. The man has consented to personal jurisdiction in Delaware.

2) A state may provide by law that a non-resident has consented to personal jurisdiction in that state if the non-resident engages in a particular activity that the

state has a substantial interest in regulating, such as driving on public roads.

EXAMPLE: A non-resident who drives a car in another state has given his implied consent to personal jurisdiction in that state, for suits arising out of his operation of a car in the state.

3) A party can also consent to federal jurisdiction by waiving her objection to personal jurisdiction. If a defendant appears in court without making a motion to dismiss for lack of personal jurisdiction, or does not include lack of personal jurisdiction in a responsive pleading, the defense is waived [Fed. R. Civ. P. 12(h)(1)]. The defendant must object to personal jurisdiction in its initial filing or appearance before the court. A defendant does not waive objections to lack of personal jurisdiction by making an appearance before the court to contest jurisdiction.

(5) **Service**

    (a) If a defendant is physically present in the jurisdiction, and is served with process while present, the court's exercise of personal jurisdiction over the defendant is constitutional.

        1) It does not matter that the defendant's presence in the jurisdiction is temporary, or that it is unrelated to the lawsuit.

        2) The defendant's presence must be voluntary, the plaintiff cannot have coaxed the defendant into the state under false pretenses. Moreover, personal jurisdiction would not be constitutional if the defendant is in the forum state to participate in a legal proceeding.

        EXAMPLE: A businessman is a resident of Missouri. While driving to Louisiana on a business trip, he stops for lunch at a restaurant in Arkansas. A process server sees him in the restaurant, and serves him with a summons and complaint for an action in federal district court in Arkansas. The court has jurisdiction over the businessman, based on service.

        EXAMPLE: A singer, a resident of Maryland, receives a telephone call telling her that she has won a prize in a raffle. In order to pick up that prize, she is told that she must go to the raffle sponsor's headquarters in Virginia. When the singer gets to the address she is given, she learns that there is no raffle prize. Instead, she is served with a summons and complaint. The court in Virginia does not have jurisdiction over the singer based on service.

(6) **Minimum Contacts**

    (a) For jurisdiction to be constitutional under a "minimum contacts" analysis, three conditions must be satisfied:

        1) the defendant must have established a minimum contact with the forum state;

        2) the claim against the defendant must arise from that contact; and

          a) A lawsuit "arises from" a defendant's contacts if the contacts played a role in causing the lawsuit.

        3) the exercise of jurisdiction must not offend traditional notions of fair play and substantial justice.

    (b) A defendant has minimum contacts with a particular state if he causes harm in the state, does business in the state or has an interest in real property in the state. Importantly, the defendant does not have to be in the state to cause the harm, do the business or have a property interest, but his contact with the state has to be purposefully established.

    (c) Therefore, for a plaintiff to establish a minimum contact, the defendant must "purposefully avail" itself to the privilege of conducting activities within the forum state [World-Wide Volkswagen Corp. v. Woodson, 444 U.S. 286 (1980)].

        1) If a defendant purposefully availed itself of the protections and benefits of the forum state, sufficient minimum contacts for personal jurisdiction will exist. Purposeful availment involves actions that are directed towards a particular state. A defendant who purposely involves himself in transactions within the state receives the benefits and privileges of that state's laws, so it is fair that he be exposed to the jurisdiction of that forum state as well.

        2) By purposefully availing itself, a party is deemed to have reasonably foreseen the possibility of being haled into court in that state to defend an action.

        3) Merely placing a product into the stream of commerce is not enough to establish purposeful availment; the defendant must also have had additional contacts with the forum state [Asahi Metal Industry Co. v. Superior Court, 480 U.S. 102 (1987)].

    (d) If a defendant has minimum contacts with the forum state, the defendant bears the burden of proving that it would be fundamentally unfair for him to litigate in that state in order to avoid the court's personal jurisdiction [Burger King v. Rudzewicz, 471 U.S. 462 (1985)].

    (e) Courts consider the following five factors when determining whether it is fair to require the defendant to litigate in the forum state [World-Wide Volkswagen Corp. v. Woodson, 444 U.S. 286 (1980)]:

1) the burden on the defendant;

2) the interests of the forum state;

3) the plaintiff's interests in obtaining relief;

4) the interstate judicial system's interest in efficiency; and

5) shared policy interests of the states.

(f) Generally, the burden on the defendant drives the analysis and must be quite substantial for a court to reject personal jurisdiction on the basis of fairness.

EXAMPLE: D, a resident of North Carolina, was driving through Rhode Island on his way to Boston when he struck P with his car. In a subsequent suit in Rhode Island, D is subject to personal jurisdiction because he caused harm in the state, the lawsuit arises from those contacts, and Rhode Island has an interest in protecting its citizens from negligent drivers and maintaining order on its roads.

EXAMPLE: P heard from a friend that D, a company in Nebraska, makes great custom tailgates for pick-up trucks. P, a resident of Kansas, called D and asked to order one. D does all its business in Nebraska but agreed to make P a tailgate and send it to him. P received the tailgate but couldn't install it because it was designed incorrectly. P can sue D in Kansas because it did business in the state, the lawsuit arose from that activity, and Kansas has an interest in protecting its citizens from breaches of contract.

EXAMPLE: P, a citizen of Texas, was driving in Connecticut when she got into a car accident with D. D is a Connecticut citizen, but spends six weeks each summer in Texas with his grandmother (and has been doing so for the past 10 years). P cannot sue D in Texas because his contacts with the state did not give rise to the lawsuit. (P could, however, wait until D comes back into the state next summer and have him served then.)

EXAMPLE: Motor MFG. manufactured an electric motor in Michigan and sold it to Golf Cart Co. in Ohio who then installed it in a golf cart. P, a resident of Georgia, purchased the cart over the phone, and Golf Car Co. then shipped it from Ohio to P at home. P was later injured when the cart's electric motor caught fire and he wants to bring suit in Georgia. Golf Cart Co. will be subject to personal jurisdiction in Georgia because it transacted business in the state or caused harm in the state, the suit arises from those acts, and fair play concerns are not implicated. In contrast, Motor MFG will not be subject to personal jurisdiction in Georgia because it did not purposefully establish any contacts with the state that gave rise to P's suit. Even if Motor MFG had sent other motors to the state in the past, personal jurisdiction is not permissible because those contacts did not give rise to P's claim.

(7) **Substantial Business**

(a) A federal court can constitutionally assert personal jurisdiction over a defendant if it is doing "substantial business" in a particular state. The Supreme Court has made clear that "substantial business" is a very high bar to clear. There is no easy definition for "substantial business" but recent opinions by the Supreme Court instruct that the business activity in a particular state must be so significant that the company is "essentially at home" in that state.

(b) A corporation would probably not be considered "essentially at home" and thus subject to general jurisdiction in a state in which it is not incorporated nor has its principal place of business [Daimler AG v. Bauman, 134 S. Ct. 746 (2014)].

(c) As a corollary to this, the Court has suggested that a company cannot be "essentially at home" in more than a couple of states.

EXAMPLE: P was vacationing in Utah when she slipped and fell in a 7-11 convenience store. After returning home to Arizona, P desired to bring suit against 7-11 in Arizona. 7-11 operates 131 stores in the state, roughly 8% of its total operations. 7-11 is not subject to personal jurisdiction in Arizona because its business, whether substantial or not, is not the sort that renders it "essentially at home" because if that was so, it would be essentially at home in all 50 states.

3. *In rem* **jurisdiction** is based on the interests of a particular piece of property or thing located within the forum state.

EXAMPLE: The courts of a state have *in rem* jurisdiction to hear an action to quiet title to a parcel of real estate in the state.

a. A federal court may exercise *in rem* jurisdiction when:

(1) there is real or personal property of value located within the state where the federal district is located;

(2) the court seizes the item; and

(a) A court's *in rem* jurisdiction cannot begin until the court has effective control of the asset.

(3) the owner of the property received proper notice of the proceeding.

b. A defendant who is no longer domiciled in the forum state may be subject to *in rem* jurisdiction if:

(1) the cause of action is of a domestic nature; and

(2) the forum state was the place of matrimonial domicile, the

defendant abandoned the plaintiff in the forum state, or an agreement or settlement for support was entered into in the forum state.

4. A federal court has ***quasi in rem* jurisdiction** in actions in which the attachment of real or personal property is part of the relief requested. The federal court located in the state in which that property is situated has *quasi in rem* jurisdiction over the property being attached.

    a. The following elements are required for *quasi in rem* jurisdiction:

        (1) there is real or personal property of value located within the state or territorial limits of the federal court;

        (2) the defendant owns the property;

        (3) the property is being attached or seized; and

        (4) the defendant has been provided proper notice of the proceedings.

    b. The court may not exercise *quasi in rem* jurisdiction unless there are minimum contacts with the forum state or territory [Shaffer v. Heitner, 433 U.S. 186 (1977)].

        (1) If the dispute concerns the parties' rights in the property itself, the presence of the property in the state will provide sufficient minimum contacts.

        (2) The minimum contacts requirements for *quasi in rem* jurisdiction are similar to those for *in personam* jurisdiction.

        (3) The minimum contacts requirements make *quasi in rem* jurisdiction a rarely used gap filler. It is used only when the constitutional requirements (minimum contacts, and a finding that the exercise of jurisdiction does not offend traditional notions of fair play and substantial justice) are satisfied, but *in personam* jurisdiction is unavailable because the long-arm statute does not authorize jurisdiction.

5. **Judgment Entered without Personal Jurisdiction**

    a. If the court entered a judgment against a defendant over whom it did not have constitutional personal jurisdiction, that judgment is void and not entitled to Full Faith and Credit by another court.

    b. However, a judgment has preclusive effect on future litigation if the defendant in the first case had the opportunity to challenge personal jurisdiction and either:

        (1) waived the personal jurisdiction challenge; or

        (2) made the personal jurisdiction challenge and lost.

D. Service of Process and Notice

1. **Commencement of an Action**

    a. A civil action in federal court is commenced by filing the complaint with the court.

    b. After the complaint is filed, the plaintiff presents a summons to the clerk for signature and seal. If the summons meets the requirements for format of a summons, the clerk certifies it and issues it to the plaintiff for service on the defendant.

c. A summons is a court document that informs the defendant that the complaint has actually been filed and that he must respond to it, or else be held in default. The process served to compel the attendance of witnesses is a subpoena [Fed. R. Civ. P. 45].

d. The formal requirements for a summons are set out in Rule 4, which requires a summons:

(1) be signed by the clerk;

(2) identify the court and the parties;

(3) be directed to the defendant;

(4) state the name and address of either the plaintiff's attorney or the plaintiff itself, if unrepresented;

(5) notify the defendant of:

(a) the time period within which it must appear or file an answer; and

(b) the potential for a default judgment if the defendant fails to appear within the time specified; and

(6) contain the seal of the court.

2. **Service of Process**

a. The plaintiff is charged with service of process.

b. A summons must be served with a copy of the complaint. Unless both the complaint and summons are served on the defendant at the same time, process has not been completed.

(1) The plaintiff is responsible for any insufficiency of either the service of process or the process itself.

c. Service of process must occur within 90 days of filing of the complaint [Fed. R. Civ. P. 3, 4(m)].

(1) If the plaintiff does not timely serve the defendant with process, the court must dismiss the suit without prejudice unless the plaintiff can show good cause why service was not timely.

d. Service may be effected by any person who is:

(1) over 18 years of age; and

(2) not a party to the suit.

e. **How Process is Served**

(1) Process can be served on the defendant (whether a natural person or corporation, partnership, or association) by following the manner prescribed by the state court in the state where the federal suit has been filed or the state court in the state where the defendant will be served [Fed. R. Civ. P. 4(e)(1)].

(2) If the defendant is a natural person, process can also be served by doing any of the following [Fed. R. Civ. P. 4(e)(2)]:

(a) personally delivering the process to the defendant himself, wherever he maybe;

   (b) leaving process at the defendant's usual place of abode with a person of suitable age and discretion who resides there; or

   (c) serving the defendant's registered agent.

  (3) If the defendant is a corporation, partnership, or association, process can also be served by delivering a copy of the summons and the complaint to [Fed. R. Civ. P. 4(h)]:

   (a) an officer;

   (b) a managing agent or general agent; or

   (c) any other agent authorized by appointment or by law to receive service of process. Note that if the agent is one authorized by law and the law requires service by mail, process must be served by personal delivery to the agent and by mail.

 f. **Waiver of Service**

  (1) A defendant may also waive service of process, upon request of the plaintiff. A waiver allows the plaintiff to save the costs of service.

  (2) Waiver of service is not a waiver of any objections the defendant may have regarding the court's subject-matter or personal jurisdiction over the suit or as to the venue of the suit.

  (3) A request for waiver of service of process must:

   (a) be in writing and addressed to the individual defendant;

    1) If the defendant is a corporation, partnership, or association, the request is addressed to an officer, manager, or authorized agent.

   (b) be sent via first-class mail or other reliable means;

   (c) be accompanied by a copy of the complaint;

   (d) identify the court where the complaint was filed;

   (e) inform the defendant of the consequences of waiving and not waiving service;

   (f) state the date on which the request was sent;

   (g) allow the defendant a reasonable time to return the waiver;

    1) at least 30 days after the request was sent; or

    2) at least 60 days after the request was sent for defendants located outside any judicial district of the United States; and

   (h) provide the defendant with an extra copy of the request, as well as prepaid postage or other means of compliance in writing.

  (4) Upon request of the plaintiff, a defendant has a duty to waive service unless the defendant is:

   (a) a minor or incompetent person;

   (b) the United States or an agency of the United States; or

   (c) a state, local, or foreign government.

  (5) A defendant who agrees to waive service need not answer the

complaint until 60 days after the waiver request. If the complaint was sent to the defendant outside of any U.S. judicial district, the defendant does not need to answer until 90 days after the waiver request.

(6) If a defendant located in the United States fails without good cause to sign and return a waiver requested by a plaintiff located within the United States, the court may impose on the defendant:

(a) expenses incurred in making service; and

(b) reasonable expenses, including attorney's fees, of any motion required to collect service expenses.

(7) Sanctions will not be imposed if the defendant had good cause for failure to waive.

(a) "Good cause" does not include a belief that the complaint is unfounded, or that the action was filed in the wrong court.

(b) Failure to receive the waiver request would constitute good cause.

g. If a plaintiff fails to effect service according to the rules, the case should be dismissed for insufficiency of service of process.

(1) A defendant may raise objections to service of process in a motion to dismiss [Fed. R. Civ. P. 12(b)].

(2) Failure to raise the objection to insufficiency of service of process in a pre-answer motion or in the answer waives the defendant's right to object.

(3) A court will dismiss an action for insufficient service of process even if the defendant received actual notice of the action by some means other than service of process.

E. **Venue, Transfer, and *Forum non Conveniens***

1. **Venue**

a. While subject matter jurisdiction dictates whether a suit can be brought in the federal court system, and personal jurisdiction informs the plaintiff what state the suit can be brought in, **venue** dictates the region within a particular state (known as a judicial district) where a suit can occur.

b. The venue of an action is the federal court in which the action is filed.

c. In any action venue is proper in [28 U.S.C. § 1391]:

(1) the district in which any defendant resides, if all of the defendants reside in the same state;

EXAMPLE: Plaintiff, a resident of Minnesota, brings a diversity action against Defendant A, a resident of Madison, Wisconsin (located in the Western District of Wisconsin), and Defendant B, a resident of Milwaukee (located in the Eastern District of Wisconsin). Venue is appropriate in either the Eastern or Western District.

(2) the district in which a substantial part of the events or omissions giving rise to the claim occurred or the district in which a substantial part of the property that is the subject of the action is located; or

EXAMPLE: Plaintiff sues Defendant, a recording artist, for copyright infringement for recording one of Plaintiff's songs without permission. The song was recorded at a studio in Nashville. Venue is proper in the Middle District of Tennessee, the district in which Nashville is located.

    (3)   the district in which any defendant would be subject to personal jurisdiction, if there is no other district in which the action could be brought.

  d.   Venue is also considered proper where a party either consents to the venue, consents to personal jurisdiction in the venue, or waives his objection by failing to raise it.

  e.   The court may raise the issue of improper venue *sua sponte*.

  f.   For purposes of venue, a defendant's place of residence is determined according to the following rules [28 U.S.C. § 1391(c)]:

    (1) **Residence of Natural Persons**

        (a)   Natural persons are deemed to reside where they are domiciled.

        (b)   This applies to aliens who are admitted to permanent residence in the United States. They are considered to reside, for venue purposes, where they are domiciled.

    (2) **Residence of Entities**

        (a)   If the entity is a plaintiff, venue is proper where that plaintiff maintains its principal place of business.

        (b)   If the entity is a defendant, venue is proper where that defendant is subject to personal jurisdiction.

        (c)   If a corporation resides in a state that has multiple districts, venue is proper in the district that would have had personal jurisdiction over that corporation had that district been its own state.

    (3) **Non-Resident Aliens**

        (a)   Venue over non-resident aliens is proper in any judicial district.

        (b)   In multi-defendant cases, we disregard non-resident aliens when computing venue.

2. Transfer of Venue

  a.   If an action was brought in a particular venue, a federal court still may transfer the action to any other district in which it might have been brought, "for the convenience of parties and witnesses, in the interest of justice" [28 U.S.C. § 1404(a)]. The court does not dismiss the action so that the plaintiff may refile, but instead transfers the action to the more appropriate judicial district.

    (1)   Courts usually give substantial deference to the plaintiff's choice of forum. The defendant bears the burden of proving that an adequate alternative forum exists, and that the plaintiff's choice of forum is significantly inappropriate.

    (2)   The burden is on the party making a motion to transfer to show that:

(a) the convenience of the parties and witnesses, the ease of access to proof, calendar congestion, and other factors favor transfer; and

(b) the court to which the action will be transferred has personal and subject-matter jurisdiction over the suit.

(3) When an action filed in a proper venue is transferred to a different court, the substantive law applied should be the same law that would have been applied by the transferor court.

EXAMPLE: Plaintiff, a resident of Oregon, brings a diversity action for wrongful termination of employment against Defendant, a corporation incorporated in Delaware but located in Washington, in U.S. District Court in Delaware. Defendant's only physical location is in Washington, and it has no assets or physical presence in Delaware. All of the records relating to Plaintiff's employment and termination are in Washington, and all of the witnesses who might be called to testify are in either Washington or Oregon. The court may transfer Plaintiff's action under Rule 1404.

b. If a case is brought in an improper venue, a federal court "shall dismiss, or if it be in the interest of justice, transfer such case to any district…in which it could have been brought" [28 U.S.C. § 1406(a)].

(1) Transfers due to improper venue are appropriate only if the action could originally have been brought in the transferee court.

(2) In an action transferred under § 1406, the action never "belonged" in the transferor court. The transferee court will therefore apply its own conflict of laws principles to determine the applicable substantive law.

3. *Forum non Conveniens*

a. The doctrine of *forum non conveniens* allows a court to decline to exercise its jurisdiction and dismiss an action if the court where the action was brought would be a seriously inconvenient forum and an adequate alternative forum exists in a foreign country.

(1) A federal court does not have the power to transfer a case to a foreign country, so the case will be dismissed. The plaintiff may then file his action in the alternative forum.

(2) Courts may give substantial weight to the possibility of any change in substantive law as a result of bringing suit in the foreign forum if the remedy is so clearly inadequate or unsatisfactory as to be no remedy at all.

(3) Any deference given to the plaintiff's forum carries less weight when the plaintiff is from a foreign country.

b. Once the court has determined that an adequate alternative forum exists, it will weigh the public and private interests to determine whether to dismiss an action under the doctrine of *forum non conveniens*.

(1) Public interests include the interests in:

       (a) resolving disputes locally and not burdening local courts with distant disputes;

       (b) avoiding application of foreign law, if the case will require applying the law of another jurisdiction; and

       (c) avoiding the imposition of jury duty for a case that would not have a substantial impact on the potential jurors' community.

(2) Private interests include:

       (a) ease of access to evidence;

       (b) cost of witness attendance at trial;

       (c) availability of compulsory process; and

       (d) any other factors that might lessen the time and expense of trial.

II. LAW APPLIED BY FEDERAL COURTS

A. **State Law in Federal Court**
  1. **Rules of Decision Act**
     a. The Rules of Decision Act states that applicable provisions of the federal Constitution, treaties, and constitutional statutes enacted by Congress always take precedence over state law [28 U.S.C. § 1652].
     b. The federal courts apply federal law when considering issues involving:
        (1) the U.S. Constitution; and
        (2) constitutional federal statutes.
  2. **The Erie Doctrine**
     a. The Erie doctrine states that a federal court that hears a state law claim in a case based on diversity or supplemental jurisdiction must apply the substantive law of the state in which the court sits [Erie R.R. Co. v. Tompkins, 304 U.S. 64 (1938)].
        (1) Under Erie, state law applies if it is a law that deals with the substantive rights of state citizens. Federal courts use federal, not state, procedural rules.
     b. The Erie doctrine applies only where the following are both present:
        (1) the court has subject-matter jurisdiction over a case, based on diversity or supplemental jurisdiction; and
        (2) the state law that would apply conflicts with the federal rule, statute, doctrine, or procedure at issue.
     c. If a valid federal statute or constitutional provision is on point, the federal court must apply the relevant provision; it is irrelevant whether the provision is substantive or procedural.
        (1) The federal rule will not apply if the federal rule abridges, modifies, or enlarges a substantive right.
        (2) If there is a valid federal rule promulgated under the Rules Enabling Act dealing with an issue, that rule is applied [28 U.S.C. § 2071, *et seq.*].
     d. If there is no valid federal statutory or constitutional law on point, the federal court will follow its ordinary practices unless doing so would lead to either a preference for one court system over another (forum shopping) or fundamental unfairness.

NOTE ▶ This part of the Erie analysis (when there is no valid federal statute or constitution provision on point) is really the substantive versus procedure law distinction. If this inquiry instructs the court to apply state law, the state law is called "substantive" regardless of its true nature. If this inquiry instructs the court to stick with ordinary federal practice, that practical is called "procedural," regardless of its true nature.

     e. Although the rules discussed above are the steps to apply in an Erie analysis, there is general agreement that certain substantive state laws should be applied in federal diversity cases.

        (1)   Federal courts in a diversity action will apply the statute of limitations of the state in which the court sits.

        (2)   Federal courts in a diversity action will apply the choice-of-law rules of the state in which the court is located.

3.   **Uncertain State Law**

    a.   If the federal court is uncertain about the state law to be followed, or if the law is unclear or unsettled, the court may:

        (1)   abstain from hearing the state law claim;

        (2)   if state law allows, certify the question to the state courts and obtain a ruling on the issue; or

        (3)   try to predict how the state courts would rule on the issue, using all available and relevant resources.

    b.   Federal circuit courts of appeal do not give deference to district courts' interpretations of unsettled state law, but review those decisions *de novo.*

B. **Federal Common Law**

   1.   **In General**

    a.   Under the Erie doctrine, there is no general federal common law. Courts apply the laws of the states in which they are located.

    b.   Federal common law now exists to interpret Congressional intent, or the meaning of statutes.

        (1)   Congress has made broad rules, with unclear or indefinite standards, for courts to interpret.

            EXAMPLE: Federal law provides that the "fair use" of copyright-protected material is not infringement; however, the statute does not define "fair use" [17 U.S.C. § 107]. The courts have thus been left to develop the parameters of the fair use defense.

        (2)   Congressional action will take precedence over common law rules.

            EXAMPLE: The Clean Air Act gives the Environmental Protection Agency authority to regulate greenhouse gases. The statutory grant of authority precludes federal common law nuisance claims against producers of those gases [American Elec. Power Co. v. Connecticut, 131 S. Ct. 2527 (2011)].

   2.   **Federal or Constitutional Interests**

    a.   Federal courts may make federal common law when [Clearfield Trust Co. v. U.S., 318 U.S. 360 (1943)]:

        (1)   federal or constitutional interests are at stake;

        (2)   Congress had inadequately addressed the situation concerned; and

        (3)   the application of individual state laws in various jurisdictions would create unacceptable levels of diversity or uncertainty.

    b.   Federal common law rules are adopted when Congress has given courts the power to make common law rules, or when Congress has been silent on a question involving federal law.

EXAMPLE: Punitive damages are available in federal maritime cases when the owner of a vessel fails to pay maintenance and cure to an injured seaman. The damages are available as a matter of federal common law, because Congress has not acted to prohibit such damages [Atlantic Sounding Co. v. Townsend, 557 U.S. 404 (2009)].

c. Generally, federal common law is confined to the following fields of law:

(1) maritime law;

(2) foreign relations;

(3) commercial rights and liabilities of the federal government; and

(4) property rights and liabilities of the federal government.

ERIE DOCTRINE

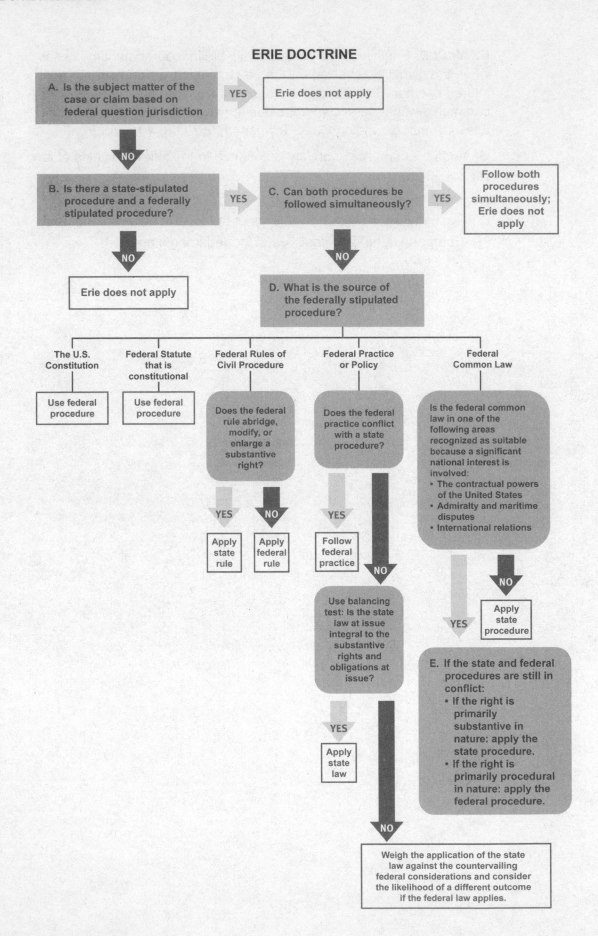

III. PRETRIAL PROCEDURES

A. Pleadings

1. **Types of Pleadings**

    a. The following types of pleadings are allowed under the Federal Rules of Civil Procedure:

    (1) complaints;

    (2) answers to complaints;

    (3) answers to counterclaims;

    (4) answers to cross-claims;

    (5) third-party complaints;

    (6) answers to third-party complaints; and

    (7) replies to answers, if ordered by the court.

2. **Rules of Pleading**

    a. To initiate a lawsuit, the first step is filing a complaint.

    b. A pleading that states a claim for relief (including a complaint), must contain [Fed. R. Civ. P. 8]:

    (1) a short and plain statement of the grounds for the court's jurisdiction;

    (2) a short and plain statement of the claim showing that the pleader is entitled to relief; and

    (a) The "short and plain statement of the claim" must include "sufficient factual matter" to state a plausible claim that is more than a "sheer possibility that a defendant has acted unlawfully" [Bell Atlantic Corp. v. Twombly, 550 U.S. 544 (2007); Ashcroft v. Iqbal, 556 U.S. 662 (2009)].

    (3) a demand for the relief sought.

    c. A pleading may make inconsistent claims or defenses. The court will allow inconsistent pleadings to be determined by the trier of facts.

    EXAMPLE: A sues B, claiming that B's dog bit him. B's answer denies that A was bitten. The answer also claims that A was bit because he provoked the dog.

    d. A party may set out two or more statements of a claim or defense alternatively or hypothetically, either in a single count or defense or in separate ones.

    EXAMPLE: C is hit by a car driven by D. C sues D, alleging that D negligently hit C. C also alleges that D intentionally hit her with his car.

    e. Generally, pleadings in federal court are to be liberally construed.

    (1) Courts are directed to ignore technical defects in pleadings, if no substantial right of the parties is prejudiced.

    (2) Note that the Twombly and Iqbal cases referenced *supra* set out heightened standards for the allegations in pleadings that may affect how pleadings are construed.

    f.   Parties must plead claims or defenses in a simple, direct, and concise manner.

        (1)   No technical pleading forms are necessary.

        (2)   Although parties should use general terms and omit evidentiary material, a pleading must contain "sufficient factual matter" to set out a plausible claim for relief.

    g.   Some cases involve special matters that must be pleaded with particularity [Fed. R. Civ. P. 9]. Those special matters are:

        (1)   capacity or authority to sue, if required to show the court has jurisdiction;

        (2)   fraud, mistake, or condition of the mind;

        (3)   conditions precedent, but only when denying that the condition has occurred;

        (4)   time and place, when testing the sufficiency of a pleading; and

        (5)   special damages.

> **EXAMPLE:** A sues B for injuries sustained in a traffic accident. A alleges that B's negligence caused her to incur medical bills, and to lose wages because she was unable to work. A must plead with specificity the amount of lost wages and the amount of her medical bills.

3. **Responsive Pleading**

    a.   An **answer** is a pleading in which the responding party admits or denies the opposing party's allegations and lists any defenses he might have.

        (1)   The responding party must admit those allegations, or parts of allegations, that are true, and deny the others [Fed. R. Civ. P. 8(b)].

        (2)   A general denial is appropriate only when the responding party intends in good faith to deny all the allegations in the pleading.

        (3)   If the defendant fails to deny an allegation, it is deemed admitted.

    b.   A party must plead certain affirmative defenses in its answer or reply to a counterclaim.

        (1)   An **affirmative defense** is a defense that relies on factual issues not presented in the complaint. It does not necessarily deny the allegations of the complaint, but pleads additional facts.

        (2)   Affirmative defenses that must be pleaded in a responsive pleading include:

           (a) accord and satisfaction;

           (b) arbitration and award;

           (c) assumption of risk;

           (d) contributory negligence;

           (e) discharge in bankruptcy;

           (f) duress;

           (g) estoppel;

           (h) failure of consideration;

           (i) fraud;

           (j) illegality;

      (k)   injury by fellow servant;

      (l)   laches;

      (m) licenses;

      (n)   payment;

      (o)   release;

      (p)   *res judicata*;

      (q)   Statute of Frauds;

      (r)   statute of limitations; and

      (s)   waiver.

   (3)   Affirmative defenses that raise objections based on jurisdiction or procedural matters may be raised either in a responsive pleading, or in a pre-answer motion.

      (a)   If an objection will be raised by a motion, rather than in a responsive pleading, the motion must be made before a responsive pleading is made [Fed. R. Civ. P. 12(b)]. These motions are therefore known as pre-answer motions.

          1)   A motion to dismiss, a motion for a more definite statement, and a motion to strike are all pre-answer motions that must be made before a responsive pleading is made.

      (b)   Objections that may be raised either by a pre-answer motion to dismiss or responsive pleading are the following:

          1)   lack of subject-matter jurisdiction;

          2)   lack of personal jurisdiction;

          3)   improper venue;

          4)   insufficient process;

          5)   insufficient service of process;

          6)   failure to state a claim upon which relief can be granted; and

          7)   failure to join a party under Rule 19.

   (4)   Failure to raise an objection in an answer or pre-answer motion to dismiss constitutes a waiver of these defenses with the exception of objections to subject-matter jurisdiction, failure to state a claim upon which relief can be granted, and failure to join a party [Fed. R. Civ. P. 12(h)(1)].

  c. **Timing of Responsive Pleading**

   (1)   An answer (or pre-answer motion) must be filed:

      (a)   within 21 days of service of process; or

NOTE The 21-day period does not include the date of service, but does include weekends and holidays. If the 21st day is on a weekend or a holiday, the answer must be filed on the next business day.

      (b)   if service was waived, within 60 days after the request for a waiver was sent, or within 90 days after it was sent to the defendant outside any judicial district of the United States.

      (2)   If the defendant responds to plaintiff's complaint by filing a pre-answer motion that is denied, the defendant must then file an answer within 14 days of the denial.

4.   **Amended and Supplemental Pleadings**

   a.   A party may amend a pleading once as a matter of course if the amendment is filed [Fed. R. Civ. P. 15]:

      (1)   within 21 days of service of the original pleading; or

      (2)   if the pleading requires a response, within 21 days after service of a responsive pleading or 21 days after service of a motion to dismiss, a motion for a more definite statement, or a motion to strike, whichever is earlier.

   b.   In situations in which a party is not entitled to amend as a matter of course, a pleading may be amended with the written consent of the opposing party, or with the leave of the court.

      (1)   Leave to amend must be freely given when justice requires. In deciding whether to grant a request to amend, the court will consider:

         (a) the reason for the delay in raising the matter to be raised by the amendment; and

         (b) the prejudice to the opposing party caused by the delay.

   c.   If a party objects at trial to evidence as not being within the scope of the issues raised in the pleadings, the court may permit the pleadings to be amended to conform to the evidence.

   d.   A response to an amended pleading is required if the original pleading required a response.

   e.   **Doctrine of Relation Back**

      (1)   Under the **doctrine of relation back**, the court will treat an amendment to a pleading as though it had been filed with the original pleading.

      (2)   An amendment to a pleading that adds a new claim will be considered filed on the date in which the original complaint was filed as long as the amendment asserts a claim or defense that arose out of the same conduct, transaction, or occurrence as the original claim [Fed. R. Civ. P. 15(c)].

      (3)   An amendment to a pleading that adds a new party will be considered filed on the date in which the original complaint was filed as long as [Id.]:

         (a) the amendment asserts a claim or defense that arose out of the same conduct, transaction, or occurrence as the original claim;

         (b) the party to be added by the amendment received notice of the original action within 90 days of service of the claim such that it will not be prejudiced in defending on the merits; and

         (c) the party to be added knew, or should have known, that the original action would have been asserted against it, but for a mistake concerning the proper party's identity.

B. Rule 11

1. Every pleading, written motion, and other paper filed with the court must be signed by at least one attorney of record in the attorney's name, or by a party personally, if the party is not represented by an attorney [Fed. R. Civ. P. 11].

   a. The signed document must state the signer's address, e-mail address, and telephone number.

   b. The court must strike an unsigned paper unless the omission is promptly corrected after it is called to the attorney's or party's attention.

   c. Rule 11 does not apply to discovery matter, whether it is a discovery request, response, motion or any other matter, although other rules may be applied to abusive discovery.

2. The attorney or unrepresented party who presents to the court a pleading, written motion, or other document certifies that to the best of the person's knowledge, information, and belief, formed after an inquiry reasonable under the circumstances that:

   a. the document is not being presented for any improper purpose, such as to harass, cause unnecessary delay, or needlessly increase the cost of litigation;

   b. the claims, defenses, and other legal contentions are warranted by existing law or by a nonfrivolous argument for extending, modifying, or reversing existing law or for establishing new law;

   c. the factual contentions have evidentiary support or will likely have evidentiary support after a reasonable opportunity for further investigation or discovery; and

   d. the denials of factual contentions are either warranted on the evidence or are reasonably based on belief or a lack of information.

   EXAMPLE: A brings a lawsuit against B for false light invasion of privacy. A's state has never recognized a cause of action for false light, but A argues that, under existing precedent, the courts of the state would likely recognize such an action. A has not violated Rule 11, even if his action is ultimately unsuccessful.

3. If the court finds that any of the above representations are untrue, it has discretion to impose sanctions on the party or the party's attorney. Sanctions are ordered after notice to the offending party and an opportunity to be heard.

   EXAMPLE: C brings a lawsuit against D for employment discrimination, claiming that C's application for employment was denied. C never applied for a job with D. The court may order sanctions against C.

   a. A party may not file a motion for sanctions without first serving the motion upon the opposing party and providing the opposing party with 21 days to withdraw or correct the offending pleading, written motion, or other paper (this is known as the **safe harbor rule**).

   b. A court may *sua sponte* issue an order to show cause why conduct described in the order does not violate Rule 11.

    c.   The nature of the sanction must be limited to "what suffices to deter repetition of the conduct or comparable conduct by others."

    d.   An order imposing sanctions must describe the sanctioned conduct and explain the basis for the sanctions.

C. Provisional Relief

1. Purpose

    a.   Provisional relief is available to maintain the status quo and prevent irreparable damage or wasting of assets during litigation or pending arbitration.

    b.   Provisional relief consists of two remedies:

        (1)   temporary restraining orders (TROs); and

        (2)   preliminary injunctions.

    c.   Both are extraordinary remedies as they are issued prior to a decision on the merits and provide immediate or quick but short-term injunctive relief.

        (1)   The temporary restraining order is used in an emergency situation, when the injunction must issue before any hearing, and lasts only a few days, generally long enough for the parties to seek a preliminary injunction.

        (2)   The preliminary injunction, if granted, will last until a decision on the merits, however long that may take.

2. Standard for Granting

    a.   A party seeking either a temporary restraining order or a preliminary injunction must first establish [Forsyth County v. United States Army Corps of Eng'rs, 633 F.3d 1032]:

        (1)   a substantial likelihood of success on the merits;

        (2)   irreparable harm will be suffered unless the remedy sought is issued;

        (3)   the harm to the plaintiff if the temporary restraining order or preliminary injunction is denied is greater than the harm to the defendant if the remedy is granted; and

        (4)   the provisional remedy, if granted, will not be adverse to the public interest.

    b.   A court may issue a temporary restraining order or a preliminary injunction only if the moving party gives security sufficient to cover the costs and damages sustained by any party who is wrongfully enjoined or restrained [Fed. R. Civ. P. 65(c)].

3. Notice

    a.   **Temporary Restraining Order**

        (1)   A court may issue a temporary restraining order without written or oral notice to the adverse party [Fed. R. Civ. P. 65(b)(1)].

            (a)   If a temporary restraining order is issued without notice, a motion for a preliminary injunction must be set for hearing at the earliest possible time, taking precedence over all other matters [Fed. R. Civ. P. 65(b)(3)].

(b) If the party who obtained the temporary restraining order does not proceed with the motion for a preliminary injunction, the restraining order must be dissolved.

(2) Temporary restraining orders will issue without notice only if:

(a) specific facts in an affidavit or verified complaint clearly show that immediate and irreparable injury, loss, or damage will result to the movant before the adverse party can be heard in opposition; and

(b) the movant's attorney certifies in writing any efforts made to give notice and the reasons why notice should not be required.

(3) Every temporary restraining order issued without notice must [Fed. R. Civ. P. 65(b)(2)]:

(a) state the date and hour it was issued;

(b) describe the injury and state why it is irreparable;

(c) state why the order was issued without notice; and

(d) be promptly filed in the clerk's office and entered in the record.

(4) A temporary restraining order issued without notice expires at the time set by the court.

(a) The time for expiration must not exceed 14 days after entry.

(b) The court may, for good cause, extend the duration for a like period or the adverse party may consent to a longer extension. The reasons for an extension must be entered in the record.

b. **Preliminary Injunction**

(1) A preliminary injunction may only be issued by a court on notice to the adverse party [Fed. R. Civ. P. 65(a)(1)].

(2) Before or after beginning a hearing on a motion for a preliminary injunction, the court may advance the trial on the merits and consolidate it with the hearing on the injunction.

(a) The court must preserve any party's right to a jury trial.

(b) Whether or not consolidation is ordered, any evidence entered on the motion for a preliminary injunction that would be admissible at trial becomes part of the trial record. This evidence need not be repeated at trial.

4. **Content and Scope of Relief**

a. Every order granting a preliminary injunction or temporary restraining order must [Fed. R. Civ. P. 65(d)(1)]:

(1) state the reasons why it was issued;

(2) state its terms specifically; and

(3) describe in reasonable detail the act or acts restrained or required. The description may not be a reference to the complaint or other document.

b. The order will only bind the following parties after actual notice is received, whether by personal service or otherwise [Fed. R. Civ. P. 65(d)(2)]:

(1) the parties;

(2)   the parties' officers, servants, agents, employees, and attorneys; and

(3)   any persons who are in active concert or participation with anyone described above otherwise.

D.   Joinder of Claims and Parties

1.   **Multiple Claims by Single Claimant against Single Defendant**

a.   A party may join as many claims in a single action as the party has against an opposing party [Fed. R. Civ. P. 18].

b.   There is no requirement that all of the claims in a complaint be related. The goal of joining all claims in one action is to achieve a complete resolution of all disputes between the parties.

(1)   If the joinder of claims would lead to jury confusion or some other prejudice, the court may sever the claims for separate trials [Fed. R. Civ. P. 42].

(2)   Federal joinder of claims is usually permissive, but it is compelled when the failure to join could result in splitting a cause of action. The doctrine of claim preclusion prevents relitigation of a claim.

(3)   Rule 18 addresses pleadings only. It cannot expand the jurisdiction of a federal court, if there is not jurisdiction over the claim otherwise. If supplemental jurisdiction is needed, then the parties must still show that their additional claims "are so related to claims in the action within such original jurisdiction that they form part of the same case or controversy" [28 U.S. Code § 1367(a)].

2.   **Counterclaims**

a.   A **counterclaim** may be brought by any party against any other opposing party and can be compulsory or permissive.

(1)   A **compulsory counterclaim** is one that arises out of the same transaction or occurrence as the original claim in the lawsuit.

EXAMPLE: Plaintiff brings a breach of contract action against Defendant, for failure to pay for construction work done by Plaintiff. Defendant's claim that the work was done negligently, and caused Defendant to sustain personal injuries, is a compulsory counterclaim.

(a)   A failure to raise a compulsory counterclaim waives the right to assert the claim in any future action.

(b)   The federal court has supplemental jurisdiction over a compulsory counterclaim even in the absence of an independent basis for federal jurisdiction [28 U.S.C. § 1367(a)].

(2)   A **permissive counterclaim** is any claim that a party has against an opposing party that does not arise out of the same transaction or occurrence that is the subject matter of the opposing party's claim.

EXAMPLE: Plaintiff sues Defendant for breach of contract for failure to paint Plaintiff's house. Defendant's personal injury claim against Plaintiff that arose out of a later traffic accident is a permissive counterclaim.

      (a)   A party is not required to assert a permissive counterclaim.

      (b)   Federal courts do not have supplemental jurisdiction over permissive counterclaims, because they do not arise out of the same transaction or occurrence as the original claim. There must be an independent ground for federal jurisdiction before the federal court will hear a permissive counterclaim.

3. **Cross-Claims**

   a.   A **cross-claim** is a claim filed by a party against a co-party (not opposing party). Cross-claims may be brought by any party against any co-party, but only when the claim arises out of the same transaction or occurrence as the original claim or a counterclaim.

      EXAMPLE: A sues B and C for failure to complete a construction project as promised. B claims that C breached a contract with B to perform certain work on the project. B may bring a cross-claim against C.

      (1)   A cross-claim may include a claim that the party against whom it is asserted is or may be liable for all or part of the claim asserted in the action against the cross-claimant.

            EXAMPLE: A sues B, a surgeon, and C, an anesthesiologist, for medical malpractice. C may bring a cross-claim against B, based on C's claim that the damages sustained by A were entirely B's fault.

      (2)   The federal court has supplemental jurisdiction over a cross-claim even in the absence of an independent basis for federal jurisdiction, because the cross-claim arises out of the same transaction or occurrence as the original claim [28 U.S.C. § 1367(a)].

4. **Impleader Claims**

   a.   After a defendant to an action has served her answer, that defendant may proceed against a non-party who may be liable for all or part of the plaintiff's claim against the defendant [Fed. R. Civ. P. 14].

   b.   Impleader thus allows a defending party to shift all or part of the liability owed to the plaintiff to a new party who is or may be liable for it.

      EXAMPLE: A sues B for injuries she sustained when B hit her while driving her car. B claims that she hit A because the steering mechanism on her car was damaged when C, a mechanic, did faulty repair work. B may proceed against C.

   c.   The two most important impleader claims are contribution and indemnity claims.

      (1)   A **contribution claim** is a claim against a joint tortfeasor that shifts part of the defendant's liability to a new party.

      (2)   An **indemnity claim** is a claim that shifts all of the defendant's liability to a new party (e.g., an insurance claim).

   d.   The defendant must file a third-party summons and complaint with the court where the original action is pending. The defendant becomes the third-party plaintiff.

(1) Service on the non-party makes that party the third-party defendant.

(2) A defendant may file a third-party complaint any time within 14 days of filing her answer. After that, third-party complaints may be filed only with leave of court.

(3) When the defendant brings in a third-party, the plaintiff may amend his original complaint to assert claims against the third-party defendant.

e. A plaintiff may file a third-party complaint to bring in a third-party defendant if a counterclaim has been asserted against the plaintiff and there is a basis for the plaintiff to argue that a third party is liable for all or part of the liability pursuant to the counterclaim.

f. Third-party defendants have the same rights as any other party to the action. These rights include the right to:

(1) service of process;

(2) file an answer to the third-party complaint (the answer may include any defenses that the third-party plaintiff asserted in his answer to the original complaint);

(3) assert counterclaims or cross-claims;

(4) implead additional non-parties by third-party complaint; and

(5) appeal orders or final judgment in the action.

g. The court may dismiss a third-party complaint without prejudice, or order a separate trial of the third-party claim or any separate issue within it, if it finds that the controversy between a third-party plaintiff and third-party defendant would unduly delay the determination of the original action or prejudice a substantial right of one of the parties.

5. **Permissive Joinder of Parties**

a. Permissive joinder allows multiple plaintiffs to join together in a single action and allows multiple defendants to be sued in a single action.

b. Multiple persons may be joined together as plaintiffs or defendants in one action if [Fed. R. Civ. P. 20]:

(1) the joined parties claim relief (if plaintiffs) or face liability (if defendants) that arises out of the same transaction or occurrence; and

(2) any question of law or fact is common to the joined parties.

EXAMPLE: A and B are injured while they are passengers on an airplane that makes a bad landing. They may join their claims in the same action.

6. **Compulsory Joinder of Parties**

a. A person who is subject to service of process and whose joinder will not deprive the court of subject-matter jurisdiction must be joined as a necessary party if [Fed. R. Civ. P. 19]:

(1) in that party's absence, the court cannot grant complete relief among existing parties; or

(2) the party claims an interest relating to the subject of the action, and an adjudication without the party may:

        (a) as a practical matter, impair or impede that party's ability to protect his interests; or

        (b) leave an existing party subject to a substantial risk of incurring double, multiple, or otherwise inconsistent obligations.

> **EXAMPLE:** P leased a valuable painting to D. P believed the lease term was 3 years, and D believed it was 4. After possessing the painting for 2.5 years, D leased the painting to X for 1 year. When the 3-year mark arrived, P brought suit to reclaim the painting. X is a necessary party because it has an interest in the subject matter of the litigation (the painting), because D could be subject to duplicative liability (D could end up being liable to both P and X) and because the court cannot order the painting returned unless the person with the painting (X) is within the jurisdiction of the court.

> **EXAMPLE:** A is injured while a passenger on a train owned and operated by B. She was injured when another train, owned and operated by C, collided with the train she was riding on. A sued B. B argues that C is a necessary party and must be joined. This argument will fail. As a rule, joint tortfeasors are not necessary parties. There is no mandatory joinder in this situation.

    b. If a person who is required to be joined cannot be joined for jurisdictional reasons, the court must determine whether, in equity and good conscience, the action should proceed among the existing parties or be dismissed. The factors for the court to consider include:

        (1) the extent to which a judgment rendered in the person's absence might prejudice that person or the existing parties;

        (2) the extent to which any prejudice could be lessened or avoided by:

            (a) protective provisions in the judgment;

            (b) shaping the relief; or

            (c) other measures;

        (3) whether a judgment rendered in the person's absence would be adequate; and

        (4) whether the plaintiff would have an adequate remedy if the action were dismissed for nonjoinder.

7. **Interpleader**

    a. **Interpleader** is used where a plaintiff has some holding that would expose the plaintiff to multiple liability from adverse claims. The stakeholding party, or "stakeholder," can commence an action for interpleader to resolve liability where there are two or more adverse claimants. Interpleader is only applicable where multiple claims demand the same thing or obligation—usually, a piece of property, prize, or, most commonly, the proceeds of an insurance policy.

b. Interpleader is either rule interpleader, authorized by the Federal Rules of Civil Procedure, or statutory interpleader.

EXAMPLE: B dies leaving a life insurance policy, the proceeds of which are claimed by his wife, ex-wife, and two children. The insurance company is the stakeholder. As a neutral third party, it may bring an action in court to determine the rights of each claimant.

c. Rule interpleader is authorized by Fed. R. Civ. P. 22.

(1) **Rule interpleader** may be initiated pursuant to Rule 22 by any person who may be exposed to multiple liability.

(2) In an interpleader under Rule 22, the stakeholder may initiate the claim or invoke the rule interpleader by his own initiative. The stakeholder may also initiate interpleader by counter-claiming or cross-claiming against a claimant in an action that has already commenced against the stakeholder.

(3) Rule interpleader has no effect on jurisdictional or venue requirements. Subject-matter jurisdiction must still be established through diversity jurisdiction, federal question jurisdiction, or supplemental jurisdiction.

d. Statutory interpleader is authorized by 28 U.S.C. § 1335.

(1) **Statutory interpleader** allows a person holding property which may be claimed, or is claimed by two or more adverse claimants, to interplead all possible claimants.

(2) Once a statutory interpleader suit is commenced, the court may restrain all of the claimants from commencing any related action or continuing any other action that has already begun.

(3) Statutory interpleader has the following advantages over rule interpleader:

(a) nationwide service of process is available for statutory interpleader, but not for rule interpleader;

(b) the federal court has diversity jurisdiction as long as there is minimal diversity between the adverse claimants and an amount in controversy over $500; and

EXAMPLE: When A died, she left $1,000 in an account with Bank. The money in the account is claimed by D, her surviving husband, and E, her daughter. D is a citizen of the same state as Bank, but E lives in a different state. The federal court has diversity jurisdiction to hear a statutory interpleader action brought by Bank.

(c) venue is established where any one of the adverse claimants resides.

8. **Intervention**

a. Intervention allows a non-party to assert a right or interest in an ongoing action. If the non-party can meet the test for intervention as a matter of right, then the court must allow the party to intervene. A non-party may also be allowed to intervene by permission of the court.

EXAMPLE: A conservation group may seek leave to intervene in an action against a developer.

b. The purpose of intervention is to enable a person outside an action to enter the suit to present an interest, a claim, or a defense relevant to the issues presented by the existing parties.

  (1) Intervention can contribute to judicial economy and protect a non-party from having its interest adversely affected by the litigation conducted without that person's participation.

  (2) Intervention can also delay or complicate the litigation by involving parties that the plaintiff chose not to join in the first instance.

c. In order to intervene in an action, a non-party's request for intervention must be timely. The factors the court may consider in deciding whether the application was timely are:

  (1) the length of time the non-party knew or should have known about its interest in the case before making the application;

  (2) the extent of prejudice that the existing parties may suffer as a result of the delay; and

  (3) the likelihood and gravity of the prejudice the non-party may suffer if the application is denied.

d. Upon a finding by the court that a non-party's application was timely, the non-party must be allowed to intervene in an action if [Fed. R. Civ. P. 24]:

  (1) a federal statute confers an absolute right of the party to intervene; or

  (2) a non-party is asserting a protectable interest relating to the property or transaction involved in the lawsuit, and:

    (a) the non-party is so situated that disposing of the action may as a practical matter impair or impede its ability to protect its interest; and

    (b) the non-party's interests are not adequately represented by existing parties.

    EXAMPLE: The United States may seek to intervene as of right in a discrimination action by students against a board of education where plaintiffs request only monetary damages and do not represent the government's interest in enforcing anti-discrimination laws.

e. If a non-party may not intervene in an action as a matter of right, the court may permit intervention if:

  (1) a federal statute allows a conditional right to intervention; or

  (2) the non-party has a claim or defense that shares a common question of law or fact with the primary action.

f. The trial court has discretion to grant permissive leave to intervene. In making its determination, the court will consider:

(1)	the complexity of the existing action and the complexity of the applicant's claim or defense;

(2)	the length of time the primary action has been pending; and

(3)	how much the existing parties will be delayed or prejudiced by the addition of the applicant's claim or defense.

9.	**Class Actions**

a.	A class action may be maintained by a party if the court finds that each of the following requirements have been met [Fed. R. Civ. P. 23]:

(1)	numerosity;

(a)	The numerosity requirement is met if the number of members of the class is so numerous that separate joinder of each member is impracticable.

(b)	No particular number is needed, nor is the number of potential class members determinative of whether the court will allow an action to proceed as a class action.

(2)	commonality;

(a)	The commonality requirement is met if there are questions of law or fact common to the class.

(b)	Rule 23 does not require that all questions of law and fact be common, nor that the common questions predominate. Instead, the party who seeks class certification must show that the class members have suffered the same injury [Wal-Mart Stores, Inc. v. Dukes, 131 S. Ct. 2541 (2011)]. Specifically, there must be a common contention that is capable of a class-wide resolution in one stroke [Id.]. Simply showing common facts or a common accusational type will not be enough to satisfy the commonality requirement.

(3)	typicality; and

(a)	The typicality requirement is met if the claims or defenses of the representative party are typical of those raised by each member of the class.

(b)	To meet this requirement, the representative's interest in prosecuting his own case must simultaneously tend to advance the interests of the absent class members. This means that the plaintiff's claim cannot be so different from the claims of potential class members that those class members' claims will not be advanced by the plaintiff's proof of his own individual claim.

(4)	adequacy of representation.

(a)	The adequacy of representation requirement is met if the representative party can fairly and adequately protect and represent the interests of each member of the class.

(b)	The representative party must have standing to bring her claim.

b.	In addition to the four requirements in Rule 23, courts will allow an action to be maintained as a class action only if at least one of the following is true:

        (1)   the prosecution of separate actions would create a risk of:

            (a)   inconsistent or varying judgments for individual class members that would establish incompatible standards of conduct for the party opposing the class, or

        (2)   judgments for individual members of the class that would substantially impede or impair the ability of other members to protect their interests; the party opposing the class has acted or refused to act on grounds that are generally applicable to the class as a whole; or

        (3)   the court finds that common questions predominate over individual questions, and class representation is superior to other methods for adjudicating the controversy. Factors used to determine common questions include:

            (a)   pending individual litigation;

            (b)   the interests of class members in individually controlling litigation of claims or defenses;

            (c)   the desirability of concentrating litigation in the forum; and

            (d)   the difficulties of managing the class action.

c.   Federal rules for class certification apply to all class actions in federal court, including those based on diversity. State laws on class certification are superseded [Shady Grove Orthopedic Associates v. Allstate Insurance Co., 559 U.S. 393 (2010)].

d.   A motion to certify a class action must be made "at an early practicable time" after the suit is commenced [Fed. R. Civ. P. 23(c)]. Local rules may provide a specific deadline for a class certification motion.

        (1)   The order permitting a class action must describe the class.

        (2)   When appropriate, the court may limit the class to those members who do not request exclusion from the class within the specified time after the notice.

            EXAMPLE: A class certification order certifies a class of all persons who bought a computer with a certain operating system who do not inform the court that they do not wish to be a part of the action within 120 days of the class certification order.

e.   An action may be brought or maintained as a class action with respect to any particular issue, or a class may be divided into subclasses with each subclass treated as a class.

f.   The court may direct appropriate notice to class members.

        (1)   For classes certified as a result of common questions of law or fact, notice is required and must include:

            (a)   the nature of the action;

            (b)   the definition of the certified class;

            (c)   the class claims, issues, or defenses;

            (d)   the ability of a class member to make an appearance;

(e) the ability of a class member to request exclusion from the class; and

(f) the binding effect of a judgment on all members of the class.

> **EXAMPLE:** Notice to potential class members in an action against the seller of computer operating systems must inform members that if they do not opt out of the class, they will be bound by the judgment in the class action, even if they did not file an individual appearance.

(2) Where a class action is brought primarily for injunctive or declaratory relief, notice need not be given to the class unless the court finds it necessary in order to protect the class.

g. In every case, the court must have personal jurisdiction over every defendant and each of the plaintiffs named in the action.

(1) The federal court is not required to have personal jurisdiction over absent members of the plaintiff class as long as they receive adequate notice of the pendency of the action and are afforded the opportunity to opt out of the class [Phillips Petroleum Co. v. Shutts, 472 U.S. 797 (1985)].

(2) It is unclear whether the court must have personal jurisdiction over the absent members of the plaintiff classes where there is no notice and/or opportunity to opt out of the class.

h. Class actions based on diversity jurisdiction are governed by the Class Action Fairness Act (CAFA) passed in 2005, which has transformed the doctrine in cases founded on diversity jurisdiction.

(1) Prior to CAFA, diversity jurisdiction required complete diversity between all of the named representative plaintiffs and all of the defendants. In addition, there was no diversity jurisdiction unless every member of the class had a claim that exceeded the amount in controversy.

(2) CAFA expands federal subject-matter jurisdiction to include classes where:

(a) the class has more than 100 persons;

(b) at least one member of the class is diverse from at least one defendant; and

(c) the total amount in controversy exceeds $5 million.

(3) CAFA's broad grant of subject-matter jurisdiction excludes local controversies, certain civil rights cases, and other categories of cases.

i. Class actions may not be dismissed or compromised without court approval. In evaluating a settlement proposal, a court must consider whether it is fair, reasonable, and in the best interests of the individuals affected by it [Fed. R. Civ. P. 23(e)].

j. A court that certifies a class action must appoint class counsel to represent the class [Fed. R. Civ. P. 23(g)]. The court may deny certification if suitable counsel is not found.

k. Counsel for the successful representative parties typically will be awarded an appropriate fee. If a fee may not be awarded pursuant to an applicable fee-shifting provision, the court may award fees out of the common fund created by the recovery from the defendant.

l. A court of appeals may permit an appeal from an order granting or denying class action certification if the petition for appeal is filed within 14 days after the order is entered [Fed. R. Civ. P. 23(f)].

E. Pretrial Conferences and Orders

1. Discovery Planning Conference

a. Rule 26(f) requires the parties to meet and have a discovery planning conference as soon as practicable, but at least 21 days before a scheduling order is to be held or is due under Rule 16(b) [Fed. R. Civ. P. 26(f)].

b. In the discovery conference, the parties must [Id.]:

(1) discuss the nature and basis of their claims and defenses and the possibilities of timely settling or resolving the case;

(2) make or arrange for the mandatory disclosures required by Rule 26(a)(1);

(3) discuss any issues about preserving discoverable information; and

(4) develop a proposed discovery plan.

c. A written report outlining the proposed discovery plan must then be submitted to the court within 14 days after the discovery conference.

2. Pretrial Conferences

a. After a Rule 26(f) conference has been held, the court may order the attorneys and any unrepresented parties to appear for one or more pretrial conferences for such purposes as [Fed. R. Civ. P. 16(a)]:

(1) expediting disposition of the action;

(2) establishing early and continuing control so that the case will not be protracted because of lack of management;

(3) discouraging wasteful pretrial activities;

(4) improving the quality of the trial through more thorough preparation; and

(5) facilitating settlement.

b. Except in categories of actions exempted by local rule, the district judge—or a magistrate judge when authorized by local rule—must issue a scheduling order that limits the time to join other parties, amend the pleadings, complete discovery, and file motions. A schedule may be modified only for good cause and with the judge's consent [Fed. R. Civ. P. 16(b)].

c. The scheduling order must be issued within the earlier of [Id.]:

(1) 90 days after any defendant has been served with the complaint; or

(2) 60 days after any defendant has appeared.

d. At any pretrial conference, the court may consider and take appropriate action on the following matters [Fed. R. Civ. P. 16(c)]:

   (1) formulating and simplifying the issues, and eliminating frivolous claims or defenses;

   (2) amending the pleadings if necessary or desirable;

   (3) obtaining admissions and stipulations about facts and documents to avoid unnecessary proof, and ruling in advance on the admissibility of evidence;

   (4) avoiding unnecessary proof and cumulative evidence, and limiting the use of testimony under the Federal Rules of Evidence;

   (5) determining the appropriateness and timing of summary adjudication;

   (6) controlling and scheduling discovery;

   (7) identifying witnesses and documents, scheduling the filing and exchange of any pretrial briefs, and setting dates for further conferences and for trial;

   (8) referring matters to a magistrate judge or a master;

   (9) settling the case and using special procedures to assist in resolving the dispute when authorized by statute or local rule;

   (10) determining the form and content of the pretrial order;

   (11) disposing of pending motions;

   (12) adopting special procedures for managing potentially difficult or protracted actions that may involve complex issues, multiple parties, difficult legal questions, or unusual proof problems;

   (13) ordering a separate trial of a claim, counterclaim, cross-claim, third-party claim, or particular issue;

   (14) ordering the presentation of evidence;

   (15) establishing a reasonable limit on the time allowed to present evidence; and

   (16) facilitating in other ways the just, speedy, and inexpensive disposition of the action.

e. After any pretrial conference, the court should issue an order reciting the action taken, which controls the course of the action unless the court modifies it [Fed. R. Civ. P. 16(d)].

f. The court may hold a final pretrial conference to formulate a trial plan, including a plan to facilitate the admission of evidence. The conference must be held as close to the start of trial as is reasonable, and must be attended by at least one attorney who will conduct the trial for each party and by any unrepresented party. The court may modify the order issued after a final pretrial conference only to prevent manifest injustice [Fed. R. Civ. P. 16(e)].

g. On motion or on its own, the court may issue sanctions if a party or its attorney:

   (1) fails to appear at a scheduling or other pretrial conference;

(2) is substantially unprepared to participate—or does not participate in good faith—in the conference; or

(3) fails to obey a scheduling or other pretrial order.

    (a) Instead of, or in addition to, any other sanction, the court must order the party, its attorney, or both to pay the reasonable expenses—including attorney's fees—incurred because of any noncompliance with this rule, unless the noncompliance was substantially justified or other circumstances make an award of expenses unjust [Fed. R. Civ. P. 16(f)].

F. Discovery

1. Overview

a. The primary purpose of the pleading stage is to provide notice to the parties; thus, the facts may not be stated in detail in the pleadings.

b. The facts surrounding a cause of action come to light during discovery.

c. The primary function of the discovery process is to provide litigants with an opportunity to obtain and review all of the pertinent evidence prior to trial.

d. There are mandatory disclosure obligations as well as specific discovery devices that are designed to elicit information within the permissible scope of discovery.

e. In general, discovery is initiated by the parties. A court will become involved only when there is a discovery dispute that cannot be resolved by the parties.

2. Mandatory Disclosures

a. Initial Disclosures

(1) With limited exceptions, parties are required to disclose some information as a matter of course upon the commencement of the litigation, without waiting for a discovery request. Mandatory disclosure is required by both parties for the following information [Fed. R. Civ. P. 26(a)(1)]:

    (a) the name (and if known, address and telephone number) of individuals likely to have discoverable information, along with the subject of that information, that the disclosing party may use to support its claims or defenses (unless the use would be solely for impeachment);

EXAMPLE: A plaintiff must disclose to the defendant the names of all witnesses to an accident that is the subject of the plaintiff's action that the plaintiff may use to support her claim.

    (b) a copy or description of all documents, electronically stored information, and tangible things that the disclosing party has in its possession, custody, or control and may use to support its claims or defenses (unless the use would be solely for impeachment);

       (c) a computation of damages claimed by the disclosing party, together with supporting materials; and

       (d) insurance agreements under which an insurance company may be liable to satisfy all or part of a possible judgment.

   (2) The initial mandatory disclosures must be made within 14 days after the Rule 26 discovery conference. A party must make these disclosures based upon the information then reasonably available.

b. Expert Disclosures

   (1) A party must also disclose the identity of any witness that may testify at trial [Fed. R. Civ. P. 26(a)(2)(A)].

   (2) If the witness is retained or specially employed to provide expert testimony in the case, or one whose duties as the party's employee regularly involve giving expert testimony, the disclosure must be accompanied by the expert's final written report. The report must contain [Fed. R. Civ. P. 26(a)(2)(B):

       (a) all opinions, including the basis and reasons for them, that the witness will testify to;

       (b) all facts and data considered by the witness in forming the opinions;

       (c) any exhibits that will be used;

       (d) the witness's qualifications, including a list of all publications authored in the previous 10 years;

       (e) a list of all cases during the previous 4 years in which witness testified as an expert; and

       (f) a statement of the compensation to be paid for the study and testimony in the case.

   (3) If the witness does not need to provide a written report, the disclosure must state [Fed. R. Civ. P. 26(a)(2)(C):

       (a) the subject matter on which the witness will testify; and

       (b) a summary of the facts and opinions that the witness will testify to.

   (4) Unless provided otherwise by court order, these disclosures must be made [Fed. R. Civ. P. 26(a)(2)(D):

       (a) at least 90 days before trial; or

       (b) if the evidence is intended solely to contradict or rebut evidence on the same subject matter identified by another party through the mandatory witness disclosure, within 30 days after the party's disclosure.

c. Pretrial Disclosures

   (1) In addition to the mandatory disclosures discussed above, at least 30 days before trial each party must provide to the other parties and promptly file the following information about evidence that it may present at trial [Fed. R. Civ. P. 26(a)(3)(A)]:

(a) the name (and if not previously provided the contact information) for each witness the party expects to present and those it may call if needed;

(b) a list of witnesses whose testimony will be presented through a deposition; and

(c) a list of documents or physical evidence the party expects to present and may present if need be.

d. **Supplementation**

   (1) A party must supplement a discovery response with any information that would have been subject to the mandatory disclosure requirement [Fed. R. Civ. P. 26(e)].

   (2) Failure to comply may lead to the exclusion of that evidence at trial [Fed. R. Civ. P. 37(c)(1)].

   EXAMPLE: Using the above example, the plaintiff must supplement its witness list if the plaintiff learns of any additional witnesses after it first discloses the list to the defendant.

3. **Scope of Discovery**

   a. In general, a party is entitled to demand the discovery of any matter that is [Fed. R. Civ. P. 26(b)]:

      (1) nonprivileged;

      (2) relevant to any party's claim or defense; and

      (3) proportional to the needs of the case.

   b. The factors to consider when determining whether a matter is proportional to the needs of the case include the importance of the issues at stake in the action, the amount in controversy, the parties' relative access to relevant information, the parties' resources, the importance of the matter sought in resolving the issues, and whether the burden or expense of the proposed discovery outweighs its likely benefit [Id.].

   c. Information is relevant if it is likely to make any fact in dispute more or less likely to be true, regardless of whether the information would be admissible at trial. A party is entitled to discovery of not only material that is relevant and admissible at trial, but also information "that appears reasonably calculated to lead to the discovery of admissible evidence" [Fed. R. Civ. P. 26(b)(1)].

   EXAMPLE: Plaintiff may question Defendant about a document even if that document would not be admissible into evidence, as long as the question is relevant.

   d. If the requested information can be obtained from another source that is more convenient, less burdensome, or less expensive, a party may be required to obtain it from the other source. A request for electronically stored information could be particularly vulnerable to this criticism.

   e. **Privilege**

      (1) Privileged matter is not discoverable.

      (2)   A privilege may arise under the laws of evidence or constitutional principles. The most frequently invoked privilege is the attorney-client privilege, which precludes the discovery of confidential communications between an attorney and her client for the purposes of obtaining or rendering legal advice.

              EXAMPLE: Defendant may object to Plaintiff's request for attorney invoices as being privileged.

      (3)   Many states also recognize some combination of the following privileges:

              (a) priest-penitent;

              (b) doctor-patient;

              (c) psychotherapist-patient; and

              (d) spousal.

f. Work-Product

      (1)   A party may not discover documents and tangible objects prepared in anticipation of litigation or for trial by or for another party or its representative, including an attorney, consultant, surety, indemnitor, insurer, or agent [Fed. R. Civ. P. 26(b)(3)(A)]. This is known as an attorney's **work-product**.

      (2)   However, such materials are still discoverable if [Id.]:

              (a) they are otherwise discoverable under Rule 26(b)(1); and

              (b) the party shows both substantial need for the material to prepare its case and it cannot, without undue hardship, obtain their substantial equivalent elsewhere.

      (3)   If the court orders the materials discoverable, the court must protect from disclosure the attorney's mental impressions, conclusions, opinions, or legal theories, which always remain privileged [Fed. R. Civ. P. 26(b)(3)(B)].

g. Experts

      (1)   A party may depose any person who has been identified as an expert who is expected to testify at trial, but only to a limited extent because communications between an attorney and his expert are considered work-product.

      (2)   Besides the information contained in the mandatory expert report (discussed above) a party can also obtain communications relating to [Fed. R. Civ. P. 26(b)(4)(C)]:

              (a) compensation for the expert's study or testimony;

              (b) any facts or data provided by the attorney to the expert that the expert considered in forming his opinion; and

              (c) any assumption the attorney provided and the expert relied on in forming his opinion.

      (3)   Expert reports that are prepared in draft (i.e., non-finalized) are also considered work-product.

(4)   A party may not, by interrogatories or deposition, obtain facts known or opinions held by an expert retained in anticipation of litigation or to prepare for trial, but who is not expected to be called to testify at trial, unless the party shows exceptional circumstances under which it is impracticable to obtain the facts or opinions by any other means, or in the case of an expert who conducts a Rule 35 examination [Fed. R. Civ. P. 26(b)(4)(D)].

4. **Objections**

a.   Parties who receive discovery requests that are beyond the scope of discovery (or are otherwise allegedly defective) can either object to the requests or request a protective order.

b.   In the event of an objection, the party requesting discovery has at least two options:

(1)   abandon or reframe the discovery request; or

(2)   bring the dispute to the attention of the court by filing a motion to compel.

c.   If the responding party requests a protective order, the party thereby brings the discovery dispute to the attention of the court.

5. **Discovery Devices**

a.   **Depositions**

(1)   Depositions permit the direct questioning of a party or witness under oath. They are typically conducted orally, and every word that is spoken is recorded verbatim and transcribed.

(2)   The witness (called the deponent) is given an opportunity to review the transcript and make technical corrections [Fed. R. Civ. P. 30(e)].

(3)   **Scheduling**

(a)   A deposition may be scheduled on reasonable notice in writing. If the deponent is a party, the deposition is scheduled by a notice of deposition served on all counsel.

(b)   The party requesting the deposition may ask the witness to bring documents to the deposition.

(c)   If the deponent is a non-party, the party requesting the deposition must also provide for the attendance of the witness, usually by serving a subpoena.

(d)   A deposition may not be used against a party at trial if the party received less than 14 days' notice of the deposition and promptly moved for a protective order that it not be taken, and the motion was still pending when the deposition was taken.

(4)   Depositions of corporations are permitted. The corporation must designate one or more persons whose answers bind the corporation and who must have completed a reasonably diligent investigation prior to testifying.

EXAMPLE: A corporation could designate its financial officer to testify at a deposition concerning the corporation's financial statements.

(5) A party may take only 10 depositions in an action as a matter of right. The primary advantages of depositions vis-à-vis other discovery techniques include engaging in a spontaneous dialogue with the witness and assessing the demeanor and credibility of potential trial witnesses. The most significant disadvantage is the expense.

b. **Interrogatories**

(1) Interrogatories are written questions that must be answered by another party in writing under oath [Fed. R. Civ. P. 33].

EXAMPLE: The defendant serves interrogatories upon the plaintiff regarding information related to the time and place of a particular accident.

(2) Interrogatories may only be served on parties to an action.

(3) Each party may submit up to 25 questions on any other party.

(4) Interrogatories must be answered in writing, under oath, within 30 days after service of the interrogatories.

c. **Document Requests**

(1) Any party may ask another party to produce documents or property for inspection and copying [Fed. R. Civ. P. 34].

(2) Documents and property may be requested from non-parties by subpoena.

EXAMPLE: A plaintiff may request minutes of the defendant's corporate board meetings for the previous five years.

d. **Requests for Admissions**

(1) A party may submit to any other party a request for admission of any matter within the scope of discovery [Fed. R. Civ. P. 36].

(2) Requests for admissions are typically "question and answer" statements that are used by either party to further explore specific contentions. Any request that is admitted is deemed established for all purposes in the litigation.

EXAMPLE: During a wrongful death lawsuit resulting from a car crash, the plaintiff may ask the defendant to admit that he was driving the Toyota involved in the crash. If the defendant makes the admission, the plaintiff will not have to prove that issue at trial.

(3) A party served with a request for admission has 30 days to respond.

e. **Physical and Mental Examinations**

(1) When a party's condition is in controversy, a physical or mental examination of the person may be requested [Fed. R. Civ. P. 35].

(2) Physical and mental examinations are the only discovery tools for which advance court approval is required. The court requires a showing of "good cause" for the examination.

> **EXAMPLE:** If the plaintiff is claiming emotional distress, the defendant may request that the plaintiff submit to a psychological exam.

6. **E-discovery**

   a. Electronic discovery (or e-discovery) refers to discovery regarding the exchange of electronically stored information, or ESI. The e-discovery process generally involves the following steps.

      (1) Electronically stored data (and their custodians) are identified by counsel as potentially relevant for further analysis and review.

      (2) ESI identified as potentially relevant is placed on a legal hold to ensure that the data cannot be destroyed.

      (3) The data is transferred from a company to its legal counsel, who will determine relevance.

      (4) Files are prepared to be loaded into a document review platform.

      (5) Documents are reviewed for responsiveness to discovery requests and for privilege.

      (6) Documents are turned over to opposing counsel, based on agreed-upon specifications.

   b. **Procedure**

      (1) A response in writing is required within 30 days after being served or, if the request was delivered under Rule 26(d)(2), within 30 days after the parties' first Rule 26(f) conference [Fed. R. Civ. P. 37(b)(2)].

      (2) Instead of permitting inspection of documents or ESI, the responding party can produce copies of the documents or the ESI. The production of the copies of ESI must take place within the same timeframe as the requested inspection or another reasonable time specified in the response [Fed. R. Civ. P. 37(b)(2)(B)]. ESI does not have to be reproduced in the form requested. If a party objects to the requested form of producing ESI, or if the form is specified in the request, the response must state the form the party intends to use [Fed. R. Civ. P. 37(b)(C)].

      (3) Unless otherwise stipulated or ordered by the court, these procedures apply to producing documents or ESI [Fed. R. Civ. P. 37(b)(E)]:

         (a) a party must produce documents as they are kept in the usual course of business or must organize and label them to correspond to the categories in the request;

         (b) if a request does not specify a form for producing ESI, a party must produce it in a form in which it is ordinarily maintained or in a reasonably usable form; and

         (c) a party need not produce the same ESI in more than one form.

   c. **Sanctions**

(1) If ESI that should have been preserved in the anticipation or conduct of litigation is lost because a party failed to take reasonable steps to preserve it, and it cannot be restored or replaced through additional discovery, the court [Fed. R. Civ. P. 37(e)]:

  (a) upon finding prejudice to another party from loss of the information, may order measures no greater than necessary to cure the prejudice; or

  (b) if the courts finds that the party acted with the intent to deprive another party of the information's use in the litigation, the court can:

    1) presume that the lost information was unfavorable to the party;

    2) instruct the jury that it may or must presume the information was unfavorable to the party; or

    3) dismiss the action or enter a default judgment.

7. **Discovery Sanctions**

  a. **Motion to Compel**

    (1) On notice to other parties and all affected persons, a party may move for an order compelling disclosure or discovery. The motion must include a certification that the movant has in good faith conferred or attempted to confer with the person or party failing to make disclosure or discovery in an effort to obtain it without court action [Fed. R. Civ. P. 37(a)].

    (2) A motion for an order to a party must be made in the court where the action is pending. A motion for an order to a non-party must be made in the court where the discovery is or will be taken.

  b. **Failure to Comply with Court Order**

    (1) If the court where the discovery is taken orders a deponent to be sworn or to answer a question and the deponent fails to obey, the failure may be treated as contempt of court [Fed. R. Civ. P. 37(b)].

    (2) If a party or a party's officer, director, or managing agent, or a designated witness, fails to obey an order to provide or permit discovery, the court where the action is pending may issue further just orders, including the following:

      (a) declaring that the facts sought are established in favor of the requesting party;

      (b) prohibiting the disobedient party from supporting or opposing designated claims or defenses, or from introducing designated matters in evidence;

      (c) striking pleadings in whole or in part;

      (d) staying further proceedings until the order is obeyed;

      (e) dismissing the action or proceeding in whole or in part;

      (f) rendering a default judgment against the disobedient party; or

        (g) treating as contempt of court the failure to obey any order except an order to submit to a physical or mental examination.

    (3) If a party fails to provide required information or identify a witness, the party is not allowed to use that information or witness to supply evidence on a motion, at a hearing, or at a trial, unless the failure was substantially justified or is harmless [Fed. R. Civ. P. 37(c)].

    (4) If a party fails to make an admission, and if the requesting party later proves a document to be genuine or the matter true, the requesting party may move that the party who failed to admit, pay the reasonable expenses, including attorney's fees, incurred in making that proof [Id.].

  c. **Additional Sanctions**

    (1) The court where the action is pending may, on motion, order sanctions if [Fed. R. Civ. P. 37(d)]:

        (a) a party or a party's officer, director, or managing agent fails, after being served with proper notice, to appear for that person's deposition; or

        (b) a party, after being properly served with interrogatories or a request for inspection, fails to serve its answers, objections, or written response.

    (2) Instead of, or in addition to, the sanctions listed above, the court must require the party failing to act, the attorney advising that party, or both, to pay the reasonable expenses, including attorney's fees, caused by the failure, unless the failure was substantially justified or other circumstances make an award of expenses unjust [Id.].

    (3) If a party or its attorney fails to participate in good faith in developing and submitting a proposed discovery plan, the court may, after giving an opportunity to be heard, require that party or attorney to pay to any other party the reasonable expenses, including attorney's fees, caused by the failure [Fed. R. Civ. P. 37(f)].

G. Adjudication without a Trial

1. Most cases do not result in a full trial. Possible methods of resolving disputes without a trial include:

  a. voluntary dismissal;

  b. involuntary dismissal;

  c. default judgments;

  d. settlements; and

  e. pretrial motions (discussed *infra*).

2. **Voluntary Dismissal**

  a. A plaintiff may voluntarily dismiss an action by filing a notice of dismissal at any time prior to service of defendant's answer or motion for summary judgment [Fed. R. Civ. P. 41(a)].

b. Before or after a responsive pleading, a plaintiff may voluntarily dismiss an action by filing a stipulation signed by all parties.

c. If the plaintiff cannot obtain another party's agreement to the dismissal, the plaintiff may make a motion for voluntary dismissal. Such a motion rests within the broad discretion of the trial court. The court will likely grant the motion unless the opponent will suffer prejudice.

d. The filing of the notice of dismissal automatically terminates the case without prejudice. If the plaintiff has already voluntarily dismissed the action once before, the notice of dismissal operates as an adjudication upon the merits.

3. **Involuntary Dismissals**

    a. **Dismissal for Failure to State a Claim**

        (1) Pleadings must contain "a short and plain statement of the claim showing that the pleader is entitled to relief" [Fed. R. Civ. P. 8(a)(2)]. If this requirement is not met, the party against whom the claim is alleged may move to dismiss for failure to state a claim for which relief can be granted [Fed. R. Civ. P. 12(b)(6)].

        EXAMPLE: Defendant may move to dismiss for failure to state a claim on the ground that the complaint fails to allege that Defendant is responsible for Plaintiff's injuries.

        (2) When an action is dismissed based on failure to state a claim, the dismissal is with prejudice unless the court states otherwise in its order [Fed. R. Civ. P. 41(b)].

        (3) A court would dismiss the claim without prejudice (or with leave to amend) in circumstances where the pleading defect can and should be rectified.

    b. **Dismissal for Failure to Prosecute**

        (1) If a plaintiff fails to prosecute or to comply with the Federal Rules or a court order, a defendant may move to dismiss. A dismissal for failure to prosecute is a dismissal with prejudice, unless the dismissal order states otherwise [Fed. R. Civ. P. 41(b)].

        EXAMPLE: Plaintiff brings a lawsuit against defendant. Eighteen months later, plaintiff has not engaged in any discovery, and has not made any efforts to move the case forward. Defendant may bring a motion to dismiss for failure to prosecute.

4. **Default Judgment**

    a. Default judgments involve two steps:

        (1) the entry of default; and

        (2) the entry of the default judgment.

    b. An **entry of default** must be entered on behalf of a party against whom a judgment for affirmative relief is sought when the party has failed to plead or otherwise defend the claim and that failure is shown by affidavit or otherwise [Fed. R. Civ. P. 55(a)].

    c. Only after an entry of default has been entered may a default judgment be entered.

d.   A **default judgment** can be entered by the clerk or the court.

(1)   If the plaintiff's claim is for a sum certain, upon the plaintiff's request and with an affidavit showing the amount due, the clerk must enter judgment for that amount and costs against a defendant who has been defaulted for not appearing [Fed. R. Civ. P. 55(b)].

> **NOTE** A clerk cannot enter default judgments against minors or incompetent persons.

(2)   In all other cases, the party must apply to the court for a default judgment to be entered.

(3)   If the party against whom a default judgment is sought has appeared personally or by a representative, that party or representative must be served with written notice of the application for default judgment at least seven days before the hearing [Id.].

(4)   The court may conduct hearings or make referrals when, to enter or effectuate judgment, it needs to [Id.]:

(a)   conduct an accounting;

(b)   determine the amount of damages;

(c)   establish the truth of any allegation by evidence; or

(d)   investigate any other matter.

e.   The court may set aside an entry of default for good cause. If the clerk or court entered a default judgment, the court may set it aside in accordance with a Rule 60(b) post-trial motion.

5.   **Settlements**

a.   Settlements may be achieved through counsel and the parties themselves, or through alternative dispute resolution (ADR) methods such as arbitration or mediation.

b.   A settlement conference is appropriate at any time. It may be held with a pretrial or discovery conference, or separately.

c.   Settlement conferences are not mandatory under the Federal Rules.

d.   A judge may, on his own or at a party's request, refer a settlement conference to another judge or magistrate.

IV. JURY TRIALS

A. Right to Jury Trial

1. The right to a jury trial in a civil action can be conferred by statute and is guaranteed by the Seventh Amendment to the U.S. Constitution.

2. Equitable actions are not triable by a jury as a matter of right. In determining whether a right to a jury trial exists, the court will consider:

   a. whether the claim more closely resembles actions in law or in equity; and

   b. whether the remedy sought is legal or equitable in nature (i.e. monetary relief or injunctive relief).

> **NOTE** If both legal and equitable relief are sought in an action, the right to a jury exists for any issue of fact underlying a damages claim, even if the resolution of that issue may also support injunctive relief.

B. Demand for a Jury Trial

1. If the right to a jury trial exists in an action, any party can exercise the right by filing with the court and serving on the other parties a written demand for a jury trial.

2. The demand for a jury trial must be made within 14 days after the service of the last pleading directed to the triable issue.

3. If the demand for a jury trial is not timely filed and served, the right to a trial by jury is waived [Fed. R. Civ. P. 38].

4. **Removal**

   a. If a party has expressly demanded a jury trial in accordance with state law prior to the case being removed to federal court, the demand need not be renewed after removal.

   b. If the state law did not require express demand, a party need not make such demand unless the court orders the parties to do so. The court may so order on its own, or must so order at a party's request [Fed. R. Civ. P. 81(c)(3)(A)].

   c. Failure to make a demand when ordered will constitute waiver [Id.].

   d. If all necessary pleadings have been served at the time of removal, a party entitled to a jury trial under Rule 38 must be given one if the party serves a demand within 14 days after [Fed. R. Civ. P. 81(c)(3)(B)]:

      (1) filing a notice of removal; or

      (2) being served with a notice of removal filed by another party.

C. Jury Selection

1. A federal jury can be composed of six to twelve members. Each juror must participate in the verdict unless excused [Fed. R. Civ. P. 48(a)].

2. The federal jury is selected by the *voir dire* process [Fed. R. Civ. P. 47]. The court may conduct the examination or permit the attorneys to question directly the prospective jurors.

3. The purpose of the *voir dire* is to explore germane factors that might expose a basis for challenge, whether for cause or peremptory.

4. Attorneys may ask the court to excuse any juror for cause. There are three categories of challenges for cause:

   a. general disqualification—a person may lose the right to sit on any jury because of a felony conviction or some other inherent disqualification;

   b. implied bias—potential jurors may be removed if the attorney believes a bias may exist; and

   EXAMPLE: A juror who has a relationship with the parties or their attorneys could be removed due to an implied bias.

   c. actual bias—jurors may be removed for cause if they indicate during *voir dire* that they would use predetermined beliefs or principles to decide the case instead of deciding the case based upon the facts.

5. **Peremptory Challenges**

   a. In federal court, each party may exercise three peremptory challenges to excuse jurors without having to state the reason before the court.

   b. Peremptory challenges may not be used to exclude jurors on the basis of race or gender.

   c. Peremptory challenges may be objected to by the opposing party only where the exclusion gives rise to an inference of racial or gender discrimination. If objected to, the excluding party must provide a nondiscriminatory explanation for the strikes or else rescind its strike of each juror involved.

D. **Jury Instructions**

   1. **Requests**

      a. At the close of the evidence or at any earlier reasonable time that the court orders, a party may file and furnish to every other party written requests for the jury instructions it wants the court to give [Fed. R. Civ. P. 51(a)].

      b. After the close of the evidence, a party may [Id.]:

         (1) file requests for instructions on issues that could not reasonably have been anticipated by an earlier time that the court set for requests; and

         (2) with the court's permission, file untimely requests for instructions on any issue.

   2. **Instructions**

      a. The court [Fed. R. Civ. P. 51(b)]:

         (1) must inform the parties of its proposed instructions and proposed action on the requests before instructing the jury and before final jury arguments;

         (2) must give the parties an opportunity to object on the record and out of the jury's hearing before the instructions and arguments are delivered; and

         (3) may instruct the jury at any time before the jury is discharged.

3. **Objections**

    a. A party who objects to an instruction or the failure to give an instruction must do so on the record, stating distinctly the matter objected to and the grounds for the objection.

    b. An objection is timely if [Fed. R. Civ. P. 51(c)]:

        (1) a party objects at the earliest opportunity as provided under Fed. R. Civ. P. 51(b)(2); or

        (2) a party was not informed of an instruction or action on a request before that opportunity to object, and the party objects promptly after learning that the instruction or request will be, or has been, given or refused.

4. **Assigning Error**

    a. A party may assign as error [Fed. R. Civ. P. 51(d)]:

        (1) an error in an instruction actually given, if that party properly objected; or

        (2) a failure to give an instruction, if that party properly requested it and—unless the court rejected the request in a definitive ruling on the record—also properly objected.

5. A court may consider a plain error in the instructions that has not been preserved as required by the Federal Rules if the error affects substantial rights [Id.].

<h1 style="text-align:center">V. MOTIONS</h1>

A.   General Rules

1.   **Requirements Regarding Form**

a.   Any applications to the court for an order shall be made by motion.

b.   A motion must:

(1)   be in writing, unless made during a hearing or trial; and

(2)   state with particularity the grounds for the request and a request for relief.

c.   All rules governing matters of form in pleadings also apply to motions.

2.   **Other Requirements**

a.   Local court rules may set out specific requirements for motion practice, such as the papers to be filed, and the timing for making a motion.

b.   The court may issue standing orders in a particular case regarding the timing of motions.

B.   Pre-Trial Motions

1.   **Motion to Dismiss**

a.   A motion to dismiss is a motion filed by a defending party seeking the dismissal of a claim filed against him.

b.   A motion to dismiss may be made on any of the following grounds [Fed. R. Civ. P. 12(b)]:

(1)   lack of subject-matter jurisdiction;

(2)   lack of personal jurisdiction;

(3)   improper venue;

(4)   insufficient process;

(5)   insufficient service of process;

(6)   failure to state a claim upon which relief can be granted; and

(7)   failure to join a party under Rule 19.

c.   A motion to dismiss based on lack of personal jurisdiction, improper venue, insufficient process, or insufficient service of process must be made in the defending party's first response to the court—either a pre-answer motion to dismiss or an answer.

(1)   If the defending party makes a motion to dismiss and one of the aforementioned defenses is not included, that defense is waived and cannot later be included in the answer.

(2)   If no pre-answer motion to dismiss is made, the defense must be in the defending party's answer, or else it is waived.

d.   A motion to dismiss based on failure to state a claim upon which relief can be granted or failure to join a necessary party can be raised at any time before the trial ends, or else it is waived.

e.   Lack of subject-matter jurisdiction is never waived, it can be raised at any time, even on appeal.

    f.   **Rule 12(b)(6) Dismissal**

        (1)   A court will dismiss a complaint for failure to state a claim upon which relief can be granted if the complaint:

            (a)   fails to state a cognizable claim;

            (b)   provides insufficient facts; or

            (c)   contains an allegation that negates one or more elements of the cause of action.

        (2)   Dismissal of a complaint under Rule 12(b)(6) is with prejudice unless the court states otherwise.

        (3)   If there is a defect in the pleading that the court deems rectifiable, the court may:

            (a)   dismiss the complaint without prejudice; or

            (b)   grant the plaintiff leave to amend the complaint.

2.   **Summary Judgment Motions**

    a.   A motion for summary judgment is a motion challenging a claim or defense on the merits. Summary judgments are intended to pierce the pleadings to determine if there is credible evidence to factually support a party's claim.

    b.   Summary judgment will be granted if the moving party "shows that there is no genuine dispute as to any material fact and the movant is entitled to judgment as a matter of law" [Fed. R. Civ. P. 56].

    c.   Any party may move for summary judgment as to any individual issue that has been joined, or as to the cause of action as a whole.

    d.   The parties may move with or without supporting affidavits for summary judgment.

    e.   Unless a local rule or court order provides otherwise:

        (1)   a party may move for summary judgment at any time before 30 days after the close of discovery;

        (2)   a party opposing a motion for summary judgment must file a response within 21 days after the motion is served or a responsive pleading is due, whichever is later; and

        (3)   a reply may be filed within 14 days after the response is served.

    f.   When a party moves for summary judgment, the court must first consider whether the moving party has shown—based on their arguments alone—that the non-moving party lacks sufficient facts and/or law to prevail on the claim or defense in question. The moving party can make this argument by either:

        (1)   pointing out holes in the opposing party's claims or defenses; or

        (2)   adducing new evidence demonstrating that the claim or defense cannot be true.

    g.   If the moving party can establish that the non-moving party lacks sufficient facts or law to prevail on the claim or defense in question, the court then turns to the non-moving party to defeat the motion.

(1) To survive summary judgment, the non-moving party must adduce evidence sufficient for a reasonable jury to find in her favor on a claim or defense.

(2) The non-moving party may not rely on allegations in the complaint to defeat a motion for summary judgment.

h. Although both plaintiffs and defendants can move for summary judgment, defendants do so far more often because it is harder for a plaintiff to prevail. For a plaintiff to prevail on her own motion for summary judgment, she must produce evidence in support of every element of her claim and the defendant must not respond with evidence of any element of the claim.

i. The evidence presented at a summary judgment motion will be viewed in the light most favorable to the non-moving party to determine whether the movant is entitled to prevail as a matter of law.

(1) A party may offer affidavits and/or evidence obtained during discovery.

(2) A party may not rely on evidence that will be inadmissible at trial to satisfy the production burden. If the evidence is in an inadmissible form at the summary judgment stage, but will be in an admissible form at trial, then the production burden is satisfied.

EXAMPLE: The inadmissibility of an affidavit that contains hearsay would be remedied by a hearsay exception of presentation of the witness who made the statement.

(3) Plaintiffs may not rely on evidence that no rational fact finder would believe or would find sufficient to establish the element.

EXAMPLE: If the only expert testimony offered by the plaintiff is "implausible," a court will enter summary judgment on behalf of the defendant [Matsushita v. Zenith, 475 U.S. 574 (1986)].

j. **Powers of the District Judge**

(1) The judge may grant or deny summary judgment in favor of or against the person asking for it.

(2) After giving notice to all parties and a reasonable time to respond, the judge can also [Fed. R. Civ. P. 56(f)]:

(a) grant summary judgment even when nobody asks for it (a *sua sponte* grant of summary judgment is proper);

(b) grant summary judgment on grounds that neither party has asked for—i.e., for completely different reasons than the moving party was seeking for summary judgment; or

(c) grant summary judgment not just for the moving party, but against the moving party and in favor of the non-moving party.

(3) Judges may grant partial summary judgment.

(4) Judges are required to state on the record the grounds for granting or denying summary judgment.

(5) Judges do not have to canvas the entire record hunting for a genuine issue of material fact. Instead, the trial judge can limit

his review on a motion for summary judgment to only those portions of the record cited by the parties.

C. Post-Trial Motions

1. **Judgment as a Matter of Law**

   a. A motion for judgment as a matter of law (JMOL) was formerly known as a motion for a directed verdict.

   b. The defendant or the plaintiff may move for JMOL after the other party closes her case. If the motion is granted, the motion results in judgment for the moving party [Fed. R. Civ. P. 50(a)].

   c. A JMOL will be granted if the court finds that a reasonable jury would not have a legally sufficient evidentiary basis to find for the non-moving party on the issue at hand [Id.].

   EXAMPLE: In an action for copyright infringement, the plaintiff fails to show that she is the owner of the copyright in question. The defendant's motion for JMOL should be granted.

   d. The analysis for JMOL motions is identical to that on a summary judgment motion.

      (1) A summary judgment motion is based on evidence that a party may introduce at trial, while the JMOL motion is based on evidence actually introduced at trial.

      (2) The evidence will be viewed in the light most favorable to the non-moving party to determine whether the movant is entitled to prevail as a matter of law.

      (3) A JMOL must specify the judgment sought and the law and facts that entitle the moving party to the judgment [Id.].

   e. Motions for JMOL are typically made at the close of the non-moving party's case, but may be made at any time after all of the non-moving party's evidence has been submitted but before the case is submitted to the jury.

   f. Most attorneys will make a motion for JMOL as a matter of course, in order to preserve the right to renew the motion at the conclusion of the trial.

2. **Renewed Motion for Judgment as a Matter of Law**

   a. A renewed motion for judgment as a matter of law was formerly known as a motion for judgment notwithstanding the verdict (JNOV, or judgment *non obstante veredicto*).

   b. Within 28 days after the entry of judgment (or discharge of the jury if the motion addresses a jury issue not decided by verdict), a party who has timely moved for JMOL may serve a motion to set aside the verdict and any judgment entered on the verdict [Fed. R. Civ. P. 50(b)].

NOTE ▶ A party that did not timely move for a JMOL during trial cannot move for a renewed JMOL.

c. A renewed motion for JMOL requires analysis identical to the JMOL motion.

    (1) Even after the jury has rendered a verdict, if a judge finds that no reasonable jury could interpret the evidence presented as supporting the verdict, a judge may grant to the party against whom the judgment was rendered JMOL.

d. In ruling on a renewed motion for JMOL, the court may [Id.]:

    (1) allow judgment on the verdict to stand, if the jury returned a verdict;

    (2) order a new trial; or

    (3) direct the entry of judgment as a matter of law.

e. When making a renewed motion for JMOL, the moving party may also move jointly or in the alternative for a new trial under Rule 59.

    (1) If the court grants the renewed motion for JMOL, it must also issue a conditional ruling on any motion for a new trial [Id.].

3. **Motion for a New Trial**

a. A new trial may be granted to all or any of the parties on all or some of the issues litigated at trial [Fed. R. Civ. P. 59].

b. A motion for a new trial must be filed within 28 days of the entry of judgment.

c. A motion for a new trial is generally made as a form of alternative relief to a renewed JMOL motion.

d. A motion for a new trial is generally appropriate in the following instances:

    (1) in order to avoid an inevitable appeal and reversal if the trial judge has committed reversible error;

    (2) when a jury verdict is so excessive or inadequate as to demonstrate that the jury has misunderstood its duty or has acted with extreme prejudice;

    (3) if evidence of jury misconduct exists, and Fed. R. Evid. 606(b) limits judicial inquiry to external influences on the deliberation process; or

    (4) when the verdict is against the clear weight of the evidence.

e. On a motion for a new trial, the court is not required to view the evidence in a light most favorable to the verdict and may grant the new trial, even though there was enough evidence to prevent JMOL or renewed JMOL.

f. The court may also consider a new trial conditioned on certain circumstances.

EXAMPLE: If the jury verdict awarded an improper or excessive amount of damages, the court may grant a new trial on the issue of damages alone. Liability would not be relitigated.

4. **Remittitur and Additur**

a. A motion for remittitur asks the judge to reduce the award of damages that are excessive. Federal courts will routinely grant motions for remittitur.

b. The converse of a remittitur is an additur, or an increase in the award of damages. Additur is unconstitutional in federal court.

5. **Motion for Relief from a Judgment or Order**

   a. The court may correct a clerical mistake or a mistake arising from oversight or omission whenever one is found in a judgment, order, or other part of the record.

      (1) The court may do so on motion of a party or on its own, with or without notice [Fed. R. Civ. P. 60(a)].

      (2) If an appeal has been docketed with the appellate court and is pending, however, the mistake may be corrected only with the appellate court's leave [Id.].

   b. On motion and on just terms, the court may grant a motion for relief form judgment for the following reasons [Fed. R. Civ. P. 60(b)(1)–(6)]:

      (1) mistake, inadvertence, surprise, or excusable neglect;

      (2) newly discovered evidence that, with reasonable diligence, could not have been discovered in time to move for a new trial under Rule 59(b);

      (3) fraud, misrepresentation, or misconduct by an opposing party;

      (4) the judgment is void;

         (a) A judgment is void where it is "so affected by a fundamental infirmity that the infirmity may be raised even after the judgment becomes final" [United States Aid Funds, Inc. v. Espinosa, 130 S. Ct. 1367 (2010)].

         (b) Rule 60(b)(4) applies only in the rare instance when a judgment is premised either on a certain type of jurisdictional error or on a violation of due process that deprived a party of notice or the opportunity to be heard. This standard does not include erroneous judgments or situations where a legal error has occurred.

      (5) the judgment has been satisfied, released, or discharged, it is based on an earlier judgment that has been reversed or vacated, or applying it prospectively is no longer equitable; or

      (6) any other reason that justifies relief.

   c. A motion under Rule 60(b) must be made within a reasonable time. If the motion is being made for any of the first three reasons listed above (mistake, new evidence or fraud), the motion must be made no more than a year after entry of the judgment, order, or the date of the proceeding.

   d. A motion for relief from judgment does not affect the finality of the judgment, nor does it suspend its operation [Fed. R. Civ. P. 60(c)].

   e. Rule 60 does not limit a court's power to entertain an independent action to relieve a party from a judgment, order, or proceeding, grant relief to a defendant who was not personally notified of the action, or set aside a judgment due to fraud on the court [Fed. R. Civ. P. 60(d)].

VI. VERDICTS AND JUDGMENTS

A. **Jury Verdicts**
   1. **In General**
      a. Unless the parties stipulate otherwise, a jury verdict must be unanimous and must be returned by a jury of at least six members [Fed. R. Civ. P. 48(b)].
      b. After a verdict is returned but before the jury is discharged, the court must on a party's request, or may on its own, poll the jurors individually. If the poll reveals a lack of unanimity or lack of assent by the number of jurors that the parties stipulated to, the court may direct the jury to deliberate further or may order a new trial [Fed. R. Civ. P. 48(c)].
   2. **General Verdicts**
      a. The court may direct the jury to return a general verdict, which simply states which party should win, the plaintiff or defendant, without addressing specific findings on each issue of fact.
   3. **Special Verdicts**
      a. The court may require a jury to return only a special verdict in the form of a special written finding on each issue of fact. The court may do so by [Fed. R. Civ. P. 49(a)(1)]:
         (1) submitting written questions susceptible of a categorical or other brief answer;
         (2) submitting written forms of the special findings that might properly be made under the pleadings and evidence; or
         (3) using any other method that the court considers appropriate.
      b. The court must give the instructions and explanations necessary to enable the jury to make its findings on each submitted issue [Fed. R. Civ. P. 49(a)(2)].
      c. A party waives the right to a jury trial on any issue of fact raised by the pleadings or evidence but not submitted to the jury unless, before the jury retires, the party demands its submission to the jury. If the party does not demand submission, the court may make a finding on the issue. If the court makes no finding, it is considered to have made a finding consistent with its judgment on the special verdict [Fed. R. Civ. P. 49(a)(3)].
   4. **General Verdict with Answers to Written Questions**
      a. The court may submit to the jury forms for a general verdict, together with written questions on one or more issues of fact that the jury must decide. The court must give the instructions and explanations necessary to enable the jury to render a general verdict and answer the questions in writing, and must direct the jury to do both [Fed. R. Civ. P. 49(b)(1)].
      b. When the general verdict and the answers are consistent, the court must approve, for entry under Rule 58, an appropriate judgment on the verdict and answers [Fed. R. Civ. P. 49(b)(2)].

c.   When the answers are consistent with each other but one or more is inconsistent with the general verdict, the court may [Fed. R. Civ. P. 49(b)(3)]:

(1)   approve for entry an appropriate judgment according to the answers, notwithstanding the general verdict;

(2)   direct the jury to further consider its answers and verdict; or

(3)   order a new trial.

d.   When the answers are inconsistent with each other and one or more is also inconsistent with the general verdict, judgment must not be entered; instead, the court must direct the jury to further consider its answers and verdict, or must order a new trial [Fed. R. Civ. P. 49(b)(4)].

B.   Judicial Findings and Conclusions

1.   In an action tried on the facts without a jury or with an advisory jury, the court must find the facts specially, and state its conclusions of law separately. The findings and conclusions may be stated on the record after the close of the evidence or may appear in an opinion or a memorandum of decision filed by the court. Judgment must be entered under Rule 58 [Fed. R. Civ. P. 52(a)(1)].

2.   In granting or refusing an interlocutory injunction, the court must similarly state the findings and conclusions that support its action [Fed. R. Civ. P. 52(a)(2)].

3.   The court is not required to state findings or conclusions when ruling on a motion to dismiss or for summary judgment or, unless these rules provide otherwise, on any other motion [Fed. R. Civ. P. 52(a)(3)].

4.   A master's findings, to the extent adopted by the court, must be considered the court's findings [Fed. R. Civ. P. 52(a)(4)].

5.   A party may later question the sufficiency of the evidence supporting the findings, whether or not the party requested findings, objected to them, moved to amend them, or moved for partial findings [Fed. R. Civ. P. 52(a)(5)].

6.   Findings of fact, whether based on oral or other evidence, must not be set aside unless clearly erroneous, and the reviewing court must give due regard to the trial court's opportunity to judge the witnesses' credibility [Fed. R. Civ. P. 52(a)(6)].

7.   On a party's motion filed no later than 28 days after the entry of judgment, the court may amend its findings—or make additional findings—and may amend the judgment accordingly. The motion may accompany a motion for a new trial [Fed. R. Civ. P. 52(b)(1)].

8.   If a party has been fully heard on an issue during a nonjury trial and the court finds against the party on that issue, the court may enter judgment against the party on a claim or defense that, under the controlling law, can be maintained or defeated only with a favorable finding on that issue. The court may, however, decline to render any judgment until the close of the evidence. A judgment on partial findings must be supported by findings of fact and conclusions of law [Fed. R. Civ. P. 52(c)].

C. **Effect of Verdicts—Claim and Issue Preclusion**
1. **Claim Preclusion**
   a. Claim preclusion (also known as *res judicata*) and issue preclusion (also known as collateral estoppel) are judicial doctrines intended to promote the policy of judicial economy and the finality of litigation. The general rule created by these doctrines is that once a case has reached a final judgment, then that case, and related claims and issues, have been decided or settled permanently and are not eligible for relitigation.
   b. The doctrine of **claim preclusion** prevents relitigation of a claim:
      (1) between the same parties and those who are in privity with them;
      (2) arising out of the same transaction or occurrence underlying the prior suit; and
      (3) that was determined on the merits by a court with proper subject-matter and personal jurisdiction.

      EXAMPLE: During trial, the jury determines that the defendant was not liable for the plaintiff's injuries arising out of a car accident. The plaintiff may not file a subsequent action against the same defendant seeking property damages resulting from the same car accident.

   c. A judgment is not on the merits if it is a dismissal for lack of personal jurisdiction, subject-matter jurisdiction, or venue. A dismissal with prejudice is considered a dismissal on the merits.
   d. Claim preclusion operates as an affirmative defense that is waived if not properly asserted. It can also be asserted as a basis for a summary judgment motion.
2. **Issue Preclusion**
   a. **Issue preclusion** prevents relitigation of issues that were fully and fairly litigated, and were necessarily decided in a proceeding that reached a final judgment on the merits.
   b. An issue is narrower than a claim. The litigation of a single claim may involve the determination of several different issues.
   c. For litigation of a particular factual issue to be precluded, four elements must be met:
      (1) the issue must have been litigated and determined in the prior suit;
      (2) the issue must have been essential to the judgment;
      (3) the prior suit must have ended in a valid final judgment on the merits; and
      (4) the party against whom preclusion is asserted must have had a full and fair opportunity and incentive to litigate the issue in the first suit.

      EXAMPLE: During a trial against John, a jury determines that the light was red when Adam crossed the street. In a subsequent action against Mark arising from the same occurrence, Adam cannot relitigate the issue of whether the light was red or green.

d. **Parties**

(1) Issue preclusion may not be used against someone who was not a party to the previous action.

(2) Although the party invoking the doctrine need not have been a party to the previous action, it would be a violation of due process to bind a non-party (or someone not in privity with a party) since that person had not yet had her day in court.

e. **Offensive Use**

(1) Issue preclusion may be used offensively by one who was not a party to the first action against one who was a party in the earlier suit.

(2) Courts are a bit reluctant to permit offensive use of issue preclusion and will base their determination on the following:

(a) whether the plaintiff in the second suit could have easily joined in the first action;

(b) whether there are procedural opportunities available to the defendant in the second suit that were unavailable in the earlier action; and

(c) whether the defendant had incentive to litigate the issue in the first action.

EXAMPLE: If the defendant was forced to defend in an inconvenient forum or was unable to engage in meaningful discovery, it may be unfair to deny the defendant the opportunity to relitigate the issue.

(3) **Use of Criminal Convictions in Civil Proceedings**

(a) If a defendant has been convicted of a crime that has an element common to an issue in a subsequent civil proceeding, the conviction may have issue preclusive effect in the civil case, provided that the issue was fully and fairly litigated and was necessarily decided.

(b) An acquittal is not likely to have issue preclusive effect in a subsequent action, as the burden of proof is more modest in a civil case.

VII. APPEALABILITY AND REVIEW

A. **Availability of Interlocutory Review**

1. **Interlocutory orders** are orders either asserting provisional relief or made upon motion or application during the trial, but which are not final adjudications on the merits. Interlocutory orders may not be reviewed before final judgment with limited exceptions.

   EXAMPLE: An order requiring a party to produce documents claimed to be protected by privilege is an interlocutory order.

2. **Collateral Order Doctrine**

   a. Appellate review is authorized for an interlocutory order rendered by a trial judge that:

      (1) conclusively determines the disputed question;

      (2) resolves an important issue completely separate from the merits of the action; and

      (3) is effectively unreviewable on appeal from a final judgment.

      EXAMPLE: An order determining that a party is immune from certain claims would be reviewable under the collateral order doctrine.

3. **Injunctive Relief**

   a. Congress has given to the federal courts subject-matter jurisdiction over appeals from an interlocutory order of the trial court that grants, denies, continues, modifies, or dissolves an injunction [28 U.S.C. § 1292(a)(1)].

   b. Interlocutory orders for injunctive relief are not appealable if a similar suit is pending in state court.

4. **Certification of Interlocutory Orders**

   a. Federal trial courts may certify an order for appeal when [28 U.S.C. § 1292(b)]:

      (1) the order involves a controlling question of law as to which a substantial ground for difference of opinion exists; and

      (2) an immediate appeal from the order may materially advance the termination of the litigation.

   b. Following the written certification, the party seeking appeal must apply to the federal court of appeals, which has discretion to grant or deny the application.

5. Federal courts of appeals have the power to issue extraordinary writs [28 U.S.C. § 1651].

6. **Multi-Claim or Multi-Party Judgments**

   a. When a final decision has been made on at least one of the claims in a multi-claim or multi-party case, the trial judge may direct the entry of a final judgment as to that claim by a finding on the record that there is no reason to delay judgment on that claim until the entire case is resolved [Fed. R. Civ. P. 54(b)].

    b.   Any party affected by the judgment may appeal the judgment while the rest of the action remains pending.

B. Final Judgment Rule

1. Congress has given to the federal courts subject-matter jurisdiction over appeals from all final decisions of the federal district trial courts [28 U.S.C. § 1291].

2. The basic principle in the federal system is that only final judgments may be taken to the appellate courts. This rule is modified by a few other principles, which when available, provide the appellant with an avenue for interlocutory appeal even though the underlying action has not gone to final judgment. Appellate courts will apply different standards of review depending on the subject matter of the appeal.

3. A final judgment is generally defined as one that disposes of all issues as to all of the parties, it disposes of the entire case.

EXAMPLE: A judgment on behalf of the plaintiff in an action for medical malpractice is a final judgment.

C. Scope of Review for Judge and Jury

1. Although an appellant may want an appeals court to review all errors alleged to have occurred at the trial court level, there are restrictions on what is reviewable:

    a.   with few exceptions, courts will not review errors that are not on the record of the trial court proceeding; and

        EXAMPLE: If the appellant did not raise or object to an error at a time when the trial court had the opportunity to correct it, the issue is not preserved and is, thus, unreviewable.

    b.   errors that do not affect substantial rights will be labeled harmless and may be unreviewable.

2. Errors will receive different levels of scrutiny upon appellate review depending on the category of error.

    a.   Conclusions of law will typically be reviewed *de novo*. *De novo* review means the appellate court will conduct a non-deferential review and address the legal issue as if it has never been addressed in the case.

    b.   Factual findings may be disturbed only if clearly erroneous.

    c.   Other discretionary determinations by the judge will be affirmed absent some indication that the judge abused his discretion.

Issue-Spotting Exercises

Question 1

Paula and Pete were hit by a truck driven by an employee of the D Corporation. The accident occurred in California, where Paula and Pete were living at the time. D's headquarters are in Florida, but its principal place of business is in Michigan. It is incorporated in Delaware. After the accident, Paula and Pete moved to Miami, Florida, where they planned to retire. After moving, they contacted a lawyer who filed suit against D in the appropriate U.S. District Court where Paula and Pete lived, alleging diversity jurisdiction. The suit alleged that each plaintiff had suffered personal injuries in excess of $75,000. D moved to dismiss the case for lack of subject matter jurisdiction.

Should D's motion be granted by the district court?

Question 2

P files suit in the U.S. District Court in Nevada alleging a federal claim (racial discrimination against him occurring in Texas). The defendant is a citizen of California, and all of the witnesses live in Texas. P lives in Nevada. The defendant moves to change the venue to California or, alternatively, to Texas.

What outcome is likely?

Question 3

P is a citizen of New York who works in New Jersey. D and E are citizens of New Jersey who work in that state. One day, D borrowed E's car, telling E that he intended to use it to pick up his sister in Trenton (the capital of New Jersey). However, D drove to New York to take a new girlfriend to Coney Island (which is in Brooklyn, New York). Unfortunately, D became involved in a traffic accident with P while driving in New York City. P brought an action against E in the proper U.S. District Court in New York for personal injuries and property damages in the amount of $85,000. A New York statute permits an action against the owner of a motor vehicle where he/she loaned the car to the person who was driving it when the incident occurred.

If E makes a motion to dismiss the action for lack of personal jurisdiction, will the court grant the motion?

Question 4

P, a citizen of Utah, was involved in an auto accident with D, a citizen of Minnesota. The accident occurred in Utah. Pursuant to the applicable Utah long-arm statute, P sued D in a Utah state court of general jurisdiction for $80,000. P also named C as a defendant. C was D's insurer. Pursuant to Utah law, this type of action was permissible. C is incorporated in Delaware and has its principal place of business in Utah. D seeks to remove the case to the applicable U.S. District Court.

Should the court grant or deny D's request?

Question 5

Denny, a citizen of Texas, leased an apartment from Polly, a citizen of California, under a one-year rental agreement at $500 per month. The rental agreement stated that Denny could sublet the premises to any person who is not of Asian ancestry. With six months remaining on the lease, Denny sublet the apartment to a Chinese person. Polly sued Denny in the appropriate U.S. District Court for breach of contract, seeking to evict Denny and recover the remaining six months' rent. The complaint stated that Denny violated the terms of the rental agreement and asserts that the clause concerning subletting does not violate the U.S. Constitution. Denny moves to dismiss the case for lack of subject matter jurisdiction.

With respect to Denny's motion, will he prevail in court on his motion to dismiss for lack of subject matter jurisdiction?

Essays

Federal Civil Procedure

In Class

You represent David Demarest. Your interview with David and your investigation reveal the following:

David grew up in Florida and has lived there all his life. Earlier this year, David took a job with Dora Enterprises, Inc., (DEI) a corporation incorporated under the laws of Delaware and having its principal place of business in Houston, Texas (in the Southern District of Texas). David obtained his job by traveling to DEI's satellite hiring office in Dallas (in the Northern District of Texas) to be interviewed. David's job was to portray the endearing cartoon character Blarney the Big Green Frog at children's birthday parties.

Several months ago, David was sent by DEI to a birthday party at the Florida home of Patrick Paulson (in the Middle District of Florida). David became so irritated by the behavior of the children at the party that David pretended to attack Patrick. Patrick was seriously injured and continues to experience ongoing pain and suffering. He recently moved to Houston, Texas (in the Southern District of Texas), where he intends to spend the rest of his life.

Last week, Patrick filed suit against DEI and David in the United States District Court for the Southern District of Texas. Patrick alleges battery under the common law of Florida and seeks damages against Patrick for his attack and against DEI under a theory of respondeat superior. In the complaint, Patrick seeks $40,000 in damages from each defendant. David was served with process at his Florida home when he received, by first-class mail, a copy of the summons and complaint. He also received a notice of the commencement of the action and a request to waive service. David did not waive service.

Assume the following procedural facts: The Texas long-arm statute for torts extends the reach of the Texas state courts to causes of action over nonresidents only if the tortious act occurs in Texas. The Texas Rules of Civil Procedure do not permit service of process by mail. The Florida Rules of Civil Procedure permit service of process by certified mail but not first-class mail. David has no contacts with Texas other than as described above.

As David's lawyer, what defenses unrelated to the merits could you raise, how could you raise them, by when would you have to raise them, and what could you argue? Be thorough and include ALL arguments in support of your defenses.

Federal Civil Procedure

In Class

I. **Lack of Subject Matter Jurisdiction**

A. **(Rule)** District courts are courts of limited jurisdiction; need federal question or diversity of citizenship
   1. Diversity jurisdiction: amount in controversy
      a. Must exceed $75,000
      b. If more than one party, cannot aggregate claims against multiple defendants in order to reach amount in controversy unless claims are common and undivided
   2. Diversity jurisdiction: dispute must involve citizens of different states
      a. Diversity measured at time suit is filed
      b. Individual is a citizen of the state of his domicile
      c. Corporation is a citizen of both the state of its incorporation and the state where it has its principal place of business
   3. Lack of subject matter jurisdiction can be raised at any time and cannot be waived

B. **(Application)**
   1. Battery is a common-law claim, so no federal question
   2. No diversity jurisdiction because:
      a. Lack of complete diversity
         i. Patrick is citizen of Texas
         ii. David is citizen of Florida
         iii. DEI is citizen of both Delaware and Texas
      b. Amount in controversy not met
         i. Patrick seeking only $40,000 from each defendant
         ii. May not aggregate claims

C. **(Conclusion)** David can successfully raise lack of subject matter jurisdiction

II. **Lack of Personal Jurisdiction**

A. **(Rule)** Defendant must meet constitutional requirements and long-arm statute
   1. For constitutional requirements, must have systematic and continuous contacts (general jurisdiction) or minimum contacts (specific jurisdiction)
   2. Court applies long-arm statute of state in which it sits
   3. Can be raised in either motion to dismiss, answer, or amended answer

B. **(Application)** David has neither systematic and continuous contacts, nor minimum contacts, and Texas long-arm statute does not permit jurisdiction
   1. David's only contact with Texas is interview in Dallas and being hired by DEI
   2. David has no minimum contacts with Texas related to Patrick's claim; Patrick's actions are not relevant and his injury was unforeseen
   3. Texas long-arm statute does not cover David because the tortious act occurred in Florida, not Texas

C. **(Conclusion)** David can successfully raise lack of personal jurisdiction

III. **Improper Venue**

A. **(Rule)** Venue in diversity actions lies in the district where any defendant resides if all defendants: reside in same state; in the district where a substantial portion of events occurred; or in the district where any defendant is subject to personal jurisdiction, but only if there is no other district where action could be brought

1. Improper venue must be raised in a motion to dismiss, answer, or amended answer

B. **(Application)** Venue is not proper in the Southern District of Texas

1. David is not a resident of Texas, so not all defendants reside in same state

2. Substantial portion of events occurred in Middle District of Florida

3. No venue under third prong because proper venue lies in Middle District of Florida

C. **(Conclusion)** David can successfully raise improper venue

IV. **Insufficient Service of Process**

A. **(Rule)**

1. Service can be made:
   a. according to state law;
   b. by personal service;
   c. by leaving the summons and complaint at the individual's dwelling; or
   d. by delivering the summons and complaint to the individual's agent

2. Defendant can waive service upon plaintiff's request

3. Insufficient service of process must be raised in a motion to dismiss, answer, or amended answer

B. **(Application)** David was not served by any permissible methods

1. First-class mail is not permitted under Florida or Texas rules

2. David never waived service

C. **(Conclusion)** David can successfully raise improper venue

Federal Civil Procedure

In Class

This sample answer would be considered above the standard expected of a 1L student.

David may raise several defenses to Patrick's suit.

First, David may raise the defense of lack of subject matter jurisdiction. Federal district courts are courts of limited jurisdiction and may hear only actions that involve federal questions or diversity of citizenship where the amount in controversy exceeds $75,000. In multiparty litigation, a claimant may not aggregate claims against multiple defendants in order to reach the threshold amount in controversy unless the claims would by substantive law appear to be common and undivided. In order for diversity to exist, the dispute must involve citizens of different states. A shared citizenship between any plaintiff and any defendant will destroy diversity jurisdiction. Diversity must be met at the time the suit is filed. An individual is a citizen of the state of his domicile; domicile requires the person to have both physical presence in the state and the intent to remain in that state indefinitely. A corporation is a citizen of both the state of its incorporation and the state where it has its principal place of business. Finally, a defendant may raise the lack of subject matter jurisdiction at any time, and this defense may not be waived.

Here, Patrick's claim for battery is a common-law claim and is, therefore, not a basis for federal question jurisdiction. Diversity jurisdiction does not exist for two reasons: (1) there is a lack of complete diversity, and (2) the required amount in controversy is not met. Patrick, the plaintiff, is a citizen of Texas because he is domiciled there—he is physically present in Texas and intends to remain there. David, one of the defendants, is a citizen of Florida because he lives there and has no intention to be domiciled anywhere else. DEI is a citizen of both Delaware (where it is incorporated) and Texas (where it has its principal place of business). Because both Patrick and DEI are citizens of Texas, complete diversity is destroyed. In addition, the required amount of controversy is not met because Patrick seeks only $40,000 from each defendant. Patrick may not aggregate claims against these two separate defendants in order to reach the required amount of $75,000. David may raise this defense at any time.

Second, David may raise the defense of lack of personal jurisdiction. The defense of lack of personal jurisdiction must be raised either in a motion to dismiss, if filed, or in the defendant's timely filed answer or amended answer filed as a matter of course, which must be filed within 21 days of service of the original answer. Personal jurisdiction is a court's authority over a defendant. In order for personal jurisdiction over a nonresident defendant to meet constitutional requirements, the defendant must either have systematic and continuous contacts with a state (such that general jurisdiction would be appropriate) or have minimum contacts with the forum state that are related to the action, such that exercising personal jurisdiction over the defendant for purposes of the instant action will not offend traditional notions of fair play and substantial justice. In addition, even if constitutional requirements are met, the applicable state long-arm statute must authorize jurisdiction over the nonresident defendant. A federal court will usually apply the personal jurisdiction statutes of the state in which it sits.

Here, David is not a resident of Texas, and his only contacts with Texas are that he interviewed for his job with DEI in Dallas and that he was then hired by DEI, a corporation whose principal place of business is in Texas. These contacts are not systematic and continuous, because David conducts no regular activities within the state, nor are they minimum contacts that are sufficiently related to Patrick's claim. Patrick's act of moving to Texas, although he is experiencing ongoing pain and suffering there, does not constitute a purposeful act on David's part, nor could David have reasonably foreseen that his behavior would have such effects in Texas. In addition, the Texas long-arm statute for torts, which will apply here because the federal court sits in Texas, only provides personal jurisdiction over nonresidents if the tortious act occurred in Texas. Here, the injury to Patrick occurred in Florida. Therefore, there is no personal jurisdiction over David in Texas.

Third, David can raise the defense of improper venue. The defense of improper venue must be raised either in a motion to dismiss, if filed, or in the defendant's timely filed answer or amended answer filed as a matter of course, which must be filed within 21 days of service of the original answer. In diversity actions, venue lies in the district where any defendant resides, provided that all defendants are located (1) in the same state; (2) in the district where a substantial portion of the events occurred, or (3) in the district where any defendant is subject to personal jurisdiction, but only if there is no other district in which the action could be brought.

Here, venue is not proper in the Southern District of Texas. Although DEI is a resident of the Southern District of Texas because it is headquartered there, venue will not lie because David is not also a resident of Texas—he is a resident of Florida. In addition, because venue would exist in the Middle District of Florida, which is where a substantial portion of the relevant events occurred, venue cannot be proper in the Southern District of Texas based on personal jurisdiction over DEI there.

Fourth, David can raise the defense of insufficient service of process. The defense of insufficient service of process must be raised either in a motion to dismiss, if filed, or in the defendant's timely filed answer or amended answer filed as a matter of course, which must be filed within 21 days of service of the original answer. An individual may be served according to the state law governing service of a summons in an action in the state in which the district court is located or where service is made, by personal service on the individual, by leaving a copy of the summons and complaint at the individual's dwelling, or by delivering a copy of the summons and complaint to the individual's agent. A defendant may also waive service of the summons upon the plaintiff's request to save the costs associated with service.

Here, David was not served by any of the permissible methods described above. He was served by first-class mail, which is not a permitted method of service under either the Florida or Texas Rules of Civil Procedure. In addition, although David received a notice of the commencement of the action and a request to waive service, he did not waive service. Therefore, the request and notice will not constitute service or a substitute for service, because David never actually waived service.

Federal Civil Procedure

In Class

This sample answer would be considered below the standard expected of a 1L student.

David can say that there is no subject matter jurisdiction. Federal courts may hear only actions that involve federal questions or diversity of citizenship where the amount in controversy exceeds $75,000. Diversity exists if the parties are citizens of different states. Diversity must be met at the time the suit is filed. Lack of subject matter jurisdiction may not be waived.

There is no basis for federal question jurisdiction because a battery claim does not present a federal question. There is also no diversity jurisdiction because the required amount in controversy is not met. The required amount of controversy is not met because Patrick seeks only $40,000 from each defendant. Patrick cannot combine his claims against two separate defendants to reach $75,000.

David can also say there is no personal jurisdiction. David can either file a motion to dismiss or raise this defense in his answer. David is not a resident of Texas, and he does not work in Texas, either. However, Patrick can argue that because he moved to Texas and is enduring ongoing pain and suffering there, personal jurisdiction does exist. However, this argument might fail because the Texas long-arm statute requires the injury to have occurred in Texas.

David might be able to say that he was not served properly. Service by mail is allowed, but only if the applicable state statute says so. Here, the Florida statute permits service of process by certified mail, but not by first-class mail. Also, David did not waive service.

Federal Civil Procedure

Homework Question 1

You represent Drake Donner (DD). Your client has been sued in federal court by Paul Pointer (PP). Federal jurisdiction exists solely under 28 U.S.C. 1332, because the parties are of diverse citizenship and more than $75,000 is in controversy. PP and DD are presently the only parties to the case. You learn that DD has three state common-law claims against Thomas P. Donald (TPD). DD and TPD are both citizens of the same state. The first of DD's claims against TPD is for contribution. If DD prevails against TPD on this claim, then TPD will be liable to DD for some of what DD may be liable to PP for. DD's second claim against TPD is for DD's damages arising from the same event that gave rise to PP's claim against DD. DD's third claim against TPD is for damages caused to DD by TPD in an event that is completely unrelated to the events that are alleged and form the basis of PP's claim against DD.

On DD's behalf, may you bring one or more of DD's claims against TPD in the case of PP v. DD? Be sure to discuss all three claims, and discuss both how any applicable joinder rules apply and how the law of federal subject matter jurisdiction applies.

Federal Civil Procedure

Homework Question 1—Outline

I. **Claim One**

    A. **Joinder**

        1. **(Rule)** Defendant can join nonparty who may be liable for all or part of plaintiff's claim

            a. Must be filed within 14 days of filing answer; after this, only by leave of court

        2. **(Application)** TPD is liable for part of the damages, so DD may file third-party complaint against TPD within 14 days of filing answer

        3. **(Conclusion)** Joinder is permissible for first claim

    B. **Jurisdiction**

        1. **(Rule)** Court must have subject matter jurisdiction over claim against nonparty

            a. Court may exercise supplemental jurisdiction over claim if arises from same case or controversy as initial claim

            b. Supplemental jurisdiction does not exist in diversity action if plaintiff is attempting to use it to circumvent diversity requirement

        2. **(Application)** Court has supplemental jurisdiction because contribution claim arises from same case or controversy

            a. Supplemental jurisdiction exists because defendant, not plaintiff, is seeking to join nonparty

            b. No independent basis for jurisdiction

        3. **(Conclusion)** There is supplemental jurisdiction over first claim

II. **Claim Two**

    A. **Joinder**

        1. **(Rule)** Party can join as many claims in single action as he has against opposing party

            a. Claims need not be related

         2. **(Application)** After TPD has been joined, DD and TPD will be parties to the action

            a. DD can then bring any claims he has against TPD

        3. **(Conclusion)** DD can bring second claim against TPD once TPD has been joined for the first claim

    B. **Jurisdiction**

        1. **(Rule)** Court must have subject matter jurisdiction over claim against nonparty

            a. Court may exercise supplemental jurisdiction over claim if arises from same case or controversy as initial claim

            b. Supplemental jurisdiction does not exist in diversity action if plaintiff is attempting to use it to circumvent diversity requirement

        2. **(Application)** Court will have supplemental jurisdiction over second claim because it is for damages arising from same event underlying PP's claim

            a. Supplemental jurisdiction will not be withdrawn (under diversity rule) because claim not made by plaintiff

   b. No independent basis for jurisdiction
3. **(Conclusion)** There is supplemental jurisdiction over the first claim

III. **Claim Three**

A. **Joinder**
1. **(Rule)** Party can join as many claims in single action as he has against opposing party
    a. Claims need not be related
2. **(Application)** After TPD has been joined, DD and TPD will be parties to the action
    a. DD can then bring any claims he has against TPD
3. **(Conclusion)** TPD can be joined under joinder rules, but no subject matter jurisdiction (discussed below)

B. **Jurisdiction**
1. **(Rule)** Court must have subject matter jurisdiction over claim against nonparty
    a. Court may exercise supplemental jurisdiction over claim if arises from same case or controversy as initial claim
2. **(Application)** No supplemental or independent basis for jurisdiction
    a. No independent basis because no federal question and lack of complete diversity
    b. No supplemental jurisdiction because claim is unrelated to basis for PP's claim against DD
3. **(Conclusion)** DD cannot join third claim against TPD in PP v. DD action

Federal Civil Procedure

Homework Question 1—Sample Answer

This sample answer would be considered above the standard expected of a 1L student.

Claim One

DD may bring the first claim against TPD in the case of PP v. DD by joining TPD as a third-party defendant. After a defendant to an action has served his answer, the defendant may proceed against a nonparty who may be liable for all or part of the plaintiff's claim against the defendant. The defendant may file a third-party complaint any time within 14 days of filing his answer. After that time, a third-party complaint may be filed only with leave of court. In order for a nonparty to be joined as a third-party defendant, the court must have subject matter jurisdiction over the defendant's claim against the nonparty. A court may exercise supplemental juris-diction over a claim against a third party if the claim arises from the same case or controversy as the initial claim. Supplemental jurisdiction may exist in diversity actions, but it will not exist if the plaintiff is attempting to use supplemental jurisdic-tion to circumvent the diversity requirement.

Here, TPD is liable for at least part of the damages for which DD is liable to PP, so DD may file a third-party complaint against TPD within 14 days of filing his answer to PP's complaint. The court will have supplemental jurisdiction over DD's claim against TPD because, as a contribution claim, it necessarily arises from the same case or controversy as PP's claim. Finally, because the defendant—and not the plaintiff—is seeking to join a nonparty, supplemental jurisdiction will exist even though the basis for subject matter jurisdiction is diversity jurisdiction. There is no independent basis for jurisdiction, because there is no federal question involved and there is not complete diversity, inasmuch as DD and TPD are citizens of the same state.

Claim Two

DD may bring the second claim against TPD once TPD has been joined as a third-party defendant as described above for the first claim. A party may join as many claims in a single action as the party has against an opposing party. There is no requirement that all claims between the parties be related. In order for a claim to be joined, the court must have subject matter jurisdiction over the claim. As noted above, a court may exercise supplemental jurisdiction over a claim if the claim arises from the same case or controversy as the initial claim. Supplemental juris-diction may exist in diversity actions, but it will not exist if the plaintiff is attempting to use supplemental jurisdiction to circumvent the diversity requirement.

Here, DD's second claim against TPD may be brought after TPD has been joined with respect to the first claim, because both DD and TPD will then be parties to the action and DD can therefore bring any claims he has against TPD. The court will have supplemental jurisdiction over the second claim because the claim is for damages arising from the same event that gave rise to PP's claim against DD. Supplemental jurisdiction will not be withdrawn, even though subject matter juris-diction is based on diversity jurisdiction, because DD's second claim is not a claim made by a plaintiff. There is no independent basis for jurisdiction over this claim, because there is no federal question involved and there is not complete diversity, because DD and TPD are citizens of the same state.

Claim Three

DD cannot bring the third claim against TPD because there is no supplemental jurisdiction over the claim. As noted above, a party may join as many claims in a single action as the party has against an opposing party. There is no requirement that all claims between the parties be related. In order for a claim to be joined, the court must have subject matter jurisdiction over the claim. A court may exercise supplemental jurisdiction over a claim if the claim arises from the same case or controversy as the initial claim.

Here, although DD may bring the third claim against TPD under the joinder rules, because a party may join all of his actions against an opposing party, there is no subject matter jurisdiction over this claim. There is no independent basis for jurisdiction over this claim, because there is no federal question involved and there is not complete diversity, because DD and TPD are citizens of the same state. There is also no supplemental jurisdiction, because the claim is completely unrelated to the events that are the basis of PP's claim against DD. Therefore, DD cannot join the third claim against TPD in the PP v. DD action.

Federal Civil Procedure

Homework Question 2

You represent Pauline Pilson (PP) in her case against her former employer, the law firm of Wellington & Graham (W & G). Her sole claim is that W & G violated her rights under the federal civil rights laws when the firm failed to admit her to partnership because she terminated a romantic relationship with Max Shipman, a senior partner at W & G. Your complaint alleges all disputed facts with particularity. W & G has filed a motion for summary judgment. The court has granted you additional time to conduct discovery, file motions, or otherwise prepare your response. With respect to each of the following items, what action or actions would you take, and/or what arguments would you make, in an attempt to defeat the motion for summary judgment?

A. *W & G has supported its motion for summary judgment with affidavits from every member of its Partnership Committee (which had the responsibility to recommend associates for partnership and which declined to recommend PP) who is still with the firm. The affidavits state that PP's relationship with Max had nothing to do with the recommendation not to admit PP to partnership and that none of the discussion of her candidacy concerned anything other than the merits of her performance as an associate at W & G. Each of the affidavits comes from someone who is currently a partner in the firm, although the affidavits do not recite this fact.*

B. *W & G supports its motion for summary judgment with an affidavit from a partner in the firm that attaches and authenticates an internal memorandum bearing a date during PP's last year as an associate and in which this partner severely criticizes her abilities and work habits. You are suspicious of this document because the first time you heard of it or saw it was when the motion for summary judgment and the supporting documentation was filed.*

C. *You learn that Jeff Franklin, a former partner in W & G and a former member of the Partnership Committee, is prepared to testify (but only if he is compelled to do so) that he was present at the meeting when PP's application received a negative recommendation, and that every member of the Partnership Committee stated at the meeting that he was voting against PP because she had had the audacity to break off her romantic relationship with their good friend Max. His testimony would be admissible direct evidence of unlawful discrimination.*

Federal Civil Procedure

Homework Question 2—Outline

I. Take depositions and submit transcripts in opposition to motion for summary judgment

    A. **(Rule)** Summary judgment is improper if evidence shows moving party's evidence will be impeached at trial such that reasonable jury could find for opposing party

        1. Court must grant summary judgment if no genuine dispute as to material fact and movant entitled to JMOL

        2. Movant entitled to JMOL if opposing party has been fully heard during jury trial and reasonable jury would not have legally sufficient evidentiary basis to find for party

        3. Party opposing summary judgment must produce evidence in support of claim

        4. Evidence will be viewed in light most favorable to party opposing summary judgment

        5. Deposition transcripts can be produced in opposition to summary judgment

    B. **(Application)** Testimony obtained via deposition can impeach partners' affidavits

        1. Question witnesses as to whether they are partners and therefore have pecuniary interest in suit

        2. Deposition testimony, once submitted to court, will impeach affidavits

        3. Reasonable jury could find for PP

    C. **(Conclusion)** Summary judgment is improper because there is evidence to impeach partner's testimony and reasonable jury could find for PP

II. File a motion to exclude the internal memorandum from being used at trial

    A. **(Rule)** Party must disclose certain documents and information, and is subject to sanctions for failing to do so

        1. Mandatory disclosure of any document or information that may be used to support claims or defenses is required within 2 weeks of initial discovery conference

        2. Supplementation required if new information becomes available

        3. Party can move to compel disclosure and for sanctions

        4. Party moving for summary judgment cannot rely on inadmissible evidence

    B. **(Application)** W & G should have disclosed document

        1. Document should have been part of W & G's initial or supplemental disclosures

        2. Because no disclosure, exclusion at trial is appropriate

        3. Because will be inadmissible at trial, cannot be relied on for summary judgment

    C. **(Conclusion)** Summary judgment is improper because cannot rely on document that was not properly disclosed

III. Subpoena Jeff for a deposition

    A. **(Rule)** A non-party must be subpoenaed for a deposition
       1. Deposition transcripts can be used to oppose summary judgment
       2. Witness is directly questioned and all statements are transcribed
       3. Rule 45 governs subpoenas

    B. **(Application)** Jeff must be subpoenaed because he will not attend voluntarily
       1. At deposition, Jeff should be questioned regarding partners' discriminatory statements
       2. Deposition transcript should be submitted in opposition to summary judgment
       3. Because testimony is direct evidence of discrimination and jury needs to determine credibility, judge cannot grant summary judgment

    C. **(Conclusion)** As jury could reasonably find for PP on this issue, summary judgment is not appropriate

Federal Civil Procedure

Homework Question 2—Sample Answer

This sample answer would be considered above the standard expected of a 1L student.

A. <u>In order to counter the affidavits from the members of the Partnership Committee, I would take the deposition of each witness who has provided an affidavit.</u>

Summary judgment, which is governed by Rule 56, is intended to pierce the pleadings to determine if there is credible evidence to factually support a party's claim. Under Rule 56(a), the court must grant summary judgment if the movant shows that there is no genuine dispute as to any material fact and the movant is entitled to judgment as a matter of law. Under Rule 50(a), a movant is entitled to judgment as a matter of law if the opposing party has been fully heard on an issue during a jury trial and the court finds that a reasonable jury would not have a legally sufficient evidentiary basis to find for the party on that issue.

Upon a motion for summary judgment by the defendant, the plaintiff must produce evidence in support of each element of its cause of action. The evidence will be viewed in the light most favorable to the plaintiff to determine whether the defendant is entitled to prevail as a matter of law. Depositions transcripts are one type of evidence that may be produced in opposition to a motion for summary judgment. Depositions permit the direct questioning of a party or witness under oath. They are typically conducted orally, and every word that is spoken is recorded verbatim and transcribed.

At the depositions, I would question each witness as to whether he or she is a partner in W & G and therefore has a pecuniary interest in the outcome of the suit. The partner-deponents will have to admit these facts. The transcripts of the depositions can then be presented to the court in opposition to the motion for summary judgment. I would then argue that the deposition testimony, as evidenced by the transcripts, impeaches the direct testimony given in the affidavits, and that at trial the jury will be entitled to disbelieve the direct testimony. Under the standard on a motion for summary judgment, which is the same as the standard on a motion for judgment as a matter of law, the court would be required to grant W & G's motion if there was no evidence presented on summary judgment to indicate that the partners' testimony would be contradicted or impeached at trial, and if the court therefore concluded that no reasonable jury could find for PP. However, the deposition testimony will demonstrate, at the very least, that the partners' testimony at trial will be impeached, and, therefore, judgment as a matter of law, and consequently summary judgment, is improper.

B. <u>I would file a motion for sanctions to exclude the internal memorandum from being used at trial.</u>

Under Rule 26(a), a party is required to disclose a copy or description of all documents, electronically stored information, and tangible things that the disclosing party has in its possession, custody, or control and may use to support its claims or defenses. Mandatory disclosures must be made within two weeks of the initial discovery conference. A party must make these disclosures based upon the information then reasonably available. In addition, a party must supplement a discovery response with any information that would have been subject to the mandatory disclosure requirement. Under Rule 37, a party may move to compel disclosure and for appropriate sanctions, which may include exclusion of that evidence at trial. In support of a motion for summary judgment, the plaintiff may not rely on evidence that will be inadmissible at trial to satisfy the production burden.

Here, this document should have been disclosed as part of W & G's initial disclosures, or, if it was not in W & G's custody or control at that time, in its supplemental disclosures, because W & G intends to use this document to support its defense against PP. Because such disclosure was not made, exclusion of the document at trial is appropriate. Furthermore, because the document will be excluded and the jury therefore will not be permitted to view or consider it at trial, the court should disregard it in connection with the motion for summary judgment.

C. I would subpoena Jeff to be deposed.

As noted above, depositions are one type of evidence that may be produced in opposition to a motion for summary judgment. Depositions permit the direct questioning of a party or witness under oath. They are typically conducted orally, and every word that is spoken is recorded verbatim and transcribed. If the deponent is a nonparty, the party requesting the deposition must also provide for the attendance of the witness, usually by serving a subpoena. Witnesses may be compelled to appear by service of a subpoena under Rule 45.

Because Jeff will not provide an affidavit or attend a deposition unless he is compelled to do so, I would serve Jeff with a subpoena to attend a deposition. At the deposition, I would ask Jeff about the meeting where the other partners' statements revealed their discriminatory intent. I would submit the transcript of the deposition in opposition to the motion for summary judgment. I would then argue to the court that the testimony is direct evidence of discrimination that should be presented to the jury at trial, and that the judge cannot render judgment as a matter of law because doing so would require a judgment as to Jeff's credibility, which is a matter for the jury and not the judge. Because a reasonable jury could have a legally sufficient evidentiary basis to find for PP on this issue, judgment as a matter of law would not be appropriate, and therefore, neither would summary judgment.

Multiple-Choice Questions

JURISDICTION AND VENUE

Question 1

Tom, a citizen of Oklahoma, filed suit against Jerry in an Oklahoma court, alleging a claim based upon a federal statute. Jerry, also a citizen of Oklahoma, filed a petition for removal to the federal court which encompasses the judicial district in which the state court is located.

Should the action be removed?

    (A) Yes, because state courts, even those of general jurisdiction, do not have subject-matter jurisdiction over federal claims.

    (B) Yes, because Tom's action arises under a federal statute.

    (C) No, because the action could not have originally been brought in the federal court to which removal has been requested.

    (D) No, because Jerry is a citizen of Oklahoma.

Question 2

D-Corp, a Michigan corporation, sells its automobiles through independent dealers. D-Corp's principal place of business is in Detroit. Each dealer has a separate dealership agreement, which they respectively executed with D-Corp at the time they were appointed to be dealers. Their agreements entitle them to sell all automobiles manufactured by D-Corp in their areas. This year, D-Corp has produced a new sports car that is a radical departure from its previous automobiles. D-Corp decided that it will not sell this car to its existing dealers, but will instead enter into agreements with new dealers to handle the new sports car line. Twelve dealers in California jointly filed actions for breach of contract, seeking an injunction against D-Corp in the appropriate U.S. District Court. D-Corp moved to dismiss the case for lack of subject-matter jurisdiction, and alternatively, moved to sever the actions.

How should the court rule on D-Corp's motions?

    (A) The court should grant D-Corp's motion to sever, because the claims arise out of the same transaction or series of transactions, and there are common issues of law and fact to all of the claims.

    (B) The court should grant D-Corp's motion to dismiss, because the plaintiffs are not diverse.

    (C) The court should deny D-Corp's motion to sever, because plaintiffs are compelled to join their actions if their claims arise out of the same transaction or series of transactions.

    (D) The court should deny D-Corp's motion to dismiss, because the diversity requirement has been met in this case.

Question 3

Twenty residents of Oklahoma and Nebraska have asserted a claim in the amount of $50,000 against XYZ Corp, a Maryland corporation. Their joinder of claims is based upon the assertion that fumes from XYZ Corp's plant in Arkansas caused them minor respiratory problems. XYZ Corp's principal place of business is in Maryland.

May the 20 persons sue XYZ Corp in a U.S. District Court?

(A) Yes, but only if their claim is based upon a federal statute.

(B) Yes, but only if the plaintiffs aggregate their claims in a class action.

(C) Yes, because diversity of citizenship exists between all plaintiffs and XYZ Corp.

(D) Yes, but only if a class action is certified and there is diversity of citizenship between the class representative and XYZ Corp.

Question 4

The plaintiff is an Alabama corporation that markets computer products of the defendant, a nationwide computer manufacturer with its headquarters in New York. The marketing agreement contained a forum-selection clause providing that any disputes arising out of the contract could only be brought in a court located in the Southern District of New York. After business relations took a turn for the worse, the plaintiff sued the defendant in the Northern District of Alabama. The complaint alleged that the defendant had breached the dealership agreement, causing more than $1 million in damages. The defendant moved the district court to transfer the case to the Southern District of New York. The Alabama court refused to do so, finding that transfer was controlled by Alabama law and that Alabama did not view contractual forum-selection clauses as enforceable. Specifically, the court found that Alabama disfavored such clauses in order to protect state court jurisdiction.

Was the Alabama court's ruling correct?

(A) Yes, because the Alabama court based its ruling on Alabama law.

(B) Yes, because such forum-selection clauses are invalid.

(C) No, because the clause was evidence of what the parties believed was convenient.

(D) No, because the defendant was a resident of New York.

Question 5

P Corp is incorporated in Delaware, but has its principal place of business in Ohio. P Corp is licensed to do business in every state except Wisconsin. P Corp filed an action against Insureco and Ernie. Insureco is a corporation existing under the laws of Michigan, where it has its principal place of business. Insureco also does business in Delaware and Ohio. Ernie is a citizen of Ontario, Canada. P Corp's claim against Ernie arises out of a fire which occurred at P Corp's plant in Delaware. P Corp's claim against Insureco is for breach of contract, based upon Insureco's refusal to pay P Corp the proceeds of a fire insurance policy that P Corp had purchased from Insureco. Both claims are for $100,000.

Which of the following is true?

(A) If the action was filed in a U.S. District Court in Ohio, subject-matter jurisdiction would not exist, and venue would not be proper.

(B) If this action was commenced in a Wisconsin court, the defendants could not remove the action to the appropriate U.S. District Court.

(C) P Corp's joinder of Insureco and Ernie in one action is proper, because P Corp is asserting two distinct causes of action.

(D) P Corp's joinder of Insureco and Ernie in one action is not proper, because Insureco and Ernie are not residents of the same state. pretrial procedures

PRETRIAL PROCEDURE

Question 6

Alice, a Colorado citizen, was injured when her car was hit by Craig, also a Colorado citizen. Craig is a minor who was illegally served drinks at a bar that is located in Wyoming and owned by Baker, a Wyoming citizen. Alice brought an action in the only U.S. District Court in Colorado against Baker, alleging negligence and breach of a statutory duty. Thirty days after answering, Baker filed a motion seeking leave to file a third-party claim (an impleader action) against Craig, based entirely upon Craig's unpaid bar bill and his failure to pay for a used car that Baker had sold to Craig.

Which of the following is true?

(A) The motion will be denied, because Baker's claim does not assert that Craig may be liable to Baker on all or part of Alice's claim.

(B) If the court finds that Baker may properly implead Craig, Baker will probably be allowed to assert any claim he has against Craig.

(C) Craig cannot be made a party to the action by Baker, because that would destroy diversity subject-matter jurisdiction.

(D) The motion will be granted, because it was properly filed.

Question 7

Tom, a citizen of Texas, is trustee of a trust set up by Garry, who is also a citizen of Texas. The beneficiaries, Adam, Bill, and Carson, are all citizens of New Jersey. The terms of the trust provide that the res is to be invested only in "community businesses." Walt persuades Tom to buy real estate for the trust, knowing that such a purchase would probably violate its terms. Walt, a citizen of Texas, had convinced Tom that the land was very valuable, but Walt actually knew that it was worthless. Tom bought the real estate for the trust for $78,000. Adam and Bill sued Tom in the only U.S. District Court in New Jersey for violating the terms of the trust. Assume that a decision in this action would, under New Jersey res judicata principles, be binding upon Carson.

Which of the following is true?

(A) The court could probably order Carson to be joined as an involuntary plaintiff.

(B) The court must dismiss the claim if Tom impleads Walt on the basis that the latter defrauded the former and the court determines that the fraud is distinct from the issue of Tom's breach of his fiduciary duties to the trust beneficiaries.

(C) Personal jurisdiction and venue requisites aside, if Tom properly impleaded Walt, the plaintiffs could not assert a claim against him for $78,000, because Walt was impleaded by Tom.

(D) Carson may join Adam and Bill in their suit against Tom only if Carson does so on his own volition.

Question 8

Carl brought an action against Don, Everett, and Flora asserting: (1) infringement of copyright, and (2) breach of contract. Copyright actions are exclusively within the subject-matter jurisdiction of federal courts. All of the claims arose from the defendants having produced a television show based upon a script that Carl had written for them. Carl seeks to recover $75,000 apiece from the defendants. All of the parties are citizens of California.

Which of the following is true?

(A) If this action was filed in a California state court, the defendants could not have it removed to federal court.

(B) If this action was filed in federal court, a dismissal for lack of subject-matter jurisdiction would be required.

(C) If this case goes to trial in a state court and judgment is entered against the defendants, they will have waived any claim of lack of subject-matter jurisdiction by failing to assert it before or during the trial.

(D) If this action was filed in a state court, the defendants would have the right to remove the action to federal court.

Question 9

Paul was rear-ended by John, a 17-year-old. The car that John was driving was owned by Mary, his mother. Paul is a citizen of Vermont. John and Mary are citizens of Maine. The accident occurred in Vermont. Paul sued Mary and John in the U.S. District Court in Maine pursuant to a Vermont statute that made parents liable for the negligent driving of their minor children. The suit demanded $90,000 in damages.

Which of the following statements is correct?

(A) Mary may assert a cross-claim against John.

(B) If Mary fails to assert a cross-claim against John, any claim by her against him will be barred.

(C) Mary may not assert a cross-claim against John.

(D) Mary may assert a counterclaim against John.

Question 10

EasyBuild, a Utah corporation, designed a building for Smith, a citizen of Idaho, six years ago. Part of that building collapsed last year, causing damages in excess of $80,000. Smith has filed an action against EasyBuild in the U.S. District Court in Utah, alleging that his damages resulted from the negligent design of the building. At the time the building was being constructed, Jones, an attorney and member of EasyBuild's board of directors who occasionally handled legal matters for EasyBuild, prepared and sent the following memorandum to the president of EasyBuild: "I have been informed by Tom Withers, an architect who used to work for EasyBuild, that the materials being used by our contractor, BuilderCorp, in constructing Smith's building are substandard." Smith filed a timely motion for the pretrial production of the Jones memorandum.

If EasyBuild asserts the work-product privilege in response to Smith's motion to compel production of Jones's memorandum, how should the reviewing court rule?

(A) The court should deny Smith's motion to compel, because the memorandum reflects Jones's impressions about EasyBuild's potential liability.

(B) The court should deny Smith's motion to compel, because Jones was an attorney.

(C) The court should grant Smith's motion to compel, because the memorandum is relevant to his action.

(D) The court should grant Smith's motion to compel, but only if Jones is not representing EasyBuild in the present action.

MOTIONS

Question 11

Pamela sued David for trespassing at her Los Angeles residence. The action was properly commenced in a U.S. District Court. David defended by claiming that he was in New York at the time that the incident allegedly took place. David intends to call Wanda as a witness to testify that she saw him in New York on the day in question. Pamela believes that Wanda is hopelessly nearsighted and could easily have mistaken someone else for David. In order to impeach Wanda's testimony, Pamela sends Wanda a Notice to Appear for Medical Examination before a licensed ophthalmologist selected by Pamela.

Which of the following is true?

(A) Wanda need not comply with the Notice to Appear, because she is not a party to the action and Pamela does not have authority to order her to submit to a medical examination.

(B) Wanda need not comply with the Notice to Appear, because physicians performing medical examinations must be selected by the judge.

(C) Wanda must comply with the Notice to Appear, because her eyesight is at issue.

(D) Wanda must comply with the Notice to Appear, but David is entitled to a copy of the ophthalmologist's findings.

Question 12

Bob sued Carol in federal district court in Wisconsin, alleging breach of contract. Bob is a resident of Michigan, and Carol is a resident of Wisconsin. Bob in good faith alleged damages in the amount of $90,000. Carol filed an answer denying, among other things, that a valid contract had been formed. At the time that she filed her answer, Carol did not raise improper service of process as a defense in her answer. Thereafter, she filed a Rule 12(b) motion alleging improper service of process. In the same motion, she moved for judgment on the pleadings pursuant to Rule 12(c).

Which of the following is true?

(A) Carol's motion must be dismissed, because Rule 12 motions must be filed before any responsive pleading.

(B) The court must determine whether service of process was proper before proceeding on any other issue.

(C) Carol's Rule 12(b) motion cannot be heard.

(D) Carol's Rule 12(b) motion may be heard.

Question 13

Joan visited Dr. Brown. After examining her, he put some drops in her left ear. She then left. However, she continued to have difficulties with her balance. Three weeks after her visit to Dr. Brown, Joan fell and sustained serious injuries. Joan sued Dr. Brown and requested a jury trial. The action was properly commenced in a U.S. District Court.

At trial, Joan testified to the foregoing, and then called Dr. Edward to the stand. Dr. Edward testified that, in his opinion: (1) he had examined Joan and found substantial damage to her inner ear; and (2) the damage was caused by a fluid containing acid. Joan then rested her case. Dr. Brown then took the stand and testified that: Joan had been suffering from an infection that affected the inner ear; and he had put some drops of perforium (an innocuous, non-acidic substance) into her ear. He further stated on cross-examination that the bottle containing perforium stood in the vicinity of a bottle containing an acidic substance. He then rested his case.

In rebuttal, Joan called Dr. Edward, who stated that the injury to Joan's inner ear was totally inconsistent with Dr. Brown's assertion of an infection. All sides then rested. Neither party moved for judgment as a matter of law. The jury returned a verdict in favor of Joan. Dr. Brown then moved for a renewed judgment as a matter of law and, in the alternative, for a new trial. The trial judge granted the motion for a renewed judgment as a matter of law, but denied the motion for a new trial. Joan then appealed the order granting a renewed judgment as a matter of law by the trial court.

What should the appellate court decide to do?

(A) Reverse the judgment and reinstate the verdict for Joan.

(B) Reverse the judgment, because a motion for a new trial cannot be joined with a renewed judgment as a matter of law.

(C) Reverse the judgment, but order a new trial.

(D) Affirm the judgment.

Question 14

Joanne visited Dr. Blue. After examining her, Dr. Blue put drops in Joanne's eyes. In the ensuing weeks, she had increasing difficulty with blurred vision. Three weeks after the drops were administered, Joanne was in a single-car accident after she experienced an episode of extreme blurred vision while driving. Joanne sued Dr. Blue in U.S. District Court and requested a jury trial.

At trial, Joanne testified to the foregoing, and then called Dr. Evans to the stand. He testified that he had examined Joanne and found substantial damage to her cornea, and that, in his opinion, the damage was caused by a fluid containing acid. Joanne rested her case. Dr. Blue then took the stand and testified that Joanne had been suffering from an infection in both eyes when she visited his office, and that he had only put saline drops (an innocuous, non-acidic substance) into her eyes. He further stated on cross-examination that the bottle containing saline stood next to a bottle containing an acidic substance. He then rested his case. In rebuttal, Joanne called Dr. Evans, who stated that the injury to Joanne's eyes was entirely inconsistent with Dr. Blue's assertion of an infection. All sides then rested.

If Joanne moves for judgment as a matter of law, how should the court decide her motion?

(A) Her motion should be denied.

(B) Her motion should be granted, because of the admission of the non-movant, Dr. Blue, that the saline bottle stood near a bottle containing an acidic substance.

(C) Her motion should be granted, but not because of the admission of the non-movant, Dr. Blue, that the saline bottle stood near a bottle containing an acidic substance.

(D) Her motion should be granted, because there is a preponderance of reasonable evidence to support her claim against Dr. Blue.

Question 15

The plaintiff was injured in a fireworks accident at a local baseball park. The plaintiff subsequently filed a complaint against the defendant baseball park that said, "On July 4, at Quahog Park in Pawtucket, RI, the plaintiff was injured by fireworks. The plaintiff suffered terrible burns, resulting in physical and mental pain, loss of earnings, and loss of consortium. The plaintiff has incurred medical expenses and losses in the sum of $150,000."

What would be the defense attorney's most appropriate response to the plaintiff's claim?

(A) Motion for summary judgment.

(B) Motion to dismiss.

(C) Motion for judgment as a matter of law.

(D) Motion for physical and mental examination.

Answer Grid

1 ⒶⒷⒸⒹ	4 ⒶⒷⒸⒹ	7 ⒶⒷⒸⒹ	10 ⒶⒷⒸⒹ	13 ⒶⒷⒸⒹ
2 ⒶⒷⒸⒹ	5 ⒶⒷⒸⒹ	8 ⒶⒷⒸⒹ	11 ⒶⒷⒸⒹ	14 ⒶⒷⒸⒹ
3 ⒶⒷⒸⒹ	6 ⒶⒷⒸⒹ	9 ⒶⒷⒸⒹ	12 ⒶⒷⒸⒹ	15 ⒶⒷⒸⒹ

Real Property

Outline

TABLE OF CONTENTS

VI.   LANDLORD / TENANT

VII.   FIXTURES

I. ESTATES IN LAND

> **NOTE** An estate in land is an interest in real property that is presently or may become possessory.

A. Present Possessory Estates

1. A freehold estate gives the owner of the estate title to or a right to hold the property. A non-freehold estate gives mere possession.

2. **Types of Freehold Estates**

   a. **Fee Simple Absolute**

      (1) A **fee simple absolute** is the largest possible estate in land, denoting the aggregate of all possible rights that a person may have in that parcel of land, including:

         (a) the unimpeded right to sell or convey all or part of the property; and

         (b) the unimpeded right to devise the property.

> **NOTE** A fee simple absolute may last in perpetuity. If the owner of a fee simple absolute dies intestate, the property will pass to the owner's heirs by intestacy.

      (2) The following words are traditionally used to create a fee simple absolute: O conveys "to A and his heirs."

         (a) **Words of purchase** describe the persons, called "purchasers," who take an interest under a grant or device. **Words of limitation** describe the nature of the estate taken by the purchasers.

            EXAMPLE: O conveys "to A and her heirs." The words "to A" are words of purchase because they indicate that A takes an interest under the grant from O. The words "and her heirs" are words of limitation because they describe the nature of the estate taken by A—in this case, a fee simple absolute.

         (b) At early common law, the words "to A and his heirs" were required to create a fee simple absolute.

         (c) However, under modern law, a fee simple absolute is generally presumed when the words "to A" are used.

   b. **Defeasible Estates**

      (1) A defeasible estate is an estate that may terminate before its maximum duration has run.

      (2) **Fee Simple Determinable**

         (a) A determinable estate terminates automatically on the happening of a named future event.

         (b) A determinable estate is described with the following words:

            1) for so long as;

            2) during;

            3) while; or

4) until.

(c) A determinable estate is created:

1) In one clause; and

2) with a limitation built into that one clause.

> **EXAMPLE:** O conveys "to A and his heirs for so long as the premises are used for educational purposes." This creates a determinable estate.

(d) A determinable estate is followed by a possibility of reverter, which may be implied.

(3) **Fee Simple Subject to a Condition Subsequent**

(a) An **estate subject to a condition subsequent** may be cut short if the estate is retaken by the grantor or a third party on the happening of a named future event.

1) The condition only gives the grantor the right to take the estate, however. It does not automatically terminate the estate (as distinguished from a determinable estate).

(b) An estate subject to a condition subsequent is described with the following words:

1) provided, however;

2) however if;

3) but if;

4) on condition that; or

5) in the event that.

(c) An estate subject to a condition subsequent is created:

1) in two separate clauses; and

2) with a condition stated in the second clause.

> **EXAMPLE:** O conveys "to A and his heirs, but if the premises are not used for educational purposes, then O has the right to reenter the premises and terminate A's estate." This creates a fee simple subject to a condition subsequent.

> **EXAMPLE:** O conveys "to A for life; provided, however, that if the premises are not used for charitable purposes, O may reenter and retake the premises." This creates a life estate subject to a condition subsequent.

(4) **Fee Simple Subject to Executory Interest**

(a) A **fee simple subject to an executory interest** is an estate that is automatically divested in favor of a third person on the happening of a named event.

> **EXAMPLE:** O conveys "to A for so long as the premises are used for charitable purposes, but if the premises cease to be used for charitable purposes, then to B."

EXAMPLE: O conveys "to A, but if the premises cease to be used for educational purposes, then to B."

1) A fee simple subject to an executory interest is followed by a shifting executory interest.

NOTE ▶ This is subject to the Rule Against Perpetuities.

(5) **Fee Tail**

(a) At early common law, a **fee tail** was a freehold estate that descended to the grantee's lineal descendants (children) only.

(b) The following words are used to create a fee tail general: O conveys "to A and the heirs of his body."

1) In a fee tail general, children of the grantee take when the grantee dies.

(c) The following words are used to create a fee tail male or female: O conveys "to A and the heirs [male]/[female] of his body."

1) In a fee tail male or female, descent is limited to the male or female heirs of the grantee.

(d) The following words are used to create a fee tail special: O conveys "to the heirs of his body by his wife B."

1) In a fee tail special, descent is limited to the grantee's descendants by a specific spouse.

(e) The fee tail is followed by a reversion in the grantor or a remainder in a third party. That future interest becomes possessory if and when the grantee's lineal line has failed.

(f) Fee tails are disfavored in modern law. Today, if the words "to A and the heirs of his body" are used:

1) in most states, the grantee gets a fee simple absolute; and

2) in some states, the grantee has a life estate, with a remainder *per stirpes* in the grantee's lineal descendants in being at the time of the life tenant's death.

(6) **Unclear Grants**

(a) If the words of the grant are not clear:

1) a covenant is preferred over a defeasible estate because the award is money damages rather than forfeiture; and

2) a fee simple subject to a condition subsequent is preferred over a fee simple determinable because in the former, forfeiture is not automatic.

c. **Life Estate**

(1) A **life estate** lasts for the duration of the grantee's life.

(2) The following words are used to create a life estate: O conveys "to A for life."

(3) A **life estate *pur autre vie*** is an estate where the duration is measured by the life of someone other than the grantee.

> **EXAMPLE:** O conveys "to A for the life of B." If B predeceases A, A's estate ends at B's death. If A predeceases B, under the modern rule, A's heirs are entitled to the use of the land until B dies.

(4) Life estates can be made defeasible.

(5) **Duty to Repair**

    (a) A life tenant has a duty to maintain the property in a reasonable state of repair, ordinary wear and tear excepted. This duty is limited to the extent of the income derived or, if he personally occupies the premises, to the extent of the reasonable rental value of the land.

    (b) A tenant for a term of years also has a duty to maintain the property in a reasonable state of repair, ordinary wear and tear excepted. However, this duty is not limited to the extent of income derived or reasonable rental value discussed above. Further, the lessee's duty is now largely governed by statutes that tend to relieve at least the residential lessee of the duty to repair.

(6) **Mortgages**

    (a) The life tenant has a duty to pay the interest on a mortgage to the extent of profits derived from the property. A tenant for years or a periodic tenant has no common law duty to make mortgage payments. However, commercial leases often require a nonresidential tenant to pay taxes, mortgages, etc., and to make specific repairs.

(7) **Taxes**

    (a) The life tenant must pay all ordinary taxes, to the extent of profits derived from the property. A tenant for years or a periodic tenant has no common law duty to pay property taxes unless:

        1) the lease is "perpetual" or for a long term with an option in the tenant and his successors to renew "forever";

        2) the tenant holds without any obligation to pay rent; or

        3) the tenant has erected improvements on the leased premises for his own benefit.

(8) **Special Assessments**

    (a) The life tenant must pay the full cost of special assessments (apparently to the extent of income derived) if the life of the public improvement is less than the duration of the life tenant's estate. Equitable apportionment is applied for improvements likely to last longer (e.g., curbs and streets). A tenant for years or a periodic tenant has no common law duty to pay carrying charges such as special assessments or insurance premiums.

d. **Non-Freehold Estates**

   (1) **Leasehold Estate**

     (a) A **leasehold estate** is an estate that is limited in duration.

       EXAMPLE: O transfers "to A for a term of 10 years."

     (b) Traditionally, the landlord was said to maintain the fee, subject to the leasehold interest.

     (c) The modern approach provides that the landlord holds a reversion following the leasehold estate.

B. **Future Interests**

  1. **Reversionary Interest**

   a. **Possibility of Reverter**

    (1) A **possibility of reverter** is a future interest in the grantor that follows a determinable estate.

    (2) The creation of a fee simple determinable estate automatically creates the possibility of reverter in the grantor.

    (3) At strict common law, a possibility of reverter could descend through intestacy but could not be devised or transferred *inter vivos*.

    (4) Today, under the modern trend, a possibility of reverter is transferable, devisable, and descendible (it can be transferred by law, will, or intestacy).

    (5) The statute of limitations begins to run on a possibility of reverter as soon as the limitation occurs, because the property automatically reverts to the grantor on the occurrence of the limitation.

    (6) A possibility of reverter is not subject to the Rule Against Perpetuities.

    EXAMPLE: O conveys "to A and her heirs for so long as liquor is not served on the premises." A has a fee simple determinable. O has a possibility of reverter, which becomes possessory automatically if liquor is served. If O then conveys her possibility of reverter to C, C's interest is still defined as a possibility of reverter, even though it is now in a third party.

   b. **Right of Entry**

    (1) A **right of entry** is a future interest in the grantor that follows a fee simple or life estate subject to a condition subsequent.

    (2) The creation of the right of entry requires a grantor to reserve this right in the conveyance either expressly or by necessary implication, where the grantor makes it clear that the estate is to terminate upon the happening of a condition.

    (3) Upon the happening of the event, the property will not automatically revert back to the grantor. The grantor has to exercise the right of entry and affirmatively retake the property.

    (4) At strict common law, a right of entry could descend through intestacy but could not be devised or transferred *inter vivos*.

(5) Today, under modern law, all states agree that a right of entry is descendible, and a majority of states agree that a right of entry is devisable, but the majority rule is that a right of entry is not transferable *inter vivos*.

(6) The statute of limitations does not begin to run against a right of entry until the grantor attempts to exercise the right. However, in some states, the statute of limitations begins to run against a right of entry when the condition occurs.

(7) A right of entry is not subject to the Rule Against Perpetuities.

EXAMPLE: O conveys "to A and his heirs, but if liquor is served on the premises, then O and his heirs may reenter and terminate A's estate." A has a fee simple subject to a condition subsequent, and O has a right of entry. If liquor is served, O must take affirmative steps before A's estate is terminated. If O transfers his right of entry to C, C's interest is still defined as a right of entry, even though it is now in a third party.

EXAMPLE: O conveys "to A; provided, however, that liquor may not be served on the premises." No right of entry has been reserved. Therefore, O cannot take the property back if liquor is served on the premises. The condition subsequent language will be stricken. Therefore, A is left with a fee simple absolute.

c. **Reversion**

(1) A reversion is a future interest retained by the grantor when the grantor transfers less than a fee interest to a third person.

(2) Under the majority rule, a reversion is transferable, devisable, and descendible.

> NOTE ▶ A reversion is not subject to the Rule Against Perpetuities.

EXAMPLE: O conveys "to A for life, then to B for life, then to C for life." The entire fee simple absolute is not accounted for in this transaction. Therefore, following all of these life estates, O has a reversion.

EXAMPLE: O conveys "to A for a term of 10 years." A has an estate for a term of 10 years. O retains a reversion.

EXAMPLE: O conveys "to A for life." O retains a reversion. If O conveys her reversion to C, C's interest is still defined as a reversion, even though it is now in a third party.

EXAMPLE: T devises "Blackacre to A for life." When T dies, A gets a present possessory life estate. T's reversion passes by the terms of his will or to T's heirs by the laws of intestacy if there is no will.

EXAMPLE: T devises Blackacre "to A for life," and T also devises "the rest and residue of my estate to B." When T dies, A gets a present possessory life estate. B gets the residue of T's estate, which includes the reversion to Blackacre.

2. **Executory Interests**

    a. An **executory interest** is a future interest in a third person that cuts short the previous estate before it would have naturally terminated.

        (1) Since a fee estate has the potential to last forever, any interest created in a third party that follows the granting of a fee will always be an executory interest.

        (2) There are two types of executory interests.

            (a) A **shifting executory interest** is an interest that cuts short a prior estate created by the same conveyance. The interest passes from one grantee to another.

            (b) A **springing executory interest** is an interest that follows a gap in possession or divests the estate of the transferor. The interest passes from a grantor to a grantee.

    b. An executory interest is transferable, descendible, and devisable.

    c. An executory interest is subject to the Rule Against Perpetuities.

    EXAMPLE: O conveys "to A, but if liquor is served on the premises, then to B and his heirs." A has a fee simple subject to an executory limitation. B has a shifting executory interest because his interest may cut short A's estate.

    EXAMPLE: O conveys "to A for life, remainder to B and her heirs one month after A's death." A has a life estate. B has a springing executory interest because her interest cannot become presently possessory until one month after the natural termination of A's life estate. O retains a reversion. After A's death, O's reversion becomes possessory. Then, one month after A's death, the fee simple springs out of O to B.

3. **Remainders**

    a. A **remainder** is a future interest created in a third person which is intended to take effect after the natural termination of the preceding estate.

    b. **Contingent Remainders**

        (1) A remainder will be contingent if:

            (a) the takers are unascertained; or

            (b) the interest is subject to a condition precedent and, therefore, does not fall in automatically on the natural termination of the previous estate.

        (2) At strict common law, a contingent remainder could descend and be devised but could not be transferred *inter vivos*.

        (3) Under modern law, a contingent remainder is transferable, descendible, and devisable (except, possibly, when the contingent remainder is in an unascertained person).

        (4) A contingent remainder is subject to the Rule Against Perpetuities.

        EXAMPLE: T devises "to A for life, remainder to A's widow and her heirs." If A is living at the time of creation, whether married or unmarried, A has a life estate and A's widow (if any) has a contingent remainder in fee simple because the taker is not yet ascertained or ascertainable. Therefore, T's estate retains a reversion.

EXAMPLE. O conveys "to A for life, remainder to B and her heirs if B reaches 21." If, at the time of creation, B is already 21, A has a life estate and B has a vested remainder in fee simple. If instead, at the time of creation, B is not yet 21, A has a life estate and B's remainder is contingent because B has not yet fulfilled the condition precedent, which is B reaching 21. Therefore, O retains a reversion.

(5) **Doctrine of Destructibility of Contingent Remainders**

(a) At common law, a contingent remainder in real property is destroyed by any of the following:

1) if it fails to vest by the natural termination of the prior vested estate;

   <u>EXAMPLE</u>: O conveys "to A for life, remainder to B and her heirs if B reaches 21." A has a life estate. If B is not yet 21, B has a contingent remainder (contingent on B reaching 21), and O retains a reversion. Assume that A dies and B is not yet 21. B's contingent remainder cannot fall in naturally at the termination of A's life estate because B has not yet met the condition precedent to vesting. B's contingent remainder is destroyed. Therefore, O's reversion will become possessory.

2) the **doctrine of merger**; or

   a) Merger occurs, and the holder of the present and future interest takes a fee simple absolute, when one party who possesses a present or future interest in the subject realty, by subsequent transactions, obtains all outstanding present and vested estates in that property. Situations in which this may occur include:

      i) by surrender of the present estate to the owner of a future estate;

      ii) by release of a future estate to the owner of a present estate; or

      iii) when all holders of present and future vested interests convey all of these interests to a third party.

      <u>EXAMPLE</u>: O conveys "to A for life, remainder to B if B earns a law degree." A has a life estate. If B has not yet earned a law degree, B has a contingent remainder in fee simple absolute. O retains a reversion. Assume that, one year later, O conveys her reversion to A, and B still has not earned a law degree. A now has both a life estate and a reversion. At common law, A's two

interests merge because they are not separated by a vested estate. A gets a fee simple absolute. B's contingent remainder is destroyed.

EXAMPLE: O conveys "to A for life, remainder to B's first-born daughter." A has a life estate. If B does not yet have a daughter, B's unborn daughter has a contingent remainder. O retains a reversion. Assume that O later devises his reversion to A and that B still does not have a daughter at the time of O's death. At O's death, A receives O's reversion. A also has her life estate. A's two interests merge because they are not separated by a vested estate. A gets a fee simple absolute, and B's first-born daughter's contingent remainder is destroyed.

3) if the holder of the present possessory estate surrenders his interest before the contingent remainder vests.

EXAMPLE: T devises "to A for life, remainder to B's widower." Assume that T's will creates this devise but does not expressly dispose of the reversion. However, T's will leaves the residue of T's estate to A. Assume further that, at the time the will takes effect (when T dies), B is alive and married. At T's death, A has a life estate and a reversion. B's widower has a contingent remainder because a person cannot have a widower until she dies. B's widower's contingent remainder is not destroyed by merger because A's interests were created at the same time and by the same instrument.

EXAMPLE: Assume that one year after T dies, A conveys her life estate and the reversion to C. C gets a life estate and a reversion. The life estate and the reversion merge. C gets a fee simple absolute. B's widower's contingent remainder is destroyed.

(6) Under modern law, many jurisdictions have abolished the rule of destructibility of contingent remainders. In those jurisdictions, if a contingent remainder has not vested at the natural termination of the prior vested estate, the contingent remainder will become an executory interest, subject to the Rule Against Perpetuities.

(7) In jurisdictions that have retained the destructibility rule, it is important to distinguish between contingent remainders, which are destructible, and executory interests, which are not destructible. If a future interest is created such that it may in some case fall in automatically at the natural termination of the previous estate, an irrebuttable presumption will arise, causing the interest to be treated for all purposes as a contingent remainder.

EXAMPLE: O conveys "to A for life, remainder to B and his heirs if B reaches 21." A has a life estate. If B is not yet 21 at the time of creation, B may not be ready to take when A dies. However, B could possibly turn 21 before A dies. Therefore, B's interest is treated as a contingent remainder rather than an executory interest and thus may be destroyed in states in which contingent remainders are still destructible.

EXAMPLE: O conveys "to A for so long as liquor is not served on the premises, but if liquor is served on the premises then to B and her heirs." A has a fee simple subject to an executory limitation. B will take only if A's estate is cut short by the service of liquor on the premises. Thus, B cannot possibly take at the natural termination of A's estate. Therefore, B has a shifting executory interest rather than a contingent remainder.

c. **Vested Remainders**

(1) A **vested remainder** requires its takers to be ascertained or ascertainable at the time that the remainder is created. A vested remainder also must fall in automatically at the natural termination of the previous estate, meaning there can be no conditions precedent to taking.

(2) A vested remainder is transferable, descendible, and devisable.

(3) A fully vested remainder is not subject to the Rule Against Perpetuities. However, a remainder that is vested subject to open is subject to the Rule Against Perpetuities.

EXAMPLE: Testator devises "to A for life, remainder to B and his heirs." A has a life estate. B has a vested remainder in fee simple because the taker is identified, and B's interest falls in automatically at the natural termination of the previous estate (when A dies).

EXAMPLE: O conveys "to A for life, remainder to B for life, remainder to C and her heirs." A has a life estate, B has a vested remainder for life, and C has a vested remainder in fee simple.

(4) **Special Types of Vested Remainders**

(a) A remainder that is **vested subject to open**, sometimes called **vested subject to partial divestment**, is a remainder that:

1) has been made to a class (e.g., "my children"); and

2) has at least one member who is ascertainable and who has satisfied any conditions precedent to vesting, but may have other members join the class later.

EXAMPLE: T devises "to A for life, remainder to A's children and their heirs." Assume that at the time of creation (T's death), A is living and has one child, B. A has a present possessory life estate and B has a vested remainder subject to open, because A could have more children. T retains nothing.

EXAMPLE: Assume further that one year later, a second child, C, is born to A. A has a life estate, B and C together have a vested remainder subject to open, and T retains nothing.

(b) A **vested remainder subject to total divestment** is presently vested but may be terminated on the happening of a future event.

EXAMPLE: O conveys "to A for life, remainder to B for so long as the premises are used for educational purposes." A has a life estate, and B has a vested remainder subject to total divestment. O retains a possibility of reverter.

C. Constructional Rules

1. **Rule in Shelley's Case**

   a. Also known as the rule against remainders in grantee's heirs, the Rule in Shelley's Case arises in grants such as the following: O conveys "to A for life, remainder to the heirs of A."

   b. The requirements for applicability of the Rule in Shelley's Case are:

      (1) A must get a freehold estate (a life estate or a fee tail);

      (2) A's heirs must get a remainder in fee (or in tail);

      (3) the same instrument must create both A's and A's heirs' interests; and

      (4) both estates must be legal or both must be equitable.

   c. If all of these requirements are met:

      (1) A gets both a life estate and a remainder; and

      (2) by merger, A gets a fee simple and thus A's heirs take nothing by virtue of the grant itself.

   d. The Rule in Shelley's Case is a rule of law, which the court must treat as creating an irrebuttable presumption.

   e. The Rule in Shelley's Case has been abolished by statute or judicial decision in most states.

2. **Doctrine of Worthier Title**

   a. Also known as the rule against remainders in grantor's heirs, the Doctrine of Worthier Title arises in grants such as the following: O conveys "to A for life, remainder to the heirs of O."

   b. The requirements for applicability of the Doctrine of Worthier Title are:

      (1) A must receive an estate less than a fee simple, such as a life estate or a term of years;

      (2) O's heirs must receive a remainder (or an executory interest, in the rare case);

      (3) both interests must be created by the same instrument; and

      (4) both interests must be legal or both must be equitable.

   c. The Doctrine of Worthier Title is a rule of construction, not law. The language leaving a remainder to O's heirs creates a rebuttable presumption that O intended to retain that interest in himself as a reversion. This presumption may be rebutted by clear express evidence that O did intend to create a remainder in his heirs. If the presumption is raised but not rebutted, A gets a life estate and O retains a reversion (and thus O's heirs take nothing on their own).

d. Under modern law, the Doctrine of Worthier Title applies to *inter vivos* transfers only (the testamentary branch of the doctrine no longer is applied).

3. **Waste**

a. The possessor of a life estate or a leasehold interest has the right to possess, use, and enjoy the property during the duration of his estate. However, he may not do anything that adversely affects the future interest that follows the life estate. An act that adversely affects the future interest is called **waste**.

b. **Voluntary waste** is the voluntary commission of an act that has more than a trivial injurious effect on or change in the property. Despite the prohibition on voluntary waste, natural resources may be consumed:

   (1) for the repair and maintenance of the property;

   (2) with permission of the grantor; or

   (3) under the open mines doctrine, which applies to both life tenants and tenants for years.

      (a) If the grantor was exploiting the natural resources of the mine, it is presumed that the grantee has the right to continue that exploitation.

c. **Involuntary** or **permissive waste** occurs if the life tenant or leasehold tenant permits the premises to fall into disrepair. Involuntary waste may also occur if the life tenant fails to pay mortgage interest payments, taxes, or the tenant's share of special assessments.

d. **Ameliorative waste** occurs if an act of a life tenant increases the value of the premises by permanently altering it. Traditionally, ameliorative waste was prohibited. However, under modern law, a life tenant is allowed to commit ameliorative waste if:

   (1) the market value of the remainderman's interest is not impaired; and

   (2) either:

      (a) it is permitted by the remainderman; or

      (b) a substantial and permanent change in the neighborhood has deprived the property of a reasonable current value.

e. A holder of a reversion has standing to sue for past or future waste. A vested remainderman also has standing to sue for past or future waste. However, a contingent remainderman has standing to sue to prevent future waste but not for damages for past waste.

4. **Restraints on Alienation**

a. A **restraint on alienation** is a condition placed on the ownership of real property that restricts the free conveyance of that property.

   (1) Under a disabling restraint, A may not convey. Disabling restraints are always void.

(2) Under a forfeiture restraint, A loses his estate if he attempts to convey. Forfeiture restraints are valid for life estates and future interests, but are not enforceable for fee simple estates.

(3) Under a promissory restraint, A promises not to convey. Promissory restraints are valid for life estates and future interests, but are not enforceable for fee simple estates. The breach of a promissory restraint does not void the conveyance; it just makes the promisor liable for breach of contract damages.

(4) Partial restraints may be enforced, with the court weighing the duration and number of persons excluded.

(5) Some courts will uphold a reasonable restraint in a commercial transaction on the theory that it appears in an agreement of the parties, is the product of their bargaining, and presumably serves a useful purpose in facilitating the parties' objectives.

5. **Rule of Convenience**

a. Under the Rule of Convenience, a class closes when a member of the class is entitled to distribution.

b. The Rule of Convenience applies to the following classes: "children," "grandchildren," "brothers," "sisters," "nephews," "nieces," "cousins," "issue," "descendants," or "family" of a designated person.

(1) If the class is already closed at the time the gift takes effect (i.e., the time of conveyance for an *inter vivos* gift or time of testator's death for a will), all members of the class at that moment will take. However, any individual later conceived or born will not be a member of the class and will not share in the estate.

(2) If, at the time the gift takes effect, the class has members entitled to take immediately but the class has not previously closed, all members of the class conceived at the time the gift is made will be included and may take; however, the class will close to the exclusion of afterborn children, who will not share in it.

(3) If the class has no members at the time the gift is made, all members of the class, whenever born, will be included and may take. The class stays open until all possible members are born.

EXAMPLE: T devises "to the children of A." If A is dead at the time of T's death, the class of A's children will be closed; therefore, all of A's children will be included and will take. If A is alive at the time of T's death and has children at that time, the children born at the time of T's death are entitled to immediate distribution. Therefore, the class will close, and all of those children will be included and may take. However, afterborn children will be excluded. If A is alive at T's death but does not have children at that time, no one is entitled to immediate distribution. Therefore, the class should remain open. All of A's children, whenever born, will be included and should be able to take. Some authorities suggest that the first-born child takes the entire estate on her birth, subject to partial divestment by the birth of later children; however, the case law on this point is sparse.

6. **Postponed Gift to a Class (with No Condition Precedent)**

   a. If the class is already closed at the time the postponement ends (e.g., at the end of a present possessory life estate), all members of the class will be included and will take.

   b. If the class has members but is not yet closed at the time the postponement ends, all members of the class conceived at the time the postponement ends will be included and may take. However, the class will close to the exclusion of afterborn children, who may not take.

   c. If the class has no members at the time the postponement ends, all members of the class, whenever born, will be included and may take.

   EXAMPLE: T devises "to A for life, remainder to the children of B." If B is dead at the time of T's death, the class of B's children will be closed; therefore, all of B's children will be included and may take. If B dies after T but before A, the class of B's children will also be closed; therefore, all of B's children will be included and may take. If B is alive at the time of A's death and B has children at that time, all children then born are included and are entitled to distribution at A's death. However, the class will close at that time to the exclusion of afterborn children. If B is alive at A's death but does not have children at that time, no child is then entitled to immediate distribution. The class should remain open. Therefore, all of B's children, whenever born, should be included and should be able to take. Again, some authorities suggest that the first-born child takes the entire estate on her birth, subject to partial divestment by the birth of later children.

7. **Immediate Gift to a Class Coupled with a Condition Precedent**

   a. An immediate gift to a class may be coupled with a condition precedent. In such a case, the class closes when the first member of the class satisfies the condition. All then-born members of the class are included and may take if and when they satisfy the condition. However, afterborn children will be excluded.

   EXAMPLE: O conveys "to B's children who reach 21." If B is dead at the time the conveyance is made, the class of B's children will be closed. Therefore, all of B's children will be included and may take if and when they reach 21. If B is alive at the time the conveyance is made, and B has a child who has reached 21, the class will close because that child is entitled to immediate distribution. All of B's then-born children will be included and may take if and when they reach 21; however, all afterborn children will be excluded. If B is alive at the time the conveyance is made, and B has one child who is, say, 15, the class will remain open. The class will close if and when a child of B reaches 21. All children of B born at the time the first child reaches 21 will be included and may take if and when they reach 21. All children born after the first child reaches 21 are excluded. If B is alive at the time the conveyance is made, and B has no children, the class will remain open. The class will close if and when a child of B reaches 21. All children of B born at the time the first child reaches 21 will be included and may take if and when they reach 21. All children born after the first child reaches 21 are excluded.

8. **Gift to a Class with a Combination of Postponements**

   a. A gift to a class may be made with a combination of postponements combined with a condition precedent. In such a case, the postponement is deemed to end, and the class closes when the last condition is satisfied. All members of the class born before the class closes are included, and they may take if and when they satisfy the condition. However, all afterborn persons are excluded.

   EXAMPLE: O conveys "to A for life, remainder to B's children who reach 21." If B is dead at the time the conveyance is made, the class of B's children will be closed. Therefore, all of B's children will be included and may take if and when they reach 21. If B is alive when the conveyance is made but dies before A, the class of B's children also will be closed. Therefore, all of B's children will be included and may take if and when they reach 21. If B is alive at the time of A's death and B has a child who is 21, that child is entitled to distribution at A's death. Therefore, the class will close at that time. All children born before A's death will be included and may take if and when they reach 21. However, children born after the class closes will be excluded. If B is alive at A's death and either has no children or has children, none of whom has reached 21, no child is entitled to distribution at A's death (which is the first postponement). Therefore, the class remains open until a child of B reaches 21 (which is the second postponement). When a child of B reaches 21, the class closes. All children conceived at the time a child of B reaches 21 will be included and may take if and when they reach 21. However, children born after the class closes are excluded.

9. **Rule Against Perpetuities**

   a. The common law Rule Against Perpetuities provides that "[n]o interest is good unless it must vest, if at all, not later than 21 years after some life-in-being at the creation of the interest."

   b. To determine whether an interest violates the common law Rule Against Perpetuities, the following analysis should be applied:

   (1) Identify the interests subject to the Rule Against Perpetuities.

       (a) Interests which are not subject to the Rule Against Perpetuities include:

           1) present possessory estates;

           2) charitable trusts;

           3) resulting trusts; and

           4) interests that are fully vested at the time of creation. The following interests are fully vested:

              a) reversionary interests; and

          b)   completely vested remainders.

    (b)   Interests which are subject to the Rule Against Perpetuities include:

        1)   options to purchase land not incident to a lease;

        2)   powers of appointment;

        3)   rights of first refusal; and

        4)   interests that are not fully vested at the time of creation, including:

           a)   remainders that are subject to open;

           b)   contingent remainders; and

           c)   executory interests.

(2)   Identify the life or lives in being, express or implied by the instrument creating interests. There is no limit on the number of lives in being, as long as they may be identified by or through the creating document. A life-in-being may, but need not, receive an interest in the document that creates the interest. However, to serve as a measuring life, a life-in-being must in some way be connected to the vesting of the interest under scrutiny.

    (a)   An express life-in-being is a person named in the document that creates the interests under scrutiny. In the grant "O conveys to A for life," O and A are express lives in being.

    (b)   An implied life-in-being is a person who is not named in, but may be implied from, the document that creates the interests under scrutiny. In the devise "to my grandchildren," the testator's children are implied lives in being.

    (c)   A class cannot be used as measuring lives unless the class is closed at the time the gifts are created.

(3)   Determine whether the interest will vest or fail within 21 years of the life or lives. Under the common law Rule Against Perpetuities, interests are analyzed under the "might have been" rule. Under the "might have been" rule, an interest violates the Rule Against Perpetuities if there is any chance, however remote, that the interest might vest more than 21 years after a life-in-being.

    (a)   Under the might-have-been rule, interests are scrutinized at the time of creation. The time of creation is the date that the creating instrument takes effect. If the interests under scrutiny are created in a deed, the time of creation is the date that the deed is delivered. If the interests under scrutiny are created in a will, the time of creation is the date of the testator's death.

(4)   Treat the part of the gift that violated the Rule Against Perpetuities as void, leaving the remainder of the gift intact.

    EXAMPLE: O conveys "to A for so long as liquor is not served on the premises, but if liquor is served, then to B." Because the vesting of the future interest is unlimited in time, it is not certain to vest or fail within 21 years of any life-in-being. Therefore, the shifting executory interest in B is void. A is left with a fee simple determinable, and O has a possibility of reverter.

EXAMPLE: O conveys "to A, but if liquor is served, then to B." Again, the shifting executory interest in B is void. However, in this case, A is left with a fee simple. Therefore, O retains nothing, and A is left with a fee simple absolute.

c. **Applications**

(1) **Fertile Octogenarian**

(a) Imagine that O conveys "to A for life, remainder to A's children for life, remainder to A's grandchildren."

(b) A's life estate is presently possessory, and therefore is not subject to the Rule Against Perpetuities. The remainder for life in A's children is either contingent or subject to open because A is conclusively presumed to be capable of having more children, and therefore is subject to the Rule Against Perpetuities. The remainder in A's grandchildren is either contingent or subject to open, and therefore is subject to the Rule Against Perpetuities.

(c) O and A are express lives-in-being. Even if children or grandchildren are already born, these persons are members of an open class and therefore cannot serve as lives-in-being. Therefore, O and A are the only possible measuring lives.

(d) A's children will take (or not take) at A's death; hence, their interest is valid. However, A's grandchildren may well take more than 21 years after O and A die. Thus, their interest violates the Rule Against Perpetuities.

(e) A retains her life estate. A's children will take for life after A dies. Because the interest in A's grandchildren is void, O retains a reversion that will become possessory after A's children die.

(2) **Unborn Widow**

(a) Imagine that O conveys "to A for life, remainder to A's widow for life, remainder to A's children living at the death of A's widow."

(b) A's life estate is presently possessory, and therefore is not subject to the Rule Against Perpetuities. The remainder for life in A's widow is contingent because there cannot be a widow of a living person, and therefore is subject to the Rule Against Perpetuities. The remainder in A's children living at the death of A's widow is contingent because there is a condition precedent to vesting, and therefore is subject to the Rule Against Perpetuities.

(c) O and A are express lives-in-being. A's widow is not a life-in-being because she has not yet been identified. A's children, even if some are already born, may not be lives-in-being because their class is open. Therefore, O and A are the only possible measuring lives.

(d) A's widow will take (or not take) at A's death; hence, her interest is valid. However, A's children may well take more than 21 years after O and A die. Thus, their interest violates the Rule Against Perpetuities.

(e) A retains his life estate. A's widow will take for life after A dies if she survives A. Because the interest in A's children is void, O retains a reversion, which will fall in when A's widow dies.

(3) **Charity-to-Charity Rule**

(a) Imagine that O conveys "to A Charity for so long as liquor is not served on the premises, but if liquor is served on the premises, then to B Charity."

(b) As illustrated above, a shifting executory interest in fee will violate the Rule Against Perpetuities, because an heir of A could violate the condition more than 21 years after the death of O, A, and B, causing the property to shift to B.

1) However, for policy public reasons, if both A and B are charities, the shifting executory interest in B Charity will be deemed to be valid under the Rule Against Perpetuities.

(4) **Rule of Convenience**

(a) Imagine that O conveys "to such of A's children as shall reach the age of 25."

1) Assume A is living at the time of this grant and has two children: B, age 26; and C, age 24. Because she is 26, B is entitled to immediate distribution. As a result, the Rule of Convenience will operate to close the class of A's children immediately. All children born as of the date the class closes (B and C) will be allowed to take upon reaching the age of 25. However, no child born after the date the class closes may take, even if he should eventually reach the age of 25.

(b) Assume that A is alive at the testator's death and has three children: B, age 24; C, age 23; and D, age 19.

1) Because no child of A has reached 25, A's children have a springing executory interest, which is subject to the Rule Against Perpetuities.

2) O and A are express lives-in-being. The class of A's children cannot be measuring lives because the class remains open; A is alive, and no child of A is entitled to immediate distribution because no child of A has reached the age of 25.

3) It is possible that a child of A could reach 25 more than 21 years after the deaths of O and A. Therefore, the springing executory interest in the children of A violates the Rule Against Perpetuities.

4) O is left with a fee simple absolute.

(5) **Uniform Statutory Rule Against Perpetuities**

(a) Some states have adopted uniform statutory revisions of the Rule Against Perpetuities ("USRAP"). Under the USRAP, a nonvested interest in real or personal property is invalid unless:

1) it satisfies the common law Rule Against Perpetuities; or

2) it vests or terminates within 90 years of its creation (this is known as the "**wait and see**" **test**). Under the wait-and-see branch of the USRAP, the court waits until the end of the prescribed period to determine whether the interest actually vested or failed within the prescribed period.

> <u>EXAMPLE:</u> In 1990, O conveys "to A for life, remainder to A's children for life, remainder to A's grandchildren." Assume that, at the time the conveyance is made, A is 55 and has one child, B, who is 16. In 1995, B marries. In 2001, C is born to B. A dies in 2004 at the age of 69. B dies in 2040 at the age of 66. C may take the property in 2040. The remainder to A's grandchildren would be void under the common law Rule Against Perpetuities; however, because C actually takes within 90 years of the conveyance, her interest is valid under the USRAP.

10. **Powers of Appointment**

a. A **general power of appointment** gives the holder of the power the right to appoint the property to anyone, including the holder of the power. Thus, a general power of appointment is considered to be equivalent to ownership of the property. To be valid under the Rule Against Perpetuities, a general power of appointment must be exercisable, but not necessarily exercised, during the period allowed by the Rule Against Perpetuities.

b. A **special power of appointment** gives the holder the right to appoint the property to a limited class of persons. To be valid under the Rule Against Perpetuities, a special power of appointment must be exercised in a manner that causes the interest in property thereby created to vest within the period of the Rule Against Perpetuities.

D. **Concurrent Estates**

1. A concurrent estate exists when two or more persons share concurrently an interest in real property. A concurrent owner is called a co-tenant.

2. **Tenancy in Common**

a. Tenancy in common is a form of concurrent ownership where each co-tenant owns an undivided interest in the whole of the property with no right of survivorship.

b. Tenancy in common is now the presumed form of co-tenancy. Therefore, no special words are required to create a tenancy in common.

EXAMPLE: O conveys "to A and B." A and B hold a fee simple absolute as tenants in common.

c. Tenancy in common requires unity of possession only. **Unity of possession** means that each tenant in common has the right to possess the whole of the property.

d. A tenant in common may transfer his interest *inter vivos*:

   (1) voluntarily, through a conveyance, lease, mortgage, or other transfer of a present possessory or future property interest; or

   (2) involuntarily, through a foreclosure on a mortgage of the tenant's interest or an execution of a judgment creditor's lien on the tenant's interest in the property.

e. A tenant in common may devise his interest, and the interest of a tenant in common may also descend by intestacy.

3. **Joint Tenancy**

   a. Joint tenancy is a form of concurrent ownership where each co-tenant owns an undivided interest in the whole of the property and has a right of survivorship.

   b. Traditionally, the following words are required to create a joint tenancy: "to A and B as joint tenants and not as tenants in common, with full right of survivorship."

   c. A joint tenancy requires the following four unities:

      (1) joint tenants must take at the same time (**unity of time**);

      (2) joint tenants must take by the same instrument (**unity of title**);

      (3) joint tenants must take equal shares of the same type (e.g., each joint tenant takes a legal fee simple) (**unity of interest**); and

      (4) each joint tenant has the right to possess the whole (**unity of possession**).

   d. Under the traditional rule, a sole owner of property cannot create a joint tenancy between himself and another person by conveying a joint interest directly to the other person. Instead, the owner must convey the property to a straw man, who then conveys the property back to the owner and the other person as joint tenants.

      (1) Some jurisdictions now do not require the unities of time and title. Under this approach, a straw man no longer is required to create a joint tenancy. Instead, a sole owner may create joint tenancy between himself and another person by conveying a joint interest directly to the other person.

   e. Each joint tenant has a right of survivorship. At the death of one joint tenant, the interest of the surviving joint tenant "grows" and absorbs the interest of the deceased joint tenant.

   EXAMPLE: O conveys Blackacre "to A and B as joint tenants and not as tenants in common, with full right of survivorship." Subsequently, A dies, leaving C as her sole heir. B's right of survivorship takes over, and B becomes the sole owner of Blackacre. C takes no interest.

f. A joint tenant may transfer his interest voluntarily or involuntarily, thereby severing the joint tenancy. However, the right of survivorship prevents a predeceasing joint tenant from devising his interest. In addition, the interest of the predeceasing joint tenant may not descend by intestacy.

g. A joint tenancy is severed if one joint tenant conveys his interest voluntarily or involuntarily. An involuntary conveyance occurs if a creditor forces a sale of a joint tenant's interest to satisfy the debt owed to the creditor by the joint tenant. If a joint tenancy is severed, the unities of time and title are destroyed. Therefore, a tenancy in common is created between the other tenant and the conveyee.

> **EXAMPLE:** O conveys Blackacre "to A and B as joint tenants and not as tenants in common, with full right of survivorship." Subsequently, A conveys her interest in Blackacre to C. The conveyance to C breaks the unities of time and title because C took by a different instrument and time from B. Therefore, B and C hold Blackacre as tenants in common.

h. If both joint tenants join in a mortgage of the subject property, the mortgage will not affect the joint tenancy. However, if only one of the joint tenants mortgages his interest, the effect of the mortgage on the joint tenancy will depend on whether the jurisdiction follows the title theory or the lien theory of mortgages.

   (1) In a **title theory** state, the execution of a mortgage by one joint tenant causes the legal interest of that co-tenant to be transferred to the mortgagee. Thus, the mortgage severs the joint tenancy because the unities have been destroyed. Most jurisdictions no longer follow the title theory.

   (2) In a **lien theory** state, the mortgagee only receives a lien on the property. Therefore, no severance occurs when the mortgage is made because the unities remain intact. However, in a lien theory state, foreclosure will sever the joint tenancy. Most jurisdictions now follow the lien theory.

> NOTE ▸ The courts are split as to whether a mortgage survives if the mortgagor/joint tenant dies before the non-mortgaging joint tenant.

> NOTE ▸ Jurisdictions are split on whether a lease severs a joint tenancy.

4. **Tenancy by the Entirety**

   a. A tenancy by the entirety is a form of concurrent ownership reserved for married couples, which gives each spouse an undivided interest in the whole of the property and a right of survivorship.

   b. Traditionally, to create a tenancy by the entirety, the following words were required: "to H and W as tenants by the entirety and not as joint tenants or tenants in common, with full right of survivorship."

   c. Today, most states have enacted statutes creating a presumption of tenancy by the entirety if a conveyance is made to a husband and wife, even if they are not identified as husband and wife in the deed.

d.   In the states that recognize tenancy by the entirety, an attempted conveyance by either spouse is wholly void.

5.   **Rights and Duties of Co-Tenants**

a.   Each co-tenant is entitled to possess the whole property.

b.   Wrongful ouster occurs when one co-tenant wrongfully excludes another co-tenant from possession of the whole or any part of the jointly held property.

c.   An out-of-possession co-tenant has the right to share in rents and net profits derived by another co-tenant from third parties, less operating expenses such as taxes, mortgages, interest, and management fees. However, an out-of-possession co-tenant does not have the right to demand rent from a co-tenant who is in actual possession of the premises, unless the co-tenant in possession has effected a wrongful ouster or has exploited the property in a manner resulting in permanent depreciation.

d.   The common law, which is still followed in some states, does not allow a co-tenant to seek contribution from another co-tenant for repairs performed on the property.

e.   However, under the modern trend, contribution may be compelled for necessary repairs if the repairs were requested by the repairing tenant and refused by the other(s).

f.   In a partition suit or an accounting suit, the costs of repairs may be credited in favor of a co-tenant who repairs.

g.   A co-tenant has no right to seek a contribution or setoff for improvements made to the premises, unless the improvements generate increased rents or profits. In that case, costs of improvements are recoverable only in a partition suit.

h.   A co-tenant who pays a mortgage or tax may seek contribution or may recover in an accounting or partition suit. However, there is no separate action to compel contribution. A co-tenant in sole possession will receive reimbursement only to the extent that his payment exceeds the market value of the property.

i.   Each co-tenant has the right to seek partition of the property.

(1)   **Voluntary partition** is usually accomplished by an exchange of mutual deeds among co-tenants or by sale of the property and division of the proceeds.

(2)   **Involuntary** (judicial) **partition** is accomplished by court action, usually at the instance of one, but not all, of the co-tenants. Involuntary partition may be either in-kind (physical division) or by sale. Traditionally, physical partition has been preferred, unless a physical partition would be impractical and the interests of the parties would be better served by a sale and division of the proceeds.

(3)   When partition cannot produce equal shares, the party receiving the larger portion must make a cash payment to the other party.

II. COMPETING CLAIMANTS

A. **Adverse Possession**
   1. Adverse possession requires proof of possession that is all of the following:
      a. open, visible, and notorious;
      b. actual;
         (1) An adverse possessor is required to possess the premises for the requisite time period. Actual possession gives notice to the world at large and the property owner in particular that someone is possessing the premises. A person **actually possesses** property when he is on the premises physically. A person may also possess the premises constructively. **Constructive adverse possession** requires color of title (usually a defective deed) and actual possession of at least a significant part of the premises. If those elements are satisfied, the possessor will constructively possess the whole property as described in deed. However, there are certain exceptions to the constructive possession rule:
            (a) if land is divided into two or more distinctive lots, constructive possession will extend only to the lot that the possessor actually occupies; and
            (b) if a third person is in possession of part of the premises, constructive possession will not extend to the portion the third party possesses.

> NOTE ▶ Many courts require some reasonable relationship between the area actually possessed and the additional area alleged to be constructively possessed.

      c. exclusive;
      d. hostile and under a claim of title or right; and
         (1) To acquire title by adverse possession, a person must possess the premises in a "hostile" manner. In this context, a person possesses **hostilely** if he holds the premises in a manner that is inconsistent with the rights of the owner.
            (a) Under the majority rule, hostility is judged objectively, which means that the possessor's state of mind is irrelevant. The element is satisfied if the possessor intends to be on the premises, regardless of whether the possessor knows that the premises are owned by someone else.
            (b) In a minority of jurisdictions, the possessor must act in good faith, which means that the possessor must believe the land is his.
            (c) A few courts require bad faith, which means that the possessor must show that he knows that the land is not his but intends to claim it nonetheless.

NOTE ▶ Adverse possession questions often involve mistaken boundaries. A typical example involves a building on one parcel of land that encroaches slightly on the adjoining parcel, often without the knowledge of the owner of the adjoining parcel. Two standards have been developed to judge those cases. Under the **objective majority** ("Maine") **view** for mistaken boundaries, possession is hostile so long as the possessor intends to claim the land as his own, even if he is unsure as to the location of the boundary. Under the **subjective minority** ("Connecticut") **view** for mistaken boundaries, the possessor must actually know that he has crossed over the boundary.

NOTE ▶ Boundary disputes may also be determined by methods other than adverse possession. An oral agreement to settle a boundary dispute is enforceable if the parties subsequently accept the line for a long period of time. Long acquiescence (perhaps for a period shorter than the statute of limitations) may also be used as evidence of an agreement between the parties to fix the boundary line. In addition, if one party makes a representation through words or acts to the other concerning the location of a common boundary, and the other party changes position in reliance on that representation, the first party may be estopped from denying the validity of his representation.

   e. continuous for the statutory period.

     (1) To acquire title by adverse possession, the possessor must show that he has possessed the property continuously for the statutory period. In some cases, a possessor may satisfy this element even if he has not been on the premises every day during the statutory period. Seasonal use may suffice if that use constitutes the best use of the property.

       EXAMPLE: The annual summer use of an unheated cabin in the north woods.

     (2) The requisite time period for adverse possession is established by statute. In many states, the common law period of 20 years has been supplanted by a shorter statutory period, which is often five, seven, or 10 years.

     (3) If an adverse possessor has not been in possession for the full statutory period, he may still meet the time period by **tacking** his possession onto possession by a previous adverse possessor. Tacking is allowed if the adverse possessor and his predecessor are in privity of estate. **Privity of estate** requires an intentional transfer of possession from one person to the next. An adverse possessor may not tack his possession onto that of a previous person if the adverse possessor dispossesses the previous possessor. If the ownership of the property changes hands during the period of adverse possession, the adverse possession continues to run uninterrupted against the subsequent owner if the two owners are in privity of estate.

EXAMPLE: In 2000, A adversely enters onto Blackacre, which is owned by O. In 2001, O conveys Blackacre to B for life, remainder to C. In 2008, B dies without ever having entered Blackacre. The jurisdiction has a five-year statute of limitations for adverse possession claims. C now seeks to quiet title against A. A entered against O before O devised to B for life, remainder to C. Therefore, the statute of limitations continued to run against both B and C. Under the five-year statute of limitations, the time period ran out in 2005; as a result, A will prevail over C.

(4) The running of a statute of limitations may be tolled in certain circumstances. **Tolling** means that the statute will not run for a period of time. For tolling to occur, a disability must be in existence at the time the adverse possessor enters. **Disability** typically includes nonage, legal incompetence, and imprisonment. Most states extend the time to bring an action to a certain period after the disability has been removed (e.g., 10 years).

EXAMPLE: In 1999, O, the owner of Blackacre, is adjudicated legally incompetent. In 2000, A enters adversely on land owned by O. In 2003, O dies without regaining legal competence; however, O leaves a valid will that devises her entire estate to B, who is under no disability at the time. The jurisdiction has a statute of limitations for adverse possession, which provides that, in the case of disability, the statutory period expires seven years after the adverse possessor enters or 10 years after the owner's disability is removed, whichever date is later. B sues to quiet title to Blackacre in 2008. The statute is tolled in this case because O was under a disability at the time that A entered the premises. O's disability was removed in 2003, when O died. The statute gives B, as the successor owner (who is in privity of estate with O through O's will), 10 years after the removal of O's disability, which means the statute would run out against B in 2013. Therefore, B will prevail over A in B's 2008 quiet title suit.

B. **Real Property Contracts**
  1. **Statute of Frauds**
     a. The Statute of Frauds requires a writing for a transfer of an interest in real property. The writing must be signed by the party to be charged and must include the following essential terms:
        (1) description of the property;
        (2) description of the parties;
        (3) price; and
        (4) any conditions of price or payment if agreed on.
     b. **Exceptions to the Statute of Frauds**
        (1) The **doctrine of part performance** may be used to enforce an otherwise invalid oral contract of sale, provided the acts of part performance unequivocally prove the existence of the contract.

To satisfy this doctrine, a showing of at least two of the following three facts must be made:

    (a) payment of all or part of the purchase price;

    (b) taking of possession; and

    (c) making substantial improvements.

(2) Equitable and, under the modern trend, promissory estoppel may also be used to prove an oral contract for the sale of land.

    (a) **Equitable estoppel** is based on an act or a representation.

    (b) **Promissory estoppel** is based on a promise.

2. Equitable Conversion

a. A purchaser becomes an equitable owner of title at the time of the execution of a binding contract.

    (1) Under the common law, the risk of loss is on the buyer on execution of a binding contract for the sale of real property. The common law rule is the majority rule.

    EXAMPLE: A house burns down after the contract is signed but before the deed is signed; the purchaser must pay the purchase price.

    (2) Under the Uniform Vendor and Purchaser Risk Act, the risk of loss is placed on the seller unless the legal title or possession of the property has passed to the buyer. The rule of the Uniform Vendor and Purchase Risk Act is the minority rule.

3. Marketable Title

a. All contracts for the sale of real property include an implied promise to convey marketable title. **Marketable title** is title that is reasonably free from doubt in both fact and law. Title is not reasonably free from doubt if it contains any of the following defects:

    (1) defects in the chain of title, such as:

        (a) adverse possession;

            1) Traditionally, title acquired by adverse possession is unmarketable.

            2) However, recent cases (though still the minority view) suggest that title acquired by adverse possession may be marketable if:

                a) the possession has been for a very long time;

                b) the risk that the record owner will sue is remote; and

                c) the probability of the record owner's success is minimal.

        (b) the defective execution of a deed; or

        (c) significant variation of the description of land from one deed to the next;

    (2) encumbrances;

        (a) For the purposes of marketable title, an **encumbrance** is a right or interest that another person has in real property that diminishes the value of the property but is consistent with the conveyance of a fee interest in the property.

    (b) In this context, encumbrances include:

        1)   mortgages;

        2)   liens;

        3)   easements; and

           a) An easement that reduces the value of the property (e.g., the burden of a right-of-way) renders title unmarketable. However, an easement that benefits the burdened estate, such as the installation of utilities, and which is visible or known to the buyer, does not render title unmarketable.

        4)   covenants and servitudes.

    (c) An encumbrance excepted in the contract may not serve as the basis for a finding that title is unmarketable.

        1)   A seller may satisfy a mortgage or lien at closing with the proceeds of the sale. If the purchase price is sufficient and satisfaction occurs simultaneously with the transfer of the land, the buyer may not complain because closing will result in marketable title.

  (3) encroachments; or

    (a) A significant encroachment renders title unmarketable.

    (b) In contrast, a slight encumbrance, such as a boundary overlap of several inches only, will not render title unmarketable.

    (c) An encroachment does not render title unmarketable if the owner says he will not rely on the encroachment as a basis for suit.

  (4) zoning restrictions.

    (a) The existence of a zoning restriction does not make title unmarketable.

    (b) However, a zoning violation may render title unmarketable.

  b. Physical defects in the property, such as termites, do not render title unmarketable.

NOTE If title is unmarketable, the purchaser may get: (1) rescission; (2) money damages for breach of contract; or (3) specific performance with an abatement of the purchase price.

4. **Duty to Disclose Defects**

  a. A seller of a residential home has a duty to disclose to the buyer material latent defects known to the seller but not readily observable and not known to the buyer.

    (1) Generally, the duty applies only to commercial builders and developers of new residential homes.

      (a) Some states extend the duty to all sellers.

(b) Real estate agents and brokers may also be included in some jurisdictions.

(2) The duty to disclose defects applies to new homes. However, some states extend the duty to used homes.

(a) In no state is the duty extended to commercial property.

b. **Material** is often limited to defects that affect the health and safety of the occupants. However, some states define material to include defects that affect value as well as health and safety.

(1) In some states, materiality is judged by an objective standard, which asks whether a reasonable person would attach importance to the defect in determining whether to purchase the home.

(2) In other states, materiality is judged by a subjective standard, which asks whether the defect actually affected the value or desirability of the property to the buyer.

c. At a minimum, **defect** means a physical defect on the premises.

(1) A few jurisdictions extend the duty to physical defects both on and off the premises (e.g., nearby environmental hazards).

(2) Some states also extend the duty to physical and nonphysical defects (e.g., noise from neighbors).

5. **Implied Warranty of Quality**

a. Most jurisdictions recognize an **implied warranty of quality**, sometimes called an implied warranty of workmanlike quality, an implied warranty of habitability, an implied warranty of fitness, or an implied warranty of suitability.

b. The implied warranty of quality generally applies to the sale of new or remodeled homes.

(1) The implied warranty of quality does not extend to commercial structures.

(2) The implied warranty is imposed on contractors, developers, and other commercial vendors of real property. The warranty covers significant latent defects caused by the defendant's poor workmanship. The defects must be discovered within a "reasonable time" of construction or remodeling.

(a) The jurisdictions are split on whether the implied warranty of quality extends to subsequent purchasers, i.e., purchasers who are not in privity of contract with the builder or remodeler. The jurisdictions are also split on whether economic loss may be recovered for breach of the implied warranty of quality.

c. Most jurisdictions permit the enforcement of an unambiguous disclaimer of the implied warranty of quality. However, some jurisdictions do not give effect to a general disclaimer (e.g., "as is") for residential premises.

d. In some jurisdictions, the statute of limitations begins to run when construction is completed. In other jurisdictions, the statute of limitations begins to run when the buyer to whom the warranty was first made takes possession of the premises, even if the buyer does not know of the breach. In other jurisdictions, the statute of limitations does not begin to run until the purchaser discovers or should have discovered the breach.

THEORY	DEFINITION	TYPE OF STRUCTURE	PARTY BOUND	TYPE OF DEFECT
Marketable Title	Title must be reasonably free and clear from doubt at closing.	Residential and commercial property.	Any seller.	Defects in title, including chain-of-title defects, encumbrances, encroachments, and zoning violations.
Duty to Disclose	Seller of residential home must disclose to buyer material latent defects known to seller but not to buyer.	• New homes. • New and used homes.	• Commercial builders and developers. • All sellers. • All brokers.	• Physical defects affecting health and safety. • Physical defects affecting health, safety, and value. • Physical and nonphysical defects.
Implied Warranty of Quality	Homes must be built and remodeled with workmanlike quality.	New and remodeled homes.	Contractors, developers, and other commercial vendors.	Significant latent defects caused by the defendant's poor workmanship.

• Denotes jurisdictional variations

C. Remedies for Breach of a Contract to Sell Real Property

1. Seller's Remedies for Buyer's Breach

a. Remedies at Law

(1) Traditionally, if the buyer breaches a contract for the sale of real property, the seller is entitled to **expectation damages**, measured by the difference between the contract price and the market price at the time of the breach. To compensate the seller in a falling market, some courts now measure expectation damages based on the difference between the contract price and the resale price.

(2) The seller may also recover **foreseeable consequential damages**, such as mortgage interest payments that the seller is required to make after the buyer's breach.

(3) The seller may recover **reasonable reliance damages**, such as repairs and the cost of inspections.

(4) Traditionally, if the buyer breaches, the seller may elect to retain the entire amount of the down payment, even in the absence of a liquidated damages provision.

    (a) Most courts now restrict the traditional rule to a down payment that equals 10% or less of the purchase price.

(b) The modern approach requires the seller to return to the buyer the amount by which the down payment exceeds the damages caused by the buyer's breach.

(5) A contract for the sale of real property may include a **liquidated damages** clause, which states that the seller may retain the entire amount of the down payment if the buyer breaches. If the contract does contain a liquidated damages clause, most courts permit the seller to retain the down payment if the clause is found to be reasonable. A liquidated damage clause is **reasonable**, and therefore is enforceable, if:

(a) the injury caused by the breach is one that is difficult or incapable of accurate estimation (traditionally judged at the time the contract was made); and

(b) the liquidated damages are a reasonable forecast of the harm caused by the breach.

NOTE ▶ Traditionally, the reasonableness of the forecast was judged at the time of the contract. Under the Second Restatement of Contracts, the reasonableness of the forecast may be judged at the time the contract was made (**anticipated harm**) or by the loss actually caused (**actual harm**).

(6) The seller may recover punitive damages if the buyer's breach was willful.

b. **Remedies in Equity**

(1) If the buyer breaches, the seller may elect to seek rescission of the contract.

(2) Traditionally, mutuality of remedy was required. Under this rule, because the buyer is entitled to specific performance, the seller is also entitled to specific performance. However, as mutuality of remedy has fallen out of favor, some courts have begun to question the general availability of specific performance for sellers.

(a) Some courts have now declined to classify a condominium unit as unique realty. Those courts refuse to grant a seller's request for specific performance.

2. **Buyer's Remedies for Seller's Breach of Contract**

a. **Remedies at Law**

(1) Traditionally, if the seller breaches a contract for the sale of real property, the buyer may recover **expectation damages**, measured by the difference between the market price at the time of the breach and the contract price. To compensate the buyer in a rising market, some courts now measure expectation damages based on the difference between the resale price and the contract price. The buyer may also recover foreseeable consequential damages, such as lost profits.

(2) The buyer may recover reasonable **reliance damages**, such as the cost of inspections.

(3) If the seller breaches a contract for the sale of real property, the buyer may seek **restitution of the down payment**.

    (a) Under the English rule, if the seller fails to deliver marketable title, the buyer may seek restitution of his down payment, plus interest and reasonable expenses incurred in investigating title. However, under the English rule, the buyer may not receive expectation damages that exceed the down payment amount unless the seller acted in bad faith or assumed the risk of failing to obtain marketable title. A slight minority of jurisdictions follow the English rule.

    (b) Under the American rule, if the seller fails to deliver marketable title, the buyer is not restricted to restitution of his down payment. Rather, the buyer may recover expectation damages plus reasonably foreseeable consequential damages. A majority of jurisdictions follow the American rule.

(4) The buyer may recover **punitive damages** if the seller's breach is willful.

b. **Remedies in Equity**

(1) If the seller breaches, the buyer may elect to seek **rescission** of the contract for sale, accompanied by restitution of the down payment.

(2) Traditionally, each piece of land is considered unique. Therefore, if the seller breaches the contract by failing to sell the property to the buyer, the buyer may seek **specific performance** of the contract for sale. If the seller fails to deliver marketable title, the buyer may elect to sue for specific performance, with an abatement in the purchase price that reflects the decrease in value caused by the title defect.

D. Passage of Property at Death

1. If the seller dies after the execution of the contract for sale but before closing, legal title passes to his heirs or devisees. However, they must honor the sales agreement, and the purchase money passes as personalty.

2. If the buyer dies after the execution of the contract for sale but before closing, the party that takes the decedent's realty may demand a closing and exoneration of liens from the personal estate of the decedent.

E. Merger

1. Traditionally, covenants in a contract of sale merge into the deed at closing. However, under the modern trend, merger does not apply to matters that are collateral to or not mentioned in the deed.

F. Conveyance of Real Property by Deed

1. **Covenants of Title**

a. The following three types of deeds are generally used in conveyances of real property.

    (1) In a **general warranty deed**, the seller warrants that no title defects have occurred during his ownership of the property. The

seller also warrants that there are no defects in the chain of title from which he derived title.

(?) In a **special warranty deed**, the seller warrants that no title defects have occurred during his ownership of the property. However, the seller does not warrant that there are no defects in the chain of title from which he derived title.

(3) In a **quitclaim deed**, the seller does not make any warranties. Instead, the grantor simply conveys whatever interest he may have.

b. A general or special warranty deed contains a series of promises or covenants, which are divided into present and future covenants.

(1) **Present covenants** are broken, if at all, at the time of conveyance. Under the American rule, present covenants are considered to be personal and do not run with the land. They include the following:

(a) in the **covenant of seisin**, the covenantor promises that he owns and possesses the estate granted;

1) The existence of an encumbrance does not breach the covenant of seisin.

(b) in the **covenant of right to convey**, the grantor promises that he has the right to convey the property; and

1) The covenant of the right to convey is often co-extensive with the covenant of seisin. However, there are several differences between the two covenants:

a) a trustee may be seised of the fee but may not have the right to convey if the trust deed prohibits the trustee from conveying; and

b) an owner of a life estate may be seised but may not have the right to convey if the life estate is subject to a valid restraint on alienation.

(c) in the **covenant against encumbrances**, the grantor promises that there are no encumbrances on the property.

1) For the purposes of the covenant against encumbrances, an encumbrance is any right in a third person that diminishes the value or limits the use of the land granted. In this context, encumbrances include:

a) mortgage and judgment liens;
b) taxes;
c) leases;
d) water rights;
e) easements; and
f) restrictions on use.

NOTE An encumbrance expressly noted in the deed cannot serve as the basis for a breach of the covenant against encumbrances. In most cases, if a defect renders title unmarketable (e.g., a mortgage or an easement), the defect also breaches the covenant against encumbrances. However, in a majority of jurisdictions, a violation of a zoning ordinance renders title unmarketable but does not breach the covenant against encumbrances. The jurisdictions are split on whether a visible or known encumbrance breaches the covenant against encumbrances.

(2) **Future covenants** may be broken after the time of the conveyance, and they run with the land. Future covenants include the following:

(a) in the **covenant of quiet enjoyment**, the grantor covenants that the grantee will not be disturbed by a superior claim;

(b) in the **covenant of warranty**, the grantor guarantees that he will assist in defending title against lawful claims and will compensate the grantee for losses sustained by an assertion of superior title; and

1) The covenant of warranty is virtually identical to the covenant of quiet enjoyment.

(c) in the **covenant of further assurances**, the grantor promises to take whatever steps may be required to perfect defects of title.

1) Under this covenant the grantor may, for example, be called on to defend a lawsuit or to execute a curative deed.

NOTE A future covenant is not breached until the grantee or his successor is evicted from the property, buys up the paramount claim to avoid suit, or is otherwise damaged.

c. **Remedies for Breach of Covenant by the Grantor**

(1) Monetary recovery is generally capped at the amount the grantor/defendant received for the property (plus interest).

(a) For breach of the covenants of seisin, right to convey, general warranty, and quiet enjoyment, the grantee may recover the full purchase price (if the conveyance is voided) or a percentage thereof (if a portion of the conveyance is voided).

(b) For breach of the covenant against encumbrances, damages are measured by the cost of removing the defect, if removal is possible, or the diminution in the value of the property if the defect cannot be removed.

NOTE In some jurisdictions, attorney's fees may also be recovered for breach of future covenants if the grantee loses the property to a lawful superior claim.

(2) Some states permit a grantee to recover damages from a remote grantor to the extent of the consideration received by the remote grantor from his immediate grantee, even if the remote grantee paid his immediate grantor less for the property. However, in some states, if the remote grantee paid less than the remote grantor received from his grantee, the remote grantee's recovery is limited to the amount the remote grantee paid to his immediate grantor.

(3) Specific performance is available for the covenant of further assurances.

    d. **Statute of Limitations**

       (1) For present covenants, the statute of limitations begins to run when the deed is delivered.

       (2) For future covenants, the statute of limitations does not begin to run until a third party asserts a superior title.

2. **Requirements for Effective Transfer**

    a. Conveyance of real property by deed requires:

       (1) donative intent;

          (a) The grantor must intend to transfer an interest immediately to the grantee. If the grantor intends the deed to take effect only on the death of the grantor, will formalities must be observed.

       (2) delivery; and

          (a) Delivery is usually accomplished through the physical act of handing the deed over to someone. However, it is possible to accomplish delivery by mere words (e.g., by a declaration of intent and relinquishment of control). A presumption of delivery arises if:

             1) the deed is later found in the grantee's possession;

             2) the deed is properly executed and recorded; or

             3) the deed contains an attestation clause that attests to delivery.

          (b) Handing the deed to the grantor's agent does not constitute valid delivery. Delivery does not occur until the grantor's agent delivers the deed to the grantee or grantee's agent, which then triggers the relation-back doctrine. However, handing the deed to the grantee's agent does constitute valid delivery.

          (c) **Doctrine of Relation Back**

             1) Handing the deed to a third party (i.e., an escrow agent) constitutes valid delivery if the grantor relinquishes all control over the deed.

             2) If a delivery is accomplished through an escrow agent, delivery will relate back to the date the grantor handed the deed to the escrow agent.

                 EXAMPLE: If the grantor dies before the escrow agent delivers the deed to the grantee, the delivery will relate back to the date the grantor handed the deed to the agent. Therefore, the deed was delivered during the lifetime of the grantor, and will formality and probate issues are avoided.

          (d) When the grantor hands the deed to the third party and places conditions on the delivery, it gives rise to concerns regarding a situation where the grantor transfers the property to someone else before the condition occurs.

             EXAMPLE: Grantor gives the deed to X, a third party, and says, "X, give this deed to Grantee if Grantee graduates from law school." A month later, Grantor conveys the property to C. At first glance, it would seem that C would win out. However, once the condition is met, the conveyance will relate back to the date Grantor gave X the deed, which was before the transfer to C.

1) The more conditions the grantor places on the conveyance, the more likely the conditioned conveyance will fail.

2) When a grantor gives the deed to a third party with instructions to deliver the deed at the grantor's death (a death escrow), the grantor is making a present transfer of a life estate with a remainder to the grantee.

EXAMPLE: Grantor gives the deed to X, the third party, and says, "X, give this deed to Grantee when I die."

(e) If the grantor expressly retains the right to reclaim the deed from the third party, transfer of title through the escrow agent will fail.

(3) acceptance.

(a) Acceptance is presumed if the conveyance is beneficial to the grantee.

b. Parol evidence is always admissible to show that a deed absolute on its face is intended as a mortgage. Parol evidence may also be used to show that the grantor did not intend the deed to have present effect.

(1) Most courts permit proof of oral conditions on deeds if delivery is to a third party.

(2) Under the majority rule, if delivery has been made to the grantee with an oral condition, the conveyance is valid, but the oral condition may not be proved. Under the minority rule, if delivery has been made to the grantee with an oral condition, the conveyance is void (particularly if the condition is delivery on the grantor's death). In a few jurisdictions, if delivery has been made to the grantee with an oral condition, the conveyance is valid, and the oral condition may be proved.

c. Natural monuments prevail over all other descriptions. Artificial monuments prevail over all descriptions except natural monuments. Courses and angles prevail over distances. All of the descriptions listed above prevail over a general description (e.g., "Blackacre"). Natural monuments, artificial monuments, courses, and distances all refer to a "metes and bounds" description. A description may also be by government survey, name of parcel, or street address.

III. RECORDING STATUTES

A. In General

1. Recordation of the deed of conveyance is not required to validate the transfer of title. However, recording becomes important when two or more parties claim that the owner has conveyed (or mortgaged) the property to them.

2. Recording statutes generally apply to conveyances of freehold interests, easements, profits, covenants, servitudes, mortgages, assignments, and liens.

3. Title based on adverse possession or prescription is not recordable.

4. Recordation will not cure defects in a deed caused by lack of delivery, forgery, or fraud.

B. First in Time, First in Right

1. Under the common law, if two persons claimed title under deeds to one parcel of real property, the property was awarded to the person who took the property first in time. The common law rule still applies if the person who took later in time fails to qualify under the relevant recording statute.

C. Types of Recording Statutes

1. **Race Statute**

   a. Under a race statute, the person who records first prevails.

   b. Typical race statutes read: "No (i) conveyance of land, or (ii) contract to convey, or (iii) option to convey, or (iv) lease of land for more than three years shall be valid to pass any property interest against lien creditors or purchasers for a valuable consideration from the donor, bargainor, or landlord but from the time of registration thereof in the county where the land lies...."

   EXAMPLE: O, the owner of Blackacre, conveys Blackacre to A, who does not record her deed. O then conveys Blackacre to B, who pays value, immediately records his deed, and has actual notice of A's deed. Although B had actual notice of A's deed, B will prevail over A because B recorded before A.

2. **Notice Statute**

   a. Under a notice statute, an unrecorded conveyance or other instrument is invalid as against a subsequent *bona fide* purchase for value and without notice.

   b. To prevail under a notice statute, a claimant of real property must prove the following three elements:

   (1) the claimant took subsequent in time to another person claiming ownership of the real property in question;

   (2) the claimant was a *bona fide* purchaser for value; and

   (3) the claimant took the property without actual, constructive, or inquiry notice.

c. A subsequent purchaser must pay value to prevail under a recording statute. Value exists if the purchaser has paid all of the purchase price. A purchaser under a contract of sale who has not yet paid any money should not be protected under the recording statute. However, if the purchaser has paid some but not all of the purchase price before receiving notice, the courts are split as to whether the purchaser is protected under the recording statute. Some courts state that partial payment is not sufficient to protect the subsequent purchaser. The majority holds that the buyer is protected *pro tanto* (so much as he has paid), which may be accomplished by:

   (1) giving the land to the holder of the outstanding interest and giving the buyer restitution (the most common method);

   (2) awarding the buyer a fractional interest in the land proportional to the amount paid prior to notice; or

   (3) allowing the buyer to complete the purchase but to pay the remaining installments to the holder of the outstanding interest.

d. **Types of Notice**

   (1) **Actual notice** exists if the claimant actually sees the deed under which the other party is claiming, or otherwise knows of the conveyance.

   (2) **Constructive** or **record notice** exists if the other party's deed is recorded in the proper place in the record books.

      (a) **Wild deeds** are deeds recorded outside of the chain of title, and which do not impart constructive notice on a subsequent purchaser.

      (b) The courts are divided on whether an easement or restriction that appears in a prior deed to one lot made by a common grantor is constructive notice to the grantee of another lot from the common grantor.

      (c) The courts are also split on whether a subsequent *bona fide* purchaser has constructive notice of a prior deed from the grantor that is recorded after a subsequent deed from the grantor is recorded.

   (3) **Inquiry notice** exists if the appearance of the property is such that the claimant should have asked more questions about the title to the property.

   (4) Lis pendens notice is notice of a pending lawsuit that will affect a particular piece of property; it is not a lien itself, but provides notice that there is or may be a lien against the property as a result of a judgment. When the lis pendens notice is properly recorded, it will serve as constructive notice to other lien holders, but does not serve to record the lien itself.

e. Typical notice statutes read: "A conveyance of an interest in land shall not be valid against any subsequent purchaser for value, without notice, unless the conveyance is recorded."

EXAMPLE: O, the owner of Blackacre, conveys Blackacre to A, who does not record her deed. O then conveys Blackacre to B, who pays value, does not have actual or inquiry notice of A's deed, and does not record his deed. Although B did not record his deed, B prevails over A because B paid value and did not have notice of A's deed; B did not have actual or inquiry notice of A's deed and B could not have constructive notice of A's deed because the deed was not recorded.

EXAMPLE: O, the owner of Blackacre, conveys Blackacre to A, who promptly records her deed. O then conveys Blackacre to B, who pays value, does not have actual or inquiry notice of A's deed, and promptly records his deed. A will prevail over B because B had constructive notice of A's deed.

3. **Race-Notice Statute**
   a. Under a race-notice statute, an unrecorded conveyance or other instrument is invalid against a subsequent *bona fide* purchaser for value, without notice, who records first.
   b. To prevail under a race-notice statute, a claimant of real property must prove the following four elements:
      (1) the claimant took subsequent in time to another person claiming ownership of the real property in question;
      (2) the claimant was a *bona fide* purchaser for value;
      (3) the claimant took the property without actual, constructive, or inquiry notice; and
      (4) the claimant recorded first.
   c. Typical race-notice statutes read: "Any conveyance of an interest in land shall not be valid against any subsequent purchaser for value, without notice, whose conveyance is first recorded."

   EXAMPLE: O, the owner of Blackacre, conveys Blackacre to A, who does not record her deed. O then conveys Blackacre to B, who pays value, does not have actual or inquiry notice of A's deed, and promptly records his deed. A then records her deed. B prevails over A because B paid value, did not have notice of A's deed, and recorded first.

   EXAMPLE: O, the owner of Blackacre, conveys Blackacre to A, who does not record her deed. O then conveys Blackacre to B, who pays value, does not have actual or inquiry notice of A's deed, and does not record his deed. A prevails over B because B did not record his deed, and therefore, A prevails under the common law rule of first-in-time, first-in-right.

4. **Title Search—Recording a Conveyance**
   a. In **tract index** jurisdictions, the searcher looks at the legal description of the tract of land followed by a chronological listing of all conveyances involving that piece of land.
      (1) This type of search always provides constructive notice of a claim to property.
      (2) A minority of jurisdictions require tract index searches.

b. In **grantor and grantee index** jurisdictions, the searcher establishes a chain of title by searching two index books.

　(1) First, the searcher looks back in time within the grantee-grantor index.

　(2) Then, the searcher looks forward in time within the grantor-grantee index to see if any grantor conveyed an interest to someone outside of the backwards chain.

　(3) A majority of jurisdictions require grantor and grantee index searches.

D. Shelter Rule

1. The **shelter rule** provides protection for a subsequent purchaser who does not satisfy the applicable recording statute. Under the shelter rule, a person who is a successor in interest to a person protected by the recording statute is also protected.

   EXAMPLE: O, the owner of Blackacre, conveys Blackacre to A, who does not record. O then conveys Blackacre to B, who pays value, records immediately, and takes without notice of A's deed. B then conveys Blackacre to C, who takes by gift. Under either a notice or a race-notice statute, C cannot prevail over A because C did not pay value. However, when B took Blackacre, B would have prevailed over A under the relevant recording statute. C may take shelter under B's protected status. Therefore, C will prevail over A under either a notice or a race-notice statute.

2. **Exceptions to Shelter Rule**

   a. A subsequent person may not take advantage of the shelter rule if that person:

   　(1) attempts to "wash" his deed by conveying to a third person and then immediately taking a reconveyance of the property; or

   　(2) commits fraud in respect to the deed.

3. Under the majority rule, estoppel by deed is an equitable remedy that is applied on a case-by-case basis. Under the minority rule, after-acquired title is a legal theory that provides for automatic flow-through of the property.

E. Marketable Title Act

1. A marketable title act provides a "cut-off" point, which limits the time period during which a subsequent purchaser is required to search the records. The cut-off point is fixed by identifying a deed that has been of record for the required period, which is usually 30 or 40 years. Any interest that is not recorded or refiled within the required period is extinguished.

   EXAMPLE: In 1960, O, the record owner of Blackacre, grants a right-of-way easement across Blackacre to A, which was recorded. In 1967, O conveys Blackacre to B in a deed that does not mention A's easement. In 2004, B conveys Blackacre to C. In 2005, A attempts to use the easement, but C prevents A from crossing over Blackacre. The jurisdiction has a 30-

year marketable title act. The 1967 deed becomes the "root of title" in 1997, when it had been recorded for 30 years. Under the marketable title act, all competing interests recorded prior to the root of title are extinguished. Therefore, A's easement was extinguished in 1997.

IV. MORTGAGES

A. **In General**

1. A **mortgage** is a conveyance of an interest in real property made to secure performance of an obligation. The obligation often arises out of a loan of money made to facilitate the purchase or development of real property. A mortgage is typically evidenced by two documents:

   a. a mortgage deed; and

   b. a promissory note (mortgage note).

2. A **mortgage deed** is a document that conveys an interest in real property designed to secure performance of a debt. Because a mortgage involves a transfer of an interest in realty, a mortgage must be evidenced by a writing (e.g., a mortgage deed) that is properly executed and delivered to the mortgagee. The mortgage deed must include, at a minimum, the following elements:

   a. the identity of the parties;

      (1) The **mortgagor** is the owner of the real property, who borrowed money and secured the debt with a mortgage on the property.

      (2) The **mortgagee** is the lender of the money borrowed, to whom the mortgage is made.

   b. a description of the property; and

      (1) The property should be described with sufficient detail to put a subsequent *bona fide* purchaser on notice of the mortgage (which may require more detail than is required to satisfy the Statute of Frauds).

   c. the intent to create a security interest.

      (1) The mortgage deed should contain evidence of an intent to create a security interest in the mortgagee.

      (2) The mortgage deed is a recordable document, which is generally subject to the terms of the applicable recording statute.

3. The **mortgage note** represents the mortgage obligation. The note is an "IOU" that creates personal liability in the mortgagor. The note typically includes, *inter alia*, the following provisions:

   a. the loan amount;

   b. the interest rate, which may be fixed (set for the term of the loan) or adjustable (it may vary over the term of the loan);

   c. the loan term (e.g., 15 or 30 years);

   d. a clause permitting prepayment but exacting a penalty for the privilege of prepayment;

   e. a clause that permits the mortgagee to declare the entire amount of the mortgage obligation due and payable if the mortgagor defaults (an **acceleration clause**); and

   f. a "due on sale" clause, which requires the entire balance due on the note to be paid before the property may be transferred by the mortgagor/seller to a buyer.

NOTE ▶ When the mortgagor satisfies (pays) the mortgage note, the mortgagee executes a document that releases the mortgage. The release document should be recorded.

B. Mortgage Theories

1. The jurisdictions are split on the nature of the interests held by mortgagor and mortgagee after the execution of the mortgage deed. The following three mortgage theories are in effect in various jurisdictions of the United States.

2. **Title Theory**

   a. The title theory is the classic common law model for determining the nature of the interests held by the mortgagor and the mortgagee. Under the traditional title theory, the mortgagee receives legal title to the mortgaged real property and has a right to take possession of and to collect rents and profits from the property. The mortgagee's title to the property is subject to a condition subsequent that divests title from the mortgagee if the mortgagor repays the loan by the due date. Until he repays the loan in a timely fashion, the mortgagor retains only an equitable interest in the property.

      (1) The traditional title theory is now the minority view. In addition, a title theory state is likely to recognize that the mortgagee holds title for security purposes only. Under this approach, the mortgagor is viewed as the owner of the land. Some title theory states have also eliminated or reduced the incidents of legal title by, *inter alia*, giving the mortgagor the right to possession until default.

3. **Lien Theory**

   a. In a lien theory jurisdiction, the mortgagee receives a lien, and the mortgagor retains legal and equitable title and possession to the mortgaged real property, unless and until foreclosure occurs. Most states now adhere to the lien theory.

4. **Intermediate Theory**

   a. In an intermediate theory jurisdiction, the mortgagor retains legal title until default occurs. After default, legal title and possession pass to the mortgagee, who may then begin to collect rents and profits. Only a few states adhere to the intermediate theory. According to the Restatement of Property, the intermediate theory differs very little from the title theory, because title theory mortgagees rarely assert a right to possession prior to default.

5. **Mortgage-Related Waste**

   a. A person holding a remainder in mortgaged property has a duty to pay the principal. A life tenant has a duty to pay the interest on a mortgage. However, the life tenant's duty is capped at:

      (1) rents and profits derived from a third person in possession of the property; or

      (2) the reasonable rental value of the premises, if the life tenant remains in possession of the property.

b. The mortgagor or a life tenant of mortgaged property also commits waste if, without the mortgagee's consent, the mortgagor or life tenant:

   (1) fails to make timely payments of property taxes or governmental assessments secured by a lien that have priority over the mortgage;

   (2) makes physical changes to the real property, negligently or intentionally, that reduce the value of the property;

   (3) fails to maintain and repair the property in a reasonable manner, except for repair of casualty damage or acts of third parties not the fault of the mortgagor;

   (4) fails to comply materially with mortgage covenants respecting the physical care, maintenance, construction, demolition, or insurance against casualty of the property or improvements on it; or

   (5) retains rents to which the mortgagee has a right of possession.

> **MORTGAGE-RELATED WASTE**
>
> **My Rubbish Makes The Castle Ruined**
>
> **M**ortgage, **R**educe Value, **M**aintain, **T**axes, **C**ovenants, **R**ents

c. The mortgagee has the following remedies if the mortgagor or life tenant commits waste:

   (1) foreclosure or the exercise of other remedies available under the mortgage for default on the secured obligation, if the waste has impaired the mortgagee's security;

   (2) an injunction prohibiting future waste or requiring correction of waste already committed, but only to the extent that the waste has impaired or threatens to impair the mortgagee's security; and

   (3) recovery of damages, limited by the amount of the waste, to the extent that the waste has impaired the mortgagee's security.

d. Absent a leasehold provision to the contrary, a tenant for years or a periodic tenant has no common law duty to make mortgage payments.

C. Foreclosure

1. In most jurisdictions, when there is a default on an obligation secured by a mortgage, the mortgagee may:

   a. obtain a judgment against any person who is personally liable on the obligation and, to the extent that the judgment is not satisfied, foreclose the mortgage on the real estate for the balance; or

   b. foreclose the mortgage and, to the extent that the proceeds of the foreclosure sale do not satisfy the obligation, obtain a judgment for the deficiency against any person who is personally liable on the obligation.

      (1) Today, a mortgagee may foreclose by forcing the sale of property secured by a mortgage after the mortgagor has defaulted on the promissory note.

      (2)   A foreclosure sale may be accomplished either through a power of sale or by court order.

         (a)   A power-of-sale foreclosure occurs without judicial action, pursuant to a power-of-sale clause included in the mortgage documents.

         (b)   A judicial foreclosure sale must:

            1)   be public;

            2)   be properly noticed;

            3)   be conducted in a reasonable manner (usually regulated by statute); and

            4)   result in a "fair" sale price.

               a)   A **fair price** is not necessarily the fair market price. Rather, it is arrived at as a result of the mortgagee's due diligence in conducting the foreclosure sale.

               b)   A foreclosure sale will not be set aside for inadequacy of the sale price unless the inadequacy is so gross as to shock the conscience.

2.   A foreclosure sale terminates the mortgagor's interest in the mortgaged real estate.

3.   The proceeds of a mortgage foreclosure sale will be distributed in the following order:

   a.   to the costs of the sale;

   b.   to the security interest foreclosed;

   c.   to junior lienholders terminated by the sale; and then

   d.   to the mortgagor, if any proceeds remain.

4.   **Junior interests** (i.e., second or later mortgages) in the property are destroyed by a foreclosure sale.

   a.   However, a junior mortgage is not extinguished if the junior mortgagee is not made a defendant in the judicial proceeding culminating in a foreclosure sale and does not receive notice of the foreclosure sale.

   b.   Senior interests not participating in the foreclosure are not affected by a foreclosure sale.

5.   If the proceeds of a foreclosure sale are not sufficient to cover the lien(s) foreclosed, the mortgagee/creditor(s) may obtain a deficiency judgment against the mortgagor (or a party that has assumed the mortgage) personally, based on the note. Some states limit deficiency judgments by:

   a.   prohibiting deficiency judgments when foreclosure is accomplished privately through a power-of-sale clause;

   b.   requiring deficiency judgments to be sought at the same time as foreclosure;

   c.   scrutinizing the fairness of the foreclosure sale, particularly if the foreclosure is accomplished by a private sale; or

   d.   requiring the mortgagee to set a minimum foreclosure sale price ("upset price").

D. Redemption

1. The mortgagor's interest in the mortgaged property is called the "equity," which is short for "equity of redemption." At any time after default but before foreclosure, the mortgagor has the right to redeem the property by paying the debt due. The right to redeem may not be waived ("clogged") at the time the mortgage is created.

   a. About one-half of the states have a fixed time period (6–12 months) after a foreclosure sale has occurred for the mortgagor to redeem (by matching the foreclosure price).

E. Priorities

1. **Purchase-Money Mortgage**

   a. A purchase-money mortgage is a mortgage given to a vendor of the real estate or to a third-party lender, to the extent that the proceeds of the loan are used to acquire title to the real estate or construct improvements on the real estate, if the mortgage is given as part of the same transaction in which title is acquired. A purchase-money mortgage, whether or not recorded, is given priority over a lien (e.g., judgment lien or a homestead claim) that attaches to the property through actions of the purchaser/mortgagor prior to the acquisition of the title, even if the lien was recorded first. However, a mortgage given the next day after the buyer acquired the property, if recorded before the purchase-money mortgage is recorded, would have priority over the purchase-money mortgage based on recording statute priority.

   b. Where the instruments are silent, a purchase-money mortgage given to the vendor of the property will have priority over one given to a third-party lender.

   EXAMPLE: Buyer acquires Blackacre by giving a purchase-money mortgage to Seller and one to Bank, and defaults on both; Seller has priority over Bank.

2. **Modification**

   a. If a senior mortgage is modified, a junior mortgage prevails over the modification if the modification materially prejudices the holder of the junior mortgage, such as by:

      (1) increasing the amount of principal; or

      (2) increasing the interest rate (if the rate under the original mortgage was fixed).

   b. Modifications that normally do not materially prejudice the holder of the junior mortgage include:

      (1) extension of the mortgage maturity date; and

      (2) rescheduling installment payments.

F. Transfers

1. **Transfer by Mortgagor**

   a. If the mortgagor transfers the property **subject to the mortgage**, and mortgage payments are not made, the mortgagee may foreclose and force the property to be sold. However, the transferee of the property does not have personal liability for the debt.

b. If the transferee of mortgaged real property **assumes the mortgage**, and mortgage payments are not made, the mortgagee may foreclose and force the property to be sold.

(1) In addition, the transferee of the mortgage has personal liability and can be held liable for any deficiency.

c. In a novation, the transferee of real property and the mortgagee agree that the transferee will assume the mortgage and the mortgagor will be released from liability.

2. **Transfer by Mortgagee**

a. The mortgagee may also transfer his interest in the mortgaged property. The mortgage generally follows the transfer of the mortgage note. If the note is negotiable, the transferee may qualify as a holder in due course, who takes free and clear of certain "personal" defenses, such as lack of consideration, duress by nonphysical threat, and fraud in the inducement. However, the transferee will take subject to "real" defenses, such as infancy, duress by physical threat, and fraud in the factum.

G. **Mortgage Alternatives**

1. In a **deed of trust**, the debtor/note-maker is the settlor, who gives a deed of trust to a trustee who is closely connected to the lender. In the event of a default, the trustee is directed to proceed with a foreclosure sale. Deeds of trust are generally treated like mortgages.

2. In an **installment land-sale contract**, the buyer takes possession under a contract of sale and makes payments to the seller. The seller delivers a deed and legal title only when the payments have been completed. If the buyer defaults, an installment land-sale contract usually provides for forfeiture of all installments paid, allowing the lender to retake the property. However, some states require a foreclosure proceeding for an installment land-sale contract. In some states, if a foreclosure occurs, the seller is required to refund to the buyer all installments already paid, as long as these payments are more than the damages suffered by the seller.

a. In many states, a buyer who defaults under an installment land-sale contract is granted a grace period to pay off the loan. The buyer may keep the land while he is paying under a new payment schedule.

b. If a seller under an installment land-sale contract has accepted late payments from the buyer, the seller may be deemed to have waived his right to demand timely payment. If this is the case, when the seller wishes the buyer to begin paying in a timely manner, he must send the buyer written notice and allow the buyer a reasonable amount of time to make back payments owed.

V. LAND USE

A. **Easements**

1. An **easement** is an interest in the land of another.

2. **Nature of Easements**

   a. Easements may be either affirmative or negative, and they may be either appurtenant or in gross.

      (1) Most easements are affirmative in nature. An **affirmative easement** gives the holder the right to do something on the land of another.

      EXAMPLE: Alpha has the right to walk across Beta's land.

      (2) A **negative easement** gives the holder the right to prevent a landowner from doing something on his land. The common law recognized only the following four types of negative easements: light, air, water, and lateral and subjacent support. A writing is always required to create a negative easement.

      EXAMPLE: Alpha may prevent Beta from building a house that blocks light to Alpha's land.

      (3) An **easement appurtenant** requires a dominant and servient tenement.

      EXAMPLE: A has the right to cross over B's property from the road to reach A's property. A has the dominant estate because the easement benefits A in the use of her property. B has the servient estate because her land is burdened with the easement. Therefore, A has an easement appurtenant.

      (4) An **easement in gross** is personal in nature, resulting in a servient but not a dominant estate.

      EXAMPLE: A utility company has the right to lay its utility cable across A's land. The cable assists the company in providing its utility services to its customers. A's land is the servient estate because it is burdened by the utility company's right to lay its cable across A's land. However, there is no dominant estate; the benefit of the easement is personal to the utility company because the easement does not benefit the company in the use of its land. Therefore, the utility company has an easement in gross.

3. **Creation of Easements**

   a. An easement may be created expressly through a writing, by implication, by prescription, or by estoppel.

      (1) An easement is an interest in land. Therefore, the Statute of Frauds generally requires a writing to create an easement.

      (2) An affirmative easement may be created by **implication** either by prior use or by necessity.

(a) An easement **implied by prior use** requires:

1) severance of title to land held in common ownership;

2) an existing, open, and continuous use while it was in single ownership (*quasi*-easement); and

    a) That use alone cannot constitute an easement because an owner cannot have an easement across his own property.

3) the common grantor manifesting intent for the *quasi*-easement to continue as a true easement after the division of land.

    a) However, some courts may require strict necessity if the implied easement is reserved and not granted.

(b) An easement **implied by necessity** requires:

1) severance of title to land held in common ownership; and

2) strict necessity for the easement at the time of severance.

EXAMPLE: O owns a large parcel of land. The parcel is bordered by a two-lane road on the east and dense forest on the north, south, and west. O lives in a house at the northwest corner of the parcel and regularly drives to and from his house on a gravel road that crosses the northeast portion of the parcel and opens onto the road. O then conveys the west half of the parcel to A. When A attempts to access the road by driving across the northeast portion of the parcel, he finds O has erected a barrier. The question is whether A has an implied easement across the portion of the parcel retained by O. O initially owned the entire tract, thereby satisfying the initial unity of ownership requirement. He then severed that unity when he conveyed the west half of the parcel to A. A has no direct access to his parcel because it is surrounded by O's parcel on the east and dense forest on the north, south, and west. The landlocked nature of A's estate should satisfy the strict necessity requirement for an implied easement by necessity.

(3) An affirmative easement may be created by **prescription**, which requires proof of the use of property that is:

(a) open and notorious;

(b) actual;

(c) continuous (the traditional period for prescription is 20 years);

(d) hostile; and

(e) exclusive.

1) Some courts require prescriptive use to be "exclusive." In this context, **exclusive** means that the use is not shared with the whole world. The user may share use of the easement with the owner.

    (4) Creation of an easement **by estoppel** requires proof of an act or representation by the owner of the burdened estate in respect to the easement, justifiable reliance on that act or representation by the owner of the benefited estate, and damages suffered by the owner of the benefited estate if the easement is not recognized.

4. **Transfer of Easements**

 a. Both the benefit and the burden of an easement may be transferred according to the following rules:

  (1) when the dominant tenement is transferred, the benefit of an easement or a profit appurtenant follows the transferred estate, even if the deed of conveyance does not specifically mention the easement or profit; or

   (a) Traditionally, the benefit of an easement in gross could not be transferred. However, the modern rule permits transfer of an easement in gross if the grantor of the easement so intends, and the easement is commercial in nature.

  (2) in the case of an express easement, transfer of the servient estate will result in an accompanying transfer of the burden, so long as the holder of the dominant tenement has complied with the provisions of the relevant recording statute.

5. **Termination of Easements**

 a. An easement may be terminated by any of the following methods:

  (1) an easement may be created for a specific term, such as 10 years;

   (a) When the time period ends, the easement is terminated.

  (2) a release occurs when the holder of the dominant estate releases his interest to the holder of the servient estate;

  (3) an easement is terminated when the dominant and servient estates come into common ownership;

  (4) an easement may be terminated by abandonment;

   (a) Abandonment requires proof of:

    1) intent to abandon; and

    2) an affirmative act in furtherance of the intent.

  (5) an easement may be terminated by estoppel;

   (a) Estoppel requires proof of:

    1) an act or representation in respect to the easement;

    2) justifiable reliance on that act or representation; and

    3) damages.

  (6) an easement may be terminated by prescription (use adverse to the easement for the statutory period); or

  (7) an easement will be terminated when a governmental body acquires the servient estate through an exercise of the eminent domain power.

B. Profits

1. A **profit à prendre** is a nonpossessory interest in land.

2. The holder of the profit has the right to take resources from the land of another.

   a. Profits, unlike easements, permit the right to remove something from the land, as opposed to mere use of the land.

   b. Examples of resources include, but are not limited to, soil, timber, and minerals.

      EXAMPLE: A has the right to take gravel from B's land.

3. Profits can only be created expressly or by prescription.

4. With the exception of creation, all rules governing alienation and termination of easements are applicable to profits.

C. License

1. A **license** is a privilege, usually to do something on someone else's property.

2. Neither a writing nor consideration is required to create a license.

3. Because a license is personal, it is not transferable unless the licensor so intends.

4. A license expires on the death of the licensor or the conveyance of the servient estate.

5. A license is generally revocable at the will of the licensor. However, a license may become irrevocable in two situations:

   a. a **license coupled with an interest** exists when one person owns personal property on the land of another and has a privilege incidental to such personal property to come on the land to use or recover the personalty; and

   b. an **executed license** is based on estoppel and often involves substantial expenditure of funds in reliance on the promisor's promise to allow the promisee to use the land. An executed license is sometimes deemed to be the equivalent of an easement.

D. Covenants that Run with the Land

1. A **covenant that runs with the land** is a promise that attaches to land. In that covenant, the covenantor promises to do or refrain from doing something on his land.

   a. In contrast to easements, most running covenants are negative in nature.

      EXAMPLE: Landowner promises that she will not build anything other than a single-family residence on her premises.

   b. Running covenants include promises to pay rent, condominium common charges, or maintenance fees.

2. For a covenant to run with the land, the following elements must be satisfied:

   a. writing;

      (1) A covenant that runs with the land is a promise that attaches to land. Therefore, a covenant that runs at law must be embodied in a writing that satisfies the Statute of Frauds.

b. intent;

   (1) The writing must include language that shows the parties' intent for the covenant to run.

   (2) Typically, the covenant will state that the covenantor promises on behalf of himself and his heirs, successors, and assigns to do or to refrain from doing something on his land for the benefit of the covenantee and his heirs, successors, and assigns.

c. privity;

   (1) **Horizontal privity** is the relationship that exists between the original covenantor and covenantee. In most jurisdictions in the United States, the horizontal privity requirement is satisfied by a conveyance of land between the covenantee and covenantor, which occurs by the same deed that includes the covenant. Horizontal privity may also exist when the covenant is created in a lease or in the transfer of an easement.

      (a) Traditionally, horizontal privity was required for both the benefit and the burden to run.

      (b) Under the modern rule, horizontal privity is not required for the benefit to run.

   (2) **Vertical privity** is the relationship that exists between an original party to a running covenant and the successor in interest to the original party. To demonstrate vertical privity, the plaintiff must show that the successor "stepped into the shoes of" the original party by taking the entire interest held by the original party. For example, if the original covenantor took a fee simple interest in land and then attempted to make a conveyance to a subsequent party, vertical privity would exist between the original covenantor and the successor only if the successor received a fee simple interest.

      (a) Traditionally, vertical privity is required for both the benefit and burden to run.

      (b) For the burden to run, privity of estate will only exist when the holder of the servient estate transfers all of his interest in the servient estate to the new owner.

      (c) For the benefit to run, privity of estate can exist when the holder of the dominant estate is transferring all or part of his interest.

d. touch and concern; and

   (1) To touch and concern, a covenant must exercise direct influence on the occupation, use, or enjoyment of the premises. The benefit touches if it increases the value of the benefited property. The burden touches if it decreases the value of the burdened property.

      (a) Traditionally, both the benefit and the burden had to touch for either side to run.

e. notice.

   (1) Originally, notice was not a requirement for a covenant to run with the land at law. However, the introduction of recording statutes

into American law caused a notice requirement to be grafted onto the requirements for a running covenant. The parameters of notice are determined according to the terms of the relevant recording statute. Notice under recording acts is necessary for the burden to run.

3. **Equitable Servitude**

   a. A court may enforce a covenant as an **equitable servitude** if:

      (1) the plaintiff can establish at law all of the elements for a covenant that runs with the land, but the plaintiff seeks equitable relief; or

      (2) the plaintiff cannot establish at law all of the elements for a covenant that runs with the land, but the plaintiff can demonstrate the relaxed requirements for an equitable servitude. These elements relate closely to the elements required for a covenant to run at law.

      (a) If the plaintiff cannot show that the covenant was embodied in a writing, the plaintiff may prove the covenant through part performance or estoppel.

      (b) If the plaintiff cannot show intent in a writing for the covenant to run, he may nevertheless establish intent by showing a common scheme. A common scheme typically exists in a subdivision. If a sufficient number of lots in the subdivision are burdened by the same covenant, the court may find that a common scheme binds all of the lots in the subdivision, including those that do not have the restriction written into the deed.

      (c) Neither horizontal nor vertical privity are required for the enforcement of an equitable servitude.

      (d) The intent element must be demonstrated for both the benefit and burden.

      (e) The touch and concern element must still be demonstrated for both the benefit and burden.

      (f) The parameters of notice for the burden to run are determined according to the terms of the relevant recording statute.

4. If the owner of two or more lots, so situated as to bear the relation, sells one with restrictions of benefit to the land retained, the servitude becomes mutual and the owner of the lot or lots retained may not do anything forbidden to the owner of the lot sold, creating an **implied reciprocal servitude**. In most jurisdictions, a negative reciprocal easement may be created by filing a declaration containing the restrictions (the "CC&Rs", which are covenants, conditions, and restrictions) before any lots are sold.

   a. The following factors may show a common scheme:

      (1) a large percentage of lots expressly burdened;

      (2) oral representations to buyers;

      (3) statements in written advertisements, sales brochures, or maps given to buyers; or

      (4) recorded plat maps or declarations.

b. In the absence of an express restriction in the deed, the burden will not be imposed on a lot conveyed before the conveyance of the first lot with an express restriction.

c. The burden will be imposed on lots (even in the absence of an express restriction in the deed to those lots) if a common scheme was evident at the time of conveyance of those lots.

d. The original subdivider may enforce a benefit unless he has sold all of the property.

e. Traditionally, a benefit could not be enforced by a buyer who purchased his subdivision lot before the conveyance of the burdened lot. In some jurisdictions, the existence of the common scheme is sufficient to show that the subdivider intended to benefit all purchasers, whether they took prior or subsequent to the conveyance that created the burden. In other jurisdictions, a previous grantee may sue as a third-party beneficiary.

f. If a common scheme is present, suit may be brought by the purchaser of a lot conveyed after the lot with the express restriction (because that restriction was for the benefit of the grantor and his heirs and assigns, and the subsequent purchaser is a successor to the grantor).

g. A condominium or subdivision association may enforce a benefit if the covenant is to benefit common land conveyed by the developer to the association.

E. Zoning

1. The state possesses the power to regulate for the health, safety, and welfare of its citizens. Through an enabling act, the state may delegate to a municipality the authority to protect the welfare of its citizens by enacting a zoning ordinance.

2. A zoning ordinance may be challenged under the Due Process and Equal Protection Clauses. A zoning ordinance may also be subject to a First Amendment challenge if it regulates billboards or aesthetics.

F. Eminent Domain

1. Constitutional Protection

a. Under the Takings Clause of the Fifth Amendment (which is made applicable to the states through the Fourteenth Amendment), private property may not be taken for a public use without just compensation.

b. The government may take a fee simple interest in property. The government may also take an easement in property or an interest in an estate in the property.

c. In the 20th century, the **public use requirement** of the Takings Clause came to be construed broadly to mean any advantage or benefit to the public. The public advantage or purpose approach permits a taking when the facility for which the property was taken provides the public with a benefit or advantage, such as the taking of property for urban renewal. Traditionally, public use has been scrutinized at the lowest level of scrutiny, which defers to the legislature. However, the Supreme Court recently opened the door for state courts to adopt a heightened level of scrutiny for takings for economic redevelopment.

d.   The **just compensation requirement** derives from equitable principles of fairness. Therefore, just compensation is generally equated with fair market value. However, just compensation does not account for intangibles such as sentimental value or special suitabilities.

(1)   Traditionally, the government is not required to pay just compensation if it takes property for nuisance prevention.

2.   **Taking**

a.   A **taking** occurs when the government exercises the eminent domain power to take private property. For example, in a condemnation proceeding, a city may use the eminent domain power to take (buy) the property of residents in a location targeted for economic redevelopment.

b.   A *per se* **taking** occurs when a government action results in a permanent physical occupation of private property. A permanent physical occupation is classified as a *per se* taking, without resort to a balancing test—for example, a governmental body enacts an ordinance that requires the owner of an apartment building to permit a cable company to install its cable wires across the owner's building.

(1)   In contrast, if a physical invasion by governmental action is temporary, a taking analysis requires a balancing of the importance of the public benefit achieved by the government action against the extent of the economic injury to the property owner.

c.   A **governmental regulation** may constitute a taking if it "goes too far." To determine whether a regulation goes too far, the court generally engages in a balancing test. The court considers the economic impact of the regulation on the property owner, the extent to which the regulation interferes with distinct investment-backed expectations, and the character of the governmental action.

3.   Money damages may be awarded for a regulatory taking. Damages may be awarded for the time period between the enactment of an ordinance and a judicial declaration of a taking.

G.   **Exaction Fee**

1.   An **exaction** is a fee or dedication that is "exacted" from a property owner who seeks to develop his property as a means of offsetting the potential impact of the development. Exactions may be monetary or nonmonetary.

2.   A **monetary exaction** is an impact or in-lieu fee that is assessed against the developer to pay for public benefits, such as roads and parks, that arise as a result of the development.

3. A **nonmonetary exaction** is a dedication of an interest in land within a subdivision for streets or parks that are needed as a result of the development.

    a. A special set of rules has been developed for nonmonetary exactions. Most experts agree that nonmonetary exactions should be judged under these rules only and that these rules should not be used for other regulatory takings.

        (1) The exaction must substantially advance a legitimate state interest. That substantial advancement can be shown only if there is an "essential nexus" between the exaction and the state interest, which means that the exaction must reasonably related to the impact alleged.

        (2) There must be a "rough proportionality" between the exaction and the impact of the development. The court must make an "individualized determination" that the exaction is related in both nature and extent to the impact of the proposed development. Thus, the burden shifts to the government to justify the exaction.

H. Nuisance

1. A **public nuisance** is an unreasonable interference with a right common to the general public. An action may interfere unreasonably with a public right if it interferes significantly with public health, safety, or convenience, or is proscribed by statute or ordinance. To recover damages or seek an injunction in an action based on a public nuisance, an individual plaintiff must have suffered harm that is different from that suffered by other members of the public exercising the right common to the general public that was the subject of interference.

2. A **private nuisance** is a substantial and unreasonable invasion (intentional or negligent) of another's interest in his use and enjoyment of land. To determine the existence of a private nuisance, a court balances the utility of the conduct against the gravity of the harm caused by the conduct.

    a. **Coming to the nuisance** is a factor that may be considered in weighing the utility of the conduct against the gravity of the harm. However, "coming to the nuisance" is not a complete bar to suit.

    b. The following persons have standing to sue for a private nuisance affecting a parcel of land:

        (1) possessors of the land;

        (2) owners of easements and profits in the land; and

        (3) owners of nonpossessory estates in the land that are detrimentally affected by interferences with its use and enjoyment.

    c. Damages and injunctive relief may be recovered in a suit for private nuisance.

I. Support Rights

1. An owner of real property has the exclusive right to use and possess the surface, airspace, and soil of the property.

2. **Lateral Support**

    a. An owner of land has no liability if a subsiding of neighboring land is caused by natural conditions on the owner's land. However, a landowner may be strictly liable if his excavation causes adjacent land to subside (sink). If the adjacent land is improved, strict liability applies only if the adjacent land would have collapsed in its natural state. Even if the adjacent land would not have collapsed in its natural state, the landowner is only liable for damages resulting from negligence. The courts are split on whether money damages may be recovered for injury to the improvements.

3. **Subjacent Support**

   a. The right of support extends to land in its natural state and buildings existing on the date when the subjacent estate is severed from the surface. However, the underground landowner is liable for damages to subsequently erected buildings only if he is negligent.

   b. An underground occupant (e.g. mining company) is liable for negligently damaging springs and wells, but an adjoining landowner is not liable for interfering with underground percolating water.

J. **Water Rights**

   1. **Riparian rights** are rights in water enjoyed by an owner of land that abuts a navigable or non-navigable natural river, stream, or lake. Several different sets of rules have been developed concerning the use of riparian water by adjoining landowners.

      a. Traditionally, a riparian owner was entitled to make only such use of riparian water as would not interrupt the natural flow of the body of water. Under the **natural flow doctrine**, a landowner may make unlimited use of riparian water for domestic or natural uses such as drinking and bathing. However, a landowner may use riparian water for artificial uses, such as irrigation, only if the use does not substantially diminish the flow of the body of water. Today, very few jurisdictions follow the natural flow doctrine.

      b. Under the **reasonable use doctrine**, a riparian owner may make reasonable use of riparian water so long as his use does not interfere unreasonably with the rights of other riparian owners. Such reasonable use is restricted to riparian land, which is defined as land lying within the watershed. Most American jurisdictions currently follow the reasonable use doctrine.

      c. The **prior appropriation doctrine** awards the right to use water to the first person to take the water for beneficial purposes. The prior appropriation doctrine was developed and is still followed in western states where water resources are scarce. Prior appropriation rules are usually set by state statute.

   2. **Diffuse surface water** is water from rain or melted snow that runs over the surface of land outside of a recognizable body of water. Several different sets of rules have been developed concerning the use of diffuse surface water.

      a. Under the **common enemy rule**, an owner may use any method available to keep diffuse surface water from coming onto his land. Traditionally, the common enemy rule was followed in crowded urban areas, primarily in northeastern states.

b.	Under the **civil law rule**, an owner was not permitted to interfere with the flow of diffuse surface water. Traditionally, the civil law rule was followed in western states with vast open spaces.

c.	Under the **reasonable use rule**, an owner may use reasonable means to alter the flow of diffuse surface water, even if surrounding land-owners are harmed.

3.	**Underground water** is water that runs beneath the surface of the land.

a.	The use of underground streams—where the water flows in a well-defined, known, and permanent channel—is governed by the rules applied to riparian waters.

b.	**Percolating underground water** is water that percolates through the subsurface of the land. The rules governing the use of percolating underground water vary from state to state.

(1)	Under the English absolute ownership doctrine, a possessor of land may take as much of the water percolating under his land as he desires. This is known as the **rule of capture**.

(2)	Some states apply the reasonable use test to percolating underground water.

(3)	A few states use a **correlative rights test**, which provides that all owners of land situated over a pool of underground water have equal rights to use the water.

(4)	In some states, prior appropriation statutes have been enacted to govern the use of percolating underground water.

## K.	Crops / Emblements

1.	The common law distinguishes between naturally growing crops, which are called *fructus naturales*, and crops produced by human labor, which are called *fructus industriales*.

a.	*Fructus naturales* are plants, such as trees, grasses, and perennial shrubs, that grow naturally on the land. Growing *fructus naturales* are considered to be part of the land. Thus, growing *fructus naturales* pass with a conveyance of the land and are subject to a mortgage on the land, unless they are specifically excluded.

(1)	The sale of growing *fructus naturales* is a conveyance of an interest in land, unless immediate severance of the crop by either the seller or the buyer is contemplated.

(2)	Because unsevered *fructus naturales* are considered real property, a conveyance of unsevered *fructus naturales* must be made by a writing that satisfies the Statute of Frauds.

(3)	If the trunks or roots of *fructus naturales* are located on the property line of adjoining landowners, the landowners own the trees as tenants in common.

b.	*Fructus industriales*, or **emblements**, are annual growing crops that result from human cultivation and labor. Under the common law, *fructus* *industriales* are considered to be part of the land and will pass with a conveyance under the land, unless the grantor expressly reserves the crop in the deed of conveyance.

    (1)   However, under the common law doctrine of emblements, a life tenant, a periodic tenant, and a tenant at will have the right to harvest *fructus industriales* planted before the end of the term. However, a tenant for a term of years has no such right.

2.   **Uniform Commercial Code**

    a.   UCC Article 2 applies to contracts for the sale of timber and growing crops apart from the land, regardless of whether the item is to be severed by the buyer or the seller. Article 2 does not distinguish between *fructus naturales* and *fructus industriales*.

    b.   Under UCC Article 9, a perfected security interest in crops growing on realty has priority over a conflicting interest of the holder of a lien on the realty or the owner of the realty if the debtor has record title to or possession of the realty.

VI. LANDLORD / TENANT

> **NOTE** A **lease** gives the tenant (lessee) exclusive possession of the premises for a period of time.

A. Creation

1. A lease may be created expressly, either orally or in writing. A writing generally is required by the Statute of Frauds for a term of more than one year.

2. An implied lease may be created by the conduct of the parties when the written lease is an invalid writing. In such a case, the resulting tenancy will be periodic. An implied lease may also be created when a holdover tenant pays rent and the landlord (lessor) accepts the rent.

B. Types of Leases

TYPES OF LEASES

Temporarily Pick Another Settlement

Term of Years, **P**eriodic, **A**t-Will, Tenancy at **S**ufferance

---

1. **Term of Years**

   a. A term of years has a definite beginning and end (e.g., until a set date or for a set number of months or years). No notice is required to terminate a lease for a term of years.

      EXAMPLE: L leases to T for a period of one year.

2. **Periodic**

   a. A periodic tenancy has a set beginning date and continues from period to period (e.g., from month to month) without a set termination date, until proper notice is given. While under the common law, notice merely has to be sufficient to show intent, some modern statutes require termination notice to be in writing.

   b. A periodic tenancy may be created expressly or by implication with a holdover tenant.

   c. Under the traditional rule, a periodic tenancy could be terminated only on the anniversary date. Improper notice was deemed ineffective, and the notice period was measured by the rent reservation clause.

   d. Under the modern statutory approach, termination may take place on any date, and the notice period is measured by the rent payment clause up to a maximum of six months.

3. **At-Will**

   a. An at-will lease has no fixed duration and lasts only as long as the landlord and tenant desire. An at-will tenancy terminates if:

            (1)   either party dies;

            (2)   the tenant commits waste;

            (3)   the tenant attempts to assign his interest;

            (4)   the landlord transfers his interest; or

            (5)   the landlord transfers the premises to a third party for a term of years.

     b.   If the lease gives the landlord a unilateral right to terminate, most courts find a tenancy at will that may be terminated by either the landlord or the tenant.

     c.   If the lease gives the tenant a unilateral right to terminate, some courts find a tenancy at will that may be terminated by either the landlord or the tenant. However, under the modern view, the tenant receives either a life estate or a fee simple, depending on the language used in the lease.

  4. **Tenancy at Sufferance / Holdover Tenancy**

     a.   A tenancy at sufferance occurs when a tenant remains in possession of the leased premises ("holds over") after the end of the lease term. A tenancy at sufferance is not a true tenancy. In most states, if a residential tenant holds over, the landlord may recover possession and receive the reasonable rental value for the holdover period.

C. Parties' Duties

  1. **Tenant's Duties**

     a. **Pay Rent**

         (1)   A tenant has a duty to pay rent. Under the common law estate theory, the tenant's duty to pay rent was not relieved if the premises were destroyed because the tenant would still have possession of the actual land. There was an exception to this common law rule where the tenant leased only a portion of the building. In that instance, if the building was destroyed, the tenant was then excused from paying rent.

         (2)   Today, there is no distinction between leasing all or part of a building. The tenant leasing all of a portion of a building may be relieved from the duty to pay rent if the premises are destroyed.

            (a) An exception to this rule exists where the tenant is not relieved from liability for rent when the tenant intentionally or negligently caused the destruction.

     b. **Waste**

         (1)   The tenant's duties in respect to waste are similar to those owed by life tenants. However, the tenant's duty not to commit permissive waste (primarily in respect to repairs) is not limited to the extent of income derived from or the reasonable rental value of the property when the tenant possesses personally.

         (2)   In addition, a tenant (except possibly a tenant for a long term) may not commit ameliorative waste, which a life tenant may be permitted to do.

c. **Repair**

(1) Under the common law estate theory, the landlord has no duty to repair the premises during the term of the lease. In contrast, the tenant had a duty not to commit waste, which includes a duty to repair the premises (i.e., not commit permissive waste). This duty extended to minor repairs that keep the building's interior safe from water and wind, but absent a covenant to the contrary, the tenant was not required to rebuild the premises if they were destroyed by an act of God. (Under the estate theory, the landlord also had no duty to rebuild).

(2) Alternatively, landlords and tenants may also agree on how to allocate repair duties. If a tenant assumes a general duty to repair, then absent a covenant to the contrary the tenant would in such a situation be responsible for repairing the premises from casualties, such as damages caused by fire and storms. The tenant would also be responsible for rebuilding or replacing the premises if they are destroyed by such casualties.

(3) Under the modern contract theory, the parties are free to covenant for duties that they would not bear under the common law estate theory.

(a) Under a general covenant to repair, the tenant is required to repair the premises. Usually, this covenant excepts ordinary wear and tear. The covenant may also except damages caused "by act of God," such as fire and weather.

(b) If the tenant covenants to repair without exception, the tenant must make all repairs, regardless of how the damage is caused.

(c) If there is no covenant in place, the landlord is required to repair damages resulting from casualties.

(4) Under the modern trend, in the absence of a contrary agreement, the tenant is not required to rebuild if the destruction was not his fault.

2. **Landlord's Duties**

a. The landlord has a duty to **deliver possession** of the premises to the tenant at the start of the lease term.

(1) The majority (English) rule requires delivery of actual possession.

(2) The minority (American) rule requires delivery of the legal right to possession only.

EXAMPLE: L and T execute a valid lease giving T a term of one year. On the date on which the lease commences, T discovers that the previous tenant is still on the premises because she has held over after the expiration of her term. Under the American rule, L has properly delivered possession because L gave T the legal right to the leased premises when L and T executed the lease. However, under the English rule, L has not properly delivered possession. The presence of the old tenant on the premises prevents L from delivering actual possession to T on the date on which the lease commences.

b. Typically, state law creates certain duties for the landlord, such as the provision of running water and heat.

c. The lease document may also create certain duties for the landlord, such as the duty to repair within the leased premises.

d. Every lease contains a **covenant of quiet enjoyment** (express or implied). In the covenant of quiet enjoyment, the landlord promises that the tenant will not be disturbed by the landlord (or someone claiming through the landlord) during his possession of the premises. A tenant may treat the lease as terminated and withhold rent if the covenant of quiet enjoyment has been breached by an actual or constructive eviction.

(1) A tenant may treat the lease as terminated and withhold rent if the landlord or someone claiming through him breaches the covenant of quiet enjoyment by **actual eviction** of the tenant.

(a) Under the majority rule, if a tenant is actually evicted from part of the premises by landlord, the tenant is relieved of all liability for rent, even if the tenant continues to occupy the rest of the premises. However, the Second Restatement of Property rejects the majority rule and calls for a rent abatement only.

(b) When a tenant is partially evicted by an act of the landlord (or his agent), rent abatement attributable to the portion from which the tenant has been evicted is appropriate.

(2) A tenant may treat the lease as terminated and withhold rent if the landlord breaches the covenant of quiet enjoyment by **constructive eviction** of the tenant. For a constructive eviction to exist:

(a) the landlord's act must substantially and permanently interfere with the tenant's use and enjoyment of the premises; and

(b) the tenant must move out.

(3) The following acts by the landlord constitute constructive eviction:

(a) withholding something essential to the full enjoyment of the property that is included within the terms of the lease, such as heat; and

(b) withholding something required by statute, such as hot and cold running water.

(4) A landlord probably constructively evicts the tenant if he breaches one of the following landlord duties created at common law:

(a) making and keeping the premises habitable in a short-term lease of a furnished dwelling;

(b) disclosing latent defects existing in the premises, known to the landlord, and undiscoverable by the tenant at the time the lease was made;

       (c)   maintaining common areas used by all tenants;

       (d)   using due care in making promised or volunteered repairs;

       (e)   refraining from making fraudulent misrepresentations concerning the condition of the leased premises; or

       (f)   in some jurisdictions, abetting immoral conduct or abetting nuisances on properties owned by the landlord that may affect the leased premises.

   (5)   Under the majority rule, if a tenant is constructively evicted from part of the premises, the tenant may receive a rent abatement but is not relieved of all liability for rent.

   (6)   In some states, if a landlord's breach of the covenant of quiet enjoyment does not constitute actual eviction or is not substantial enough to constitute constructive eviction, the tenant who remains on the premises can seek money damages from the landlord.

e.   Under the modern trend, the landlord is deemed to have impliedly warranted that the residential premises are fit for habitation. The **implied warranty of habitability** guarantees that the landlord will deliver and maintain premises that are safe, clean, and fit for human habitation.

   (1)   To prove that the landlord has breached this warranty, the tenant must show a defect in essential residential facilities.

       (a)   In the majority of jurisdictions, the defect may be patent (obvious) or latent (nonobvious).

       (b)   Some jurisdictions exclude patent defects from the scope of the implied warranty of habitability.

   (2)   To claim a breach of the implied warranty of habitability, the tenant must:

       (a)   provide the landlord with notice of the defect; and

       (b)   allow the landlord reasonable time to make necessary repairs.

> **NOTE** The implied warranty of habitability applies to residential leases. Commercial leases are not covered by the warranty. The following leases may also be excluded from coverage under the implied warranty of habitability: leases for single-family residences, agricultural leases, long-term leases, and casual leases made by non-merchant landlords.

f.   In some jurisdictions, a housing code violation automatically breaches the implied warranty of habitability. In other jurisdictions, the housing code provides the standard; however, substantial compliance with the code is sufficient so long as habitability is not affected. In some jurisdictions, the standard for the implied warranty is found in the common law, even in the absence of a housing code. In those jurisdictions, a breach of the warranty may be found if the premises are uninhabitable in the view of a reasonable person.

   (1)   If the landlord breaches the implied warranty of habitability:

       (a)   the tenant is excused from further performance under the lease;

       (b)   the tenant may, but need not, vacate the premises;

(c)   the tenant may treat the lease as canceled, and the rent is abated;

(d)   the tenant may seek money damages; and

1)   Some courts use the contract measure of damages for breach of warranty, which is the value of the premises as warranted less the value of the premises as received, and agreed rent is evidence of the rental value.

2)   Other jurisdictions measure damages by finding the difference between the agreed rent and the fair rental value of the premises received.

(e)   the tenant may seek reformation or other traditional contract or tort remedies.

D.   Remedies for Breach of Duty

1.   Landlord's Remedies for Tenant's Breach of Duty

a.   If the tenant fails to pay rent or commits another material breach of the lease, the landlord may seek:

(1)   to evict the tenant; and/or

(2)   to recover damages for the tenant's breach.

b.   Traditionally, acceleration of rent was not available to the landlord for anticipatory breach of a lease by the tenant. However, the modern rule permits the use of **rent acceleration clauses** in leases.

(1)   In an action for rent, the tenant may defend on the grounds of non-compliance by the landlord or on the ground of destruction of the premises.

c.   A tenant **abandons** the premises if he vacates the premises without intent to return and fails to pay rent. Traditionally, if the tenant abandons the premises, the landlord may:

(1)   retake the premises;

(2)   ignore an abandonment and continue to hold the tenant liable for rent; or

(3)   reenter and relet the premises.

(a)   Under the traditional view, if the tenant abandons the premises, the landlord has no duty to mitigate by attempting to relet the premises. However, under the modern view, the landlord has a duty to mitigate if the tenant abandons. If mitigation is required, the burden of proof is placed on the landlord to show that he attempted to mitigate his losses.

d.   Traditionally, a landlord was allowed to use **self**-help to remove a breaching tenant from the premises. However, under the modern approach, self-help is prohibited or carefully constrained. The landlord must seek court action to reenter the premises.

e.   A security deposit may be retained by a landlord only to the extent necessary to cover actual loss that the deposit was intended to secure (e.g., unpaid rent, damage).

f. **Retaliatory eviction** (e.g., eviction in response to tenant's complaints about landlord) is prohibited in most states.

CONSTRUCTIVE EVICTION AND BREACH OF IMPLIED WARRANTY OF HABITABILITY			
Theory	Basis for Cause of Action	Effects of Breach on the Lease	Remedies Available
Constructive Eviction (Breach of Covenant of Quiet Enjoyment)	The tenant must show an interference with beneficial use and enjoyment of the premises serious enough to amount to an eviction.	The tenant is excused from further performance under the lease. The tenant must vacate the premises within a reasonable time.	The tenant may treat the lease as canceled. Rent is abated.
Breach of Implied Warranty of Habitability	The tenant must show a patent or latent defect in essential residential facilities.	The tenant is excused from further performance under the lease. The tenant may, but need not, vacate the premises.	The tenant may treat the lease as canceled. Rent is abated. The tenant may seek money damages, reformation, or other traditional contract or tort remedies.

2. **Tenant's Remedies for Landlord's Breach of Duty**

   a. A tenant may seek money damages for the landlord's breach of the lease.

      (1) Traditionally, a tenant may vacate the premises and terminate the lease if the tenant has been evicted by the landlord, actually or constructively.

      (2) Statutes in many jurisdictions provide the tenant with the following statutory remedies:

         (a) withholding rent; or

         (b) repairing the premises and deducting the cost of repair from subsequent rent payments.

   b. A landlord is not liable to the tenant or others on the premises with the consent of the tenant for injuries caused by a condition of the premises, except in the following situations:

      (1) an undisclosed dangerous condition exists that is known or should have been known to the landlord but is unknown to the tenant;

      (2) a condition exists that is dangerous to persons outside of the premises;

      (3) the premises are leased for admission to the public;

      (4) parts of land are retained in the landlord's control but are available for use by the tenant;

      (5) the landlord has contracted to repair; or

      (6) the landlord has been negligent in making repairs.

E. **Assignments and Subleases**

   1.   An **assignment** occurs when the tenant transfers to a third person (the assignee) all of his rights, title, and interest in the leased premises. An assignee comes into privity of estate with the landlord.

       a.   Therefore, if the rent is not paid, the landlord may sue the assignee, so long as the assignee remains on the premises. However, the landlord may not sue the assignee after the assignee has transferred the premises to another third person, unless the assignee had assumed the duty to pay rent.

   2.   A **sublease** occurs when the tenant transfers to a third person (the subtenant or sublessee) less than all of his rights, title, and interest in the leased premises. A subtenant does not come into privity of estate with the landlord. Therefore, absent an express assumption of the duty to pay rent, the landlord may not sue the subtenant directly for rent due.

   3.   Covenants against assignments and/or subleases are construed strictly against the landlord.

       a.   Under the **Rule in Dumpor's Case**, once waived, a covenant against assignment is unenforceable as to the next assignment.

           (1)   The Rule in Dumpor's Case does not apply to subleases.

VII. FIXTURES

A. **In General**

1. A **fixture** is a chattel that has become so connected to real property that a disinterested observer would consider the chattel to be part of the realty.

    EXAMPLE: If a homeowner attaches a bookshelf to the wall of her home, it retains its separate identity after the attachment, and thus is not a fixture. However, the same bookshelf built into the wall becomes part of the realty, and thus is a fixture.

2. When one person owns a chattel and the land to which the chattel is to be fixed, the chattel becomes a fixture if:

    a. it is annexed to the real property;

    b. it has been appropriated to the use of the land; and

    c. the annexor intends it to be a fixture.

3. A chattel may be deemed annexed to the land if:

    a. it is permanently attached to real property or to something appurtenant to the real property;

    EXAMPLE: A chain-link fence may be deemed annexed to the land if it is erected around a parcel of land by placing posts into holes in the ground.

    b. it would be difficult to move solely based on its own weight; or

    EXAMPLE: A large, heavy statue may be deemed annexed to the land if it is placed on the ground in a backyard garden.

    c. it is constructively annexed to the property by being specially designed for the property or a fixture on the property.

    EXAMPLE: Hurricane shutters custom designed for a house may be classified as annexed to the house, even if they are removed and stored in the garage during winter months.

4. An annexed chattel may become a fixture if the chattel is so necessary or convenient to the use of the land that it is commonly regarded as part of the land. In determining whether a chattel has been appropriated to the use of the land, the court will consider the nature of the land or structure to which the chattel is affixed.

    EXAMPLE: Chairs in a movie theater will be deemed appropriated to the use of the land, while chairs placed in the kitchen of an apartment may not be regarded as such.

5. Intent to annex a chattel is a question of fact that is judged objectively, according to a reasonable person standard. The finder of fact considers the nature of the chattel, the degree of annexation, and the appropriateness of the chattel to the property's use.

B. Transfers, Severance, and Change of Ownership

1. When both the chattel and the land are owned by the same person, a deed to the real property will transfer all of the fixtures on the property. However, the buyer and seller may agree that the seller may remove certain fixtures from the property before title is transferred to the buyer.

    EXAMPLE: A deed describing a lot of land also transfers the house on the lot and the plumbing fixtures in the house.

2. An owner of a chattel may affix it to land also owned by that person which later becomes encumbered by a mortgage. In that case, the mortgage extends to both the land and the fixture. If the chattel is attached to land already encumbered by a mortgage, the prior mortgage also encompasses the chattel, even though the mortgagee thereby receives a security interest that is greater than the one bargained for by the mortgagee.

3. If a fixture and the land to which it is attached are subject to common ownership, the owner is free to sever the chattel physically and permanently from the premises. In that case, the fixture regains its status as personal property. A constructive severance of a fixture may occur when the owner of the land expressly reserves the fixture in a contract of sale for the land or deed of conveyance of the land.

4. Under Article 2 of the Uniform Commercial Code, a contract for the sale of a structure to be removed from realty is a contract for the sale of goods if the structure is to be severed from the land by the seller. Article 2 also applies to contracts for the sale of other things attached to realty and capable of severance without material harm to the land, regardless of whether the item is to be severed by the buyer or by the seller.

C. Trade Fixture

1. A **trade fixture** is a chattel that is annexed to the land by a tenant (i.e., a life tenant, tenant for a term, periodic tenant, or tenant at will) to advance his business or trade during his tenancy.

2. During a tenancy, a tenant is free to remove a trade fixture. If a tenant removes a trade fixture, he is responsible for repairing damages caused by its removal. In some states, the trade fixture exception has been broadened to include domestic and/or ornamental fixtures.

3. At common law, if the tenancy is for a definite term and ends on a certain day, trade fixtures must be removed before the end of the term or they become part of the realty.

    a. Most states refuse to follow the common law rule that a tenant forfeits his trade fixtures by failing to remove them before expiration of the lease term. To encourage trade and industry, a tenant is permitted to remove trade fixtures within a reasonable time after the expiration of a lease.

        EXAMPLE: L leases Blackacre to T as a store for three years, with a set termination date. During the term, T firmly affixes shelves to the floor of the store building. These shelves are still standing the day after the lease terminates. Under the common law rule, the shelves remain fixtures on the property and belong to L because T did not remove them before the end of the term. However, under the modern view, T has not yet forfeited his interest in the shelves. Instead, T will be given a reasonable time after the termination date to remove the shelves.

D. Security Interest

1. A security interest may be created if a chattel becomes or already is a fixture [UCC § 9-334(a)]. Often, the land to which the chattel is affixed is encumbered with a mortgage.

2. Under the common law, priority of recording will determine priority between a security interest in a fixture and a conflicting security interest in the realty to which the fixture is attached.

3. Under Uniform Commercial Code Section 9-334, a security interest in a fixture is subordinate to a mortgage or other lien on the land to which the fixture is attached. However, in the following cases, a lien on the fixture may be given priority:

    a. a purchase-money security interest in a fixture will have priority over a conflicting lien on the real property to which the fixture is attached if [UCC § 9-334(d)]:

        (1) the purchaser of the fixture has record title to or possession of the real property to which the fixture is attached; and

        (2) the security interest in the chattel:

            (a) attaches before the chattel becomes affixed to the land; and

            (b) is perfected by a fixture filing before the goods are attached or within 20 days of the attachment;

    b. a non-purchase-money security interest in a fixture will have priority over a conflicting lien on the real property to which the fixture is attached if the purchaser of the fixture has record title to or possession of the real property and the security interest in the chattel [UCC § 9-334(e)(1)]:

        (1) is perfected by a fixture filing before the interest of the holder of the lien on the real property or the owner is recorded; and

        (2) has priority over any conflicting interest of a predecessor of the lien holder or the owner;

    c. a security interest in readily movable goods (e.g., office machines) has priority if it is perfected by any method permitted by Article 9 [UCC § 9-334(e)(2)]; and

    d. a security interest in a fixture also has priority over a lien on the realty to which the fixture is attached if the real property lien was obtained by legal or equitable proceedings after the security interest in the fixture was perfected by any means permitted under Article 9 [UCC § 9-334(e)(3)].

EXAMPLE: Buyer purchases an item from Seller on credit. Buyer grants Seller a security interest in the item. Buyer then affixes the item to her real property, which is encumbered by a mortgage previously executed by Buyer. Under the common law, between Seller and the mortgagee of the land, priority will be given to the party that records first. However, under UCC Section 9-334, the result is different. Under this section, if Seller perfects his interest by a fixture filing within 20 days after Buyer affixes the item to her land, Seller will prevail over the mortgagee of the Buyer's land.

Issue-Spotting Exercises

Question 1

Grantor was the owner in fee simple of a ten-acre tract of land. In 1993, Grantor executed a warranty deed purporting to convey the land "to Grantee, his heirs, and assigns, in fee simple, but if Grantee or his successors shall use the property for other than residential purposes during the next 30 years, then the Grantor or his successors may re-enter and resume the former estate."

After Grantee took possession, he constructed a home and resided on the property with his family. In 2008, Grantee and his wife died, leaving Son as their sole heir. Son took sole possession and built an addition on the dwelling, which he converted into an office. One day, Grantor, who was still alive, was driving past the property and noticed that Son was operating a law office on the property. Thereupon, Grantor demanded that Son surrender possession because the non-residential use meant that Grantor once again owned the property in fee simple.

Is the Grantor correct?

Question 2

Hernandez owned Casa de Sol, a beautiful 12-acre hacienda estate, in San Antonio. Hernandez was the record title owner in fee simple absolute. In 2005, Hernandez conveyed Casa de Sol to Gomez for life with remainder to Tampica, Hernandez's daughter. Gomez took possession and two years later sold the property to Tavarez for $200,000. The following year, Tampica died and was survived by her sole heir, Xavier. Tavarez has now indicated a desire to sell the property. A dispute has arisen as to legal title to the property.

Hernandez, Gomez, and Xavier are still alive. What is the state of title to Casa de Sol?

Question 3

Landlord owned an apartment, which he leased to Abel for a three-year term beginning December 1, for a monthly rental of $1,000, to be payable on the first of each month. After Abel resided in the apartment for six months, he assigned his interest in the premises to Baker on June 1. Baker paid the rental on the apartment for two months and then assigned his interest to Carr. Carr took possession on August 1, and paid the rental for August, but did not pay the rental for the next three months of occupancy.

Then on December 1, Carr assigned the premises to Dave, who took possession, but didn't pay any rental to Landlord during the period of his occupancy from December 1 to April 1 of the following year. On April 2, Landlord now brings an action against Dave to recover the outstanding rent that is due on the premises.

Dave is liable for what amount?

Question 4

A brother and sister inherited their childhood home from their father. They thereby became tenants in common. The property had never been used as anything except a residence. The brother had been residing on the property with his father at the time his father died. The sister had been residing in a distant city. After their father's funeral, the brother continued to live on the property. There was no discussion between the brother and the sister concerning their common ownership, nor had there ever been any administration of their father's estate.

The brother paid all taxes, insurance, and other carrying charges on the property. He paid no rent or other compensation to his sister, nor did she request any such payment. Thirty years later, a series of disputes arose between the siblings for the first time concerning their respective rights. The jurisdiction where the land is located recognizes the usual common-law types of co-tenancies, and there is no applicable legislation on the subject. The jurisdiction has an ordinary 20-year adverse possession statute.

The brother now claims fee simple title and brings an action against the sister to quiet title in himself. For whom should the court rule?

Question 5

The State of Blue has the following recording statute in effect:

"No conveyance is good against a subsequent purchaser for a valuable consideration and without notice, unless the same be recorded prior to subsequent purchase."

Lau is the owner in fee simple of a 20-acre tract of unimproved land in State Blue. On May 1, Lau sold the property to Eto for the purchase price of $40,000 under a quitclaim deed. Eto did not record the deed. On May 5, Lau died leaving a valid will by which he devised the property to his son, Landon. After the administration of Lau's estate, Landon, in consideration of the sum of $75,000, conveyed the property to Fong by warranty deed. This transaction took place on August 1. When Fong acquired title, he had no actual knowledge of Eto's deed (which was still unrecorded). On August 10, Eto recorded his deed. Fong did not record the deed he received from Landon until August 15.

In an appropriate action to quiet title, in which all interested parties have been joined, who owns title to the property?

Essays

Real Property

In Class

Part A:

Joe Snidely owns two buildings in the city of Harmony Hills. The first is a high-rise apartment building, Harmony Towers. The second is a two-story commercial building, the bottom of which is rented to Myra King, who operates a dress shop. The upper floor is rented to Lois Parker, who runs a bakery and tearoom. Harmony Hills is located in a modern jurisdiction.

Arthur Willis rents unit 212 in Harmony Towers. He has a written lease that runs from January 1, 2010 to January 1, 2011. According to the lease, both Snidely and Willis must give 30-days written notice of intention not to renew. Rent is $1,200 per month, payable on the 15th of every month. The lease prohibits assignments without the landlord's approval.

In June 2010, Willis decides to move in with his brother to save money. Without informing Snidely, he assigns unit 212 to his girlfriend, Connie. Connie makes timely rental payments to Willis in June, July, and August, and Willis in turn pays Snidely on the 15th of each month. On September 1, Connie begins experiencing water problems, namely a lack of hot water from both the kitchen and bathroom taps. The cold water that comes from the taps has taken on a brownish color. Willis informs Snidely, who promises to "see to it immediately." Two weeks later, the water situation has not improved, so Connie and Willis decide to withhold the rent for September. On October 14, Snidely finally comes to repair the plumbing and discovers Connie, who admits that she has been subletting from Willis since June. She offers Snidely a check for the October rent, which he accepts, saying, "I don't care who pays me, as long as I get paid on time."

The next morning, Connie attempts to shower. When she turns on the faucet marked "cold," she is severely scalded because Snidely accidentally switched the taps while repairing the plumbing. Connie immediately vacates the premises and goes to the nearest hospital for treatment. No further rent is forthcoming for the remainder of the lease term.

1. Snidely sues both Willis and Connie for rent payments due in September, November, and December. Discuss the outcome, including the validity of Snidely's claims against both parties and any relevant defenses that could be raised by Willis and/or Connie.

2. Connie sues Snidely for her injuries. Explain the probable result.

Part B:

Meanwhile, in the commercial building, Lois Parker's bakery and tearoom closes its doors due to lack of business. There are 14 months remaining on Lois's two-year lease with Snidely, with rent set at $2,000 per month. Lois defaults on her rent, but Snidely makes no effort to find a new tenant. Finally, six months later, Myra King approaches Snidely with an offer to rent the upper floor to expand her clothing store.

Snidely agrees to lease the upper story to Myra for $1,500 per month, effective immediately, but Lois is still in possession and refuses to vacate "until she is good and ready." Lois finally leaves the premises, but before she vacates, she removes her commercial oven, leaving a gaping hole in the wall.

1. If Snidely sues Lois for the rents due for the remainder of her lease term, discuss the probable result.

2. If Snidely sues Lois for the wall damage, discuss the probable result.

3. If Myra demands an abatement of her first month's rent, what will be the probable result?

Real Property

In Class Question

Snidely v. Willis and/or Connie

I. **Was there privity between Snidely and Willis?**

    A. **(Rule)** A lease gives a tenant exclusive possession of the premises for a period of time
        1. A writing is required by the Statute of Frauds for a term of more than year
    B. **(Application)** Willis entered into written lease
    C. **(Conclusion)** Willis is in privity with Snidely

II. **Was there a valid assignment of the lease?**

    A. **(Rule)** An assignment occurs when tenant transfers to a third person all of his right, title, and interest in leased premises
        1. Lease expressly prohibits assignments without landlord's approval
    B. **(Application)** Such covenants against assignments and/or subleases are construed strictly against landlord
        1. Willis continued to pay Snidely for rent due on 15th of each month
        2. Willis did not intend to transfer to Connie all of his right, title, and interest in leased premises
    C. **(Conclusion)** Assignment was invalid

III. **Was there privity between Snidely and Connie?**

    A. **(Rule)** A sublease occurs when the tenant transfers to a third person less than all of his right, title, and interest in leased premises
        1. A subtenant does not come into privity of estate with landlord absent an express assumption of duty to pay rent
    B. **(Application)** Although Snidely accepted rent payment from Connie for October, does not rise to the level of an express assumption of duty to pay rent
        1. Willis continued to pay rent for June, July, and August
    C. **(Conclusion)** Connie is a subtenant
        1. No privity for Snidely to sue Connie

IV. **Did Willis have duty to pay rent?**

    A. **(Rule)** A tenant has a duty to pay rent
        1. Under common law, tenant's duty is not relieved if premises are destroyed
        2. Under modern theory, tenant may be relieved from duty if premises are destroyed, unless tenant intentionally or negligently caused destruction
        3. Under the modern contract theory, parties are free to take on duties that they would not bear under common-law estate theory
    B. **(Application)** Leased property was not destroyed; rather, the tenant began experiencing water problems that required repair
    C. **(Conclusion)** Unless Snidely agreed to take on a duty of repair, Willis had duty to pay rent

V. **Was there a constructive eviction?**

A. **(Rule)** Constructive eviction—landlord's act must substantially and permanently interfere with tenant's use and enjoyment of premises, and tenant must move out
   1. Every lease contains a covenant of quiet enjoyment
   2. Landlord promises tenant will not be disturbed by landlord (or someone claiming through him) during his possession of premises
   3. Tenant may treat lease as terminated and withhold rent if covenant of quiet enjoyment breached by actual or constructive eviction
   4. State law creates obligation on landlord to provide running water and heat

B. **(Application)** Withholding of hot water and failure to exercise due care in making promised or volunteered repairs likely constitute constructive eviction
   1. Willis opted not to move out

C. **(Conclusion)** No constructive eviction because elements have not been met

VI. **Can Willis assert any defenses?**

A. **(Rule)** Under modern trend, landlord impliedly warrants that residential premises are fit for habitation
   1. Implied warranty of habitability applies to residential leases and guarantees that landlord will deliver and maintain premises that are safe, clean, and fit for human habitation
   2. To prove breach, tenant must show defect in essential residential facilities and: (1) provide the landlord with notice of defect, and (2) allow landlord reasonable time to make necessary repairs
   3. If landlord breaches: (1) tenant is excused from performance under lease; (2) tenant may, but need not, vacate the premises; (3) tenant may treat the lease as canceled, and rent is abated; (4) tenant may seek money damages; and (5) tenant may seek reformation or other traditional contract or tort remedies
   4. Traditionally, tenant's remedies entailed vacating premises and terminating lease
   5. Many jurisdictions provide statutory remedies, including withholding of rent or repairing and deducting cost of repair from subsequent rent payments

B. **(Application)** Plumbing problems began in September
   1. Clean, hot, running water falls within landlord's implied warranty of habitability
   2. Willis provided timely notice on September 1
   3. Snidely promised to "see to it immediately"
   4. Did not address plumbing problems until month and a half later

C. **(Conclusion)** Willis has valid defense to withhold rent

Connie v. Snidely

I. **Can Connie recover for her injuries?**

A. **(Rule)** Landlord not liable to tenant, or others on the premises with consent of tenant, for injuries caused by a condition of premises, except where landlord negligent in making repairs

B. **(Application)** Snidely was negligent in his repairs of plumbing
   1. He accidentally switched taps, resulting in Connie's being severely scalded in shower
   2. Connie was on leased premises with Willis' express consent
C. **(Conclusion)** Connie can recover money damages for her injuries

Snidely v. Lois

I. **Did Lois have a duty to pay rent for the remainder of her lease?**

A. **(Rule)** A tenant has a duty to pay rent
   1. Tenant abandons premises if she vacates without intent to return and fails to pay rent
   2. Traditionally, if tenant abandons, landlord may retake premises, ignore abandonment and continue to hold tenant liable for rent, or reenter and relet premises
   3. Under traditional view, if tenant abandons, landlord has no duty to mitigate
   4. Under modern view, landlord has duty to mitigate.
   5. Burden of proof is on landlord to show that he attempted to mitigate his losses
B. **(Application)** Lois failed to pay rent for six months before ultimately abandoning premises
   1. Did not indicate any intent to abandon for several months
   2. Remained in possession and refused to vacate "until she is good and ready"
   3. Mere failure to pay rent does not rise to level of abandonment
C. **(Conclusion)** Snidely acted appropriately in seeking to mitigate by allowing Myra as a replacement tenant
   1. Lois liable for rents due for remainder of lease term

II. **Was Lois liable for wall damages caused by removal of oven?**

A. **(Rule)** Fixture is a chattel so connected to real property that disinterested observer would consider it to be part of the realty
   1. Chattel becomes a fixture if (1) it is annexed to real property, (2) it has been appropriated to use of land, and (3) the annexor intends it to be fixture
   2. Chattel annexed to land if (1) it is permanently attached to real property, or to something appurtenant to real property; (2) it would be difficult to move solely based on its own weight; or (3) it is constructively annexed to property by being specially designed for property or a fixture on the property
   3. Annexed chattel may become a fixture if so necessary or convenient to land that it is commonly regarded as part of land
   4. Court will consider nature of land or structure to which chattel is affixed
   5. Intent to annex a chattel is a question of fact that is judged objectively, according to a reasonable person standard
      a. Finder of fact considers nature of chattel, degree of annexation, and appropriateness of chattel to property's use
   6. A trade fixture is a chattel annexed to the land by a tenant to advance her business or trade during tenancy

7. Tenant is free to remove a trade fixture
   a. She is responsible for repairing damages caused by its removal
B. **(Application)** Commercial oven constituted annexed chattel that became a fixture
   1. Permanently attached to the real property
   2. So connected and specially designed for land that it left a gaping hole in wall
   3. Difficult to move based on its weight
   4. Annexed to land by Lois to advance her bakery and tearoom business during her tenancy
C. **(Conclusion)** Lois liable for wall damages caused by her removal of commercial oven
   1. Chattel was so necessary or convenient to property's use that it constituted a trade fixture

Myra v. Snidely

I. **Was Myra entitled to an abatement of first month's rent?**

A. **(Rule)** Landlord has duty to deliver possession of premises to tenant at the start of lease term
   1. Majority rule requires delivery of actual possession
   2. Minority rule requires delivery of legal right to possession only
B. **(Application)** Snidely agreed to lease upper story to Myra effective immediately
   1. At that time, Lois was still in possession pursuant to her lease
   2. Although Lois defaulted on her rent payment, she did not intend to abandon at time Snidely agreed to lease to Myra
   3. Lois still had 14 months remaining on her two-year lease
   4. Lois was entitled to remain in possession of leased property
C. **(Conclusion)** Snidely failed to deliver possession to Myra at start of her lease term
   1. Myra entitled to an abatement of first month's rent

Real Property

In Class Question

This sample answer would be considered above the standard expected of a 1L student.

Part A:

1. The issues are (1) whether Snidely has any valid claims against Willis and/or Connie for unpaid rent where an assignment of the lease took place without Snidely's consent, and (2) whether Willis and Connie may assert a defense of constructive eviction.

    A lease gives a tenant exclusive possession of the premises for a period of time. Here, Willis entered into a written lease with Snidely that runs from January 1, 2010 to January 1, 2011. A writing is required by the Statute of Frauds for a term of more than year. This term-of-years lease was in writing, thereby satisfying the Statute of Frauds. Thus, Willis is in privity with Snidely.

    However, in June 2010, Willis attempted to assign the lease to Connie. An assignment occurs when the tenant transfers to a third person all of his right, title, and interest in the leased premises. The lease expressly prohibits assignments without the landlord's approval. Although such covenants against assignments and/or subleases are construed strictly against the landlord, it is likely that the court will nevertheless find that the assignment was invalid. The fact that Willis continued to pay Snidely for the rent due on the 15th of each month demonstrates that Willis did not intend to transfer to Connie all of his right, title, and interest in the leased premises. Because the assignment was invalid, there is no privity between Connie and Snidely.

    The issue now becomes whether there is any privity at all for Snidely to sue Connie. A sublease occurs when the tenant transfers to a third person less than all of his right, title, and interest in the leased premises. Connie is merely a subtenant of unit 212. A subtenant does not come into privity of estate with the landlord absent an express assumption of the duty to pay rent. Although Snidely accepted rent payment from Connie for the month of October, the court would likely hold that such conduct does not rise to the level of an express assumption of the duty to pay rent. Indeed, Willis continued to make timely rental payments for the months of June, July, and August. Thus, the mere production of a check from Connie for October's rent does not constitute an express assumption of the duty to pay rent. Accordingly, there is no privity for Snidely to sue Connie. Snidely may proceed with his claim for rents due in September, November, and December against Willis only.

    A tenant has a duty to pay rent. Under the common-law estate theory, the tenant's duty to pay rent is not relieved if the premises are destroyed. Conversely, pursuant to modern theory, the tenant may be relieved from the duty to pay rent if the premises are destroyed, unless the tenant intentionally or negligently caused the destruction. Here, the leased property was not destroyed; rather, the tenant began experiencing water problems that required repair. Under the common-law estate theory, the landlord had no duty to repair the premises during the term of the lease. In contrast, the tenant had a duty not to commit waste, which included a duty to repair the premises. Under the modern contract theory, however, the parties are free to take on duties that they would not bear under the common-law estate theory. Thus, unless Snidely agreed to take on a duty of repair, the duty presumably fell on Willis.

However, every lease also contains a covenant of quiet enjoyment where the landlord promises that the tenant will not be disturbed by the landlord (or someone claiming through him) during his possession of the premises. A tenant may treat the lease as terminated and withhold rent if the covenant of quiet enjoyment has been breached by an actual or a constructive eviction. Here, the issue arises as to whether a constructive eviction occurred by Snidely's failure to make timely repairs to the leased premises. For a constructive eviction to exist, the landlord's act must substantially and permanently interfere with the tenant's use and enjoyment of the premises, and the tenant must move out. State law typically creates an obligation on the landlord to provide running water and heat. Thus, the withholding of hot water and the failure to exercise due care in making promised or volunteered repairs would likely constitute a constructive eviction by Snidely. However, although the court will likely hold that there was sufficient evidence to demonstrate a constructive eviction, Willis nevertheless opted not to move out. As a result, Willis's withholding of rent under the defense of a constructive eviction will likely fail because the elements establishing such a defense have not been met.

The question now becomes whether Willis can assert any defenses against Snidely's claim for the recovery of unpaid rent. Under the modern trend, a landlord is deemed to have warranted impliedly that residential premises are fit for habitation. The implied warranty of habitability applies to residential leases and guarantees that the landlord will deliver and maintain premises that are safe, clean, and fit for human habitation. To prove that the landlord has breached this warranty, the tenant must show a defect in essential residential facilities. To claim a breach of the implied warranty of habitability, the tenant must (1) provide the landlord with notice of the defect, and (2) allow the landlord reasonable time to make necessary repairs. If the landlord breaches the implied warranty of habitability, (1) the tenant is excused from performance under the lease; (2) the tenant may, but need not, vacate the premises; (3) the tenant may treat the lease as canceled, and the rent is abated; (4) the tenant may seek money damages; and (5) the tenant may seek reformation or other traditional contract or tort remedies.

Here, plumbing problems began in the leased premises in September. The provision of clean, hot, running water falls within a landlord's implied warranty of habitability. Willis provided timely notice to Snidely of the defect in essential residential facilities on September 1. Upon receiving notice, Snidely was entitled to a reasonable amount of time to make necessary repairs, and he promised to "see to it immediately." Yet, Snidely did not address the plumbing problems until nearly a month and a half later on October 14—a period of time well outside the scope of reasonableness for making such necessary repairs.

Traditionally, a tenant's remedies entailed vacating the premises and terminating the lease. Many jurisdictions now provide the tenant with statutory remedies, including the withholding of rent or repairing the premises and deducting the cost of repair from subsequent rent payments. Thus, Willis has a valid defense to the withholding of rent for the month of September in which Snidely failed to timely implement the necessary repairs. Moreover, because the water issues were not even effectively resolved, Snidely continued to breach the implied warranty of habitability. Accordingly, Willis is excused from performance under the lease. Snidely's claim against Willis for unpaid rent for the months of November and December will similarly fail.

2. The issue is whether Connie will be successful in her claim for injuries caused by Snidely's negligent repairs on the leased premises. A landlord is not liable to the tenant, or others on the premises with the consent of the tenant, for injuries caused by a condition of the premises, except where the landlord has been negligent in making repairs. Here, the court will likely hold that Snidely was negligent in his repairs of the plumbing, inasmuch as he had accidentally switched the taps, resulting in Connie's being severely scalded in the shower. Connie was on the leased premises with the express consent of Willis. Thus, Connie will likely succeed in her claim against Snidely, thereby recovering money damages for the injuries sustained by his negligent repairs.

Part B:

1. The issue is whether Snidely may assert a claim against Lois for rents due for the remainder of her lease term. A tenant has a duty to pay rent. A tenant abandons the premises if she vacates the premises without intent to return and fails to pay rent. Here, Lois failed to pay rent for six months before ultimately abandoning the premises in breach of the lease.

    Traditionally, if the tenant abandons the premises, the landlord may retake the premises, ignore an abandonment, thereby continuing to hold the tenant liable for rent, or reenter and relet the premises. Under the traditional view, if the tenant abandons the premises, the landlord has no duty to mitigate by attempting to relet the premises. Under the modern view, however, the landlord has a duty to mitigate if the tenant abandons. Because mitigation is required in this modern jurisdiction, the burden of proof is placed on the landlord to show that he attempted to mitigate his losses. Here, Lois did not indicate any intent to abandon the premises for several months, inasmuch as she remained in possession of the property. In fact, she made it clear that she refused to vacate "until she is good and ready." Her mere failure to pay rent does not rise to the level of abandonment. Thus, the court will likely hold that Snidely acted appropriately in seeking to mitigate his damages by allowing Myra to lease the property as a replacement tenant. Thus, Snidely will likely succeed in his claim for rents due from Lois for the remainder of her lease term.

2. The issue now becomes whether Snidely may recover for damages to the wall caused by Lois's removal of the commercial oven. A fixture is a chattel that has become so connected to real property that a disinterested observer would consider the chattel to be part of the realty. A chattel becomes a fixture if (1) it is annexed to the real property, (2) it has been appropriated to the use of the land, and (3) the annexor intends it to be a fixture. A chattel may be deemed annexed to the land if (1) it is permanently attached to real property, or to something appurtenant to the real property; (2) it would be difficult to move solely based on its own weight; or (3) it is constructively annexed to the property by being specially designed for the property or a fixture on the property. An annexed chattel may become a fixture if the chattel is so necessary or convenient to the use of the land that it is commonly regarded as part of the land. In determining whether a chattel has been appropriated to the use of the land, the court will consider the nature of the land or structure to which the chattel is affixed. Intent to annex a chattel is a question of fact that is judged objectively, according to a reasonable person standard. The

finder of fact considers the nature of the chattel, the degree of annexation, and the appropriateness of the chattel to the property's use.

Here, the court will almost certainly hold that the commercial oven constituted an annexed chattel that became a fixture, because the oven was permanently attached to the real property. In fact, it was so connected to the property and specially designed for the land that the oven left a gaping hole in the wall. Moreover, it is difficult to move based on its weight. The court will likely hold that the chattel was so necessary or convenient to the property's use that it constituted a fixture.

A trade fixture is a chattel that is annexed to the land by a tenant to advance her business or trade during her tenancy. Clearly, the commercial oven was annexed to the land by Lois to advance her bakery and tearoom business during her tenancy. A tenant is free to remove a trade fixture during her tenancy. However, if a tenant does remove a trade fixture, she is responsible for repairing damages caused by its removal. Accordingly, the court will hold Lois liable for wall damages caused by her removal of the commercial oven.

3. The final issue is whether Myra will succeed in her claim against Snidely for an abatement of her first month's rent. A landlord has a duty to deliver possession of the premises to the tenant at the start of the lease term. The majority rule requires delivery of actual possession. The minority rule requires delivery of the legal right to possession only. Here, Snidely agreed to lease the upper story to Myra effective immediately. However, at that time, Lois was still in possession of the premises pursuant to her lease. A tenant abandons the premises if she vacates the premises without intent to return and fails to pay rent. Although Lois may have defaulted on her rent payment, she did not intend to abandon the premises at the time that Snidely agreed to lease the upper story to Myra. Indeed, Lois still had 14 months remaining on her two-year lease. Moreover, a tenancy at sufferance occurs when a tenant remains in possession of the leased premises after the end of the lease term. Here, Lois does not constitute a tenant at sufferance, inasmuch as she did not convey any intent to anticipatorily breach her lease at the time that Snidely agreed to lease the premises to Myra. It is entirely possible that Lois intended to open a new business using the same space. Thus, she was entitled to remain in possession of the leased property.

When a tenant fails to pay rent, the landlord may seek to evict the tenant. Traditionally, a landlord was allowed to use self-help to remove a breaching tenant from the premises. However, under the modern approach, self-help is prohibited or carefully constrained. The landlord must seek court action to reenter the premises. Thus, the forcible removal of Lois from the property was not permissible without first seeking court action. Accordingly, Snidely failed to deliver possession of the premises to Myra at the start of her lease term. As a result, Myra will be successful in her claim for an abatement of her first month's rent.

Real Property

In Class Question

This sample answer would be considered below the standard expected of a 1L student.

Part A:

1. The issues are (1) whether Snidely's claims are valid against Willis and Connie for unpaid rent; and (2) what, if any, are the relevant defenses that Willis and Connie could raise.

   An assignment occurs when the tenant transfers to a third person all of his right, title, and interest in the leased premises. In June 2010, Willis assigned the lease to Connie. The lease expressly prohibits assignments without the landlord's approval. Because the assignment was invalid, there is no privity between Connie and Snidely.

   Under the common-law estate theory, the landlord had no duty to repair the premises during the term of the lease. Under the modern contract theory, the parties are free to take on duties that they would not bear under the common-law estate theory. Thus, unless Snidely agreed to take on a duty of repair, the duty fell on Willis.

   However, a tenant may treat the lease as terminated and withhold rent if the covenant of quiet enjoyment has been breached by an actual or a constructive eviction. Here, the issue arises as to whether a constructive eviction occurred by Snidely's failure to make timely repairs to the leased premises. State law typically creates an obligation on the landlord to provide running water and heat. Thus, the withholding of hot water and the failure to exercise due care in making promised or volunteered repairs would likely constitute a constructive eviction by Snidely.

2. The issue is whether Connie will be successful in her claim for injuries caused by Snidely's negligent repairs on the leased premises. A landlord is not liable to the tenant for injuries caused by a condition of the premises, except where the landlord has been negligent in making repairs. Here, Snidely negligently repaired the plumbing. However, because Connie was not the tenant, there is no privity between Connie and Snidely. Therefore, Connie will not succeed in her claim against Snidely for the injuries sustained by his negligent repairs.

Part B:

1. A tenant has a duty to pay rent. Here, Lois failed to pay rent for six months. Thus, Lois owes Snidely for rents due for the remainder of her lease term.

2. The issue is whether Snidely may recover for damages to the wall caused by Lois's removal of the commercial oven. A fixture is a chattel that has become so connected to real property that a disinterested observer would consider the chattel to be part of the realty. Chattel becomes a fixture if (1) it is annexed to the real property, (2) it has been appropriated to the use of the land, and (3) the annexor intends it to be a fixture. An annexed chattel may become a fixture if the chattel is so necessary or convenient to the use of the land that it is commonly regarded as part of the land. Here, the commercial oven constituted an annexed chattel that became a fixture.

3. A landlord has a duty to deliver possession of the premises to the tenant at the start of the lease term. Here, Snidely agreed to lease the upper story to Myra effective immediately. Yet, he failed to deliver possession of the premises to Myra at the start of her lease term. As a result, Myra will be entitled to an abatement of her first month's rent.

Real Property

Homework Question 1

Gerry owned an empty lot (Lot A) in Funville. The lot was 200 yards away from a pair of mountains with a pond at its base. Gerry lived in the next town over from Lot A. She used Lot A for growing pine trees and for parking her car when she went ice skating on the pond or hiking in the mountains.

Twenty-five years ago, Gerry delivered to Lori a deed. The deed read in its entirety:

> Gerry hereby conveys Lot A in Funville to the grantee under a general warranty deed.

Gerry's signature was immediately below the quoted paragraph. Gerry's signature was notarized. The deed was never recorded.

For the next 12 years, Lori used the land for a multitude of purposes. Every summer, she planted corn on the land for personal consumption; every winter, she cut down pine trees for the holidays; and throughout the year, she parked her car on the lot when going swimming in the pond or hiking in the mountains. She allowed her friends and family to also use the land to park their cars when visiting the mountains and pond. She thought about building a cabana house with a bathroom on the property, but the expense was too much. She also considered fencing the property and posting "no trespassing" signs, but never got around to it.

Lori also paid the annual property taxes on the land, even though the tax bills were sent to Gerry. Lori did not get a tax bill in her name because the deed was never recorded, and as a result, title was still in Gerry's name.

Eight years ago Lori's husband's job transferred the family to another state, Gainsville. Since the move, Lori has not returned to Funville. She has not used Lot A or granted others permission to use Lot A. It appears that Lot A has remained unoccupied for the last eight years.

Earlier this year, Gerry died intestate and left her son, Gino, as her only heir. Gino conveyed Lot A to Fern by valid deed for fair market value. Neither party knew about the deed from Gerry to Lori. Both Gino and Fern believed that Gerry was the owner of Lot A at the time of her death. Fern immediately recorded the deed and took possession of Lot A.

A month ago, Lori finalized her divorce from her husband, and last week, she returned to Funville. She wants to build a home on Lot A—the only place she has ever felt happy. When she finds Fern in possession of Lot A, she sues Fern for possession.

Funville has enacted the following statutes:

Any action to recover possession of real property must be brought within 10 years after the cause of action accrues.

Any conveyance or mortgage of real property is not good against subsequent purchasers for value and without notice unless said conveyance or mortgage has been recorded in accordance with the law.

Who is entitled to possession of Lot A? Discuss.

Real Property

Homework Question 1—Outline

I.   Did Gerry's deed convey fee simple title to Lori?

    A.   **(Rule)** A valid deed requires inclusion of the names of the buyer and seller, description of land, indication of present intent to convey title, and signature of grantor

       1.   Some courts will uphold a deed absent buyer's name if conveyance document clearly indicates enough information about the grantee so that the court can identify

    B.   **(Application)** Gerry signed over title to Lot A to Lori, but Lori is not specifically named in deed

       1.   Deed names Gerry as grantor

       2.   Deed names Lot A in Funville

       3.   Gerry "hereby conveys" indicates intent to transfer

    C.   **(Conclusion)** There is no inclusion of Lori's name as grantee in the conveyance, and there is no information from which a court could identify Lori as the grantee. Lori did not receive fee simple absolute

II.   May Lori claim title to Lot A through adverse possession?

    A.   **(Rule)** Title over real property can occur through adverse possession if claimant can prove (i) open, visible, and notorious; (ii) actual control; (iii) exclusive; (iv) hostile possession of land; (v) continuously for designated time in jurisdiction

       1.   Occupancy unnecessary

          a.   Depends on circumstances and nature of land

          b.   Some jurisdictions require payment of taxes by hostile landholder

       2.   Title by adverse possession as good as title traceable to prior record owner

    B.   **(Application)** Funville has adverse possession time of 10 years

       1.   Lori used land actively and openly for 12 years

          a.   Seasonal planting, parking vehicles by family and friends

          b.   Lori paid property taxes

          c.   Permitted use by friends evidences exclusive use not open to public

       2.   No facts that Gerry objected to Lori's use of land

       3.   Lori used land more than Gerry did

    C.   **(Conclusion)** Lori can likely establish ownership of Lot A through adverse possession

III. Who has title to Lot A?

    A.   **(Rule)** Title by adverse possession is as valid as title held by former owner

       1.   Statute protects purchasers against interest holders who had opportunity to record interest in land, but failed to do so

          a.   Equitable doctrine to help subsequent purchasers who obtain property without notice of prior interest

       2.   Exception—adverse possession

          a.   Title through adverse possession prevails over later conveyance by prior record title owner

B. **(Application)** In Funville, a subsequent *bona fide* purchaser (BFP) prevails against a prior donee or purchaser if BFP had no knowledge of prior donor or purchaser's interest

    1. Gino, Gerry's heir, sells Lot A to Fern, a BFP

        a. Fern and Gino unaware of Gerry's conveyance to Lori because not recorded

    2. Lot A not used for eight years, so no constructive notice of Lori's possession

    3. Lori contests Fern's title

C. **(Conclusion)** If there is a judicial decree of adverse possession, Lori owns land superior to Fern's claim. If adverse possession not found, Fern as BFP has title because no actual or constructive notice of Lori's possession

Real Property

Homework Question 1—Sample Answer

This sample answer would be considered above the standard expected of a 1L student.

I. <u>Lori has no fee simple absolute interest because she was not named as grantee in the deed.</u>

The issue is whether the omission of Lori's name on the deed invalidates her title in Lot A in Funville. To be legally valid, a deed of conveyance must include the name of the grantee or buyer, the grantor or seller, a description of the land, an indication of a present intent to convey title, and signature of the grantor. If a deed fails to include the name of the buyer or grantee, the courts are willing to consider a deed valid if the court can easily determine who the grantee is in the conveyance document.

The deed at issue delineates that Gerry, as seller and grantor, conveys Lot A. The deed specifically describes the land as "Lot A in Funville," and is evidence of a clear intent to convey title. However, the deed does not specify the grantee or buyer of Lot A, and there are no clues as to whom it might be. Accordingly, a court would be unable to deduce from the deed that Gerry conveyed her property to Lori.

Without the inclusion of Lori's name as buyer or grantee in the deed, Lori did not receive fee simple absolute.

II. <u>Lori may have acquired title in Lot A by adverse possession.</u>

The issue is whether Lori's use of Lot A for 12 years gives her adverse possession of the property. Title over property can be established by adverse possession if the claimant can prove open, visible, and notorious possession, and actual ownership that is exclusive, hostile, and continuous for the time designated in the jurisdiction.

Actual possession does not require occupancy of the land, but equates to dominion or control over the land. Open, visible, and notorious possession is conduct pertaining to the land that places the owner on notice that the claimant is holding himself out as owner of the property. When a claimant's conduct generally excludes others, ownership is said to be exclusive and distinct. The claimant's use need not be entirely exclusive, but of a nature that is in line with an owner's use of that land. The element of hostility is that the claimant's ownership is such that it generally excludes others. Finally, the claimant must use the land continuously for a specific and minimum number of years. State B's adverse possession time is 10 years.

Here, for 12 years, Lori seasonally planted corn and cut pine trees on Lot A. She also parked vehicles on the land when she visited the nearby mountains and pond. She permitted her friends to park cars on Lot A as well. All of this establishes actual possession. Although Lori did not erect any physical boundaries, post signs, or build on Lot A, to anyone who looked, the land was occupied. Lori's use of the land was thus open and notorious, as well as exclusive and distinct in that permission from Lori was necessary to make use of the land.

Gerry's conveyance of her title to the land to Lori and Lori's payment of the annual property taxes further establish that Lori considers the land her own. Finally, Lori's use of Lot A was consistent for 12 years before she moved to Gainsville and ceased visiting Lot A.

Accordingly, Lori has been in adverse possession of Lot A for 12 years. Lori likely has title to Lot A through adverse possession.

III. Determination of whether Fern or Lori has title to Lot A depends on the court's ruling on Lori's adverse possession.

The issue is whether Fern or Lori has title to Lot A. The statute protects subsequent purchasers without any notice of other potential claims of ownership against an interest holder who had an opportunity to record his interest in the land but failed to do so. It is an equitable principle to help purchasers who are unaware of and without notice of the prior interest.

An exception to this general rule is title through adverse possession. Because no document is available for recordation of title obtained through adverse possession, title obtained through adverse possession prevails over a later conveyance of the land by the prior or record title owner.

In Funville, a subsequent *bona fide* purchaser (BFP) prevails against a prior donee or purchaser if the BFP had no knowledge of the prior donor or purchaser's interest.

Here, Gino, Gerry's heir, sells Lot A to Fern, a BFP. Neither Fern nor Gino is aware of Gerry's conveyance to Lori because that deed was not recorded. Thus, there was no actual notice. Lori did not use Lot A for eight years, so there was also no constructive notice of Lori's possession.

If Lori contests Fern's title and acquires a judicial decree of adverse possession, Lori owns the land superior to Fern's claim. If there is no adverse possession found, Fern as BFP has title because she had no actual or constructive notice of Lori's ownership or use of the land.

Real Property

Homework Question 2

Alexis is the owner of two adjoining parcels of land in Greenvillage. Parcel A consists of undeveloped forest land. Alexis lives on Parcel B in one unit of a two-family home. The house was constructed in 1960. Parcel B does not have a driveway for directly entering or exiting the property. As a result, Alexis uses a driveway that runs across Parcel A in order to access the road.

One day, while driving around looking at various properties, Martha spots the house on Parcel B. As an avid hiker, Martha has always dreamed of living in a home next to the woods. She immediately agreed to purchase Parcel B from Alexis, inasmuch as she knew she would need to rely on extra income derived from renting out the other unit in the two-family home. Alexis informs Martha that because there was no other access to the road, Martha could use the driveway across Parcel A.

After the sale of Parcel B to Martha, Alexis decides to build a new home on Parcel A before selling Parcel A to Julie. In search of greater privacy for her home, Julie erects a six-foot mound on Parcel A, which is lined with eight-foot-high shrubs. The new fence interferes with Martha's view of the woods while also obstructing access to the driveway across Parcel A.

Deciding to take advantage of her forest property, Julie decides to start a woodcutting business in her yard. The woodcutting area is extremely noisy and emits giant plumes of wood particles in the air. Given the trajectory of the wind, the wood particles are constantly blown onto Martha's property. Martha can no longer use her yard because everything is blanketed by the thick dust and makes breathing extremely difficult and sometimes impossible when outdoors.

In the interest of preserving the natural beauty of the woodlands, Greenvillage had enacted an ordinance prohibiting the construction of any fence over five feet tall.

Martha has recently received a citation from Greenvillage's zoning officer for violating the 1999 zoning ordinance that prohibits the construction of multiple-family dwellings where Parcel B is located.

Martha seeks your legal advice to assess what causes of action may be available to her.

Prepare a memorandum explaining Martha's rights and obligations.

Real Property

Homework Question 2—Outline

Driveway Across Parcel A

I. **Was there an express easement across Parcel A?**

    A. **(Rule)** An easement is an interest in land of another
1. Created expressly through a writing, by implication, by prescription, or by estoppel
2. Easement is expressly created when dominant landowner grants servient landowner an easement to use land
3. Statute of Frauds requires a writing to create an easement.
4. Express easements must be recorded in order to put others on notice

    B. **(Application)** No indication in Julie's deed that an express easement had been granted to Martha
1. Oral grant of an easement is not sufficient to satisfy Statute of Frauds
2. Julie's deed did not expressly state that such an easement had ever been expressly created
3. Julie not required to allow Martha continued access to driveway
4. Mere fact that Alexis orally promised Martha use of driveway does not rise to the level of an express easement

    C. **(Conclusion)** In the absence of a recorded writing, no express easement

II. **Was there an easement by implication by prior use?**

    A. **(Rule)** Easement implied by prior use requires (1) severance of title to land held in common ownership; (2) an existing, apparent, and continuous use when severance occurs; and (3) the parties' intended use to continue after division of land because use is reasonable necessity for enjoyment of dominant part at time of severance

    B. **(Application)** Alexis was owner of adjoining parcels, Parcels A and B
1. When Martha purchased Parcel B, Alexis advised her to use the driveway across Parcel A because no other way to access road
2. Martha's use was existing, apparent, and continuous when severance occurred
3. Alexis and Martha intended for use of driveway to continue because it was reasonably necessary for use of her property
4. Existence of the continuing implied easement was evident
5. Julie erected a mound and fence that blocked access

    C. **(Conclusion)** Easement by implication by prior use created
1. Martha permitted to continue accessing driveway
2. Easement had not been terminated

III. **Was there an easement by implication by necessity?**

    A. **(Rule)** Easement implied by necessity requires (1) severance of title to land held in common ownership, and (2) strict necessity for easement at the time of severance

B. **(Application)** Parcel B was landlocked; required use of driveway easement to access road

    1. Once adjoining parcels divided by Alexis, Martha had strict necessity for easement

C. **(Conclusion)** Easement created by implication by necessity

Mound on Parcel A

I. **Are any remedies available to Martha concerning the mound on Parcel A?**

A. **(Rule)** Landowner has right to use her property in any manner that is reasonable

    1. Use is not reasonable when it interferes with property rights of neighbors or others in the vicinity

    2. Greenvillage enacted ordinance prohibiting construction of any fence over five feet tall

B. **(Application)** Martha has right to use implied easement driveway across Parcel A; Julie cannot unreasonably interfere with access

    1. A six-foot mound and eight-foot-high shrubs blocks and prohibits Martha's use of easement

    2. Mound also interferes with quiet enjoyment of Martha's use of property Martha specifically purchased land because it was adjacent to woods

       a. Mound and shrubs now thwart or impede any view of woods that she once enjoyed

    3. Municipality sought to protect such views by enacting an ordinance designed to prevent such obstructions

C. **(Conclusion)** Martha will succeed in claim for injunction to prevent further interference with easement by Julie

    1. Because mound and shrubs violate spirit and purpose of ordinance, Julie must remove obstruction

Woodcutting Business

I. **Does Julie's woodcutting business constitute a nuisance?**

A. **(Rule)** Private nuisance is a substantial and unreasonable invasion (intentional or negligent) of another's interest in her use and enjoyment of land

    1. Court balances utility of the conduct against gravity of harm caused by conduct

    2. The following persons have standing to sue for a private nuisance: (1) possessors of land, (2) owners of easements and profits in land, and (3) owners of non-possessory estates in land that are detrimentally affected by interferences with its use and enjoyment

    3. Damages and injunctive relief may be recovered in a suit for private nuisance.

B. **(Application)** Woodcutting business produced excessive noise and giant plumes of wood particles that descended upon Martha's property

    1. Martha cannot use property because everything "is blanketed by the thick dust and makes breathing extremely difficult and sometimes impossible when outdoors"

    2. Substantial and unreasonable invasion of Martha's use and enjoyment of land

3. Woodcutting business further interferes with public's use and enjoyment of the forest space

4. Burden substantially outweighs any benefit

C. **(Conclusion)** Damages or equitable relief available to Martha

1. Because money damages may be obtained only where equitable relief is not available, Martha should seek injunction to cease woodcutting activity

Zoning Officer's Citation

I. **Must Martha comply with the 1999 zoning ordinance?**

A. **(Rule)** State has power to regulate for health, safety, and welfare of its citizens

1. Through an enabling act, state may delegate to a municipality authority to protect welfare of its citizens by enacting a zoning ordinance

2. Municipality may not unreasonably require compliance with an ordinance where there is a preexisting, non-conforming use

B. **(Application)** Two-family home on Parcel B was constructed in 1960

1. Zoning ordinance prohibiting multiple-family dwellings was enacted in 1999, 39 years after construction of the home

2. Two-family home qualifies as a preexisting, non-conforming use

3. Only way Martha can comply would be to destroy her home and construct a new one

C. **(Conclusion)** Martha's multiple-family dwelling constitutes a preexisting, non-conforming use that is exempt from the zoning ordinance

Real Property

Homework Question 2—Sample Answer

This sample answer would be considered above the standard expected of a 1L student.

MEMORANDUM

To: Martha
From: Lawyer
Re: Martha's rights and obligations concerning Parcel A

Driveway Across Parcel A

The first issue is whether Martha has the right to continued use of an easement across Parcel A. An easement is an interest in the land of another. Easements may be either affirmative or negative, and they may be either appurtenant or in gross. Most easements are affirmative in nature. An affirmative easement gives the holder the right to do something on the land of another. An easement appurtenant requires a dominant and servient tenement. Here, Parcel A would be the servient tenement while Parcel B would be the dominant tenement if an easement had been created for Martha's use.

An easement may be created expressly through a writing, by implication, by prescription, or by estoppel. An easement is expressly created when the dominant landowner grants the servient landowner an easement to use the land. Here, Martha may claim that an express easement had been created. However, such a claim will likely fail inasmuch as there is no indication in Julie's deed that an express easement had been granted to Martha. An oral grant of an easement is not sufficient to satisfy the writing required by the Statute of Frauds. The Statute of Frauds requires a writing to create an easement. Moreover, express easements must be recorded in order to put others on notice. Although Martha relied on the continued use of the driveway across Parcel A in order to access the road, Julie will likely be able to argue that her deed did not expressly state that such an easement had ever been expressly created. As a result, Julie may not be required to allow Martha continued access to the driveway. The mere fact that Alexis orally promised Martha that she may use the driveway does not rise to the level of an express easement. In the absence of a recorded writing, Martha's claim of an express easement is likely to fail.

The issue then becomes whether an affirmative easement was created by implication, either by prior use or by necessity. An easement implied by prior use requires (1) severance of title to land held in common ownership; (2) an existing, apparent, and continuous use when severance occurs; and (3) the parties' intended use to continue after division of land because use is reasonable necessity for the enjoyment of the dominant part at the time of severance. Here, Alexis was the owner of the two adjoining parcels of land, Parcels A and B. When Martha purchased Parcel B, Alexis advised her to use the driveway across Parcel A because there was no way to access the road otherwise. Thus, Martha's use of the driveway easement was existing, apparent, and continuous when severance of the adjoining parcels occurred. The facts indicate that both Alexis and Martha intended for Martha to continue use of the driveway after division of the land because it was reasonably necessary for her to use her property. Thereafter, Julie purchased

Parcel A from Alexis. A cursory survey of the property would have been evidence of the existence of the continuing implied easement across Parcel A. Yet, Julie nevertheless erected a mound and fence on her property that subsequently blocked access to the driveway easement. However, because the court will likely hold that an easement had been created by implication by prior use, Martha will be permitted to continue accessing the driveway.

In addition, Martha will likely succeed in arguing that an implied easement existed by necessity as well. An easement implied by necessity requires (1) severance of title to land held in common ownership, and (2) strict necessity for the easement at the time of severance. Parcel B was a landlocked piece of property that required use of the driveway easement across Parcel A in order to access the road. Once the adjoining parcels had been divided by Alexis, the court will hold that Martha clearly had a strict necessity for the easement at the time of severance. Thus, Martha will likely succeed in establishing that an easement had been created by implication, both by prior use and by necessity.

Mound on Parcel A

The next issue is whether Martha would be able to seek any relief concerning the six-foot mound on Parcel A, which is lined with eight-foot-high shrubs. In general, a landowner has the right to use her property in any manner that is reasonable. However, such use is not reasonable when it interferes with the property rights of her neighbors or others in the vicinity. Here, because Martha has the right to use the implied easement driveway across Parcel A, Julie cannot unreasonably interfere with access to this necessary path. The erection of a six-foot mound and eight-foot-high shrubs across this driveway blocks and prohibits Martha's use of this easement. Therefore, Martha will likely succeed in a claim for an injunction to prevent further interference with the easement by Julie.

Furthermore, the mound and shrubs further interfere with the quiet enjoyment of Martha's use and enjoyment of her property. Martha specifically purchased this land because it was adjacent to the woods. The mound and shrubs now clearly thwart or impede any view of the woods that she once enjoyed. Indeed, the municipality sought to protect such views by enacting an ordinance designed to prevent such obstructions. Here, "[i]n the interest of preserving the natural beauty of the woodlands," Greenvillage had enacted an ordinance prohibiting the construction of any fence over five feet tall. Thus, because Julie's installation of the mound and shrubs also violates the spirit and purpose of the ordinance, the court will likely require her to remove such an obstruction.

Woodcutting Business

The issue is whether Julie's woodcutting business rises to the level of a nuisance, thereby entitling Martha to any equitable relief. A private nuisance is a substantial and unreasonable invasion (intentional or negligent) of another's interest in her use and enjoyment of land. To determine the existence of a private nuisance, a court balances the utility of the conduct against the gravity of the harm caused by the conduct. The following persons have standing to sue for a private nuisance affecting a parcel of land: (1) possessors of the land, (2) owners of easements and profits in the land, and (3) owners of non-possessory estates in the land that are detrimentally affected by interferences with its use and enjoyment. Damages and injunctive relief may be recovered in a suit for private nuisance.

Here, Julie commenced a woodcutting business on her property, which resulted in excessive noise and giant plumes of wood particles that would constantly descend upon Martha's property. As a result, Martha can no longer use her property because everything in her yard is covered in dust and breathing is difficult. The court will likely hold that such detrimental effects constitute a substantial and unreasonable invasion of Martha's use and enjoyment of her land. Moreover, in determining whether a private nuisance exists, the court will balance the benefits of Julie's woodcutting business against the harm and burden caused by it. Not only does Julie's woodcutting business negatively impact Martha's use and enjoyment of her property as well as her health, but the activity further interferes with the public's use and enjoyment of the forest space as well. Thus, the burden substantially outweighs any benefit of permitting Julie to maintain her woodcutting business. As such, Martha will likely succeed in obtaining either damages or equitable relief against Julie's woodcutting activity. Because money damages may be obtained only where equitable relief is not available, Martha should seek an injunction to cease Julie's woodcutting activity and to prevent any further interference with the use and enjoyment of her property.

Zoning Officer's Citation

The final issue is whether Martha is obligated to comply with a 1999 zoning ordinance that prohibits the construction of multiple-family dwellings when her home had been constructed in 1960. The state possesses the power to regulate for the health, safety, and welfare of its citizens. Through an enabling act, the state may delegate to a municipality the authority to protect the welfare of its citizens by enacting a zoning ordinance. However, a municipality may not unreasonably require compliance with an ordinance where there is a preexisting, non-conforming use. Here, the two-family home located on Parcel B was constructed in 1960. The zoning ordinance prohibiting multiple-family dwellings was enacted in 1999, 39 years after construction of the home. As such, the two-family home on Parcel B qualifies as a preexisting, non-conforming use of the land. The only way Martha may come into compliance with the ordinance at this time would be to unreasonably require her to destroy her home and construct a new one. As a result, Martha will likely succeed in arguing that her multiple-family dwelling constitutes a preexisting, non-conforming use that is exempt from the zoning ordinance.

Multiple-Choice Questions

ADVERSE POSSESSION

Question 1

A homeowner obtained and moved onto a large plot of land, occupying a significant portion of the property. The homeowner lived on that portion of the land for more than 22 years, believing that the whole plot was his own. Recently, however, the homeowner learned that the deed he had acquired was in fact defective. Now, a person with a valid deed is claiming the entire plot of land for himself. The statutory period for adverse possession in this jurisdiction is 20 years.

What rights, if any, does the homeowner have with respect to the plot of land?

(A) The homeowner owns the whole plot of land, because he acquired title to the land by adverse possession.

(B) The homeowner owns the portion of the property on which he lived, but not the whole plot, because he did not possess the whole plot.

(C) The homeowner does not own any part of the land, because his possession was not hostile.

(D) The homeowner does not own any part of the land, because he did not possess the whole plot of land.

Question 2

While hunting on public grounds, an outdoorsman crossed over onto adjoining private property. The outdoorsman soon came upon a log cabin, which had obviously been abandoned some time ago and was in great disrepair. On inspection, the outdoorsman found the cabin to be generally well built, except that the lock on the front door was broken, the windows needed to be replaced, and some shrubs and bushes had nearly overgrown the front porch. The outdoorsman cleared out the overgrown bushes from the cabin, replaced the lock on the front door, and installed new windows.

For the next year, the outdoorsman stayed in the cabin nearly every weekend. After the first year, the outdoorsman moved into the cabin. For the next 10 years, he lived in the cabin nine months out of the year, leaving only during the harsh winter months, as the cabin had no heating system apart from a small fireplace, and snow and ice in the area made it unsuitable for hunting or camping. During the winter, the outdoorsman locked up the cabin and left it unattended. No one other than the outdoorsman ever occupied the cabin during this period. The outdoorsman received no word from the owner until almost 11 years after first discovering the cabin, when, one Saturday morning, a man claiming to be the owner showed up, pounding on the door and demanding that the outdoorsman vacate the premises immediately. The applicable statutory period for acquiring title by adverse possession is seven years.

If the outdoorsman files an action to quiet title to the cabin, will he prevail?

(A) Yes, because the outdoorsman was the only person to occupy the cabin for a period of more than 10 years, and he held himself out to be the owner.

(B) Yes, because the outdoorsman made substantial improvements to the cabin.

(C) No, because the outdoorsman did not possess the cabin continuously for the statutory time period.

(D) No, because the outdoorsman took possession of the cabin in bad faith, knowing that it belonged to someone else, but intending to claim it nonetheless.

Question 3

Developer purchased a lot in the downtown business district of a city. For years, the lot had been used as a fee-pay parking lot. Developer obtained the required city zoning approvals and building permits to construct an office building on the lot. The proposed office building would be twice as tall as an older high-rise apartment building on an adjacent lot. Believing that his tenants would be unhappy about the loss of light and of their former view of a large city park on the other side of Developer's lot, the owner of the apartment building brought an action to enjoin the construction of the office building.

Will the owner succeed in obtaining injunctive relief?

(A) Yes, because a subsequent use of property must not unreasonably interfere with the light and air of existing adjacent uses.

(B) Yes, if the parking lot and any prior uses of Developer's property permitted light and air to reach the apartment building for the statutory period required for adverse possession.

(C) No, unless the owner has a cognizable property interest in light and air.

(D) No, because Developer received the necessary city approvals and permits.

Question 4

A handyman owned a two-story hardware store on the main street of a town. The hardware store was located on a corner lot, next to a retail building owned by a lawyer. At the rear of the hardware store was a narrow alley, wide enough to accommodate a car or small truck. The handyman gave the lawyer oral permission to use the alley behind the handyman's store to access the narrow space behind the lawyer's building, where the lawyer parked his truck every weekday.

The lawyer later sold his building to a dentist, who insisted on having an off-street parking space. At the time of the conveyance, the lawyer negotiated with the handyman and obtained an express easement in favor of the retail building for a right-of-way through the alley. The dentist subsequently took over the retail building and parked behind the building on weekdays and Saturdays until his vehicle was vandalized, at which point he began to park it in a secured lot.

After five years, the dentist sold the building to a pharmacy conglomerate that purchased the hardware store from the handyman at the same time, intending to renovate the two buildings into one large retail space. Almost immediately, the pharmacy conglomerate found a more attractive location at which to carry out its plans, and sold the hardware store and retail building to two separate small business owners. The new owner of the hardware store placed a dumpster in the alleyway, thereby blocking access to the space behind the retail building. The new owner of the retail building would like to park his car in this space.

If the new owner of the retail building seeks a court order requiring the new owner of the hardware store to remove the dumpster, what is the likely outcome?

(A) The new owner of the retail building will prevail, because an easement by prescription exists.

(B) The new owner of the retail building will prevail, because the easement has not been abandoned.

(C) The new owner of the hardware store will prevail, because the easement merged with the fee when the pharmacy conglomerate purchased both buildings.

(D) The new owner of the hardware store will prevail, because the new owner of the retail building is estopped from asserting rights under the easement.

Question 5

Ethan owned a 50-acre parcel of land, 40 acres of which was swampland. Ethan lived in a house on a five-acre area in the northeast corner of the land, and used the rest of the dry land as a Christmas tree farm. In 1968, he planted new trees in the portion of the dry land furthest from his house. Because he was not a very good farmer, Ethan planted the trees so close together that he ended up having a thick forest in his backyard, which blocked his view of the swamp.

Meanwhile, Mike advertised "Prime Vacation Land" for sale in the back of *Get Rich Quick* magazine. The page touted the temperate climate, the abundance of water, and the resale possibilities. Gus purchased the land sight unseen and received a warranty deed from Mike in 1969. Unknown to Gus or Ethan, the "Prime Vacation Land" was the 40 acres of swampland owned by Ethan. In 1970, Gus gave a quitclaim deed to the land to Donald as payment for gambling debts. Donald intended to fill the swamp and develop an amusement park, but he was prevented from doing so when a local environmental protection group obtained an injunction ordering him not to disturb the swamp. Not wishing to keep property he could not use, in 1971, Donald donated the swampland to a charitable organization called Save Our Swamps (SOS).

In order to raise funds to support its efforts, SOS gave canoe tours of the swamp. The tours never went outside of the southwest 15 acres of land, because a notoriously large and vicious alligator prevented any further incursion by humans. In 1992, Ethan returned for the first time to the area where he planted the trees in 1968. Having heard of the legendary alligator, Ethan took a large-bore shotgun with him. While standing on the edge of the swamp, Ethan was attacked by the alligator. Firing in self-defense, Ethan missed the alligator and shot the ground. High-grade crude oil bubbled up, and Ethan concluded that he was now the very wealthy owner of valuable mineral rights.

Very soon after his discovery, Ethan contracted with Junior's Oil Drilling Service. Junior determined that the best approach to the oil was from the southwest corner. At the first sign of Junior's equipment, SOS filed for an injunction, claiming that they owned the entire 40 acres of swamp. The statutory period for obtaining title by adverse possession in this jurisdiction is 20 years.

Will SOS be successful?

(A) No, because their claim to ownership descends from Gus, who never had good title.

(B) No, because they occupied only the southwest 15 acres, and therefore cannot claim title to the entire 40 acres.

(C) Yes, because SOS is a charitable organization that is exempt from the rules of adverse possession.

(D) Yes, because SOS fulfilled the requirements for adverse possession.

INTERESTS IN LAND

Question 6

At the start of the basketball season, a team's coach decided not to start a player who was a long-time fan favorite. As the team started to lose on a consistent basis, one season ticket holder became disgusted with the coach and began wearing a T-shirt suggesting that people stop attending the team's games. During the games, the fan would walk in front of TV cameras with his T-shirt slogan prominently displayed.

As the season progressed, many other fans joined in heckling the coach and wearing similar T-shirts. Soon thereafter, the fan received a notice from the team's management revoking his season tickets. The fan was informed that he would not be allowed to attend any more games, but would receive full reimbursement for all remaining games.

If the fan brings an appropriate action against the team challenging the revocation of his season tickets, will he prevail?

    (A) Yes, because he was entitled to express his rights of free speech.

    (B) Yes, because he had paid for the tickets for the whole season.

    (C) No, because his license to attend games was revocable.

    (D) No, because obscene speech is not constitutionally protected.

Question 7

Alvin held a life estate in a commercial building, where he ran a music store. His sister Belva held a contingent remainder in the building. Alvin insisted that vinyl records would be popular again in the future, and so he spent all of his money stocking up on old rock and roll records. Over the years, Alvin allowed the premises to become dilapidated—the ceiling sagged, the basement had water damage, and one of the main structural walls showed significant cracking. Belva visited the music store and was horrified to see the condition of "her" building. She subsequently sued Alvin to prevent future damage to the building.

Should the court rule in favor of Belva?

    (A) Yes, because Alvin committed voluntary waste.

    (B) Yes, because a remainderman has standing to sue to prevent future waste.

    (C) No, because a remainderman does not have standing to sue for damages.

    (D) No, because a life tenant is not responsible for permissive waste.

Question 8

A farmer and his business associate owned a large farm as joint tenants with right of survivorship. Their primary crop was corn. Following a general decline in the market price of corn, the business associate suggested making wheat their primary crop. The farmer agreed that such a change would make sense under the circumstances, and he and the business associate implemented the change. However, shortly before the first wheat crop was to be harvested, the farmer told his business associate that he preferred growing corn, and that he would be conveying his one-half interest in the farm to an interested buyer. The farmer's deed of conveyance to the buyer made no mention of the wheat crop growing on the land.

What interest will the buyer own in the farm and/or the wheat crop following the farmer's conveyance of his one-half joint tenancy interest?

(A) The buyer will own a one-half share of the farm as a tenant-in-common with the business associate, and the buyer will not own a one-half interest in the wheat crop growing on the land.

(B) The buyer will own a one-half share of the farm as a tenant-in-common with the business associate, and the buyer will own a one-half interest in the wheat crop growing on the land.

(C) The buyer will own a one-half share of the farm as a joint tenant with the business associate, and the buyer will own a one-half interest in the wheat crop growing on the land.

(D) The buyer will own a one-half share of the farm as a joint tenant with the business associate, and the buyer will not own a one-half interest in the wheat crop growing on the land.

Question 9

An 80-year-old farmer had a successful cattle farm. The farmer had little family, and wanted to ensure that the farm would continue to be operated by someone who appreciated the farm's history and enjoyed working with cattle. The farmer only had one son, who was 45 years old and as yet had no children of his own. One of the farmer's employees had started working on the farm during high school. The employee had shown a great interest in cattle and was a loyal and hardworking employee. That employee was now in his early twenties. To ensure that the farm would continue operating after his death, the farmer included a clause in his will that provided that upon the farmer's death, the farm would go to his son for life, and then upon the son's death, the farm would pass to the son's children. The will further provided that if the son had no children at the time of his death, then the farm would pass to the valued employee. The farmer died two years later, at which time his son still had no children. The employee was still working on the farm.

Does the employee have a remainder interest in the farm?

(A) No, the employee has a fee simple interest subject to a condition subsequent.

(B) No, the employee has an executory interest.

(C) Yes, the employee has a contingent remainder interest subject to a condition precedent.

(D) Yes, the employee has a vested remainder interest subject to open.

Question 10

A landowner conveyed his property "to A, her heirs and assigns, so long as it is used by the people to gather for purposes of public assembly and debate, then to B and his heirs."

Which of the following best describes A's interest in the property?

(A) A fee simple absolute.

(B) A fee simple determinable.

(C) A fee simple subject to a condition subsequent.

(D) A fee simple subject to an executory interest.

Question 11

A caterer owned a large, undeveloped area of grassland and rolling hills. A mining company wished to extract coal from the land without having to purchase the property. The mining company offered to pay the caterer for the right to mine as much coal as it wished from the land in exchange for the payment of a specified sum plus a royalty per ton of coal removed. The caterer agreed and executed a document granting the requested rights for a period of 10 years, renewable upon renegotiation of the royalty payment for an additional 10 years. The mining company promptly recorded this agreement.

The document further stated that the caterer agreed not to grant a similar right to any other party during the pendency of the agreement, although he could continue to use the land for his own purposes, including the removal of coal. For the next three years, the mining company removed coal from the land. However, a dam was subsequently constructed at the southern end of the valley in which the land was located, and the state asserted its power of eminent domain to buy all the lands in the soon-to-be-flooded valley. The caterer negotiated a price and sold the land to the state.

If the mining company sues the caterer to compel him to pay it a portion of the price that the state paid for the land, who will prevail?

(A) The caterer, because the mining company owns a license, which is not a property right protected by the Due Process Clause.

(B) The caterer, because the mining company owns a profit a prendre, which is not a property right protected by the Due Process Clause.

(C) The mining company, because it owns a license, which is a property right protected by the Due Process Clause.

(D) The mining company, because it owns a profit a prendre, which is a property right protected by the Due Process Clause.

LANDLORD-TENANT

Question 12

A married couple entered into a two-year lease. The neighborhood consisted primarily of vehicle repair shops and older couples. For the first year, the landlord never visited the property, and the couple paid the rent as directed. In the second year, the couple had a child and decided to use the spare room beside the master bedroom as the nursery.

Rather than leave the master bedroom each time to enter the nursery, the couple decided to hire a local man to add a doorway to the wall between the two rooms. The man, a certified building contractor, checked the wall to make sure it was not a load-bearing wall, to which local ordinances preclude any kind of alterations.

When the lease was about to end, the landlord inspected the premises and noticed the doorway between the two rooms. He remarked that it was a nice touch, and even conceded that it made the home more valuable, because the neighborhood—particularly over the past year—had begun to accommodate many younger couples starting families. The couple vacated the property at the expiration of the lease without restoring the wall. The landlord then sent the couple a bill for the estimated cost to restore the wall to its original state. The couple refused to pay the bill, and the landlord filed suit to recover this amount.

What type of waste has the couple created?

(A) Permissive waste.

(B) Voluntary waste.

(C) Ameliorative waste.

(D) No waste, because the value of the property was improved.

Question 13

A landowner conveyed a large estate "to my daughter, her heirs and assigns, on condition that she produce an heir with her husband, but if she dies without such an heir, then to my personal assistant." Five years after the landowner conveyed the estate to her daughter, the personal assistant and the landowner got into a serious dispute, which resulted in the personal assistant's decision to set up her own rival business. At the same time, the landowner's daughter and her husband divorced. Three years later, the husband died of a stroke brought on by undiagnosed high blood pressure. The daughter remarried to a new business protégé of her father. The estate was a heavily forested property with a number of stands of maple trees. The daughter and her new husband walked the property and marked stands to be harvested for wood. The daughter then exploited the timber on the estate for a large profit.

Which of the following best describes the daughter's act of exploiting the timber for profit?

(A) Impermissible as affirmative waste, because the daughter was only a life tenant of the estate.

(B) Impermissible as trespass, because the personal assistant owns the estate in fee simple absolute.

(C) Impermissible, because the daughter has not produced an heir with her first husband.

(D) Permissible, because the daughter holds in fee simple.

Question 14

A man entered into a lease for a period of five years. Planning to open a hardware store, the man hired a contractor, who installed overhead lighting and built wooden shelves that were nailed into the walls. The contractor also constructed freestanding tables for displaying merchandise. In addition, the man hired a builder to construct a second-floor loft that was structurally attached to the main building. At the expiration of the lease, the man decided to vacate the premises and remove the improvements that he made. He began disassembling the loft and started removing the lighting, shelving, and freestanding tables. The landlord immediately filed suit seeking to enjoin the man from removing these items.

The court will most likely allow the man to remove what items?

(A) Everything.

(B) Everything except the loft.

(C) Everything except the loft and the lighting.

(D) The freestanding tables only.

Question 15

A landlord and a tenant signed a lease agreement for a one-year term. One month into the lease term, the tenant changed jobs and abandoned the apartment, because his new job was an inconvenient commute from the apartment. The landlord did not find a replacement tenant. At the end of the lease term, the landlord sent the tenant a bill for the unpaid rent.

In determining how much tenant owes, to which of the following would most courts give the greatest weight?

(A) How burdensome the tenant's new commute is.

(B) Whether the lease contained a covenant of quiet enjoyment.

(C) Whether the landlord has met his burden of showing that he attempted to find a replacement tenant.

(D) Whether the tenant has met his burden of showing that the landlord failed to attempt to find a replacement tenant.

Question 16

The owner of a two-bedroom beachfront cottage leased the dwelling to a couple for an occupancy period terminating on March 20. On March 10, the owner leased the property to a college student for six months. According to the written lease agreement, the tenancy would begin on April 1 and extend through September 30.

On April 1, the couple was still in possession and refused to vacate the premises despite the fact that the lease had expired. As a result, the student was prevented from taking possession. Unable to take possession, the student refused to pay the owner the rent for the month of April. The owner has instituted a suit against the student seeking to enforce their lease agreement and recover rent for the month of April.

In accordance with relevant Anglo-Saxon case law, which party will most likely prevail?

- (A) The owner, because the student's only cause of action is against the couple who are the holdover tenants.

- (B) The owner, because the landlord is under no obligation to deliver possession of the premises to the tenant.

- (C) The student, because the owner cannot deliver possession at the inception of the leasehold.

- (D) There is a split of authority, and the outcome will depend upon which rule of law is followed in this jurisdiction.

Answer Grid

1 (A) (B) (C) (D)   5 (A) (B) (C) (D)   9 (A) (B) (C) (D)   13 (A) (B) (C) (D)
2 (A) (B) (C) (D)   6 (A) (B) (C) (D)   10 (A) (B) (C) (D)   14 (A) (B) (C) (D)
3 (A) (B) (C) (D)   7 (A) (B) (C) (D)   11 (A) (B) (C) (D)   15 (A) (B) (C) (D)
4 (A) (B) (C) (D)   8 (A) (B) (C) (D)   12 (A) (B) (C) (D)   16 (A) (B) (C) (D)

Torts

Outline

TABLE OF CONTENTS

I. INTENTIONAL TORTS

A. **Elements of Intentional Torts**
   1. An intentional tort consists of the following elements:
      a. a **voluntary act**;
         (1) A defendant is not liable in tort for acts that are not voluntary. Acts are not voluntary if they are a product of pure reflex or if the defendant is unconscious when the act is performed.

         EXAMPLE: Dex, during a sudden epileptic seizure, hits Pon. While Dex did not intend the harm, there is also no liability because there was no voluntary act by Dex.

      b. **intent**;
         (1) All intentional torts require the defendant to have a certain mental state when he performs the wrongful act. This mental state is called **intent**. For most intentional torts, intent is established if the defendant either:
            (a) desires that his act will cause the harmful result described by the tort; or
            (b) knows that it is substantially certain that such a result will occur.
         (2) **Incompetency**
            (a) The fact that a defendant is mentally incompetent or a minor does not preclude a finding that he possessed the intent to commit an intentional tort, but incompetency may affect whether such intent actually existed.
         (3) **Transferred Intent**
            (a) If a defendant acts with the necessary intent to inflict certain intentional torts, but for some reason causes injury to a different victim than intended, the defendant's intent is "transferred" to the actual victim. This **transfer of intent** applies only to assault, battery, false imprisonment, and trespass to land or to chattels.

            EXAMPLE: Darryl swung a baseball bat, intending to strike Astrid. However, the person Darryl hit was Plato. Darryl's intent to cause a harmful touching of Astrid will be "transferred" to Plato so that Darryl will be liable for committing a battery against Plato.

      c. **causation**;
         (1) As to intentional torts, the defendant's act or a force set in motion by that act must cause the plaintiff's injury.
      d. **harm**; and
      e. **lack of a privilege or defense**.

B. Battery

1. A **battery** is an intentional act that causes a harmful or offensive contact with the plaintiff or with something closely connected thereto.

2. The defendant must either:
   a. desire to cause an immediate harmful or offensive contact; or
   b. know such contact is substantially certain to occur.

   EXAMPLE: Dagwood intentionally swings his fist into Pickles' face, intending to hit Pickles. Dagwood has committed a battery.

3. The harmful or offensive contact element is satisfied if the contact would inflict pain or impairment of any body function, or if a reasonable person would regard it as offensive.
   a. It is sufficient for a battery if the defendant causes a contact with something close to the plaintiff, as where the defendant snatches a hat from the plaintiff's hand.
   b. Unlike assault, plaintiff need not be aware of the contact.

   EXAMPLE: Ryan intentionally spits on Prudence while she is asleep. Several weeks later, Prudence learns of Ryan's act. Ryan is liable for battery.

C. Assault

1. An **assault** is an intentional act that causes the plaintiff to experience a reasonable apprehension of an immediate harmful or offensive contact.

2. The defendant must act with the desire to cause an immediate harmful or offensive contact or the immediate apprehension of such a contact, or know that such a result is substantially certain to occur.

3. Liability for assault will not be found unless a reasonable person in the same position as a plaintiff would have experienced the same apprehension. However, if the plaintiff's apprehension is reasonable, the fact that the defendant lacked the actual ability to cause the harmful or offensive contact does not defeat liability.

   EXAMPLE: An assault is committed if Delson points an unloaded gun at Paulson, as long as Paulson reasonably thought the gun was loaded.

4. This element is satisfied if the contact threatened would inflict pain or impairment of any body function or if a reasonable person would regard it as offensive.

   EXAMPLE: Donahue holds a knife to Petunia's throat and threatens to hurt her. He is liable for assault and battery.

   EXAMPLE: Delilah, a bank robber, points a gun into a crowded bank and says, "Everyone lie down and keep quiet or else I'll shoot." This conditional threat is an assault.

D. **False Imprisonment**

1. **False imprisonment** is an intentional act that causes a plaintiff to be confined or restrained to a bounded area against the plaintiff's will, and the plaintiff knows of the confinement or is injured thereby.

   a. The defendant has the requisite intent for false imprisonment if he:

      (1) desires to confine or restrain the plaintiff to a bounded area; or

      (2) knows that such confinement is virtually certain to occur.

   b. The plaintiff may be confined by the use of physical barriers (e.g., locking the plaintiff in a room), by failing to release the plaintiff where the defendant has a legal duty to do so, or by the invalid assertion of legal authority. No duration of confinement is required—a very brief confinement will suffice, though the duration of the confinement may affect the amount of damages.

      (1) The plaintiff is under no duty to resist if the defendant uses or makes a credible threat to use physical force. A plaintiff is not "confined" if there is a reasonable means of escape of which he is actually aware.

      EXAMPLE: Stuart takes all of Susan's clothes and leaves her in the middle of the woods. Because Susan does not have a means of escape, Stuart has falsely imprisoned her.

      (2) In general, the plaintiff must be aware of the confinement or must suffer actual harm as a result of the confinement. Some cases have held that infants or incompetents who are incapable of being aware of their confinement can, nevertheless, recover for false imprisonment.

E. **Intentional Infliction of Emotional Distress**

1. **Intentional infliction of emotional distress** is an intentional or reckless act amounting to extreme and outrageous conduct that causes the plaintiff severe mental distress.

   a. The defendant must act with intent to cause severe mental distress or be reckless in creating the risk of emotional distress.

      (1) Recovery for infliction of emotional distress is allowed where a defendant acts **recklessly**, meaning that the defendant acts in deliberate disregard of a high degree of probability that the emotional distress will follow. This is contrary to the general notion that reckless conduct is somehow "less wrongful" than intentional conduct, and should be considered an exception limited to this tort.

   b. The element of **extreme and outrageous conduct** is satisfied if the defendant's conduct is beyond the bounds of decency—conduct that a civilized society will not tolerate.

      (1) Offensive or insulting language is generally not considered outrageous, except in cases involving defendants who are common carriers or innkeepers, or plaintiffs with known sensitivity, such as the elderly, children, or pregnant women.

(2) There is a trend toward permitting recovery for offensive insults made by one in a position of authority (e.g., a workplace supervisor).

EXAMPLE. Damien, who does not like children, dresses up like a monster and runs into a kindergarten classroom shouting, "I'm going to eat all of you little children!" Damien's conduct may be extreme and outrageous.

c. The plaintiff must prove that the distress suffered was **severe**—more than the level of mental distress a reasonable person could be expected to endure. The emotional distress must be substantial, not trivial or transitory. The more outrageous the defendant's conduct, the easier it will be for plaintiff to establish the requisite mental injury.

(1) Most states no longer require the plaintiff to show that actual physical injury accompanied the severe emotional distress.

2. Where the defendant's conduct is directed at a third party, the defendant is subject to liability to a plaintiff, assuming the other elements of the tort are satisfied, if the defendant intentionally or recklessly causes severe emotional distress:

a. to a plaintiff who is an immediate family member or close relative of the third party, where the plaintiff is present at the time and the defendant is aware of the plaintiff's presence; or

(1) Recovery is available whether or not such distress results in bodily harm.

b. to any other plaintiff (regardless of relationship) who is present at the time, if such distress results in bodily harm and the defendant is aware of the plaintiff's presence.

F. Trespass to Land

1. **Trespass to land** is an intentional act that causes a physical invasion of the plaintiff's land.

a. A defendant need only act with intent to cause a physical invasion of a particular piece of land, not the specific intent to invade the plaintiff's land. Intentional entry onto land is a trespass even though the defendant does not realize he has crossed a boundary line, or has a good faith belief that his entry is lawful. In other words, mistake is not a defense as to a trespass action.

EXAMPLE: Don is out for a walk with his dog, Rover. Believing that he is the rightful owner of a grove of pecan trees near his property line, Don allows Rover to wander into the trees to "do his business." The trees are actually on Pam's property. Although Don is mistaken about his ownership of the trees, he may still be liable for trespass.

b. In order to bring an action for trespass, the plaintiff must be in actual possession or have the right to immediate possession of that land. It is important to distinguish "possession" from "ownership"—an adverse possessor or a lessee may maintain a trespass action against a defendant entering wrongfully onto land possessed, but not owned, by them.

However, if the person who holds legal title to the land is not in possession, that person may not maintain a trespass action as to that land.

c. The element of physical invasion is satisfied if the defendant enters or causes a third person or object to enter onto the plaintiff's land, enters onto the plaintiff's land lawfully but then remains when under a legal duty to leave, or fails to remove an object from the plaintiff's land when under a legal duty to do so.

EXAMPLE: Don is hitting baseballs in his backyard. For kicks, he decides to see if he can hit a baseball into his neighbor Paxton's yard, 100 feet away. If he succeeds in hitting a baseball over the fence into Paxton's yard, absent Paxton's consent, Don is liable for trespass.

EXAMPLE: Paxton calls Don and asks him to remove a baseball that Don accidentally hit onto his land. If Don fails to remove the baseball, he may be liable for trespass.

2. Some events that might logically be considered intrusions onto land, such as airborne pesticides that float onto a plaintiff's land from the defendant's crop dusting of adjacent property, were traditionally addressed by tort law under nuisance or strict liability principles. Some jurisdictions have begun treating such invasions as trespasses to land if actual harm was caused.

> EXAM TIP ▶ Consider nuisance and strict liability, along with trespass to land, whenever there are facts involving something entering the plaintiff's land and causing harm.

3. **Plaintiff's land** includes the area both above and beneath the surface. Traditionally, plaintiff's land was thought to include the airspace and the subsurface to a level that the plaintiff did or could make beneficial use of.

EXAMPLE: Debbie loves to climb trees. She regularly climbs a tall tree in her backyard. One day, she climbs high into the tree and out onto a limb that overhangs onto Peggy's property. Debbie may be liable for trespass.

EXAMPLE: Dirk digs a tunnel to escape from his basement bedroom, where his mother thinks he is sleeping. As he digs, he digs under his own house and under the neighbor's yard. Dirk may be liable for trespass.

a. Aircraft flying at or above normal flight altitude do not "trespass" on the land above which they are flying. An intrusion into a plaintiff's "airspace" may be trespassory if it both enters into the "immediate reaches" of that airspace and interferes substantially with the use and enjoyment of the plaintiff's land.

4. Traditionally, nominal damages are recoverable where the defendant trespasses but causes no real injury, as a way to vindicate the land possessor's rights. If the trespasser causes injury during the trespass, however, he is liable for that harm as well. Further, where the defendant acts willfully or maliciously, he may be liable for punitive damages.

EXAMPLE: Dex drives onto Paula's land, believing wrongly that he has permission to do so. While on the land, driving with all possible care, Dex hits a concealed pothole, loses control of the car, and destroys a rare and expensive bush on Paula's property. Dex is liable for the harm to the bush.

5   **Ejectment**

a.   **Ejectment** is an action at law to recover possession of real property.

b.   The following elements are required for ejectment:

(1)   proof of legal title;

(2)   proof of the plaintiff's right to possession; and

(3)   wrongful possession by the defendant.

c.   A successful plaintiff is entitled to judgment for recovery of the property and for *mesne* damages. *Mesne* **damages** compensate for the loss of use of the land and are measured by the rental value of the property or the benefit gained by the wrongful possessor, whichever is greater.

d.   At common law, where the defendant mistakenly trespasses on or takes possession of the plaintiff's property and makes improvements thereon, the plaintiff is entitled to recover the property and need not compensate the defendant for these improvements. This is true even though the defendant acted in good faith, believing that he had rightful possession of the property.

G.   **Trespass to Chattels**

1.   **Trespass to chattels** is an intentional act by the defendant that interferes with the plaintiff's chattel, causing harm.

a.   Intent is satisfied when the defendant intentionally performs the physical act that interferes with the plaintiff's chattel. The defendant is liable even though he did not intend or recognize the legal significance of his act. Mistake is not a defense to trespass to chattels.

EXAMPLE: Dorothy needs a black evening bag to carry to her sorority formal. Without asking Paula's permission, Dorothy goes into Paula's room in the sorority house, takes Paula's black bag, carries it to the formal, then returns it to Paula's closet the next morning. Because Dorothy has Paula's bag, Paula does not have a bag to carry to the formal. Dorothy may be liable for trespass to chattels.

b.   **Chattel** means tangible personal property or intangible property that has a physical representation, such as a promissory note, or documents in which title to a chattel are merged, such as warehouse receipts or bills of lading.

c.   Interference with plaintiff's chattel is actionable if it constitutes dispossession or intermeddling. More serious interferences with the plaintiff's chattel may amount to a conversion, discussed below.

(1)   **Dispossession** is a direct interference with the plaintiff's possession, such as where a defendant temporarily takes the plaintiff's chattel or wrongfully refuses to return it.

(2)   **Intermeddling** is an interference with a chattel that does not directly affect the plaintiff's possession.

<u>**EXAMPLE:**</u> Smearing mud on the plaintiff's truck or kicking the plaintiff's dog.

2.　In order to bring a trespass to chattel action, the plaintiff must have been in actual possession or have had the right to immediate possession of the chattel.

3.　Unlike other intentional torts, proof of actual damages is an element of the cause of action for trespass to chattels. **Actual damages** would include the value of loss of use (e.g., rental value) of the chattel during a dispossession or the cost to remedy an intermeddling.

H.　Conversion

1.　**Conversion** is an intentional act by a defendant that causes the destruction of or a serious and substantial interference with the plaintiff's chattel.

　　a.　As with trespass to chattels, mistake is not a defense to conversion. A defendant is liable even though he did not intend or recognize the legal significance of his act.

　　　<u>**EXAMPLE:**</u> Drew sees Peter's 1978 Volkswagen Bug parked by the curb. Drew has always wanted to drive a vintage Bug, so she decides to hotwire it and take it for a spin. Seven hours later, she returns the Bug to the same parking spot where she found it, full of gas and in perfect condition. Drew may be liable for conversion. If, while Drew is driving the car, the Bug is hit and totaled, Drew is liable for conversion, even if the accident is not Drew's fault.

　　b.　"Destruction" or "serious and substantial interference" with a plaintiff's chattel is alternatively described as "the exercise by defendant of dominion and control" over the chattel. This is an interference with the plaintiff's property interest that is more serious than in a trespass to chattels. In distinguishing between the two torts, the longer the period of interference and the greater the use of the chattel by the defendant, the more likely it will be considered a conversion rather than a trespass to chattels. The following types of acts are likely to be classified as conversions:

　　　(1)　wrongful acquisition (e.g., theft, embezzlement, and receiving stolen property);

　　　(2)　wrongful transfer (e.g., selling, misdelivering, or pledging);

　　　(3)　wrongful detention (withholding from owner);

　　　(4)　loss, destruction, or severe damage;

　　　(5)　material alteration; or

　　　(6)　significant misuse.

　　c.　In determining the seriousness of the interference and the justice of requiring the defendant to pay the full value, the following factors are important:

　　　(1)　the extent and duration of the defendant's exercise of dominion or control;

　　　(2)　the defendant's intent to assert a right inconsistent with the other's right of control;

　　　(3)　the defendant's good faith;

(4) the extent and duration of the resulting interference with the plaintiff's right of control;

(5) the harm done to the chattel; and

(6) the inconvenience and expense caused to the plaintiff.

2. The plaintiff is generally permitted to elect either recovery of damages, usually fair market value at the time of conversion plus consequential losses, or replevin/detinue/claim and delivery, compelling the defendant to return a converted chattel, with recovery of damages attributable to its wrongful detention.

3. If the defendant offers to return the plaintiff's chattel, this does not alleviate the conversion, and the plaintiff need not accept the return. Such an offer might be considered in mitigation of damages by a defendant who "innocently" converted the plaintiff's chattel (e.g., the defendant unknowingly received property stolen from the plaintiff by a third person).

TRESPASS TO CHATTELS	CONVERSION
Intentional tort.	Intentional tort.
Committed by intentionally dispossessing or intermeddling with a chattel in the possession of another.	Committed by intentionally exercising dominion or control over a chattel and seriously interfering with the rights of the owner.
Defendant is liable for damage or diminished value of chattel.	Defendant is liable for the full value of the chattel at the time of the conversion.

EXAMPLE: On leaving a restaurant, A mistakenly takes B's hat from the rack, believing it to be his own. When he reaches the sidewalk, A puts on the hat, discovers his mistake, and immediately reenters the restaurant and returns the hat to the rack. This is not a conversion. However, if A keeps the hat for six months before discovering his mistake and returning it, this is a conversion. If A reaches the sidewalk, puts on the hat, and a sudden gust of wind blows it off his head and into an open manhole, this is also a conversion. If A takes B's hat from the rack intending to steal it, and he approaches the door, sees a policeman outside, and immediately returns the hat to the rack, this too is a conversion.

4. **Replevin**

a. **Replevin** is an action at law for the recovery of specific chattels that have been wrongfully taken or detained. It is also called "claim and delivery" in some states.

b. Replevin is a possessory action that permits the plaintiff to recover immediate possession of the property (at the beginning of the action).

(1) When the plaintiff seeks to recover the chattel at the beginning of the action, he must post a bond as security against the possibility that judgment will be found for the defendant. Note that the defendant may post bond if he wishes to retain the chattel until the action has concluded.

        (2)   No seizure of the chattel is allowed until a hearing has taken place to determine the plaintiff's entitlement to the chattel [Fuentes v. Shevin, 407 U.S. 67 (1972)].

    c.   Any damages suffered from the deprivation may also be recovered.

        (1)   The measure of damages is either the market value of the chattel at the time of the deprivation minus the market value at the time the action is commenced (if the chattel is held for sale) or the value of lost use (rental value or lost profits).

        (2)   Where judgment is for plaintiff but the chattel is not returned, the plaintiff recovers the present value of the chattel as established at trial.

    d.   If the defendant has hidden the chattel or removed it from the jurisdiction, and it cannot be seized, then an injunction for equitable replevin may issue.

    e.   Replevin may be brought only to recover tangible personal property; it is not available for recovery of real property or intangible personal property.

        (1)   Under the Uniform Commercial Code, the buyer has a right of replevin for goods identified to the contract if [UCC § 2-716(3)]:

            (a)   after reasonable effort he is unable to effect cover for such goods;

            (b)   the circumstances reasonably indicate that such effort will be unavailing; or

            (c)   if the goods have been shipped under reservation and satisfaction of the security interest in them has been made or tendered.

        (2)   In the case of goods bought for personal, family, or household purposes, the buyer's right of replevin under Article 2 vests upon acquisition of a special property interest, even if the seller had not then repudiated or failed to deliver.

    f.   Article 2 of the UCC also provides for restitution of amounts paid in sales of goods. Where the seller justifiably withholds delivery of goods because of the buyer's breach, the buyer is entitled to restitution of any amount by which the sum of his payments exceeds [UCC § 2-718(2)]:

        (1)   the amount to which the seller is entitled by virtue of terms liquidating the seller's damages; or

        (2)   in the absence of such terms, 20% of the value of the total performance for which the buyer is obligated under the contract or $500, whichever is smaller.

I.   Defenses and Privileges to Intentional Torts

DEFENSES
POPCANS
Privilege, Defense of **O**thers, Defense of **P**roperty, **C**onsent, **A**uthority, **N**ecessity, **S**elf-Defense

1. **Privilege**
   a. Under certain circumstances, a defendant may not be liable for conduct that would ordinarily subject him to liability.
   b. A **privilege** may exist where:
      (1) the person affected by the defendant's conduct consents;
      (2) some important personal or public interest will be protected by the defendant's ordinarily prohibited conduct, and this interest justifies the harm caused or threatened by the defendant's conduct; and
      (3) the defendant must act freely in order to perform an essential function.

      EXAMPLE: Delbert looks out his window and see his neighbor's house on fire. He grabs his hose and goes over to the house, putting out the fire. Delbert's entry onto his neighbor's land will be privileged.

   c. The defendant has the burden of proving the existence of a privilege and that the privilege was exercised reasonably under the circumstances.

2. **Consent**
   a. Even though a defendant has otherwise committed an intentional tort, he is not liable if the plaintiff consented to the act which constituted the tort. In order to invoke this defense, the consent must be effective, and the defendant must not exceed the scope of the consent.
   b. A plaintiff can manifest consent expressly, by implication, or as a matter of law.
      (1) **Express consent** exists where the plaintiff affirmatively communicates permission for a defendant to act.
      (2) Consent is **implied** under circumstances where a reasonable person would interpret the plaintiff's conduct as evidencing permission to act.

      EXAMPLE: David, a football player, tackles Pat, a player on the other team. Because the boys are engaged in a football game, it is apparent from Pat's conduct that he consents to the tackle.

      (3) Consent may be found to exist as a matter of law where the plaintiff is unable to consent, and:
         (a) emergency action is necessary to prevent his death or serious injury;
         (b) a reasonable person would be expected to consent under the circumstances; and
         (c) no reason exists to believe that the plaintiff would not consent.

         EXAMPLE: Della falls and hits her head, splitting it open. She is unconscious. A surgeon may operate to repair the damage under the premise that Della would have consented had she been awake.

   c. **Defenses to Consent**
      (1) Even where consent is expressly or impliedly given by the plaintiff, the circumstances may be such that this consent is ineffective

and will not operate as a defense for the defendant. The most frequently tested situations involve mistake, fraud, duress, incapacity, and violation of criminal statutes.

(2) **Mistake**

    (a) Consent is not effective if:

        1) it is the product of a mistake of fact or law as to the nature or consequences of the defendant's act; and

        2) the defendant is aware of the mistake.

(3) **Fraud**

    (a) Consent is not effective if it is induced by the defendant's intentional deceit as to the essential nature or consequence of his act. If the fraud relates to a collateral matter, the consent may still be effective, but the fraud itself may be independently tortious as to a plaintiff.

(4) **Duress**

    (a) Consent is not effective if it is induced by a threat of imminent harm to the plaintiff or by a false assertion of lawful authority over the plaintiff. The same principle operates if the threat or false assertion of authority is made as to a member of the plaintiff's immediate family.

(5) **Incapacity**

    (a) As a matter of law, young children and people whose mental capacities are impaired by mental disease, mental defect, or intoxication are incapable of consenting to tortious conduct. Without particular knowledge, the defendant may interpret a plaintiff's actions as manifesting consent.

(6) **Violation of Criminal Statute**

    (a) Most jurisdictions treat consent as ineffective where the defendant's tortious conduct also constitutes a crime. A minority of jurisdictions and the Restatement regard consent to a criminal act as effective for purposes of civil liability for that conduct.

        1) Minority rule jurisdictions consider consent to be effective, for tort law purposes, to an act that is also a violation of a criminal statute, so long as the defendant's act does not constitute a breach of the peace. The majority rule is that a person cannot consent to a crime. The minority rule (Restatement rule) is that a person can consent to a crime, provided it is not a crime that is also a breach of the peace (in other words, a person cannot consent for everyone). In addition, a person cannot consent to a violation of a criminal statute that was meant to protect him (i.e., consent is not a defense to statutory rape).

        2) All jurisdictions regard consent as ineffective if the plaintiff is a member of the class of persons protected by the

violated criminal statute. This is thus an "exception" to the minority/Restatement approach as well as the "no breach of peace" principle in a majority jurisdiction.

d. While a physician's treatment of a patient without the patient's informed consent is typically treated as a form of negligence liability, there remain situations where there is such a gross deviation on the part of the defendant-doctor that a battery action will lie.

EXAMPLE: Parth gives Dr. Darth permission to remove his tonsils. Parth awakes from surgery to find that Dr. Darth cut off one of his toes instead. This would likely be a battery, as Dr. Darth far exceeded the consent given to her.

e. If the defendant's conduct substantially exceeds, in degree or nature, the scope of the plaintiff's otherwise effective consent, the defendant may still be held liable for his tortious actions.

3. **Self-Defense**

a. A defendant charged with an intentional tort may defend on grounds that he used reasonable force to prevent the plaintiff from engaging in an imminent and unprivileged attack.

(1) A defendant otherwise acting in self-defense may only use the degree of force reasonably necessary to avoid the harm threatened by the plaintiff. A defendant could not successfully assert self-defense if he used deadly force against a plaintiff whose conduct did not threaten death or serious bodily harm to that defendant.

EXAMPLE: Dylan sees Percy approaching him in a bar with a baseball bat poised to hit him. Percy shouts, "I'm going to get you, Dylan!" If necessary, Dylan may tackle Percy to the ground or grab his arms to prevent Percy from hitting him. However, if Dylan sees Percy approaching him with a flyswatter, Dylan may not shoot Percy, as he would be meeting non-deadly force with deadly force.

(2) A defendant cannot successfully assert self-defense when the purported threat represented by the plaintiff's conduct is not about to happen, has been averted, or has ended.

EXAMPLE: Percy says to Dylan, "I'm going to come back here tomorrow and kill you."

(3) Where the plaintiff's conduct, which purportedly threatens an imminent attack, is privileged, a defendant may not invoke self-defense and will be liable for any tortious acts committed toward the plaintiff.

EXAMPLE: police officer makes a lawful arrest of defendant.

(4) A defendant cannot successfully assert self-defense if he used force to defend himself when he knew an impending attack was based on a mistake as to his identity, and he would have had time to correct the mistake and prevent the attack.

b. Even where there is actually no harm threatened against the defendant, he may successfully assert self-defense if a reasonable person in the same circumstance would have believed that he was under attack. Thus, so long as the defendant subjectively (i.e., honestly and in good faith) believes that a sufficient threat exists to justify defensive force, and there is an objective basis for that belief (i.e., a reasonable person would believe so under the circumstances), self-defense is available.

c. In a majority of jurisdictions, a defendant acting in self-defense has no duty to retreat; even if a safe retreat is possible, the defendant may choose to use reasonable force against the attacking plaintiff. In a minority of states, a defendant outside his home must retreat before using deadly force if that is safely possible; if inside his own home or where safe retreat is not possible, use of defensive force is permitted.

d. Where a defendant otherwise properly acts in self-defense, he is not liable for an intentional tort if he thereby inadvertently inflicts injuries on innocent third persons. However, that defendant will be liable if he deliberately injures a third party, and may be liable for negligence if he unreasonably inflicts such injuries in the course of defending himself against an attack by the plaintiff.

4. **Defense of Others**

a. A defendant is entitled to defend another person from an attack by the plaintiff to the same extent that the third person would be lawfully entitled to defend himself from that plaintiff.

EXAMPLE: Dora and Terry are walking down the street. Dora sees Terry's ex-girlfriend, Phoebe, coming toward Terry with a knife. Realizing that Terry does not see Phoebe, Dora jumps out and grabs Phoebe's wrist, wrestling the knife from her. Because Terry could have been injured, Dora is privileged to protect him.

b. In many jurisdictions, a defendant who makes a mistake about whether defense of a third person is justified, or as to the degree of force that is reasonable, cannot assert the defense and will be liable to the plaintiff for an intentional tort. Other jurisdictions apply a **reasonable mistake doctrine**, which states that a defendant is relieved of liability where the third person would not be permitted to assert self-defense against the plaintiff if a reasonable person in the defendant's position would have believed that defense of the third person was justified, and that the defendant's action was necessary to prevent harm to the third person.

EXAMPLE: Dakota sees Xenobia run out of a doorway pursued by Patton. Patton tackles Xenobia and they struggle. Xenobia cries out, "Help, he's hurting me!" Dakota seizes Patton and forces him to release Xenobia. It is subsequently established that Xenobia had robbed Patton of his wallet and Patton was lawfully seeking to restrain Xenobia. In some jurisdictions, Dakota is liable to Patton for battery. In other jurisdictions, Dakota will not be liable to Patton for battery if a reasonable person in Dakota's position would have believed that Xenobia was entitled to exert force in defense against Patton.

b. **Defense of Property**

a. A defendant is permitted to use reasonable force to prevent a plaintiff from committing a tort against the defendant's property.

(1) The defendant must first demand that the plaintiff desist the conduct that threatens injury to his property before he can use force in defense, unless it would be futile or dangerous to make such a demand.

(2) The amount of force used by the defendant must be no greater than necessary to prevent the threatened harm. In addition, it is never permissible to use deadly force to protect one's property from injury.

(a) A defendant may not indirectly use a greater degree of force than would be justified if he were acting personally against a plaintiff. Thus, use of dogs or mechanical devices to protect property will generally result in liability, even if the plaintiff's conduct is otherwise tortious, because such force inflicted on the plaintiff is almost always considered unreasonable.

b. A defendant may use reasonable force to promptly recover his personal property if tortiously dispossessed of that property by the plaintiff. The defendant may also use reasonable force to recover such property from a guilty third party (one who took possession knowing of the tortious dispossession).

(1) The defendant may apply only such force against the plaintiff as is reasonably necessary to recover the property. A defendant may never use deadly force to recover property.

(2) A defendant must act with reasonable diligence to discover the dispossession and to recover his property. This has often been described by the courts as a requirement that the defendant be "in hot pursuit" of the tortiously dispossessing plaintiff or the guilty third party.

(3) Before being otherwise entitled to use force to recover personal property, the defendant must demand that it be returned by the wrongfully dispossessing plaintiff or guilty third party in wrongful possession.

EXAMPLE: Pam takes Darla's gold bracelet. Pam knows that the bracelet belongs to Darla, but she really likes it, so she takes it. Darla asks Pam to give it back, but Pam refuses. Darla may go up and grab the bracelet away from Pam.

(4) Even if otherwise proper, a defendant may not use force to recover property as to which the plaintiff came into possession under a claim of right.

EXAMPLE: Defendant may not use force to recover property from a withholding bailee or a purchaser on credit who has defaulted on the obligation to pay.

(5) A defendant cannot successfully assert the defense of recovery of property if he is mistaken about the fact that he was tortiously dispossessed of it by the plaintiff. This is so even if the mistake is reasonable.

(6) If otherwise proper for the defendant to use reasonable force to recover property, that defendant may enter upon the land of the plaintiff or guilty third party in order to effectuate the recovery. Such entry must be at a reasonable time and must be accomplished in a reasonable manner. The same rule applies if the property is on the land of an innocent possessor. However, the defendant will be held liable for any actual damage such entry causes.

EXCEPTION: Defendant may not enter upon the land of an innocent party and recover tortiously dispossessed property if that property is so situated as a result of the defendant's fault.

c. **Recovery of Wrongfully Dispossessed Land**

(1) In the majority of jurisdictions, the modern rule is that a defendant may never use force to recover land of which he has been wrongfully dispossessed. Such jurisdictions provide civil statutes that offer prompt judicial remedies and thus avoid any necessity for violent confrontations over possession of land.

(2) A minority of states still apparently follow the traditional rule that permits a defendant to use reasonable, non-deadly force to recover tortiously dispossessed land, so long as he acts promptly after discovering the dispossession.

6. **Necessity**

a. A defendant is permitted to injure a plaintiff's property if this is reasonably necessary to avoid a substantially greater harm to the public, to himself, or to his property.

(1) A defendant may successfully assert this defense if a reasonable person in the same circumstance would believe it necessary to injure the plaintiff's property. This is an objective standard.

(2) If the defendant reasonably but mistakenly believes that his actions are justified under the objective standard set forth, he is privileged to act, even if it subsequently is established that there was no actual necessity.

(3) If the defendant is acting to protect private, individual interests, he is justified in doing so if the threatened harm he is acting to avoid is substantially greater than the harm that will result from the action he actually takes.

(4) If the defendant is acting to protect the public interest, he is justified in doing so only if the threatened harm is severe—essentially, a disaster (e.g., the 1906 San Francisco earthquake and fire).

(5) In most jurisdictions, when a defendant acts out of private necessity, the defendant is still liable for any actual damage to the

plaintiff's property, but is not liable for any technical tort (such as trespass). In some jurisdictions, necessity is a complete defense.

(0) If a defendant acts out of public necessity, he incurs no liability whatsoever for damage to the plaintiff's property.

7. **Authority**

   a. **Arrest**

      (1) Where the defendant is a police officer acting pursuant to a duly issued warrant, valid on its face, he is not liable in tort for the fact of arrest. This rule applies to both felony and misdemeanor arrests, and applies even if the warrant is subsequently held to be invalid by a court.

         (a) This defense is available even though the arrested plaintiff is not the person against whom the warrant was issued, so long as the defendant-police officer's mistake as to the identity of the person to be arrested was reasonable.

      (2) Where a police officer or private citizen acts to prevent a felony that is being committed or appears about to be committed in his presence, he is not liable for an intentional tort based upon such an arrest.

         (a) The defendant may assert the defense even though he was mistaken in his belief that a felony was being or about to be committed, so long as the mistake is reasonable.

      (3) Both police officers and private citizens may assert the defense for arrest of a person who has, in fact, committed a felony. Treatment varies where a mistake is made as to either the fact that a felony has been committed or the identity of the felon, depending upon whether the defendant is a police officer or not.

         (a) A police officer is not liable in tort for a warrantless felony arrest, even if he makes a mistake about whether a felony was committed or about the identity of the person who committed the felony, so long as the mistake is reasonable.

         (b) Where a private citizen makes a felony arrest but makes a mistake about whether a felony was committed the defense of authority is not available, even if the mistake is reasonable. If a felony was committed but the private citizen makes a mistake about the identity of the person who committed the felony, the defense of authority is available if defendant's mistake as to identity is reasonable.

      (4) A police officer or private citizen is not liable for an arrest made without a warrant as to a breach of the peace (e.g., a misdemeanor involving violence) that is committed or appears about to be committed in his presence.

         (a) A defendant may assert this defense even though mistaken in his belief that a breach of the peace was being or about to be committed, so long as the mistake is reasonable.

(5) In the majority of jurisdictions, a defendant may not assert the defense of authority if he makes a warrantless arrest for commission of a misdemeanor not involving a breach of the peace.

   (a) Statutes in a few jurisdictions give police officers the authority to make warrantless misdemeanor arrests not involving a breach of the peace if the misdemeanor is committed in their presence.

(6) If a defendant is otherwise entitled to make an arrest, the defendant may also enter upon the plaintiff-arrestee's land to effectuate the arrest.

b. Shopkeeper's Privilege

(1) A defendant-shopkeeper is not liable for false imprisonment or a related tort if he has a reasonable suspicion that the plaintiff has stolen goods, uses reasonable force to detain the person, and detains the plaintiff for a reasonable period and in a reasonable manner, either on the premises or in the immediate vicinity.

   (a) The defendant-shopkeeper may assert the defense, even if the detained plaintiff has not, in fact, stolen any property, so long as the defendant's mistake is reasonable. It is often stated that the shopkeeper must have a **reasonable suspicion** that goods were stolen and that the detained plaintiff was the person who stole them.

c. Discipline

(1) If a defendant is charged with maintaining discipline (e.g., a parent or teacher), he may use reasonable force to perform this duty.

   (a) Force that is reasonably necessary to maintain discipline varies according to the circumstances. Factors considered include the nature of the misconduct; the age, sex, and physical condition of the disciplined plaintiff; and the motivation under which the defendant acted.

II. NEGLIGENCE

A. **Duty**

1. The element of **duty** is usually described as an obligation, recognized by law, requiring the defendant to conform to a certain standard of conduct for the protection of others against unreasonable risk. Where the defendant engages in conduct that is claimed to have injured the plaintiff, the issue can be framed as: did the defendant have a duty to the plaintiff to conform to a certain standard of conduct?

2. In some situations the general duty rule will not apply.

3. **Foreseeable Plaintiffs**

   a. In the famous Palsgraf case, Justice Cardozo articulated the rule that a defendant owes a duty only to **foreseeable plaintiffs** [Palsgraf v. Long Island R.R. Co., 162 N.E. 99 (N.Y. 1928)]. (Justice Andrews' dissent in that case argued that "[e]veryone owes to the world at large the duty of refraining from those acts which unreasonably threaten the safety of others.")

      (1) Justice Cardozo's view is the prevailing view.

      (2) If taken literally, the Cardozo view that a duty is owed only to foreseeable plaintiffs could prevent some worthy persons from recovering for negligence. A key example of a worthy plaintiff is a rescuer who is injured due to a person's negligence. Cardozo claimed, and virtually all jurisdictions have agreed, that rescuers are *per se* foreseeable plaintiffs, and thus are owed a duty.

   b. The traditional rule is that there is no affirmative duty to take action to aid or protect a plaintiff who is at risk of injury unless such action is taken. This is based on the distinction between nonfeasance and misfeasance. The law does recognize certain situations, however, in which a duty to take action does arise.

      EXAMPLE: Darren sees Polly injured by the side of the road. Late for an appointment, Darren does not stop to help Polly. Polly bleeds to death. Polly's estate does not have a cause of action against Darren.

      (1) If the defendant's conduct is responsible for placing the plaintiff in a position where he requires aid, the defendant has a duty to take action to aid the plaintiff.

         (a) A **negligent omission** occurs when the defendant fails to do something that a reasonable person would have done, such as stopping at a stop sign. Negligent omissions are treated as misfeasance for which a duty is typically owed.

         (b) The traditional application of this exception recognized a duty to act only when a defendant's conduct that caused a plaintiff to be in peril was itself negligent. The modern approach, which is still a minority view, is to recognize a duty to take action even when a defendant's conduct creating the peril was not tortious.

EXAMPLE: Danielle is on her way to the bar exam. She is worried about being late, so she is speeding. As she turns a corner, she fails to notice Pedro on his bike. Her car strikes Pedro's bike and causes Pedro to fall into the road and become trapped under his bicycle. Pedro sustains a broken ankle. Danielle must stop and help Pedro out of the road so that another car will not hit him.

(2) Although a defendant has no general duty to take affirmative action to aid a plaintiff, in many jurisdictions, once a defendant actually takes such action, he has a duty to exercise due care as to his subsequent conduct.

    (a) Some jurisdictions state that if a person undertakes to act, he is liable if he leaves the plaintiff-victim in a worse position.

    (b) As a general rule, a rescuer must act reasonably in effecting the rescue. Many jurisdictions, however, have Good Samaritan statutes which limit the liability of rescuers who provide emergency aid. For example, some only impose liability for reckless or intentional wrongdoing on the part of the rescuer.

    (c) The majority rule is that a defendant who gratuitously promises to take action to aid a plaintiff has no duty to actually take the promised action. This is so even if the plaintiff relied on the promise to his detriment. This is often referred to as **nonfeasance**, a complete failure to render the promised aid.

    (d) If a defendant gratuitously promises to aid a plaintiff, once the defendant attempts to give the promised aid, the defendant has a duty to exercise reasonable care in doing so. Due to the perceived harshness of the nonfeasance rule, courts readily find that a defendant who makes a gratuitous promise to aid a plaintiff has subsequently taken action that constitutes an attempted performance of the promise.

    (e) In a minority of jurisdictions, a defendant is liable for a complete failure to perform a gratuitous promise of aid if the plaintiff relied on the promise to his detriment (e.g., by foregoing other aid).

(3) The defendant has a duty to take affirmative action in aid of a plaintiff where a **special relationship** exists between the defendant and plaintiff.

    (a) If the defendant derives or occupies a position of power over the plaintiff (e.g., the plaintiff is particularly vulnerable and dependent upon the defendant), there is a duty to take action. The following relationships have been generally recognized as triggering the duty to care for the plaintiff:

        1) employer-employee during and in the scope of employment;

        2) common carrier- and innkeeper-customer;

        3) school-pupil;

        4) parent-child;

5) business-patron; and

6) jailer-prisoner.

(4) Duty to control third parties

(a) There is no duty to control the conduct of a third person as to prevent him from causing physical harm to another, unless:

1) a special relationship exists between the defendant and the third party that imposes a duty upon the defendant to control the third party's conduct; or

EXAMPLE: Dean is in a movie theater sitting next to Perry. Dean and Perry do not know one another; they just happen to be sitting in adjacent seats. Perry gets very angry with the usher because the usher tells him to take his feet off the seat in front of him. If Perry decides to slug the usher, Dean has no duty to control him.

2) a special relationship exists between the defendant and the third party that gives the third party a right of protection.

EXAMPLE: Dean is in the movie theater sitting next to his son when Eliza enters. Eliza takes one look at Dean's son, realizes that he is the kid who bit her child on the playground, and lunges at him. Dean has a duty to protect his son from Eliza and to control her conduct.

(b) A parent is under a duty to exercise reasonable care to control his minor child so as to prevent the child from intentionally harming others or creating an unreasonable risk of bodily harm to them, if the parent:

1) knows or has reason to know that he has the ability to control his child; and

2) knows or should know of the necessity and opportunity for exercising such control.

EXAMPLE: Milly and Erica, two 13-year-olds, are building bombs in Milly's garage. Their parents do not supervise their free time and giggle when they find bomb-making manuals in the house, saying, "Kids will be kids!" If Milly and Erica bomb their school and kill many of their classmates and teachers, their parents may be liable.

(c) A master is under a duty to exercise reasonable care to control his servant while acting outside the scope of his employment in order to prevent the servant from intentionally harming others or creating unreasonable risk of bodily harm to them, if:

1) the servant:

a) is upon the master's premises or premises upon which the servant is privileged to enter only as his servant; or

b) is using a chattel of the master; and

2) the master:

    a) knows or has reason to know that he has the ability to control his servant; and

    b) knows or should know of the necessity and opportunity for exercising such control.

> **EXAMPLE:** Darnell owns Silver Skates, an ice-skating rink in Coldville. Ellie is a skating teacher at the rink. Darnell is in the office overlooking the rink one day when he sees Ellie, who is supposed be taking the day off, doing skating lifts with skaters that Darnell knows to be beginners. Darnell knows that beginning skaters are not ready to do lifts and can really hurt themselves if they do. Darnell has a duty to intervene to protect the students if he is able to do so.

(d) The defendant-employer has a duty to a plaintiff to exercise reasonable care in hiring employees, such that a defendant may be liable to a plaintiff if an employee subsequently injures the plaintiff. This is distinguished from the vicarious liability of an employer for his employee's torts—*respondeat superior*, where the negligent conduct is that of the employee and liability is attributed by law to the employer. In negligent hiring, the employer is liable for his own negligence in hiring the employee, not vicariously liable for the wrongful conduct of the employee.

(e) Where a defendant permits a third person to use his personal property, the defendant has a duty to control such use and to exercise due care in permitting the third person to use the property. The context in which this issue is frequently tested is an auto owner-defendant who permits a member of his family to drive his car.

(f) In some jurisdictions, a defendant who has the requisite special relationship with a third person and who becomes aware that the third person intends to do specific harm to an identified plaintiff has a duty to warn the plaintiff of the harm. The special relationships that have been recognized as triggering this duty include:

1) psychotherapist-patient; and

2) custodian-prisoner.

> **EXAMPLE:** Zazu tells his therapist, Dr. Drew, that he intends to kill his ex-wife, Pru. Dr. Drew takes no action to warn Pru of the threat, which Dr. Drew believes to be credible. Pru is killed. In a negligence action against Dr. Drew, most jurisdictions would find that he had a duty to take reasonable steps to warn Pru of the impending danger based on his relationship with Zazu, his patient.

(5) Based on the distinction between nonfeasance and misfeasance, one generally does not have a duty to protect a person from third party criminal conduct. In certain circumstances, however, a special relationship (such as a landlord-tenant or business-invitee) will trigger a duty. Jurisdictions vary on the amount of foreseeability that must exist before a court will find a duty to protect.

   (a) Some jurisdictions will only find a duty to protect where there were **prior similar incidents**, making the third-party criminal conduct particularly foreseeable. Others use a more flexible **totality of the circumstances test**, while some others balance the degree of foreseeability against the burden that would be placed on the defendant to protect the plaintiff from harm.

c. When the defendant is a governmental entity, the question of whether the defendant owes a duty to the plaintiff will depend on the function the government is fulfilling that gives rise to the cause of action.

   (1) If the governmental entity is acting in a **proprietary function**– that is, acting in an area traditionally occupied by private entities– the government will be treated as any other defendant for the purpose of determining duty.

   (2) When the governmental entity is engaged in a **discretionary activity**–that is, where the governmental entity is using judgment and allocating resources–the courts will not find a duty.

   (3) When the governmental entity is acting in a **ministerial function**, courts will find a duty; once the governmental entity has undertaken to act, it must do so non-negligently.

      (a) Under the **public duty doctrine**, when a government agency (e.g., the police or fire department) is sued for failing to provide an adequate response, courts will find no duty unless:

         1) there has been reliance on the response of the agency;

         2) there is a special relationship between the plaintiff and the agency; or

         3) the agency has increased the danger beyond what would otherwise exist.

            EXAMPLE: Paul's third-story apartment catches fire, and he calls 911. Paul asks the dispatcher if he should jump out the window, and she tells him that the fire department is only a minute away, and he should wait for the firemen to arrive so that he can climb down the ladder. In reality, the firemen have stopped off to grab a snack before responding, and by the time they arrive the fire has spread, blocking Paul's access to the window to jump.

      (b) If the defendant is a utility, courts have refused to impose duty beyond those who are in privity of contract to the utility.

4. **Negligent Infliction of Emotional Distress**

    a.   If the plaintiff's injury is not personal injury or property damage, duty issues arise.

    b.   Courts have traditionally been reluctant to allow liability for emotional distress, and apply special rules for claims for pure emotional distress.

> **NOTE** Pain and suffering, though emotional damages, are not subject to the limitations placed on claims for pure emotional distress.

    c.   **Direct Claims**

        (1)   In most jurisdictions, to recover for emotional distress the plaintiff must:

            (a)   have been in the **zone of danger**—that is, the area in which he was at risk of being physically injured; and

                EXAMPLE: Paula and Peter are crossing the street when Dexter comes driving down the road at twice the speed limit. Paula manages to get out of the way, but Peter is hit by Dexter. Paula was in the zone of danger and may have a cause of action for emotional distress.

            (b)   have suffered some accompanying physical manifestation of the emotional distress.

        (2)   Two exceptions exist to the zone of danger and physical manifestation requirements:

            (a)   if the defendant negligently transmits a telegram announcing the death of a loved one; and

            (b)   if the defendant negligently mishandles a corpse.

        (3)   In a minority of jurisdictions, if the defendant has a preexisting duty to the plaintiff, the plaintiff may recover for negligent infliction of emotional distress.

        (4)   Some jurisdictions have eliminated the requirement of physical manifestation of emotional distress and allow plaintiffs to prevail based on a showing of severe emotional distress without accompanying physical symptoms.

    d.   **Bystander Actions**

        (1)   In a bystander action, the physical harm occurs to a loved one, and the plaintiff sues for his emotional distress as a result of the injury to another. It is premised upon the defendant's violation of the duty not to negligently cause emotional distress to people who observe the conduct which causes harm to another.

        (2)   The majority rule is that a plaintiff may recover for negligent infliction of emotional distress under a **bystander theory** if he:

            (a)   was located near the scene of an accident;

            (b)   suffered a severe emotional distress ("shock") resulting from the sensory and contemporaneous observance of the accident; and

            (c)   had a close relationship with the victim.

(3) Before the recognition of bystander liability, American courts permitted a person to recover for negligently caused emotional disturbance only if the person suffered physical impact due to the defendant's negligent conduct or, later, was personally in the **zone of danger** created by the defendant's negligent conduct. Most American courts have now adopted some version of the bystander liability rule.

(4) Bystander emotional distress is a derivative claim in most jurisdictions. As a result, the bystander's recovery may be reduced proportionally if the injured party is found to be comparatively negligent.

> **EXAM TIP** ▸ The requirements for negligent infliction of emotional distress ("NIED") are different than the requirements for intentional infliction of emotional distress ("IIED"). IIED is covered in depth earlier in this outline. See the chart below for a recap of the different elements required for both NIED and IIED.

INTENTIONAL INFLICTION OF EMOTIONAL DISTRESS		
Elements Required for Plaintiff Recovery When Conduct Directed at Third-Party		
Theory 1		**Theory 2**
1. Plaintiff must be **present** when conduct occurs to third party/victim; 2. Plaintiff must be a **close relative** of the third party/victim; 3. Defendant is **aware of plaintiff's presence**; and 4. Plaintiff suffers **severe emotional distress** (whether or not it results in bodily harm).	**OR**	1. Plaintiff (no special relation to the third party/victim required) must be **present** when conduct occurs; 2. Plaintiff suffers **actual bodily harm** (a physical manifestation of the emotional distress); and 3. Defendant is **aware of plaintiff's presence**.

NEGLIGENT INFLICTION OF EMOTIONAL DISTRESS		
Elements Required for Recovery		
Theory 1: Direct Claim		**Theory 2: Bystander Action**
1. Plaintiff is within the **"zone of danger"**; and 2. Plaintiff suffers **emotional distress** and some accompanying **physical manifestation** of the emotional distress.	**OR**	1. Plaintiff is **present** at the scene and **witnesses** the event; 2. Plaintiff is a **close relative** of the third party/victim; and 3. Plaintiff suffers **severe emotional distress**.

5. **Wrongful Conception, Wrongful Birth, Wrongful Life**

a. **Wrongful conception** applies where the injury is the birth of a healthy child.

(1) Generally, wrongful conception actions arise where the plaintiff has had a negligently performed vasectomy or other negligently administered form of birth control.

(2) Damages typically involve the cost of the birth and the cost to rectify the ineffective contraceptive measure.

(3) Courts are very reluctant to award the costs of raising a child through the age of majority.

b. **Wrongful birth** is the claim of the parents for the birth of an unhealthy child.

(1) Wrongful birth claims generally stem from a physician's failure to diagnose a disability in the fetus, which the plaintiff claims would have led her to not give birth to the child.

(2) Many courts will not recognize a claim for wrongful birth.

(3) Some courts will award the extraordinary costs of having a child with special needs, but the jury may offset this award by the benefit obtained from having the child.

c. **Wrongful life** is the child's action for having been born unhealthy.

(1) Most courts will not award damages for wrongful life.

(2) A small number of courts have awarded damages for the costs of the child's special needs after the age of majority.

6. **Land Possessor Liability**

a. The standard of care applied to owners and occupiers of land varies according to which of three categories of danger or activity were involved in the injury to the plaintiff. These categories are:

(1) activities—the injury to the plaintiff derived from the conduct of persons on the land;

(2) artificial conditions—the injury to the plaintiff derived from circumstances created by persons on the land, such as buildings, excavations, cultivation, etc.; and

(3) natural conditions—the injury to the plaintiff derived from circumstances not created by persons but existing on the land, such as natural bodies of water, trees occurring naturally, falling boulders, etc.

b. In addition to considering the category of danger or activity that injured the plaintiff, the analysis of the standard of care varies according to the categories of the plaintiffs who claim injury.

c. **Plaintiffs on the land**

(1) **Invitees**

(a) An **invitee** is a person who enters onto the defendant's land at the defendant's express or implied invitation, and who enters for a purpose relating to the defendant's interests or activities. Invitees are classified as either business invitees or public invitees.

1) A **business invitee** is an invitee who enters onto the defendant's land for a purpose related to the defendant's business activities or interests.

EXAMPLE: Customers and persons accompanying them, delivery persons, salespersons (if reasonable for them to expect that someone on the non-private, non-residential premises may be interested in purchasing), and job applicants (it reasonable for them to expect that employment may be available) are examples of business invitees.

2) A **public invitee** is a member of the public who enters onto the defendant's land for a purpose as to which the land is held open to the public.

EXAMPLE: Visitors to airports and visitors to churches.

a) In a minority of jurisdictions, the classification of public invitee is not recognized. However, courts in such jurisdictions readily find a business purpose in visits by persons who would otherwise be considered public invitees.

(b) A defendant has a duty to exercise reasonable care to prevent injuries to invitees caused by activities conducted on his land.

(c) The defendant also has a duty to exercise reasonable care to discover dangerous artificial conditions that invitees would not reasonably be aware of, and to warn invitees of the existence of such conditions or to make the conditions safe. If it would be insufficient to make the dangerous condition reasonably safe by providing only a warning, the defendant's duty includes a duty of reasonable care to provide other precautions.

(d) The defendant's duty to invitees with regard to dangerous natural conditions is the same as that applicable to artificial conditions.

(e) An invitee may be regarded as a licensee or even as a trespasser if the invitee enters areas of the defendant's property to which his invitation does not extend, or if the invitee stays in a permitted area longer than was contemplated by the invitation.

(2) **Licensees**

(a) A **licensee** is a person who enters onto the defendant's land with the defendant's express or implied permission, and who does not enter for a purpose benefiting the defendant or the defendant's activities.

EXAMPLE: Visiting relatives, social guests, and door-to-door salespersons.

NOTE ▸ Invitees who exceed the scope of defendant's invitation are treated as licensees.

(b) As to licensees, a defendant has a duty to exercise reasonable care to protect them from injury arising from activities conducted by the defendant or on the defendant's behalf. It is usually sufficient for the defendant to warn the plaintiff-licensee, but the defendant's duty includes the exercise of reasonable care to discover licensees of whom he is not aware.

(c) A defendant has a duty to exercise reasonable care to warn of any artificial conditions of which he is aware, which present an unreasonable danger, and of which the plaintiff-licensee is unaware and unlikely to discover. The defendant has no duty to inspect his land for such dangerous artificial conditions.

  1) The standard of care applicable to licensees requires defendant to protect them from dangerous natural conditions to the same extent required for artificial conditions.

(3) Trespassers

(a) If a plaintiff enters onto a defendant's land without the defendant's permission or without a privilege to so enter, the plaintiff is classified as a **trespasser**.

EXAMPLE: Demi wants to see the great view of the Mississippi from the top of Blueberry Hill. Blueberry Hill is entirely on Philip's property. If Demi hikes up Blueberry Hill without Philip's permission, she is a trespasser.

(b) The trespasser category is further broken down into four subcategories, as to which the standard of care may vary.

  1) **Unknown**

    a) A defendant has no duty of care as to a trespasser whose presence is unknown to him. The defendant also has no duty to inspect his land to attempt to discover unknown trespassers.

  2) **Known**

    a) If the defendant becomes aware that a particular plaintiff has trespassed on his property or becomes aware of facts from which he should reasonably conclude that a plaintiff has trespassed, the plaintiff is regarded as a **known trespasser**. The applicable standard of care varies according to the category of danger.

    b) Most jurisdictions require the defendant to exercise reasonable care to protect a known trespasser from injuries deriving from activities conducted on his land.

    c) The defendant must exercise reasonable care to warn a known trespasser of hidden dangers of which the defendant is aware and the known trespasser is unaware.

    d) The defendant has no duty to protect a known trespasser from injuries deriving from natural conditions on his land.

  3) **Frequent**

    a) If the defendant knows or reasonably should know that trespassers frequently enter upon a portion of his land, the standard may be higher than that normally applicable to unknown trespassers. For example, if the defendant observed that a beaten path cuts across his property, he would be alerted to the presence of frequent trespassers. Frequent trespassers are owed the same duty of care owed to known trespassers, even if the defendant is not aware that a particular plaintiff is present on his land or has ever previously trespassed upon his land.

4) **Children**

a) Where activities and natural conditions are involved, the standard of care as to children who trespass is the same as that for the applicable category of adult trespassers. A heightened standard of care may apply as to artificial conditions on the defendant's land.

b) If the heightened standard of care as to children trespassers is invoked, a defendant has a duty to exercise reasonable care to prevent injury to the children, applicable to dangerous artificial conditions. The heightened standard of care set forth above arises if four prerequisites are shown to exist:

  i) the artificial condition is a foreseeable risk of unreasonable danger to trespassing children;

    a. An artificial condition on a defendant's land poses a foreseeable, unreasonable risk of danger to children trespassers if a defendant knows or reasonably should know of the existence and nature of the artificial condition. A defendant has no independent duty to inspect the land to discover such artificial conditions.

    b. It is relevant to whether a condition poses a foreseeably unreasonable danger to children trespassers that the danger is one which a child might ordinarily be expected to recognize. Thus, a child old enough to play without immediate parental supervision can ordinarily be expected to recognize the danger represented by water, fire, and falling.

  ii) it is foreseeable that children are likely to trespass where the artificial condition is located;

    c. If a defendant has no reason to anticipate that children are likely to trespass where an artificial condition is located, the heightened standard of care is not triggered. Foreseeability of the likelihood of children trespassers may arise from a defendant's knowledge of past trespasses, proximity to places where children are likely to be, accessibility to the artificial condition, and other relevant factors. Thus, if the artificial condition is located near a park, playground, or street, or is easily climbed, a defendant should reasonably know that children are likely to trespass there. It was from this aspect of foreseeability that the traditional label **attractive nuisance doctrine** was derived.

 iii) the child trespasser is unaware of the risk; and

  d. This prerequisite is satisfied if the child trespasser, because of his age or immaturity, did not discover the condition or appreciate the danger it represented. If the child trespasser is aware of the condition, understands the risk of danger it poses, and is able to avoid that risk, the defendant owes no heightened duty to prevent injury to that child (i.e., the child is treated as if he were an adult trespasser).

 iv) the risk of danger of the artificial condition outweighs its utility.

  e. It is said that the utility of maintaining the dangerous artificial condition must be "slight" compared to the risk to trespassing children in order for this prerequisite to be satisfied. This is similar to the negligence calculus (cost of precautions balanced against probability and gravity of harm considering social utility).

EXAMPLE: Paloma is a six-year-old girl who frequently trespasses on Donatella's land. Donatella knows that Paloma sometimes trespasses on her land. If there is a dangerous dumpsite on Donatella's land, Donatella must make it safe. If there is an abandoned car that is rusty and dangerous on Donatella's land, Donatella should remove it or cover it to prevent Paloma from injuring herself. However, Donatella does not have to build a fence around her pond, as natural bodies of water are generally not included within the rule.

(4) **Privileged entrants**

 (a) Where there has been no express or implied permission or invitation extended by a defendant, certain persons are nevertheless privileged by law to enter onto the defendant's land. These include police officers or firefighters responding in an emergency, census takers, or private persons exercising a privilege (e.g., where unauthorized entry is necessary to avoid a greater harm). **Privileged entrants** are classified as either licensees or invitees, usually depending on the purpose for which they entered.

(b) If the public purpose for which the privileged entrant was acting has a connection with the defendant's activities conducted on the premises, the privileged entrant is regarded as an invitee for standard of care purposes. Courts readily find that such a connection exists.

(c) Police and firefighters entering onto the premises have traditionally been regarded by the courts as licensees. As set forth above, a defendant has no duty to inspect and discover dangerous conditions as to licensees.

(d) A private person entering onto a defendant's land under some legal privilege is regarded as a licensee.

STATUS	DUTY OWED
Trespasser— Undiscovered	No duty.
Trespasser— Known or Anticipated	Ordinary care—duty to warn of dangerous conditions that are known to possessor (**exception**: no duty to warn of obvious natural conditions of the land (e.g., lake)).
Licensee	Ordinary care—duty to warn of dangerous conditions which are known to possessor.
Invitee	Ordinary care—duty to (1) inspect premises and/or land; and (2) make safe for protection of invitees who enter.

d. **Plaintiffs not on the land (But Adjacent to It)**

(1) A defendant must exercise reasonable care to prevent a plaintiff not on his land from an injury deriving from the defendant's activities or the activities of others conducted on his land.

(2) A defendant must exercise reasonable care to prevent a plaintiff not on his land from an injury deriving from unreasonably dangerous artificial conditions that abut or protrude onto adjacent land. A defendant must also exercise reasonable care to protect passersby on a public street from injury deriving from dangerous artificial conditions on his land.

(3) A majority of jurisdictions impose no duty on a defendant to protect a plaintiff not on the defendant's land from dangers deriving from natural conditions on his land. The minority rule

is that the defendant must exercise reasonable care to prevent injury to a plaintiff not on his land from dangers deriving from natural conditions on his land.

(4) Many jurisdictions require that in urban areas, a defendant must exercise reasonable care to protect a plaintiff passing by his land on adjacent public streets from injury deriving from native trees on his land.

(5) The defendant to whom the standard of care is applied is the person in possession of the land, which includes the owner, a tenant, a purchaser, or an adverse possessor. The standard of care may also vary if the possessor of land is a landlord or seller of land.

(6) A substantial number of jurisdictions have eliminated the distinctions between the various classes of persons entering the land, and simply hold the landowner to a "reasonable under the circumstances" test. In applying the test, the nature of the entry is simply one factor in determining foreseeability and reasonability.

e. **Landlords and Tenants**

(1) The standard of care applicable to owners and occupiers of land is invoked in connection with possession of land. Thus, the appropriate standard of care (determined as discussed above) applies when a defendant is a tenant in possession of leased premises. Areas retained in the landlord's possession, such as common areas in multiple housing units, remain the landlord's responsibility. Under certain circumstances, however, a landlord may be liable to the tenant or to third persons for injuries they suffer in areas to which the landlord has surrendered possession to the tenant.

(a) The nature and extent of the landlord's duty to protect a tenant in possession from harm arising from a dangerous condition on the premises varies according to whether the defect was patent or latent, or whether it arose after the transfer of possession.

1) Dangerous natural or artificial conditions that are or should be reasonably apparent to the tenant upon transfer of possession are called **patent defects**. The landlord is under no duty to warn of or repair such obvious conditions.

2) Dangerous natural or artificial conditions of which the tenant is unaware and which are not reasonably apparent to him, and of which the landlord is aware, are classified as **latent defects**. The landlord has a duty to warn the tenant of such dangers or repair them. The landlord has no duty to inspect the premises for latent dangers.

3) The landlord has no duty to exercise reasonable care as to dangerous conditions that arise after possession has been transferred to the tenant, unless the landlord actually undertakes to repair such conditions or covenants to repair them. This latter view is a modern minority position, imposing liability where the tenant is injured

because the landlord failed to perform a contractual duty to repair a dangerous condition of which the landlord knew or should have known and as to which the landlord had a reasonable opportunity to repair.

(b) Under the traditional view, a landlord had no duty to protect third persons from injuries arising from dangerous conditions or activities on the leased premises. Today, many jurisdictions treat third persons who would otherwise be classified as licensees or invitees of the tenant as though they were tenants themselves in assessing the tort liability of the landlord.

1) Even under the traditional view, if the landlord knew that the tenant intended to open the leased premises to the public, the landlord had a duty to prevent injury to members of the public who came onto the premises. This standard of care required the landlord to exercise reasonable care to discover and repair any dangerous natural or artificial conditions existing at the time of transfer of possession.

f. **Sellers of Land**

(1) Where a defendant transfers both possession and ownership of land to another, there is generally no further duty to protect anyone from injuries arising from the conditions of the land or activities conducted thereon. Under limited circumstances, however, the vendor-seller of land has a continuing duty even after the transfer of possession and title.

(a) A defendant-seller has a duty to disclose to the purchaser of land any hidden dangerous natural or artificial conditions of which the seller knows or reasonably should know and which the seller reasonably could anticipate the purchaser will not discover. The duty to disclose hidden dangers continues until the purchaser has had a reasonable chance to discover and remedy the dangers.

(b) The seller's duty to disclose hidden dangerous conditions applies to the purchaser and the purchaser's invitees and licensees as to injuries occurring on the land, and to persons not on the land if the dangerous conditions create an unreasonable risk to such persons.

(c) Where the defendant-seller actively conceals the existence of a dangerous condition, the duty to disclose continues until the purchaser actually discovers the dangerous condition and remedies it (i.e., the seller may not argue that the purchaser reasonably should have discovered the condition).

(d) In many jurisdictions, the builder of a residence has a tort law duty to exercise reasonable care in construction so that such builder remains liable for defects in its construction.

B. Standard of Care

1. **Reasonably Prudent Person under the Same or Similar Circumstances**

   a. In general, a defendant breaches the duty to a plaintiff if he fails to conduct himself as a reasonable person would in the same circumstances.

   (1) **Exceptions**

   (a) The reasonable person standard is applied as though the reasonable person possessed the same physical characteristics as the defendant. Thus, the trier of fact assesses what conduct a reasonable person of the same height, weight, ability to see or hear, and disabilities as the defendant would have engaged in under the circumstances.

   EXAMPLE: Del, blind since birth, is walking down the street using a cane. He knocks into Pol, injuring him. In Pol's negligence action against Del, Del will be held to the standard of care of a reasonably prudent blind person.

   > **NOTE** The reasonable person standard is not altered to account for a defendant's physical disability if the disability is the result of the defendant's voluntary intoxication.

   (b) For purposes of analyzing a negligence action, the conduct of defendants whose cognitive abilities are diminished due to mental illness, mental disability, or intoxication is assessed without such diminishment of abilities.

   1) However, to the extent that a defendant possessed greater knowledge or expertise than the average person, the "reasonable" person to whom the defendant is compared is thought of as also possessing that greater knowledge or expertise.

   EXAMPLE: Dennis has an IQ of 75. Dennis places a large number of rocks in the back of his pickup truck but does not tie them down. When he drives his truck on the highway, a lot of rocks fall out of the back of the truck, causing a pile-up accident behind him. In a negligence analysis, Dennis's actions will be compared with persons of average intelligence, not those of other people with mental challenges.

   (c) Where a defendant's conduct occurs in an emergency situation, it is recognized that a reasonable person might accept greater risk or have less opportunity for reflection in determining the reasonable course of action. The defendant must act as a reasonable person would behave in the emergency situation.

   1) If a defendant's own negligent conduct is responsible for creating the emergency situation, the above principle is not applied in assessing the reasonableness of the defendant's conduct during the emergency.

(2)   In determining whether a defendant's conduct constituted a breach of duty under the "reasonable person" standard, Judge Learned Hand offered the following analysis. If the burden (or cost) to the defendant of taking precautions against the threatened risk was outweighed by the likelihood (or probability) that the plaintiff would be injured by the risk-producing activity, considering also the gravity (or severity) of the injury to the plaintiff if the risk manifests itself, and considering the social utility of the activity in which the defendant is engaged, then the defendant failed to act as a reasonable person would. In short, if the burden of taking precautions is less than the probability of injury "times" the severity of that injury, plus the social utility of the defendant's activity, the defendant breached his duty of care by not taking such precautions. Although legal problems cannot be reduced to simple mathematical formulae, this is a useful way to remember and to articulate the relevant considerations.

(a)   The greater the benefit society derives, viewed in the aggregate, from the activity engaged in by a defendant, the more likely the defendant will not be found to have breached a duty to a plaintiff merely by engaging in such an activity or by not undertaking certain precautions.

EXAMPLE: Driving a car presents a fairly high probability of colliding with others and a relatively severe danger of death or great injury, which might be thought to justify significant precautions, such as driving very slowly or avoiding driving at all when there is great congestion or pedestrian activity. However, the social utility of driving is also very great, so that such precautions are considered to be "outweighed" in the Learned Hand calculus, and a reasonable person would not undertake them. Less burdensome precautions, such as remaining alert and operating the vehicle competently, are regarded as sufficient to fulfill the duty of care.

(b)   The determination of whether a person has acted unreasonably is very fact-intensive. Use Hand's formula as a guide in asking whether the probability of harm multiplied by the likely magnitude of that harm outweighs the burden of avoidance.

(c)   The reasonable person standard of care is an objective one. In other words, the standard is applied as though the reasonable person possessed the experience, knowledge, and mental capabilities of an average member of the community, even if the defendant did not himself actually possess it.

(d)   In determining how a reasonable person would behave under the circumstances, it is relevant how a person engaging in the defendant's activity would customarily behave. However, evidence of custom is not conclusive; the trier of fact may find either that the customary manner of behavior was not reasonable under the circumstances or that a reasonable person would have engaged in behavior other than what is customary.

1) A plaintiff may submit evidence of a defendant's deviation from custom as evidence of the defendant's unreasonable conduct. Conversely, a defendant may put on evidence of compliance with custom to show the reasonableness of his conduct.

EXAMPLE: In trying to show that her landlord, Darv, was negligent for failing to install unbreakable glass in her shower, Penny may put on evidence that most landlords use unbreakable glass. This evidence is persuasive, as it suggests that the burden of using that glass is not too great.

2. **Children**

a. The reasonable person standard specifically takes account of age when a defendant is a minor.

(1) In the majority of jurisdictions, a minor defendant's conduct is assessed according to what a reasonable child of the same age, education, intelligence, and experience would have done.

(2) A minority of states follow the traditional rule, which divided minors into three age levels:

(a) age six and below, as to which the defendant was conclusively presumed incapable of being negligent;

(b) ages seven to 13, as to which it was rebuttably presumed that the defendant was not negligent; and

(c) age 14 and up, as to which it was rebuttably presumed that the defendant was capable of being negligent.

EXAMPLE: Darlene is seven years old and is very intelligent. One day, she leaves her roller skates on the front walk. Patrick, who is walking down the walk, does not see the skates and slips and falls on them, breaking his leg. If Patrick sues Darlene, her act of leaving the skates on the walk will be compared with that of a seven-year-old with similar experience and intelligence.

b. Children engaging in adult activities (e.g., operating an automobile, boat, or airplane), however, are required to conform to an adult standard of care.

EXAMPLE: Nine-year-old Dilbert takes his dad's motorboat out for a spin. While driving the boat across the bay, he hits Patricia, a swimmer, and knocks her unconscious. Patricia drowns. If Patricia's estate sues Dilbert, he will not be compared with other children's standard of care. Instead, he will be held to the objective, adult reasonable person's standard of care.

3. **Statutory**

   a. A statute that provides for civil liability supersedes the common law of torts. A defendant's civil liability will be determined by the specific statutory provisions. Such civil statutes are rare.

      EXAMPLE: A legislature could enact a statute stating that anyone injured in a car accident who was not wearing a seatbelt is barred from pursuing a negligence action.

   b. Where a defendant's conduct also violates a statute that does not provide for civil liability (usually a criminal statute), the statute may establish the standard of conduct for breach of duty purposes. In a majority of jurisdictions, this means that an unexcused violation conclusively establishes that the defendant breached his duty to the plaintiff (often referred to as **negligence *per se***).

      (1) Other (minority) jurisdictions regard a qualifying violation of statute by a defendant as either raising a rebuttable presumption (so that the plaintiff wins unless the defendant introduces enough evidence to overcome the presumption) or as *prima facie* evidence (so that the plaintiff wins unless the defendant introduces any evidence, but the plaintiff retains the burden of proof if the defendant offers evidence) that the defendant's conduct breached the duty of care owed to the plaintiff.

   c. In a jurisdiction that has adopted a negligence *per se* rule, a defendant's violation of a criminal statute has the effect of establishing the standard of care only when all of the following three conditions are present:

      (1) the injury caused by the defendant's conduct is the type that the statute was intended to prevent;

      (2) the plaintiff is a member of the class intended to be protected by the statute; and

      (3) the defendant's violation of the statute is not excused.

   d. A defendant's violation of an applicable statute is excused if compliance with the statute:

      (1) would have resulted in a harm greater than the harm produced by the violation; or

      (2) would have been impossible.

   e. A few statutes are regarded as so important that their violation cannot be excused as a matter of law (e.g., the statutory obligation to maintain a vehicle's brakes in proper working order).

      EXAMPLE: To prevent children from getting poisoned, the legislature passes a law making it a crime to sell toxic substances without a child-proof cap. DunCo fails to put a child-proof cap on its rat poison. Four-year-old Pablum finds the rat poison, drinks it, and suffers harm. Even though the statute is criminal in nature, in most states it would become the standard of care because it was designed to protect children from ingesting poison. Breach would be the violation of that statute—i.e., not putting a child-proof cap on the poison. The plaintiff must still prove the other elements of negligence.

f. Compliance with a statute is regarded as mere evidence on the issue of whether a defendant breached his duty of care, and does not raise any presumption in the defendant's favor.

4. **Professionals**

a. Historically, defendants who engaged in certain activities were held to a higher standard of care to the public or to their customers.

(1) Common carriers (e.g., trains, bus lines, etc.) were traditionally said to have a duty to avoid harm to their passengers through exercise of "the highest degree of vigilance, care and precaution," or "the utmost caution characteristic of very careful, prudent persons."

(2) Some jurisdictions utilize the same standard of care for assessing the conduct of innkeepers toward their customers as that applied to a common carrier regarding its passengers.

(3) The dangerous products or services dispensed by public utilities (e.g., electricity, and gas) caused many jurisdictions to impose a duty of care which required that such utilities "take every reasonable precaution suggested by experience or prudence" to avoid injury to the public.

b. Professionals are treated differently from other defendants in negligence. For most defendants, custom is only evidence related to providing breach of duty. For professionals, such as doctors, lawyers, and accountants, custom is everything. The customary practice of professionals in good standing sets the standard of care. If the defendant deviates from that custom, he has breached his duty; if he has complied with that custom, he cannot be found to have breached his duty.

EXAMPLE: Dr. Dell uses a certain procedure to remove Penn's tonsils, and in so doing causes Penn harm. In Penn's malpractice action against Dr. Dell, if it is established that Dr. Dell performed as other doctors in good standing would have performed, she is free from liability. Conversely, if the evidence is that Dr. Dell deviated from the customary way tonsils are removed, even if she did so in good faith, she will have committed malpractice.

(1) The effect of this rule is that a defendant will be found to have breached the standard of care if he did not conduct himself as would a competent member of the profession with minimally adequate knowledge and expertise. If the defendant is a specialist within a profession, the standard of care is applied according to the standards appropriate to that specialty.

(a) Where there are several accepted ways of acting, the defendant's compliance with any of these accepted schools of thought protects him from liability.

(2) Traditionally, the conduct of a defendant with specialized skill or expertise was assessed for reasonable person/breach of

duty purposes with regard to the community in which the defendant practiced his profession. Some jurisdictions apply a more modern, national standard, recognizing that technology permits communication and exchange of knowledge that transcends traditional geographic limitations. Specialists are particularly likely to be held to a national standard.

c. Traditionally, a physician was liable for the intentional tort of battery if he failed to properly inform a plaintiff-patient about the risks and alternatives of a proposed medical procedure or treatment; the plaintiff's consent was said to be negated by the lack of disclosure. This is still the case where there is a gross deviation from consent, such as where a patient agrees to a tonsillectomy, but her leg is amputated instead. Most jurisdictions now treat nondisclosure as a form of malpractice.

(1) In some jurisdictions, malpractice based on the failure to disclose is treated like any other kind of medical malpractice. The physician-defendant must disclose risks that doctors in good standing customarily divulge. The failure to do so is malpractice.

(2) The trend, based on recognition of patient autonomy, has been to require physicians to divulge all material risks—that is, risks that a reasonable patient would want to know in deciding whether to undergo a specific procedure. The failure to divulge a material risk is malpractice provided the patient can show that he would have refused the procedure had the risk been divulged.

C. Breach of Duty

1. *Res Ipsa Loquitur*

a. A plaintiff generally meets his burden of proving breach of duty by establishing that the defendant's conduct fails to conform to the applicable standard of care. This is rendered difficult or impossible where a plaintiff does not know and cannot effectively determine specifically what a defendant's injurious conduct was. The doctrine of *res ipsa loquitur* ("the thing speaks for itself") helps the plaintiff in such situations.

(1) In the majority of jurisdictions, if a plaintiff makes a qualifying showing of *res ipsa loquitur*, he has produced evidence sufficient, if believed by the jury, to support a finding that a defendant breached his duty. *Res ipsa loquitur* is thus merely a means of adducing evidence of breach of duty to satisfy the burdens of producing evidence and persuasion. In most jurisdictions, *res ipsa loquitur* permits the jury to infer the defendant's breach of duty.

(2) A small minority of jurisdictions regard a qualifying showing of *res ipsa loquitur* as shifting the burden of producing evidence to the defendant as to the issue of breach of duty. The defendant must then produce sufficient evidence to support a verdict in his favor, or the court will instruct the jury that breach of duty is established. If the defendant produces qualifying evidence, the burden of

persuasion remains on the plaintiff, and the jury may find for the defendant if the plaintiff has not established breach of duty by a preponderance of the evidence.

    (3)   Some jurisdictions—another small minority—give a qualifying showing of *res ipsa loquitur* the effect of shifting the burden of persuasion to the defendant. If the defendant does not then persuade the jury, by a preponderance of the evidence, that he did meet the applicable standard of care, breach of duty is established.

  b.   A plaintiff must establish that three requisites are present in order to invoke the doctrine of *res ipsa loquitur*:

    (1)   the event that caused the plaintiff's injury was one which would not ordinarily occur in the absence of negligence;

       (a)   The trier of fact may determine whether an event is one that would not ordinarily occur in the absence of negligence with reference to common experience, or if that is not sufficient, by resort to evidence provided by the plaintiff. Expert testimony may be required to establish that negligence is the likely cause of the injury-causing event. The plaintiff is not required to show that negligence is the only possible cause of the injury-causing event; it is enough if the trier of fact finds that negligence was more likely than not the cause.

    (2)   it is more likely than not that it was the defendant's negligence that was responsible for the injury-causing event; and

       (a)   Traditionally, a plaintiff was required to show that the defendant was in exclusive control of the instrumentality that inflicted injury upon the plaintiff. Today, this requirement has become less rigid in many states. In some states, for instance, it is sufficient if a plaintiff shows that it is more likely than not that the defendant is responsible for the negligent event. Control, either exclusive or not, is merely a circumstance relevant to determination of the defendant's responsibility.

    (3)   the plaintiff was not responsible for the event that caused injury.

       (a)   A plaintiff must demonstrate that he did not set in motion the forces that resulted in his injury. However, it is immaterial that the plaintiff placed himself in a situation of peril or that he did not take precautions to avoid injury. In light of the current move to comparative fault, this element has become less important.

D. Cause-in-Fact (Actual Cause)

  1.   The element of cause-in-fact ties the defendant's breach of duty to the plaintiff's injury. Without proof of this element by a preponderance of the evidence, the plaintiff loses his negligence claim.

     EXAMPLE: Dorkas fails to use his headlights after dusk, as required by statute, and hits Petunia when she comes running out between two parked cars. Even though Dorkas has breached the duty he owes to Petunia, she would lose her negligence claim if the jury determines that he still would have hit Petunia even if his lights had been on.

2. **"But-For" Test**

   a. A defendant's conduct was the cause-in-fact of an event if that event would not have occurred but for the existence of the conduct.

   EXAMPLE: City negligently mixes its drinking-water line with its sewage-water line. Pyn, who drinks City-provided water, contracts typhoid. Pyn may recover if he can show that it is more likely than not that "but for" the negligent mixing of the water lines, he would not have contracted typhoid.

3. **"Substantial Factor" Test**

   a. A defendant's conduct is also the cause-in-fact of a plaintiff's injury if that conduct was a substantial factor in bringing about the injury. This accounts for the situation where the conduct of two or more defendants results in injury to the plaintiff, and each individual defendant's conduct, taken alone, would have been sufficient to directly cause the injury. A mechanical application of the "but-for" test would permit each defendant to claim that the plaintiff's injury would have occurred whether he acted or not and thus "but for" causation did not exist.

   EXAMPLE: Kramer negligently sets a fire that would have burned down Jerry's house on its own. Separately, Elaine negligently set a fire that also would have destroyed Jerry's house. The fires combine and burn down Jerry's house. Each fire is a substantial factor of the harm and both Kramer and Elaine are the cause-in-fact of the harm. Note that the "but-for" test doesn't work where there are multiple causes, either of which would have brought about the harm.

   b. Where there are multiple negligent parties, each of whom contributes to the plaintiff's indivisible harm, they are jointly and severally liable. That means that the plaintiff may recover fully against any of the defendants, and those defendants can sue each other for contribution.

   EXAMPLE: If Jerry's torched house is worth $1 million, he could sue just Elaine to recover that amount. Elaine could then sue Kramer, a joint tortfeasor, for contribution (partial repayment of that judgment). Note that Jerry cannot recover more than the total amount of his damages—$1 million.

4. **Alternative Liability Theory**

   a. Where a plaintiff's injury arises from the negligent conduct of two or more independently acting defendants, only one of whom can actually be responsible, and the plaintiff is unable to establish which defendant is in fact responsible, each and every defendant's conduct is regarded as a cause-in-fact of the injury unless a defendant can prove that he did not cause the plaintiff's injury. In effect, the burden of proof as to cause-in-fact is shifted from the plaintiff to the defendant [Summers v. Tice, 199 P.2d 1 (Cal. 1948)].

EXAMPLE: Wyn negligently shoots in the direction of a rustling bush at the same moment that Fahn does. One bullet hits Pantaloon, who cannot identify which gun the bullet came from. Because both Wyn and Fahn breached a duty owed to Pantaloon, and because both are before the court, the court will shift the burden of proof on the element of cause-in-fact. If Wyn and Fahn cannot prove they were not the responsible party, they will be jointly and severally liable.

5. Where a plaintiff demonstrates that the injury resulted from the conduct of several defendants, each acting independently, but cannot identify which particular defendant's conduct actually injured him, each defendant's conduct may be regarded as a cause-in-fact of the plaintiff's injury. Liability is apportioned among the defendants based upon the economic benefit, as measured by percentage or market share, each defendant derived from the risk-producing conduct. Market share liability applies only to generic products such as DES.

6. As a general matter, like the other *prima facie* elements of negligence, the plaintiff must prove cause-in-fact by a preponderance of the evidence (i.e., by more than 50%). This has led to the result that where a doctor commits malpractice on a patient who, due to illness, had a likelihood of death, the doctor escapes liability for his malpractice. A growing number of jurisdictions allow the plaintiff to proceed by recharacterizing the injury as "loss of chance."

EXAMPLE: Dr. Dyl commits malpractice and fails to diagnose cancer in his patient, Prax. Had Dr. Dyl done so, Prax would have had a 40% chance of survival. By the time the cancer is found, the cancer is incurable. Under the traditional cause-in-fact rule, Prax loses his malpractice case because he cannot show that it is more likely than not that, but for Dr. Dyl's malpractice, he would have survived. however, some jurisdictions would allow the case to proceed, finding that it is more likely than not that, but for Dr. Dyl's malpractice, Prax would not have lost his 40% chance of survival.

a. Statutes in many jurisdictions reduce the duty of care owed by the driver of an automobile to a **guest** (a non-paying passenger) in that auto. Such statutes frequently provide that the driver of an auto is not liable for injuries suffered by the guest unless the driver's wrongful conduct amounted to gross negligence or recklessness.

b. **Slip-and-Fall Cases**

(1) In cases where a person is injured because of a fall on the defendant's premises, the plaintiff must show evidence from which a jury may reasonably infer unreasonable conduct on the part of the defendant. Typically, the plaintiff must put on evidence about the condition of the item on which he fell so that a jury may infer that the object was there long enough that the defendant was unreasonable in not discovering and remedying the dangerous condition.

EXAMPLE: Pashanda is injured when she slips on a grape on the floor in the produce section of Dexto's market. If this is all the evidence she presents, Pashanda's negligence claim will be thrown out. If she can show, however, that the grape on which she slipped was blackened and gritty, she will proceed to a jury because there is circumstantial evidence that would permit the jury to find that the grape had been on the floor long enough that Dexto's should have discovered it.

E. **Proximate (Legal) Cause**

1. In addition to being a cause-in-fact of a plaintiff's harm, the defendant's conduct must also be a proximate, or legal, cause of the injury.

    a. A defendant owes a duty of reasonable care only to **foreseeable plaintiffs** (i.e., those individuals who are within the risk of harm created by the defendant's unreasonable conduct). The majority view holds that a defendant only owes a duty of care to foreseeable plaintiffs who are within the **zone of danger** (i.e., under the circumstances, a reasonable defendant would have foreseen a risk of harm to the plaintiff). The broader minority view allows recovery to any person thereby harmed due to a breach of the defendant's duty of care.

2. Not all injuries "actually" caused by the defendant will be deemed to have been proximately caused by his acts. As such, the doctrine of proximate or legal cause deals with a limitation of liability with respect to persons and consequences that bear some reasonable relationship to a defendant's tortious conduct.

    a. **Unforeseeable Extent of Harm**

        (1) If the defendant's conduct is a substantial factor in bringing about the harm to another, the mere fact that the defendant neither foresaw nor should have foreseen the extent of the harm does not prevent him from being liable.

        (2) Under the so-called **thin-skulled** or **eggshell plaintiff rule**, a defendant is liable for the full consequences of a plaintiff's injury, even though, due to the plaintiff's peculiar susceptibility to harm (of which the defendant was unaware), those consequences were more severe than they would have been in a normal person.

        EXAMPLE: Peyton is a hemophiliac. Derek leaves a bunch of paper and boxes lying around in the hall just outside his cubicle. When Peyton walks by, he falls and hits his head on the side of Derek's desk. He begins to bleed heavily. Eventually, he loses so much blood that he must be hospitalized. Derek will be liable to Peyton for the full extent of Peyton's injuries, even if he did not know about Peyton's inability to clot blood.

    b. **Unforeseeable Type or Manner of Harm**

        (1) **Superseding Cause**

            (a) A **superseding cause** is an unforeseeable, intervening cause that breaks the chain of causation between the initial wrongful act and the ultimate injury, and thus relieves the original tortfeasor of any further liability.

(b) Commonly occurring examples of superseding causes:

1) naturally occurring phenomena;

2) criminal acts of third persons;

3) intentional torts of third persons; or

4) extraordinary forms of negligent conduct.

(c) An **intervening force** is one that actively operates in producing harm to another after the actor has already committed his negligent act or omission.

1) As a general rule, a defendant will be held liable for harm caused by foreseeable intervening forces.

2) Because rescuers are foreseeable, the original tortfeasors will be held liable for the ordinary negligence of the rescuer.

   EXAMPLE: Don is throwing balls around at a playground. Don hits Poppy in the head, causing her to lose consciousness. Casey arrives and tries to resuscitate Poppy, breaking Poppy's ribs while doing compressions. Because Casey was merely negligent, Don will be liable for both Poppy's head injury and broken ribs.

3) The original tortfeasor is usually held liable for the ordinary negligence of the plaintiff's treating physician or nurse.

   EXAMPLE: When Poppy is hit in the head, Casey does not come to her aid. Instead, an ambulance takes her to the hospital. The triage nurse does not examine Poppy carefully and concludes that she does not need medical attention. The nurse keeps Poppy lying on a gurney in the hallway for eight hours. During that time, Poppy has a cerebral hemorrhage and sustains irreversible brain damage. Don will be liable for Poppy's brain hemorrhage and the strike on the head.

4) The original tortfeasor is usually held liable for diseases contracted or subsequent injuries sustained because of the impairment of the plaintiff's health resulting from the original injury caused by the defendant's tortious conduct.

   EXAMPLE: When Don hits Poppy in the head, her sinuses are affected. As a result, Poppy becomes much more susceptible to sinus infections. She must go to the doctor frequently and take expensive medications. Don will be liable for both the head injury and the sinus infections.

5) A defendant will be held liable for negligent efforts on the part of persons to protect life or property interests endangered by his negligence.

6) In situations where the plaintiff suffers a subsequent injury after the original injury, and the original injury was

a substantial factor in causing the second accident, the original tortfeasor is held liable for damages.

EXAMPLE: Doug negligently fractures Prudence's left leg. while walking on crutches, Prudence trips and falls, breaking her right leg. Doug will be liable for both leg injuries.

    (d) Considerations of importance in determining whether an intervening force is a superseding cause of harm to another include:

        1) the fact that its intervention brings about a harm different in kind from that which would otherwise have resulted from the defendant's negligence;

        2) the fact that its operation or the consequences thereof appear to be extraordinary and unforeseeable after the event; and

        3) the fact that the intervening force is operating independently of any situation created by the defendant's negligence.

   3. Another highly tested area of proximate causation deals with rescuers. A negligent defendant owes an independent duty of care to a rescuer. Even where the rescue efforts are done negligently (but provided they are not wanton), the negligent defendant will be liable for both personal injury and property damage, whether the rescuer succeeds in injuring himself, the person rescued, or a stranger.

	FORESEEABLE	UNFORESEEABLE (I.E., SUPERSEDING)
Effect	Chain of proximate causation unbroken—original defendant remains liable.	Chain of proximate causation broken—original defendant's liability cut off for consequences of antecedent conduct.
Typical Examples	• Subsequent medical malpractice, including aggravation of plaintiff's condition. • Subsequent disease or accident, including all illnesses and injuries resulting from plaintiff's weakened condition, but not deadly, rare diseases. • Negligent rescue efforts.	• Criminal acts and intentional torts of third parties, but only where they are unforeseeable under the facts or circumstances. • Highly extraordinary harm arising from defendant's conduct, as viewed by the court, including grossly negligent conduct of third parties. • Unforeseeable, naturally occurring phenomena.

F. Damages

   1. A plaintiff must affirmatively prove **actual damages**. Nominal damages are not available, and punitive damages generally are not allowed.

   2. Personal injury and property damages are recoverable. Included are general and special damages, past and future pain and suffering, medical expenses, lost wages, and loss of consortium, but not attorney's fees. The plaintiff's duty to mitigate damages applies.

3. Payments made to or benefits conferred on the injured party-plaintiff from other (i.e., collateral) sources are not credited against the tortfeasor's liability, even where they cover all or a part of the harm for which the tort-feasor is liable. This is known as the **collateral source rule**.

    a. The rule that collateral benefits are not subtracted from the plaintiff's recovery applies to the following types of benefits:

        (1) insurance policies, whether maintained by the plaintiff or a third party;

        (2) employment benefits;

        (3) gratuities, including cash gratuities and the rendering of services; and

        (4) social legislative benefits.

        EXAMPLE: Della negligently injures Pasha when she sets off firecrackers incorrectly. Pasha has second-degree burns over most of her body. If Pasha collects disability or health insurance benefits, these will not be subtracted from the amount of damages that Della owes Pasha.

        EXCEPTION: Payments made by a tortfeasor or by a person acting for him (e.g., the defendant's insurance company) to the injured plaintiff are credited against the defendant's tort liability.

4. **Punitive Damages**

    a. **Punitive damages** are an amount over and above the compensation needed to make the plaintiff whole. They are intended to punish the defendant for egregious conduct and to act as a deterrent against future conduct by the defendant or others, and are thus also called "exemplary" damages.

    b. Punitive damages are available in tort cases when there has been willful, wanton, or malicious conduct. They are generally not available in negligence actions or in contract actions.

    c. A plaintiff is never entitled to an award of punitive damages, but a jury may award them at its discretion. Jury rewards may be reversed or overturned if excessive. Due process requires that punitive damage awards not be grossly excessive on three measures [State Farm Mut. Auto. Ins. Co. v. Campbell, 538 U.S. 408 (2003); BMW of No. America v. Gore, 517 U.S. 559 (1996)]:

        (1) the degree of reprehensibility of the defendant's conduct, considering such factors as whether:

           (a) the defendant acted intentionally, maliciously, or with reckless disregard for harm;

           (b) such conduct was repeated or isolated; and

           (c) the harm caused to the plaintiff was economic or noneconomic (e.g., lost profits or personal injury);

        (2) the ratio between the plaintiff's compensatory damages and the amount of the punitive damages (presumptively, punitive damages should not exceed 10 times the compensatory damage award); and

(3)   the difference between the punitive damage award and the civil or criminal sanctions that could be imposed for comparable misconduct.

d.   There may also be specific limitations on entitlement to punitive damages under state law.

G. Defenses to Negligence

1. Contributory Negligence

a.   Tort law requires a plaintiff to exercise due care to protect himself from injury by the defendant. Thus, the plaintiff's own negligence—called **contributory negligence** at common law—may bar the plaintiff's recovery. The analysis is similar to that for the defendant's negligence—whether the plaintiff acted as a reasonable person would under the same circumstances. Contributory negligence is conduct on the part of the plaintiff that falls below the standard to which he should conform for his own protection, and which is a legally contributing cause cooperating with the defendant's negligence in bringing about the plaintiff's harm.

b.   To show contributory negligence, the defendant must prove by a preponderance of the evidence that the plaintiff fell below the relevant standard of care and that this failure was the cause-in-fact and proximate cause of the plaintiff's damages.

    (1)   Traditionally, if a plaintiff is found to have engaged in contributory negligence, he is barred from recovery for a defendant's otherwise negligent conduct, even if the plaintiff is only 1% at fault.

        EXAMPLE: Delbert, who is speeding, hits Pol's car one night. Pol will be barred from recovery because he is contributorily negligent *per se* if he was hit because, in violation of the statute, Pol did not have his headlights on.

    (2)   Contributory negligence does not bar recovery if the plaintiff's theory is intentional tort, recklessness, or strict liability.

c.   Risks or dangerous acts undertaken by a plaintiff that might otherwise be regarded as contributory negligence are often viewed as reasonable in an emergency (i.e., the plaintiff is threatened with immediate danger of bodily harm or death because of the defendant's negligence) or if the plaintiff is attempting to rescue someone.

d.   The analysis of whether a child plaintiff is contributorily negligent is similar to the negligence analysis for children generally.

    (1)   A majority of jurisdictions apply the "reasonable child" standard—whether a child of the same age, education, intelligence, and experience, in the same circumstances, would have acted as the plaintiff did.

    (2)   A minority of states utilize the traditional age categories:

        (a)   below age six, contributory negligence is precluded as a matter of law;

        (b)   ages seven to 13, the child-plaintiff is rebuttably presumed incapable of contributory negligence; and

(c) 14 and older, the child-plaintiff is rebuttably presumed capable of contributory negligence.

e. The concept of negligence *per se* is applicable to the plaintiff in a contributory negligence situation.

(1) Contributory negligence is not available, even though the plaintiff's conduct violates a statute, where the defendant's negligent act violates the same statute, the plaintiff is a member of the class of persons the statute was intended to protect, and the harm suffered by the plaintiff is the type the statute was intended to avoid.

EXAMPLE: 15-year-old Pasha, who was hired by DunCo in violation of a statute prohibiting the hiring of children, will not be found to be contributorily negligent.

f. In order to invoke contributory negligence, a defendant must prove that the plaintiff's conduct is the actual and proximate cause of the injuries suffered by the plaintiff.

g. In two limited situations, the contributory negligence of a third person may be imputed to the plaintiff so as to bar recovery against the defendant:

(1) the plaintiff and the contributorily negligent third person are sufficiently related such that the plaintiff would be vicariously liable for the third person's negligence (e.g., partners and joint enterprisers, employers and employees); and

(2) the plaintiff's claim against the defendant is completely derivative of the third person who was contributorily negligent (e.g., wrongful death, loss of consortium).

(a) A minority of states do not impute one spouse's contributory negligence to another in an action against a defendant for loss of consortium.

h. The **last clear chance doctrine** provides a basis for recovery even where a plaintiff is otherwise contributorily negligent. The focus is on the time period after the plaintiff has engaged in contributory negligence. If injury to the plaintiff could still have been avoided through a subsequent exercise of due care by the defendant, then the defendant is said to have had the last clear chance to avoid harm, and the plaintiff's contributory fault will not bar recovery.

(1) If the defendant is aware that his breach of duty has placed the plaintiff in danger, the last clear chance doctrine is always available to the plaintiff. The majority of jurisdictions deny a plaintiff the benefit of the last clear chance doctrine if the defendant is not aware that the plaintiff is in danger, and the plaintiff is in "helpless peril" rather than "inattentive peril."

(a) A plaintiff is in **helpless peril** when his negligence has placed him in a position of danger from which he cannot extricate himself. A plaintiff is in **inattentive peril** when his contributory negligence has placed him in a position of danger from which he could escape if observant enough to recognize his peril.

(b) In a majority of jurisdictions, if a defendant is under a duty to discover danger to the plaintiff (e.g., an owner/occupier of land has duty to exercise due care in discover dangerous conditions and protect invitees from them), no distinction is made between helpless and inattentive danger.

2. **Comparative Negligence**

   a. Under a modern comparative negligence regime, where a plaintiff's negligence has contributed to his own injuries, the total damages caused by the defendant may be apportioned based upon a determination of the relative fault of each party. Virtually every state has adopted a comparative negligence system, either by statute or judicial decision. The analysis of comparative fault is identical to the analysis of contributory negligence, though the effect is different.

      (1) Some states have adopted a **pure comparative negligence** scheme. In such states, apportionment of damages tracks apportionment of fault perfectly—if a defendant is 25% responsible and a plaintiff is 75% responsible, plaintiff recovers from the defendant 25% of the total damages he suffered.

      (2) Other states have adopted a **partial comparative negligence** system. Here, damages are apportioned only if the defendant's responsibility exceeds the plaintiff's responsibility. The plaintiff is denied any recovery if he is responsible for 50% or more of his own damages.

      (3) If there are two or more defendants who are not jointly liable, two different systems of comparative negligence have been developed—the "aggregate" system and the "individual equality" system.

         (a) In an **aggregate system**, the plaintiff does not recover anything if his responsibility exceeds the total percentage responsibility of all the defendants combined. Thus, if two defendants each contributed 24% of a plaintiff's damages, totaling 48%, and the plaintiff contributed 52%, he would not recover.

         (b) Under an **individual equality system**, a plaintiff does not recover anything if his responsibility exceeds that of any single defendant. Thus, if two defendants each contributed 33% of a plaintiff's damages, and the plaintiff contributed 34%, the plaintiff would be barred from recovery.

EXAM TIP▶ On the MBE, assume that a pure comparative negligence system applies unless the question states otherwise.

3. **Assumption of Risk**

   a. A plaintiff "assumes the risk" of injury from a defendant's negligence if the plaintiff expressly or impliedly consents to undergo the risk created by the defendant's conduct.

      (1) A plaintiff is barred from negligence recovery when he has, by written or oral words, expressly relieved the defendant of his

obligation to act non-negligently toward the plaintiff. As long as the waiver is not void as against public policy and the language is clear, the waiver will be enforced by most courts.

(2) A plaintiff may also impliedly assume the risk of a defendant's conduct.

(a) A plaintiff is barred from recovery, or recovery will be, reduced under the assumption of the risk doctrine if the defendant establishes that:

1) the plaintiff had knowledge of and appreciated the nature of the danger involved;

a) This is a subjective standard. Youth, lack of information, or lack of experience may justify a finding that a plaintiff actually failed to comprehend the risk involved. If so, there can be no assumption of the risk, even if a "reasonable plaintiff" would have recognized the danger under similar circumstances.

2) the plaintiff appreciated the specific danger that injured him; and

EXAMPLE: A plaintiff who knowingly agrees to ride in a car where the driver is speeding does not assume the risk that the driver might also be intoxicated.

a) Some risks are regarded as so obvious that any competent adult is expected to be aware of them.

EXAMPLE: The danger of falling through an unguarded opening, slipping on ice, or being struck by a baseball at a baseball game.

3) the plaintiff voluntarily chose to subject himself to that danger.

a) Voluntariness can be established by express consent (e.g., an exculpatory clause in a contract providing that one party will hold the other party harmless for injuries caused by the first party), or consent may be implied from the fact that the plaintiff continued in the face of a known danger. With regard to implied assumption of the risk, courts closely examine whether behavior is voluntary when there is a lack of alternatives.

(b) In some circumstances, a court will determine that a defendant has no obligation to be non-negligent toward the plaintiff because of the nature of the activity that they are engaged in. The most common context is sports.

(c) Assumption of the risk may not be asserted where a plaintiff is a member of a class intended to be protected by a statute, and the defendant's conduct both violates the statute and threatens the risk the statute was designed to prevent. In some states, any risk-creating violation by a defendant of a public safety statute has the above effect.

EXAMPLE: Petunia and Drucilla are playing basketball. Petunia's eye is severely injured when Drucilla pokes Petunia in the face trying to get a rebound. Even if Drucilla was negligent, many courts would conclude that the harm that befell Petunia was an inherent risk of the game, and thus Drucilla had no duty to avoid such harm. However, if a court found Drucilla's conduct to be more than negligent, Petunia would be permitted to proceed with her tort claim.

III. STRICT LIABILITY

A. In General

1. In strict liability, a defendant is liable for injuring a plaintiff whether or not the defendant exercised due care. As to certain activities, the policy of the law is to impose liability regardless of how carefully a defendant conducted himself.

B. Categories

1. A defendant may be held strictly liable as to two categories of activities:

   a. **possession of animals**; and

      (1) The analysis of strict liability in connection with the possession of animals varies according to the nature of the plaintiff's injury and whether the animal is wild or domestic.

      (2) A defendant can be held strictly liable for personal injuries inflicted by his animal if it has "known dangerous propensities."

         (a) This is, in part, a "scienter-like" element, in that the defendant is subject to strict liability only if he knew or had reason to know of the dangerous quality of the animal.

            1) Wild animals generally have "known dangerous propensities" for this purpose. A **wild animal** is one not customarily devoted to the service of humankind at the time and in the place where it is kept.

            2) Domestic animals have "known dangerous propensities" only if a reasonable owner would realize that the animal presented a danger of death or injury. The classic example of a domestic animal with known dangerous propensities is a dog that has previously bitten a human being (the "one bite" rule—after one bite, the owner is presumed to know that the dog is dangerous).

               a) Strict liability does not apply to possession of domestic animals as to which dangerous propensities are normal, such as bulls, stallions, mules, rams, and bees.

               EXAMPLE: Parker is seriously injured when bitten by Damien's pet tiger. Damien is strictly liable for this injury even if Damien's tiger has been as gentle as a kitten until that moment. If Parker had been bitten by Damien's cat, Damien is only strictly liable once Damien should have known of his cat's dangerous propensity.

         (b) If the plaintiff is an unknown trespasser, most jurisdictions do not impose any liability for injuries inflicted by a defendant's animals while the plaintiff is on the defendant's land, even as to animals with known dangerous propensities. If the plaintiff is any other type of trespasser (known, frequent, or child), a defendant is liable only for negligence. The plaintiff must establish that the defendant failed to exercise due care to warn of or protect the trespasser from his animal.

    (3)   A defendant is held strictly liable for any trespass to the land or chattels of a plaintiff by wild animals if of a kind likely to escape, trespass, and do damage, or by "livestock" possessed by the defendant. Domestic pets (e.g., dogs and cats) are not considered livestock.

    b. **abnormally dangerous activities**.

        (1)   A judge determines whether an activity is abnormally dangerous by considering if:

            (a)   the activity creates a risk of serious injury as to the plaintiff, his land, or his chattels;

            (b)   this risk cannot be eliminated by the exercise of due care; and

            (c)   the activity is not usually conducted in that area. Such things as dynamiting, crop-dusting, and exterminating have been found to be abnormally dangerous.

        (2)   Principles of causation generally applicable to negligence are also applied in a strict liability analysis.

        (3)   In order for strict liability to apply, the harm to the plaintiff must have resulted from the type of danger that justified classifying the animal or activity as dangerous.

        (4)   An unforeseeable, intervening force could relieve a strictly liable defendant of liability as well.

C. Defenses

    1. **Contributory Negligence**

        a.   Where strict liability is applicable, a defendant generally may not raise contributory negligence as a defense.

            EXCEPTION: Where a plaintiff knew of the danger that justified imposition of strict liability, and his contributory negligence caused exactly that danger to be manifested, such contributory negligence will bar the plaintiff's recovery, assuming the jurisdiction applies the traditional contributory negligence doctrine.

            EXAMPLE: If Pat O'Pheline stands next to a circus tiger's cage knowing that the tiger is dangerous and can reach between the bars of the cage, and despite seeing and understanding warning signs and ropes posted to keep circus patrons at a safe distance, he may be barred from recovery by the doctrine of contributory negligence if the tiger claws him.

NOTE ▶ Contributory negligence is not a complete defense to strict liability; it can only reduce recovery.

    2. **Comparative Negligence**

        a.   Some states that have adopted comparative fault systems reduce the recovery of plaintiffs whose negligence contributes to their own injuries involving strict liability situations.

3. **Assumption of Risk**

   a. A plaintiff may be found to have assumed the risk of injury and be completely barred from recovery in a strict liability situation if the plaintiff knows of and appreciates the danger justifying imposition of strict liability and voluntarily exposes himself to such danger.

IV. PRODUCTS LIABILITY

A. Strict Products Liability in Tort

1. Strict products liability is invoked when a defective product, for which an appropriate defendant is responsible, injures an appropriate plaintiff. To analyze an action for strict products liability, it is necessary to consider certain specific factors.

2. **Proper Plaintiff**

   a. In general, if strict liability is otherwise applicable, any plaintiff injured while using a defective product may recover damages from an appropriate defendant. This includes purchasers and consumers, as well as families, friends, guests, and employees.

   b. There is a modern trend to permit one not using a defective product to invoke strict liability against an appropriate defendant if it was reasonably foreseeable that such a plaintiff might be injured by the defective product. Examples include bystanders (e.g., the plaintiff was a pedestrian injured when an automobile manufactured by the defendant with defective steering went out of control and struck him) and rescuers (e.g., the plaintiff attempted to rescue a third person who was endangered by a defective product manufactured by the defendant).

3. **Proper Defendant**

   a. Commercial suppliers at all levels of the distribution chain (i.e., the manufacturer, distributor, or retailer) as well as commercial lessors, new home developers, and sellers of used goods are all potential defendants. Occasional sellers and those supplying services (i.e., an optometrist) cannot be strictly liable, but may be sued for negligence.

      (1) A person who assembles component parts into a finished product is strictly liable for defects in the components used. The manufacturer of the component part is also strictly liable for defects in the component. If the finished product is defective not because of a defect in a component part but because the assembler put the component to a use for which it was not suited, the component manufacturer is generally not liable unless the component manufacturer knew or should have known that his component was being misused. A person who rebuilds or reconditions used goods is often held to be the equivalent of a manufacturer, and may be subject to strict liability for injuries caused by defects in the rebuilt or reconditioned goods.

      EXAMPLE: Dunlop Tire Co. manufactured a tire that proves to be defective. Ford Motor Company purchases Dunlop tires to put onto its new car model, the Stallion. Ford sells a Stallion to Jen Smyth Ford, a car retailer. While driving a Stallion purchased by Paxtona at Jen Smyth Ford, Penelope is physically injured because of the defect in the tire. Dunlop, Ford, and Jen Smyth are all proper defendants for a strict products liability claim because they are all in the business of dealing with this product and part of the marketing chain. Note that these defendants are liable even though there is likely no fault on their part.

b. Retailers and commercial lessors are subject to strict liability for defects in new goods that they sell or lease. Commercial lessors are subject to strict liability for defective used goods leased, but there is a split in authority as to whether a retailer of used goods is strictly liable for defects in those goods.

c. Most jurisdictions hold sellers of mass-marketed new residences strictly liable for defects in those homes. There is a split in authority as to whether other new home sellers, such as custom builders who construct a few houses at a time or building contractors who construct residences under specific contracts, may be held strictly liable for defects in those constructions. No court has imposed strict liability on a defendant who sold a home he did not construct.

d. Occasional or one-time sellers are not proper defendants for purposes of strict products liability because they are not in the position to further the goals of the tort—safer products and cost-spreading.

    EXAMPLE: Pumpkin is injured as a result of a defect in a new widget she bought at Della's garage sale. Della is not a proper defendant for strict products liability. To recover, Pumpkin will have to prove negligence or a breach of warranty.

e. A few states have imposed strict liability on a franchisor, at least where it was found that the franchisor exercised substantial control over the operations of the franchisee.

4. **Proper Context for Strict Products Liability**

    a. Generally, providers of services are not held strictly liable for injuries received by their customers. If defective goods are supplied along with services, strict liability is still not applicable so long as the goods supplied were merely "incidental" to rendition of the services. In this regard, restaurants are frequently regarded as sellers of goods (food) subject to strict liability. Doctors, dentists, and blood banks are usually regarded as primarily providing services, so defective products (medicines, blood, etc.) provided are incidental and not subject to strict liability.

5. **Defect**

    a. Almost all jurisdictions impose strict liability where a product is "in a defective condition unreasonably dangerous."

    b. Formulations of liability occur under three categories of defects.

        (1) **Manufacturing Defects**

             (a) A product manufactured in a form other than the manufacturer intended contains a **manufacturing defect**. All jurisdictions impose strict liability on the manufacturer and everyone else in the chain of distribution for personal injury or property damage to a plaintiff caused by a manufacturing defect.

EXAMPLE: Pachina cuts her lip on a piece of metal in the tuna fish she was eating. The tuna fish was manufactured by Tuna-of-the-Ocean and purchased from Delmon Grocery. Because Tuna-of-the-Ocean did not intend for there to be a piece of metal in the tuna fish, this is a manufacturing defect. They, along with Delmon as part of the marketing chain, will be strictly liable to Pachina for her personal injury.

(2) **Design Defects**

(a) A product manufactured as the manufacturer intended, but that still presents a danger of personal injury or property damage to a plaintiff, suffers from a **design defect**. The analysis of whether such a defect is sufficient to invoke strict liability is complex.

1) Under the **consumer expectation test** standard, a product is in an unreasonably dangerous defective condition when it is more dangerous than would be contemplated by the ordinary consumer who purchases it, with the ordinary knowledge common to the community as to its characteristics. Thus, a product is dangerously defective if a reasonably foreseeable purchaser would not have expected it to present the danger that resulted in his injury.

a) One interpretation of the consumer expectations test would hold that obvious danger could not be a dangerous defect because it would not be unexpected to a reasonable consumer.

b) Many jurisdictions that apply the consumer expectation test expand "consumer" to include a nonpurchasing user. A product is thus considered defective and unreasonably dangerous if more dangerous than a reasonable user would have expected.

2) Under the **danger-utility test** approach, a product is defective if a jury determines that the danger it threatens (the cost in human injury and property damage) outweighs its utility to society. The danger-utility test balances the likelihood, nature, and potential severity of injuries caused by a product against the usefulness of the product, considering the availability and cost of safer alternative designs. A product's design is usually defective under this test if an alternative design could have reduced the danger at about the same cost.

a) Almost all jurisdictions that utilize the danger-utility test apply it so that the inquiry as to the availability of alternative designs focuses on the time the product was put on the market rather than considering alternatives that were discovered in the period up until trial.

3) Under the **hindsight-negligence test**, a product is defective if a reasonable person, knowing of the danger it presented, would not have placed it in the stream of commerce. This test imposes constructive prior knowledge of the defect on the defendant, in effect presuming that the defendant knew of the risk, whether or not he actually did know or reasonably could have known of it.

EXAMPLE: Dun Motors manufactures a new lightweight, fuel-efficient car, the Stallion, which because of the placement of the gas tank proves to be vulnerable to explosion upon a low-speed rear-end collision. Pafto is injured when the Stallion he is driving is rear-ended and explodes due to the placement of the gas tank. This is a design defect because the product is in the condition intended by the manufacturer. It may be defective if it is more dangerous than an ordinary consumer would expect when using the car in its intended or foreseeable manner. However, a consumer may have no particular expectations about the placement of the gas tank, so many jurisdictions would permit Pafto to show that the car was defective because the risk of the car with the gas tank placed where it was outweighs the benefit of such a design.

(3) **Absence of Warnings**

(a) A product may be considered dangerously defective when it is accompanied by an **inadequate warning**—for example, its message to the user (e.g., a child who cannot read) fails to sufficiently describe the danger, fails to mention all dangers, or is inconsistent with the instructions for use of the product.

(b) A defendant's failure to warn a plaintiff that a product presents a threat of personal injury or property damage may be considered a defect. Where a plaintiff establishes that the manufacturer of a product knew or reasonably should have known of a danger presented by the product and failed to take the precautions a reasonable person would have taken to warn adequately of that danger, the absence of such warning is sufficient to impose strict liability.

1) Certain products are regarded as so obviously dangerous that a warning is considered unnecessary, (e.g., a sharp knife).

2) Whether absence of a warning of allergic or other adverse reactions is a dangerous defect depends upon the severity of the potential reaction and the number of people expected to be affected. A small number of reactions justifies a warning if the adverse reaction threatens death or serious illness. A mild reaction

might require a warning if a substantial number of people likely will experience it.

6. **Cause-in-Fact**

   a. That the injury is attributable to the defendant is usually proven by showing that the defect that injured plaintiff was in existence at the time it left defendant's control. It may be necessary in this regard to establish that intermediate handlers (distributors and suppliers) did not mistreat or alter the product.

   b. Plaintiff shows that the injury was caused by the defect by proving that the defect was a substantial factor in bringing about his injury.

   c. Warning defect claims often pose difficult issues of causation because the plaintiff must prove that she would not have been injured by the product had there been a warning on the product or had the warning been adequate. Some jurisdictions employ a "heeding presumption," which puts the burden of proof on the defendant to prove that a warning or adequate warning would not have made a difference.

7. **Proximate Cause**

   a. Principles of legal or proximate cause relevant to negligence are applied in like fashion to strict products liability, except for where the intervening conduct of third persons occurs.

   b. The negligent handling of a product by a third party after it leaves the defendant's control is regarded as foreseeable and is not a superseding intervening force. This includes negligent handling not directly affecting the defectiveness of product, e.g., where a third party negligently collides with plaintiff's car, which is dangerously defective in a manner attributable to defendant.

   c. A defendant will be relieved of strict products liability where an intervening force is the sole proximate cause of the harm. In other words, the intervening force will sever the defendant's liability where it is such that the injury would not have been suffered but for that superseding or intervening force, independently of the act or omission which constituted the defendant's negligence.

   d. A third party's criminal or intentionally tortious conduct is regarded as an unforeseeable intervening force that supersedes a defendant's wrongdoing, unless the defect somehow increased the risk that a third party would engage in such conduct.

8. **Damages**

   a. General principles of tort damages apply to strict liability, except for the following:

      (1) In a majority of jurisdictions, pure economic losses, such as loss of profits due to the defective product not performing as expected, additional expenses incurred in obtaining replacement equipment or materials, etc., may not be recovered by a plaintiff in strict liability. However, most jurisdictions permit recovery of

economic losses as derivative elements of otherwise appropriate personal injury or property damage claims.

(2) Some jurisdictions look to the nature of the harm threatened by the defect to determine the availability of damages in strict liability, rather than distinguishing between property damage and economic losses. Under this approach, any loss suffered is recoverable if caused by a defect that threatened personal injury, even if the actual loss did not include personal injury. If the defect was not such that it would threaten personal injury, no property damage or economic losses are recoverable in strict liability.

9. **Defenses**

a. **Misuse**

(1) If a plaintiff uses a product in a manner that is neither intended nor foreseeable, he has misused the product and it cannot be defective.

EXAMPLE: Parker stands on a chair manufactured by DrekCo to reach a pot in his kitchen. The chair collapses under him. While sitting is the intended use of a chair, it is foreseeable that a person would stand on a chair, and thus, there is no misuse. If Parker was using the chair as part of an act in which he has an elephant balance on the chair, this would be a misuse because it would be an unforeseeable use of the chair.

b. **Contributory Negligence**

(1) As initially conceived, a plaintiff's unreasonable conduct was not a defense to a strict products liability action unless the plaintiff knew of the defect, comprehended the risks posed by the defect, and voluntarily elected to expose himself to those risks. That is, only an assumption of the risk was a defense to strict products liability.

EXAMPLE: Because of a defect, Parker's television set, manufactured by DuMont, starts to spark. A reasonable person would have noticed this, but Parker, because he is totally engrossed in his favorite sitcom, does not. DuMont has no defense.

(2) A plaintiff's continued use of a product which the plaintiff knows to be defective is not voluntary, and thus not an assumption of the risk, if there are no practicable alternatives to such use.

EXAMPLE: If while in the desert hundreds of miles from a city, Plaintiff discovers that his car has a dangerous steering defect, it would not be an assumption of the risk that Plaintiff continued to use the car to drive back to civilization.

(3) Where a defendant can show that his product was subsequently altered in an unforeseeable manner by someone in the chain of distribution or a third party, courts usually relieve that defendant of liability.

c. **Comparative Negligence**

   (1) Some jurisdictions that have adopted a comparative negligence system as to negligence also apply that system to strict liability. A plaintiff's wrongful conduct that contributes, along with the defective product, to his own injury reduces his recovery in some amount. This is usually limited to misuse, abnormal use, or independent negligence situations (i.e., not where the plaintiff's wrongful conduct is a failure to discover the defect).

   (2) In some jurisdictions that permit comparative fault, the plaintiff's unreasonable conduct in failing to discover and guard against the defect is not a defense.

B. **Products Liability on a Negligence Theory**

   1. **Proper Defendants**

      a. If negligence, rather than strict liability, is the theory of recovery in a products liability action, the plaintiff must establish a greater personal degree of fault. Negligent conduct should result in liability for the following:

         (1) a defendant selling used goods (i.e., a commercial seller of used goods unreasonably passes on a defective product or negligently fails to discover a dangerous defect);

         (2) a defendant repairing used goods (i.e., where the negligent repair of used goods renders or leaves them dangerously defective);

         (3) a defendant leasing real property;

         (4) a defendant providing services; and

         (5) franchisors.

   2. **Elements**

      a. The elements of a products liability claim based in negligence are the same elements that are part of the negligence cause of action in general.

      b. **Duty**

         (1) A duty is owed to any foreseeable plaintiff. No contractual relationship is required.

              EXAMPLE: If Tom buys a car negligently manufactured by Ford for his wife, Katie, she may bring a negligence claim against Ford, as she is a foreseeable plaintiff.

      c. **Breach of Duty**

         (1) The defendant will typically be judged by the reasonable person standard of care, and breach of duty will be unreasonable conduct on the part of the defendant. On a negligence theory, proof that a product is defective does not automatically establish that each defendant in the chain of distribution breached a duty. The plaintiff must therefore establish that each defendant failed to exercise due care.

         (2) If a reasonable person would have realized that a product was dangerous in normal use, a defendant's failure to inspect and

discover the defect is a breach of duty under negligence principles. It is relevant to consider the nature of the product, the source of the product, and the extent of information available to the defendant.

(3) In general, a failure to inspect packaged goods for defects is not a breach of duty if they come from a reputable manufacturer or distributor. If the goods are manufactured or otherwise supplied by a previously unknown or questionable source, a defendant's unreasonable failure to inspect is a breach of duty. It likely would be a breach of duty not to inspect a particular product as to which a defendant had received or otherwise became aware of complaints from customers.

(4) If the defendant inspects or becomes aware of a defect, his subsequent failure to find the defect or to take reasonable precautions is judged by the reasonable person standard.

d. **Cause-in-Fact and Proximate Cause**

(1) The principles of actual (cause-in-fact) and legal (proximate) causation which govern a negligence analysis generally apply equally to products liability claims where negligence is the theory of recovery.

e. **Damages**

(1) Damages in negligence products liability are assessed according to the same principles applicable to strict liability.

f. **Defenses**

(1) Those defenses generally applicable to negligence are also available in products liability sounding in negligence.

C. **Products Liability on a Warranty Theory**

1. Today, there is little left of the historical requirement for products liability on a warranty theory that the parties be in privity. Only where a plaintiff seeks recovery for pure economic losses and the theory of recovery is implied warranty is privity a relevant consideration. **Privity** in this context refers to the relationship between the injured plaintiff and the last commercial seller in the chain of distribution of the defective product.

2. UCC Section 2-318 offers three alternatives regarding privity (a legislature could enact any one of the three). Each provides that if the purchaser of goods was the beneficiary of a warranty, privity extends to:

   a. members of the purchaser's family or household, plus guests of the purchaser, if they suffer personal injury;

   b. any natural persons who may reasonably be expected to use, consume, or be affected by the goods, if they suffer personal injury; and

   c. any persons who may reasonably be expected to use, consume, or be affected by the goods, if they suffer personal injury.

3. On a warranty products liability theory, liability arises from the fact that a product is not as represented (i.e., it breaches a warranty made either expressly or impliedly by the defendant). The plaintiff must establish that a warranty existed as to the product and that the product does not conform to the warranty.

a. An **express warranty** exists where the defendant made a representation as to the nature or quality of the product. This can occur via advertising, during negotiations for purchase, or as a provision of the contract of sale.

b. The UCC provides that an express warranty may be created by a defendant's promise, by affirmation of fact, by description, or by use of a sample or model [UCC § 2-313].

c. An **implied warranty** may arise under a variety of circumstances.

   (1) The UCC is limited by its own terms to the sale of goods. There are two types of warranties that may be implied under the proper circumstances:

      (a) where a merchant deals in goods of a particular kind, the sale of such goods constitutes an implied warranty that those goods will be merchantable—that is, they are of average quality for goods of that kind and generally fit for the purpose for which such goods are normally used [UCC § 2-314(1)]; and

      (b) where a defendant knows or has reason to know that [UCC § 2-315]:

         1) the plaintiff is purchasing the goods for a particular purpose; and

         2) the plaintiff is relying upon the defendant's skill or judgment to furnish appropriate goods—sale of the goods will constitute an implied warranty that those goods will actually be fit for the plaintiff's purpose.

   (2) Many states recognize judicially created implied warranties of merchantability and fitness for a particular purpose that apply to leased goods.

   (3) The decisional law of a small minority of states extends the implied warranties applicable to sales of goods to real property as well.

4. Recovery of damages for breach of warranty is governed by the same principles applicable to strict liability in tort, except that pure economic losses are recoverable (e.g., loss of profits, cost of obtaining replacement equipment or materials, etc.). The plaintiff must also be in privity with the defendant, as discussed above.

5. **Defenses**

   a. **Disclaimer**

      (1) The UCC enables a defendant to disclaim or limit the applicability of all warranties by a sufficiently conspicuous writing.

      (2) The UCC provides that it is *prima facie* unconscionable for a seller to attempt to limit the remedies available for breach of warranty so as to exclude recovery for personal injuries (e.g., by limiting responsibility for breach to repair or replacement) where consumer goods are involved.

      (3) Where goods are sold "as is," it is often implied that the seller is disclaiming any warranties, implied or express.

      (4) Federal law provides that a seller who gives a written warranty to a consumer may not thereby disclaim any implied warranties.

b. **Failure to Notify Seller**

(1) The UCC provides that a plaintiff-buyer must notify a defendant-seller of the breach of warranty within a reasonable time after the buyer discovers or should have discovered it. This provision is often not applied where the plaintiff is a bystander who suffers personal injury.

c. **Contributory and Comparative Negligence**

(1) With respect to personal injury or injury to property, contributory negligence and comparative fault defenses are available where warranty is the theory on a similar basis to strict liability in tort.

d. **Assumption of Risk**

(1) As to products liability in warranty, this defense is similar in application to strict products liability in tort. If the plaintiff voluntarily and unreasonably continues to use a product after he discovers that it is not fit for the purpose purchased or not of merchantable quality, the defendant is exonerated from liability for personal injuries or property damage suffered by the plaintiff.

V. NUISANCE

A. **Types of Nuisance**
  1. **Public Nuisance**
     a. A **public nuisance** is an unreasonable interference with a right common to the general public.
     b. Circumstances that may sustain a holding that an interference with a public right is unreasonable include the following:
        (1) whether the conduct involves a significant interference with the public health, safety, peace, comfort, or convenience;
        (2) whether the conduct is proscribed by a statute, ordinance, or administrative regulation; and
        (3) whether the conduct is of a continuing nature or has produced a permanent or long-lasting effect, and as the actor knows or has reason to know, has a significant effect upon the public right.
     c. To recover damages in an individual action for a public nuisance, a plaintiff must have suffered harm of a kind different from that suffered by other members of the public.
     d. To maintain a proceeding to enjoin or abate a public nuisance, a plaintiff must:
        (1) have the right to recover damages;
        (2) have authority as a public official or public agency to represent the state or a political subdivision in the matter; and
        (3) have standing to sue as a representative of the general public, as a citizen in a citizen's action, or as a member of a class in a class action.
  2. **Private Nuisance**
     a. A **private nuisance** is a thing or activity that substantially and unreasonably interferes with the plaintiff's use and enjoyment of his land.
     b. The interference with the plaintiff's use and enjoyment must be substantial. This means that it must be offensive, inconvenient, or annoying to an average person in the community. A plaintiff cannot, by devoting his land to an unusually sensitive use, complain of a nuisance based on conduct that would otherwise be relatively harmless.
     c. The interference must be unreasonable, which means that either:
        (1) the gravity of the plaintiff's harm outweighs the utility of the defendant's conduct; or
        (2) if intentional, the harm caused by the defendant's conduct is substantial and the financial burden of compensating for this and other harms does not render unfeasible the continuation of the conduct.
     d. A trespass is an invasion of a plaintiff's interest in the exclusive possession of land (e.g., an entry of something tangible onto the property). On the other hand, a nuisance is an interference with a plaintiff's interest in the use and enjoyment of the land, which does not necessarily require a physical intrusion.

> **EXAMPLE:** Amanda is a writer. Every day, she tries to get work done in the morning. If her neighbor, Callie, calls her every morning, this will not be a private nuisance. However, if Callie calls her fifteen times a morning after Amanda has asked her not to, this may be a private nuisance.

   e.   For a private nuisance, there is liability only to those who have property rights and privileges in respect to the use and employment of the land affected, including:

      (1)   possessors of the land;

      (2)   owners of easements and profits in the land; and

      (3)   owners of nonpossessory estates in the land that are detrimentally affected by interferences with its use and enjoyment.

   f.   A defendant is subject to liability for a private nuisance if, but only if, his conduct is a legal cause of an invasion of another's interest in the private use and enjoyment of land, and the invasion is either:

      (1)   intentional and unreasonable; or

      (2)   unintentional and otherwise actionable under the rules controlling liability for negligent or reckless conduct.

> **EXAM TIP** ▸ Often the key determination on an examination question is to evaluate the reasonableness or unreasonableness of the defendant's conduct. This analysis involves weighing the gravity of the harm done to the plaintiff against the utility of the defendant's activity. Unlike in trespass, the court will balance several factors: compliance with applicable zoning ordinances; priority of occupation; the frequency and extent of the interference, applied objectively to normal persons; and the utility and social value of the defendant's activity.

TRESPASS ON LAND	NUISANCE
A defendant who intentionally, negligently, or recklessly enters the land in the possession of another or causes a thing or a third person to do so is subject to liability.	Substantial and unreasonable interference with the plaintiff's use and enjoyment of the land; basis of nuisance may be intentional, negligent, or absolute.
Consists of intrusions upon, beneath, and above the surface of the earth.	Consists of: (1) interference with the physical condition of the land (such as by vibrations or blasting which damages a house, the destruction of crops, the flooding or pollution of a stream, etc.); or (2) a disturbance of the comfort or convenience of the occupant (such as by unpleasant odors, smoke, dust, loud noise, excessive light, or even repeated telephone calls).

B. **Defenses**

1. **Contributory Negligence**

   a. When a nuisance results from negligent conduct of the defendant, the **contributory negligence** of the plaintiff is a defense to the same extent as in other actions founded on negligence.

   b. When the harm is intentional or the result of recklessness, contributory negligence is not a defense.

   c. When the nuisance results from an abnormally dangerous condition or activity, contributory negligence is a defense only if the plaintiff has voluntarily and unreasonably subjected himself to the risk of harm.

2. **Assumption of Risk**

   a. In an action for a nuisance, the plaintiff's assumption of risk is a defense to the same extent as in other tort actions.

3. **Coming to the Nuisance**

   a. The fact that the plaintiff has acquired or improved his land after a nuisance will not by itself bar his action, but it is a factor to be considered in determining whether the nuisance is actionable.

4. **Compliance with Statute**

   a. A relevant and persuasive, but not absolute, defense to nuisance arises upon evidence that the defendant's conduct was consistent with applicable administrative regulations (i.e., a zoning ordinance or pollution control regulation).

C. **Remedies**

1. For a private or public nuisance, the usual remedy is damages.

2. Where the legal remedy (i.e., money damages) is inadequate or unavailable, courts may grant injunctive relief. The legal remedy may be deemed to be inadequate for a number of reasons (e.g., the nuisance is a continuing wrong or the nuisance is of a kind which will cause irreparable harm). In determining whether an injunction will be granted, the court will undertake to balance the equities, namely taking into account:

   a. the relative economic hardship to the parties for granting or denying the injunction; and

   b. the public interest in the defendant's activity continuing.

EXAM TIP Keep in mind that a court may require the defendant to pay damages while denying injunctive relief.

3. A plaintiff has the privilege to enter upon the defendant's land and personally abate the nuisance after notice to the defendant and his refusal to act. The privilege extends to the use of all reasonable action that is necessary to terminate the nuisance, even to the destruction of valuable property, provided the damage done is not greatly disproportionate to the threatened harm, but does not extend to unnecessary or unreasonable damage. There will be liability for any excess.

EXAMPLE: It may not be justifiable, for instance, to destroy a house merely because it is used for prostitution.

4. A plaintiff who has suffered some unique damage has a similar privilege to abate a public nuisance by self-help. However, a public nuisance may be abated by a private individual only when it causes or threatens special damage to himself apart from that to the general public, and then only to the extent necessary to protect his own interests.

5. **Injunctions**

    a. **Nature and Forms**

        (1) The injunction is the most common form of equitable remedy. An **injunction** is a court order directed to a person or entity, usually to refrain from doing a particular act (a **prohibitory injunction**).

        (2) Less commonly, a court may issue an order to do a particular act (a **mandatory injunction**). Requests for mandatory injunctions are subject to heightened scrutiny, requiring a showing that the facts and law clearly favor the moving party [Dahl v. HEM Pharmaceuticals Corp., 7 F.3d 1399 (9th Cir. 1993)].

            EXAMPLE: Plaintiff, a 30-year-old male, brings an action against Health Club, an all-women's health facility, to allow him to take aerobics classes there. If the court requires the health club to admit him, it may do so in the form of a mandatory injunction.

            EXAMPLE: Plaintiff, a women's health clinic, brings an action against Defendant, an anti-abortion group, to enjoin it from harassing patients and passersby on the sidewalk in front of the clinic. If the court enjoins Defendant, it will do so in the form of a prohibitory injunction.

    b. **Availability**

        (1) In accordance with the general rules on the availability of equitable remedies, injunctive relief is generally available when money damages would not afford adequate relief, such as where it would be extremely difficult to ascertain the amount of compensation that would afford adequate relief or where injunctive relief is necessary to prevent a multiplicity of judicial proceedings.

            EXAMPLE: Injunctive relief has been the primary remedy in civil rights litigation because a deprivation of the individual's constitutional rights is not deemed remediable by money damages.

            EXAMPLE: If the defendant repeatedly trespasses on the plaintiff's land, equity may enjoin the trespass rather than force repeated actions at law to redress the injury.

        (2) The plaintiff who seeks an injunction must specifically show that:

            (a) he is about to suffer or will continue to suffer an irreparable injury for which money damages would be inadequate compensation;

        (b)   the balance of hardships between the plaintiff and defendant supports an equitable remedy; and

        (c)   the public interest would not be disserved by the grant of an injunction.

    (3)   Injunctive relief is generally not available to:

        (a)   stay court proceedings, unless necessary to prevent a multiplicity of proceedings;

        (b)   enforce the criminal laws other than those that restrain a public nuisance; or

        (c)   prevent the breach of a contract that is not specifically enforceable, such as where the terms of the agreement are not sufficiently certain to make the precise act which is to be done clearly ascertainable.

  c. **Temporary Restraining Orders and Preliminary Injunctions**

    (1) **Showing Required**

        (a)   Courts apply a number of other factors to determine whether preliminary injunctive relief is appropriate. The following criteria are the most commonly applied:

           1)   the plaintiff is likely to succeed on the merits of the underlying claim;

           2)   the complaint shows that the plaintiff is entitled to the relief demanded (restraining the commission or continuance of the act complained of) either for a limited period or perpetually;

           3)   denial of injunctive relief would produce waste, or great or irreparable injury, to the plaintiff, such as where it appears, during litigation, that a party to the action is doing or is about to do some act in violation of the rights of another party to the action that would tend to render the judgment ineffectual; and

           4)   the public interest as well as the balancing of hardships between the parties favors the grant of an injunction.

    (2) **Notice Requirements**

        (a)   A preliminary injunction may not be granted without notice to the other party. During the time required for notice and hearing on the preliminary injunction, however, the moving party may seek immediate relief through a temporary restraining order ("TRO").

    (3) **Duration**

        (a)   A TRO granted without notice remains in effect for only a specified period of time, generally 10 to 20 days (a TRO issued without notice in a federal court is effective for a maximum of 14 days [Fed. R. Civ. P. 65(b)(2)]).

d. **Permanent Injunctions**

(1) The plaintiff must have prevailed on the substantive claim and shown a need for continuing protection to be eligible for permanent injunctive relief.

   (a) **EXAMPLE:** When a claimant who insisted the famous lawyer Johnnie Cochran owed him money, and picketed Cochran's office with signs containing insults and obscenities, indicated that he would continue to engage in the activity absent a court order, the court permanently enjoined the claimant from making defamatory statements about Cochran and his firm in any public forum [Tory v. Cochran, 544 U.S. 734 (2005)].

(2) Unlike the interlocutory temporary injunction, a permanent injunction is a final judgment and continues in force until dissolved, but the permanent injunction need not be perpetual—it may be set to expire by its own terms.

VI. DEFAMATION

A. In General

1. For a defamation action, a plaintiff must establish that the defendant published defamatory material concerning the plaintiff that caused reputational damage. In analyzing an action for defamation, one must check for:

    a. a defamatory message;

    b. certain pleading problems;

    c. publication of the message;

    d. the type of defamation;

    e. damages;

    f. common law defenses; and

    g. constitutional issues.

B. Defamatory Message

1. A message is **defamatory** if it lowers a plaintiff in the esteem of the community or discourages third persons from associating with him.

    a. A **defamatory message** has been characterized as one that holds a plaintiff up to hatred, ridicule, contempt, or scorn. Whether or not a defendant's statement includes this notion of disgrace, it should be actionable if it causes third persons to avoid contact with the plaintiff. A message is also defamatory to an entity if it causes customers to stop doing business with the entity, causes persons to stop making charitable contributions to it, or causes them to avoid membership.

2. In general, only statements of fact are actionable as defamatory. However, expressions of opinion which imply that the speaker knows certain facts to be true, or which imply that such facts exist, may be sufficient to classify the messages as defamatory. If a reasonable person would interpret a statement as one of fact, considering the context and the nature of the utterance, a jury may find that the message is defamatory.

    a. A statement is more likely to be regarded as a statement of fact rather than opinion to the extent that it is more specific and detailed. It is not sufficient to change what is otherwise a statement of fact to one of opinion by adding qualifiers such as, "I think…" or "It is my opinion…."

       EXAMPLE: The Daily may be subject to defamation liability to Paxton for stating falsely: "In our opinion, Paxton was involved in the planning of the assassination of Robert F. Kennedy." The Daily cannot be liable for publishing: "Paxton was once a very stylish dresser, but this year his clothes seem drab."

3. A message is defamatory if it has the required injurious effect on any substantial minority of reasonable people. If a negligible number of people are affected, or only those whose views are too antisocial, the message is not defamatory.

    a. A messages is defamatory *per se* if it is apparent on the face of the message that it will injure the plaintiff's reputation. If the message at issue does not on its face seem injurious to the plaintiff's reputation, or defamation *per quod*, the plaintiff must plead additional, extrinsic facts that render the message defamatory. The plaintiff must also explain how the message, with the extrinsic facts, injures his reputation. Where a statement is defamatory only upon a showing of extrinsic facts, the plaintiff must:

(1) plead and prove inducement;

(2) establish a defamatory meaning by innuendo; and

(3) show that he himself was the intended plaintiff by colloquium.

> **EXAMPLE:** The Daily prints, "Petunia married Donald yesterday." This does not appear reputation-harming on its face, but it may become so through the inducement that Petunia is already married to someone else.

4. The defamatory message must be understood by the person who receives it. A judge decides whether a communication could be understood as defamatory, and the jury decides whether it was defamatory in the case before it.

EXAMPLE: The Daily falsely states in an article that Penelope used to be best friends with a drug addict. A judge may determine that a false statement that a person was once friends with a person who was addicted to drugs is not capable of causing reputational harm. If the judge instead determines that it could be harmful, then it would be up to the jury to determine if such a statement harmed Penelope's reputation in the situation before it.

C. Pleading Problems

1. To bring an action for defamation, the party suffering the defamation must have been a living person or an existing organization.

   a. A defamatory message published about a third person is actionable only to the extent that it also defames the plaintiff. A defamatory message concerning only a third person, even one closely related to the plaintiff, cannot defame the plaintiff.

   b. Where a defendant makes an otherwise defamatory statement about a group of persons, his liability to individual plaintiffs varies according to the size of the group and the nature of the defamatory message.

      (1) A defamatory message made concerning all members of a large group does not create a right of action in favor of any particular member of that group. However, if the circumstances would indicate to a reasonable person that a particular plaintiff is the actual subject of the defamatory message, the fact that the message is spoken of the group does not relieve the defendant of liability.

      (2) If the group that is the subject of the defendant's defamatory message is sufficiently small, each member of the group is generally regarded as sufficiently identified so that each could bring an action for defamation.

      > **EXAMPLE:** In a case involving a sportswriter who published an article stating that all 20 members of the University football team

had used illegal steroids, each member of that team was permitted to bring an action against the sportswriter for defamation.

(3) Traditionally, no individual member of a small group was permitted to bring an action for defamation where the defendant defamed some but not all of them. Today, whether a particular member was sufficiently identified is examined on a case-by-case basis, considering all the circumstances.

D. Publication

1. A defamatory message is commonly a spoken or written statement. Any form of communication may be defamatory, however, including television and radio broadcasts, films, plays, novels, cartoons, sculpture, etc.

   a. A plaintiff must prove that some reasonable third person who received the defamatory message understood it to refer to the plaintiff. Thus, if the plaintiff is not specifically named in the allegedly defamatory communication, he must allege through colloquium that some people will interpret the communication to be about him.

   EXAMPLE: The Daily states that the longest serving Torts professor at Acme School of Law does not know the difference between battery and assault. Pinnafore may proceed in his action for defamation by alleging and proving that he is the longest serving Torts professor at Acme.

2. It is not actionable to utter a defamatory message to the plaintiff alone. For the defendant's message concerning the plaintiff to constitute defamation, it must be communicated to a third person, who receives and understands it.

   a. In most situations, it is apparent that the defendant desired that third persons receive the defamatory message. However, a message is "published" if the defendant negligently permitted it to be communicated to third persons. If it is reasonably foreseeable that an eavesdropper might overhear a message, for example, and one does so, there is a sufficient publication.

3. In addition to the defendant who originates the defamatory message, other persons who repeat it may be liable to the plaintiff, varying according to their relationship to the original publisher. Such republication may also increase the originator's liability to the plaintiff.

   a. All persons who participate in originating a defamatory message are liable as primary publishers.

   EXAMPLE: The author of a book defamatory to a plaintiff, the editor who selected it for publication and provided editorial services, and the company that employed the editor and printed the book would all be liable as primary publishers.

   b. Any person who repeats the defamatory message is liable as a publisher. This is so even where the repetition is qualified by such terms as "alleged" or is said not to be the opinion of the republisher.

      (1)   Where the original publisher could reasonably foresee that the defamatory message would be republished, he is liable to the plaintiff for additional damages caused by the republications.

    c.   A person who distributes the original defamatory message as a commodity (e.g., a bookseller, newspaper vendor, retailer, etc.) is liable only if he knew or should have known that the material distributed contained the defamatory message.

E. Type of Defamation

1.   Historically, **libel** was a written form of defamation. Today, a defamatory message embodied in any relatively permanent form is a libel.

    <u>EXAMPLE:</u> A sound recording, video recording, picture, sculpture, etc.

    a.   **Libel *per quod*** is a libel as to which it is not apparent on the face of the communication that it is defamatory. A plaintiff must plead and establish extrinsic facts to establish that the libel was defamatory and that it referred to the plaintiff. A large minority of jurisdictions require proof of special damages for libel *per quod*.

2.   Historically, **slander** was defamation in spoken, rather than written, form. Today, a defamatory message not preserved in permanent form is classified as slander.

    a.   **Slander *per se*** is a type of slander historically regarded as so harmful that it was presumed that the plaintiff suffered damage from the very fact of its utterance. Four types of slander were so classified:

        (1)   a slander that imputed to the plaintiff the commission of a crime involving moral turpitude or infamous punishment (imprisonment or death);

        (2)   allegations of the plaintiff having a loathsome disease are slander;

           (a)   Historically, a loathsome disease was one that was incurable and persisted over time, such as venereal disease or leprosy. Allegations of insanity or tuberculosis have been held not within the slander *per se* category.

        (3)   slander which imputes to the plaintiff behavior or characteristics that are incompatible with the proper conduct of his business, profession, or office; and

        (4)   it was slander *per se* to falsely impute unchastity to a woman.

           (a)   Scholars have concluded that the same conclusion would follow if the target of the defamation were a man, but no case has so held. The Restatement defines this form of slander *per se* in terms of false imputation of "serious sexual misconduct" to any person. A small minority of jurisdictions hold it slander *per se* to falsely impute impotency to a man. In addition, commentators have suggested that false imputation of deviant sexual behavior might fall within this category.

3.   Where it is not clear whether a defamatory message is libel or slander, factors to distinguish the two include:

    a.   the permanence of the form;

b.   the area of dissemination; and

c.   the extent to which the message was planned rather than spontaneous.

   (1)   The more permanent the form, widely disseminated, and planned a defamatory message is, the more likely it is to be considered libel.

F.   Damages

1.   Three different types of damages are potentially recoverable for defamation. In some situations, the need for actual proof of damages is affected by the type of defamation involved.

   a.   **Pecuniary damages** are quantifiable monetary losses suffered by the plaintiff due to the injury to his reputation. Examples include loss of customers, loss of a job, or other diminishment of economic advantage. The plaintiff must present evidence of specific actual monetary losses in order to recover pecuniary damages.

      (1)   Proof of pecuniary damages is necessary to establish a *prima facie* case if the form of defamation is slander and, in some states, if it is libel *per quod*. Once pecuniary damages are established, presumed damages are also available.

   b.   In certain circumstances, the jury is permitted to presume that plaintiff suffered **general damages** as a result of the defendant's defamatory statement. These include nonpecuniary aspects of the injury to reputation, such as humiliation, loss of friends, etc. The jury is instructed to estimate the amount of presumed damages based upon the extent of injury to the plaintiff's reputation.

      (1)   It is "presumed" that the plaintiff suffered general damages, and thus no proof of actual damage need be offered, when the form of defamation is slander *per se* or "ordinary" libel (i.e., not libel *per quod*).

   c.   Damages that are assessed against the defendant to punish and deter future wrongful conduct are called **punitive damages**. The plaintiff must make some additional evidentiary showing of vexatiousness or evil intent (i.e., common law malice) to recover punitive damages.

G.   Common Law Defenses

1.   **Truth**

   a.   Historically, falsity was presumed once the plaintiff established the publication of a defamatory communication. In other words, truth was a substantial defense. The defendant had to prove that the communication was "substantially true."

   b.   Now, in all defamation cases except possibly those where the plaintiff is a private plaintiff and the matter is of private concern, the plaintiff must prove falsity as part of his *prima facie* case.

2.   **Absolute Privilege**

   a.   Where an **absolute privilege** applies, the defendant may not be held liable for an otherwise defamatory message as a matter of law.

(1) A legislator is not liable for a defamatory message uttered while on the floor of the legislature or during hearings or committee proceedings. The nature or content of the defamatory message or its relationship to any matter before the legislature is immaterial to availability of this privilege.

(2) A participant in judicial proceedings (e.g., a judge, attorney, witness, or juror) is not liable for any defamatory message that is reasonably related to the proceedings.

(3) The privilege for statements made during judicial proceedings arises upon filing of the complaint and continues until final termination of the action. It includes pleadings, pretrial proceedings, and discovery, and may include settlement negotiations occurring prior to the filing of the litigation. *Quasi*-judicial administrative hearings are considered judicial proceedings for this privilege.

(4) An absolute privilege from liability for defamation applies to policy-making officials of the executive branches of state and federal governments, so long as the defamatory utterance was made in the course of their duties and was relevant to those duties.

(5) A defamatory message communicated by one spouse to another is absolutely privileged from defamation liability.

(6) The U.S. Supreme Court has held that a broadcast media defendant compelled by the fairness doctrine to permit a third person to utilize its facilities is absolutely privileged as to defamatory statements made by the third person. Commentators suggest the same rule might be applied to a newspaper compelled by law to print public notices.

b. The defendant has the burden of establishing that an absolute privilege applies to his defamatory message.

3. **Qualified Privilege**

a. If a **qualified privilege** is applicable, a defendant is not held liable for otherwise defamatory messages he utters unless he loses the protection of the privilege.

b. A defendant is qualifiedly immune from liability for defamatory messages made in a communication that appears reasonably necessary to protect or advance the defendant's own legitimate interests.

c. A defendant who communicates on a matter of interest to the recipient of the communication or a third person is qualifiedly immune from liability for defamatory messages in the communication.

EXAMPLE: Duncan was employed for seven years with ABC Company. After being terminated, he sought employment with XYZ Company. XYZ contacted ABC and asked for a recommendation. The president of ABC stated, "If I were you, I wouldn't hire Duncan—he's a thief." As long as the speaker reasonably believed the information to be true, there is a qualified privilege to act in the interest of others. Thus, ABC would not be liable for defamation.

d. A defendant who communicates concerning a matter of public interest to one empowered to protect that interest is qualifiedly privileged as to a defamatory message contained in the communication.

e. A defendant has a qualified privilege as to defamatory messages contained in a criticism of a matter of public interest.

f. A defendant is qualifiedly immune from liability for defamatory messages that are republished in a report of public hearings or meetings, so long as the defendant's report is fair and accurate.

g. The defendant bears the burden of establishing that a qualified privilege is available.

h. The defendant loses an otherwise available qualified privilege if:

(1) he acts out of malice;

(a) **Malice** is present if the defendant's primary motive in publishing the defamatory message was something other than furthering the interest that justified the privilege.

(2) he exceeds the scope of the privilege; or

(a) A qualified privilege may be lost if the defamatory message includes matters not relevant to the interests protected by the privilege or is published in a manner or to persons outside the legitimate scope of the privilege.

(3) he does not believe the truth of the defamatory communication.

(a) A qualified privilege is lost if the defendant does not possess an honest belief in the truth of the defamatory message. Some states also require that the defendant have a reasonable, honest belief.

i. While a defendant bears the burden of establishing that a qualified privilege is applicable, a plaintiff bears the burden of establishing that conditions exist under which the privilege is lost.

4. **Consent**

a. Generally applicable principles relating to the defense of consent apply to defamation.

H. Constitutional Issues

1. Decisions interpreting the Free Speech Clause of the First Amendment have altered the common law of defamation with regard to:

a. the degree of fault required of a defendant;

(1) At common law, defamation was a strict liability offense, in the sense that the plaintiff need only establish that the defamatory statement was made in order to recover (all other elements being present), not that defendant had any particular mental state or degree of fault.

b. the nature of the plaintiff;

(1) Where a plaintiff is a public official or a public figure, the plaintiff must establish that the defendant acted with "malice" before any recovery may be had [New York Times v. Sullivan, 376 U.S. 254 (1964)].

(a) A **public official** is a government official who has or appears to have substantial responsibility over governmental operations. While this does not include every public employee, courts have, for example, generally included police officers among public officials.

(b) A **public figure** is a person who has either:

1) achieved such pervasive fame or notoriety such that he becomes a public figure for all purposes (e.g., a celebrity); or

2) voluntarily injected himself or allowed himself to be drawn into a particular public controversy such that he becomes a public figure as to the limited issues present in that controversy.

(c) **Malice**, for this purpose, is defined as knowing falsity or recklessness as to truth or falsity. In order for malice to exist, the defendant must have actually known the defamatory message was false or actually entertained serious doubts about its truth (i.e., had reckless disregard) [Id.].

(d) The plaintiff must establish malice with "convincing clarity." Commentators have analogized this language from New York Times v. Sullivan to the "clear and convincing" evidence standard, which requires something more than proof by a preponderance of the evidence, and something less than the "beyond a reasonable doubt" standard used in criminal matters.

c. the subject matter of the defamatory statement;

(1) Where the plaintiff is neither a public official nor public figure, constitutional protection of free speech still precludes application of the common law strict liability scheme if the subject matter of the defamation is a matter of public concern. In such a case, the defendant must be shown to have exhibited some degree of fault higher than strict liability, which presumably means negligence. However, actual malice must be proved for presumed or punitive damages.

(2) Where a private plaintiff sues in defamation and the subject matter is also private (i.e., not a matter of public concern), the U.S. Constitution does not require that the plaintiff prove actual malice to recover presumed or punitive damages.

(3) This can be a blurry line, but the test is to look at the "form, content, and context" of the communication. As a practical matter, if the defendant is a member of the media, or if the communication is widely disseminated, it is probably of public concern. Conversely, if the case involves slander that is shared with only very few people, it might be a matter of private concern.

d. the availability of presumed and punitive damages; and

(1) General damages may be presumed if otherwise available under defamation law, and punitive damages may be awarded upon proper proof in two situations:

           (a)   in any case where the plaintiff establishes that the defendant acted with malice; and

           (b)   where the common law still applies—that is, where a private plaintiff sues for defamation as to a matter not of public concern.

      (2)   Where negligence is the applicable degree of fault required by constitutional principles and the plaintiff does not show malice, the plaintiff may only recover actual damages.

      (3)   **Actual damages** are broader and more inclusive than the common law pecuniary damages, and include all injuries to the plaintiff's reputation. They need not be supported by evidence of quantifiable monetary losses, but there must be introduction of some evidence as proof.

      (4)   The U.S. Supreme Court has held that speech such as parodies, cartoons, and other satirical utterances cannot be actionable as an intentional infliction of emotional distress unless they contain false statements of fact made with malice.

  e.   the media status of the defendant.

VII. INVASION OF PRIVACY

A. **Intrusion into Seclusion**

1. This form of invasion of privacy is present when a defendant unreasonably intrudes into the plaintiff's seclusion.

   a. The wrongful conduct is an interference with the plaintiff's seclusion, including physical intrusions (placing a webcam in the plaintiff's bathroom) and non-physical intrusions (i.e., photographing the plaintiff in his backyard from off the property).

   b. To be actionable, the defendant's intrusion must be one that would be highly objectionable to a reasonable person.

   c. **Seclusion** refers to a plaintiff's right to physical solitude or to the privacy of personal affairs or concerns. In circumstances where the plaintiff has no reasonable expectation of solitude or privacy, conduct by the defendant that might otherwise be intrusive is not an invasion of seclusion (e.g., eavesdropping on a conversation between the plaintiff and another person as they walk down a public sidewalk).

2. Damages recoverable for invasion of seclusion include compensatory damages (e.g., mental distress unaccompanied by physical injury) and, under appropriate circumstances, punitive damages.

B. **Appropriation of Identity or Likeness**

1. **Appropriation** is an unauthorized use of the plaintiff's identity or likeness for the defendant's commercial advantage.

   a. The plaintiff bears the burden of proving that he did not consent to the defendant's use of his identity or likeness.

   b. Use of "identity or likeness" is present if the defendant uses any object or characteristic sufficient to identify the plaintiff. Use of an object or characteristic that does not identify the plaintiff is not actionable.

   c. The wrongful use of the plaintiff's identity or likeness must be in connection with the promotion of a product or service. The fact that the defendant derived economic benefit from the use of the plaintiff's identity is not enough alone to constitute a violation (e.g., a biographer paid to write an unauthorized book about a famous plaintiff).

2. Compensatory damages are recoverable, measured by the reasonable value of the use of the plaintiff's identity or likeness. Punitive damages should be recoverable on a proper showing.

   EXAMPLE: Jonathan wishes to advertise a weight-loss product. Without asking her permission, Jonathan puts Calista Flockhart's photo in an ad for the product. Flockhart will have a cause of action against Jonathan.

C. **Public Disclosure of Private Facts**

1. This form of invasion of privacy is present when a defendant unreasonably discloses private facts about a plaintiff to the public.

a. Disclosure is actionable if it would be highly offensive to a reasonable person and not of legitimate public concern.

b. The private facts must be disseminated to the public. Communicating them to a third person is not sufficient to constitute this tort (as distinguished from defamation, where communication to a single third person is a sufficient publication).

c. The information or material disclosed by the defendant must be an aspect or component of the plaintiff's life not open to public view or inspection and not a matter of public record.

2. The plaintiff can recover compensatory damages, including mental distress unaccompanied by physical injury.

3. Public disclosure of private facts is not actionable where the publication is newsworthy. This broad defense can apply to pictures published in newspapers as well as magazine articles on former celebrities and public figures. Private matters contained in public records are absolutely privileged.

D. Portrayal in a False Light

1. This tort is present when a defendant publishes matters that portray a plaintiff in a false light.

a. The defendant must communicate the material to a substantial number of people.

b. **Portraying in a false light** means attributing to the plaintiff views he does not hold or attributing actions to him that he did not take. In addition, the false light in which the plaintiff is placed must be such that a reasonable person would find it highly offensive.

(1) This is a "lesser" form of offensive falseness than required for defamation.

2. The plaintiff can recover compensatory and, in a proper case, punitive damages.

E. Defenses and Privileges

1. **Truth**

a. Truth is not a defense to appropriation or intrusion, since truth or falsity is not a relevant issue. However, truth is a complete defense to portrayal in a false light.

2. **Consent**

a. Consent is a defense to disclosure, intrusion, and false light to the same extent it is to any other intentional tort.

b. The plaintiff is required to prove lack of his consent as an element of his *prima facie* case for appropriation.

3. **Privilege**

a. The absolute and conditional privileges applicable to defamation should be available as to public disclosure of private facts and portrayal in a false light.

F. Constitutional Principles

1. Where a plaintiff is portrayed in a false light as to a matter of public interest, the plaintiff must prove that the defendant had acted with malice—knowledge of falsity or reckless disregard for truth or falsity—in order to recover.

VIII. WRONGFUL INSTITUTION OF LEGAL PROCEEDINGS

A. **Malicious Prosecution**

1. **Malicious prosecution** is the institution of criminal proceedings by a defendant, done for an improper purpose and without probable cause, that terminate favorably for the plaintiff and cause the plaintiff damages.

   a. The wrongful conduct is the taking of action that results in the commencement of the criminal prosecution of the plaintiff. Such actions include persuading a prosecutor to bring charges against a plaintiff, signing an affidavit for a warrant, or giving false information to the authorities with knowledge of its falsity. It does not constitute malicious prosecution to give information to authorities while relying upon their discretion as to whether to prosecute.

   b. The defendant must act for a primary purpose other than to bring a guilty person to justice. That there was no probable cause supporting the initiation of proceedings is evidence that the defendant's purpose was improper.

   c. The defendant lacks probable cause for initiation of criminal proceedings when either:

      (1) a reasonable person possessing the same facts as the defendant would not have believed that the plaintiff was guilty of the charged offense; or

      (2) defendant did not actually believe that the plaintiff was guilty.

      EXAMPLE: Dahlia is still angry with her former boyfriend, Preston. Dahlia contacts the police and has Preston arrested on suspicion of being a terrorist. Preston is not a terrorist, and Dahlia knows this fact. A judge eventually dismisses the case. Preston will have a cause of action against Dahlia for malicious prosecution.

   d. A grand jury indictment returned against a plaintiff after the defendant's action or a magistrate holding the plaintiff to answer after a preliminary hearing are *prima facie* evidence that probable cause existed to believe the plaintiff was guilty. A plaintiff's conviction on criminal charges is conclusive evidence of probable cause, even if the conviction is subsequently reversed on appeal.

   e. An attorney's advice to the defendant to institute criminal proceedings conclusively establishes probable cause in most jurisdictions, at least where the defendant made a full and fair disclosure of all relevant facts, and the attorney is competent and duly admitted to practice in the jurisdiction or otherwise qualified to render an opinion.

   f. The criminal prosecution must have terminated in a fashion indicating that the plaintiff was innocent of the charges. Terminations on the merits (i.e., acquittal after trial or court dismissal for lack of sufficient evidence) are sufficient in this regard; terminations based on procedural or technical defects, prosecutorial discretion, or similar grounds are not.

2. When a plaintiff establishes the essential elements of a cause of action for malicious prosecution, he is entitled to recover damages for:

   a. the harm to his reputation resulting from the accusation brought against him; and

   b. the emotional distress resulting from the bringing of the proceedings.

3. **Defenses**

   a. **Privilege**

      (1) Judges, prosecutors, and other law enforcement officials are absolutely privileged as to malicious prosecution.

   b. A defendant may prevail in a malicious prosecution action by a plaintiff if the defendant can establish by a preponderance of the evidence that the plaintiff was actually guilty of the crime for which the plaintiff was prosecuted.

      (1) A termination of the criminal proceeding in favor of the plaintiff does not preclude this result, having no *res judicata* effect due to the higher standard of proof in criminal proceedings (because the prosecution must prove the defendant's guilt beyond a reasonable doubt).

B. **Wrongful Institution of Civil Proceedings**

   1. A person who takes an active part in the initiation, continuation, or procurement of civil proceedings against another is subject to liability to the other for wrongful civil proceedings, if:

      a. he acts without basis and primarily for a purpose other than that of securing the proper adjudication of the claim on which the proceedings are based; and

      b. except when they are *ex parte*, the proceedings have terminated in favor of the person against whom they are brought.

      EXAMPLE: Deborah dislikes her new neighbor, Parker. To try to get him to move out of the neighborhood, Deborah sues Parker for private nuisance, alleging that his music is too loud. Deborah knows that Parker rarely plays his music so that it can be heard outside of his home and he always turns it down if asked. When the court hears the evidence against Parker, it dismisses the case. Parker has a cause of action against Deborah for the wrongful institution of civil proceedings.

C. **Abuse of Process**

   1. Abuse of process exists where a defendant intentionally misuses a judicial process (whether civil or criminal) for a purpose other than that for which the process is intended. This tort also parallels malicious prosecution.

   2. The plaintiff need not show the defendant's lack of probable cause, as proof of the defendant's improper purpose serves the same function.

IX. ECONOMIC TORTS

A. Intentional Misrepresentation (Fraud)

1. An **intentional misrepresentation** by a defendant, made with scienter, which is material and justifiably relied upon by a plaintiff and which causes damages to the plaintiff, is actionable.

2. An actionable **misrepresentation** is an assertion of a false past or present fact. The generally cited principle that a misrepresentation of opinion is not actionable is subject to exceptions, which are discussed in connection with reliance.

3. A misrepresentation can consist of:

    a. a false, affirmative assertion;

    b. active concealment; or

        (1) In a majority of jurisdictions, a defendant cannot be liable for active concealment if his transaction with the plaintiff is stated to be "as is," or the plaintiff is otherwise put on notice as to the concealed facts.

    c. an omission of fact (i.e., a failure to disclose).

        (1) Traditionally, a defendant was not liable for misrepresentation if his only wrongdoing was the omission of facts. Many exceptions have been developed over the years, including:

            (a) where the defendant is a fiduciary for the plaintiff;

            (b) where the defendant makes an assertion believing it to be true, subsequently discovers that it was false or that circumstances have changed, and fails to disclose the truth or changed circumstances;

            (c) where the defendant makes an incomplete or ambiguous assertion, omitting additional facts that render his assertion misleading;

            (d) where the defendant makes a false assertion not intending that anyone rely upon it, subsequently discovers that the plaintiff intends to act in reliance upon the false assertion, and fails to disclose that the assertion was false; and

            (e) where the plaintiff reasonably expects disclosure.

                1) A minority of modern jurisdictions impose liability on a defendant for the omission of facts where, under the circumstances, the plaintiff could reasonably expect disclosure. Factors to consider include:

                    a) the relation of the parties;

                    b) the nature of the undisclosed facts; and

                    c) the nature of the transaction.

4. The defendant must intend that the plaintiff or a class of persons of which the plaintiff is a member will act or fail to act in reliance on his misrepresentation.

    EXCEPTION: Any plaintiff may recover for misrepresentation regardless of defendant's intent if the misrepresentation is characterized as ongoing (e.g., a mislabeled product).

a. Some cases have found liability for misrepresentation in any situation where the defendant could reasonably foresee that someone would rely upon his misrepresentation, regardless of whether the defendant intended that the particular plaintiff rely on it.

5. Scienter is present when the defendant makes a misrepresentation knowing it to be false or recklessly possessing insufficient information as to its truth or falsity.

6. A representation or omission is material if it would influence a reasonable person in determining his course of action in the particular transaction at issue. A fact is also material, even if a reasonable person would not regard it as important, if the defendant knows that the plaintiff actually regards it as important.

7. The plaintiff must rely on the defendant's misrepresentation, and that reliance must be justified. In general, reliance on an assertion is justified if a reasonable person would have relied upon it. Factors considered in this analysis include the nature of the misrepresentation, the parties, and the relationship of the parties.

    a. Reliance on a misrepresentation of fact is generally regarded as justified except where the representation is patently false. A plaintiff has no duty to investigate, even where not burdensome to do so. If the plaintiff actually investigates, he may not rely on representations inconsistent with what he actually or might reasonably have discovered.

    b. In general, reliance on a misrepresentation of opinion is not justified. There are numerous exceptions to this principle, however.

        (1) A plaintiff's reliance on a defendant's assertion of opinion is justified where the defendant owes the plaintiff a fiduciary duty.

        (2) In circumstances not amounting to a fiduciary relation, but where a defendant has the confidence of a plaintiff (e.g., the defendant is the plaintiff's uncle), reliance on the defendant's misrepresentations may be justified.

        (3) Reliance on a defendant's opinion is more likely to be justified if the defendant possesses much greater expertise than the plaintiff as to the subject of the transaction.

        (4) If the defendant has an interest that he fails to disclose to the plaintiff, it is justifiable for the plaintiff to rely on the defendant's expression of opinion on the subject of that interest.

    c. Traditionally, representations of law were regarded as expressions of opinion, and thus a plaintiff's reliance was not justified. Today, courts apply the principles discussed above. In addition, courts are quite willing to find implied statements of fact in legal opinions.

8. The element of causation is met if a defendant's misrepresentation played a substantial part in inducing the plaintiff to act as he did.

9. A plaintiff may recover compensatory damages for the value of what he would have received if not for the misrepresentation. A plaintiff may also recover punitive damages upon a showing that the defendant acted with common law malice.

B. **Negligent Misrepresentation**

1. The traditional rule, followed by a majority of jurisdictions, is that **negligent misrepresentations** are not actionable. Many of these jurisdictions neverthe-less allow recovery where there is arguably no intentional misrepresentation by resorting to legal fictions that permit their courts to find intent because a defendant's honestly held belief in the truth of his assertion is unreasonable.

    a. Many jurisdictions impose liability for negligent misrepresentation only in certain situations where a special relationship exists between the defendant and the plaintiff, and the nature of the defendant's activity justifies holding the defendant liable for a failure to exercise due care. The most widely recognized circumstance involves a defendant in the business of supplying information to be used by others in making economically significant deci-sions (e.g., accountants, title abstractors, or lawyers). Such defendants are liable if they fail to exercise due care in determining the truth or falsity of the representations they make. The elements of this cause of action are identical to those for fraud, with the following differences:

        (1) The mental state a defendant must have for liability under negli-gent misrepresentation is the same for negligence analysis generally. Thus, a defendant's representations, made in good faith, are not actionable if they are inaccurate because the defen-dant failed to exercise due care.

        (2) A defendant is liable for a negligent misrepresentation only to:

            (a) the person to whom the misrepresentation was made; and

            (b) to any other specific persons or identifiable group of persons that the defendant knew would rely upon the misrepresentation.

                1) Note the absence of foreseeability, a common negli-gence concept; courts expanding the reach of fraud into negligent misrepresentation sought to limit the class of potential plaintiffs.

C. **Interference with Contractual Relations**

1. The main type of interference with economic relations that has been marked out by the courts and regarded as a separate tort is referred to as **inducing breach of contract** or **interference with contract**.

2. Virtually any type of contract may be the basis for this type of tort action. The contract must:

    a. be in force and effect;

    b. be legal; and

    c. not be opposed to public policy.

3. For reasons that have not been clearly stated, contracts to marry have received special treatment, and almost without exception the courts have refused to hold that it is a tort to induce the parties to break them.

4. To be held liable for interference with a contract, the defendant must be shown to have caused the interference. It is not enough that he merely has

d. Lan and Patrick's Individual Claims

Lan and Patrick would sue on their own behalf for loss of consortium. Loss of consortium compensates a plaintiff for the loss of the injured loved one's love and affection. These awards have traditionally been limited to spouses of the injured party, specifically as compensation for loss of conjugal relations. In modern times, the definition has generally broadened to include companionship more generally. The relationship to the injured party, as well as the closeness of the relationship, factor into a determination on loss of consortium. Patrick, as Xena's spouse, has a strong claim for loss of consortium provided the damages can be proved. Lan, as Xena's father, has a basis for recovery in a few jurisdictions that allow a parent to sue for loss of consortium, although it is diminished somewhat by the fact that Xena is now an adult and presumably independent of her father.

Torts

In Class Question

This sample answer would be considered below the standard expected of a 1L student.

I.   Actions Against Dau

a.   Battery

A battery is an intentional act that causes a harmful or offensive contact with the plaintiff.

Dau did not intend to harm Xena; however, he opened his door into a designated bike lane without looking to see if a bike was approaching. Dau likely would succeed in arguing that he was merely exiting his legally parked vehicle and did not mean to come into contact with anyone.

There is no question that Dau's act in opening the door caused the harmful contact with Xena. But for his actions, Xena would not have hit his car door and fallen off of her bike.

Xena clearly suffered harmful contact, because she fell to the pavement, breaking her arm.

Dau is likely not liable for battery because he did not intend to harm Xena.

b.   Negligence

Negligence is a breach of a duty that causes harm to the plaintiff.

Duty is owed only to foreseeable plaintiffs. Here, Dau owed a duty of reasonable care in exiting his vehicle to anyone in the vicinity, which included Xena.

The standard of conduct required is judged by the reasonable person standard. A reasonable person would look around at the bike lane before opening his door.

To recover in negligence, a defendant's conduct must also be the cause of the plaintiff's injuries. The defendant's conduct was the cause of an event if that event would not have occurred but for the existence of the conduct. Here, Xena would not have crashed into the car door and fallen to the pavement but for Dau's opening the door into her path. Xena was also a foreseeable plaintiff because she was riding in the marked bike lane. There also was no superseding cause here.

Negligence *per se* is when a defendant violates a statute that is intended to protect plaintiffs from the type of harm suffered. Here, a section of the Vehicle Code provides: "No person shall open the door of a vehicle on the side available to moving traffic unless it is reasonably safe to do so. Failure to do so is a misdemeanor punishable by a fine not to exceed $1,000."

For negligence *per se* to apply, the injury caused by the defendant's conduct must be of the type that the statute was intended to prevent, and the plaintiff must be a member of the class intended to be protected by the statute. This statute seems to be designed to protect bikers such as Xena from injuries sustained by colliding with an opening car door. Thus, Xena could recover for negligence *per se*.

There are three available defenses to negligence: contributory negligence, comparative negligence. and assumption of the risk. A plaintiff's negligence may completely bar recovery under common-law contributory negligence. The reasonable person standard discussed above applies to plaintiffs in a contributory negligence analysis. Here, Dau may argue that Xena was contributorily negligent by failing to swerve out of the way to avoid the car door. However, we do not know if she could have swerved out of the way, because it appears that she may not have had any time to react to the opening door.

Comparative negligence reduces the plaintiff's recovery by the percentage of his or her contributing fault. Xena might be considered a little at fault for not swerving out of the way, and her damages would be reduced.

The plaintiff does not seem to have assumed the risk of being hit by Dau's opening his car door.

Xena has a strong likelihood of success in a negligence claim against Dau.

II. Actions Against BF and HelmetCo

a. Negligence

The negligence analysis here is similar to that discussed above. Anyone who places a product into the marketing chain owes a duty of reasonable care to all foreseeable plaintiffs. HelmetCo is subject to this by virtue of manufacturing the helmet Xena was wearing, and BF, by virtue of renting out the helmet. Xena is a foreseeable plaintiff as to both defendants.

Plaintiff must establish that each defendant failed to exercise due care. Here, it appears that even the exercise of reasonable care would not have revealed the "imperceptible" defect in the helmet; thus, it is likely that HelmetCo and BF are not liable to Xena under a negligence claim.

It is obvious that this breach would be the cause of injury to Xena. The facts state that she most likely would not have sustained a head injury if the helmet had not cracked.

The three defenses to negligence discussed above apply here as well. It is likely that Xena was not contributorily or comparatively negligent, and HelmetCo does not have an argument that Xena assumed the risk of injury. However, BF may claim that Xena explicitly assumed the risk of injury by signing the waiver relieving BF from liability for harm "…even such harm resulted from Bike Fun's negligence or other culpable conduct." Such waivers are generally upheld, as long as they are not void as against public policy and the language is clear. Here there does not appear to be a compelling public policy argument in favor of voiding the waiver.

It is likely that HelmetCo and BF are not liable to Xena in negligence because even the use of reasonable care would not have revealed the imperceptible crack in the helmet. Furthermore, BF is likely absolved from negligence by the waiver Xena signed.

b. **Strict Products Liability**

In strict liability, defendant is liable for injuring plaintiff whether or not defendant exercised due care. There are three categories of product defect: manufacturing defect, design defect, and failure to warn. Here, the helmet contained a manufacturing flaw because of the crack.

Xena needs to prove that the manufacturing flaw existed when the helmet left HelmetCo's control.

Defenses to a products liability claim include misuse, contributory negligence, and comparative negligence. If a plaintiff uses a product in a manner that is neither intended nor foreseeable, she has misused the product, and it cannot be defective. Here, Xena clearly used the helmet as intended; therefore, the defense of misuse does not apply.

Common-law contributory negligence would apply to bar a strict products liability claim if the plaintiff was negligent while wearing the helmet. Xena was probably not contributorily negligent.

Comparative negligence will reduce the damages awarded to plaintiff if she misuses the product. However, Xena was wearing the helmet normally.

III. **Damages**

a. **Xena's Compensatory Damages**

Xena can recover personal injury and property damages, as well as past and future pain and suffering, medical expenses, lost wages, and loss of consortium. Here, Xena would be entitled to recover all medical costs related to her injuries. Xena would also be able to recover lost wages for any time she misses from work, at the rate of $30,000 per year. Xena can argue that her future lost wages should be doubled to account for her increased earning capacity when she graduates. However, she would need to prove that she could get a higher paying job.

b. **Punitive Damages as to Dau**

Punitive damages may be available in tort cases when there has been willful, wanton, or malicious conduct. In general, courts look to the potential deterrent effect punitive damages would have on defendant's conduct, as well as the appropriateness of a punitive damage award in reference to any civil liabilities imposed on the behavior. Here, Dau's actions do not seem willful or wanton and probably do not rise to the level of justifying punitive damages as a deterrent against future such behavior. The statute Dau violated in opening the car door subjects him to conviction on a misdemeanor and a maximum fine of $1,000. This relatively modest penalty suggests that, at most, a very small punitive damage award would be justified.

c. **Collateral Source Rule**

The collateral source rule prevents defendants from reducing their liability in tort by showing that plaintiff got money from collateral sources. These sources typically include insurance policies, employment benefits, gratuities, and social legislative benefits. This rule should be retained because defendants should not be rewarded for being fortunate enough to injure a plaintiff with collateral sources of recovery. The defendant should still have to pay the full damages he caused.

d. **Lan and Patrick's Individual Claims**

Lan and Patrick would sue on their own behalf for loss of consortium. Lan, as Xena's father, has a basis for recovery, although it is diminished somewhat by the fact that Xena is now an adult and presumably independent of her father. Patrick, on the other hand, is Xena's spouse. Lan may be able to obtain a modest loss of consortium award, and Patrick stands to win a more substantial award.

Torts

Homework Question 1

Jon's (J) father rented an apartment from Dora (D). Jon, 12 years old, lives in the apartment with his father and his six-year-old sister, Maya. J is somewhat developmentally disabled with a subnormal IQ. J attends regular classes in public school, but because he has been kept back twice, he attends fourth grade rather than sixth grade.

On November 15, the hot water heater that served J's apartment broke. The apartment building was designed so that one water heater served each floor of the eight-story apartment building. Although not required by law, it is common for landlords to have yearly inspections made of older hot water heaters to ensure that rust is not getting into the water, thereby posing a possible health risk to tenants. Three years had passed since D last had the relatively old water heaters in her building inspected. Had there been a timely inspection, there is a good chance that the deteriorating condition of the water heater in question would have been discovered so that repairs could have been made to preclude the hot water heater from breaking. The required repairs cost about $500. The inspection costs $75.

When the water heater broke, J's father and other tenants served by the broken hot water heater immediately called D to inform her of the problem. Despite repeated requests from J's father and other tenants, no repairs were made for three weeks. Thus, the affected tenants had no hot water available for three weeks.

During the period in which there was no running hot water, J observed his father regularly heat pots of water in the kitchen for bathing, washing dishes, shaving, and the like. On November 30, during the start of the third week in which there was no hot water, J's father left home briefly in order to retrieve his car from the auto repair shop where it had been left for repairs. J was instructed to watch his younger sister, something that J had done on many instances without incident. J was playing with a paint set that he had received as a gift, and he spilled some paint onto his arm and leg. Thinking his father would get angry at J if J's father returned home to see J covered in paint, J decided he had better take a bath. Although his father had instructed J never to use the stove, J heated water in a large pot on the stove as he had observed his father doing on numerous occasions. J filled the pot until it was nearly full. As J was carrying the pot of hot water toward the bathroom, Maya bolted out of her room and collided with J. The pot of scalding water spilled on J causing serious burns. J's father never filled the pot as full as J did out of concern that the hot water might spill.

J has filed a legal action against D. D does not deny the lack of running hot water at the time of the accident, nor does D deny that she had not inspected the water heater for three years prior to the accident. D does claim, however, that due to several vacancies in the building and because some tenants were behind in their rent (not J's father, however), she would not have been able to pay for the repairs to the hot water heater even if they had been discovered earlier. Further, D points to the lease agreement, which J's father signed after reading its terms, providing that "Landlord shall not be liable to Tenant for any conduct or omissions, negligent or non-negligent, on Landlord's part."

Analyze J's negligence action against D, including any defenses D may assert. You should assume that D owes a duty to J, and that, to the extent relevant, the jurisdiction has adopted pure comparative fault.

Torts

Homework Question 1—Outline

I. **Standard of Care and Breach of Duty**

  A. **(Rule)** Standard of care is that of reasonable person in same circumstances
   1. If burden outweighed by likelihood of injury, considering gravity of injury and social utility of activity in which defendant is engaged, then defendant failed to act as a reasonable person would

  B. **(Application)** Two possible breaches: failure to inspect water heaters and failure to repair water heater in timely manner
   1. First breach
     a. Burden to landlord of yearly inspection is $600
     b. Probability of harm is fairly high: older water heaters more likely to allow rust to leach into water
     c. Gravity of harm is low: rusty water poses few health risks
     d. Custom likely not relevant because yearly inspections done to prevent rusty water, not harm that occurred here
   2. Second breach
     a. Burden to landlord is $500—minimal in terms of care and maintenance of large residential building
     b. Probability of harm is high—many apartments and tenants affected by lack of hot water
     c. Gravity of injury is high, because scalding water can cause severe burns
     d. No social utility in failing to promptly inspect and fix broken water heater
     e. Defendant's personal financial situation is subjective and therefore irrelevant because standard is what a reasonable landlord would do

  C. **(Conclusion)** As to both breaches, burden on defendant is low and probability of harm is moderate to high, so defendant likely breached duty

II. **Cause-in-Fact**

  A. **(Rule)** To prove negligence, defendant's conduct must be both cause-in-fact and proximate cause of plaintiff's injuries
   1. Defendant's conduct is cause-in-fact of an event if event would not have occurred but for the conduct

  B. **(Application)**
   1. Had there been timely inspection, there is good chance that deteriorating water heater would have been discovered and water heater could have been fixed before it broke
     a. "Good chance" is sufficient because plaintiff need only prove negligence by preponderance
     b. But for defendant's failure to inspect water heaters in timely manner, plaintiff would not have been burned, because J would not have transported scalding hot water
   2. Also, if water heater had been repaired promptly, before third week, plaintiff would not have been burned, because there would have been no need to transport hot water

  C. **(Conclusion)** J can prove cause-in-fact for both breaches warning was sufficient to adequately warn its customers. CheapChili clearly knew its chili presented a risk of burns because it had settled hundreds of burn cases previously, and more basically, because it placed a warning on its bowl. It will argue that it had adequately warned of the danger. Paul can argue that a more prominent or forceful warning was required to ensure that he fully appreciated the risk. For example, the warning could have been in larger type, placed on the lid of the bowl, in addition to the bowl itself, and/or included a warning about the risk of third-degree burns.

As in negligence, a plaintiff in a strict products liability action must show that the defect was the cause-in-fact and proximate cause of his injury. While the hot chili certainly caused Paul's burns, it is less clear that the possibly inadequate warning did, as discussed previously.

Proximate cause is likely present here, because Paul is a proper, or foreseeable, plaintiff, and his injuries are foreseeable for one handling hot chili.

Defenses to a products liability claim include misuse, contributory negligence, and comparative negligence. If a plaintiff uses a product in a manner that is neither intended nor foreseeable, she has misused the product and it cannot be defective. Here, misuse is not really relevant as Paul did not intend to spill the chili onto his lap.

Common law contributory negligence would apply to bar a strict products liability claim where plaintiff knew of the defect, comprehended the risks posed by the defect, and voluntarily elected to expose himself to those risks. It is not clear that Paul knew the extent of the risk posed by the hot chili, namely, third-degree burns, and is probably not barred from recovery on this basis.

Comparative negligence is applied in some jurisdictions that have adopted it for negligence actions, such that wrongful conduct that contributes, along with the defective product, to his own injury reduces his recovery in some amount. This is usually limited to misuse or abnormal use or independent negligence situations (i.e., where the plaintiff's negligence is not simply failure to identify the defect). Paul might be deemed partially responsible for his injuries by choosing to remove the lid of the chili in a moving car.

While there are challenges in both the design defect and failure to warn claims, they are likely to be successful, although recovery may be reduced somewhat in a comparative negligence jurisdiction.

d. Negligent Infliction of Emotional Distress

Frank may have a cause of action for negligent infliction of emotional distress. The majority rule for negligent infliction of emotional distress is that a plaintiff may recover under a bystander theory if he was located near the scene of an accident, suffered a severe emotional distress ("shock") resulting from the sensory and contemporaneous observance of the accident, and had a close relationship with the victim. The first and last elements are clear here—Frank was sitting next to Paul at the time of the accident, and Paul is his son. As to the second element, Frank suffered a panic attack at the time of the accident, continues to have nightmares, and is under the treatment of a psychologist. These injuries would appear to be sufficient for severe emotional distress.

Frank probably can recover for negligent infliction of emotional distress, although as a claim derivative of Paul's, his recovery would be reduced in proportion to any reduction in Paul's claims by virtue of his comparative negligence, if any.

Multiple-Choice Questions

INTENTIONAL TORTS

Question 1

A man purchased a new bike. One day, he rode the new bike to a local movie theater for the eight o'clock show and parked his bike out front. As it was a small town, he felt comfortable leaving his bike on the rack without locking it. While the man was in the movie theater, the ticket agent decided to take the bike out for a spin. The ticket agent rode the bike once around the block before placing it back in the rack just as the man had left it. As the ticket agent was placing the bike back in the rack, the handlebars gently rubbed against the rail. After the movie, the man retrieved the bike, and had no idea that it had been moved until he noticed a small scratch on the handlebars.

If the man files suit against the ticket agent, will he prevail?

(A) No, because the man was unaware of the ticket agent's use.

(B) No, because there was insufficient damage to the man's bike.

(C) Yes, for trespass to a chattel.

(D) Yes, for conversion.

Question 2

An artist and a firefighter were neighbors who had been feuding for some time. One afternoon, the artist found some trash in her yard next to the fence that separated her and the firefighter's properties. Convinced that the firefighter had deposited the trash on her property, the artist picked it up and threw it onto the firefighter's property. The firefighter saw the artist throw the trash onto his property and immediately ran up to the artist with a sledgehammer in his hand, got to within inches of the artist's face, and shouted, "If you ever do something like that again, I'll break your leg!" The firefighter then stormed off, leaving the artist shaken by the encounter. The artist subsequently brought an action against the firefighter for intentional infliction of emotional distress.

What is the likely outcome of the case?

(A) Judgment for the firefighter, because he did not threaten any immediate physical harm.

(B) Judgment for the firefighter, as long as the artist experienced no physical harm as a result of the firefighter's actions.

(C) Judgment for the artist, if the firefighter intended that the artist experience an apprehension of a harmful physical contact.

(D) Judgment for the artist, if she suffered severe emotional distress as a result of the firefighter's actions.

Question 3

A father and son decided to celebrate the Fourth of July by shooting off some fireworks in their backyard. As they stood in the center of their yard, the father carefully proceeded to place the device in the ground and light the fuse of a new type of rocket.

The rocket was supposed to shoot three rainbow-colored streams into the air, one straight up and the other two to the sides. On the box, a warning stated, "As a safety precaution, launch this rocket only on level ground." Due to a slight downhill slope in the yard, one "stream" of the rocket veered sideways and entered the neighbors' yard. The neighbors' young daughter was startled by the rocket, and ran into the house crying. The burned-out shell of the rocket landed harmlessly three feet away from where the child had stood, but charred a small portion of the lawn.

If the neighbors bring an action on behalf of themselves and their daughter, will they prevail?

(A) Yes, for assault.

(B) Yes, for trespass.

(C) Yes, based on strict liability.

(D) Yes, for arson.

Question 4

A woman worked as a hostess at a local restaurant. One evening, she was getting ready to leave for work when her boyfriend stopped by to surprise her. Because she was running a little late, she asked her boyfriend to come back later, after her shift was over. The boyfriend laughed and said that he just needed a minute of her time, because he wanted to give her something. Despite her objections, the boyfriend gently pushed the woman into her kitchen and locked the door so that he could retrieve something from the front step. The woman was annoyed because she did not want to be late for work. She couldn't unlock the kitchen door, but she also didn't want to go out the back door of the building, because she would then have to walk all the way around the apartment complex to get to her car. The boyfriend returned shortly thereafter and released the woman, who refused to accept his gift.

If the woman were to bring an action against her boyfriend for false imprisonment, who would prevail?

(A) The boyfriend, because the confinement was brief and he was joking around.

(B) The boyfriend, because the woman could have left through the back door.

(C) The woman, because her boyfriend knew he was confining her against her will.

(D) The woman, because she did not have a reasonable means of escape.

Question 5

A real estate agent was having an affair with his neighbor's wife. The neighbor learned of the affair and decided to confront the real estate agent. The neighbor stormed over to the real estate agent's house carrying a loaded gun. The real estate agent refused to open the door, instead yelling at his neighbor through the closed door. Enraged at the real estate agent's refusal to open the door, the neighbor fired a warning shot through the top of the door. The neighbor did not intend to injure the real estate agent, but simply to scare him. However, the door shattered and several long, wooden shards flew off, becoming lodged in the real estate agent's chest and shoulder. The real estate agent sued the neighbor for battery.

Who should prevail?

(A) The neighbor, because he did not intend for the shards to strike the real estate agent.

(B) The neighbor, because he did not intend to injure the real estate agent.

(C) The real estate agent, because the neighbor failed to act as a reasonably prudent person.

(D) The real estate agent, because the neighbor intended to shoot the gun.

NEGLIGENCE

Question 6

A man went to see a play at the local theater operated by a local theater company. The man bought a ticket which assigned him to sit in Seat 24 in Row 30. When the man handed his ticket to the usher, the usher glanced at the ticket and lead the man to what he believed was the appropriate seat. However, the usher mistakenly took the man to Seat 23 in Row 30. The man occupied Seat 23 in Row 30, failing to notice it was not the seat listed on his ticket. During the second act of the play, the seat which the man was occupying suddenly collapsed, causing the man several injuries. A subsequent investigation failed to determine why the seat collapsed.

If the man brings an action for negligence against the theater company, which of the following is the most accurate statement?

(A) In order to prove breach of due care, the man must show that the usher acted unreasonably in leading him to the wrong seat.

(B) Under the doctrine of *res ipsa loquitur*, the fact that the seat collapsed is sufficient to establish that the theater company breached its duty of care.

(C) In order to prove that the theater company breached its duty of care, the man must demonstrate why the seat collapsed.

(D) Because the investigation failed to determine why the seat collapsed, the man cannot prevail in a negligence action against the theater company.

Question 7

A young woman felt crushed after her boyfriend of two years broke up with her. Feeling despondent, she consumed several bottles of wine. Now drunk, the woman decided that it would be a good idea to fry up some bacon. Once she got the bacon frying, however, the woman lost interest in the food, and instead sat on her couch to watch television. Within minutes, the woman passed out, leaving her food burning on the stove. Before long, the apartment filled with smoke, causing the fire alarm to go off.

Luckily, the woman's neighbor saw the smoke and called 911. Within a few minutes of the call, the fire department arrived at the woman's house. However, because the smoke was so thick inside the house, one of the firemen suffered smoke inhalation and had to be taken to the hospital.

If the fireman asserts a claim against the woman to recover for his injuries, will he prevail?

(A) No, because the woman did not intend to harm the fireman.

(B) No, because the firefighter's rule treats emergency personnel as licensees.

(C) Yes, because the woman intentionally placed herself in a position of peril.

(D) Yes, because the fireman succeeded in saving the woman's life.

Question 8

The day before Christmas, a shuttle-bus driver began making trips to and from the airport beginning at 4:00 a.m., and by 5:00 p.m., he had already worked 13 hours. As tired as he was, the shuttle-bus driver continued picking up and dropping off passengers, heading out with a nearly full shuttle to retrieve his last group of passengers and return to the airport. As the shuttle pulled up to the next bus stop, a masked man shoved his way past the waiting passengers and onto the shuttle wielding a large handgun.

The masked man loudly demanded that the driver and passengers empty their wallets and hand over their cash. At that very moment, a passenger who had been waiting to board the shuttle dove on top of the gunman, knocking him to the ground. As the passenger attempted to wrestle the handgun from the masked man, a shot rang out. The gunman jumped to his feet and scrambled out the door. The passenger lay on the floor of the shuttle groaning, having been shot in the stomach.

If the passenger sues the shuttle-bus driver, what is the shuttle-bus driver's best defense?

(A) The shuttle-bus driver owed passengers a duty only to use reasonable care to prevent injuries caused by his employees.

(B) The shuttle-bus driver owed passengers a duty only to protect them from foreseeable danger.

(C) The shuttle-bus driver had no duty to control the acts of third parties.

(D) The shuttle-bus driver was not the legal cause of the passenger's injury.

Question 9

A man owned an independent grocery store in an upscale urban area. The grocer prided himself on his high-end deli meats and cheeses and his large selection of expensive wines. The grocer had recently noticed, however, that one of the freezers in the store leaked from time to time, causing the tiles underneath the freezer to become wet. The grocer had called the freezer company to repair the freezer, but the freezer company had not yet sent a technician to repair it.

While the grocer was preparing for the lunchtime rush, a man came into the store and slipped on a portion of the floor that was wet due to the freezer leakage. The man landed awkwardly on his knee, shattering his kneecap.

If the man brings suit against the grocer, how should the court rule?

(A) Judgment for the grocer, because by calling the freezer company to fix the freezer, the grocer took reasonable care to prevent the injury.

(B) Judgment for the man, but only if the grocer knew that the leakage had expanded to the area around the freezer.

(C) Judgment for the man, if the grocer could have discovered the risk posed by the freezer leakage by a reasonable inspection of his property.

(D) Judgment for the man, because the grocer is liable for any condition on his premises that injures a customer.

Question 10

Sunday was generally family day at the shopping mall. One Sunday, like many others, two parents took their two children, a six-month-old daughter and a seven-year-old son, to the mall. At their son's insistence, the parents decided to let him push the courtesy stroller provided by the mall that was carrying the daughter, while the father held the handle. The son proudly pushed the stroller, grinning from ear to ear as he walked along the main promenade.

The father's former high school basketball coach smiled as he passed the family. Ten minutes later, the coach passed the family again. At that moment, the father let go of the handle of the stroller in order to bend down and pick up the daughter's pacifier, and the son became temporarily distracted. In his moment of distraction, the son ran the stroller into the coach. The collision caused the coach to fall to the ground, and he sustained a broken elbow.

If the coach sues the son, what is the son's best defense?

(A) The coach assumed the risk when he saw the son pushing the stroller.

(B) The son was exercising the care appropriate for a reasonable child of like age, knowledge, and experience.

(C) A seven-year-old is presumed incapable of negligence.

(D) The son did not intend to strike the coach.

STRICT LIABILITY

Question 11

A chef had equipped his home kitchen with the latest cutting-edge appliances, including a brand-new cappuccino machine. One night, when the chef was at work and the nanny was at the home with the chef's two small children, the nanny decided to use the cappuccino machine. The nanny knew that the chef preferred that she not tamper with his equipment other than to use the microwave oven to reheat the dinners which he prepared every day for his children. However, it was a particularly chilly night, and the nanny was relatively certain that she knew how to operate the machine. The nanny was unaware, however, that the machine had been recalled by the manufacturer for a design defect that caused one of the handles to overheat, creating a risk of severe burns. The chef knew of the recall but had not thought to warn the nanny. While using the cappuccino machine, the nanny burned her hand on the overheated handle and had to seek medical treatment.

If the nanny files a strict products liability action against the manufacturer of the cappuccino machine, is she likely to prevail?

(A) Yes, if the nanny demonstrates that the defect was the result of unreasonable design by the manufacturer.

(B) Yes, because the cappuccino machine was defective when it left the manufacturer.

(C) No, because the nanny was not supposed to use the chef's equipment.

(D) No, because the nanny was not the purchaser of the cappuccino machine.

Question 12

A ski instructor purchased a new brand of sunscreen made especially for the sensitive skin on a person's face and neck. He took the unopened product to his first ski class of the day and offered it to one of his students, who had forgotten her own sunscreen. When the student opened the sunscreen, all of the skiers in her vicinity noticed a very strong chemical odor. The student didn't believe that the unpleasant smell came from the product, though, and applied the sunscreen to her face and neck. Within minutes, a painful rash had broken out on the student's face. It was later determined that the manufacturer of the sunscreen had inadvertently included a harsh cleaning agent in the batch of sunscreen used by the student. The student filed a strict products liability claim against the manufacturer. The manufacturer claims that the student should not recover because she assumed the risk by applying a sunscreen with such a strong chemical odor.

Is the manufacturer likely to succeed in asserting this defense?

(A) No, because the student did not comprehend the risk.

(B) No, because a plaintiff's conduct cannot negate or reduce the plaintiff's strict products liability claim.

(C) Yes, because the student could smell the chemical odor and exposed herself to it nonetheless.

(D) Yes, because the student assumed the risk by applying the sunscreen.

Question 13

A bar manager told one of his bartenders that there was a new type of home blender on the market that could handle the ingredients of any drink, as well as the ingredients to make salsa and other chopped foods. The manager intended to wait in line to buy the blender at a special sale, and the bartender asked the manager to pick an additional blender up for the bartender as well. The manager purchased three blenders, and kept one for himself. He sold one to the bartender for the sale purchase price, and gave the third to his sister as a gift. Two weeks later, the manager came across information on the Internet that the blender manufacturer was recalling the blenders because the motors could overheat and throw sparks, causing a fire. The manager called his sister right away and left a message, but she didn't get it in time. Her blender sparked, causing a fire in her kitchen that burned her right hand and caused major property damage. The bartender was also burned by his blender, although he didn't suffer nearly as much property damage. The manager apologized to the bartender for not having told him about the recall.

If the sister and the bartender file a strict products liability action against the manager for damages, what is the likely outcome?

(A) The bartender and the sister will prevail against the manager, because the manager is strictly liable.

(B) The bartender, but not the sister, will prevail against the manager, because the manager failed to warn the bartender about the recall.

(C) Neither the bartender nor the sister will prevail against the manager, because the manager is not a commercial seller.

(D) Neither the bartender nor the sister will prevail against the manager, because the manager did not tamper with the blender.

Question 14

In preparing for her law school examinations, a student invited a few classmates to her apartment for a study group. The student, who loved spiders, kept a pet tarantula caged in her apartment. When the student purchased the tarantula, she had the poisonous venom removed so that it would be harmless.

During the study group session, the student brought out the cage with the tarantula to show her friends. When she was placing the cage down on the kitchen counter, the student carelessly left the cage door slightly ajar. Moments later, the tarantula crawled out of the cage and crept toward one of the classmates. The classmate, who was deathly afraid of spiders, saw the tarantula and tried to run away. As she did so, she tripped over a chair and fell down, fracturing her wrist.

If the classmate files suit against the student to recover damages for her injury, who will prevail?

(A) The classmate, because the student was negligent in leaving the cage door open.

(B) The classmate, because the student is strictly liable.

(C) The student, because the spider did not directly cause the classmate's injury.

(D) The student, because a spider is not a wild animal.

Question 15

A company was engaged in transporting liquids. As is normal, the company was hired to deliver a container of highly flammable chemicals to a local plant. The company required all of its employees to engage in extensive training. On the day of the delivery, the trucker hauling the chemicals noticed a stalled car ahead of him in the right lane. There was no way for the trucker to avoid the car. As he tried to maneuver around it, some of the chemicals spilled out of the container and ended up on the car. The car's driver, who had been smoking a cigarette with his windows rolled down while waiting for a tow truck, quickly caught fire, and later died. The driver's estate now brings a strict liability action.

Will the company be liable for the injuries caused to the car's driver?

    (A) No, because the trucker and the company exercised due care.

    (B) No, because the driver should have removed the car from the road.

    (C) Yes, because transporting flammable liquid is an abnormally dangerous activity.

    (D) Yes, because transporting flammable liquid is illegal.

Answer Grid

1 (A)(B)(C)(D)	4 (A)(B)(C)(D)	7 (A)(B)(C)(D)	10 (A)(B)(C)(D)	13 (A)(B)(C)(D)
2 (A)(B)(C)(D)	5 (A)(B)(C)(D)	8 (A)(B)(C)(D)	11 (A)(B)(C)(D)	14 (A)(B)(C)(D)
3 (A)(B)(C)(D)	6 (A)(B)(C)(D)	9 (A)(B)(C)(D)	12 (A)(B)(C)(D)	15 (A)(B)(C)(D)